THE LAST OF THE RULING
REPTILES · *Alligators, Crocodiles, and Their Kin*

The Last of the Ruling Reptiles

ALLIGATORS, CROCODILES, AND THEIR KIN *by Wilfred T. Neill*

1971 COLUMBIA UNIVERSITY PRESS

New York and London

TO COLLEAGUES still active or lately departed,
who have contributed outstandingly to a knowledge of the crocodilians:

Robert Mertens	*Heinz Wermuth*
Karl P. Schmidt	*Hugh M. Cott*
Fred Medem	*P. E. P. Deraniyagala*
Charles C. Mook	*Albert M. Reese*

CONTENTS

INTRODUCTION

WE HAVE TODAY a remarkably detailed knowledge of life and its characteristics, its processes, its present diversity, and its history over more than 3,000 million years. But much remains unknown; and the biologist, whatever his specialty within the life sciences, usually looks ahead, toward fresh research problems whose solution will further refine and augment biological knowledge. Still, he finds it sometimes useful, and often entertaining, to look back occasionally. To look back, for example, at the 1700s and 1800s, when the physical world was being explored for plants and animals, and when the world of ideas was being searched for biological principles—principles revolutionary then, although commonplace today. Or to look even further back, to the time when men of great intellectual stature were establishing the objectives of research, the viewpoints appropriate to the research worker.

About three centuries ago, the English prelate Thomas Sprat penned a statement that could scarcely be improved upon as an introduction to a scientific work, whether the work be a highly technical account intended to do no more than edify a few specialists, or whether it be (like the present book) a review of some broad topic, written with the hope that it will be not only useful to the specialist but also revealing to the layman who is interested in the world about him. Sprat was a member of the Royal

Society of London, which had been incorporated by Charles II, Stuart king of England, in 1662. The society had been formed "for the promotion of natural knowledge"; and to this end it issued journals in which research workers could publish their findings, and held meetings at which scientists could present their views. In any civilized country today, such activities would be regarded as commendable and in fact indispensable, but they were disturbing to many people in the latter 1600s; for the scientific Renaissance had just gotten well under way, sparked by the Reformation and by Francis Bacon's assertion that the natural world should be interpreted not in the murky twilight of ancient writings, but in the sharp, clear sunlight of observation and experiment. And so the Royal Society, a few years after its incorporation, was moved to prepare an account of its "history." The Society was too young to have much of a history, in the usual sense of the term, and the account would in actuality be a statement of purpose and objectives. To Sprat fell the task of drawing up that statement.

"Their Purpose is, in short, to make faithful *Records* of all the Works of *Nature*," Sprat wrote of the society's membership,

> . . . so the present Age, and Posterity, may be able to put a Mark on the Errors, which have been strengthened by long Prescription; to restore the Truths, that have lain neglected; to push on those, which are already known, to more various Uses; and to make the way more passable, to what remains unreveal'd. This is the Compass of their Design. And to accomplish this, they have endeavour'd to separate the Knowledge of *Nature*, from the Colours *Rhetorick*, the Devices of *Fancy*, or the delightful Deceit of *Fables*.

Although Sprat's statement is familiar to many scientists, it does not become trite by repetition.

Since the first appearance in print of *History of the Royal Society*, thousands of research workers have, through adherence to the principles enunciated so clearly therein, brought the biological sciences up to a level that could scarcely have been imagined in Sprat's day.

Sprat and his scientifically-minded contemporaries might not easily understand what we now mean by DNA, DDT, antibiotics, cholesterol, viruses, interferon, mutation, territoriality, fluoridation, or leukemia, but they would grasp quite readily that today's dramatic biological achievements have stemmed from, and have of necessity been preceded by, basic research into plant and animal structure, function, development, classification, inheritance, and adjustment to environment.

Usually the biologist has added to the pool of biological information through research into a specialized topic that has particular appeal for him: perhaps the behavior of birds, or the classification of ferns, the body chemistry of mammals, the fossil history of the flowering plants, the anatomy of fishes, the factors controlling plant and animal distribution, the mechanisms of inheritance, the effect of environment on living things, the life histories of parasites, the microscopy of cells and tissues, the embryological development of reptiles, or others. But the many possible lines of basic research have not all progressed at the same rate. There are some topics that have gone largely uninvestigated, some groups of living things that are still very poorly known. One such group is the Crocodilia—the alligators, crocodiles, and their kin.

If a living dinosaur turned up today on some remote island, what a stir there would be among scientists to learn its ways, and to discover why it had persisted so much longer than any of its relatives. Yet, the crocodilians, who were contemporaries of the dinosaurs and of common ancestry with them, have gone largely unstudied. The American alligator is the only crocodilian species to have received much attention; and even in this case, unfortunately, a great deal of misinformation has entered into the published accounts. This is especially true of accounts dealing with the alligator's courtship and nesting, egg-laying and hatching, guarding of the nest and young, feeding, fighting, and attacks on man. Herpetologists, scientists who study crocodilians along with certain other groups of animal life, are careful in their researches, but seldom do they have chance to know these reptiles in the wild; and so when they are called upon to write about the alligator or other crocodilians, they can do little more than offer an uncritical compilation of the published literature. This literature is riddled with half-truths and misinterpretations, many of which have not been discovered; it is still beset with folktales, legends, and myths, many of which have gone unrecognized as such. Accordingly, the old fallacies are perpetuated, and lent a spurious air of authenticity, through frequent repetition in modern books and articles.

The present book is the first one that tries to cover most aspects of crocodilian biology, and to interpret available data in the light of modern concepts. It is the first book whose preparation called for a winnowing of all the early literature relating to crocodilians, in the hope of discovering grains of truth amid a predictably large quantity of chaff. The research worker knows, and the layman can imagine, that in any long-continued line of investigation, there must be a constant re-evaluation of earlier ideas, some of which have to be abandoned; abandoned at no discredit to their proponents, for it is also a contribution to show that some alluring trail leads not to a goal but to a dead end. A writer in a scientific field commonly finds that an unsatisfactory body of earlier literature has already been rejected for him by a host of authors in the scientific journals; and if he does not so find, he might simply omit reference to older works, or disavow them all in a single sentence. But there is a good reason why the older writings about crocodilians should not be so summarily dismissed, even when they are a good bit less than scientific. Ideally, a life history account is based upon observations that were made objectively by modern techniques, and interpreted in the light of up-to-date scientific knowledge; but such observations have not often been made on crocodilians. These reptiles appear slated for rapid extermination at the hands of man, and many aspects of their biology may never receive more than casual attention. Indeed, some aspects are no longer amenable to direct investigation, for the geographic ranges of crocodilians in most cases have been reduced in modern times, and the original habitats disturbed or completely removed. The nature of a crocodilian's prey has been altered in many areas through the recent introduction of foreign animals and the extirpation of native ones, as well as through modifications of the environment and the concomitant changes in the relative abundance of prey species. Introductions, extirpations, and alterations of a pre-existing balance also have lately exposed crocodilians to a new set of predators and competitors. The maximum size and average size of most crocodilians have declined, simply because most individuals are shot before they are fullgrown. And, as a result of constant hunting, most populations of crocodilians throughout the world have become abnormally shy. Thus, some questions about crocodilians will never be answered more fully than they are answered in the older writings.

Indeed, I suspect that the present book will be not only the first to deal broadly with crocodilian biology, but also the last; the last, that is, to be written by someone who had chance to see almost all of the modern species in life, and a majority of them in their natural habitats. Throughout the entire world, the natural landscape is being altered and the wildlife exterminated at a rapid rate. In the highly urbanized and industrialized lands of Europe and the United States, we often like to imagine that the tropics (the home of most crocodilians) are pristine, undisturbed. Nothing could be further from the truth. Along the larger rivers of the tropics, virgin rainforest is no longer to be seen, for the great trees have been cut for timber and charcoal; many of the tropical lands suffer from the effects of erosion, deforestation, indiscriminate burning, over-grazing, and improvident agriculture to a greater degree than most parts of the United States. Living things usually maintain a rather delicate balance with their environment, by which I mean not just the physical environment but also the other organisms with which they must exist and interact; and man's profound alteration of the environment presages the rapid disappearance not just of the animal life that he kills for pleasure or economic gain, but also of many "innocent bystanders" in both the plant and animal kingdoms. I doubt that any crocodilian species will persist in nature much beyond the present century. Even if there is an abrupt surge of interest in the activities of crocodilians, these survivors from the Age of Reptiles are likely to vanish before their biology is even half understood. The next reviewer of the crocodilians will probably find himself relying almost wholly on earlier publications for any information that cannot be derived from museum skins and skulls.

This is not to say that all aspects of crocodilian biology have been neglected to the same degree, or that all of them are befogged by early misconceptions. The paleontologists, students of ancient life, have uncovered substantial portions of the fossil record of these reptiles. Taxonomists, students of biological classification, have shown how the living species of crocodilians are related among themselves and to the extinct species. There have been many useful studies on the anatomy of the crocodilian skull, although other parts of the body have not been investigated to a comparable extent. Something is known about the development of the embryo in a few of the species, and some attention has lately been given to the body chemistry of crocodilians. A good many internal parasites of these reptiles have been discovered. There have also been a few studies on the responses of crocodilians to various stimuli in captivity. The great and depressing gap in our knowledge relates to the habits of crocodilians in the wild. It was in the reporting of crocodilian habits that the early writers went so often astray, and thus came to lead modern students similarly astray.

The present book is divided into six sections. It is the job of the first section, Chapters 1–4, "to put a mark upon the Errors, which have been strengthened by long Prescription"; to reveal where the earlier literature, whose influence is strong in modern writings about crocodilians, actually was colored by rhetoric, embellished with sheer fancy, and clouded by fables of insidious appeal. From the early 1500s through 1935, there were written about a hundred books and shorter articles that have affected our present view of crocodilian natural history—adversely affected in many cases, I am bound to state. Many of the old publications are hard to come by today, and so I have not simply referred to them, but have quoted directly from most of them. I believe that even the professional herpetologist will be surprised to see, from these quotations, just how much so-called information about crocodilians, purveyed by modern handbooks and guides to the reptiles, must be traced back only to the rhetoric, fancies, and fables of an earlier time, and not to any scientifically dispassionate observation. And I believe that the general reader will enjoy, especially, the older quotations relating to the alligator; for these, even when of limited value to science, paint for us a picture of a bygone America, its wilderness inhabited by settlers who were sturdy and naive, by naturalist-explorers who were brave and credulous, and by shadowy beasts whose presence was somehow disturbing.

With the fallacies disavowed, and the dubieties at least challenged, the way is opened for the presentation of the more factual material. The second section of the book, Chapters 5–9, supplies some necessary background information about the crocodilians, their place in nature, their distinguishing features, and the convenient scheme by which they are classified. The section then describes the fossil history of crocodilians. It is astonishing to note the length of this history: more than 200 million years. It is astonishing, also, to see how diverse the Crocodilia have been in the past ages: the world has known horned alligators, great crocodiles capable of feeding on dinosaurs, tiny crocodilians less than a foot long, fin-backed sea-crocodiles, fearsomely toothed crocodilians that hunted their prey on land, "duck-billed" and nearly toothless crocodilians whose food must only be guessed. Just as these and other crocodilians preceded the modern ones in time, so a presentation of crocodilian evolutionary history would seem a desirable prelude to a review of the living species.

What would we not give for a firsthand look at the Mesozic Era, that remote time when reptiles, often of great size and grotesque mien, walked the earth, swam in the fresh waters and the seas, even glided through the air on leathery wings. But we are vouchsafed no such look, and we must cast about among the sciences for scraps of information that might supplement paleontological data. The students of ancient reptile life have rarely turned to the study of living reptiles as a source of stimulating ideas. Probably the circumstance reflects the original development of paleontology as a science not closely allied with any other except geology; and surely it reflects the special concern of paleontologists with bones and teeth, tanglible relics in need of study and identification. At any rate, the third section of the book attempts to analyze some puzzling episodes of crocodilian history in the light of what is known about certain modern reptiles. Chief among these episodes is the evolution of crocodilians, flying reptiles, a bewildering diversity of dinosaurs, and some other organisms, all from one group of small reptiles most of which scampered bipedally over the ground. I have kept this third section short, only two chapters, 10–11.

With the fossil history of the crocodilians accounted for, and various links established between ancient species and modern ones, the discussion proceeds to the natural history of a living crocodilian, the American alligator. In the fourth section of the book, Chapters 12–19, I have tried to indicate not just what we know about the alligator, but also what we should hasten to find out about this reptile in the few decades of existence that remain to it. The account of the alligator's activities is as broad as I could make it, for I also wanted to show what topics any crocodilian life history could and should cover. It is perturbing to see that our knowledge of all the other living crocodilians, at least our knowledge of their life histories, can be summarized in a single and not over-long section, the fifth portion of the book, Chapters 20–27. The sixth and concluding section is the bibliography, intended to document parts of the text as well as to guide the advanced student to the widely scattered literature of the crocodilians.

The arrangement of the text needs no further comment, but certain aspects of my approach perhaps need explanation here. I have had unusually good opportunity to study crocodilians in both captivity and the wild. It is customary for the writer of a scientific book to efface himself from his narrative, restricting first-person usages to an introduction in which aims and outlook are stated; but I have offered in the text a good many new observations or interpretations, and so have deemed it better to indicate, without circumlocution, that these are my responsibility.

When Thomas Sprat penned the lines I have quoted, the Western world had just become fully awake after a thousand years of intellectual stagnation. The questions to be asked then were the basic ones, "what, where, how." It is still useful to ask similar questions: What kinds of crocodilians exist? Where does each live? How does each feed? But today, with much more data at our command, the really stimulating question is "why." Why did crocodilians survive past the Age of Reptiles, when their relatives the dinosaurs failed to do so? Why does an adult alligator bellow, a hatchling grunt? Why should the American alligator have its closest relative in China, halfway around the world? Why does the male alligator, courting in the water, blow a stream of bubbles past the cheeks of his prospective mate? Why does the stomach of a crocodilian so often contain rocks or gravel? Why are the teeth and bones of a certain extinct crocodilian usually associated with deposits of phosphate in the southeastern United States? Why do crocodilians have five toes on the front foot but only four on the hind? Why cannot the crocodiles live outside the tropics, as the alligators do? Some questions of this kind cannot yet be answered, but others can. To answer only the "what, where, how," while ignoring the "why," is rather like pointing out the red threads, the blue threads, and the yellow threads of a tapestry, while saying no words about a grand and complex design into which they are woven. Thus, I have had no hesitancy in looking at times beyond the bare facts and to some broad concepts; at looking beyond the threads to some portion of the design.

For assistance in the preparation of this book, I am indebted to several people. Richard Thomas brought to my attention many publications on crocodilians, and some unusual caimans he had found on Trinidad. Joseph T. Collins provided a set of *Herpetological Review,* a publication devoted to the bibliography of amphibians and reptiles. Rhodes Fairbridge, through Robert J. Tilley, supplied references to Kingsley Fairbridge's experience with an estuarine crocodile in New Guinea. M. C. Downes and H. Robert Bustard sent information about the present status of crocodiles in New Guinea. All these people have my thanks.

I am especially indebted to Ross Allen. For a dozen years I directed a program of biological and archeological research, sponsored by his Reptile Institute at Silver Springs, Florida; and the present book has profited in several ways from that association. There was frequent opportunity to talk with Mr. Allen about the alligator's habits, a subject on which no one could speak with more authority than he. There was also chance to accompany him on trips to various parts of the New World tropics in search of caimans and crocodiles, trips that were a valuable supplement to my own quests for Old World crocodilians. There was chance to study captive examples of almost every crocodilian species that lives today. Finally, it was possible to secure many photographs of crocodilians, both in captivity and in the wild.

Wilfred T. Neill

New Port Richey, Florida
March 5, 1970

THE LAST OF THE RULING
REPTILES · *Alligators, Crocodiles,*
and Their Kin

PART I *Little-Known Survivors from an Ancient Day*

1 THE FABLED ALLIGATOR

ON THE EAST COAST of Florida, about half-way down the peninsula, a small and sandy cape noses bluntly into the Atlantic Ocean. In 1961 the cape still bore its 400-year-old name of Canaveral, "place where the reed-grass grows." The canebrakes had long since vanished, together with the Spanish explorers who had dubbed them *cañaveral*. Gone, too, were the Timucua Indians who once plaited the split cane into baskets, mats, shields, and fish traps; gone the pioneer white settlers who set the brakes afire in the dry season to hear the exciting crackle. In 1961 Cape Canaveral and nearby Merritt Island had sprouted a forest of man-made structures, some of them squat, others pointing toward the heavens. In the spring of that year, the cape and its environs shook to a thunderous roar, a roar that was carried around the globe by radio and television. It was a new sound in the world, the sound of a mighty rocket boosting America's first astronaut into space.

Before that sound had died away, there arose from swamps on Merritt Island an answering roar, a deep and vibrant rumble that set the swamp water to quivering so that droplets danced atop the surface. This was an old sound in the world. It was the bellow of an alligator, and it was an old

1

sound ages before man began to chip at flint and wonder about the stars. Survival to the present is the astonishing feature of the crocodilians, the reptile group that includes alligators and crocodiles among others. The crocodilians, the grotesque flying reptiles, and the dinosaurs—collectively known as Ruling Reptiles—together dominated the earth for 100 million years. Their long reign ended 63 million years ago; dinosaurs vanished from the land, the flying reptiles from the air, and other reptilian types from the sea. Yet, the crocodilians somehow escaped the extinctions that terminated the Age of Reptiles. The survival of crocodilians in general is remarkable enough; but almost incredible is the persistence of one of them, the American alligator, into the opening decade of the Space Age, and this in a country where so much other wildlife has been extirpated by man. Scarcely less remarkable is the survival of another species of alligator in China, in a thickly populated region where reptiles and all their parts are variously prized as food, leather, or nostrums.

However, as emphasized in the Introduction, all the crocodilians are now in danger of extinction, and some aspects of their biology may never be investigated adequately. It is needful to "make the way more passable," as Thomas Sprat long ago phrased it, "to what remains unreveal'd"; and this can scarcely be done without first expunging a considerable number of misconceptions that have adversely influenced the study of these reptiles.

Of course, a folklore about crocodilians has grown up wherever these reptiles exist; but folk fallacies, usually transmitted orally, command our attention only when they have been incorporated into the biological litera- ture. In the case of two species—the Nile crocodile and the American alliga- tor—the folk fallacies have modified scientific thinking to a degree that is truly intolerable; and the misconceptions relating to the Nilotic reptile were in most cases transferred to the American one. Thus, the opening section centers around the alligator, and some of the published accounts that have helped to mold the currently accepted (but largely inaccurate) version of its life history and activities. Chapter 1 merely samples the falla- cies that have somehow come to involve the American alligator. The sam- ple is intended primarily to show the diversity of these fallacies as well as the diversity of the milieus in which they exist. The chapter traces a few misconceptions back to their approximate sources, in order to reveal that the legends and myths may be as diverse in origin as in content; but such tracing, at least in detail, is left to Chapters 2, 3, and 4.

A myth is often defined as a widely held belief that stems from pure imagination, with no factual basis whatsoever. Of myths relating to the American alligator, the most widely accepted one asserts that only the male bellows. This is a logical supposition, to be sure, for in some living things the male is more vocal. Male frogs set up a noisy chorus, male birds sing from high perches while the females nest quietly in the shrubbery, roosters crow loudly while hens merely cackle and cluck. Accordingly, the modern accounts of the alligator, almost without exception, regard bellowing as an activity of the male only. Yet any schoolboy, earning a few dollars by summer work on a Florida "alligator farm," knows that when the captive alligators begin to bellow, the females join in as thunderously as any male of equal size (Fig. 1). The sex of an alligator is not often obvious, except perhaps to another of its species; but those that build the nests and lay the eggs will do their share of roaring. They are surely female.

A legend is often defined as a belief whose somewhat factual basis has been altered imaginatively. In this category, perhaps, we should place the assertion (still encountered in some biology texts) that crocodilians

Figure 1. Bellowing alligators: a photograph that helps dispel several myths. Both males and females bellow, on land or in water, by day as well as by night. Bellowers show no hostility toward each other. [Ross Allen's Reptile Institute]

Figure 2. Alligators do not replace their teeth indefinitely. Few teeth remain to this individual, a male about 35 years old. [*Ross Allen's Reptile Institute*]

continue to replace their teeth indefinitely throughout life. It is true that the alligator can replace its teeth a number of times; each functional tooth is backed up by a series of replacement teeth, the largest of which will grow into place as the functional tooth is lost. But this process does not continue indefinitely. The American alligator is described as having 80 teeth (40 in each jaw), but the description is applicable mainly to young or middle-aged specimens; in old alligators the tooth count is less, showing that some teeth are no longer being replaced. A very old alligator is nearly toothless (Fig. 2). Such near-toothless oldsters have lived for years in captivity, feeding heartily but developing no more teeth in their bony jaws.

The most exciting biological work of recent times—perhaps, ultimately, the most important scientific advance of the twentieth century—has been the unraveling of the "genetic code" that determines cellular growth into tissues and organs. The ramifications of this work are numerous, and one of them involves the regeneration of lost parts. Most salamanders can regenerate a lost tail; a newt can regrow the hyoid apparatus (to which tongue muscles attach); a frog can replace surgically removed lungs; a tadpole may regrow amputated gills. In some lizards a new tail (or several new ones) may grow from the stump of the old; yet in other lizards, and in most if not all snakes, the stump of an amputated tail merely heals over. A man cannot regrow a lost finger or toe, yet a certain larval salamander can regenerate an entire limb. Why do such differences exist among the various groups of backboned animals? Investigations into this problem are obviously important. Equally obvious is the desirability of knowing

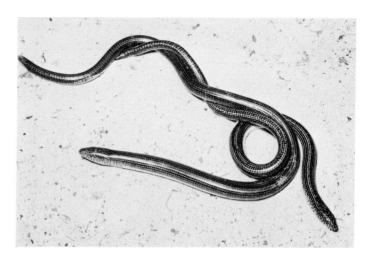

Figure 3. Much biological interest now attaches to regeneration of lost parts. A salamander (upper) can regenerate a tail, and so can a glass-lizard (center); but a watersnake (lower) cannot. [Ross Allen's Reptile Institue, Tony Stevens, and W. T. Neill]

beforehand the extent to which different animals can regenerate lost parts. Biological texts declare that in crocodilians there is no regeneration of any lost appendage beyond the healing over of the stump. This is not precisely the case. If a major portion of an alligator's tail is amputated, the stump merely heals over as predicted by the literature; but if only the tail-tip is lost a new structure is regenerated (Fig. 4). The new tail-tip may soon grow as long as the original one, but remains comparatively formless for a year or two at least, and redevelops only a few scales during this period. It is suspected that, with the passage of years, the regenerated structure becomes more tail-like; an occasional adult alligator appears to have regrown a moderately good replica of a tail-tip (Fig. 9).

It has been stated that the female alligator does not guard her nest; if she is found near it, she is merely sunning. This observation will scarcely

Figure 4. An alligator, having lost most of his tail when a hatchling, years later shows no regeneration (at right). Yet, when only the last part of the tail is lost, regeneration soon begins (below). [Ross Allen's Reptile Institute and W. T. Neill]

impress the considerable number of people whose curiosity about an alligator nest has been terminated abruptly by the threatening lunge of the guardian female. Female alligators, kept for years in artificial pens and exposed to people every day, might very well lose the impulse to defend the nest; and the aforesaid statement stemmed from observations made under just such captive conditions. Also, in parts of the wild where alligators have been continually hunted, and so have become exceptionally shy, the females rarely expose themselves even if someone approaches the nest. But in the remoter wilds, or in spacious pens with limited disturbance and a fairly natural environment, the female will defend her nest most effectively, even against man. It might be added that if penned alligators nest in the bright sun it is probably because they have no other choice. In the wild, alligators usually nest in the shade, frequently in deep shade.

Figure 5. A widely credenced myth asserts that the alligator uses its tail as a weapon. People who actually know the alligator have no fear of the tail, but make sure the jaws are secured. [W. T. Neill]

Another fallacy is the insistence that the tail of the alligator is a weapon as formidable as the jaws. Actually, an alligator that has been over-powered may thrash, twist, or roll in efforts to escape; at such times a bystander could accidentally be struck by the reptile's tail, but that appendage delivers no aimed or intentional blow. People who actually catch large alligators in the wild, or forcibly move the unwilling .reptiles from pen to pen in captivity, pay little attention to the tail (Figs. 5 and 18). Nor does the alligator make any use of the tail when capturing prey. Prey is taken and an enemy confronted by the alligator's strong, tooth-studded jaws.

The use of the tail by the alligator, whether for offense or defense, is a myth. In later chapters we shall see that this myth and several others, originally applied more than 2,400 years ago to the Nile crocodile, were eventually transferred to the American alligator, and finally incorporated into the biological literature along with folktales of more recent coinage. Fallacious beliefs about crocodilians flourished in 1935, when an amateur naturalist, E. A. McIlhenny, proffered a book, "The Alligator's Life History." His account was based for the most part on casual observations, boy-hood recollections, and the beliefs of local rustics, along with elaborations upon old myths and legends. Yet, the great majority of subsequent workers, having little personal familiarity with the actual facts about the alligator's life history, have made McIlhenny's book the most frequently cited reference in the field of crocodilian behavior. Thus, it has seemed necessary in the present chapter, and in the three that follow, to quote some widely accepted statements from McIlhenny's account, and to contrast these statements with what I take to be the reality of the situation. McIlhenny declared, among other things, that the lens of an alligator's eye is a vertical slit, and that at night, in the rays of a flashlight, the eyes of a "bull" alligator glow reddish, those of a female or juvenile a "greenish or bluish yellow." He went on to say that the teeth of a full-grown alligator are nearly solid, while those of a young specimen are hollow; that bullfrogs could not possibly swallow a baby alligator; and that a child walks faster than an alligator can run on land. He observed that an alligator, having eaten some mammal, thoroughly digests the bones and hair along with the meat. He repeated the widespread fiction that only the male alligator will bellow, regarded its bellowing as a challenge to other males, and asserted that bellowing is not done on land but only in the water. He further asserted that the high-pitched grunt of the baby alligator is also voiced by adults, and is given by the female to call her young or to warn them of danger.

Actually, it is the pupil of the alligator's eye, not the lens, that forms a vertical slit in the light; the pupil becomes round in the dark and during the act of bellowing. Contrary to some authors, bellowing is not solely a nocturnal activity (see Figs. 1 and 10). In the southeastern United States, backwoodsmen often assert that the eye of a male alligator has a particularly reddish glow by reflected light. This sounds plausible until one asks how one can pronounce as assuredly male all those alligators whose eyes are noted to shine redly. The sex of a young alligator is hard to determine even with dissection; the comparatively undeveloped penis and testes of the small male are difficult to distinguish from the clitoris and ovaries of a small female. Male and female alligators differ on the average (but not trenchantly) in the arrangement of the scales around the vent; the sex of a young adult may be determined by bending the reptile backward across one's knee and opening the vent to reveal a penis if one is present; the sex of a large adult may be determined by probing into its vent. Such methods of sex determination are not employed by those who play a flashlight by night over a swamp or marsh where alligators dwell. When a flashlight is so played, some distant eyes are seen to glow reddish, others bluish or greenish. Closer investigation would reveal that the reddish or reddish-orange reflections are attributable to alligators, the more bluish or greenish ones to bullfrogs, pig frogs, or leopard frogs, which are usually present in the alligator's habitat.

The teeth from the largest alligator skulls are hollow, and show no sign of unusual thickening or solidification. The hollow tooth of a very large alligator was prized in pioneer times; it was made into a charger and used to dip up a measured amount of gunpowder. Not only bullfrogs but also the smaller leopard frogs are definitely known to have gulped down baby alligators; and as for the speed of an alligator on land, a small or medium-sized one can fairly dash across the ground, at least for 15 or 20 feet. This flurry of activity is seen in the wild only when the alligator is surprised on land, and flees to nearby water. Regarding total digestion of prey, it is quite true that an alligator has powerful digestive fluids; but their action is not unlimited. On one occasion, autopsy revealed a large alligator to have died because its intestine had been completely blocked

Figure 6. By night, in the rays of a flashlamp, the eye of an alligator has a bright, reddish gleam. [Ross Allen's Reptile Institute]

Figure 7. The pig-frog is an associate (and often a food) of the alligator. Its bright, blue-green eye-shine, in the rays of a flashlamp, is often mistaken for that of an alligator. [W. T. Neill]

by a ball-like mass of hog's hair. Young alligators voice a so-called grunt, actually a high-pitched call; when about 4 feet long they make their first attempt at bellowing, and thereafter grunt no more; male and female adults will bellow on land as well as in the water (Fig. 1).

Needless to say, misconceptions about the American alligator are by no means limited to written accounts; they have always abounded among the general public. Most people would be surprised to learn that the so-called alligator farms scattered over the southern United States are not farms in the sense that a marketable surplus of alligators is profitably raised in captivity. The profits of an "alligator farm" come mostly from tourist admission fees and the sale of gimcracks, not from the natural increase of the captive reptiles. Alligators sometimes breed in captivity, but the purchase of wildcaught alligators is the main source of larger ones on display throughout the country. As these reptiles are fairly long-lived, and are moderately hardy in captivity, only at long intervals may it be necessary to purchase a few more large specimens.

This is not to say, however, that alligators reach the great age so often ascribed to them. In some "farms" the pen of a 10-foot alligator may bear a sign imputing an age of 1,000 years to the captive; and a 12-foot alligator may be assigned an age of 2,000 years. Actually, the 10-foot specimen could be no more than eleven years old, the 12-foot one no more than sixteen years. Toothlessness and other signs of senility are evident in alligators that have lived for about fifty years, and the maximum age is not much beyond this. It is certain that the alligator, on the average, does not live as long as man.

In some "farms" an attendant will point out a large alligator, and then remark, "He's so old he has moss growing on his back!" Most tourists seem to regard this as particularly impressive evidence of the reptile's vast age. Actually, the growth is not moss but algae, and it can sprout in a few days' time. Even very small alligators, if ailing or improperly cared for, may develop a greenish coat of algae. An alligator or other crocodilian, if heavily infested with algae, will usually die. Much interest attaches to this algal growth, which will be considered in a later chapter; but it has nothing to do with a reptile's age.

Of all popular fallacies relating to crocodilians, the most widespread asserts that the upper jaw is hinged and moveable in the crocodile, the lower jaw in the alligator. But in truth, all the crocodilians—the two living species of alligators, the five living species of caimans, the fourteen of crocodiles, the "false gavial" of Malaya, the unique gharial of India, and a great variety of extinct species—exhibit the same basic jaw structure. In all, the upper jaw is a prolongation of the skull to which it is rigidly attached, while the lower jaw is hinged and moveable. Obviously a crocodilian, resting with its lower jaw on the ground, could open its mouth only by tilting the entire skull backward and so lifting the upper jaw. (A man, resting with his chin on a mantelpiece, could open his mouth in the same fashion.) Interestingly, the fallacious view of the crocodile jaw goes back to Classical times. Herodotus, the "Father of History," writing in the fifth century B.C., knew nothing of alligators, but he had visited the Egyptian home of the Nile crocodile. He reported that the reptile's lower jaw was fixed immoveably, the upper jaw being hinged. The longevity of a myth is amusingly demonstrated by the use in recent motion pictures of imitation crocodiles complete with hinged upper jaw; as the sham reptiles float down upon their supposed victim, their upper jaws pop open to reveal white teeth and a mouth painted bright scarlet.

Not only were mistaken notions about the Nile crocodile transferred to the American alligator but a local mythology also grew up about this latter reptile. Throughout the backwoods of the southeastern United States, where the alligator still leads its precarious existence, many a present-day native will proclaim the gastronomic excellence of what he calls "'gator tail." A long strip of meat, about 2 inches wide, is cut from each side of the reptile's tail. The length of the strip depends, of course, on the size of the alligator. The strip is cut into short segments; these are rolled in salted and peppered flour, and then fried quickly in butter. Alternatively, the floured segments are browned in butter, then simmered for about two hours in water and the juice of a lemon. Either procedure results in excellent fare; but how senseless to take two little strips from the tail and throw the rest of the meat away! As a matter of fact, a filet from the alligator's tail is less savory than certain other cuts. In the tail musculature there may be many thin sheets of fat, and these slightly impair the flavor of the meat. Yet, for probably 200 years in the southern backwoods most of the meat of slaughtered alligators has gone to waste. In 1935 E. A. McIlhenny remarked, "The flesh of the tail of the young alligator is excellent." More than a century before, the traveler James Forbes, in his 1821 account of Florida, stated, "The rattlesnake and the tail part of the alligator are sometimes eaten by the hungry traveler." Christian Schultz, writing from Louisiana in 1808, described "the tail part of a young alligator" as "that delicious morsel." According to an 1802 account, Captain Matthew Phelps saw alligators on the Big Black River of Mississippi in the 1770s; he killed many, "on the tails of which the inhabitants make an agreeable repast." Andrew Ellicott, surveying the Georgia-Florida border in 1800, remarked in his journal that alligator tails were eaten; "Mr. Bowles [the English adventurer William Augustus Bowles] informed me that he thought them one of the greatest delicacies." This curious emphasis on the edibility of an alligator's tail, as opposed to the rest of the carcass, can be traced back at least to 1791. In that year John Pope, visiting Bayou St. John near New Orleans, counted 73 alligators in the bayou; and in his diary he wrote, "The tail part of this animal yields a very nutritious food." An old European myth attributed aphrodisiac qualities to meat from the tail of a crocodile; and certain Indian tribes of the southeastern United States ate strips from the powerfully muscled tail of a large alligator in the hope of thereby acquiring some of its strength. The two superstitions may have misled pioneer whites into believing that the rest of the carcass was valueless as food.

Some aspects of crocodilian behavior have given rise to a variety of mistaken beliefs in different parts of the world. Take, for example, the explanations that have been advanced to account for the occurrence of a few stones and other hard objects in a crocodilian's stomach. In the zoological literature, such objects are called gastroliths. They are not, however, gastroliths in the medical sense of being pathological concretions; they are items ingested by the reptile. The actual function of gastroliths has never become widely known, and the literature provides various explanations of their function. An old legend, supposedly of African origin, states that a crocodile swallows a stone for every person it eats, thereby keeping a tally of depredations. Another legend relates that a crocodile swallows one stone a year, thus keeping track of its birthdays and permitting determination of its age. In 1841 William Byrd of Virginia expressed a less ridiculous, but still erroneous, belief of his day. Writing of crocodiles generally, he commented, "They swallow great stones, the weight of which being added to their strength, enables them to tug a moderate cow under water." Actually, the total weight of gastroliths in even a large crocodile does not exceed a few pounds, a negligible burden.

Within the range of the American alligator, stones are not wholly lacking from river and lake bottoms, but they are perhaps a bit less common than hard objects of other kinds. In that region, it is widely believed that the alligator swallows a "literd knot" (pine lightwood knot) in the fall in order to "give its stomach something to work on" during the hibernation period when prey is not accepted. This legend can be traced back at least to the year 1800, when Andrew Ellicott killed and then cut open two large alligators, "to examine the truth of the report of their swallowing pine knots in the fall of the year to serve them (on account of their difficult digestion) during the term of their torpor." Ellicott found both stomachs to contain pine and other knots, along with wood chips; one stomach also held some charcoal, but neither contained food remains.

John James Audubon, famous nineteenth-century painter of birds, started a new legend about gastroliths.

> Opening alligators to see the contents of the stomach . . . I regularly have found round masses of a hard substance, resembling petrified wood. . . . I have broken some of them . . . and found them brittle, and hard as stones. . . . And, as neither our lakes nor rivers . . . afford even a pebble as large as a common egg, I have not been able to conceive how they are procured by the animals, if positively stones, or by what power wood can become stones in their stomachs.

Audubon's remarks were contained in a letter that was not published until 1927. In 1929 the U. S. Department of Agriculture issued a bulletin about alligators; and its author, Remington Kellogg, quoted Audubon. E. A. McIlhenny, in his 1935 work, had read Kellogg's pamphlet, and remarked,

> Some writers claim to have found in alligators' stomachs round pieces of wood or other foreign substances . . . closer examination of the substances would probably have proven them to be reminant [sic] of food that had remained in the stomach after hibernation had begun, and during the several months of inactivity had been molded by the muscular actions of the stomach into a solid mass, dark brown in color and in texture much resembling wood. I have found such objects from the size of a walnut to ones larger than my fist. . . .

McIlhenny went on to say that "pieces of wood and other foreign substances are frequently swallowed by alligators . . . in catching their food." He denied that hard objects are ever swallowed intentionally by alligators.

Actually, the deliberate ingestion of hard objects, including wood chips and knots, does take place among both wild and captive alligators. On one occasion a medium-sized alligator, killed in northern Florida, proved to have in its stomach numerous chips of fresh pine, both wood and bark. In the area from which the reptile came, the large pines had just been made available to turpentiners, who use a special kind of axe to cut a series of deep channels in each tree that is tapped. Chips thus removed were picked up by the alligator, presumably from the water rather than from the land. Other hard items, reliably reported as having been found in the stomachs of wild alligators, include charred wood, dead wood, cinders, shotgun shells, and cartridge cases. Pebbles and small stones of both quartz and limestone are (in spite of Audubon's belief) widespread in the range of the alligator; and they are often ingested. Alligator stomachs often contain plant material, some of which, being hard, might have been swallowed as gastroliths. In this category are lotus seeds and hickory nuts. The bony scales of garfish, along with fragments of turtle shell, occur in alligators' stomachs, probably because garfish and turtles were captured for food; but the hard parts of such prey should function for a time as gastroliths. Small alligators often have gravel in the stomach.

The alligator's custom of swallowing hard objects is perhaps best known to operators of alligator "farms" where in each day's lot of tourists there are many who, unless closely watched, will throw soft-drink bottles, tin cans, sticks, and rocks into the pens to see what will happen. Usually nothing happens at the time; but if not removed, the thrown objects will eventually be swallowed by the penned alligator. They are ingested from the surface if they float, or from the bottom if they do not. Captive alligators, if exposed to the public, often ingest flashbulbs discarded by photographers. The alligator's method of swallowing a potential gastrolith is different from the method of taking food; the hard object is engulfed with considerable care, and even thin-walled bottles are not crushed. However, a potential gastrolith, too large to be swallowed whole, may first be crushed or broken and then swallowed.

Captive crocodiles of several species will also ingest hard objects. For example, at the Cincinnati Zoo a large Nile crocodile was seen to swallow a soft-drink bottle. Fearing injury to a valuable specimen, the zoo's veterinarian operated on it and removed from its stomach the bottle; he also discovered and removed five other bottles, 39 stones, three marbles, a porcelain elephant, two cartridge cases, and a metal whistle. At the New

York Zoological Park, a small crocodile was found to contain more than a pound of coins, stones, glass, broken pottery, bits of plastic, tire-tube caps, and fine gravel. Three species of crocodiles have been studied in the wild, and found to contain gastroliths. Some recent students have likened the stones to ballast, and ascribed to them a hydrostatic function. But this would seem improbable. The crocodilian stomach is divided into two parts; and the larger of these, into which the esophagus opens, is essentially a gizzard, a tough-walled, muscular structure much like the gizzard of various birds such as the chicken. Indeed, in the anatomical literature the larger or left-hand portion of the crocodilian stomach has actually been called a gizzard, and the contained stones rather convincingly equated with the coarse grit that grinds food in the gizzard of a chicken.

A few old fables, attached originally to the Nile crocodile, have nearly vanished; yet, they still merit our attention for reasons that will become apparent. From Classical sources comes the story that a crocodile will lure a man by piteous sobbing, or else will weep copious tears over its victim. In actuality crocodiles do not weep, and hypocrisy is characteristic of man only. Yet, the notion of crocodilian deception captured the European mind in Elizabethan times. Shakespeare and Spenser made literary allusion to it. Appropriately, the fable of the hypocritical crocodile was brought to the New World by John Hawkins, a slave trader who, with his vessel the *Jesus of Lubeck*, built up such a profitable traffic in human beings that he was knighted by Queen Elizabeth I. In May of 1564 the *Jesus of Lubeck* was anchored off the coast of Colombia, in the mouth of a river whose strong flow here freshened the waters of the Caribbean. The slavers saw many crocodiles, and these could only have been the American crocodile, the same species that ranges northward into southern Florida. John Sparke the younger, who kept the journal of the voyage, had no hesitancy in ascribing to this New World reptile the same deceptive character that had long been imputed to the Nile crocodile:

> His nature is ever when hee would have his prey, to cry and sobbe like a Christian body, to provoke them to come to him, and then hee snatcheth at them, and thereupon came this proverbe that is applied unto women when they weepe, Lachrymae Crocodili, the meaning whereof is, that as the Crocodile when hee crieth, goeth then about most to deceive, so doeth a woman most commonly when she weepeth.

John Swan, in *Speculum Mundi* (1635), had this to say: ". . . the crocodile, when he hath devoured a man and eaten up all but the head, will sit and weep over it as if he expressed a great portion of sorrow for his cruel feast, but it is nothing so, for when he weeps it is because his hungrie paunch wants such another prey." This was an iconoclastic view for its day; general opinion held that a crocodile, having once eaten human flesh, remained forever inconsolable even though likely to take another victim when opportunity arose. What is gained by a repetition of such absurd and nearly vanished fables? Just this: the old beliefs warn of man's deep-seated tendency to interpret an animal's behavior in terms of his own. Some legends may have become moribund, but the tendency to anthropomorphize has not. In children's books, in newspaper articles, in popular magazines from the primmest to the most sensational, on television and in the motion pictures, animal activities are customarily portrayed as though they resulted from human emotions, human forethought, human freedom to select between alternative courses of action. It is easy to speak of a "bloodthirsty" weasel, a "sly" fox, a "courageous" bird defending its nest against a "malevolent" serpent, a "cowardly" jackal or hyena, a paroquet "mourning" its dead mate, an "enraged" crocodile. This approach is sterile of scientific results. The behavior of an animal is in greatest part stereotyped. When we come to discuss such topics as alligator courtship, nesting, and feeding habits, or attacks on man, we must remember that a crocodilian acts instinctively in an almost mechanical response to environmental stimuli and to the demands of its own internal rhythms.

2 OUR LEGACY
OF CROCODILIAN LEGENDS

IN THE PRECEDING chapter, a quick look was taken at a scattering of myths and legends, primarily to reveal their diversity. The complexity of crocodilian biology was suggested, also. Now we may trace in some detail the growth and spread of a dozen or so fallacies relating to the American alligator. Some of these fallacies are still thriving, some are vanishing, and some are gone; but taken together they show how easily a misconception, of folk or individual origin, can come to modify the technical literature.

The alligator first came to the notice of European and American writers in the days when the Nile crocodile was still a fabled reptile. At that time the name "alligator" was regarded as a mere vulgarism (it was a backwoods Anglicization of the Spanish *el lagarto,* meaning "the lizard"); the American species was held by more cultured people to be a crocodile, upon which could be fastened the fables originally inspired by the Nilotic species. Baron Lahontan wrote in 1703, "The crocodiles of the Mississippi are exactly the same as those of the Nile and other places." William Byrd, writing of the American alligator in South Carolina around 1728, said the reptile was "a smaller kind of crocodile, being the same shape exactly, only the crocodile of the Nile is twice as long." A 1776 history of North America phrased the situation this way: "Some of the rivers breed a kind of crocodile that differs but little from those of the Nile." And from Alexander Hewatt, 1799: "The alligator [is] probably a species of crocodile."

Thomas Ashe, who supposedly navigated the Mississippi River in 1806, had evidently heard about the sobbing attributed to the Nile crocodile. He therefore wrote, "I was started up by the most lamentable cries that ever assailed the human ear . . . [The cries] expressed such a variety and number of persons afflicted with the deepest grief. . . . At times the cries sank into the feeble plaints of expiring infancy, and again . . . rose into the full and melancholy swell of an adult tortured by fiends. . . . The lamentations, turn by turn, touched every string capable to vibrate excess of misery . . . [I heard] sobs, sighs, and tears, and moans of inexpressible anguish and length." After much more in this same vein, Ashe described his discovery of the wailers: "They were a host of alligators."

The myth of the sobbing crocodilian did not persist long into the nineteenth century; but its repetition, by Ashe and others of his ilk, gave impetus to the practice of describing alligator activities in terms of ancient, Old World beliefs. We shall hear more of Ashe later. Let us turn now to William Bartram, the writer-naturalist who rambled about the southeastern United States from 1773 to 1777. He believed the American reptile to be a crocodile, "alligator being the country name." So feeling, he had no hesitancy in transferring to the alligator many of the old legends about the Nile crocodile, legends widely known and accepted by literate people in his day. The Nilotic reptile was supposed to lay an enormous number of eggs, and these were said to be deposited in layers or tiers within the nest. And so in his journal, Bartram provided this description of an alligator's nest:

> The nests . . . are of the form of an obtuse cone, four feet high and four or five feet in diameter at their bases; they are constructed with mud, grass, and herbage: at first they lay a floor of this kind of tempered mortar on the ground, upon which they deposit a layer of eggs, and upon this a stratum of mortar seven or eight inches in thickness, and then another layer of eggs, and in this manner one stratum upon another, nearly to the top: I believe they commonly lay from one hundred to two hundred eggs in a nest: these are hatched I suppose by the heat of the sun, and perhaps the vegetable substances mixed with the earth, being acted upon by the sun, may cause a small degree of fermentation, and so increase the heat in those hillocks.

Out of fairness to Bartram it should be emphasized that his comments on the number of eggs, and on their incubation, were identified by him as being speculative. He also realized that the alligator builds a nest that is well elevated above the level of the ground.

Bartram's journal was published in 1791. The 1808 work of Thomas Ashe had this to say about the alligator's reproductive habits:

> . . . their nests . . . are in the form of an obtuse cone, about four feet high, and from four to five feet in diameter at their bases. They are constructed with a sort of mortar, blended with grass and herbage. First they lay a floor of this composition, on which they deposit a layer of eggs; and upon this a stratum of mortar, seven or eight inches thick, then another layer of eggs; and in this manner one stratum upon another nearly to the top of the nest. They lay from one hundred to two hundred eggs in a nest. These are hatched by the heat of the sun, assisted by the fermentations of the vegetable mortar.

Thus Ashe furthered the legend of the many-tiered nest, and elevated Bartram's speculations to the status of fact. Unlike Ashe, John Lee Wil-

liams at least acknowledged a literary indebtedness to Bartram. In an 1837 account of Florida, Williams said this of the alligator:

> Their nests are truly described by Bartram. . . . Their eggs are usually laid in five or seven tiers, one above another, with layers of green vegetables and mud between each; the whole is then plastered over with mud, and forms a cone of four feet high, and as many in thickness. The heat of the fermenting vegetables and the sun's rays hatch the eggs.

Just as ignorant people today have a superstitious dread of the number 13, so did even the better educated people of Williams's day regard certain numbers as "better" or "more fundamental" than others. The numbers 5 and 7 were regarded as especially significant, and to pervade the natural world; the superstition no doubt accounts for Williams's decision that alligator eggs were laid in "five or seven tiers." General George McCall, in an 1886 account of experiences at Tampa, Florida, during the Seminole Wars, also claimed to have first-hand knowledge of an alligator's nest and its contents: "I removed the top which was composed of bulrushes and

Figure 8. A typical alligator nest is less than a yard high (at left). The eggs are clustered within the nest (above). [*Ross Allen's Reptile Institute*]

mud to the height of four feet. Throwing off layer after layer, I found between each two a layer of eggs." Bartram's misinformation, after various other repetitions, was eventually embalmed for posterity in an 1893 bulletin of the U. S. Fish Commission: "The maternal alligator . . . builds a small mound. The foundation of the mound is mud and grass, and on this she lays some eggs. She covers the deposit with another stratum of grass and mud upon which she deposits some more eggs. Thus she proceeds until she has laid one hundred to two hundred eggs." The author of this version, Hugh M. Smith, was an outstanding biologist but in this case too credulous. His stature was such that the author of a 1931 bulletin, issued by the Louisiana Conservation Department, had no hesitancy in declaring, "She carries the . . . marsh vegetation in her mouth and piles it into a rounded heap. . . . This first layer completed, the first eggs are laid, and then grass is added and more eggs laid [etc.]."

By the middle 1930s it was generally evident that alligators actually lay about 30 to 50 eggs, occasionally a few more or less; that a nest is usually under a yard high; and that the supposedly tiered structure of the nest is mere fantasy, the eggs being deposited in a cluster (Fig. 8).

However, the aforesaid 1935 account of the alligator's life history, and later works, have continued to maintain the fiction that the eggs are "incubated" by the sun and the heat of the decaying vegetation. Chicken eggs are incubated, it is true; but a chicken maintains its body temperature at a level that would be fatal to an alligator. Even a large alligator cannot long withstand a body temperature of 38 degrees Centigrade (about 100 degrees Fahrenheit), and will not voluntarily accept a body temperature above 35 degrees Centigrade (95 degrees Fahrenheit). It is most unlikely that the tiny embryo should be substantially more heat-hardy than the adult. Damp, rotting plant material can indeed generate heat, but the alligator's problem is to minimize this effect, not encourage it; for during the breeding season, in most parts of the alligator's range, air temperatures almost daily exceed the maximum body temperature that would be accepted by the adult. It is perhaps significant that, at an actual temperature of 35 degrees Centigrade, the interior of an alligator's nest will feel quite warm to the human hand; in the absence of a thermometer, the temperature within the nest could easily be overestimated.

It is amusing to see, wholly within the twentieth century, the growth of a new legend about the alligator's nest: that the female carries the nesting material in her mouth. This fiction was begun unwittingly by Albert M. Reese, a competent and objective student of the alligator. He was the first worker to report accurately on the size and interior construction of the alligator's nest, as well as on the number and arrangement of eggs therein. He never witnessed nest-building, but guessed that the nesting female alligator "proceeds to collect, probably biting it off with her teeth, a great mass of whatever vegetation happens to be abundant. . . . This mass of flags or of marsh grass is piled into a conical or rounded heap. . . ." This speculation, offered by Reese in 1907, was repeated by him, still as speculation, in a 1915 book. Later workers sometimes accepted his unfortunate guess as an established fact. It was added to the Bartramian fallacies by the aforesaid 1931 booklet. McIlhenny in 1935 freely enlarged upon Reese's unfortunate surmise:

> After the eggs are laid . . . they are covered by the alligator's taking the loose material needed for covering them in its mouth and dropping it on top of the eggs. . . . When I got near the [nesting] spot, she was making considerable noise biting off the growth. . . . When I

Figure 9. A female alligator uses her body and hind feet to build a nest. In the absence of leaf litter, she builds of sand. [Ross Allen's Reptile Institute]

first saw her at work she was scooping up, from the outside edges of her trash pile, in her mouth, twigs and leaves, and holding them firmly, would [drop] her burden on top of the mound. . . . She would then go forward and get another mouthful . . . four Alder trees [up to] three inches in diameter, had been broken off. [The alligator] tore off the limbs by crushing them in her jaws and with violent shakes of her head. After the limbs were stripped off, the trunks were carried by mouth to the side of the clearing and discarded. Occasionally she would . . . grasp in her jaws a mouthful of whatever the standing growth might be. . . ."

Actually, the female alligator scrapes dirt and ground debris together by lateral movements of body and tail. If debris is lacking, as might be the case in a pen, she scrapes dirt alone. She shapes the nesting mound by crawling over it, by crawling around it and pushing against it with her flanks, and by scraping and pushing the material with a hind foot (Fig. 9).

The hind foot is also used to scoop out the cavity in the top of the mound, to manipulate and arrange the eggs as they are being deposited, and to cover the eggs at the conclusion of the operation. The mouth is not used to gather nesting material or to shape it.

According to McIlhenny.

> the old alligator crawls over the nest and evacuates a considerable amount of water on top of the nest so as to keep the nest-material wet and the eggs damp. This wetting down is done with great regularity each day or night during periods of drought. . . . Many times in the following days I visited the nest [and] on the days when it did not rain, the old alligator would crawl over the top of the nest and liberally wet it by voiding water through her vent in order to keep the nest-material and the eggs moist. On very hot, dry days this wetting was done twice a day.

It is widely believed, both by rustics and authors, that the female alligator urinates on her nest to keep the eggs moist. The misconception would not be so widespread if every writer on alligators knew that these reptiles have no urinary bladder; and that, like barnyard chickens, they excrete much of their nitrogenous wastes as uric acid in a minimum of water. Actually, the female alligator makes many trips between her nest and the water. Each time she returns to the nest, water pours off her as she emerges, but some is retained a little longer, especially in numerous small concavities of the dorsal armor. Trips between nest and water may be more frequent in hot, dry weather, and possibly function at times to prevent desiccation of the nest's material; but these are mere speculations.

In several species of crocodilians, a soggy path is formed by the movements of the dripping female between the water and the nest. Aelian's *De Animalium Natura*, written early in the third century, observed that the Nile crocodile fills his mouth with water, then spews it to make the path slippery for a prospective victim. In 1524 Desiderius Erasmus repeated the story. Fortunately it died out before it was transferred *in toto* to the American alligator. However, its probable influence can still be detected. It was amusing to see, in the "outdoors" column of a 1968 newspaper, the statement, "Should the nest dry out, mama [alligator] spews a mouthful of water on it."

In the modern literature relating to the life history of the American alligator, a good many fallacies can be traced to Bartram. Within a few years of its publication in Philadelphia, Bartram's narrative had become famous in Europe. The writings of Coleridge and Wordsworth were influenced by it. In later years Carlyle wrote to Emerson about it: "Do you know Bartram's 'Travels'? Treats of Florida chiefly, has a wonderful kind of floundering eloquence in it; and has grown immeasureably old. All American libraries ought to provide themselves with that kind of book; and keep them as a future *biblical* article." Bartram's comments were indeed taken to have scriptural authority. They were passed from one author to the next, sometimes credited to Bartram but other times offered as personal experience. We may follow a few more Bartramian myths. Bartram is writing of alligators, which he took to be crocodiles, in Florida:

> Behold his rushing forth from the flags and reeds. His enormous body swells. His plaited tail brandished high, floats upon the lake. The waters like a cataract descend from his opening jaws. Clouds of smoke issue from his dilated nostrils. The earth trembles with his thunder. . . . I was attacked on all sides, several [alligators] endeavoring to overset the canoe . . . two very large ones attacked me closely . . . roaring terribly and belching floods of water over me.

Bartram's imaginative approach is especially well revealed by the following passage. He had made camp at nightfall by a lagoon where fishes and alligators lived.

> I may say hundreds of thousands of [fishes] were caught and swallowed by the devouring alligators . . . the alligators were in such incredible numbers, and so close together from shore to shore, that it would have been easy to have walked across on their heads, had the animals been harmless. . . . The horrid noise of their closing jaws, their plunging amidst the broken banks of fish, and rising with their prey some feet upright above the water, the floods of water and blood rushing out of their mouths, and the clouds of vapor issuing from their wide nostrils, were truly frightful. This scene continued at intervals during the night.

As this episode took place by night, the scientist must ask by what light it was observed in such exciting detail. The report must have been constructed in large part from the imaginative interpretation of night sounds.

To continue with Bartram's story:

. . . a huge alligator rushed out of the reeds, and with a tremendous roar, came up, darted as swift as an arrow under my boat, emerging upright on my lea [*sic*] quarter, with open jaws, and belching water and smoke that fell upon me like rain in a hurricane; I laid soundly about his head with my club and beat him off. . . . [Another] monster came up with the usual roar and menaces, and . . . I could distinctly see a young brood of alligators, to the number of one hundred or more, following after her in a long train. They kept close together in a column without straggling off to one side or the other; the young appeared to be of an equal size, about fifteen inches in length. . . . [Alligator] nests being so great a curiosity to me, I was determined at all events . . . to land and examine them.

Bartram next originates the myth of the many-tiered alligator nest, and then continues,

. . . certain it is that the young are not left to shift for themselves; having had frequent opportunities of seeing the female alligator, leading about the shores her train of young ones, just like a hen does her brood of chickens; and she is equally assiduous and courageous in defending the young, which are under her care, and providing for their subsistence. . . . I believe but few of the brood live to the years of full growth and magnitude, as the old feed on the young as long

Figure 10. When the alligator bellows, there is no emanation from its mouth or nostrils, and no eversion of the throat glands. The pupil of the eye seems to dilate. [Ross Allen's Reptile Institute]

as they can make prey of them. . . . Only the upper jaw moves, which they raise almost perpendicular, so as to form a straight angle with the lower one . . . he now swells himself by drawing in wind and water through his mouth, which causes a loud sonorous rattling in his throat for near a minute, but it is immediately forced out again through his mouth and nostrils, with a loud noise, brandishing his tail in the air, and the vapour ascending from his nostrils like smoke.

In the above few sentences, abstracted from ten pages of highly sensational material, Bartram created a whole new mythology. At no time in reality is there any visible emanation from the alligator's nostrils, or from glands that open to the surface on the under side of the lower jaw (Fig. 10); and even the comparatively credulous readers of Bartram's day were not much taken with his hint that the alligator was a sort of dragon, spewing clouds of smoke from dilated nostrils. (The nostril of an alligator is valvular, closing to a slit or opening to a near circle. In a very large specimen, the circle is about ½ inch in diameter.) Priscilla Wakefield, the first woman to write about the alligator, was one of the few authors to follow Bartram even in having this reptile snorting. In her 1806 account of a visit to St. Augustine, Florida, she claimed to have been rescued by a heroic Indian who, armed with mere club and tomahawk, killed an 18-foot alligator that attacked her as she sat on a rock. The large rock overhung the water, and the reptile lurked beneath it. "In one dreadful moment he had darted out of the water, opened his terrific jaw, spouted both wind and water out of his nostrils." Adam Hodgson, in an 1824 description of his trip to America, paraphrased Bartram with due credit, or blame. "Bartram . . . gives the following amusing account, which, although it partakes a little of the mock-heroic, I cannot forbear copying: '. . . two very large [alligators] attacked me closely . . . roaring terribly, and belching floods of water over me.' Note; this account appears to partake a little of the marvellous." Hodgson was remarkably astute. Not so Charles Cist, 1846: "In such places [sand bars] will they bask and blow off, with a loud noise, the inflated air and water, that would seem to expand within them as if confined in an iron pipe." After Cist, writers abandoned the Bartramian fancy of the alligator that spouted vapor, water, or smoke.

However, a large part of Bartram's farrago was seized upon by later writers, and is still with us. Thomas Ashe, he of the sobbing alligators, in

his account of an 1806 trip on the Mississippi, claimed to have killed one
of these reptiles.

> I heard . . . cries issuing from several voices in deep distress . . . so
> plaintive that they could not but reach the heart. The dawn disclosed
> the cause of this lamentation which never ceased throughout the night.
> On going on shore, I found the alligator I had killed attended by six-
> teen or seventeen young ones, who were solicitously engaged about
> the dead body, running over it and around it in great agitation, and
> whining and moaning, because they discovered it without animation
> and destitute of all symptoms of life. . . . The mother, for it seems
> it was a female we killed, is nineteen feet in length. . . . The upper
> jaw only moves.

Ashe next supplied the Bartramian description of an alligator's nest, 4 feet
high, many-tiered, with 100 to 200 eggs. He then continued,

> [The female alligator] takes her brood under her care, and leads them
> about the shores as a hen does her chickens, and is equally courageous
> in defending them in time of danger. When she lies basking on the
> warm banks with her brood around her, the young ones may be heard
> whining and crying like young infants. The old feed on the young
> alligators till they get so large that they cannot make a prey of them;
> so that fortunately, but few of the brood survive the age of a year.

From Henry Ker, 1816: "The younger ones are often destroyed by the cata-
mount . . . many are likewise devoured by the larger alligators, and thus
nature has provided a way to destroy these dangerous beasts, and keep their
number down, which would otherwise render the country uninhabitable."
Mrs. F. E. M. Trollope, the second woman to write about alligators, out-
did Bartram in an 1832 description of the American settlers. She related
how an alligator entered a cabin at night and ate three children while the
rest of the family slept; awakened by a "faint cry," the husband "beheld
relics of three of his children scattered over the floor, and an enormous
crocodile with several of her young ones around her, occupied in devouring the remnants of their horrid meal." The husband slipped out a window
to get help; when he returned, he found the reptile had eaten his wife and
two more children. ". . . the hut had been constructed close to the mouth
of a large hole, almost a cavern, where the monster had hatched her hateful brood." Timothy Flint, describing the Mississippi Valley in 1832, said

of young alligators, "When they are hatched, the turkey buzzards and the parents are said alike to prey upon them." In 1837 John Lee Williams remarked, "But it is in his wallow . . . that the alligator is quite at home, surrounded by a hundred young imps of ugliness, all barking like young puppies, and constantly pursued by the male for food." After repeating Bartram's description of an alligator nest, Williams continued, ". . . the young whelps, about six inches long, crawl, in succession, from a hole near the top of the nest, and instinctively seek their mother in some neighboring wallow." J. S. Buckingham, visiting the Augusta, Georgia, area about 1840, described alligators in the Savannah River.

> It is said that they devour and feed upon their own offspring; and it is from this that many account for their not increasing very much; since in their retreats, or nests, called alligator-holes, as large a brood as a hundred are seen at a time; but they do not come to maturity, as the numbers remain nearly stationary through a series of years, or diminish rather than increase.

Bartram's fable, about the mother alligator who leads her brood around the lake, and watches over them like a mother hen over chicks, has survived into modern times. The 1935 version of it, in McIlhenny's account of the alligator's life history, ran as follows:

> . . . the young . . . feed sparingly . . . in the limited area in which their mother keeps them. I have seen mother alligators catch large fish, large snakes, and turtles in their jaws and crush them to a pulp, holding them at the surface of the water between their jaws, so that the young could gather bits of food from the crushed flesh.

This work described the purported investigation of an alligator nest in which the eggs had just hatched. The guardian female was roped and tied to a tree. The babies were examined and put back in the nest.

> . . . after freeing the mother and giving her a few pieces of raw meat, which she readily took, I left the nest . . . and saw that the old alligator was crawling around the nest making low grunts, sounding very much like a large pig, and the young could be heard answering. [The babies] ran in a most lively way to the mother. . . . Her little ones took to the water alongside of her and she slowly backed out of sight into the rushes with them on each side and following.

Figure 11. Captive alligators may struggle over food. The circumstance does not mean that one alligator would attack another in nature, however. [Ross Allen's Reptile Institute]

In reality an alligator inherits its pattern of actions, just as it inherits its anatomical structure. A given action, like an anatomical organ, has evolved because it is favorable to the success and survival of the species; it is absurd to think that an alligator on the one hand has evolved a pattern of action involving intensive care of the young and on the other hand a pattern involving predation upon these same young. Two alligators of roughly comparable size will struggle with each other over food. In captivity, where dozens of equal-sized alligators are crowded into a small pen, several might be injured in a struggle over food (Fig. 11). But in both captivity and in the wild, the smaller alligators—those from hatchling size up to about four feet long—are tolerated by adults and in fact are generally ignored by them (Fig. 12).

It seems customary (following Bartram, Ashe, and others) to refer to the alligator as "greedy" or "voracious"; but as shown in a later chapter, the food intake of this reptile is astonishingly small. In captivity, an

Figure 12. Small alligators, dispersing immediately after hatching, rest briefly on the nose and tail of an adult male. The hatchlings are perfectly safe. [Ross Allen's Reptile Institute]

alligator becomes accustomed to seizing chunks of meat or dead fish thrown to it, and so will bite down hastily on almost anything that is tossed into the water of its pen. This often-witnessed occurrence has obscured the fact that the alligator is remarkably discriminating in its feeding. In Florida the alligator will discriminate between two species of garfish, eating one and avoiding the other. It will distinguish between a harmless water snake and a superficially similar, but venomous, cottonmouth moccasin; and will utilize different techniques when preying upon these two serpents. An alligator, foraging on the bottom of a body of water, will distinguish a tiny bit of water-soaked food from all the surrounding pebbles, silt, algae, twigs, dead leaves, and other bottom debris. How it does so is material for another chapter; suffice it at this point to say that in the wild a hatchling alligator is in no danger of being mistaken for a food item by its male parent or any other adult of its species. Even under the abnormal conditions of captivity, it is most unusual for an alligator actually to eat another of its kind. In captivity or the wild, one alligator will sometimes eat the rotting carcass of a smaller alligator, but such a carcass is probably recognized only as a chunk of rotting meat.

Care of baby alligators by their mother is a subject of great importance. Some major differences between reptile and mammal are those involved with care of the young. A mammal has flexible lips, a character correlated with suckling; the female has milk glands, nurses her young, and (in the case of many carnivores) brings them meat after they are weaned. In contrast, a reptile has comparatively inflexible lips; the female has no milk glands; the young do not nurse, receive little or no parental care, and are hatched (or born, in the case of some lizards and snakes) fully capable of foraging for themselves. There is no reliable evidence that the female alligator is mammal-like in caring for the young after they have hatched. She does guard the nest, under normal circumstances. (Guarding of the nest is not an unusual activity among reptiles; it is carried on by some snakes and many lizards.) In spite of assertions to the contrary, there is no evidence that the female opens the nest in any fashion. The young wriggle out of the nest without help, and make their own way to water. As declared by a manuscript in the files of the U. S. Biological Survey (predecessor of the Fish and Wildlife Service), "The prevailing idea that the mother destroys the nest to let the young escape is erroneous. I have seen dozens of nests from which the young had escaped and the small hole in the top was the only opening." The female alligator is likely to be present when the young ones emerge, and chance observation of the group at this time, colored by Bartramian legends, might lead to the assumption that the hatchlings were remaining under their mother's care. A similar assumption might be derived from the simultaneous disappearance of an adult and some young upon the approach of an observer. In Florida and Georgia, the brood rapidly disperses upon reaching water. It is possible that in the coldest parts of the alligator's range the last broods to emerge do not immediately disperse, but instead make their way to water (perhaps by chance to a nearby "'gator hole," not necessarily the mother's), remaining more or less as a group over the winter and dispersing the following spring. This has not been demonstrated, however. As an adult alligator, perhaps because of satiety, occasionally lies for hours with some large item of food in its mouth, and as the presence of a hatchling is tolerated by an adult, it is possible that someone really did see one or two small juveniles trying to feed from a crushed carcass held by a larger alligator. But it should be noted that in the wild the observer could not be sure that the adult was a female, much less the mother of the young; nor could the fortuitous nature of the association be disavowed. It is also possible that someone was impressed by the way in which an adult alligator is automatically attracted to the "distress call" of the young, and charges in its direction. This action could be misinterpreted as maternal care (or at least parental care if the observer did not care to guess at the sex of the adult), but actually any adult, male or female, will react to the call of any hatchling or juvenile. The adults can also be made to react to an imitation of the distress call, given by the human voice.

3 CROCODILIAN BIOLOGY VS. HUMAN PSYCHOLOGY

WE HAVE NOT YET reviewed all the Bartramian legends. In a small alligator, no tooth stands out as being conspicuously enlarged. In a large one the fourth tooth of the lower jaw is somewhat enlarged, and the fourth of the upper jaw even more so. These

Figure 13. In the adult alligator, several pairs of teeth are conspicuously larger than all the others. [Ross Allen's Reptile Institute]

fourth teeth, upper and lower, are somewhat reminiscent of mammalian canines in their enlargement and anterior position. But unlike any mammal, the adult alligator has yet another enlarged, canine-like tooth farther back in the tooth row (Fig. 13). This is the eighth of the upper jaw, and it is the largest of all. (The eighth of the lower jaw is very small.) The teeth are stained to some degree in nature, but when large ones are kept as curios they are usually polished to ivory whiteness. Bartram described this dentition as follows: ". . . just under the nostrils, are two very large, thick strong teeth or tusks [having] the shape of a cone, these are white as the finest polished ivory." Thomas Ashe, in 1808, describing a large alligator he claimed to have killed, said, "The jaws . . . are furnished with two large conical tusks as white as ivory." Writer after writer subsequently mentioned the alligator's "ivory tusks," and so revealed a probable familiarity with Bartram's famous account.

The modern literature has not been importantly affected by Bartram's description of alligator "tusks," but it still feels the impact of various myths that Bartram transferred from the Nile crocodile to the American reptile. As already noted, in Bartram's time there was scarcely any doubt about the identity of the American alligator: it was really the Nile crocodile, or essentially so; and it should therefore behave in the fashion outlined by the writers of Classical antiquity. One ancient myth, still credenced in Bartram's day, averred that the Nile crocodile uses its tail to knock prey into its waiting jaws. Accordingly, Bartram claimed that while he was scaling fishes he saw "a very large alligator, moving slowly towards me. I instantly stepped back, when, with a sweep of his tail, he brushed off several of my fish." From Timothy Flint, 1832, on alligators: "They strike with their tails, coiled into a section of a circle, and this blow has great power. The animal stricken is by the same blow propelled toward their mouth to be devoured. . . . They have large, ivory teeth." John Lee Williams, 1837, said, "The female [defending her brood from the devouring male] then adds rage to her natural deformity and often kills her whelps by the strokes of her tail, while fighting in their defence." From J. H. Hinton, 1846: "They strike with their tails coiled into the section of a circle; this blow has great power, and the animal stricken is, by the same blow, propelled toward their mouth to be devoured. . . . They have large ivory teeth."

From E. A. McIlhenny, 1935: "I have seen [alligators] lie in wait for fish . . . they wait until a school of fish . . . comes between their tail and the bank, when with a quick sweep of the tail some of the fish may be thrown onto the bank." This comment, like several others proffered by McIlhenny, seems to reflect the influence of J. J. Audubon, who in 1827 presented his own version of the alligator's life history in Louisiana. Audubon wrote, "When alligators are fishing, the flapping of their tails about the water may be heard at half a mile. . . . The alligators thrash them and devour them [the fishes]. . . . You plainly see the tails of the alligators moving to and fro, splashing, and now and then, when missing a fish, throwing it up into the air."

McIlhenny managed to retain the old myth even though he knew that prey was seized directly by the alligator's jaws. He continued,

> In feeding, alligators make no attempt to kill their prey with their tails. . . . They use their powerful tails only when their intended prey is in such a position that it cannot be readily grasped with its jaws. It then strikes at its intended victim with its tail. As the tail sweeps in an arch [sic] towards the head, the head is thrown in the same direction. Thus, if the victim is struck with the tail, it will be swept into grabbing distance of the jaws.

According to the original myth, the prey that was batted into the crocodile's mouth was often a person; and Raymond L. Ditmars, popularizing North American reptiles in a series of books from 1907 to 1936, did not omit the exciting detail when he applied the myth to the alligator: ". . . the reptile bends its entire body, in bowlike fashion, reaching sideways at an enemy, this motion bringing the tail around toward the head with force enough to knock a man from his feet and sweep him in the direction of the infuriated brute's crushing powers." The myth of alligator defense by tail slap was mentioned in Chapter 1. As noted there, the alligator defends itself with its jaws; however the tail may slap about, it delivers no aimed blow. Nor does the American alligator secure food with its tail. In the water, an alligator will often take prey by a short, lateral snap of the jaws; but if the tail is deliberately moved during this predation, it is only to compensate for the abrupt movement, or otherwise to alter the reptile's position in the water.

Bartram was also parroting older legends about the Nile crocodile when he said that the alligator's upper jaw was hinged and lifted perpendicularly to the lower jaw. The ramifications of this story, after its application to the American alligator, show how folk fallacies can, with sufficient uncritical repetition, acquire an unmerited air of authenticity. Occasionally, the Nile crocodile may rest with jaws somewhat agape even when the observer is at a considerable distance. The alligator hardly ever does this. Once in a while a large alligator, resting undisturbed and with closed jaws, becomes aware that someone or something is approaching; and the reptile then opens its mouth. This conspicuous movement, which discloses the huge teeth, may function to discourage an enemy from further approach; so-called warning behavior (in some cases mere bluff), involving the opening of the mouth at the approach of an intruder, is widespread in other reptile groups, including snakes, lizards, and turtles (Fig. 14). The few alligators seen to rest open-mouthed may have sensed the presence of an intruder. But early writers, holding the alligator to be a crocodile, blandly imputed to it the habit of resting customarily with the jaws agape. For example, Francis Baily, visiting Louisiana around 1796, mentioned "enormous alligators which we saw basking in the sun on logs near the shore. Here they would expose themselves, lying with their monstrous jaws wide open, and apparently asleep." An observation made between 1797 and 1811, quoted by John Bernard, 1887:

> Once . . . through a telescope, I surveyed [an alligator] who was enjoying himself in a manner truly Oriental, stretched upon a couch of the downiest mud, . . . his jaws extended to receive all chance contributions of flies and insects. . . . The amusement, for instance, of extending his jaws until his tongue was spread like a blister with

Figure 14. *Reptiles often automatically confront an enemy with opened mouth. Shown are a hog-nosed snake (above), a Cuban giant anole (at right) and an alligator snapping-turtle (below).* [Tod Swalm and Ross' Allen's Reptile Institute]

Spanish flies and then suddenly dropping the gates upon the innocents, was a villainy that nothing could excuse.

And this from Thomas Ashe, 1806: "They open their mouths while they lay basking in the sun, on the banks of rivers and creeks, and when filled with all manner of insects, they suddenly let fall their upper jaw with surprising noise, and thus secure their prey." Ashe's reference to a "surprising noise" stemmed from remarks of Bartram: ". . . their jaws clap together, re-echoing through the deep surrounding forests. . . . They struck their jaws together so close to my ears, as almost to stun me . . . when they clap their jaws together it causes a surprising noise." Henry Ker, describing his American travels in 1816, reported: "As they lie thus basking in the sun, they throw open their upper jaw, which forms a right angle with the lower one; in this manner they lie as if they were lifeless until a sufficient quantity of insects, bugs, and the like are collected within their peaceful jaws; then suddenly dropping the jaw, they enclose their prey and swallow them whole."

From Charles Cist, 1846: ". . . they are in the height of their glory, stretched out upon the sand-bar, in the meridian sun, when the summer heat pours down. . . . When thus disposed of, and after the first nap is taken, they amuse themselves with opening their huge jaws to their widest extent, upon the inside of which instinctively settle thousands of mosquitoes and other noxious insects that infest the abode of the alligator. When the inside of the mouth is thus covered, the reptile brings his jaws together with inconceivable velocity, gives a gulp or two, and again sets his formidable trap for this small game." F. W. True, in an 1884 account of United States fisheries, said,

> It would appear that they [alligators] are also expert fly-catchers. The quaint allusion of Exquemelin [in 1684] to this subject is too interesting to be omitted. 'The *Caymanes*,' he says, 'are ordinarily busied in hunting and catching flies, which they eagerly devour . . .' The existence of this habit, I have recently been informed, has been frequently confirmed in Louisiana by reliable observers.

In 1930 Francis Harper wrote, "Lone Thrift, an elderly hunter of [Okefinokee Swamp] astounded me by telling with circumstantial detail, out of his own experience, how [the alligator] opens its mouth while resting upon a log . . . until its tongue becomes covered with mosquitoes,

Figure 15. *The alligator normally rests with jaws closed (above);
but when an enemy approaches, it opens the mouth (below).*
[Bruce Mozert]

whereupon it brings its jaws together with a resounding smack and so makes an end, if not a meal, of the buzzing pests." Unfortunately, Harper continued, "Scoff at the tale? Far from it. Long association with the men of the Okefinokee engenders faith in their words." Actually, residence in Okefinokee may lend a certain glamour to a backwoods "Cracker," but it lends no particular veracity to his stories. He will also relate in circumstantial detail how he was chased by a hoop-snake, which took its tail in its mouth and rolled at him, missing him and imbedding its venomous tail-spine in a tree, which promptly dropped all its leaves. Without a trace of guile he will tell how he saw a tie-snake, 18 feet 4½ inches long, tie his grandfather to a tree and whip the old man almost to death, occasionally sticking its tail up the oldster's nose and whipping him some more if this act evoked a sneeze. He will further tell how he struck a joint-snake with a hoe handle, and watched its scattered fragments reassemble and crawl away; how a ground dove called in the yard one morning, and someone in the house died that night; how crops must be planted, stock gelded, and hogs butchered only when the moon is "right"; how he watched a pilot-snake lead a rattlesnake to a cozy den for the winter; how one can make it rain by hanging a dead snake over a fence or a branch; how his cousin was bitten by a "skarpin" (a harmless lizard of the genus Eumeces) and nearly died. The southern backwoodsman believes that the ruby-throated hummingbird and the Amphiuma salamander are highly venomous; that the dragonfly (which he calls a "snake-doctor") will tend injured snakes, and will "sew up your ears." He is sure that "if'n a mudpuppy barks six times at you, you'll die 'fore sundown." His biological naiveté is incredible. He will insist that the garfish is a "cross" between a male alligator and a female cottonmouth moccasin; and that the reciprocal cross, one involving a male moccasin and a female alligator, will produce a snapping-turtle. With particular reference to crocodilians, Okefinokee dwellers believe in the local existence of two species. In one of these the eyes shine reddish, and the upper jaw is "the onliest one that moves"; the other species, admitted to be an alligator, is said to have yellowish or greenish eye-shine and a movable lower jaw!

I have collected reptiles all over the backwoods of Georgia (in which state I was born and raised), and have heard the same tiresome yarns—the fly-catching alligator, the narrow escape from the hoop-snake, the tie-snake episode, the ground dove whose call presaged a death, and so on

Figure 16. An alligator lies in a Florida spring-run, and takes its body temperature chiefly from the water. The reptile lies in the sun, but perhaps only coincidentally so. [Dick Morris]

—related over and over again, usually as personal observation. Most of the stories have spread throughout the Southeast if not beyond; and in this spread they have retained a remarkably rigid structure, so that one can hear the same folktales in widely separated areas.

The myth of the open-mouthed alligator may be followed a bit further. From McIlhenny's 1935 book:

> While taking sunbaths on the bank, it is usual for alligators to hold their mouths partly open. I have never in all my experience seen them snap their jaws together at such times, although flies and mosquitoes swarm around them. I believe the reason they open their mouths is to let the leeches and small water lice which frequently attach themselves inside of their mouths along the tongue to have a chance to dry out in the hot sunlight, which perhaps would rid them of these pests.

Karl P. Schmidt, who greatly advanced our knowledge of crocodilians through his laboratory examination of skins and skulls preserved in museum collections, wrote in 1944, "All crocodilians sun themselves on river banks, often lying with their jaws wide open. This habit has been explained as a means of drying up the leeches with which their mouths are usually infested." Schmidt's comments have been widely quoted or paraphrased.

Now for the facts. It is true that, in captivity, almost any crocodilian may lie in the sun; but the circumstance might reflect only an absence of shade, or the exposure of the penned reptile to cooler air or water temperature than it would voluntarily accept. A few of the crocodilians are restricted in nature to ponds, lakes, swamps, or marshes; as they do not frequent rivers, they do not sun on river banks, assuming that they sun at all. Sunning in nature, whether on river banks or elsewhere, may be widespread but has been reliably reported for only five species of crocodilians among the 23 species that exist today. And if a crocodilian is seen lying in the sun, might not this be happenstance? (See Fig. 16.) Need the sunlight have anything to do with the matter? Might not the sunniness of the "basking" spot simply reflect the circumstance that the crocodilian lies where locomotion and vision are not impeded by brush? In the tropics, to which all but a few crocodilians are confined, a reptile should usually be able to maintain its optimum body temperature without sunning; and in nature, apparent basking could have nothing to do with heat absorption. Perhaps an overheated crocodilian emerges from the water dripping wet, and automatically seeks a spot where it can be cooled by unimpeded wind currents which hasten evaporation. Again, perhaps insolation is involved with Vitamin D metabolism, or with the timing of the reproductive cycle. Other possibilities also come to mind. A selection among them can be made, and in a later chapter we shall do so; but in the meanwhile, nothing is gained by the continued assertion that all of the crocodilians, or any of them, are given to deliberate sunning.

As for the idea that any crocodilian will voluntarily lie for hours in the hot sun, I can do no better than quote from H. Hediger's 1942 book, *Wildtiere in Gefangenschaft*. Dr. Hediger stated (in translation from the German), "It is often believed that crocodiles grill themselves for hours in the burning tropical sun, and can stand any amount of sunshine. Yet, collectors who want to kill these animals without damaging them use the simple method of laying the captured crocodile out in the sun, where it

Figure 17. An American crocodile rests with closed jaws (at left); but when it senses the presence of an observer, it opens the jaws (at right), and may leave them open for hours. [George Bushman]

dies after a short time." In 1934 Hediger reported the death of an estuarine crocodile after only two hours exposure to direct sun; and in 1939 H. Böker found a small American crocodile to be killed by 25 minutes exposure to strong sunlight. The American alligator is less tolerant of high temperatures than is any crocodile. Also, the alligator will sunburn, will blister and "peel" along the back, if forced to remain over-long in the sun, even on a cool day when the ambient temperatures are tolerable by the reptile.

As for gaping, only two species of crocodilians have been reported to rest in the wild with the jaws somewhat agape at a time when the observer is presumably outside the reptile's radius of awareness. Even with these two—the Nile crocodile and the American crocodile—it is possible that the gaping reptile has actually sensed something disturbing, perhaps an odor or the vibration of a boat's engine, at a considerable distance (Fig. 17).

As for leeches, there is one casual and somewhat unsatisfactory reference to the presence of these parasites in the mouth of an emaciated and presumably ailing alligator. Otherwise, the occurrence of leeches in an alligator's mouth has merely been assumed, not demonstrated. Once again, a "fact" about the alligator's biology rests chiefly on a statement of Herodotus about the Nile crocodile. Herodotus claimed that as the Nile crocodile basked with open mouth, an unidentified bird would enter its mouth to pick off "blood-sucking insects." In 1898 John Anderson pointed out that Herodotus could have meant leeches, not mosquitos or flies. On this basis it has been assumed that the American alligator must often be attacked by leeches, and will sun itself, open-mouthed, to kill them! (Ironically, Herodotus's actual reference was almost surely to the tsetse fly, an African insect that does suck the blood of the Nile crocodile.)

On many occasions I have seen leeches on aquatic turtles, but never on an alligator. Perhaps the alligator is on rare occasions parasitized by leeches, but obviously any assertion to that effect should await actual proof. Leeches, attached to an aquatic turtle, have been noted to survive several days' drying when the host reptile is kept out of water; and so if any crocodilian is really attacked by leeches, the parasites could probably withstand desiccation longer than the host could withstand the high body temperature that would result from prolonged sunning. As for so-called water lice, this name is a vernacular one widely used in the southern United States and elsewhere for certain small, aquatic, parasitic crustaceans. In textbooks they are called fish lice, argulid branchiurans, or simply argulids. A few species of argulids have been found on tadpoles, and one on an aquatic salamander; but otherwise, argulids live on fishes of the fresh water and the sea. The actual discovery of argulids on a reptile would be of much biological interest, as would be their discovery on any organism that was not fully aquatic. It is not expected that such discoveries will be made.

An alligator, cruising in the water with uplifted head, occasionally will bang its jaws together at the approach of an intruder; and if cornered on land will sometimes interrupt its open-mouthed hissing with a snapping of the jaws. The resultant sound is loud and sharp, "a surprising noise" as Bartram put it. Jaw-banging could easily be misinterpreted as fly-catching, especially by those who subscribe to the old legend.

It is remarkable how a train of thought, and sometimes even its phraseology, may be handed down from one author to another. Note, for example, the repetition of the concepts that make up the legend of the open-mouthed alligator: midsummer, a blazing sun, a river bank or sand bar, a crocodilian motionless and somnolent, basking, its jaws gaping wide, insects swarming. Apparently this scene has had wide psychological appeal. Indeed, much that passes for crocodilian biology reflects little more than human psychology, human nature, human emotions and attitudes. Some fallacies about the crocodilians might be called fables. In the myths and legends that beset the literature, the reptiles do not converse with each other in the fashion of Aesop's beasts, but otherwise they are often human personalities. The crocodile who is most predatory when weeping, or the crocodile who endlessly bewails its evil deed although quite ready to repeat it—these are not reptiles but people. The mother alligator anxiously defending her brood from their father, a father who, blustering and roaring on the outskirts of the family group, yearns to make away with his own offspring —this is the family life not of reptiles but of peasants. The crocodile or alligator basking sleepily in the warm sun, and provided with choice tidbits by the mere act of dropping its jaw upon them—this is a picture of sybaritic ease toward which many people would yearn. In Charles Cist's version of the picture, the alligator has become a voluptuous Oriental potentate, a popular stereotype of Cist's day.

In the references so far mentioned, from Gent in 1682 to McIlhenny in 1935, alligators were characterized individually or collectively as being ravenous, voracious, remorseless, greedy, fierce, timorous, crafty, subtle, proud, triumphant, courageous, impudent, avid, warlike, lordly, intrepid, enraged, solicitous, vicious, disappointed, lazy, luxury-loving, mean, villainous, affable, proprietous, liberal-hearted, sociable, ferocious, happy, unhappy, and resentful. Later works, even though they might have a higher ratio of fact to fiction, add such adjectives as satyriac, friendly, angry, amorous, irascible, and sullen. These terms are applicable to people, but not to alligators except by very misleading analogy. The literaure relating to crocodilian activities has been further modified by the psychology of authors who, in many cases, have been reluctant to abandon tradition or even question it, and who have sometimes tried to seem knowledgeable by presenting the old folk fallacies as though they were personal observations. Even actual observations on crocodilians have been modified by the beliefs of the observer. Finally, crocodilian activities have at best been described chiefly in anecdotal fashion; and human recollection of an event inevitably alters with time.

Let us take some observations that have been presented as factual, and see how human nature has entered the picture. An excellent subject in this connection is the "musky" scent supposedly given off by alligators at various times. McIlhenny in 1935 stated that he saw an alligator kill a cow, one of a herd of cattle crossing a marsh. "I shot the alligator . . .

killing it instantly. . . . He [*sic*] measured ten feet ten inches, and had a piece, perhaps two and a half to three feet long, missing from its tail." After describing the condition of the cow, McIlhenny continued, "During this encounter, the alligator had thrown off such a quantity of musk that the water and bank was strongly scented with it. The cattle-men tried several times to force the herd past this spot in the water, but it was useless, as they would not pass." McIlhenny explained the source of alligator "musk" as follows:

> When a bull alligator roars, it, on raising its head above the water, opens the two musk glands located [on the under side] of the lower jaw, and throws off a considerable quantity of sweet pungent-smelling musk that not only scents the air but the surface of the water as well, and lingers as a strong perfume in the vicinity for some hours. There is positively nothing visable [*sic*] in the throwing off of this musk. . . . The female does not seem to make use of the jaw musk glands of the under neck, except when fighting to protect her nest or young or herself, but does throw off, during the mating season, a considerable amount of strong sweet-smelling musk from two musk glands located in the inside wall on each side of the cloaca.

These observations seem plausible, and have been accepted into the herpetological literature; but they raise certain questions. How can one be sure that a roaring alligator is a "bull"? There being no visible emanation from the glands under the jaw, how does one know that they are producing an odor? How does one know that the anal glands are producing an odor in alligators guessed to be female? If the anal glands are inside the cloaca, and if the glands under the throat produce no visible emanation (and if an odor really arose from an alligator defending its nest or a juvenile or itself), how does one know which pair of glands is producing the aroma? As both sexes are provided with similar glands, why should females use the anal pair and males the gular pair (assuming the sex of each specimen to have been guessed accurately)? What is the empiric basis for the assertion that the sexes differ in the use of the glands? It is conceivable that cattle might be reluctant to ford a stream at a point where one of their number was recently pulled down by a crocodilian; but does a scent have anything to do with the matter? And how can the observer know the stimulus to which the cattle are reacting?

The truth of the situation is that small alligators (and small crocodilians of other species), if seized and handled roughly, will usually evert the glands of the under jaw. The action produces no odor detectable to human nostrils, not even if the experimenter brings his nose to within an inch or so of the everted glands. The function of these glandular structures is unknown. The throat glands are not everted during bellowing, by male or female (see Fig. 10). The anal glands perhaps leave a scent trail perceptible to another alligator; but this is a mere guess, bolstered by a small amount of experimental work on the function of anal glands in snakes. When alligators court, copulate, bellow, or fight, they give off no scent detectable by man. At such times the observer usually cannot approach more closely than about 20 or 25 feet (if that), for at nearer approach the reptiles desist in their activities. When the reptiles have moved on, they leave no scent of their own at the scene of action (Figs. 18, 19). Swamp water has odors produced by microorganisms and by chemical reactions, especially in bottom debris. When alligators court, bellow, fight, or dig a den, they usually roil the water, and the aforesaid odors may be briefly intensified, just as they may be intensified when a man wades through a mucky swamp, or disturbs bottom debris with a boat paddle. The swamps of the southeastern United States are in fact full of odors, produced by fungi, slime-molds, terrestrial and aquatic microorganisms, dead

Figure 18. From the time it was noosed until it was brought to land with jaws bound, this struggling alligator gave off no scent detectable by man. Note also that the captors, familiar with alligators, take no heed of the reptile's tail. [Ross Allen's Reptile Institute]

Figure 19. A female alligator, full of eggs, and her mate (in foreground) together kill a third alligator which intruded into their domain. The contest was watched for more than an hour; no combatant gave off a scent detectable by man. [André de la Varre]

leaves and living ones, and the decay of various organic substances. Some of these odors—especially the sharp, sweetish ones—are commonly ascribed to alligators (or else to snakes); but the field biologist knows better, and can often trace an odor to its true source.

When the anal glands are removed from a freshly killed alligator, they have an odor detectable a foot or two away. The throat glands have a similar but less pronounced odor. The carcass of an alligator has an aroma which is no more pronounced than the odor of, say, a raccoon or opossum carcass. A freshly butchered hen is more odoriferous than a living or dead alligator, even a large one. An overfed, dyspeptic house dog imparts to its owners' house an odor far more noticeable than the largest alligator imparts to its own immediate surroundings. As for the "muskiness" of the alligator's faint odor, who knows what someone else means by "musky"? How many people using the term actually know what musk smells like, or even what it is? At best, odors are hard to categorize and describe objectively.

Thus, McIlhenny's account appears to stem not so much from crocodilian biology as from the vagaries of human nature. This conclusion is bolstered by another circumstance. A Classical legend is the actual basis for the story of the crocodilian whose odor warns off cattle. The legend was still popular when America was being settled, and at that time it was strongly allegorical: a Divine Providence benevolently gave the evil crocodile an odor from which the cattle could take warning. In this form the legend was transferred to the American alligator (and to cattle whose ancestry was quite different from that of Egyptian stock). We may follow the growth and spread of the story, and related aspects of alligator "muskiness," in the literature. It should be kept in mind that the authors of this literature were in most cases influenced not only by their predecessors but also by the then current folk beliefs.

René Goulain de Laudonnière, who attempted to found a colony in Florida in the sixteenth century, wrote that the Indians "eat willingly the flesh of the crocodile: and indeed it is fair and white: and were it not that it savoureth too much like musk we would oftentimes have eaten thereof." Human reaction to an odor is usually a matter of cultural conditioning; an odor considered nauseating or intolerable in one part of town may be acceptable or unnoticed in another part where a different ethnic group or social class predominates. Laudonnière, unlike the Indians, showed the widespread, irrational abhorrence of reptiles; the rejection of alligator meat was rationalized by over-emphasis of its supposed odor. The next reference to the alligator's scent, by T. Ashe Gent in 1682, is interesting. Speaking of these reptiles in South Carolina, he says, "Nature by instinct has given most creatures timely caution to avoid them by their strong musky smell, which at a considerable distance is perceivable, which the poor cattle for their own preservation make use of." Here is the first appearance in the New World of McIlhenny's story (or more accurately, the story of some ancient Egyptian, transferred millennia later to a New World setting). Gent continued, ". . . the young ones are eatable; the flesh of the older smells so strong of musk that it nauseates: their stones at least so called, are commended for a rich lasting perfume." Gent, repeating the folk beliefs of his milieu, did not connect the "stones so called"— the anal glands—with the supposed musky odor of the flesh. Also in 1682, Robert Cavelier, the Sieur de la Salle, was in Louisiana, where he shot an alligator. According to an account of the episode, ". . . our soldiers, who had good stomachs, boiled and ate the alligator M. de la Salle had killed. The flesh of it was white, and had a taste of musk, for which reason I could not eat it." In 1687 Richard Blome wrote of the American crocodile in Jamaica, but his remarks show his familiarity with legends relating to the alligator.

> . . . they have in them musk-cods, stronger scented than those of the East Indies: by which strong scent they are discovered and avoided and it is supposed that the cattle, by an instinct of nature, are likewise sensible of it, and do by that means often shun them. . . . Those that are bred in fresh water smell of musk, and that so strongly that they perfume the very air an hundred paces round about them, and scent the very water in which they live; those of them that live in the sea have not so strong a scent.

The crocodilian of Jamaica is the American crocodile, a reptile of the coastal situations; Blome probably had heard the legends that were growing up about the alligator in the fresh waters of Florida. Blome's account was widely read, and influenced much of the later literature. The seventeenth-century writers were interested in musk glands because musk was a highly expensive import; it was used not only in perfume-making but as a medicine and supposed aphrodisiac.

Around 1728 William Byrd wrote, "In the Santee River, as in several others of Carolina, a small kind of alligator is frequently seen, which perfumes the water with a musky smell." A 1741 account of the British Empire in America said that "They have bags of musk stronger and more odorous than that of the East Indies, the smell is so great and so searching that it is easy by it to discover where they lie, and avoid them before a man sees them; even the cattle by a natural instinct smell them, and run away from them." Thus, Blome's work was paraphrased more than a half-century later. It was still exciting to think that the British possessions in the New World might some day be made to yield that valuable natural resource, musk. Antoiné S. Le Page du Pratz, in a 1774 account of Louisiana, claimed to have killed, with a single musket ball, an alligator 19 feet in length. "It infected the whole air with the odor of musk." From Andrew Ellicott's 1803 writings:

> Alligators appear to abound plentifully in musk, the smell of which is sometimes perceptible to a considerable distance, when they are wounded or killed; but whether the musk is contained in a receptacle for that purpose, and secreted by a particular gland or glands, or generally diffuses through the system appears somewhat uncertain: and I confess their appearance was so disagreeable and offensive to me, that I feel no inclination to undertake the dissection of one of them.

Writing in New Orleans in 1808, Christian Schultz claimed to have examined a large, dead alligator. "I found this animal to be strongly impregnated with musk, the whole place being perfumed with that odor. I had it opened, and every part examined, but found nothing which appeared to contain the effluvia; and am therefore of opinion that it is diffused through the whole system of the animal." Henry Ker, who in 1816 perpetuated a variety of legends, remarked, "The smell of the alligator is very disagreeable; it is between that of the musk and the pole cat." Timothy Flint, another legend-monger, stated in 1832, "The animal, when slain, emits an intolerable smell of musk; and it is asserted, that its head contains a quantity of that drug." This may have been the first reference to musk in the alligator's head rather than the cloacal region. The Reverend Adiel Sherwood, in his 1837 gazetteer of Georgia, commented, "When killed, the body emits an intolerable smell of musk, and it is asserted that its head contains a quantity of that drug." J. H. Hinton, in an 1846 history of the United States, supplied the by now familiar observation that "The animal, when slain, emits an intolerable odor of musk; and it is asserted that its head contains a quantity of that drug."

The latter half of the nineteenth century saw comparatively little publication on the activities of the alligator. The swamps and the wildlife of the southeastern United States were rapidly losing their mystery as settlement progressed, and other subjects—the American Civil War, westward expansion, the Indian Wars in the west—occupied the public mind. By the early twentieth century the crocodilians had become the subject of more scientific writings, but the authors of these works seldom had personal familiarity with the reptiles in nature. In 1901 there appeared the *Amphibia and Reptiles* volume of the Cambridge Natural History, an influential work. Hans Gadow, author of this volume, said that all crocodilians had a pair of throat glands and a pair of anal glands, "both [pairs] secreting musk." He went on to say that the throat gland contains "a concentrated essence of musk, much prized by natives. The secretion is most active during the rutting time, when the glands are partly everted." Gadow then mentioned the anal glands. Referring either to these glands alone, or to both pairs of glands, he guessed that "The use of these strongly scented organs, which are possessed by both sexes, is obviously hedonic. The sexes are probably able to follow and find each other, thanks to the streak of scented water left behind each individual." Guesswork aside, Gadow's actual observations on the use of either pair of glands was as follows: "My young Crocodiles and Alligators often turned [the throat glands] inside-out, like the finger of a glove, when they were taken up and held by force." In 1921 Albert M. Reese published an anatomical and embryological study of the throat glands and anal glands of the alligator and some unidentified species of caiman. The study was based on preserved embryos taken from eggs, so Reese could not supply any original observation on the function of the glands. However, he quoted Gadow's guess, and closed his own work with a paraphrase of Gadow: "The secretion . . . is doubtless used by the sexes, both of which produce it, in locating and following each other during the breed-season [sic] when the glands are said to be most active."

K. P. Schmidt, in his 1922 museum bulletin, remarked, "During the mating season the bellowing of the males is heard. . . . A strong musky odor is discharged from the scent-glands at the sides of the throat when they are excited." R. Kellogg's 1929 bulletin stated that "At the time of bellowing fine jets of a musky-smelling fluid are ejected from glands on the chin of the male, and this ejection is commonly associated with the period of courtship." McIlhenny's 1935 remarks have been quoted. R. L. Ditmars's account of North American reptiles, in its 1936 edition, put the situation this way: "As the patriarch gives voice to his roars the scent glands—on the under surface of the chin—are opened, and fine, steamy jets of a powerful, musky-smelling fluid float off into the heavy, miasmatic atmosphere of the bayou. The odor may be carried for miles."

Figure 20. An alligator, bellowing in the water, waves its tail as though wafting a scent from the anal glands. However, no scent is detectable by man. [Ross Allen's Reptile Institute]

Ignoring guesses, and limiting discussion to factual reports, we can say that both anal and throat glands are present in most crocodilian species, and probably all of them; that in several species of crocodilians the throat glands are often everted by a juvenile when molested; that the anal gland has a faint odor, and the throat gland a fainter odor, when dissected from the freshly killed alligator. We can further say that in the alligator both kinds of glands will at times contain a waxy substance; but that the anatomical structure of the glands has been investigated in only a few species, and these mostly on the basis of embryonic material. Finally, we can say that the odor of an alligator does not perfume its surroundings, is very faint in the quiescent or recently killed alligator, and is not intensified during courtship, copulation, bellowing, or fighting. But what an elaborate edifice has been constructed upon the folktales of ancient Egyptians and American rustics by authors following their respective bents!

4 THE LEGENDS' HATEFUL BROOD

IN THE SCIENTIFIC literature, fallacies are undesirable per se, and so are unsupported guesses when they are offered as demonstrated fact. Worse yet, a myth or legend that goes unchallenged may come to spawn a whole new crop of misconceptions. One illustration of this point may be cited. As noted previously, a majority of authors have mistakenly agreed that only the male alligator bellows. Let us see how this fallacy has ramified. The idea seems to have developed slowly, and, unlike much that passes for the alligator's biology, cannot be traced to Classical beliefs about the Nile crocodile; for in crocodiles the adult voice (where known to exist) is a hoarse, loud, hissing, not an impressive thundering as in the alligator. Probably the fallacious idea (along with several others) was influenced by observations on familiar domestic animals. Young alligators, dutifully following their mother around Bartram's lake or into McIlhenny's bulrushes, are really chicks following the hen around the barnyard; and it is hardly coincidental that McIlhenny's alligators are called "bulls" and are said to "bellow." The misconception of Bartram about the alligator's "distended nostrils," and of McIlhenny's Cajun neighbors about the eye shine, may reflect a conscious or subconscious effort to find some parallel with domestic cattle, in which the aroused, bellowing bull is supposedly red-eyed, and distended of nostril.

Jacques Le Moyne in 1564 was the first to describe the bellowing of the alligator. He said only that if the reptiles could find no prey, "they make such a frightful noise that it can be heard for half a mile." Referring to the Mississippi in 1721, Pierre F. X. Charlevoix wrote in his journal, "There are many caymans in this river. . . . We hear them seldom but in the night, and their cry so much resembles the bellowing of bulls, that it deceives one." Thus, Father Charlevoix introduced the bull into the story. Actually, the alligator's roar does not resemble the bellowing of a bull. It is a single deep note, repeated about five to eight times. The note, which has a vibratory quality, is produced by and prolonged throughout one exhalation of the reptile's breath, and the interval between repetitions corresponds to an inhalation. Thus the complete vocalization, the same deep note uttered about five to eight times at precise intervals, has a quality of mechanical repetition quite unlike the coloratura effort of a bull. Charlevoix also was the first to describe bellowing as a nocturnal activity of alligators. However, it is not especially so, unless disturbance by man is considerable by day and much reduced by night. Le Page du Pratz wrote in 1774: "The voice is as strong as that of a bull." William Bartram in 1791 had alligators "roaring" (and blowing smoke from dilated nostrils) as a prelude to combat; see the lengthy quotation in Chapter 2. Actually, bellowing is not followed by combat, and an alligator fight is not preceded by bellowing; but Bartram's guess, or flight of fancy, was seized upon by later authors. Bartram also commented, "It was by this time dusk, and the alligators had nearly ceased their roar." Here he seemed to regard bellowing as a daytime activity. The (imaginary) female alligator that led a hundred or more young alligators beneath his boat also "roared" at him; so Bartram evidently did not regard sound production as possible to males only. He further mentioned "the incredible loud and terrifying roar, which they are capable of making, especially in the spring season, their breeding time." Thus, by guess he originated the myth that bellowing is involved with alligator courtship in the spring. The myth still exists in the literature. Actually, the bellow is given occasionally in the spring and the fall, but more often in summer after courtship has ceased and the eggs have been laid.

Francis Baily, writing of Louisiana in 1796, said, "These animals make a tremendous howling, or rather bellowing, when they first come out of the dens, or at the approach of bad weather. I have heard them continue this during the whole night, and that in such numbers that it has been dismal to hear them." It is tempting to think that Baily had actually heard the astonishingly loud frog choruses that develop in the spring, or during rainy weather, throughout much of the alligator's range. (Even today, the noc-

Figure. 21. Feeding accidents, common among captive reptiles, throw little light on behavior in nature. Here a Florida watersnake, through a feeding accident, has chanced to engulf two others of its kind; yet the Florida watersnake is not normally cannibalistic. [W. T. Neill]

turnal grunting of the pig frog is almost invariably ascribed by the layman to alligators.) Alligator choruses, unlike many frog choruses, do not continue all night but last for only a few minutes. It is not true that bellowing among alligators is more frequent in the period immediately following hibernation. Nor is it particularly associated with rainy weather, except that alligators are occasionally stimulated to bellow in immediate response to a thunderclap. Today they bellow in response to the engine of a logging truck, or the roar of a sawmill. In Florida distant blasting at limestone quarries frequently sets captive alligators to bellowing. Thomas Ashe's 1808 account of alligator vocalizations, quoted in Chapter 2, is mere fiction derived from legends of Classical antiquity. E. Montule, visiting New Orleans in 1817, claimed to have wounded an alligator; "being nearly suffocated by the effusion of blood, it roared like a bull." When much disturbed or hurt, the adult alligator hisses loudly but does not bellow. In 1836 C. J. Latrobe wrote, "Now and then a sound like a long drawn sigh is heard in the direction of the swamp notifying the presence of the alligator: but his proper time for singing is about dawn, when you may hear him and his brethren roaring like a distant herd of bulls." Latrobe used a masculine pronoun for the bellowers, and introduced the fallacious idea that vocalization is mostly at dawn. Charles Cist observed in 1846: "Scattered about in every direction, yet hidden by the darkness, [the traveler at nightfall] hears their huge jaws open and shut with a force that makes a noise, when numbers are congregated, like echoing thunder." Cist was the only author to assume that the alligator's jaw-banging, reported by Bartram, was the source of the thunderous noise also reported by Bartram.

Within the present century, R. L. Ditmars, in various writings from 1907 on, emphasized only the louder voice of larger individuals, and did not refer to the sex of a bellowing alligator beyond calling a large one a "patriarch." In 1922 K. P. Schmidt said, "During the mating season the bellowing of the males is heard, and from the frequent mutilations of large specimens, it is presumed that fighting takes place between them at this time. The voices may be heard at a distance of a mile or more." Thus Schmidt proffered several fallacies: that bellowing is done by the male only, that it is a strongly seasonal activity, that it is involved with courtship, and that it is somehow linked with male combat. Schmidt also repeated the legend that alligators often maim each other in the wild. Of several authors so remarking, not one gives evidence of having examined any number of recently captured alligators in order to determine, first of all, whether these reptiles actually are maimed in nature to any significant degree. And if scars and injuries are found, how can they be attributed definitely to a bite from another alligator? The truth of the matter is that under conditions of abnormal crowding in captivity an alligator may be accidentally injured in a struggle over food that is tossed into the pen. Such a happenstance is not surprising; accidents at feeding time are frequent among many reptiles, including kinds that are normally unaggressive toward members of their own species (Fig. 21). A large, captive, adult

Figure 22. Many reptiles are often found scarred or mutilated as a result of predation or an encounter with man. Shown is a gopher tortoise that had survived a serious injury of unknown origin. [Bruce Mozert]

Figure 23. The Florida panther is among the animals that have been reported to molest the alligator. [Tod Swalm]

Figure 24. The raccoon, shown here in Okefinokee Swamp, is an important predator on small alligators. [Tod Swalm]

alligator may attack a smaller adult that is introduced into the same pen; but in nature a smaller adult is not forced into close proximity with a larger one, nor is a wild alligator prevented from fleeing if a larger individual behaves aggressively. In the wild, few alligators are maimed or scarred. Within the alligator's geographic range, some common harmless reptiles —for example the ground skink, the southeastern five-lined skink, the southern blacksnake, the yellow ratsnake, the brown watersnake, the banded watersnake, the gopher tortoise—are scarred in nature more frequently than the alligator is. Scars and mutilations among alligators should in many cases represent narrow escapes of juveniles from snapping turtles, softshell turtles, raccoons, opossums, otters, minks, panthers, bears, great blue herons, various hawks and owls, garfishes, and other carnivores within the alligator's range (Figs. 23–25). Also, people who visit the swamps with a rifle or shotgun, be they such people as hide-hunters, local rustics, sportsmen, or youths on an outing, can seldom resist the temptation to fire at an alligator (Fig. 26). The narrow escape of juvenile alligators from predators,

Figure 25. The black bear, shown here in Okefinokee Swamp, probably molests the alligator at times. [Tod Swalm]

Figure 26. When any crocodilian is found with a missing foot, the injury is usually ascribed to "fighting." But the Florida crocodile shown here is known to have had its foot shot off by man. [Paul Browning]

Figure 27. This alligator was blinded by a gunshot. A common resting position of the alligator, with forelimb turned backward, shows how this limb could be hit by a shot that was aimed at the reptile's chest region. [Harold Piel]

and of adult alligators from man, adequately account for the small number of injuries noted among these reptiles in the wild. Bellowing has nothing to do with mutilations.

Also debatable is the assertion that the bellow can be heard a mile or more away. This idea developed in the twentieth century, and is not to be found in earlier works. Schmidt probably adopted his phraseology from some early edition of *The Reptile Book*, in which R. L. Ditmars stated, "Among reptiles, the alligator is unique in giving voice to a loud noise or 'bellow.' In the southern swamps the night air carries the call of a large individual for a mile or more." The distance at which a sound may be heard by a person depends on the person and the environment, as well as on the loudness and pitch of the sound. Perhaps a listener of keen hearing could, on a perfectly still day, detect the bellow of a large alligator across a mile of perfectly open country. However, the average person will, in the usual swamp habitat of the alligator, detect a bellow from a distance no greater than about one-tenth of a mile. (The average listener will also grossly overestimate his distance from the bellower.) The deep note of the alligator does not "carry" nearly as far as the bellowing of a bull or even the bawling of a cow.

In the previous chapter, in connection with alligator "muskiness," a brief quotation was offered from R. Kellogg's 1929 bulletin. In this same work Kellogg noted that "The male alligator is unique among reptiles in being able to produce a loud noise or bellow that may be heard at a distance of a mile or more." This remark obviously was taken from Ditmars. Kellogg continued, "On cloudy days or evenings of spring and early summer the bellowing of these creatures is most surprising to one unaccustomed to it." The comment suggests that of Baily, but with modifications. Kellogg went on to say, "Opinions differ as to the purpose of the raucous bellow of an old bull alligator, some considering it a challenge or a warning to near-by bulls, and others a call to attract the attention of females." Kellogg next repeated the legend that the bellowing male ejects "fine jets" of a musky-smelling "fluid" from glands on the "chin" [*sic*], the ejection being "commonly associated with the period of courtship. The voice of the female is less tremulous, and that of the young may be described as a weak grunt. . . . When alligators in captivity are annoyed they [inflate with air], discharging the air through the throat with a hissing bellow that may be repeated several times a minute." Actually, as noted, the bellow is not likely to be heard a mile; the female bellows as loudly as a male of the same size; bellowing is not done more frequently on cloudy days or in the evening; it is not done more frequently in the spring and early summer; the throat glands are not known to function at all during bellowing, and they certainly do not eject fine jets of fluid at such times. Kellogg's reference to the "less tremulous" voice of the female apparently related to the warning hiss, which he did not distinguish clearly from the bellow.

Finally, a 1960 encyclopedia of science, under the heading "Crocodilia," stated, "During the breeding season male crocodilians set up territories on land which they defend against intruders of the same species. During this period their loud roars are frequently heard at night." And so the unsuspecting modern herpetologist, knowing little of crocodilians in nature, and relying too heavily on the legend-mongers for his information, was led to offer eleven fallacies or dubieties at once. Six of these are old legends: that bellowing is done by males only; that it is done mostly by night; that it is done in special connection with the breeding season; that it is done in connection with combats; that combats regularly take place; and that males are more combative than females. Five new dubieties are also created here, for the American alligator is the only crocodilian known to voice what might be called a loud roar; while bellowing may be linked with territoriality (the impulse of an individual to defend a limited area against intrusion by another of its kind), this has not actually been demonstrated; indeed, the existence of territoriality has never been demonstrated for any crocodilian (it might be inferred for the American alligator, although in the face of some contrary observations); if any crocodilian sets up a territory, it is surely not on land; and in the possibly territorial alligator, there is no evidence that the males are more inclined than the females to defend an area.

Mrs. Trollope's man-eating alligator had reared, she said, a hateful brood. No more hateful, however, than the brood of myths, legends, and dubieties that have been spawned in the present century by several of the older fallacies about crocodilians.

A high percentage of the legends, both the old ones and their modern derivatives, center around the alligator's reproductive behavior. Authors are especially confused and confusing about this reptile's activities during the period from the onset of courtship to the dispersal of the young. The remainder of this chapter will deal with some of the current misconceptions about these activities. It may be mentioned in passing that many of an animal's adaptations, both anatomical and behavioral, are closely linked with reproduction, with the processes and activities that determine the survival of the species through the continued production of new generations. Many topics can be obscured when reproductive behavior is erroneously described. In dealing with the alligator's reproduction, therefore, one must be exceptionally wary of those authors whose approach to the subject has been casual.

In the very near future when the numbers of the American alligator will have declined almost to the vanishing point, there will probably be an upsurge of interest in the conservation of this reptile. A fallacious view of the alligator's life history could seriously hinder conservation. One illustration of this point will be advanced. McIlhenny, to whom so many modern students have turned in the hope of obtaining information about the alligator, said,

> The young remain with, and are guarded by, the mother from the time of hatching all through the Winter, and until the next spring's mating period. At this time the female wanders off in search of a mate, and the young, being then about sixteen or eighteen inches in length and well able to care care of themselves, spread over the surrounding marshes and bayous.

This statement, like McIlhenny's claim that the mother alligator feeds her brood, may reflect the influence of Bartramian fictions. At any rate, one would suppose from McIlhenny's widely credenced account that alligators under about 18 inches are well protected by their mother. The actual situation is quite different. In the first place, the babies disperse upon hatching, as do newly hatched or newborn reptiles generally. From the very beginning of the alligator's hatching season until the advent of cold weather, the young of the year are widely scattered, often in ponds, shallow lagoons, and other situations where the adults are lacking. The number of young in a backwater, lagoon, marsh, stretch of river, or other circumscribed body of water is easily determined with considerable accuracy, for the brilliant eye-shine renders each baby alligator very conspicuous when a flashlight is played over the water by night. In the spring, within a given body of water, the number of juveniles to be seen is about one-tenth of the number that were present at the end of the previous hatching season. It is not contended that this figure of one-tenth is exact, but it is a close approximation. In other words, about nine-tenths of the alligators that hatch will die within the first eight or nine months of life. While there could be some deaths from defects of anatomy or behavior, almost surely predation accounts for the greater part of this juvenile mortality. Many organisms are definitely known to prey upon small alligators, making off with the young reptiles before their distress cries can summon an adult. The juveniles that survive through the first winter are not markedly reduced in numbers during the following spring and summer. Therefore, if conservationists ever attempt to increase the numbers of an alligator population, they should bear in mind that individuals under about 18 inches in length, far from receiving protection from their mother, are in the greatest danger of predation. Wildlife authorities will of course not be surprised to learn that the juvenile mortality rate is high; this is a common situation among a great variety of living things.

The uncritical acceptance of earlier writings can also obscure certain matters of wide biological interest. One illustration of this point will be advanced, drawn again from misconceptions about the alligator's reproductive habits. McIlhenny's account of these habits was highly imaginative, a compound of old legends, local folk beliefs, and some embellishments that were *sui generis*. C. H. Pope, in a 1955 book treating the world's reptiles in popular vein, unfortunately took his own review of the alligator's reproduction mainly from McIlhenny, broke McIlhenny's version of nest-building activities into ten numbered steps, and so lent the farrago an unmerited air of authenticity. From McIlhenny's and Pope's accounts, the alligator's reproductive habits would appear to be unique within the animal kingdom: a very large area is cleared off for a nesting site (a Bartramian fiction, originally), mud and trash is brought by mouth for use as nesting material, the female urinates on the nest regularly when the weather is dry, she bites the top off her nest when the eggs hatch, the babies follow her about and are fed by her until they are almost yearlings. Now let us ignore legends and guesses, concentrate on what the alligator has actually been seen to do, and compare this behavior with that of an aquatic turtle.

For comparison we may select the yellow-bellied turtle, a common associate of the alligator in many parts of the latter's range. In the spring, both the turtle and the alligator emerge from winter retreats, and soon begin courtship. The turtle courts in the water; the male swims backward in front of the female, and vibrates his elongated fingernails against her cheeks. Eventually she is aroused; the male then approaches her from the rear, and she moves her tail to one side as he accomplishes intromission. The alligator, meanwhile, is carrying on a similar but somewhat more elaborate courtship, which takes place in the water and which may continue for days. The male lies alongside the female and strokes her repeatedly along the upper sides. A row of glands, unknown in function, lies in the area that is stroked. Later, however, the male approaches the female from the front, in much the fashion of the courting turtles. The male alligator ducks his head beneath the female's lower jaw, rubs her there by movements of his head, and blows great streams of bubbles past her cheeks. Finally the female is aroused; the male approaches her from the rear, and she moves her tail upward and aside while he accomplishes intromission.

Next comes nesting. The gravid female turtle leaves the water, and finds a nesting spot on high ground where the eggs will be in little danger from flooding. The spot must offer fairly moist soil, however, for turtle eggs are not wholly resistant to desiccation. The female digs a nesting hole in a surprising fashion: she faces away from the nesting site, and uses her hind feet to push the sand about, and to dig with remarkable dexterity. As she begins to deposit eggs in the hole she has dug, she keeps one or both hind feet near her vent; the eggs are thus not dropped abruptly into the hole, but are slowed in their fall by the "palm" of her hind foot. When she has finished laying, she covers the hole, using her hind feet but also pushing

Figure 28. Like the alligator, many turtles dig a nesting cavity with the hind foot, and use the hind foot to manipulate the eggs. Shown is a nesting female of the Florida turtle. [Ross Allen]

with the side of her shell against the dirt. Finally she crawls back and forth over the filled hole, smoothing the surface of the nest. She is incapable of defending the clutch against a predator, and after nesting she goes back to the water. When the eggs hatch, the baby turtles make their own way out of the nest and to the water, where they disperse rapidly. The gravid female alligator also leaves the water to nest, but usually does not go onto high ground. Instead, using her flanks and hind feet, she pushes together a mound of dirt and vegetation at some spot not far from the water's edge. In the top of this mound she digs a nesting hole in surprising fashion: she faces away from the mound, and uses her hind feet to push the dirt and debris about, and to dig with remarkable dexterity. As she lays eggs in the hole she has formed in the mound, she keeps one or both hind feet near her vent, and the eggs are prevented from dropping abruptly into the hole. She looks as though she were trying to lay each egg into the "palm" of a hind foot. When she has finished laying, she covers the hole in the mound, using her hind feet but also pushing with her flanks against the dirt and vegetation. Next she crawls back and forth over the sides of the nest, smoothing its surface. Under normal conditions she stays near the nest and guards it against predators, something she is fully capable of doing. Her movements to and from the water keep the nest area damp, perhaps only coincidentally. When the eggs hatch, the baby alligators make their own way out of the nest and to the water where they begin to disperse.

In short, the reproductive behavior of a crocodilian, as exemplified by the American alligator, is remarkably like that of a freshwater turtle. Almost surely the crocodilians and the turtles inherited this behavior from some common ancestor, just as they both inherited certain reptilian anatomical characteristics. To find a probable common ancestor of crocodilians and turtles one must go back a good 280 million years, to some of the earliest reptiles. The basic crocodilian-turtle pattern of reproductive behavior thus appears to have been an ancient, conservative, and highly successful one.

The legend-mongers have not gone wholly undetected. A. M. Reese in 1910 published a photograph showing the actual arrangement of eggs in an alligator's nest. In 1918 Reese reported the serving of alligator meat to about thirty people, who agreed that the entire animal was "delicious." Percy Viosca, Jr., a field herpetologist without peer, in 1925 remarked, ". . . it is by no means certain that alligators pay any attention to their young after they make their way into the water." He also contrasted the greenish eye-shine of the bullfrog with the reddish eye-shine of the alligator. Francis Harper, in 1930, while perpetuating various fallacies of Bartram and the local rustics, reported hearing the bellow of the alligator in Okefinokee from May through September, most often in mid-morning; and he concluded that such vocalization could not be primarily associated with breeding. Ross Allen in 1952 pointed out that the nesting material is scraped together, that the young alligators disperse shortly after hatching, and that they are not fed by the female parent. Clifford B. Moore in 1954 emphasized that captive alligators give off no odor, and mentioned the insistence of many untrained observers that certain plant odors are of animal origin. Dick Bothwell in 1962 invoked common sense in his discussion of the "ballast" theory of crocodilian gastroliths: "It would be surprising to say the least to find that nature, after equipping the crocodilian so superbly in every other manner, should have neglected to throw in proper balance." But these and similarly veracious observations (to be summarized in Part IV), appearing mostly in semitechnical magazines, or else in journals of general science or of wildlife management, were inadequate to counteract the more flamboyant and captivating efforts of the legend-mongers, who had impressed their stamp almost indelibly on herpetological thinking.

PART II *Two Hundred Million Years of Crocodilian History*

5 THE CROCODILIANS AND THEIR KIN

THE PRECEDING SECTION of this book did not present all of the misstatements that have distorted the current view of the alligator's life history. It did present the more significant misstatements, and now it might seem logical to pass from fallacies about the alligator to truths about it. In a sense we shall do this. However, it is not desirable at this point to begin a review of the alligator's life history. A life history study, one in the modern tradition, will touch upon and try to integrate a variety of subjects. Among these subjects are the geographic range of the organism studied, the habitat in which it lives, and the factors that keep it within its range and habitat. The courtship and mating, the nesting and hatching (or birth if the organism is a live-bearer), the growth and longevity—these, too, are life history topics. So are sensory perceptions, the wandering of individuals and their method of orientation, sound production (if any) and its role in the organism's life, the composition of a population as regards the age and sex of the individuals that make it up, and social relationships such as combat or adult protection of the young. Still other life history topics include territoriality where present, the food and its procurement, the defense (if any) of nest, young and self, predators and parasites upon the organism, competitors with it, and the modifications of its biology in consequence of man's activities. Many aspects of a crocodilian's life history will reflect the circumstance that a crocodilian is a reptile, with both the possibilities and the drawbacks that are inherent in the reptilian grade or level of biological organization. Other aspects may reflect evolutionary history, the time when and place where a group of crocodilians originated, and the environmental vicissitudes to which that group was exposed as millennia went by. A crocodilian's activities, as much as its anatomical structures, are largely innate, and so to a considerable degree will reflect an inheritance from some earlier stock. Thus, a detailed account of the alligator, and of the other surviving crocodilians, becomes more meaningful if preceded by some general remarks on these reptiles, their characteristic anatomical structures, their astonishing history throughout the ages, and their position in the scheme whereby all living things are classified.

One person in his lifetime can see little change in the climate, in the height of mountains, or in the relation of sea to land. Thus, it is difficult to realize just how profoundly the surface of the earth has been remodeled, not once but many times, throughout the ages. The origin of the crocodilians dates back to a time when the world was greatly different from the one we know. It dates back to what geologists call the Triassic Period, which began some 230 million years ago. In that remote time the land masses of the world did not have their familiar modern outlines. Geologists have come to believe that the continents we know today were originally fragmented from a single, primordial supercontinent dubbed Pangaea; or else from no more than two supercontinents. Long before the Triassic began, there were two supercontinents separated by an east-west trending seaway, the Tethys Sea. The two great land masses have been named Gondwanaland and Laurasia. Gondwanaland, somewhat the larger of the two, was also more diverse of environment. Lying mostly in the southern hemisphere, it stretched from equatorial to south-polar latitudes. Laurasia lay mostly in the northern hemisphere, stretching from the equatorial region northward through warm-temperate latitudes. Gondwanaland was destined eventually to break up into the land masses we now call South America, Africa, Antarctica, the Indian peninsula, and Australia; Laurasia into North America, Greenland, and Eurasia (minus the Indian peninsula). The fragments would drift apart and to their present positions. It is uncertain how far this continental drift had proceeded when the Triassic Period opened. There is mounting evidence that the land was still grouped into two super-continents at that time. Thus, amazingly, the history of the crocodilians dates back to a time before any of the modern continents had been formed.

The two supercontinents of the early Triassic must have offered a diversity of environments, with streams, swampy lowlands, perhaps chilly uplands, and surely a cold region in the south of Gondwanaland. However, most of the land was warm, and some of it must have been dry. Even in this remote period the world was not new. Glaciers, great ice sheets, had already formed, spread across the land, and melted away again; vast mountain ranges had already been thrust up and then eroded back into hills and plains. Life was not new either; for when the Triassic opened living things had already been evolving for 3,000 million years. Many groups of organisms had arisen, flourished for some millions of years, and then become extinct. The trilobites (which resembled the modern horseshoe crab), the seascorpions, the squid-like nautiloids, a variety of marine and freshwater fishes, early amphibians, some reptilian types, scale-trees, giant horsetails, seedferns—these and many other groups had vanished or else had fallen into marked decline by the Triassic. Forests were mostly of conifers, cone-bearing trees related to the living Araucaria and Podo-carpus. The invertebrates—the lower animals without a backbone—were thriving. In the Triassic seas there were jellyfishes, corals, sponges, snails, bivalve mollusks, squids, lamp shells, sea cucumbers, bryozoans, starfishes, crustaceans, sea-urchins, jointed worms, and sea-lilies. On the land were scorpions, millipedes, centipedes, mites, spiders, and a great variety of insects—in fact most or all of the major invertebrate groups that occupy the land today. Of the vertebrates, the higher or backboned animals, the sharks and true fishes were flourishing. The amphibians were declining in over-all view, yet in the Triassic were establishing one new and successful line of descent, the frogs. The reptiles, which had evolved in an earlier period from amphibian ancestors, were the highest form of life when the Triassic opened.

Early reptiles were advanced over their amphibian ancestors chiefly in matters relating to reproduction. The usual amphibian life history involves the deposition of gelatinous eggs in water. The eggs hatch into a gilled, aquatic larva, which must for a time lead a fish-like existence before transforming into an adult. Almost every one is familiar with the sequence that

Figure 29. Unlike reptiles, most amphibians
have a free-living larval stage that differs greatly
from the adult. Shown is the tadpole larva
(at right) and the adult (above) of the river-
frog. (The adult is devouring a newborn
diamondback rattlesnake.) Amphibians must
also lay their eggs in water or wet places. The
female Amphiuma salamander (below) lays her
gelatinous eggs in a very wet spot, and moves
them to safety if drying threatens. [W. T. Neill
and Ross Allen's Reptile Institute]

Figure 30. Reptile eggs have a leathery or hard shell that protects them to some degree from water loss. Shown are eggs of the reticulated python (at left), laid in captivity; and eggs of the alligator (at right). The alligator eggs have been cleared of nest debris, to reveal them more clearly. [Ross Allen's Reptile Institute]

leads from a gelatinous egg to a wriggling, aquatic tadpole and finally to an adult frog that hops about in damp places on land. A minority of living amphibians pass the larval stage in the egg, which is laid on land; but it must be laid in a constantly moist spot, for it desiccates easily. The adult amphibian may be able to live on land, but its soft, moist skin does little to prevent water loss from the body. Thus, the adult, even if terrestrial, is generally excluded from the really dry habitats by the likelihood of desiccation there. In their early life history stages, that is, egg and larva, the amphibians strongly suggest their fish ancestors. The reptiles, in contrast, typically deposit leathery-shelled or hard-shelled eggs on land. A minority of reptiles went further and developed a live-bearing condition. Within the reptile egg, the developing embryo rests in a liquid medium, surrounded by a membrane called the amnion. Extending from the embryo is a sacklike membranous structure, the allantois, which serves as a respiratory organ and as a place for the storage of wastes produced by the growing embryo. A mass of yolk, functioning to nourish the embryo, is surrounded by another membrane called the yolk sac. Embryo, amnion, allantois, yolk, and yolk sac are all encapsulated by still another membrane, the chorion. In some reptiles, the crocodilians among them, a space between the egg shell and the chorion is filled with a watery albumen. An egg of this kind, while not absolutely immune to water loss, can be deposited in a variety of terrestrial situations, and its evolutionary development was a great forward step in the emancipation of life from the water.

The development of such an egg required simultaneous, or perhaps even antecedent, modifications of anatomy and behavior. Among many fishes and amphibians, the unfertilized eggs are deposited in the water by the female, and the male then discharges his sperm over them. Nothing like this is possible to reptiles, whose eggs must be fertilized before the

Figure 31. Rainbow snake eggs (at right) and alligator eggs (below) hatching. The alligator eggs have been removed from the nest. Unlike most amphibians, reptiles do not have a free-living larva that differs markedly from the adult. [Ross Allen's Reptile Institute]

tough shell is secreted. In short, reptile fertilization must be internal. Among the vertebrates, several methods of internal fertilization have evolved. In some living salamanders, for example, the male deposits a sperm packet which the female then inserts into her cloaca before her eggs are laid. However, the most effective device for internal fertilization is a penis, and this was evolved by the reptiles. In the North American "tailed frog," an inhabitant of swift streams that would wash sperm away, a tail-like prolongation of the vent serves the male as a copulatory organ, and in some fishes the anal fin is modified into a tube that permits internal fertilization; but such structures are anatomically quite unlike a penis, which makes its first appearance with the reptiles. Invasion of the dry habitats also necessitates a skin that is resistant to water loss, and the reptile skin is usually covered with protective scales.

Geologists once held that the Triassic, as well as the preceding Permian, had been marked by widespread aridity. Such environmental conditions would help account for the rise and diversification of reptiles, because their closest relatives and principal competitors, the amphibians, would have been barred from such Permian and Triassic land by an inability to depart the wet places. Extensive Permian-Triassic aridity is not now visualized, but emancipation from the water must have had a great deal to do with reptilian takeover before the Triassic was past.

Figure 32. Internal fertilization, by a male intromittent organ, was a reptilian evolutionary advance over the Amphibia. Shown are a copulating pair of the green anole, a lizard [Tod Swalm]

Figure 33. The scaly skin of a reptile was an evolutionary advance over the soft, moist skin of an amphibian. Some reptiles inhabit desert areas, seemingly with little danger of water loss. Shown are two desert lizards, a Gila monster (upper) and a Mexican horned lizard (lower). [Orin G. Fogle]

Of special interest is a group of Triassic reptiles called the Thecodontia. The term "thecodont" means "having socketed teeth"; the teeth of these reptiles were set in deep sockets of the jawbone (as is the case with crocodilians and mammals today). The early thecodontians were, in the main, rather small reptiles, not over 4 or 5 feet long. Half or more of this length was taken up by a long, stout tail. The head was long, the snout often compressed laterally, the jaws armed with sharp teeth. The back was protected by rows of small, bony plates. The hind legs were much larger and stronger than the front ones. Many of the thecodontians, and perhaps most of them, were bipedal in gait. They scampered across the Triassic landscape on powerful hind legs, their forward-leaning bodies counterbalanced by their long, heavy tails. In these bipedal reptiles, the middle toe of the hind foot was enlarged and strengthened. The forelimbs were so reduced as to be of limited usefulness; and the pelvis, the bony structure of the hip region, was strengthened and modified for an upright posture. The foregoing description relates to the thecodontian norm. Departures from it included quadrupedal gait, aquatic habitat, larger size, strongly beaked jaws, and spiny armor. Some descendants of the theocodontians also reverted to the quadrupedal gait, or went back to the water, or both. But even in these the skeletal traces of thecodontian ancestry can be detected.

In the Triassic, and in the two geological periods that followed (the Jurrassic and then the Cretaceous), a great variety of reptiles evolved from thecodontian stock. Among them were small dinosaurs that ran swiftly on their hind legs, and some bulkier upright dinosaurs that wallowed in marshes or that stalked about to browse on vegetation. From thecodontians there also evolved the great, bipedal, carnivorous dinosaurs, the most fearsome predators ever to walk the earth. Other descendants of the Thecodontia included lumbering, quadrupedal dinosaurs with fantastic horns or armor plates; and gigantic, long-necked, quadrupedal dinosaurs, the largest weighing 50 tons. Also descending from the thecodontians were the flying reptiles, some no bigger than a sparrow and others with a wingspread of 25 feet or more. But of all reptile groups that evolved from thecodontian stock, the most successful proved to be the crocodilians.

Casting about for a name to cover all these walking, running, swimming, and flying reptiles, scientists hit upon the name Archosauria. Scientific names are in Latin, or at least Latinized from some other language, and in this case the name was constructed and Latinized from Greek rootwords meaning (in rough translation) the Ruling Reptiles. The designation was appropriate enough, for descendants of the Thecodontia would hold undisputed sway over the earth for many millions of years. The various dinosaurs, the flying reptiles, and the crocodilians, along with their thecodontian ancestors, are collectively referred to as archosaurs.

Dinosaurs, flying reptiles, crocodilians—these may seem a remarkably diverse lot of reptiles to have descended from one stock. However, it must be remembered that in the Triassic no higher animals stood in the way of reptilian rise, or of thecodontian radiation into all environments. Also, we

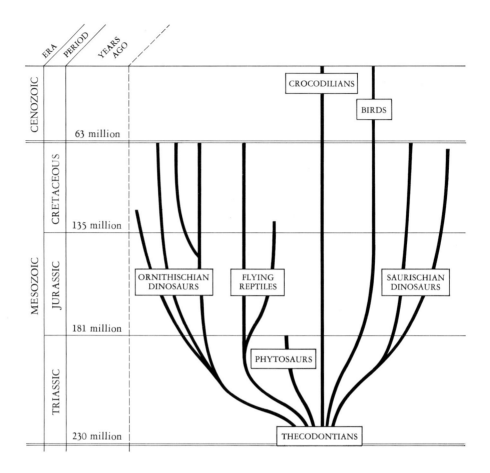

Figure 34. A "family tree" of the thecodontians and their descendants. The chart shows only the major lines of descent. Dates are approximate.

have compressed into a few paragraphs the evolutionary events that took place over a great span of time. The Triassic, during which the thecodontians established the main lines of archosaur evolution, lasted for 49 million years; the Jurassic, in which these lines diversified, lasted for another 46 million years; and the Cretaceous, during which the archosaurs reached their greatest variety, provided 72 million years more. Dinosaurs and flying reptiles did not survive beyond the Cretaceous; but the crocodilians did so, and continued to evolve for another 50 million years.

Actually, the thecodontian capacity to diversity was not limited to the production of dinosaurs, flying reptiles, and crocodilians. During the early to middle Triassic, certain thecodontians developed into long-snouted, aquatic reptiles called phytosaurs which looked, superficially, much like the crocodilians, and which must have been similar in habits. Whereas a crocodilian has the nostrils situated near the end of the snout, in a phytosaur they were located atop the head, almost between the eyes. In some of the phytosaurs the nostrils occupied the top of a cone-shaped elevation. Presumably this was a modification that permitted breathing when most of the reptile was submerged. The phytosaur nasal passages opened into the back of the mouth, not a highly satisfactory arrangement for a reptile that might have to fight or catch prey under the water. (Crocodilians improved on this arrangement, as we shall see.) The phytosaurs were not on the line of crocodilian ancestry; they were an independent offshoot from the early thecodontians. One might say that a crocodilian-like build, and certain habits appropriate thereto, were evolved at least twice from thecodontian stock. But only the true crocodilians were successful; the phytosaurs did not survive beyond the Triassic. Phytosaurs are usually regarded as specialized thecodontians, and as such are to be listed as primitive archosaurs; but their "rule" lasted only 25 million years or so. (Not a bad record, really, especially when one recalls that man's domination of the earth is to be measured in mere thousands of years.)

Amazingly, the theocodontians also gave rise to birds. The finest and most famous specimen of reptile-bird comes from the Jurassic of Germany. This specimen, intermediate between a bird and an archosaur, was given the name of Archaeopteryx ("ancient wing"). Archaeopteryx was about the size of a crow. It had a long neck, a long reptilian tail, and a reptilian head with socketed teeth in upper and lower jaw. The hindlimbs were not very different from those of a modern bird. Three toes were directed forwardly, a fourth backwardly. But the forelimbs of the reptile-bird had not evolved fully into wings; they still bore three long fingers, each tipped with a claw. The fine-grained rock, in which Archaeopteryx chanced to be fossilized, had preserved the detailed impression of the reptile-bird's feathers. The lizard-like tail was provided with a row of feathers along each side. The forelimbs were feathered, constituting short wings. The reptile-birds were not descendants of the flying reptiles; the two groups were independent offshoots of the Thecodontia. In other words, the remarkable thecodontians invaded the air on two separate occasions.

The thecodontians and their multifarious descendants were not the only reptilian types of the Triassic, Jurassic, or Cretaceous. Most of the other reptile groups need not enter into our story at this point, but one of them should be discussed. This was a group of medium-sized or fairly large reptiles called the Synapsida. The synapsidans were among the earliest of reptiles, and flourished before the Triassic. They were chunky, and moved clumsily on short legs. As the millennia went by, the synapsidans evolved some improvements in their gait, but always in the direction of more effective quadrupedal locomation; they never showed the thecodontian trend toward a bipedal gait. The teeth of the Synapsida exhibit a striking departure from the reptilian norm: the tooth row includes sharp anterior teeth that might be called incisors; an enlarged canine tooth, useful in defense or in the retention of struggling prey; and a series of chewing teeth farther back in the row. A majority of the Synapsida were carnivores, although some were plant-eaters.

On at least two occasions the early synapsidans evolved a high fin on the back, a curious sail-like organ supported by bony spines. There is evidence that this structure was well supplied with blood vessels, and helped to regulate the body temperature. That is to say, the reptile may have raised its temperature by spreading the fin to the sun, or lowered its temperature by moving into a cool, shady spot where the fin would lose heat. The synapsidan fin draws attention to a dilemma that has confronted every reptile, including the crocodilians living or fossil. Reptiles have no effective internal mechanism for maintaining a constant body temperature, and so must take on the temperature of their surroundings. Yet in many regions the range of environmental temperatures is greater than the range of body temperatures at which a reptile will carry on its normal and necessary activities. Although there is some variation from one reptile group to another, it is probably safe to say that most reptilian activity takes place at body temperatures above 15 degrees Centigrade (59 degrees Fahrenheit) and below 30 degrees Centigrade (about 86 degrees Fahrenheit). These rough figures are based on the study of modern reptiles, but a similar problem of temperature regulation beset the ancient types.

We shall see in another chapter how the crocodilians met this problem. Suffice it to say that the fin-backed synapsidans had not evolved an ideal solution to it. The fin-backs and many other synapsidans had vanished by the time the Triassic opened. However, one finless group of the Synapsida, persisting into the Triassic, met the problem in a new way: through modification of the internal anatomy, and especially of the circulatory system, they began the approach to a condition of constant warm-blooded-ness. They also developed a secondary palate, a bony plate in the roof of the mouth, separating the nasal cavity from the mouth cavity. The croco-dilians were independently evolving a similar structure. The advanced synapsidans continued with the specialization of the dentition into inci-sors, canines, and cheek teeth. Some time in the late Triassic, while the archosaurs were beginning their radiation, certain Synapsida had become essentially mammalian. There are indications that, by the latter Triassic, descendants of the Synapsida had evolved a moist snout, facial vibrissae ("whiskers"), and flexible lips perhaps correlated with the mammalian trait of suckling. It would be millions of years before the mammals amounted to much. The Age of Reptiles would end before the Age of Mammals began. Still, the warm-blooded mammalian condition was an evolutionary develop-ment of enormous potential.

The present chapter has devoted considerable space to living things other than the crocodilians. But the crocodilians have never existed in iso-lation; at all times they have interacted with the world about them. To understand the rise and astonishing persistence of the crocodilians, as well as details of their life history, it is useful to know something about their environment through the ages, and about the other life-forms with which they have competed.

The Triassic was a crucial time in vertebrate evolution, and we cannot see the period with anything like the desired clarity. Amphibians were declining, reptiles attaining domination, mammals and birds rising. Among Triassic and later fossils, similar evolutionary trends can be detected in groups that were not closely related to each other. The crocodilian-like build evolved twice, once as phytosaurs and again as true crocodilians. The air was invaded twice, once by the flying reptiles and again by the reptile-birds that became true birds. Some thecodontians and some dinosaurs were bipedal; so, probably, were the immediate ancestors of the reptile-birds. Warm-bloodedness developed at least twice, the developments culminating in birds and mammals; but the condition has also been suspected for some dinosaurs and flying reptiles. The crocodilian circulatory system evolved in a direction that could have led to, but did not quite attain, the condition of warm-bloodedness. Scales were replaced by hair somewhere around the synapsidan-mammalian boundary, and hairiness is generally considered a typically mammalian character; yet a small flying reptile, fossilized in sediments that preserved some fine details of external anatomy, was scale-less and seemingly provided with hair-like structures. The paleontologist, the student of ancient life, would not be surprised by the discovery of a little, bipedal archosaur with feathers, perhaps adequate only for insulation and not flight. Indeed, if chance had not preserved an imprint of feathers, the reptile-bird Archaeopteryx would probably be listed simply as another small archosaur. A secondary palate became better developed in crocodilians than in synapsidans or even mammals. The middle-ear cavity of the croco-dilians became mammalian-like in the extent to which it encroached upon the surrounding skull bones. Specialization of the dentition into incisors, canines, and cheek teeth took place not only in the advanced synapsidans and their mammalian descendants but also in various synapsidans that were off the line leading to the mammals. The same condition was approached in the crocodilians. The crocodilian penis finds its closest counterpart among the mammals; the crocodilian egg is not substantially different from the hen's egg of the breakfast table.

Some of these parallel developments can be accounted for in part by common ancestry; but in all cases we must consider the Triassic environ-ment, the opportunities it offered for exploitation by suitably endowed organisms, the impasses it placed in the way of unsuitably endowed ones. Crocodilian history is interesting enough per se, but gains in meaning when viewed as part of a vastly larger story, the interaction of living things with each other and with the physical environment.

6 THE CROCODILIANS IN BIOLOGICAL CLASSIFICATION

AS IS WIDELY KNOWN, biologists have at-tempted to give to each species of living thing a binomial designation that is in Latin, or that is at least Latinized if from some other language. The binominal system of nomenclature is often called the Linnaean system, after the famed Carolus Linnaeus, pioneer student of plant and animal classification. Our present system of zoological nomenclature is considered to date from the tenth (1758) edition of Linneaus's *Systema Naturae*, in which Linnaeus used a binorial designation for every living species that he could recognize. By that time he had been able to examine several species of crocodilians; and so the classification of these reptiles has an official beginning in 1758 (although some of the species were known to science long before then).

Linneaus, primarily a botanist, was not enthusiastic about reptiles. He lumped them with amphibians, and described the composite group as "foul and loathesome animals . . . abhorrent because of their cold body, pale color, cartilaginous skeleton, fierce aspect, calculating eye, offensive smell, harsh voice, squalid habitation, and terrible venom. . . ." Linnaeus carefully dissected flower blossoms and counted all their parts; but when it came to reptiles and amphibians, his mind was a jumble of recollections: the sliminess of a salamander, the coldness of a frog, the awesome gape of a crocodilian, the unwinking gaze of a snake, the raucous call of a toad, the secretive habits of many amphibians, the venom of some snakes, the sharp odor given off by many snakes when disturbed. Perhaps he recalled vaguely the cartilaginous skeleton of a shark, the pallid coloration of worms and grubs beneath a rock. Nearly two centuries have elapsed since Linnaeus's death; and needless to say, great strides have been made in classification. Linnaeus would find little unfamiliar in our present scheme whereby groups of related species are combined into a genus, of related genera into a family, of families into an order, orders into a class, classes into a phylum, and phyla into a kingdom. However, only in comparatively modern times have anatomical and paleontological studies revealed how crocodilians should be placed within this hierarchy.

The crocodilians belong to the Animal kingdom, within which there are 26 phyla. The animal phylum that concerns us is the Chordata, which includes all the backboned animals as well as some little marine organisms called lancelets and sea-squirts. Within the phylum Chordata, the backboned animals make up the important subphylum Vertebrata, the vertebrates or higher animals. The subphylum Vertebrata includes seven classes. Three of these classes are necessary to accommodate the diversity of fishes; a fourth serves for all the amphibians (salamanders, frogs, caecilians, and their relatives), a fifth for all the reptiles, a sixth for the birds, and the seventh for the mammals. Crocodilians are a part of the class Reptilia, the reptiles. A previous chapter came close to defining the reptiles, but the description may now be amplified a bit.

In general, reptiles have epidermal scales but no feathers or fur. If limbs are present, they do not have the structure of fins. (Certain reptiles—snakes and a minority of the lizards—are essentially limbless. In a minority of the turtles, the limbs are more or less flipper-like.) Unless the limbs are much reduced, at least some of the fingers and toes will terminate in a horny claw. The reptile skin is not markedly glandular, and does not stay moist like that of a frog or salamander. The thin outer layer of the skin does much to inhibit the loss of moisture from the body. This layer, called the stratum corneum, is periodically sloughed, or else is worn away and replaced. Reptilian respiration is accomplished by lungs, just one lung in the case of some snakes, but in any event not by gills or through the skin. Some turtles can take water into the throat, or into the cloaca, and extract oxygen from it; such pharyngeal or cloacal respiration supplements the work of the lungs in several aquatic species. Except in crocodilians, there is no muscular diaphragm separating a lung cavity from the rest of the body cavity. In no reptile is there a sharp distinction between a ribbed thoracic region with closed lung cavities, and a ribless abdominal region. The heart is three-chambered, except in the crocodilians, which have a four-chambered heart. Reptiles have no internal mechanism for maintaining a constant body temperature, but partly compensate for this lack by restricting their activities to situations where favorable temperatures exist. Attention has already been drawn to certain important features of reptilian reproduction: internal fertilization by means of an intromittent organ; an egg that is provided with an amnion, much yolk, and a shell; eggs not laid in the water; no free-living larval stage; no suckling of the young. The reptilian kidney is of an advanced type; a duct, involved solely with excretory function, carries urine from the kidney to the cloaca. The latter chamber opens to the outside through a slit called the vent. Most reptiles, like birds, excrete the greater part of their nitrogenous wastes as uric acid rather than urea or ammonia. (The American alligator excretes a good bit of ammonia; other crocodilians may prove to do the same.)

The foregoing list of reptilian characteristics is based upon the groups that exist today. The list could be extended to include various other features of the skeletal, muscular, digestive, circulatory, and nervous systems, but there is no need here to take such a lengthy detour into the complexities of anatomy. Nor is there need to trace all the known departures from the reptilian norm made during the 300 million years that the class Reptilia has been in existence. It will be seen that there is in living reptiles (and inferentially in extict ones) a close integration of form and function, body chemistry, life history, and activities. Since Linnaeus's time, anatomy has been the chief basis of biological classification, but increasing use is being made today of other taxonomic criteria such as behavior.

In the classificatory scheme, the crocodilians have been traced through the Animal kingdom, the phylum Chordata, the subphylum Vertebrata, and the class Reptilia. This class is divided into seven subclasses, four of them extinct. Only one of the completely vanished four has so far entered our story: the ancient subclass Synapsida, the mammal-like reptiles described previously. The other three extinct subclasses will make a brief appearance in the story, and may be introduced now.

Thus, the subclass Ichthyopterygia has been erected for some spectacular reptiles that swam in the Triassic, Jurassic, and Cretaceous seas. Often called ichthyosaurs ("fish-lizards"), the reptiles of this subclass had evolved a streamlined, fish-like shape. The snout was elongated, the limbs reduced to flippers. At least some ichthyosaurs were provided with a huge tail fin and a triangular dorsal fin. Some and probably all ichthyosaurs were live-bearers, as shown by an occasional, well-developed "baby" fossilized within its mother. Fossilized stomach contents imply an ichthyosaurian diet of squid-like organisms, but fishes were probably eaten also. Another extinct subclass, the Euryapsida, included terrestrial, semiaquatic, and fully aquatic types. A few small euryapsidans may have lived in fresh water; others inhabited coastal waters but were capable (to judge from their limbs) of moving about on land. Of greater concern here were the marine euryapsidans with paddle-like flippers. Best known of these marine types were the Jurassic and Cretaceous plesiosaurs, with a stout body and a snake-like neck. The fourth and last extinct subclass is the Mesosauria. The mesosaurs lived during the Permian, the geological period that preceded the Triassic. A mesosaur had the general conformation of a small crocodilian. The slender snout was armed with long, delicate, needle-like, socketed teeth along the jawbones. There were also teeth on the palate. The unique dentition implies an unusual diet, and it may be significant that fossil beds with mesosaur remains often have a remarkable abundance of small crustaceans as well. Along the midsection of the mesosaur tail, each vertebra had a "breaking point." If some enemy pounced on a mesosaur, the tail would

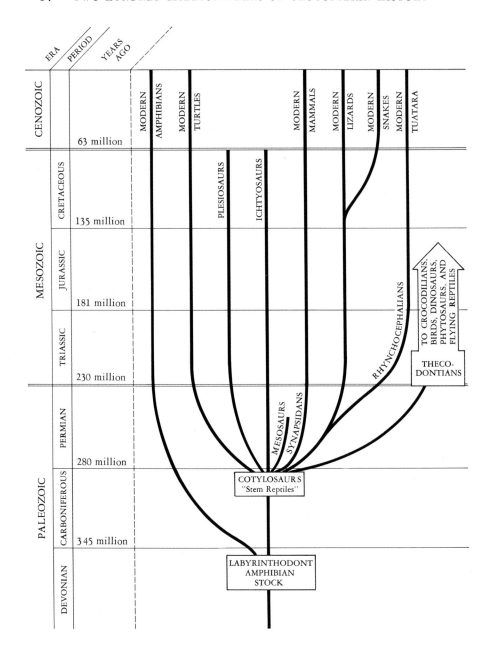

Figure 35. Evolutionary relationships of the reptiles. Diagrammatic. Many side lines are omitted; ages are approximate. Descendants of the thecodontians are shown in detail on another diagram (Figure 34).

Figure 36. This alligator's pose reveals several characteristic features of crocodilian anatomy: long tail, long snout with valvular nasal openings near tip, dorsal armor, two reduced outer toes on fore foot, slight specialization of dentition, and flap covering eardrum (behind eye). [Ross Allen's Reptile Institute]

break off; the enemy might be distracted at least momentarily by the writhing appendage, while the abbreviated mesosaur made its escape. Modern lizards often have a similarly breakable tail, and can grow a new appendage as needed.

Three reptilian subclasses have survived to the present. All of them include extinct groups as well as living ones. Of these three, the subclass Anapsida embraces all the turtles, as well as the long-extinct Paleozoic cotylosaurs or "stem reptiles." The second surviving subclass is the Lepidosauria; it includes the lizards and their close relatives the snakes, along with the unique tuatara, a "living fossil" of New Zealand. To the Lepidosauria belong, also, a number of extinct groups. Most interesting of the vanished lepidosaurians were the mosasaurs of the Cretaceous Period. They were, essentially, marine lizards that reached a great size. With elongate body, paddle-like limbs, and fearsomely toothed jaws, the mosasaurs included diving, surface-dwelling, and high-seas types. A third reptilian subclass, with extinct members and modern survivors, is the Archosauria, the archosaurs or Ruling Reptiles. As already shown, archosaurs persist only in the crocodilians. To put previous discussion on a more formal basis, in the subclass Archosauria there are five orders, four of them extinct. The vanished orders are the ancestral Thecodontia, of which much has already been said; the Pterosauria or flying reptiles; and two orders (Ornithischia and Saurischia) necessary to cover the diversity of dinosaur types. The only living order of the subclass Archosauria is the order Crocodilia, the crocodilians.

How is the order Crocodilia to be distinguished from other reptiles? A succinct characterization is more readily made when the view is limited to modern crocodilians. These are medium-sized or large reptiles with four limbs and a long, stout tail. Toward its tip, the tail becomes progressively more flattened in a vertical plane. The hindlimbs are longer than the forelimbs. The snout is moderately to very long, while the remainder of the skull is somewhat broadened and flattened. Almost the entire external skull surface is sculptured. There are two openings in the temporal region of the skull. The upper of these openings may be much reduced or even virtually closed, but the lower is well developed and forms part of a trough in which the ear apparatus is set. The external nares (nasal openings) lie near the tip of the snout, within a bony orifice. A secondary palate is highly developed. Involving the premaxillary, maxillary, palatine, and pterygoid bones of the skull, the secondary palate forms a shelf that extends backward parallel to the roof of the mouth. The nasal passages, extending backward above the secondary palate, open posteriorly not into the mouth cavity but into the throat. The throat can be closed off from the mouth cavity by a flap of skin. The pterygoid and quadrate bones of the skull are tightly plastered to the lateral walls of the brain case, an arrangement making for rigidity in this part of the head. The antithesis of this arrangement is seen in the snakes, among which the jaw and palate apparatus are very flexibly attached to the skull. Certain bones of the crocodilian skull are somewhat lightened by air spaces within them. The crocodilian dentition is thecodont, the teeth being set in deep sockets of the jawbone. In other living reptiles the teeth may be absent, fused with the jawbone, set rather superficially atop it, or set along the edge of it. Specialization of the crocodilian dentition is not marked, but enlarged canines are often evident, and blunt posterior teeth may contrast with sharper anterior ones. The mandible (a bone complex forming a right or left half of the lower jaw) is strongly fused to its fellow of the opposite side. The fusion takes place near the tip of the lower jaw. If the snout chances to be very narrow, then the symphysis (the longitudinal line of mandibular fusion) may be very long.

Characteristic features of the living Crocodilia are not limited to those of general conformation and head skeleton. Mention should be made of a vertebral column divisible into five regions. The cervical (neck) vertebrae bear short ribs that do not attach to the sternum (breastbone). Behind the cervicals, the thoracic vertebrae bear longer ribs; the more anterior of these thoracic ribs do attach to the sternum. Behind the thoracics are a few lumbar vertebrae without ribs. Next come two sacral vertebrae, flattened and attached to the pelvic girdle. Finally there is a series of caudal (tail) vertebrae. These five regions are not as sharply defined as in the mammals, but they are more sharply defined than in any other living reptiles. The thoracic ribs, and a few nearby cervical ribs, each bear a curved structure (the uncinate process) that extends posteriorly to overlap the rib behind; thus the body wall is given extra strength. Small bones called gastralia lie in the body wall between the ribs and the pelvis. The latter, a complex of bones forming the hip region, has a triradiate structure (a short ilium, a slender pubis, a short and broad ischium). The pubis is excluded from the acetabulum (the cup-shaped cavity that receives the head of the thigh bone) by the ischium. In advance of the pelvic region, each vertebra is concave anteriorly and convex posteriorly. Bony plates, imbedded in the skin, form a dorsal armor (Fig. 37). There may also be small, poorly developed, bony platelets in the skin of the under surfaces, especially toward the throat. (Hide dealers call these ventral platelets "buttons," and thoroughly despise them because their somewhat unpredictable development ocassionally lowers the value of a crocodilian skin.) The front foot bears five toes, the outer two being somewhat reduced (note Fig. 36). The hind foot seems, externally, to bear only four toes; a fifth is represented internally by a mere stump of bone.

Distinguishing characters of the modern Crocodilia involve more than those of the skeleton. For example, the heart is four-chambered, as in mammals but not in other living reptiles. However, the crocodilian circulatory system does not attain a complete separation of oxygenated blood from

Figure 37. A bony scute lies within each scale of the crocodilian's dorsal armor. Shown here is an alligator scute. [Tod Swalm]

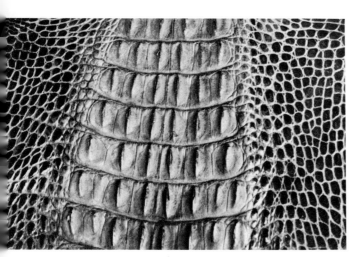

Figure 38. The crocodilian's skin is fairly thick, the epidermis thrown up into non-overlapping scales (at left). The dorsal scales, with their bony scutes, form an armor. In a few species, some of the ventral scales (below) may bear bony platelets. [W. T. Neill]

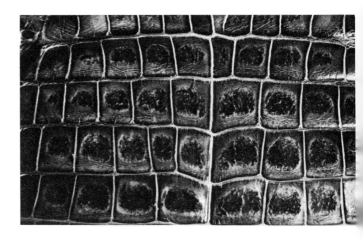

Figure 39. In this submerged alligator, the transparent "third eyelid" is drawn across the eye. The reptile can see without getting water in its eyes (upper). An American crocodile shows the "aquatic profile"; eyes and nostrils are above the general level of the head (lower). [Ross Allen's Reptile Institute]

blood that has lost oxygen during its passage through the body. A major arterial structure (the right aortic arch), carrying oxygenated blood from one side of the heart, fuses with a counterpart arterial structure (the left aortic arch) that carries deoxygenated blood. Thus the fused structure (the dorsal aorta) results in some circulatory inefficiency. The crocodilian dermis—the thickest and deepest skin layer—is well developed. (If it were not, there would be less demand for alligator shoes and handbags.) The skin is covered with epidermal scales which do not overlap each other. The stratum corneum, or thin outermost layer of the skin, is not sloughed entire or in large patches; it wears away and is replaced. There is a pair of gland-like structures on the under side of the lower jaw, another pair of glands just inside the cloacal opening, and a row of glands down either side of the back between the first and second rows of plates. Oral glands, which help moisten prey in preparation for swallowing, are poorly developed. There is a counterpart of the mammalian diaphragm, the body cavity being divided by a muscular septum into lung cavity and peritoneal cavity; the arrangement makes for more efficient breathing. The tongue lies on the floor of the mouth, and is not protrusible. A part of the stomach is modified to form a muscular, gizzard-like organ in which stones and other hard objects may accumulate. A colic caecum, or pocket at the junction of large and small intestine, is lacking. The vent, the external opening of the cloaca, is a longitudinal slit. There is no urinary bladder. The ovaries are paired structures lying in the body cavity. Ovarian structure is solid as in higher vertebrates, not saccular as in amphibians. The egg is "cleidoic"; that is, rather effectively closed off from the environment in which it is laid. In the upper part of the oviduct are glands that secrete albumen about the egg. The egg shell is calcified but somewhat flexible. The male crocodilian has paired testes suspended in the body cavity. There is a single penis, erectile and provided with a glans; except during copulation, the organ is retracted within the cloaca. The crocodilian eye has upper and lower lids. There is also a transparent "third eyelid" or nictitating membrane, which can cover the eye while yet permitting vision (Fig. 39). In the dark, the pupil of the eye expands to a large circle; in bright light it contracts to a vertical slit. The ear drum lies beneath a protective flap. The nostrils are valvular, closing when the reptile submerges. The brain is noteworthy for the presence of a true cerebral cortex.

It would be possible to lengthen this characterization of the modern crocodilians. The skeletal features of the group, in particular, could be treated at greater length. Such features are of particular interest to the paleontologist, who rarely has anything else to guide him in his study of a vertebrate fossil. One scrap might be precisely what is needed to permit identification of fragmentary remains. It must not be supposed, however, that the foregoing description, based on the living members of the group, is wholly applicable to extinct ones also. The distinguishing characters of a major taxonomic group do not all develop abruptly; most if not all of them evolve slowly. Living crocodilians are removed by 200 million years from the earliest representatives of their order, and have evolved some departures from the ancestral types. For example, very early crocodiles did not have such a highly developed secondary palate as do the modern ones. The discrepancy in size between hindlimb and forelimb was most evident in early types, possibly because they were related to (or even derived from) bipedal

thecodontians. A presacral vertebra of an early crocodilian was slightly concave at both ends, not concave anteriorly and convex posteriorly. In some of
the extinct crocodilians, bony plates formed an armor not only dorsally but
also ventrally. All the living crocodilians exhibit the "aquatic profile," with
nostrils and eyes elevated above the general level of the head; but not so
some extinct kinds, in which the eyes were directed laterally. Furthermore,
the living crocodiles represent somewhat conservative and generalized stocks
within the order. Within this same order, various extinct groups had evolved
certain anatomical specializations, surprising departures from the crocodilian
norm. The major specializations are noted in subsequent chapters that deal
with crocodilian history.

7 CROCODILIAN HISTORY: THE FIRST 137 MILLION YEARS

THE BINOMIAL system of biological nomen-
clature is applicable to fossil species just as it is to living ones. In a cursory
survey of fossil crocodilians, attention is focused chiefly on genera and
higher taxonomic categories. Until the crocodilian story nears modern
times, there is no need to supply the full, Latinized, and italicized names of
every species involved. The earliest known crocodilian has been named
Proterochampsa barrionuevoi, but one may call the reptile Proterochampsa,
just as one might write of a Magnolia, an Iris, an Aster, a Narcissus, a
Chrysanthemum, or a Petunia (generic names all).

The oldest and most primitive crocodilian was discovered in western
Argentina in fossil beds dating from the middle part of the Triassic. The
name given it, Proterochampsa, appropriately means "forerunning crocodile." The jaws of Proterochampsa bore the usual tooth rows, but in addition there were extra teeth on the palatines, the bones that form the back
of the roof of the mouth. This was a very primitive character. Throughout
the history of the vertebrates, from the fishes through the mammals, there

has been a trend toward a reduction in the number of locations where teeth might develop. Fishes may have teeth almost anywhere in the mouth or even back in the gullet. There are fishes with teeth on the tongue, the hyoid arch (which serves also to anchor the tongue muscles), or the gill arches, as well as on the roof of the mouth and along the jawbones. Among the amphibians, teeth are usually located not only on the jawbones but also on various other bones that make up the roof of the mouth. A comparatively primitive type of dentition, with teeth on the roof of the mouth as well as along the jawbones, has been retained to the present day by some reptile groups. Most snakes, for example, have nearly as many teeth in the roof of the mouth as along the upper jawbones. Some early thecodontians retained palatine teeth. In the reptile-birds and the early, toothed birds (whose modern descendants have only a toothless, horny beak), the teeth were restricted to the jawbones; the same is true of the modern crocodiles and of the mammals. Proterochampsa thus suggested a primitive thecodontian in the location of its teeth. It was also thecodontian-like in several

Figure 40. Africa and South America were formerly joined in the fashion shown at the right. Early crocodilians and other organisms could have moved from one of these continents to the other, without having passed through any more northerly lands. Below, the former fit of Australia, Tasmania, and Antarctica. Diagrammatic. A few modern place names have been added to facilitate orientation.

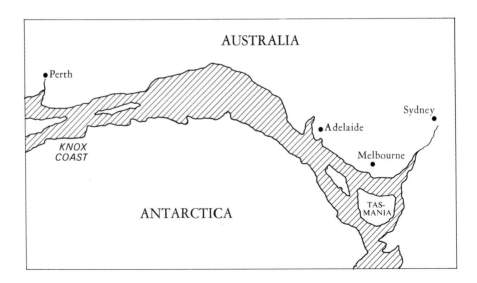

other details of skull structure, although the skull was crocodilian-like in a majority of features. Proterochampsa was so distinctive that it was assigned to a family of its own, the Proterochampsidae.

This is not to say that the family Proterochampsidae stands wholly apart from all other crocodilians. It is related to another family, the Notochampsidae, from the late Triassic of southern Africa. These two families are grouped as a suborder, Archeosuchia ("ancient crocodiles"), distinct from all later types. Two genera of the Notochampsidae have so far been discovered: Notochampsa and Erythrochampsa. These early crocodilians had lost palatine teeth, but resembled Proterochampsa in having (among other things) eyes that were directed somewhat laterally. This is an unspecialized character among crocodilians. As previously remarked, the modern species have evolved the "aquatic profile:" nostrils and eyes rise above the general level of the head, permitting vision and respiration when the body and most of the head are hidden beneath the water. Like Proterochampsa, the notochampsids were small crocodilians with a fairly long and

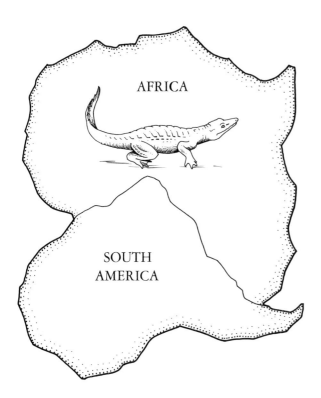

slender snout. Both archeosuchian families were well armored. The dorsal armor consisted of a single row of quadrangular, bony plates to each side of the dorsal midline.

The restriction of the suborder Archeosuchia to South America and southern Africa is interesting. How did archeosuchians get from one of these areas to the other? It must not be forgotten that, in the early Triassic, the two supercontinents of Laurasia and Gondwanaland had not split into the continental masses we know today. Although there is some uncertainty about the exact order in which the land masses were split away, it seems clear that the last splitting sundered Africa from South America, and took place well after the Triassic. (Long before geologists, geophysicists, and oceanographers attacked the problem of continental drift, several people were impressed to note that the east coast of South America very neatly duplicates in reverse the west coast of Africa; and that if the two continents were pushed together like two pieces of a jigsaw puzzle, certain geological formations would coincide just as would the coastlines.) Archeosuchians passed between South America and Africa without crossing an ocean or moving through the northern continents.

If archeosuchians could so spread, then other living things should also have been able to do so. Various ancient groups of reptiles and other organisms should be represented in South America and Africa, without trace in the fossil record of Eurasia or North America. Such groups do exist. A review of them is outside the scope of the present work, but it is not amiss to mention the mesosaurs, little reptiles that were described as making up the subclass Mesosauria. Living far back in the Permian, the period preceding the Triassic, they left their fossil remains only in South America and southern Africa. The African and South American mesosaurs all belonged to a single genus, Mesosaurus. A comparable pattern of distribution has been noted in certain groups of the reptilian subclass Synapsida. The most mammal-like synapsidans have been set apart as the order Therapsida (and occasionally placed with the mammals instead of with the reptiles). The therapsidan family Cynognathidae is represented in the Triassic of South America and southern Africa; the therapsidan family Diademodontidae in the Triassic of South America, southern Africa, and eastern Africa.

Returning to the order Crocodilia, from northern Arizona come the remains of an interesting little reptile called Protosuchus. Of the late

Triassic, this crocodilian was about a yard in length. It had a comparatively blunt snout and a high head. In other words it was not streamlined, and probably was not a water dweller. It had seventeen well-spaced teeth along each side of the upper jaw, and an equal number along each side of the lower jaw. Protosuchus was well armored. To each side of the dorsal midline was a row of broad plates; the belly was protected by an oval shield made up of small plates in sixteen transverse rows; the tail was completely sheathed in bony armor. This reptile must have been somewhat lizard-like in habits, pursuing its prey on land. However, one must not visualize it as inhabiting deserts like those of present-day Arizona. Protosuchus lived more than 160 million years before Arizona turned to desert. This small, ancient crocodilian has been given a family of its own, the Protosuchidae, and a suborder of its own, the Protosuchia ("ancestral crocodiles"). From Wales, in the British Isles, come the remains of a crocodilian perhaps allied to Protosuchus.

Southern Africa has yielded the fragmentary remains of a late Triassic reptile dubbed Sphenosuchus. It might have been a thecodontian, a comparatively unchanged African remnant of the stock that elsewhere gave rise to crocodilians. Alternatively, it might have been a true, albeit primitive, crocodilian. It was unarmored, and had a rather short, deep head like Protosuchus. Sphenosuchus is given a family of its own, the Sphenosuchidae, and tentatively placed in the suborder Protosuchia.

Crocodilians are very scarce in the Triassic of the northern continents, and the one or two known kinds seem to have been terrestrial rather than aquatic. At this point one can see how the phytosaurs, described previously, may fit into the crocodilian story. It will be remembered that the phytosaurs were regarded as specialized thecodontians, and that they resembled aquatic crocodilians in superficial appearance and general way of life. The oldest known phytosaur comes from the early Triassic of Europe, and is older than any crocodilian. During the Triassic, phytosaurs became widespread from Europe to North America (then combined as parts of Laurasia). Being firmly established in the aquatic habitats of what are now the northern continents, phytosaurs probably stood in the way of crocodilian radiation northward. Crocodilians reached Laurasia and were eventually able to replace phytosaurs in aquatic situations there, but this later procedure was a slow one and was not accomplished during the Triassic. In that period, the only crocodilians to invade phytosaur territory were small, land-dwelling kinds, which did not have to compete with the bigger and more aquatic phytosaurs.

Some Triassic crocodilian history may be concealed beneath the Antarctic ice. Today the southernmost continent is ice-locked and nearly barren, but it was forested during the Triassic-Jurassic-Cretaceous span, as well as during periods earlier and later. The best known Antarctic fossil plant is called Glossopteris. It and some other plants occurred together so consistently that paleobotanists, students of ancient plant life, speak of the "Glossopteris flora." This flora dates from around the earliest part of the Permian. Plants of the Glossopteris flora were fossilized into coal beds on several parts of Antarctica. Coal deposits, with Glossopteris leaves and conifer needles, have been found within 250 miles of the South Pole. The Glossopteris flora included big trees with annual growth rings, a circumstance perhaps implying a temperate climate and a cycle of the seasons. This flora is mentioned because its existence reveals Antarctica to have had in former times a climate that reptiles might have tolerated. Also, the Glossopteris flora has been discovered not only in Antarctica but in South America, Australia, Africa, and India as well. This distribution is suggestive of former land connections in the southern hemisphere. Modern computer technology has revealed the former connection of Antarctica with Australia; the southeastern end of Australia, along with Tasmania, once fit into what is now the Ross Sea, and the southwestern end of Australia reached to what is now the Knox Coast of Antarctica. Most interestingly, Glossopteris deposits in Antarctica have yielded the fossilized trackways of what was either an amphibian or a reptile.

The Glossopteris flora had vanished by the Triassic, but Antarctica was still vegetated in that period. Excavations in the Transantarctic Mountains, about 325 miles from the pole, revealed the bed of a Triassic stream, and the remains of an amphibian. It was one of the so-called labyrinthodonts, and must have been about a yard long. It had early Triassic relatives in Australia and southern Africa. Of all vertebrate classes, the Amphibia are the least tolerant of salt water, and their discovery on Antarctica accords well with the concept of former land connections in the southern hemisphere. An ancient stream bed in the Alexandra Range, near the South Pole, yielded the remains of a therapsid reptile called Lystrosaurus. This genus was present in Asia and Africa during the early Triassic. In its proportions and probable semiaquatic way of life, Lystrosaurus has been likened to a hippopotamus, although it was much smaller. The fragmentary remains of a thecodontian were also found along with the Antarctic Lystrosaurus. Evidently, an important part of vertebrate evolution is hidden beneath the south polar ice cap.

Birds may have arisen on Antarctica, a circumstance to explain why reptile-bird intermediates (in contrast with reptile-mammal intermediates) are so scarce in the fossil record of the more accessible continents. Turtles, too, may have evolved on Antarctica. Turtles, complete with shell and various other features of their order, appear rather suddenly in the latter Triassic of Europe, but must have had a lengthy evolution in some undisclosed region. Just one known reptile, Eunotosaurus from the Permian of southern Africa, might possibly be regarded as directly ancestral to turtles. Pterosaurs, highly specialized flying reptiles, appear abruptly in the early Jurassic of Europe; they show anatomical evidence of a thecodontian ancestry, but thecodontian-pterosaur intermediates have not come to light anywhere. Could their remains likewise lie beneath Antarctic ice?

About 181 million years ago the Triassic passed into the Jurassic. Early and middle Jurassic deposits, except marine ones, are scarce throughout most of the world. During this period some of the crocodilians took to the sea, and left their remains in marine sediments. The marine crocodilians of the family Teleosauridae had a long, narrow snout that was set off sharply from the posterior part of the skull. The modern gharial of India, with a similar head shape, feeds by lying motionless on the bottom of a river and slashing sideways at passing fishes; the water offers little resistance to the narrow snout, and a darting fish is snapped up with astonishing speed and accuracy. The teleosaurs probably fed in the same way, although in salt water. Teleosaur teeth were very long and slender, a circumstance compatible with fish-eating habits. The hind legs were about twice as long as the fore legs. The back was protected by a paired row of overlapping bony plates, and the belly was armored also. Against what enemies might the teleosaurs have been armored? The Jurassic seas harbored other reptilian carnivores: marine lepidosaurians, ichthyosaurs in variety, and euryapsidans such as the plesiosaurs and their kin. There were also sharks and bony fishes, big enough to menace at least a young teleosaur if not a grown one. The weight of bony armor was probably not much of a drawback in the sea. Salt water is more buoyant than fresh, and a little extra weight could have helped the teleosaur to submerge without expelling all the air from the lungs. Swimming speed would have been reduced by armor, but it is inferred that teleosaurs, like the gharial, captured prey by lurking rather than by pursuing. To judge from their anatomy, teleosaurs were quite capable of movement on land. Probably they inhabited coastal waters, and came up on sandy beaches to nest. The Teleosauridae thrived from the Jurassic well into the succeeding Cretaceous, and during this time its members reached such diverse places as Europe, South America, and Madagascar.

Allied to the teleosaurs are the reptiles of the family Metriorhynchidae. Called sea-crocodiles, they represent the only invasion of the high seas by any archosaur. Metriorhynchids were rather elongate crocodilians. The snout was slender, but not set off abruptly from the rest of the head. The limbs had taken on a paddle-like structure. The end of the tail was angled downward to form the support and lower edge of a tail fin. There may also have been a small, fleshy fin on the back. Metriorhynchid teeth were laterally compressed, the ones of the upper jaw meeting those of the lower jaw with a shearing action. This dentition probably served to chop up sizeable fishes. Bony armor had been lost, sacrificed in favor of swimming speed. Sculpturing of the skull bones had also been lost. A sea-crocodile gives the impression of having been a sleek and streamlined reptile, capable of arrow-like progression through the water, and of catching fishes or eluding enemies by virtue of superior speed. Reproductive habits of the metriorhynchids are unknown. Did they live in deep waters but return to the beach for egg-laying, or were they live-bearers? (On this subject, more later.) Sea-crocodiles are known from such widely separated areas as South America and Europe. Flourishing in the Jurassic, they survived well into the next period, the Cretaceous.

In sea-crocodiles and at least some teleosaurs small plates of bone formed a ring about the eyeball. A "scleral ring" of this kind is present in many reptiles, in fact in most vertebrates except mammals and shark-like fishes. However, it is lacking in modern crocodilians. The function of the ring is uncertain. In marine crocodilians it may have preserved the eyeball from deformation by water pressure when the reptile made a deep dive. This assumption is not ruled out by the occurrence of a scleral ring in various nonaquatic reptiles. In modern crocodilians the skull is so solidly constructed that eyeballs are not put under pressure when food is taken, but certain other reptiles become quite pop-eyed in their efforts to engulf proportionately large prey. A scleral ring has also been regarded as serving to counteract the intraocular pressure of fluids.

Although the Jurassic seas were invaded by several different reptile groups, it must not be supposed that the marine habitat was open simply for the taking. Reptiles in general are poorly equipped for existence in the sea, and must evolve special adaptations if they are to do more than visit a saltwater habitat from nearby land or fresh water. Life in a salt solution offers problems whose nature may not be readily apparent. For example, water tends to diffuse in the direction of greater salt concentration. A minnow from a brook will usually shrivel and die if kept in salt water, for the water of its tissues will be lost to the surrounding medium. Many a marine organism will bloat and die if placed in fresh water, where the water of its tissues is saltier than, and therefore invaded by, the surrounding medium. Marine fishes maintain a proper water balance in several ways, depending on kind. Sharks do not excrete their urea but store it in the blood. A urea concentration acts like a salt concentration in preventing diffusion of water from the tissues into the sea. In the higher or bony fishes of marine habitat, the salt concentration in the tissues is kept down to about one-third that of sea water. This is possible because excess salt can be removed through the gills with little loss of body water. Such physiological and anatomical adaptations are not possible to reptiles. A further complication is that some movement of water into the system is needed to carry away nitrogenous waste products. How could a reptile obtain drinking water in the sea? If it drank salt water, what could it do with the excess salt? Kidneys might in theory remove salt, but would remove needed water as well. The reptile kidney cannot excrete urine that is saltier than the blood. A diet of fishes would be productive of some water, but such a highly proteinous diet would also increase the amount of water needed for excretion.

In various living marine reptiles (and sea birds) some gland of the head region is modified into a "salt gland" which extracts salt from the blood, and liberates a concentrated salt solution to the outside. In a partially marine lizard, the salt-concentrating gland is the nasal gland, and its secretion reaches the outside by way of the nasal passage. The venomous sea-snakes have a unique structure, the natrial gland, opening into the roof of the mouth. This structure is believed to be the salt gland, for a concentrated salt solution is produced from the reptile's mouth. In sea turtles the Harderian gland is the salt gland, and discharges its secretion beneath the eyelid. Although the modern crocodilians have not been intensively studied, it is believed that they (or some of them) remove excess salt by the same route that exists in sea turtles. In the American crocodile, which often lives in estuaries and coastal situations, a salt solution more concentrated than sea water has been collected from the eye region. Invasion of the sea by some ancient reptile group might have been contingent in part upon the evolution of an efficient salt gland. Teleosaurs and metriorhynchids probably had a salt gland.

But many other factors are involved with reptilian existence in marine habitats. There is, for example, the matter of reproduction. A reptile egg cannot have a completely impermeable shell, for the embryo has to breathe. Blood vessels in the allantois, the respiratory membrane within the egg, take up oxygen that has diffused through the shell, and pass carbon dioxide in the opposite direction. The oxygen requirements of a reptile embryo are not high, but they do exist; and a reptile egg cannot be laid in salt water or any other water. A marine reptile must return to land for nesting, or else be a live-bearer. The necessity to move overland, if only to a nesting spot on the beach above storm tides, is not compatible with thoroughgoing adaptation to marine existence, for the reptile must retain some capacity for terrestrial locomotion. Also, some part of the body must remain suitable for digging a nesting hole. (Modern sea turtles dig mostly with the hindlimb, which is much less paddle-like than the forelimb.) As for the live-bearing condition, it need not develop simply because it might prove useful. Evolution is not directive but opportunistic. At its simplest it depends on the innate capacity of an organism to vary, and the continued selection in nature of the more useful variations—immediately useful ones, that is. It is therefore surprising that crocodilians were ever able to invade the high seas, especially since the marine habitats had been taken over by invertebrates and fishes long before the Age of Reptiles began. Yet, the metriorhynchids survived in the oceans for 70 million years. So did the teleosaurs, although they probably frequented the inshore waters rather than the high seas where the metriorhynchids lived.

While these two families were evolving in the sea, other crocodilians must have existed in freshwater and terrestrial habitats. Their remains have not been found, for known deposits of early and middle Jurassic age are marine in large part, as already noted. However, non-marine crocodilians reappear in the fossil record during the latter Jurassic, which provides the appropriate non-marine deposits. Terrestrial and freshwater crocodilians of the latter Jurassic were not derived from the specialized teleosaurs or metriorhynchids, but rather from some more generalized stock. Most important of the late Jurassic crocodilians were those of the family Goniopholidae. This group probably originated in the Old World during the middle Jurassic. By late Jurassic times the family was present in North America, Europe, and Asia; and it survived into the Cretaceous in all these areas. During the Cretaceous it spread also into South America and Africa. Goniopholids were not marine. Most of them probably were semi-aquatic in fresh water, and not very different in their habits from the modern crocodilians. Toward the back of the goniopholid jaws, the teeth were stout and blunt, adapted for crushing. What might have been crushed by the heavy jaws and blunt teeth? Probably turtle shells, for living crocodilians with similar dentition often prey heavily on turtles. Goniopholids were armored above and below. In some the dorsal plates were fastened together by a sort of peg-and-socket articulation, an arrangement producing a continuous yet flexible sheet of dorsal armor. Presumably the goniopholids were menaced by mightier carnivores. Meat-eating dinosaurs could have taken a toll of these crocodilians. However, far less spectacular predators might have threatened the hatchlings. (A later chapter will note that baby alligators are eaten by birds, fishes, and even frogs.) Goniopholids seem to represent the central line of crocodilian ancestry, the line that led eventually to the modern species.

Obviously, the crocodilians have been far more varied in the past than they are today. We have scarcely begun to describe the diversity of types that have existed within the order Crocodilia. Among the extremes were two late Jurassic families, Theriosuchidae and Atoposauridae, both of them probably derived from goniopholid ancestors. Theriosuchids, known only from the late Jurassic of Europe, resembled goniopholids but were much smaller. The largest theriosuchids probably did not exceed a yard in total length. Atoposaurs were even smaller; some of them were scarcely a foot long, no bigger than the "baby alligators" that tourists bring back from Florida. Atoposaurs were unarmored below, but were provided with one row of broadened plates to each side of the dorsal midline. These pygmy crocodilians are definitely known only from the late Jurassic of Europe, but one possible atoposaur has been reported from China and another from North America. (It should be clear why some fossils cannot be placed exactly in the taxonomic scheme. They are fragmentary when found, and the most diagnostic structures may be missing. A tentative identification must suffice until better specimens are unearthed.)

It would not be surprising to find unmistakable atoposaur remains in Asia and North America as well as Europe. Among vertebrates of the land and fresh water, one of the commonest patterns of distribution has been the Eurasian-North American. This circumstance in part reflects a former continuity of land at the time before Laurasia was fragmented. Even after this fragmentation, there was a broad land connection across the North Atlantic from eastern North America to western Europe. It was long after the Jurassic that this connection was broken. There has also been a land connection between western North America and eastern Asia. Today these two areas are separated by only 56 miles of water, the Bering Strait; and the strait is broken by islands. The land connection that preceded the Bering Strait is often called Bering Bridge. It was a broad highway, up to 1,300 miles wide, across which plants and animals passed during several geological periods. The present cold climate of the Bering Strait region is a fairly new development, from a geological and paleontological standpoint; cooling began rather gradually around 27 million years ago. There have been great spans of time during which not only mammals and birds but also reptiles and amphibians could pass between Eurasia and North America, undeterred by climatic rigors. Some freshwater fishes also made the passage, in streams that flowed between North America and Asia.

Neither the theriosuchids nor the atoposaurs survived beyond the Jurassic. However, another crocodilian family, the Pholidosauridae, proved more successful. Pholidosaurs appeared in the late Jurassic of Europe and Asia. Before the period was out, they had reached North America, which still had land connections with Eurasia at that time. The pholidosaurs were notably long-snouted, but otherwise they were rather generalized crocodilians. They were armored both dorsally and ventrally. By early Cretaceous times the family had reached northern Africa, and had given rise to a gigantic crocodilian in what is now the Sahara Desert. The Sahara region was not a desert then, but a well-watered land, capable of supporting enormous, aquatic crocodilians and their prey. By late Cretaceous times the pholidosaurs were vanishing from northern continents, but were establishing a new line of descent in Africa. This pholidosaur line, whose members are sometimes called the dyrosaurs, originated in the latter Cretaceous, persisted through the succeeding Paleocene, and survived even into the next period (the Eocene). Dyrosaurs were exceedingly long-snouted. Their eyes were directed more laterally than upwardly.

Two other crocodilian families warrant mention: the Notosuchidae from the late Cretaceous of South America and the Libycosuchidae from the same time period of northern Africa. Both families are made up of short-snouted, deep-skulled types. One supposes that they were not primarily aquatic. Notosuchus of South America was unarmored, and had only ten or eleven teeth in each side of the jaw, upper or lower. Libycosuchus of northern Africa was practically toothless, and its food is unknown. Perhaps it grubbed in the mud for worms and insect larvae.

Eight families discussed in the present chapter—the sea-dwelling Metriorhynchidae and Teleosauridae, the freshwater Goniopholidae, the dwarfed Theriosuchidae and even more dwarfed Atoposauridae, the long-snouted Pholidosauridae, the high-headed Notosuchidae, and the puzzlingly toothless Libycosuchidae—are placed in one suborder, the Mesosuchia or "intermediate crocodiles." The sea-crocodiles are so distinctive that they have at times been removed from the suborder Mesosuchia and given a suborder of their own, Thalattosuchia. However, they seem close enough to teleosaurs and pholidosaurs to be retained in the Mesosuchia.

To recapitulate briefly: Crocodilians originated with the thecodontian-like Proterochampsa, from the middle Triassic of South America. Its family, the Proterochampsidae, had relatives, the Notochampsidae, in the latter Triassic of southern Africa. The two families make up the suborder Archeosuchia or "ancient crocodiles." Protosuchus, the small, land-dwelling crocodilian from the late Triassic of Arizona, has its own family, Protosuchidae, and its own suborder, Protosuchia or "ancestral crocodiles." Protosuchus may have had relatives in Wales. The problematic family Sphenosuchidae, from the late Triassic of southern Africa, is tentatively placed in the Protosuchia. The suborder Mesosuchia includes eight families of "intermediate crocodiles," ranging from marine and freshwater to land-dwelling, from diminutive to gigantic.

With the exception of dyrosaurs in Africa, the crocodilians so far discussed did not persist beyond the Cretaceous, if they survived to that period. (Some families vanished earlier, as noted.) Two crocodilian suborders, not mentioned so far, originated in the Cretaceous but survived long past it, one of them to the present. These two suborders will bring the crocodilian story up to modern times.

8 CROCODILIANS AT THE END OF AN ERA

THE TRIASSIC, Jurassic, and Cretaceous Periods collectively make up the Mesozoic Era (the Age of Reptiles in popular usage). Mesozoic means "of intermediate life." The era is thus contrasted with the preceding one, the Paleozoic ("of ancient life"), and with the succeeding one, the Cenozoic ("of recent life"). Of periods composing the Paleozoic Era, only one has required mention: the last one, the Permian.

When a geological deposit is being formed, new material is continuously or sporadically laid down atop the old, and the upper levels of the deposit will therefore be younger than the lower. Accordingly, geologists and paleontologists may speak of "Upper" and "Lower" divisions of a period; but it suffices in the present work to use more informal designations such as "latter" or "early."

In general, eras and periods were established on the basis of geological and paleontological episodes in the marine waters of Europe and North America. That is to say, boundaries between periods were set up at points where there seemed to be important breaks in the record of marine sedimentation, and significant changes in the marine invertebrate life. But depositional events in one area need not be paralleled exactly by events in some other area; and a marked change in marine invertebrate life does not necessarily mean a simultaneous and comparable change in land or freshwater vertebrate life. When the view is limited to one vertebrate group, such as the class Reptilia, period boundaries may appear far less significant than they do in broad view. For example, the transition from the Permian Period to the Triassic—in other words from the Paleozoic Era to the Mesozoic—did not signal a major change in reptile life. The reptile fauna of the early Triassic was essentially Paleozoic in aspect, and not until the latter Triassic did important new groups appear.

The transition from Mesozoic to Cenozoic was important in reptilian history, important not especially for the development of new groups of reptiles but rather for the extinction of some old ones. However, the faunal turnover at the end of the Mesozoic was not as abrupt, sweeping, or in-explicable as brief accounts might lead one to think. The disappearance of the dinosaurs has perhaps been over-emphasized in the literature. The extinction of the dinosaurs at the end of the Mesozoic was hardly more remarkable than the disappearance at earlier times of scale-trees, trilobites, sea-scorpions, ammonites, armored fishes, various amphibians and reptiles, or hundreds of other plant and animal groups. Dinosaurs (or at least cer-tain well-publicized ones) were very large, and provided either with enormous teeth or fantastic armament. Man is still impressed by size, teeth, talons, horns, and spines, and so he attaches great significance to the disappearance of the dinosaurs. Yet, the history of life is typified by these reptiles. Groups of living things arise, flourish, and diversify, then decline, and finally vanish to be replaced by better adapted groups.

It does seem as though extinctions and replacements are hastened or multiplied in times of marked geologic and climatic changes. This is not surprising, for many living things might not be able to keep pace with environmental changes, and so would yield to the ones that could. The Cretaceous ended with the so-called Laramide revolution, a time of moun-tain building. The Rockies began to rise in North America, and other mountain chains elsewhere. During the Cretaceous a great arm of the sea had split North America into eastern and western components; but as the land continued to rise, the sea retreated. Vast new lands were ex-posed in several parts of the world, changing the direction of ocean cur-rents. Countless swamps and lagoons vanished as former lowlands were elevated. There were climatic shifts, documented by marked changes in the flora. All these are conditions under which numerous extinctions and replacements are to be expected.

It should already be clear that, of the reptile groups mentioned in previous chapters, some disappeared long before the end of the Cretaceous and others long after. It is interesting to note the times at which these groups actually became extinct. The Thecodontia did not persist as such beyond the Triassic, but they evolved into archosaurs and birds. In like fashion the Synapsida persisted in part, as mammals. The phytosaurs, specialized thecodontians with crocodilian-like build, did not survive past

Figure 41. "Cretaceous" means chalky; the Cretaceous Period got its name from the famed white cliffs of the English south coast. [British Travel Association]

the Triassic. Mesosaurs lived only in the Permian. One group of flying reptiles and one of armored dinosaurs vanished in the early Cretaceous. A second group of flying reptiles and the rest of the dinosaurs became extinct at the end of the Cretaceous, as did the marine ichthyosaurs and plesiosaurs. Turtles persisted into modern times. Among the Lepidosauria, the mosasaurs and allied types became extinct at the end of the Cretaceous; but lizards, snakes, and the lone tuatara survive to the present. Interestingly, the subclass Lepidosauria produced one superficially crocodilian-like offshoot in the Cretaceous, the genus Champsosaurus, which persisted from the latter Cretaceous through the Eocene in both North America and Europe.

As for extinctions among the Crocodilia, there probably was a continuity of descent from the Archeosuchia through the Protosuchia to the Mesosuchia. This line of descent had sterile side-branches, but not all of these were terminated with the end of the Cretaceous. The atoposaurs and theriosuchids vanished at the end of the Jurassic, the teleosaurs and sea-crocodiles in mid-Cretaceous, the pholidosaurs long after the Cretaceous. The goniopholids disappeared as such at the end of the Cretaceous, but not before giving rise to a new and successful suborder to be discussed presently. The Notosuchidae and Libycosuchidae did indeed vanish as the Age of Reptiles drew to a close. At this point in the story, it looks as though the Mesozoic-Cenozoic transition was not particularly important in crocodilian history. However, before offering this conclusion flatly we must review two more crocodilian suborders, both of which originated in the Cretaceous but continued beyond that period.

From the latter Cretaceous of South America comes a crocodilian family, the Baurusuchidae, quite unlike anything so far discussed. The baurusuchid skull was high and narrow, yet rather long-snouted. Baurusuchid teeth were reduced in number, but the ones that remained were large, some of them almost tusk-like. The cheek teeth were laterally flattened, with serrate anterior and posterior ridges. (Serrations on the edges of a tooth, like those on the edge of a steak knife, permit more effective cutting of meat.) In both head shape and teeth, baurusuchids remind the paleontologist of a carnivorous dinosaur. These crocodilians must have been predators on land. Specimens are few and fragmentary, so unfortunately we know little of their body structure. Descended from the Baurusuchidae is the family Sebecidae, also South American. Sebecids are Cenozoic crocodilians. They persisted in their homeland from the Paleocene through the Eocene, the Oligocene, and the Miocene. As a later chapter will try to show, these land-dwelling crocodilians may have finally vanished through inability to compete with a horde of mammalian carnivores. The Baurusuchidae and Sebecidae make up the suborder Sebecosuchia ("Sebecus-like crocodiles," from Sebek, a malignant, crocodile-headed deity of ancient Egypt). The distinctiveness of this suborder implies that it diverged from other crocodilians at a very early time, perhaps in the little-known early Jurassic; and the high head of the sebecosuchians may indicate descent from a protosuchian. Sebecosuchians probably developed their characteristics during a very lengthy isolation in South America. However, this is a speculation that may have to be revised. Scattered teeth, apparently of sebecosuchians, have lately been reported from several continents; and if the identifications are correct, the suborder was nearly world-wide and not just South American. To judge from the rarity of sebecosuchian remains, these reptiles inhabited situations not conducive to fossilization. Tropical forest comes to mind in this connection. On the damp floor of the forest, dead animals rot quickly, and seldom have chance to fossilize; bones are softened by the acids of the humus, and only the enamel-coated teeth may persist. Tropical forest was once more widespread than it is today, and began to fall back around the midportion of the Cenozoic.

In the preceding chapter it was noted that the goniopholids, belonging to the suborder Mesosuchia, were on the central line of crocodilian descent. There arose from goniopholid stock, probably in the latter Jurassic, a new suborder, the Eusuchia ("true crocodiles"). The earliest eusuchians are those of the family Hylaeochampsidae, from the early Cretaceous of Europe. Hylaeochampsids were small crocodilians with a fully developed secondary palate. The family did not persist, as such, to the end of the Cretaceous, but probably gave rise to all the other, and later, eusuchian families. By late Cretaceous times the eusuchians had become quite diverse.

Most important of eusuchian families was the Crocodylidae. Originating probably from hylaeochampsid stock in the early Cretaceous, the crocodylids first appear in the latter Cretaceous. We shall briefly postpone a discussion of them in order to dispose of two families derived, probably, from the Crocodylidae.

One might think that, well before the advent of the eusuchians, the crocodilians had reached the limit of their adaptive possibilities. There had been sea-crocodiles, diminutive atoposaurs, oversized pholidosaurs, toothless libycosuchids, and dinosaur-headed sebecosuchians, along with more generalized types. However, with the family Stomatosuchidae crocodilian evolution explored yet another pathway. The stomatosuchids were probably derived from some early Crocodylidae that reached Africa by late Cretaceous times. Stomatosuchus, on which the family name was based, was truly gigantic, perhaps 50 or 60 feet long. Its head was flattened and widened; the snout was spatulate; the eyes were set far back and directed upward. The upper jaw bore many small teeth; the weakly constructed lower jaw was toothless. Whatever the food of the duck-billed crocodile, this huge reptile must have inhabited very large rivers or the lakes along them. Such waters did exist in the North African home of the duck-billed crocodile during the latter Cretaceous. The Stomatosuchidae vanished at the end of that period.

In India there lives today an enormous but harmless fish-eating crocodilian called by the Hindustani name of gharial. Through an unfortunate misreading, the name was improperly rendered "gavial," and the reptile given the generic name of Gavialis. This genus is so distinctive as to merit a family of its own, the Gavialidae. The fossil history of the family is just beginning to come to light. The group is believed to have branched off from the Crocodylidae around the late Cretaceous. Fossil material to prove this is lacking, and the view is a fairly new one. The gharial differs from other living crocodilians in several details of skull structure. The differences were once thought to be very important, and to indicate for the Gavialidae a taxonomic position remote from the Crocodylidade. It has even been suggested that gavialids were derived from the long-snouted teleosaurs. By this interpretation, the eusuchian characters of the gharial would have evolved independently of the other families that make up the suborder Eusuchia. Fortunately, some fossil material has turned up to guide our thinking about the ancestry of the Gavialidae. India has yielded a sequence of gharials, from the Miocene to the present. The sequence reveals a prolongation of the snout with time, along with a regular change in skull profile; also, the teeth become more numerous and closer together as the Periods go by. And so to find a possible ancestor of the Gavialidae we do not have to look only among the long-snouted crocodilians.

Just when Indian material was beginning to clarify at least the Miocene-to-recent history of the Gavialidae, there came the surprising discovery of a pre-Miocene gavialid—not in India but in South America. The South American reptile, although of Oligocene age, was a long-snouted species of essentially "modern" aspect, a circumstance no one has attempted to explain. Gavialids have also been found in the Miocene and Pliocene of South America. The South American specimens reveal that one skull character (elongation of the snout by extension of the maxillary bones but not the nasals), formerly taken to set the Gavialidae far apart from the Crocodylidae, is a specialization that arose in the Indian branch of the family but not the South American one. The South American gavialids draw attention to a situation that is common in science: a surprising new discovery will help solve an old problem while raising several new ones.

Certain aspects of gavialid history can be clarified only when more specimens are discovered, but the broader outlines of this history are amenable to interpretation. A previous chapter noted that the peninsula of India was originally a part of Gondwanaland, the more southerly supercontinent. With the breaking up of Gondwanaland, this part drifted northward, finally ramming Asia and pushing up great "wrinkles" which we call the Himalayas. At the time of the Mesozoic-Cenozoic transition, India had broken away from Gondwanaland, but lay closer to Africa than to Asia. Viewed in the light of this continental drift, the distribution of the Gavialidae makes sense. The group had its origin in some part of Gondwanaland. A portion of the early gavialid stock was carried north with drifting India, another portion remained behind. The two components evolved in roughly parallel fashion, but not at the same rate. Perhaps both components became highly specialized fish-stalkers because no other way of life was left open as other crocodilians spread.

In the time when Gondwanaland was still intact, and at a later time when its fragments had not drifted far apart, Africa lay between India and South America. Gavialid remains should someday be discovered in Africa. In fact, there has been a tentative report of a gavialid from the African Pliocene, but the fragmentary nature of the material makes a definite statement impossible. The African stay of the Gavialidae could have been brief, and terminated by the expansion of the pholidosaurs. As noted in a preceding chapter, at the beginning of the Cenozoic the pholidosaurs underwent a surprising new radiation in Africa, producing the so-called dyrosaurs. The very long-snouted dyrosaurs, for some reason highly successful in the early Cenozoic of Africa, could have ousted their competitors, including gavialids.

The Gavialidae will not be described in detail here, for a subsequent account of the living gharial will suffice to characterize the group. It is worth noting, however, that an extinct gharial of India reached a length of 60 feet, and was one of the longest members of the entire order Crocodilia. This giant belonged to the same genus, Gavialis, as the modern gharial.

Thus, the family Crocodylidae produced one sterile offshoot, the Stomatosuchidae, and a more successful offshoot, the Gavialidae. Before the Cretaceous had ended, the main line of the Crocodylidae had begun to ramify further, the ramifications resulting in three distinct lines of descent. One of these tended toward a comparatively short and blunt snout, while a second tended toward a very long and slender snout. The third line was more or less intermediate between these extremes in the matter of snout shape. The three lines of descent do not differ among themselves sufficiently to warrant the erection of as many families; but since they represent definite groups within the family Crocodylidae, they have been given the status of subfamilies under that family name. The blunt-snouted subfamily is the Alligatorinae, the long-snouted one the

Tomistominae, the more generalized one the Crocodylinae. All three lines survive today.

Subsequent remarks on crocodilian history will involve the tracing, as far as possible, of these three crocodylid lineages. We can now return to the question of crocodilian survival past the Cretaceous. Only three crocodilian families vanished completely, and without descendants, at the end of the Mesozoic Era. These were the Notosuchidae of South America, and the Libycosuchidae and Stomatosuchidae of northern Africa. All three were highly atypical crocodilians. The notosuchids were small, unarmored land-dwellers with reduced dentition; the libycosuchids were small and nearly toothless land-dwellers; the stomatosuchids were duck-billed giants confined to large rivers or lakes. The Goniopholidae vanished as such at the end of the Cretaceous, but not before the family had given rise to eusuchians. The Mesozoic-Cenozoic transition was successfully passed by the Alligatorinae, Crocodylinae, and Tomistominae, of the Crocodylidae; inferentially by the Gavialidae; by the dyrosaur group of the Pholidosauri-

Figure 42. Three distinct lines of crocodilian descent are represented by the American crocodile (left), the gharial (center), and the American alligator (right). [Ross Allen's Reptile Institute]

dae; and by the Sebecosuchia. How did these crocodilians manage to escape the extinction that overtook other archosaurs at the end of the Cretaceous? This question cannot be answered with any degree of certainty. Too little is known about the needs and tolerances of the extinct groups, and about environmental changes at the end of the Mesozoic Era. However, the Mesozoic-Cenozoic transition separated the Age of Reptiles from the succeeding Age of Mammals, and it is tempting to believe that crocodilians survived the transition partly because they were notably mammal-like in several regards. In Chapter 6, crocodilians were noted to depart from the reptilian norm in certain major features. The departures are usually in the direction of the mammalian norm. A four-chambered heart, a muscular septum between lung cavity and peritoneal cavity, a complete secondary palate, encroachment of the middle-ear cavity upon surrounding bones, division of the vertebral column into five distinguishable regions, a single penis with glans, a true cerebral cortex, socketed teeth, a periodontal membrane, a slight specialization of the dentition into incisors, canines, and cheek teeth—these features show at least some approach to the mammalian condition. Just as improvements in circulatory, respiratory, reproductive, and other systems presumably led to the rise of the mammals, so the foreshadowing of these improvements must have abetted the survival of crocodilians.

Some anatomical features, for example the socketed teeth, set the crocodilians apart from other living reptiles but not from other archosaurs. As soft parts are rarely fossilized, we do not know how closely the dinosaurs and flying reptiles, or various extinct nonarchosaurian reptiles, may have aproached the mammals in certain details of anatomy. In any event, structural advances alone will probably not suffice to explain crocodilian persistence; habits and habitat could also have been involved. Discussion of this point will be deferred to a later chapter.

9 CROCODILIAN HISTORY: THE LAST 63 MILLION YEARS

WE LEFT the Crocodylidae in the latter Cretaceous, during which time the family was diverging into three subfamilies. The subfamily Tomistominae is the easiest to trace. This line of narrow-snouted crocodilians originated probably in Eurasia in the latter Cretaceous. Before the period was out, tomistomines had spread into North America. The genus Thoracosaurus is known from the latter Cretaceous of both Europe and North America, and had a close relative in China at the same time. Another genus, Holops, comes from the latter Cretaceous of North America. This radiation of tomistomines continued past the Mesozoic-Cenozoic boundary without significant interruption. It resulted in such genera as Dollosuchus and Eosuchus from the Eocene of Europe, and Eotomistoma from the Eocene of Asia. Holops persisted into the Eocene of North America. The distribution pattern of the early Tomistominae is the familiar Eurasian-North American one. Fossil remains of early tomistomines are found mostly in sediments that were deposited in estuarine waters. These large, active crocodilians did not frequent the small streams or the still waters of the interior, nor did they venture far into the sea.

By the Eocene, the Tomistominae had reached Africa, where they spread widely, and from where they began a second radiation. In the Oligocene or early Miocene, this African stock invaded Europe. In other words, the early tomistomines had moved into Africa from Eurasia, but the later ones pushed in the opposite direction. During the Miocene these reptiles became widespread, mostly in estuarine situations, in both Europe and Africa. They also moved across Asia and into North America. This line of descent may even have eventually reached South America, for a possible tomistomine has been reported from the Pliocene or Pleistocene of Brazil.

In North America, the late tomistomine line was present at least during the first part of the Pliocene, vanished before the end of that period, and seemingly never invaded inland waters. In its simplicity the foregoing comment is not unlike remarks that have been made herein about other crocodilian groups. The simplicity is deceptive, however. Geographic distribution, time of existence, habitat, survival or extinction—these are complicated subjects in actuality, and may be linked in complicated ways. For want of space, or more often for lack of information, complex interactions sometimes must be discussed only in terms of their apparent outcome. Fortunately, it is possible to take a closer look at a North American tomistomine, a member of the later radiation.

By the Pliocene if not earlier, the late tomistomine genus Gavialosuchus had spread from Eurasia into North America. *Gavialosuchus eggenburgense,* from the Miocene of Austria, is very similar to *Gavialosuchus americanus* from the Pliocene of the southeastern United States. Remains of the latter were first discovered in a Florida phosphate mine. Quite a few additional Florida specimens have come to light. They have varied in completeness from a dorsal plate, a few teeth, or a mere skull fragment to well-nigh an entire skeleton. A majority of these specimens have come from pebble phosphate deposits. The distribution of Gavialosuchus has been traced northward into lower South Carolina, where again some of the remains were discovered in phosphate beds. Obviously this crocodilian was somehow associated with deposits of phosphate. What is the origin of such deposits? What natural agency could concentrate vast quantities of phosphorus compounds in small areas? Sea birds were (and in places still are) the agency. Phosphorus compounds occur in the sea, where they are taken up especially by tiny, plant-like organisms that drift in the upper waters. These organisms are fed upon by tiny fishes and crustaceans, which in turn fall prey to somewhat larger fishes. Many of the latter, in their turn, go to nourish sea birds. The concentration of phosphorus compounds can be seen today on certain islets and shores, where terns, gulls, and other sea birds alight by the thousands, some of them to form nesting colonies. Such birds can drop an astonishing quantity of phosphorus-rich excrement. Boating in Gulf waters near my Florida home, I have noted with interest the "Bird Racks," as they are locally known. Before chemical fertilizers became readily available, someone had thought it commercially profitable to build a long line of elevated platforms three miles out in the

Figure 43. Sea-birds, such as these gannets, often nest communally, and concentrate phosphorus about their rookeries. In more southerly climes, "guano islands" are produced by accumulated droppings. One ancient crocodilian lived about guano islands. [Canadian Government Bureau]

Figure 44. The largest tooth of a very large alligator (specimen at left) is dwarfed by a tooth of Gavialosuchus, extinct crocodilian of the southeastern United States. Gavialosuchus tooth is blackened by mineralization. [W. T. Neill]

ocean, and to collect the bird droppings from them. On the Chincha and Lobos Islands, off the coast of Peru, the droppings of pelicans, cormorants, gannets, petrels, and other sea birds once formed deposits 200 feet thick. Similar but less impressive "guano islands" have existed off the coasts of Bolivia, Chile, southeastern Argentina, western Africa, southeastern Saudi Arabia, and western Australia. On such islands the chemical fate of the guano depends on the climate. In areas of low rainfall, almost all the nitrogenous and phosphatic compounds remain; but where rainfall is somewhat higher, the more soluble constituents are lost, and little remains except the relatively insoluble phosphates such as those of calcium and magnesium. Under conditions of even higher rainfall, these phosphates themselves dissolve and trickle down into the sands, where they may later come out of solution and begin to form little concretions. This is the origin, apparently, of pebble phosphates such as those mined in Florida; and the phosphate deposits of that state yield the fossilized remains of birds belonging to groups that produce guano on various islands today.

During much if not all of the Pliocene, some of Florida was under water, and so were some of the present southeastern lowlands. Here and there were small peninsulas or groups of islets, along whose shores the sea birds congregated, and around which the fishes teemed. Gavialosuchus lived chiefly about the Pliocene guano islands or shores, where it could find an abundance of food. It was a huge crocodilian, reaching a length of perhaps 45 feet. Although it may have preyed at times on small fishes and sea birds, it probably subsisted mainly on large, predatory fishes such as sharks. Even though Gavialosuchus had a comparatively narrow snout, its teeth were enormous, a circumstance implying a diet of large organisms. While collecting fossils about the phosphate pits in central Florida, I found a Gavialosuchus tooth which, although broken off or reabsorbed at the base, measured more than 5 inches in length, and 6½ inches in basal circumference (Fig. 44). In contrast, the largest tooth from the largest known alligator skull measures about 4 inches in length, and a little less than that in basal circumference.

As the Pliocene continued, more land was exposed in what are now the lowlands of the southeastern United States. As the seas withdrew, birds no longer congregated in such vast numbers on small coastal islands and peninsular shores; at least, the deposition of phosphates seemingly did not continue much beyond the mid-Pliocene. Nor has *Gavialosuchus americanus* appeared in fossil beds clearly postdating the Florida phosphate deposits.

Thus, the environmental relationships of this crocodilian were diverse and intricately connected. Ecology, the study of organisms in relation to their environment, reveals complex interactions everywhere. Gavialosuchus was singled out for discussion because its way of life was a bit less obscure than that of most extinct species.

An apparently critical time in the history of the Tomistominae was the withdrawal of seas around the latter Miocene or the early Pliocene. In both Europe and North America, tomistomines vanished as the seas withdrew; in Africa and Asia some of these reptiles persisted, but were able to do so only in fresh water. One genus, Tomistoma, survived in rivers of Africa through the early Pleistocene, but then vanished from that continent. This same genus has survived to the present day in Asia. Its sole remaining species, *Tomistoma schlegeli*, the "false gavial," is confined to streams on Sumatra, Borneo, and the southern part of the Malay peninsula. This reptile will be described in another section of the book.

As for the broad-snouted Alligatorinae, their place of origin is uncertain. Either they originated in Asia and spread to North America, or the reverse. A reptile called Paralligator was discovered in the late Cretaceous of China. It would be considered ancestral to the alligatorines were not its presacral vertebrae concave at both ends. Among Cretaceous crocodilians, such biconcave vertebrae characterize the suborder Mesosuchia. In the Eusuchia, a presacral vertebra should be concave on its anterior face and ball-like posteriorly. It is not out of the question that a mesosuchian type of vertebra was retained as a primitive character among some very early Crocodylidae; but it might be wise to await additional work before deciding whether or not Paralligator should be placed with the Alligatorinae. Even if so placed by further studies, it is clearly off the main lines of alligatorine descent.

From the late Cretaceous of North America comes a medium-sized, chunky crocodilian dubbed Brachychampsa. It was found in the Hell Creek fossil beds of Montana. Brachychampsa seems too specialized to have been a direct ancestor of the Alligatorinae, but may have been an offshoot from the original alligatorine stock. It may be placed tentatively in the Alligatorinae.

By the Paleocene, this subfamily had reached South America, where it diversified and became the dominant crocodilians. South America had one alligatorine genus, Notocaiman, in the Paleocene. Two are known from the Eocene. One of these, Eocaiman, may have been ancestral to Caiman, Paleosuchus, and Melanosuchus, the three alligatorine genera that exist in South America today. The South American Alligatorinae probably reached their greatest diversity in the Miocene, when at least four genera were present. Also in the Miocene of South America, there arose from alligatorine stock a group so distinctive as to be accorded a family of its own, the Nettosuchidae. The nettosuchids had a long, flattened head, with spatulate snout and reduced dentition. These reptiles were, in fact, "duck-billed" crocodilians reminiscent of the African stomatosuchids. Yet, the two duck-billed families were not closely related to each other; they were independent offshoots from the more generalized family Crocodylidae, the African group having vanished 44 million years before the South American one began to rise. The similarity of a nettosuchid to an African stomatosu-chid probably reflects similar feeding habits. The discoverer of the Netto-suchidae wondered if these reptiles could even have been plant-eaters. (It would be more accurate to say "one of the discoverers" of the Nettosu-chidae; by a coincidence, two paleontologists independently discovered and named the only known genus of this family. One dubbed it Mourasuchus, the other Nettosuchus.) A herbivorous crocodilian sounds a bit improbable. True, some modern crocodilians occasionally swallow plant material; but they do so accidentally, or through secondary ingestion (described in Chapter 16), or as gastroliths. More significantly, crocodilians cannot digest starches, sugars, or cellulose, and so would receive little nourishment from ingested plant material. Fortunately, there exist today certain reptiles and amphibians that have evolved a curiously flattened snout and lost the teeth or comparable dental armament. From these living species (of turtles and frogs) we get a clue to the probable feeding habits of the Nettosuchidae (and of the Stomatosuchidae). The mata-mata turtle of South America has a flattened head (Fig. 45); and its delicate, unarmored jaws cannot even deliver a painful pinch. Thoroughly aquatic, the mata-mata stalks little fishes and other small game in the water. Nearing its prey, it suddenly opens its mouth and the prey is swept into that cavity along with a rush of water. The Surinam "toad" (Fig. 45), also of South America, feeds in much the same way. The mata-mata and the Surinam "toad" are highly specialized for the aforesaid method of feeding. Some other turtles and

Figure 45. *The mata-mata turtle (at left) and the Surinam toad (right) both have a flattened head and unarmored jaws. Their unusual method of feeding may throw light on the feeding behavior of extinct "duck-billed" crocodilians with unarmored jaws.* [Ross Allen's Reptile Institute]

frogs are less specialized for it, but resort to it at times. It is not surprising that crocodilians, with their remarkable capacity for adaptive radiation in past ages, evolved the same technique of engulfing fishes and other small aquatic organisms.

The alligatorine genus Caiman made its appearance in the Pliocene of South America. Caiman is represented today by two small species, but some Pliocene members of the genus were giants, perhaps up to 50 feet in length. One of these giant Caiman had a remarkably long, narrow snout for an alligatorine. There were also extinct species of Caiman with short head, broadened snout, and heavy teeth. The wide-snouted line of descent is represented today by *Caiman latirostris*, the broad-nosed caiman of Brazil. This latter reaches a length of about 7 feet, but some of its broad-headed, Pliocene relatives tripled that measurement. Yet another line of descent, within the genus Caiman, culminated in *Caiman sclerops*, the spectacled caiman of the New World tropics. Throughout most of its range, *Caiman sclerops* has a moderately wide snout. However, even within this single species, one can see the crocodilian tendency to produce lineages that are divergent in snout shape. In the upper drainage of the Rio Apaporis, in southern Colombia, the local population of *Caiman sclerops* is remarkably narrow-snouted as compared with populations of the same species elsewhere. The spectacled caiman is also noteworthy in having extended its range a remarkably long distance northward, to Oaxaca in Mexico, as well as southward to the mouth of the Paraná River in Argentina.

The South American alligatorine genus Paleosuchus also appeared in the Pliocene. It likewise diverged into two lines of descent, characterized by a difference in snout shape and correlated habits. The living *Paleosuchus trigonatus*, Schneider's smooth-fronted caiman of northern South America, has a much narrower snout than *Paleosuchus palpebrosus*, Cuvier's smooth-fronted caiman from the same region. The genus Melanosuchus, represented today only by the South American *Melanosuchus niger*, the black caiman, has not been recognized in the fossil record. Melanosuchus is not highly differentiated from Caiman, and some fragmentary remains, now ascribed to the latter genus, probably represent the black caiman or some close relative thereof. The living caimans—one species of Melanosuchus, two of Paleosuchus, and two of Caiman—will be described in a later section.

In the Old World, the Alligatorinae were confined largely to Europe and to northern Asia. At this and other points in the book, the term northern Asia means that portion of the Asian continent lying north of the present tropics. In the Paleocene, northern Asia was the only part of the Old World to have an alligatorine. In the Eocene, three genera of the subfamily inhabited Europe. At least one of these genera seemingly was also present in the Eocene of North America. A European alligatorine may also have invaded northern Africa. During the Oligocene, Europe had three genera of the Alligatorinae, one of them present in northern Asia also. But by the time the Miocene had gotten well under way, alligatorines had vanished from all of the Old World except northern Asia, where one genus remained. The subfamily never managed to enter the vast area that today makes up the Old World tropics. In northern Asia, where the Alligatorinae remained throughout the Cenozoic, no more than one genus was present in any one period.

The North American history of the Alligatorinae is exceptionally interesting. Brachychampsa, from the late Cretaceous of Montana, may not have been a direct ancestor of later alligatorines, but the subfamily had become diverse in North America by Paleocene times. One North American

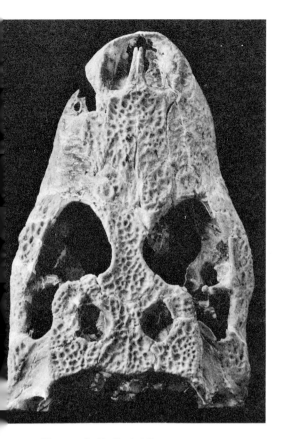

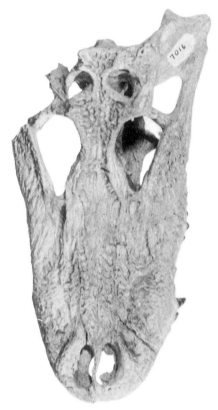

Figure 46. Skull of Alligator mcgrewi, extinct alligator from the Miocene of Nebraska. From K. P. Schmidt, Geol. Ser.—Field Museum of Natural History 8 (4).

Figure 47. Fragmentary skull of Alligator mefferdi, extinct alligator from the Pliocene of Nebraska. From C. C. Mook, 1946, American Museum Novitates No. 1311.

Paleocene genus, Allognathosuchus, persisted into the Eocene. (This genus, or something close to it, may have been ancestral to the South American Eocaiman, which in turn may have been ancestral to the three living alligatorine genera of the New World tropics.) In Allognathosuchus, the hindlimbs were much longer than the forelimbs. The rear teeth were so enlarged that each was crowded against the next. The dentition and the rather heavy jaws suggest that much of the food was crushed. Once again, turtles come to mind as the most likely victims, although other prey could have been taken as well. Allognathosuchus inhabited the southwestern United States, a lush area in the Paleocene.

Ceratosuchus, from the Paleocene of Colorado, was a remarkable alligatorine, and has been called a "horned alligator." The squamosals, bones at the rear of the skull behind the eyes, were enlarged and heightened to form a pair of blunt, triangular horns. The function of this armament is unknown. It may have helped to protect the head-neck juncture (a vulnerable spot) from attack. What might have attacked the horned alligator? Dinosaurs had vanished by the end of the Cretaceous, but the mammals, small and few in that period, were diversifying rapidly in the Paleocene. There were carnivorous mammals in the Paleocene of North America, some of them as big as a bear. In Ceratosuchus, oddly, horn size bore no set relationship to body size. That is to say, two individuals of equal size might differ considerably in horn size. Perhaps the males were provided with larger horns than the females. Ceratosuchus was short-snouted, with enlarged rear teeth like those of Allognathosuchus.

In Eocene times, North America had at least four alligatorine genera. One or more of these may also have reached Europe, as noted. Among the American Eocene alligatorine genera, Procaimanoidea is of particular interest. Known from Utah and Wyoming, Procaimanoidea resembled modern caimans and alligators in several anatomical features. Conceivably, Procaimanoidea was ancestral to Alligator, which was one of three closely related alligatorine genera that appeared in the Oligocene of North America. Of these three, Alligator was the only one to survive past the Oligocene. Alligator is, of course, the genus to which the modern alligators belong, and so merits special comment.

The genus Alligator, first appearing in the Oligocene of North America, is represented therein by a species called *Alligator prenasalis*. This broad-headed reptile lay on or very near the basal stock from which all later alligators developed. By the Miocene, this stock had diverged into three lines of descent. One of these lines is represented by *Alligator mcgrewi*, from the Miocene of Nebraska (Fig. 46). An extremely broad-headed and short-snouted reptile, *Alligator mcgrewi* was an evolutionary "dead end," with no descendants beyond the Miocene. But *Alligator olseni*, from the Miocene of northern Florida, was probably the direct ancestor of the living *Alligator mississipiensis*, the American alligator. In this case the modern species is much larger than its ancestor; *Alligator olseni* seemingly did not exceed 8 feet in total length. The third Miocene species, *Alligator thomsoni* from Nebraska, is not like the American alligator, but is very much like the living *Alligator sinensis,* the Chinese alligator. Eveidently some near relative of *Alligator thomsoni* pushed into northern Asia, perhaps in the early Miocene, and was ancestral to the Chinese alligator. *Alligator thomsoni* also gave rise to a descendant in North America; this was *Alligator mefferdi,* known from the Pliocene of Nebraska (Fig. 47). Yet, the *thomsoni* lineage, in spite of its success in China, did not survive past the Pliocene in North America.

The two surviving alligators, the American and the Chinese, are discussed in other sections of this book.

Finally, we come to the subfamily Crocodylinae, characterized as being more or less intermediate between the Tomistominae and the Alligatorinae in matters of snout shape. The characterization is a very general one, and refers only to the crocodyline norm. The living *Crocodylus cataphractus,* the African sharp-nosed crocodile, is about as narrow-snouted as a tomistomine, while the living *Crocodylus palustris,* the mugger of southern Asia, is as broad-snouted as some alligatorines. However, such species represent extremes of divergence within the subfamily.

The Crocodylinae arose in the late Cretaceous, either in Eurasia or North America (probably the former). Spread was rapid from the original homeland. Before the Cretaceous was out, crocodylines were present in northern Asia, Europe, Africa, and southern Asia, as well as in both North and South America. At this time the subfamily was most diverse in North America, where five genera existed.

The crocodylines made their poorest showing in South America, where the alligatorines held sway. The Crocodylinae are represented in South America by no more than two genera in any geological Period. The only crocodylines to thrive in South America, during any Period, were long-snouted ones, very different from alligatorines in head shape, and inferentially different in habitat and diet. Most of these long-snouted reptiles did not evolve their characteristics in South America, but invaded that region from the north. Only one reptile even hints that the crocodylines could also have undergone a significant amount of evolution within South America. This one is Charactosuchus, from the latter Miocene of Colombia. Unfortunately, its remains are fragmentary. Charactosuchus had a long, narrow snout, and its teeth were longitudinally ribbed or fluted. Ribbed teeth occur among several modern crocodylines, such as the African sharp-nosed and the New Guinea crocodiles; and a crocodyline affinity is suspected for Charactosuchus (although tomistomine affinity is also possible). But even this reptile genus may not have been strictly South American. From South Carolina there comes a fragmentary jaw of a crocodilian that had a long, narrow snout with ribbed teeth. Similar teeth have been found at scattered localities along the Atlantic slope of the United States from New Jersey to Florida.

The most important of the late Cretaceous crocodyline genera was Crocodylus. Even though dating back to the Cretaceous, it persists today and has twelve living species scattered over the tropics of the world. Only one other genus of living reptiles is of Cretaceous age: Podocnemis, "side-necked" turtles of South America and Madagascar. Crocodylus probably originated in Eurasia. Its earliest known species comes from the late Cretaceous of Europe. From a Eurasian center the genus spread rapidly, reaching Africa and North America by the Eocene.

Africa today has two species of Crocodylus. One of these is *Crocodylus niloticus*, the Nile crocodile, a very large reptile inhabiting streams and estuaries; the other is *Crocodylus cataphractus*, the slender-snouted crocodile mentioned previously. Africa also harbors another genus of crocodylines, Osteolaemus, but its origin is unknown. Called dwarf crocodiles, the two living species of Osteolaemus superficially resemble the caimans of the genus Paleosuchus.

From North America, Crocodylus spread into South America but was never very successful there. Today South America has two species of this genus. *Crocodylus acutus*, the American crocodile, is narrow-snouted and estuarine; it inhabits Caribbean shores, and also ranges to the southern tip of Florida. *Crocodylus intermedius*, the Orinoco crocodile, is a very long-snouted species confined to the Orinoco drainage. In the New World tropics, but outside alligatorine range, there live two more species of Crocodylus. *Crocodylus rhombifer*, the Cuban crocodile, inhabits Cuba and the Isle of Pines; *Crocodylus moreleti*, Morelet's crocodile, is known from the Atlantic drainage of southern Mexico and northern Central America, from Tamaulipas to Guatemala.

As the Cenozoic climate continued to deteriorate, crocodylines vanished from more northerly lands. The Miocene was the last period in which Crocodylus, or any other crocodyline genus, inhabited Europe. But the tropical mainland of southern Asia, and the tropical archipelagos to the south thereof, formed a refuge area for Crocodylus. Today the

Asiatic tropics harbor *Crocodylus siamensis*, the Siamese crocodile; *Crocodylus palustris*, the mugger; *Crocodylus mindorensis*, the Mindoro crocodile; and *Crocodylus porosus*, the estuarine crocodile. Asiatic stocks of Crocodylus also pushed down into New Guinea and Australia. The living *Crocodylus novae-guineae*, the New Guinea crocodile, is related to the Mindoro species. *Crocodylus johnstoni*, the Australian crocodile, is a long-nosed species of unknown affinity. The estuarine crocodile of southern Asia also ranges southward to New Guinea and northern Australia. Little is known of the fossil history of crocodiles in the Australia-New Guinea region. Back in the 1880s, a Pleistocene crocodile was discovered in Australia and named Palimnarchus. Today it appears as though it might have been a species of Crocodylus. It was very heavily armored, and had keeled scutes dorsally, with flattened scutes laterally and perhaps ventrally.

The discussion of the Crocodylinae has concentrated on Crocodylus because this genus persists today. There have been many other and less successful crocodyline genera in various parts of the world. The subfamily became quite diverse in Europe during the early Cenozoic, but vanished from that region by the end of the Miocene. In Africa there were several mid-Cenozoic genera of crocodylines, but all of these except Crocodylus (and inferentially Osteolaemus) disappeared by the end of the Pliocene if not sooner. In southern Asia there were also several mid-Cenozoic genera of crocodylines; but of these, only Crocodylus survived past the Pliocene. In northern Asia, the Crocodylinae were most diverse in the Eocene, when three genera were present. After the Eocene, northern Asia seemingly had no crocodylines, only alligatorines. As noted, South America had but few crocodylines, and after the Pliocene it had only Crocodylus.

North America had a rich crocodyline fauna in the late Cretaceous and early Cenozoic. Its most remarkable component was Deinosuchus of the late Cretaceous. This genus came to light when some crocodilian bones, gigantic in size, were discovered in the Judith River fossil beds of Montana. There were some vertebrae, ribs, the pelvis, bony plates, and bone fragments—not the complete skeleton, but enough of it to reveal the important nature of the find. The bones indicated a crocodilian larger than any other known from North America, and the species was named *Deinosuchus hatcheri*. A second species of Deinosuchus was discovered in late Cretaceous fossil beds of Big Bend National Park, Texas, and was named *Deinosuchus riograndensis*. Its remains were less fragmentary, and included much of the skull along with the lower jaw. "Deinosuchus" means "terrible crocodile," an appropriate name; the Texas specimen must have been 50 feet long in life, and there is no particular reason to think that it was of record length for its species. It was stoutly built for a crocodyline, and the massive jaws were armed with great, pointed teeth. The back was shielded with heavy plates of bone. The tip of the snout looked as if it had four nostril openings, a large pair lying external to the normal pair. The two large, extra openings probably had nothing to do with breathing, however. In some dinosaurs, various skull openings served merely to reduce the weight of an enormous head; and this might also have been the case with Deinosuchus. Certainly the head of this crocodyline was heavy; and the neck vertebrae were enlarged, to accommodate the skull along with its muscular attachments. Deinosuchus was fossilized in company with a variety of dinosaurs: armored and three-horned ones, "duck-billed" bipedal kinds, and long-necked quadrupedal giants. About the Cretaceous marshes of western North America, dinosaurs were almost the only very large prey, and Deinosuchus evidently fed upon them.

Among crocodyline genera from the late Cretaceous of North America, another interesting one was Leidyosuchus. This genus, which survived into the Paleocene, included several species in the northwestern United States and in Saskatchewan. The distribution is evidence that these areas, which today lie more than 3,000 miles north of the tropics, once had a warm climate. This is also demonstrated by fossil floras. Even long after the Cretaceous, there were figs, laurels, avocados, and magnolias in Oregon, Washington, and Nevada; breadfruits, figs, laurels, and magnolias in Wyoming. Palms and cycads grew in British Columbia and on islands off the coast of southern Alaska, while forests of maples, beeches, ashes, sycamores, alders, and basswoods grew on Greenland. Until the last few years, students of animal and plant distribution had to suppose that, during the Mesozoic and early Cenozoic, tropical climate extended into much higher latitudes than it does today. This is still not out of the question; but very recent studies on continental drift also imply that North American and Eurasia, the continents derived from Laurasia, formerly lay south of their present locations. It is of course beyond the scope of the present work to discuss the factors that may have modified the climate of any given region throughout the ages, but it is not amiss here to emphasize that crocodilians are excellent indicators of past warm climates. A few crocodilians (all of them alligatorines) have been able to invade warm-temperature lands; but other-wise, the order Crocodilia seems always to have been restricted to the tropics. When fossil remains of these reptiles turn up in areas that today are cold-temperate or even colder, one can be sure that these areas were tropical or nearly so in the days when they were inhabited by crocodilians.

Returning now to the chronological review of the Crocodylinae, the Eocene was the last period in which that subfamily was diverse in North America. Five North American genera are known for that period. One of them, Brachyuranochampsa, is illustrated (Fig. 48). North America has yielded but one crocodyline genus, Crocodylus, from post-Eocene fossil beds.

With the foregoing account of the Crocodylinae, the various lineages of the order Crocodilia have been brought up to modern times. Like the living gavialid, tomistomine, and alligatorines, the living crocodylines—two species of Osteolaemus and twelve of Crocodylus—will be described in a later portion of this work. But first, some questions remain to be answered about crocodilian evolution. These are questions that have so far been passed over lest they lead discussion too far from taxonomy and fossil his-tory, the subjects with which Part II has been chiefly concerned. Part III analyzes some episodes of the crocodilian story in the light of broad bio-logical concepts, concepts that should be applicable to ancient reptiles just as to modern ones.

Figure 48. Skull of Brachyurano-champsa, extinct crocodile from the Eocene of Wyoming. After R. Zangerl, 1944, Annals of the Carnegie Museum 30, Art. 7.

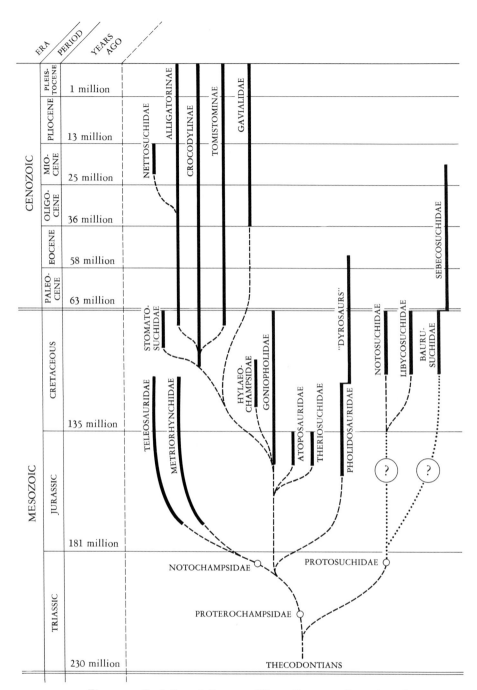

Figure 49. Evolution of the crocodilians; diagrammatic, and partly conjectural. In general, solid lines are moderately well documented by fossils; dashed lines are inferences based on anatomical similarities; and dotted lines, leading from the Protosuchidae, are highly speculative. Ages are approximate.

PART III *A Little Light on Some Ancient Episodes*

10 THE PROBLEM OF ANCIENT BIPEDALITY

THE FOREGOING review of crocodilian history raises several questions. Some of these must be tabled until more fossil material is discovered, but others can be answered, tentatively at least, through observations on living reptiles.

To begin at the very beginning of crocodilian history, how likely is it that the order Crocodilia descended (as some have thought) from thecodontians that were actually bipedal? We might expect the development of a bipedal gait to be correlated with a strong trend toward terrestrialism. How might we account for the curious interweaving, among thecodontians and some of their descendants, of trends toward bipedality and toward an aquatic rather than a terrestrial existence? What can be inferred about the habits, habitats, and locomotion of early thecodontians, those ancestral to crocodilians and other reptile groups?

Some of the thecodontians, with enormous hindlimbs and tiny forelimbs, could only have been bipedal, but these highly specialized types were not on the direct line of crocodilian ancestry. The early crocodilians, to judge from their anatomy, were descended from a somewhat more generalized thecodontian in which there was considerable difference in size between hindlimb and forelimb, but not the great disparity that is met with among the fully bipedal stocks. The fossil record of thecodontians is surprisingly good for such rather small and exceedingly ancient reptiles—they must have been widespread, abundant, and successful in their day—but the more generalized types are poorly known as compared with the specialized ones. It is usually an extreme specialization that leaves its unmistakable brand on a reptile's skeletal anatomy. Less extreme specializations may leave marks, but we cannot interpret them with much assurance unless other lines of evidence can be brought to bear on the problem. Fortunately, speculations upon the activities of a long-extinct reptile do not always have to be based upon its anatomy alone. Our thinking can at times be guided by the nature of the deposits in which a fossil reptile is found (whether freshwater, marine, or terrestrial deposits, for example); by our knowledge of other organisms fossilized in the same deposits; by well-marked evolutionary trends within the group to which the reptile belongs; and by investigations into the activities of living reptiles, especially those related to or anatomically similar to the extinct one.

Paleontologists, discussing the upright posture of some thecodontians and dinosaurs, have looked hopefully at certain modern lizards for clues to the development of bipedality; for these lizards, too, are capable of running upright, and do so occasionally. The desired clues have not been forthcoming, however, and it is easy to see why, for the habits, habitats, and locomotion of these lizards have in most cases been reported inadequately. No previous attempt has been made to review all the lizards whose lifeways might throw some light on the development of bipedality; no generalizations about lizard bipedality have been offered in the herpetological literature, beyond the unproven assertion that this method of locomotion simply permits a greater speed. A discussion of bipedal lizards, merely to analyze the evolution of an upright posture in various reptiles, would be somewhat out of place or unduly tangential in a book about crocodilians. But as it happens, such a discussion provides clues not only to the origin of reptilian bipedality but also to a more pertinent problem, the otherwise puzzling evolution of aquatic, quadrupedal crocodilians from an essentially bipedal stock. And as a bonus, from a brief look at the bipedal lizards and their kin we can see how a small group of reptiles, its members all fairly similar in conformation and general way of life, could give rise simultaneously to aquatic, terrestrial, and flying descendants. In short, the earliest part of the crocodilian story, the part that is dimmest to our vision, is clarified when attention is turned not only to the bones of long-dead reptiles, but also to the activities of some living ones. Thus, we are justified in devoting a few pages to certain lizards. Through a fortunate coincidence, a discussion of these lizards introduces certain concepts—warning behavior, sex recognition, courtship display, ritual combat, escape behavior—that will engage our attention again, when we come to review the life histories of the living crocodilians.

Lizards and thecodontians are not closely related, belonging as they do to different subclasses of the class Reptilia. But within the limits of a class, or even within much broader limits, a similarity of gross anatomy is likely to be correlated with a similarity of habitat, locomotion, and general way of life. The biological literature cites numerous instances of the "adaptive convergence" of unrelated organisms. Since form and function are often correlated, and since the activities of thecodontians cannot be observed directly, it is not amiss here to consider the activities of lizards that are somewhat thecodontian-like in conformation.

Twelve lizard genera are of special interest in this connection. Five of these genera—Physignathus, Hydrosaurus, Chlamydosaurus, Gonyocephalus, and Draco—belong to the family Agamidae. The remaining seven—Enyalioides, Iguana, Anolis, Deiroptyx, Corytophanes, Basiliscus, and Crotaphytus—belong to the Iguanidae, a family closely related to the Agamidae. (The term "iguanian" is used to cover both iguanids and agamids.) The members of these genera are all characterized by a long tail, and by hindlimbs that are larger than the forelimbs. A few of the species are a bit smaller than any adult thecodontian; but in general, the size range within the order Thecodontia is approximately the same as in the iguanians. Species of all the above-mentioned genera are known to me in their respective natural habitats. The account of these genera departs from taxonomic arrangement in order to emphasize specializations of locomotion and habits.

The tamacuaré, a species of Enyalioides, was seen at La Pedrera, Amazonas, Colombia. The adult is about 14 inches long, including the long, slender tail. The snout is of moderate proportions. These lizards were found to inhabit waterside vegetation. They were inclined to rest motionless, well camouflaged by markings of rich green and dark brown. However, when closely approached they would run on tree trunks and jump about among leaves and twigs. On the ground (which they rarely visited) they ran quadrupedally. When pursued they made off arboreally, not diving or running into the water. Their seeming restriction to waterside vegetation is not surprising; in the forested tropics, many lizards are concentrated at the edges of lakes, streams, clearings, roads, and trails—places where the much-needed sunlight is available.

The water-lizard, a species of Physignathus, was studied near Port Moresby, Papua. The adult is about 16 inches long, including the long, slender tail. The snout is of moderate length and breadth. These lizards were numerous in bushes and on fallen trees bordering or overhanging swampy lakes. They leaped about agilely in the vegetation. When disturbed they would promptly dive into the water, usually from heights of about 5 to 10 feet. When surprised on the ground, they would dash into the water and "skitter" across the surface for as much as 15 or 20 feet before submerging. Herpetologists use the phrase "skittering locomotion" to denote the rapid movement of certain lizards and frogs across the surface of water. The dash for the water seemed to be accomplished quadrupedally, the body of the scurrying water-lizard remaining parallel to the ground. When resting undisturbed on the ground, a branch, or a log, a water-lizard would fold the hindlimbs, but stretch the forelimbs to their fullest extent. In this resting posture the head is elevated, and the axis of the body makes an angle of about 45 degrees with the ground. Water-lizards were also found miles from water, on dry, dusty hillsides where they scampered around the boles of the scattered trees and dashed up the trunks when approached. They were likewise encountered on the coast in mangrove swamp, where they ran over the mud flats. Although the flats had numerous water-filled holes, the lizards ignored these when disturbed, and climbed a mangrove to escape pursuit. In addition, water-lizards were seen in shrubby vegetation bordering ponds in the savanna woodland. Here they would run into the water and skitter across the surface. The diversity of habitat was astonishing. A lizard species is usually able to inhabit only a few, or perhaps even just one, of the environmental situations that exist within its range. Restriction to a limited variety of situations is particularly characteristic of tropical lizards, and few of them would be expected to occupy such a diversity of environments as does the water-lizard.

The striped basilisk, a species of Basiliscus, was studied at many localities in British Honduras. The male of the striped basilisk bears a high crest of skin on the back of the neck, but otherwise the reptile has the general conformation of the water-lizard. The Basiliscus is a little longer than the Physignathus, and has a somewhat longer snout. Striped basilisks were abundant in open forest along the Mopan River near the Guatemala border. Here they lived on bushes and tree trunks, leaping through this vegetation with great agility when disturbed, and making no effort to enter the swift river. However, at both Augustine and Roaring Creek, a few individuals ran into a small creek and skittered across the surface. As the running lizard nears the water, it rises to a bipedal position, and maintains this while skittering. Striped basilisks were also found in mangrove swamp; at Stann Creek one individual ran into the flooded burrow of a crab when pursued. Others were seen about towns on fences and trees; along the strand; in fields of high grass; in sunny openings of the forest; and in treeless wet savanna. As with the water-lizard, the variety of habitats was surprising.

The striped basilisk is the smallest and least aquatic member of its genus. The other and larger species are noteworthy for the elaborate development in the males of a crest on the head and neck, another on the back, and a third on the tail. A large species of Basiliscus was seen near Turrialba, Costa Rica. Adults were resting on branches overhanging a river, into which they dived when disturbed. Small individuals were occasionally surprised

Figure 50. Although essentially arboreal, the striped basilisk will enter the water readily, and can run bipedally on land. [Ross Allen's Reptile Institute]

on the ground, and would run bipedally into the water and skitter across the surface.

The sail-tail, a species of Hydrosaurus, was observed near Lingayen, Luzon, Philippine Islands. This is the largest agamid, reaching a length of about 4 feet. The snout is somewhat elongated. The tail bears a high crest (higher in males), and is vertically flattened toward the tip. Sail-tails were seen resting on branches of trees overhanging ponds. They were always on lower branches, roughly 10 to 15 feet above the water. When disturbed, they would run a pace or two on the branch, dive into the water, and swim off submerged. Other observers have reported these lizards to run bipedally into the water and then skitter across the surface. Those I saw, all large adults, were too heavy to skitter. At this locality the sail-tails had a strong "fishy" odor like that of the stagnant ponds about which they lived, and it is likely that they often entered the water for purposes other than escape from an occasional predator.

The water-dragon, a species of Physignathus, was observed near Sydney, New South Wales, Australia. The water-dragon reaches a total length of about 3½ feet, and so is a much larger reptile than its congener the water-lizard. The water-dragon has a proportionately longer snout, and its vertically flattened tail is quite unlike that of the water-lizard. The few specimens seen were all clinging to small branches overhanging a creek, except for one that had climbed a snag protruding from the water. When approached, the reptiles dropped into the creek and swam off submerged. Other students have surprised water-dragons on land, and noted them to dash bipedally into nearby water. Captive ones often rest crocodilian-fashion in the water, with only the top of the head above the surface. ("Gippsland crocodile" was an old vernacular name for this reptile.) Oviferous females are reported to leave the water and seek high ground for a nesting site. Among most climbing iguanians, the color pattern provides concealment when the reptile is among leaves and twigs, or on branches and tree trunks; but the water-dragon is patterned in a fashion adapted primarily for concealment in the water. Above, the water-dragon is dark greenish, with many narrow, pale crossbars. These transverse markings become interrupted and obscure on the sides of the body, but continue boldly down the sides of the tail. The dark limbs are also marked with pale crossbands. The pattern is reminiscent of a young alligator or black caiman.

The foregoing iguanian sequence began with a reptile (the tamacuaré) that is largely arboreal, although terrestrial at times. It runs only in quadrupedal fashion, and is but casually or coincidentally associated with the water, by virtue of occurrence in streamside vegetation. From this we passed to an arboreal-terrestrial-aquatic reptile, quadrupedal at most if not all times, not restricted to the vicinity of water, but utilizing water as an escape route whenever possible (the water-lizard). Next came an arboreal-terrestrial-aquatic reptile, bipedal at times, not restricted to the vicinity of water but utilizing water as an escape route whenever possible (the striped basilisk). Then came an arboreal-terrestrial-aquatic reptile, bipedal at times, utilizing water as an escape route and never going far from it (a larger basilisk). From there we passed to an arboreal-terrestrial-aquatic reptile, bipedal at times, restricted to the immediate vicinity of water, entering the water not only when disturbed but probably at other times as well, too heavy as an adult to leap among twigs, and with partly flattened tail (the sail-tail). Finally we came to an arboreal-terrestrial-aquatic reptile, bipedal at times, restricted to the immediate vicinity of water, spending much time in the water, climbing mostly upon snags and waterside branches, and with a tail that is flattened throughout most of its length (the water-dragon). A roughly comparable sequence of life-ways might well have accompanied the evolution of certain early thecodontians, those destined to give rise to crocodilians.

Thecodontian-iguanian comparisons become more convincing by the demonstration that iguanians have paralleled thecodontians in several additional ways. Of interest in this connection are the iguanian genera Anolis and Draco. The green anole (popularly miscalled "chameleon"), a species

Figure 51. The green anole sleeps at night on vegetation, especially vegetation overhanging water [Tod Swalm]

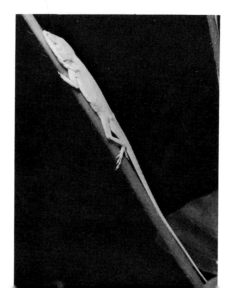

Figure 52. A male anole, reacting to the approach of another male, displays a brightly colored throat-fan, and erects a low crest on the back of the neck. [Tod Swalm]

Figure 53. Among reptiles, combat is often ritualized and without bloodshed. A male green anole seizes an intruding male by the head (at left), twists the intruder over (below), and flings him away (below right). The intruder departs, not really hurt. [Tod Swalm]

of Anolis, was observed at many localities throughout its wide range in the southeastern United States. Smaller than any of the other lizards so far mentioned, it is about 7 inches in total length. The snout is proportionately long (Fig. 51). The green anole inhabits a variety of situations: hardwood forests, old fields grown up in weeds, river swamps, lake shores, dry sandhills covered with stunted oaks and pines, suburban gardens, and others. However, the optimum habitat is waterside vegetation. Each year many thousands of these lizards are collected for the "pet" trade, most of them collected while they are sleeping by night on the leaves and stems of plants that grow beside the water. Green anoles do not automatically leap into the water when an enemy arrives on the scene, but they will unhesitatingly dive in if other escape routes are cut off; and they swim fairly well. Sometimes they run on the ground, quadrupedally but with occasional hops for which the hindlimbs supply most of the propulsive force. Usually, however, they leap about in vegetation. They have a slight ability to glide. Green anoles often drop from trees, usually into brush but sometimes to the ground. Generally they fall not straight down and thrashing wildly, but in a rigid attitude and at a slight angle from the vertical. Often in shrubbery they make a leap downward and outward, a well-aimed leap so prodigious as to suggest some buoying by the air. In short the green anole, whose anatomy would imply nothing more than a specialization for arboreal life, has actually taken the first minute step toward invasion of the air. Some ancient thecodontian must have taken a comparable step, for thecodontians

gave rise to the flying reptiles, and to the reptile-birds which became true birds.

As for the iguanian genus Draco, its various species are called flying-dragons. They are noteworthy for a wing-like expanse of skin on each side of the body. These "wings," which are supported by ribs, can be folded back or can be expanded. When they are expanded, a flying-dragon can glide through the air. A species of Draco was observed near Lingayen, Luzon. The habitat had been greatly disturbed by man. Most of the trees had long since been removed, but a few very large ones had been left standing, and some of these supported colonies of flying-dragons. Scampering over the branches with "wings" folded, these small lizards were reminiscent of various small, comparatively unspecialized, arboreal agamids. About the big trees, no Draco was seen to glide; but on the outskirts of the town of Lingayen a small individual glided from a ceiling joist of an open shed to the shoulder of a man. Only a flash of "wings" could be seen, the structures being folded away again the moment the reptile landed. Another species of Draco has been reported to glide 60 feet, and to catch an insect while in the air.

In many iguanians, the male is brightly colored on surfaces that are usually concealed except during courtship or combat. When courting, the male may distend a brightly colored dewlap that is normally folded back, or elevate the head to reveal a brightly colored throat and chest. Such actions are involved especially with sex recognition during the breeding season. The display of a male evokes a hostile reaction from another male but not from a female. The displaying males engage in combat, more accurately a "ritual combat" in which little physical damage is done, and which is terminated by the hasty departure of one of the combatants, presumably the weaker or less aggressive one. In the only species of Draco that has received much study, the courting male flashes the "wings" and distends the enormous dewlap; both structures are garishly colored when thus displayed. The wing-like expanses permit gliding, and the dewlap has been likened to the vertical stabilizer of an airplane; yet, both structures, in an earlier and less developed state, could have functioned not at all in connection with aerial locomotion but solely with the more ordinary iguanian activities of the breeding season. Thus, iguanians reveal a theoretical evolutionary pathway along which aerial reptiles could have developed from arboreal-terrestrial ones.

Let us consider the life-ways of a few other iguanians, long-tailed ones

Figure 54. The abbess lizard (at left) runs bipedally but slowly. Its associate, the rainbow ameiva (right) runs quadrupedally but very rapidly. [Anthony Wolffsohn]

with enlarged hindlimbs. Of special interest is the abbess lizard, a species of Corytophanes (spelled Corythophanes by some). The abbess lizard was seen at a few localities in the southern half of British Honduras. It is a small reptile, its head bearing a high crest and a prominent dewlap. The body is flattened in a vertical plane, and the lizard's shape is leaf-like. The color is that of a dead or dying leaf; the pattern suggests leaf venation; a ridge down the side of the body resembles the midrib of a leaf. The abbess lizard is in fact a leaf mimic. It inhabits leafy thickets beneath forest trees, and has not been found in waterside vegetation. Like other leaf mimics, the abbess lizards moved slowly among the twigs and branches. (In any leaf mimic, an impulse to leap about would negate the effectiveness of the mimicry.) When approached, the lizards were inclined to "freeze" rather than flee, another habit widespread among leaf mimics. When moving undisturbed through twigs and leaves, an abbess lizard would occasionally rear up, hesitate for a moment, and then leap with perfect aim to some higher perch. This movement, while bipedal, was a hopping rather than a running one. In the wild, no individual was seen on the ground. Captives, provided with leafy branches, stayed among them during the day, but spent the night on the cage floor, resting or sleeping motionless in a straddle-legged posture. Surprisingly, these slow-moving, arboreal leaf mimics turned out to be the most impressively bipedal of all iguanians. An abbess lizard, seized and then released on the ground, would run off bipedally. The fleeing reptile would not try to escape by leaping into the bushes, but would continue running bipedally as long as it was pursued. The posture was nearly erect, not forwardly leaning as in other bipedal iguanians; and the pace was slower than in the other species. If cornered or hard pressed, the fleeing abbess lizard would stop, turn the flat side of its body toward the enemy, and make a series of quadrupedal, sideways hops. During this performance the head was bent over, displaying the crest to its fullest extent; the dewlap was expanded; and the tail was thrashed about. When seized, the lizard would squeak.

It has often been assumed that bipedality is closely linked with a terrestrial way of life, but the habits of Corytophanes lead us to question this assumption. The abbess lizard is exceptionally skillful at bipedal running, yet is highly specialized in form and behavior for life in the trees rather than on the ground.

The collared lizard, a species of Crotaphytus, was seen at various localities in eastern New Mexico. It is a small lizard with proportionately large head and stout body. It inhabited dry, rocky hillsides with very sparse vegetation. When undisturbed, the collared lizards ran about quadrupedally. They were not given to climbing the faces of boulders. When approached, they usually hid under rocks; but if routed out from these retreats, they would run off, sometimes rising to a vertical posture while fleeing. If cornered, they would assume a bipedal stance, and open the mouth to disclose its startlingly black interior.

The frilled lizard, the only species of Chlamydosaurus, was seen near Charters Towers, Queensland, Australia. The habitat here was a hilly, open woodland, further opened by the felling of trees. This reptile receives its name from a wide frill or ruff which nearly encircles its neck. Familiar photographs of the frilled lizard would lead one to expect a huge, dinosaurian reptile that habitually stands upright. Actually, few of these lizards exceed 2 feet in length, including the long tail; and the usual gait is quadrupedal, with the frill folded back across the shoulders. When pursued across an open space, the lizards would rise to a bipedal stance as they ran off. The bipedal dash often brought them near a tree, up which they would run. However, if hard pressed they would turn suddenly, open the brightly colored mouth, expand the even more brightly colored (yellow, orange, and red) ruff, and hiss.

In the abbess, collared, and frilled lizards we see adaptive trends unlike any so far mentioned. These three have no inclination or need to live near the water. The Corytophanes is a highly specialized leaf mimic; the Chlamydosaurus is somewhat more terrestrial than arboreal, and can exist where trees are scattered; the Crotaphytus lives outside the tropics, in dry, rocky places where trees are few or lacking. As noted previously, the habits of Corytophanes lead us to question the assumption that bipedality is necessarily linked with terrestrialism. When Corytophanes, Crotaphytus, and Chlamydosaurus are considered together, we can go a bit further, and question the assumption that bipedality has evolved in iguanians primarily as an improved—in other words faster—method of locomotion. Of all the iguanians so far discussed, the most accomplished at bipedal running are the abbess, collared, and frilled lizards. That is to say, in the basilisks, the sail-tail, and the water-dragon (as well as in the water-lizard if it ever departs from a quadrupedal stance), the bipedal dash is almost invariably a very short one to the safety of water, or to climbable vegetation such as a bush or tree. In contrast, the abbess, collared, and frilled lizards are inclined to make longer bipedal dashes; they do not escape into water, and none of them habitually or predictably runs bipedally to some nearby climbable vegetation. Yet, even these last three species are not particularly speedy when running upright.

Among iguanians, one may chase another during the breeding season; perhaps a male chases a coy female, or a male chases a rival male. But in any event bipedal running has never been reported to accompany such antics. Nor has any iguanian, in captivity or in the wild, been reported to run bipedally in pursuit of an insect or other active prey. A lizard might be expected to run as fast as it could when pursuing food, a mate, or a rival; but only one circumstance evokes from bipedal iguanians the impulse to rise to the upright position: the arrival and advance of an enemy, a potential predator. The escape behavior of an iguanian (and of many other animals) involves a series of actions in sequence, as needed. Thus, an iguanian, first sensing the presence of a potential enemy, might run a few yards quadrupedally, and do no more if not actually attacked. But if the enemy advances in actual or apparent pursuit, the fleeing lizard may next rise to a bipedal stance. If the enemy is discouraged from further pursuit by this sudden change in the prey's appearance, the lizard will carry its escape behavior no further. If the predator continues the chase, however, the lizard will stop, turn, and confront its pursuer with some apparently

Figure 55. When disturbed, the harmless larva of a walnut-moth rears menacingly (above); a harmless South American snake flattens the neck and inflates the throat (at right).
[C. M. Binder, Jr. and Tony Stevens]

menacing attitude. If the pursuer is discouraged by this second change in the prey's appearance, the lizard once again will carry the escape behavior no further. But if the predator, undeterred, pounces on its prey, the lizard may squeak, bite, and defecate. These actions, the last in the series, may cause a predator to drop its prey, which then has a new chance for freedom.

This account of iguanian escape behavior is generalized; various modifications of it are known, and others are to be expected. Such modifications will not be discussed; the intention here is simply to emphasize that in an iguanian, bipedal running is part of a linked series of actions, collectively termed the escape behavior. This behavior is complex, and involves a good deal more than the mere outrunning of a predator. Important to escape behavior are actions that alter the prey's image. Especially important, perhaps, are actions that make the prey look much taller.

Figure 56. When the harmless hog-nosed snake (above) is menaced by an enemy, it goes through a series of actions that function to disconcert this enemy. The series begins with a flattening of the head and neck (below). [Ross Allen's Reptile Institute and Bruce Mozert]

A great many organisms, both vertebrate and invertebrate, when closely approached by an enemy will adopt an unusual stance, make an unusual movement, flash a previously concealed color, or carry on several of these actions simultaneously. For example, several harmless snakes will elevate the tail and coil it into a corkscrew shape when disturbed; other harmless snakes inflate the throat and flatten it vertically, presenting the flat side to the enemy. The common hog-nosed snake, an inoffensive species, will swell with air, spread a hood, hiss loudly, and make threatening lunges of the head; then, if the enemy is not discouraged by these actions, the snake will roll onto its back, writhe a few times, extrude its tongue, evert the cloaca to emit a mixture of fecal material and the contents of the anal scent glands, and seemingly die. One monitor lizard and several of the true chameleons are known to rear up when cornered. The juvenile of the mata-mata turtle will elevate the hindquarters, lower the forequarters, and make an upward lunge of the head, displaying the red-striped throat. The Louisiana newt, disturbed in winter when chilled and incapable of fleeing, will stand on its head and curl the uplifted tail into a spiral. Many other examples could be cited of actions that suddenly alter the appearance of an animal when it is menaced by an enemy. And there is evidence that a predator may be discouraged, at least for a few important moments, when its intended prey suddenly changes orientation, color, scent, or other characteristic. The terms "discouraged" and "intended" are used without implication of human emotion or forethought; predator and prey are regarded as responding automatically to stimuli. Since bipedal running is utilized by iguanians only as a part of the escape behavior, such running probably evolved not as an improved method of locomotion, speedier than the quadrupedal, but as one of many activities serving to disconcert a predator.

Iguanians reveal an evolutionary pathway along which truly bipedal reptiles might have developed from more or less quadrupedal, arboreal-terrestrial ones. The first hint of bipedality is seen in the water-lizard, which habitually sits with head and forequarters elevated, and the forelimbs barely touching the substratum. The next stage in the development of bipedality is exemplified by the basilisks, the sail-tail, and the water-dragon, as well as by the abbess, collared, and frilled lizards. In these species, the ordinary lizard activities such as courtship and the pursuit of prey are still carried on quadrupedally; the stimulus to rise upright is provided only by the attack of an enemy. In some of these lizards, the impulse to adopt a bipedal posture accompanies not only the flight from, but also the in-place confrontation of, the enemy. It might be said that the collared lizard, and certain desert iguanians to be described shortly, represent a still further development of bipedality, in that they have abandoned the wooded situations, the typical iguanian habitat. However, iguanians of the open country have retreats such as rocky crevices and ground burrows, just as other iguanians have trees and ponds in which to find safety.

A further development of bipedality is not to be found among iguanians. In this connection it may be significant that lizards arose at a comparatively late date in the history of reptiles. The latter Jurassic yields a few possible lizard ancestors, and the early Cretaceous some aquatic types; but most lines of lizard descent, including the agamid and iguanid, can be traced back only to the latter Cretaceous. The adaptive radiation of lizards, unlike that of thecodontians and dinosaurs, has been carried on mostly in a world already occupied by mammals and birds, many of them highly effective as predators on or competitors with the reptiles. Lizards must have been barred from many ways of life that were open to thecodontians and dinosaurs.

Development of bipedality beyond the iguanian stage would involve an increased dependence on the hindlimbs, and concomitant modifications of anatomy making for more effective locomotion in an upright position. A final stage would be a reptile with enormous hindlimbs, a heavy tail to counterbalance the body, and much-reduced forelimbs that play no part in locomotion. These stages can be detected among the dinosaurs, and need not be discussed further. From observations on the living iguanians, and from the fossil record of various dinosaur groups, it is clear that almost any stage in the development of bipedality is compatible with a semi-aquatic existence. Only in the case of the fully bipedal thecodontians and dinosaurs might we be justified in guessing that their way of life was thoroughly terrestrial. And even these reptiles could regularly have fled into the water, or hunted food there.

Heretofore, the thecodontians have puzzled us by trends toward both an aquatic life and bipedality, trends oddly intermingled in some of their descendants. Yet, in iguanians these traits are not only compatible but are even correlated to some degree. Two genera of agamids and five of iguanids have been reported to include aquatic members; both of the agamid genera and one of the iguanid include bipedal members as well.

Of all the major evolutionary trends detectable among thecodontians and their descendants, the commonest one leads a bipedal reptile to the water, where it reverts to the more usual reptilian gait. This rather strange sequence has been postulated for the line of descent that led to the crocodilians. The last part of the sequence, eventual loss of bipedality, is readily explained, for an aquatic reptile, moving often in the water but seldom on land, would be expected to improve its tail-sculling aquatic locomotion while losing some of any pre-existing ability to run terrestrially. But the beginning of the sequence is clarified by nothing but observations on the living iguanians.

Thus, a consideration of the Iguanidae and Agamidae has opened a storehouse of ideas. The supply of ideas has not been exhausted; a few more iguanians repay study as we puzzle over the derivation and early history of the crocodilians.

As mentioned previously, the habit of running bipedally has been reported for certain lizards of the desert. More specifically, it has been reported for a few iguanids of the southwestern United States and northern Mexico: the crested lizard (Dipsosaurus), the zebra-tail (Callisaurus), and the sand lizards (several species of Uma). These iguanians are very interesting in their own right; but they are highly specialized reptiles of the arid environments, and as such they do not provide much insight into the problems that concern us here. We need say but little about them. The zebra-tail and the sand lizards are very fast runners quadrupedally, and so bipedally as well. The actions of these lizards (so much more familiar than the actions of the tropical iguanians) have done much to bolster the idea that bipedality is nothing but a very rapid method of locomotion employed by a lizard only to attain high speed. If any of the desert lizards ran faster bipedally than quadrupedally (and this is not proven), the situation would establish no more than a secondary relationship between bipedality and speed; for in these lizards, as in other bipedal iguanians, bipedal running is part of a stereotyped series of actions making up the escape behavior, and is not resorted to when one lizard chases another or some fast-moving insect prey. Dipsosaurus, Callisaurus, and Uma are of interest in showing the diversity of habitats that may be occupied by lizards with some tendency toward bipedal running. This method of locomotion, which not only carries a reptile away from danger but also disconcerts at least some predatory pursuers, has been useful to iguanians in many habitats, from tropical forests and grasslands to temperate deserts and rocky canyons.

For the sake of completeness, mention should be made of the casque-

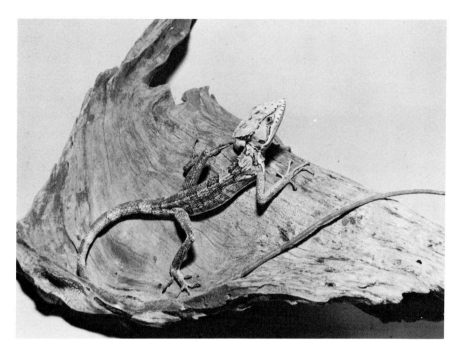

Figure 57. A casque-headed basilisk from Quintana Roo. Casque-heads can run bipedally, yet seldom do so. [Ross Allen's Reptile Institute]

headed basilisks, members of the iguanid genus Laemanctus (Fig. 57). This genus, restricted to southern Mexico and northern Central America, is closely related to Corytophanes. Casque-heads are not well known, but it is clear, from a few but quite reliable accounts, that they can run bipedally. Yet, they do so only when menaced on the ground by some enemy, and they make off by jumping through the branches of shrubs whenever such an escape route is available. There are also some vague reports of bipedality in one or two species of race-runner lizards, genus Cnemidophorus, from the southwestern United States. (The genus Cnemidophorus belongs to the family Teiidae, and so is not iguanian.) As far as I can learn, the aforesaid reports of teiidae bipedality rest on the dubious inference that since the lizards run very rapidly over the sand they must be running bipedally!

Three more genera—Gonyocephalus of the Agamidae, Iguana and Deiroptyx of the Iguanidae—will round out the review of those iguanians whose habits may throw light on the adaptive radiation of ancient thecodontians. The numerous species of Gonyocephalus are called angle-heads. They are small lizards, about 9 to 18 inches in total length, with blunt head, very long hindlimbs, and long, thin tail. One species of angle-head was seen on the island of Morotai in the Moluccas, Indonesia. Here the lizards were found along a sandy coast, on the ground in a strip between the high-tide mark and the coconut zone. When approached, they fled quadrupedally, but with a marked tendency to hop over tussocks and other small obstacles. ("Hopping" involves use of the hindlimbs simultaneously, not alternatively.) When chased into brush, they would progress through it by a series of long, skillfully aimed hops from twig to twig. At Lae, Northeast New Guinea, another species of Gonyocephalus was seen on brush-covered hillsides. These lizards fled quadrupedally over the ground, but made hops over, into, and through the twiggy vegetation. Yet another species of this genus has been reported to live on the ground and to ignore trees when fleeing from an enemy.

As noted, the abbess lizard may hop from one arboreal perch to another. Basilisks will do the same, and so will the "cameleão pequeno," a small, slow-moving, arboreal iguanid of South America (genus Polychrus). The collared lizard will hop across a gully or from rock to rock, and the green anole may hop when amid grass or twigs; both of these are inclined to use the forelimbs at least when alighting. Several (if not all) of the angle-heads are unique among iguanians in showing some tendency toward a hopping gait not just in the bushes but also on the ground. However, no lizard, not even an angle-head, has taken to hopping over the ground bipedally in the familiar fashion of a kangaroo. The angle-head's hop is rather

Figure 58. An iguana. Although primarily arboreal, this large reptile will dive into the water from some tree-top perch. [Ross Allen's Reptile Institute]

Figure 59. A water-anole (at right). These reptiles were seen to dive into a Cuban brook (above). [Dorothy Claussen and Tod Swalm]

sprawling or straddle-legged, often with one hindlimb lifted or extended more than the other, and with the forelimbs outstretched and playing at least some small part in the locomotion.

As for bipedal thecodontians and dinosaurs, in many cases it is hard to say whether a particular species progressed by striding or by hopping. Trackways, series of fossilized footprints, indicate that at least some of the ancient, bipedal reptiles moved their limbs in alternate fashion. This is not surprising. In the "standard" quadrupedal gait of terrestrial reptiles, the hindlimbs are moved alternately, and the shift from quadrupedality to partial or full bipedality does not necessitate a rejection of the basic alternate movements. One dinosaurian order produced gigantic bipeds, stoutly built and with massive hindlimbs; and in such heavy reptiles, striding is a much more likely gait than hopping. Both dinosaurian orders produced bulky, more or less bipedal types that lived in and about the water, feeding upon vegetation; and these heavy reptiles are more likely to have waded through the muck than to have hopped in it. The chances are good that among ancient reptiles, as among the living iguanians, the bipedal gait generally involved use of the hindlimbs alternately.

Further parallels between thecodontians and iguanians are suggested by observations on Iguana and Deiroptyx. The Central American iguana, a species of the genus Iguana, was studied along the Mopan River from Succoths to Benque Viejo, British Honduras. A large lizard, larger than many thecodontians, the iguana in Central America reaches a length of 6 feet. The bright green juveniles were seen climbing about in leafy vegetation, approximately 10 to 20 feet above the ground. They were most abundant in, but not confined to, the streamside thickets. The adults, in contrast, formed colonies in large trees whose branches overhung the river. Sometimes the adults descended to the ground and lay on the sand of the river bank. Surprised at such times, they never dashed for the water but rather for a tree to climb. However, when a collector went up the tree after them, they would dive into the river and swim away submerged. It was astonishing to see a large reptile leap into a swift, rocky stream from a height of 50 feet, and swim twice that distance before coming to the surface. The iguana swims in the fashion of a crocodilian; the legs are folded back, and the propulsive force is supplied by lateral movements of the tail. The gait on land is quadrupedal.

Thus, the Central American iguana differs from the basilisks and the bigger agamids in having no impulse to flee over the ground into the water or to run bipedally. Yet, the iguana reveals, once again, the evolution of aquatic tendencies and abilities in a reptile that is primarily arboreal.

Finally, the water-anole, a species of Deiroptyx, was studied at Rancho Mundito, at that time the Batista estate in low mountains near Consolación del Sur, Cuba. The genus Deiroptyx is close to Anolis, within which some workers would place it. A Deiroptyx may be thought of as an anole that has become specialized for a semi-aquatic life. The water-anole is larger than the green anole, reaching a total length of about 15 inches. The very long snout of the water-anole suggests a crocodilian in miniature. (The local name for this lizard was *caiman*.) Individuals were found to live in colonies along a small, swift brook, where they clung to logs and branches overhanging the water. They did not leap about but lay motionless, camouflaged by color and pattern. On being approached, they dropped into the water and dived to the bottom, where they hid under stones of the stream bed. They would remain submerged for about fifteen minutes. Like a crocodilian, the water-lizard draws the transparent "third eye-lid" across the eye when submerged; water is kept out of the eyes, yet vision is permitted. Captured water-lizards, liberated on land, would run quadrupedally to the water and skitter across the surface. A cornered individual would flatten the body in a vertical plane, distend the throat, erect a low crest on the back of the neck, and turn sideways to the enemy. In this position the reptile would bob up and down a few times, and then make an open-mouthed lunge at the enemy, accompanying this movement by a high-pitched squeak. When seized, some would merely try to bite; others would squeak or mew, very loudly for a lizard; still others would "play dead."

Thus, in its habits the water-anole on the one hand differs from the iguana, on the other from the basilisks and the larger agamids. But once again, arboreal life has led a reptile to the water. Physignathus and Hydrosaurus possibly inherited their aquatic tendencies from a common ancestor; but Basiliscus, Iguana, and Deiroptyx have all developed such tendencies independently, for they represent separate evolutionary lines within the largely nonaquatic iguanians.

As mentioned previously, seven genera of iguanians include species that are inclined to enter the water. Five of these genera—Physignathus and Hydrosaurus of the Agamidae, along with Basiliscus, Iguana, and Deiroptyx of the Iguanidae—have been discussed. In southern Mexico, a species of Anolis has been reported to drop from vegetation into water when alarmed; and in the Galapagos Islands, the gigantic marine iguana (Amblyrhynchus) eats the seaweed from intertidal rocks, and swims across protected coves. Amblyrhynchus, oriented toward the sea, need not concern us further. The iguanian genera that invade fresh water are, without exception, primarily arboreal ones. Iguanians seemingly are led to the water by an evolutionary pathway that begins in the trees.

The paleontological literature is noncommittal on the likelihood of arboreal habits in the thecodontians, which display such obvious trends toward bipedality and an aquatic life. But the iguanians reveal that aquatic and bipedal tendencies, separately or in combination, are compatible with a primarily arboreal existence. Thecodontians and iguanians parallel each other in general conformation and adaptive trends. In iguanians, the trends have culminated in the partly aerial flying dragons, the largely aquatic water-dragon, and a variety of occasionally bipedal types; while the thecodontians, diversifying in a world that had not yet been usurped by mammals and birds, carried the comparable trends much further to produce the flying reptiles, the highly aquatic crocodilians, and a variety of fully bipedal types. But the problems that concern us most are not those relating to the more highly specialized thecodontians, for their life-ways may be inferred, at least in broad outline, from anatomical modifications. The puzzle has been the kind of life that was led by early thecodontians, those that somehow managed to have aerial, aquatic, and bipedal descendants. The iguanians reveal what this way of life could have been.

As the Paleozoic was drawing to a close, forests of coniferous trees were spreading over the earth, replacing the ferns and other lower plants which had previously dominated the landscape. When the Mesozoic opened, the rapidly burgeoning reptiles were presented with a new environment; and it is inconceivable that some reptilian group did not seize the evolutionary opportunity to take over a major habitat, the trees. Of all the Triassic groups, only the thecodontians display the slim, counter-balancing tail and the enlarged hindlimbs expected of reptiles that leap about in vegetation. And, improbable as it would seem if we had no chance to observe iguanian activities, a primarily arboreal habitat is precisely the one that can lead a reptile group to bipedality, to invasion of the air, and to crocodilian-like existence in the water.

To judge from their structure, the early thecodontians were active reptiles. The crocodilians must have had some agile ancestors. This idea would not come to mind from casual observation of a large crocodilian in its usual resting pose, belly to ground. But a crocodilian can do some surprising things. In moving over land, it does not drag itself clumsily along, but lifts the body well off the ground, and makes away in the gait a horseman would call a "walk." When a crocodilian walks, only the latter half of its tail drags the ground; this portion flops left and then right, back and forth, in a rhythm matched to the stride. In the crocodiles, particularly, the rump of the walking reptile is conspicuously higher than the shoulders, the hindlimbs being longer than the forelimbs. The gait is not plantigrade, not flatfooted as in a bear or a man, but digitigrade, up on the toes, the heel of the hind foot not touching the ground. At least one modern species, the Cuban crocodile, not uncommonly rests in the posture described for the water-lizard, its hindlimbs flexed, and its forelimbs straightened to their fullest extent. Very small alligators occasionally assume this posture, also.

Young crocodilians, and even medium-sized adults, can and will climb agilely. Baby alligators are almost lizard-like in their ability to scale a fence of wire mesh. I have seen a foot-long baby alligator escape from a smooth wooden box twenty inches deep by clawing its way up a corner. In the wild, small alligators will occasionally climb onto snags, and I saw one resting in a loop of Berchemia vine that dangled into the water from a recently toppled tree. A captive alligator, nearly four feet long, habitually climbed a large, much-branched Yucca that adorned an artificial islet in its pen. The reptile would come to rest at a point about four feet above the water, where its movements had flattened the spine-tipped Yucca leaves into a horizontal perch. A hatchling alligator, when the substratum became too warm, would climb into a potted Philodendron that decorated its pen.

Figure 60. When walking, the alligator holds the body well off the ground.
[Ross Allen's Reptile Institute]

On one occasion a captive American crocodile, about seven feet long, made a scrambling leap over a four-foot fence, in automatic response to my imitation of the juvenile's distress call. Several of the crocodilians can leap upward, the movement being accomplished chiefly by a powerful thrust of the hindlimbs. The leap may be directed toward a larger enemy, or toward food. In nature, several of the crocodiles are accomplished at climbing up steep banks, and at leaping from them into the water. Such actions are often necessary in the dry season, when the reptiles' customary resting places are left high and dry as the water table falls. In the upper Amazon drainage, floods may leave a great mass of flotsam hanging in streamside vegetation; and Cuvier's smooth-fronted caiman sometimes rests at night not in the water but 6 or 8 feet above it in this tangle of roots, vines, branches, and debris.

The behavior of crocodilians, studied in detail, makes it easier to credence their evolution from reptiles that were given to leaping and climbing; for among reptiles, even small details of behavior are likely to be inherited, to be genetically determined in the same fashion as small but consistent details of anatomy.

Somewhere in the remote ancestry of the crocodilians there may have been little thecodontians that behaved much like, say, a Basiliscus, living principally in waterside vegetation, leaping among twigs, diving or running into the water when alarmed, and rising on occasion to a bipedal position. But 30 million years would go by before this early reptilian stock would become more crocodilian than thecodontian, and during that span the stock would carry bipedality farther than any iguanian would ever do.

Theocodontians were themselves descended from very early reptiles with five toes, and with a clumsy, quadrupedal gait in which the feet were turned outward to some degree. Correlated with the thecodontian trend toward bipedality were evolutionary changes in the anatomy of the hindlimbs, pelvic girdle, and tail. In a biped the body could not be supported efficiently by hindlimbs that were spread apart; and one of the evolutionary changes involved the turning forward of the hindlimbs, giving them a fore-and-aft swing. Concomitantly, the hindlimbs became larger and straighter; essentially they formed two long pillars upholding the reptile's body. With the turning forward of the hindlimb, the foot pointed forward; the reptile's weight was brought to bear chiefly on the middle toe; the first (innermost) and the fifth (outermost) toe became comparatively unimportant in locomotion. The evolutionary outcome of this situation among reptilian bipeds was the enlargement of the second, third, and fourth toes, especially the third (middle) one; the first toe was reduced and in some cases turned backward as a sort of prop; the useless fifth toe was lost. (The three-toed foot of a chicken differs in no important anatomical respect from that of a bipedal dinosaur.) In the crocodilians, the fifth toe has pratically vanished; externally it is not evident, and skeletally it is represented by a mere nubbin of bone. No such reduction has taken place among the iguanians, and this is one reason for believing that the ancestors of the crocodilians were more thoroughly bipedal than modern lizards.

Yet, the ancestors of the crocodilians probably were not fully bipedal, for the crocodilian forelimb does not exhibit the degree of reduction that would be expected if it had once been completely withdrawn from locomotion. Although smaller than the hindlimb, the forelimb is still a well-developed structure. The forefoot is small for the reptile's size. (Hide-hunters in Florida often confess an unrealized ambition to kill an alligator so large that its forefeet, skinned, could be worn for gloves.) There are five digits. The fourth digit is made up of four bones (one less than in the primitive reptilian norm); both the fourth and fifth digits are clawless. Otherwise, the forefoot shows no significant reduction in anatomical complexity.

The hindfoot of a crocodilian is noteworthy for the presence of a true "heel bone" (a tuber calcanei in technical parlance). This structure, more characteristic of mammals than of reptiles, serves for the attachment of certain muscles that flex the hindlimb, and its development makes for improvement in walking and running. Its presence in crocodilians suggests that the ancestors of these reptiles were accomplished at terrestrial locomotion, but does not reveal the extent to which this locomotion was bipedal. The forelimb throws light on the latter problem. In reptiles generally, several small bones lie between the wrist and the digits; in the crocodilians, two of these bones are notably elongated, in effect adding an extra segment to the limb. Such elongation is a modification associated with digitigrade running, and we are led to think that the ancestors of the crocodilians made use of the forelimbs when moving about on land. Considerable use of the forelimbs, even in a reptile capable of walking bipedally, is not at all unlikely. A temporarily quadrupedal position would be advantageous in drinking, and often in feeding. Also, it must not be forgotten that various modern reptiles locate prey, or a mate in the breeding season, by following scent trails across the ground. Scent plays a highly important role in the life of most and probably all reptiles. A bipedal reptile, walking always with its head in the air, has cut itself off from a potential source of information about its environment and associates. Perhaps this is why the ornithischian dinosaurs, an entire order descending from thecodontians, never carried bipedal walking beyond the stage we have inferred for the ancestors of the crocodilians.

11 MORE PROBLEMS IN CROCODILIAN HISTORY

THUS, THE SCIENCES of paleontology, anatomy, herpetology, and animal behavior have combined to throw at least a little light on that early period when crocodilians and other archosaurs were evolving from thecodontian forebears. A later period in crocodilian history, the early and middle Jurassic, is scarcely amenable to any kind of analysis; for, as noted in Chapter 7, this time span is known chiefly from marine deposits and the fossil remains of sea-dwelling organisms. The Jurassic gap in the fossil record is unfortunate, for it obscures a very important part of crocodilian history. During the Triassic, the crocodilians were a minor group; except for two marine families, the group vanishes from sight at the beginning of the Jurassic; it reappears in the latter Jurassic as the Mesosuchia, a diverse lot of families. It was during the early and middle Jurassic that crocodilians became an important group, spread widely, and accomplished much of their adaptive radiation; and so we should welcome any clues to the events of that time period.

Only a few clues exist. As we have seen in Chapter 7, eight crocodalian families have been combined as the suborder Mesosuchia. This has been done chiefly because in certain details of skull and vertebrae these families are all comparably intermediate between the early crocodilian suborders and the advanced Eusuchia. But among the archosaurs it is not unusual for two groups to exhibit parallel trends in the evolution of certain anatomical structures; and it is not out of the question that the mesosuchians actually represent two major lines of descent. Proto-suchus, the little crocodilian from the latter Triassic of Arizona, is short-snouted and high-skulled, a terrestrial type. It is possible that a line of descent led from the Protosuchidae to the short-snouted, high-skulled Notosuchidae and Libycosuchidae, perhaps even to the suborder Sebeco-suchia, whose fossil history is just beginning to emerge. By this inter-pretation, the "suborder Mesosuchia" would actually be a composite, de-scended in part from the suborder Protosuchia and in part from the suborder Archeosuchia. Adoption of this view would not wholly negate the usefulness of the term Mesosuchia; for the eight families now placed in this suborder do represent a certain level or grade of evolutionary ad-vancement within the Crocodilia, whether they attained this level by one pathway or two. The suborder Mesosuchia is by no means the only pale-ontological grouping than may prove to be based more on evolutionary grade than on close relationship. A conservative course would be to recognize but a single group until the discovery of additional fossil material demonstrates the existence of two or more distinct lineages.

The taxonomic position of the metriorhynchid sea crocodiles is a matter of approach. Retention of them in the Mesosuchia emphasizes their basic resemblances to other crocodilians, such as the pholidosaurs; placing them in a suborder of their own, the Thalattosuchia, emphasizes their unique adaptations for marine existence. We have followed the former course; but more interesting than exact taxonomic position is the question of why metriorhynchids were the only crocodilians—in fact the only archo-saurs—ever to become highly specialized, anatomically, for life in the sea. Teleosaurs and some tomistomines lived in the sea, and some modern crocodiles are species of the salt water more than of the fresh. Yet, these reptiles exhibit much the same general conformation as a freshwater croco-dilian. The gross anatomy of a freshwater crocodilian represents a sort of compromise; the reptile is about as thoroughly adapted for aquatic life as it could be, short of losing the ability to move over land, as it must, at least to nest. But metriorhynchids evolved a conformation unique among crocodilians. The limbs were paddle-shaped, the back finned, the tail tip angled downward to support a tail fin. It is hard to escape the conclusion that the metriorhynchids, alone among archosaurs, had managed to break all ties with the land. This would mean, of course, that they did not even come to land to nest. As suggested by Chapter 4, in the modern crocodilians the hind foot is used to dig the nest and manipulate the eggs; and there is reason to believe that this pattern of behavior is exceedingly ancient, antedating even the rise of the thecodontians. In the metriorhynchids the hindlimb was even more paddle-like than the forelimb; it was an excellent structure for swimming and steering in the water, but not for digging a hole. We are led to suggest that the sea-crocodiles had become live-bearers. Actual proof of viviparity, the live-bearing condition, would come only with the discovery of a foetus fossilized within its mother. Such a discovery has not been made, but this situation is not very significant; the extinct ichthyosaurs, live-bearing reptiles of the Triassic, Jurassic, and Cretaceous seas, were known for a long while before chance revealed the fossilized remains of a gravid female and her young. In the absence of direct information, a little speculation is not amiss; for much biological interest attaches to viviparity in the Animal kingdom.

Biologists have often puzzled over the development of viviparity among certain reptiles but not others. Some have emphasized the fact that the living crocodilians and turtles, as well as the taxonomically isolated tuatara, are all egg-layers, and that they all secrete albumen about the egg; whereas the living snakes and lizards, which even if egg-laying do not secrete albumen, on a good many separate occasions have evolved the live-bearing condition from the egg-laying one. Albumen supplies moisture to the developing embryo; and so it might be reasoned that the eggs of snakes and lizards, once they are laid, could well be in greater danger of desiccation than the eggs of crocodilians, turtles, and the tuatara. Thus, among snakes and lizards, more often than among other reptiles, natural selection

Figure 61. In the green sea-turtle, the forelimb is much more paddle-like than the hindlimb. Although primarily marine, sea-turtles are still bound to the land by the necessity of nesting on beaches. [Ross Allen's Reptile Institute]

Figure 62. Some snakes, such as the pine snake (above), lay eggs; others, such as the anaconda (below), give birth to young. [Kurt Severin and Ross Allen's Reptile Institute]

might favor retention of the eggs in the assuredly moist environment of the female's oviducts.

Yet, the topic of viviparity is complex. Of all living reptiles, the snakes are the ones to have developed the live-bearing condition most often. Among the snakes, this condition seems to develop when eggs in the nest are endangered more than eggs in the female's oviducts. Under these circumstances, natural selection favors progressively longer retention of the eggs by the female, regardless of what menaces eggs in the nest. The danger of desiccation seems to have little to do with the matter; there is no unusually high percentage of live-bearers among snakes of the desert. But viviparity is of frequent occurrence among aquatic snakes, in whose habitat eggs might be menaced by excess of moisture, and among snakes of the high latitudes and altitudes, where eggs would be endangered by cold weather. It also seems that viviparity can develop not only when eggs in the nest are menaced to some exceptional degree, but also when the adult has exceptional ability to guard itself (and therefore the eggs within the gravid female) from the hazards of existence. Thus, viviparity has been a frequent development among venomous snakes.

Lizards have developed viviparity less often than snakes, and so provide less information about the condition. However, observations on live-bearing lizards are compatible with the above conclusions based on a study of the snakes. Lizards and snakes are not closely related to crocodilians, but our attention must be directed toward them because they provide the only information about the circumstances that foster reptilian viviparity.

Of interest is a group of closely related, viviparous South American snake genera. This group includes two (Tomodon and Pseudotomodon) whose members are swamp-dwelling frog-eaters; one (Tachymenis) that has invaded high altitudes of the Andes; and one (Thamnodynastes) with species that live in bushes and trees, and that do not have to venture to the forest floor for egg-laying. These genera probably inherited viviparity from a common ancestor, just as they inherited anatomical structures that lead us to describe them as a closely related group. Whatever caused the ancestral stock to evolve the live-bearing condition, the descendants of that stock moved into several of the environmental situations where viviparity is of especial value. The point is that a live-bearing reptile need not have become viviparous in the habitat where we now find it. If metriorhynchid sea-crocodiles were viviparous, it would seem possible and indeed probable that the live-bearing condition evolved in a freshwater archeosuchian whose eggs were menaced to an unusual degree by some component of the physical environment or by some predator. The descendants of such an archeosuchian would be "preadapted" (as the biologist would phrase it) for life in the high seas. In other words, the hypothetical archeosuchian ancestor of the metriorhynchids would be provided beforehand with an evolutionary adjustment that is almost indispensable if a reptile is to become thoroughly marine.

Among the snakes there can be found all the stages leading from the oviparous or egg-laying condition to the viviparous one (Fig. 62). Typically among oviparous snakes, the embryo is not far advanced when the eggs are laid, and the clutch reposes in the nest for three or four months. A first step toward viviparity is the longer retention of the eggs by the female, thus shortening the time they must spend in the nest. For example, the female of the smooth green snake (Opheodrys) in the Chicago area may retain the eggs until they are within a month of hatching. In northern Michigan, smooth green snake eggs would often be endangered in the nest by the brevity of the warm season, but the female could lengthen her active season by basking in the sun or taking cover from the cold; and in this area, the smooth green snake's eggs are usually retained to within ten or fifteen days of hatching. One female of this species even retained her eggs to within four days of hatching. (A comparable case is that of a Eurasian lizard, a species of Lacerta ranging from the Pyrenees and the Alps to southeastern Siberia. It is a live-bearer in most areas; but in the southern part of its range, where the warm season is sufficiently long to permit the hatching of eggs, it is oviparous like all of its numerous congeners. The southern population of this lizard maintains the primitive method of reproduction, while the northern one has developed viviparity presumably in response to the brevity of the warm season.) A further advance is shown by a large number of snakes in which the eggs are retained by the female to the point of hatching, and the egg shell is reduced to a mere membrane about the newborn young. Finally, in some of the live-bearing snakes a placenta-like structure has developed, a connection between the bloodstream of the gravid female and that of the embryo (although the latter is still nourished in large part by yolk material).

An evolutionary trend, once established in some taxonomic group, may proceed apace if it continues to be advantageous. The initial establishment of an evolutionary trend is quite another matter. The modern crocodilians are surely not live-bearers, and as far as is known their eggs repose for a long while in a nest. But the question we should ask is whether crocodilians show any possibility of taking that first critical step toward viviparity, the prolonged retention of the eggs by the female.

Of interest in this connection are the experiences of an embryologist, Samuel F. Clarke, in the 1890s, and the rather similar experiences of Albert M. Reese twenty years later. Each of these men came to Florida to collect material that would throw light on the embryonic development of the alligator, and each had great difficulty in obtaining alligator eggs that would show the earliest stages of embryonic development. Reese watched newly made nests, took the eggs within a few hours of their deposition, and found them to be well advanced in their development. Next he killed gravid females, but discovered even their eggs to be well along embryonically. He finally obtained from a freshly killed female some eggs that were in a fairly early stage of embryonic development, roughly the stage reached by a chicken embryo after 24 hours' incubation. About the time Clarke was in Florida, A. Voeltzkow had difficulty in obtaining early embryonic stages of the Nile crocodile; for the eggs of this reptile also seemed to be well advanced even at the time they were laid. Voeltzkow made several trips to Africa, and finally, to accomplish his embryological aims, he had to tie a gravid female and periodically remove the eggs from her oviducts through a slit cut in the body wall.

We do not know whether retention of the eggs by the alligator, or by any other crocodilian, is a frequent occurrence, an occasional one, or a rare one. Reese thought he was dealing with an unusual or exceptional situation. During one of his summers in Florida, he made some highly important observations. The weather had been unusually dry; ponds and other bodies of shallow water had vanished; "'gator holes" had been reduced to puddles. The female alligators built their nests at the usual season, but these nests sat empty for two weeks. At the end of that time the drought broke, and all the female alligators immediately began laying. When the eggs were finally layed, the embryos were in an advanced stage. Reese was meticulous in his work, and no doubt the sequence of events was precisely as he reported it. But did excessive dryness lead the females to retain their eggs even though nests had been built? Did the arrival of rain lead the females to lay at last?

In the absence of experimental data on crocodilians, we can only turn to some other reptile group. If a gravid female of some oviparous snake is captured during the egg-laying season of her species, and is thereafter kept in a barren, wood-floored cage, she will usually retain her eggs for weeks or even months. I have known gravid female snakes, kept under such conditions, suddenly to lay their long-retained eggs on the damp spot formed by accidental spillage from a water pan. Of course many species have not been investigated; but retention of the eggs, under the conditions outlined above, is widespread among oviparous snakes. Adjustments of physiology and behavior are necessary if eggs, ready for deposition, can be retained in the female's oviducts when some environmental condition would menace them in the nest. Snakes indicate that such adjustments are possible within the reptilian evolutionary level. The chances are good that Reese's interpretations were correct.

The problem may be approached from another angle. The gravid females in the alligator population studied by Reese withheld their eggs far beyond the normal laying time. They did not do so capriciously or with human foresight; for, as emphasized in other chapters, alligators act more or less automatically in response to stimuli coming from their environment or from their internal rhythms. Such responses have a genetic basis. When Reese's alligators finally layed, the eggs contained well-advanced embryos without obvious abnormalities. In other words some stimulus— an environmental rather than an individual one, since it affected many females over a sizeable area—caused Reese's alligators to withhold their eggs; and embryonic development was not inhibited thereby. Even ignoring evidence from snakes, and ignoring the probability that drought was the environmental stimulus leading to the egg retention that was noted by Reese, it still appears that the all-important first step toward viviparity is not denied the alligator, and the experiences of Voeltzkow suggest that it is not denied the Nile crocodile.

Thus, the weight of evidence favors the view that, under the proper circumstances, crocodilians could become viviparous. The requisite circumstances might be a shift toward a drier climate, to the point where rainfall was unpredictable even during the rainiest time of year; with eggs in the nest frequently harmed by the drying up of swamps and waterside situations, natural selection would put a high premium on the progressively longer retention of the eggs by the gravid female. And as we have seen, a viviparous reptile of the fresh waters is preadapted for successful invasion of the sea. There would seem to be an evolutionary pathway whereby crocodilians of the high seas could have been derived from stock with ordinary oviparous habits and an ordinary freshwater habitat. The pathway is to a considerable degree theoretical, but it is consistent with all the pertinent data that can be gathered from a study of reptiles ancient and modern. We may never have the fossil material to reveal in strictly empiric fashion the way in which one line of crocodilian descent managed to become highly adapted for life in the sea.

Some problems of much interest are not ever to be solved through the mere stock-piling of specimens, but rather through the analysis of data in the light of the appropriate biological concepts. For example, competition in the biological sense of the term has been invoked to explain various peculiarities of crocodilian history. At several points in the account of that history, it was suggested that one reptile group exerted an important effect on the distribution and spread of another group. Thus, as noted, the northward spread of aquatic crocodilians might at first have been slowed by the prior establishment of phytosaurs in the aquatic habitat. But crocodilians, better adapted anatomically, finally displaced the phytosaurs, which became extinct. The poor showing of the Crocodylinae in South America was attributed tentatively to the firm and prior establishment of the Alligatorinae there. The success of crocodylines in southern Asia, the present Asiatic tropics, probably had much to do with the failure of alligatorines to invade that area. The presence of dyrosaurs might have kept Africa from becoming a major center of gavialid evolution. If these views are correct, then competition has played a major role in crocodilian history, and the concept merits further discussion.

We often speak of competition between two taxonomic groups of animals, but the actual competition is between two species that live in the same area. The outcome of many interspecific struggles might be the disappearance of all the species belonging to one group, and their replacement by members of some other and better-adapted group. Only in this sense do groups compete. One might easily jump to the conclusion, especially where crocodilians are involved, that a competitive relationship between two species has something to do with physical combat. It is conceivable that a more aggressive species might extirpate a less aggressive one, but more often than not competition involves no physical contact.

Imagine a limited tract capable of supporting a population of, say, 1,000 crocodilians. The tract provides everything that is necessary to maintain a crocodilian population of this size. Why could not this population be made up of 500 crocodilians of one species and 500 of another? Such an arrangement would not last over many generations, for the two species would have to be exactly equal both in their needs and in their abilities to fill these needs. Let us concentrate on the most obvious need, food, and assume both species to require the same amount. One species would probably be somewhat better than the other at capturing whatever prey animals existed in the tract. Perhaps one species, at the outset making up 50 per cent of the population, could capture 60 percent of the available food. The other and less fortunate species could not continue to make up 50 per cent of the population when getting only 40 per cent of the food, and so its numbers would decline. The better-adapted species might soon come to make up 60 per cent of the population. But remember that this species, even at the time when it made up only 50 per cent of the population, could capture 60 per cent of the food; so now that it make up 60 per cent of the population, it will capture more than 60 per cent of the food. The process will continue; the better adapted species will take over the entire tract, while the other will vanish. The two species of our imaginary tract could compete not only for food, but for anything that was both necessary and in limited supply. Needs might include such things as waterholes for denning, open spots for resting, islets for nesting, or adequate room if the species were territorial.

But between these two species there would go on another and more subtle interaction, which we could term competition only by granting that the two are (in effect) competing for sole occupancy of the entire tract. For example, one of the two species might be more resistant to the local parasites, or better able to escape the local predators; it might guard the nest more effectively, or lay eggs that were more resistant to desiccation. In any of these circumstances, and in many others that are imaginable, one species would come to outnumber the other, and eventually usurp the entire tract. Thus, one species may oust another through competition over the utilization of one or more tangible components of the environment, or through a superior ability to cope with the problems of that environment.

Might not one of the two species be, say, the poorer at getting food but the better at defending the nest, so that the ability of one species cancels out the different ability of another species? Could not two coexisting species reach some kind of balance? But if a balance were reached under some set of environmental conditions in nature, it would be nonetheless impermanent because the conditions would change. Climate becomes cooler or warmer, drier or wetter. As climate changes, so does the nature of the vegetation. Different types of vegetation ameliorate in different ways such climatic rigors as droughts, freezes, hard winds, and rainwater run-off. Soil is modified by the vegetation that covers it. As the landscape is being remodeled, some living things are vanishing from the affected area and new ones moving in. There may be new parasites, new predators upon the young crocodilians, and new competitors with the adults, as well as new climatic hazards. And apart from the local effect of climatic shifts, distant environmental changes may open a corridor between two formerly separated areas, loosing one fauna upon another and forming new animal and plant associations with many new interrelationships.

Competition exists everywhere in nature. Even plants compete fiercely with each other for soil moisture and nutrients, for space, and for the sunlight that triggers photosynthesis (the food-making process of a green plant). Yet, the natural world is not solely one of struggle. There is a way in which two related species (or even more) might live in the same geographic area. That is, they might be restricted for the most part to two different habitats. This is a commonly occurring situation among reptiles (Fig. 63). One might enunciate a rule that would be applicable to almost all the snakes, lizards, turtles, and crocodilians in the world: If two species are closely related, belonging usually in the same genus, their respective geographic ranges will not overlap; or if there is some area where the ranges do overlap, in that area the two species will occupy different habitats; or if two species are found in both the same area and the same habitat (an infrequent situation), then they eat different foods. The few exceptions to this rule seem mostly to reflect profound disturbances of the environment by modern man, who, through such activities as timbering, farming, burning, and stock raising, creates new habitats in which the pre-existing interrelationships of living things are set all awry.

How does such a rule work in practice? Let us take an area in north-central Florida, where the reptile life is diverse. The herpetologist here would find the red-headed skink (a lizard of the genus Eumeces) mostly on the trunks of big trees in the damp forests that border the rivers and creeks. The southeastern five-lined skink, another Eumeces, might occasionally turn up in the same places; but usually it would be found on the dry sandhills, in the flatwoods, and in the sand pine scrub. It would be seen mostly on the ground, or about stumps and logs. A third Eumeces, the red-tailed skink, would hardly ever be seen above ground; it lives in the upper sands, where it inhabits beetle burrows and the sand "push-ups" made by burrowing animals. Naturally, it would be concentrated in areas of loose, dry soil. Of the local species of Ophisaurus, the island glass-lizard would be found only in sand pine scrub and the drier flatwoods; the eastern glass-lizard in damp, grassy or weedy places such as lake margins, low-lying meadows, moist forests, and the wetter flatwoods; the slender glass-lizard in dry, grassy or brushy places such as broomsedge fields and the sandhills. Years of reptile collecting might never reveal even one glass-lizard "off sides." The eastern and island glass-lizards do overlap in certain flatwoods which offer a gradient from damp to dry; but the eastern glass-lizard is more of a burrower than its congener, and there is some environmental separation of the two even where they occupy the same major habitat. The mud snake (Farancia) would be found mostly in vegetation-choked ponds, bogs, and swamps, where the water is still and and acid; its near relative, the rainbow snake, mostly in the larger streams with alkaline or neutral waters. The mud snake as an adult feeds mainly on large, aquatic, eel-like salamanders, the rainbow snake on the common eel, a fish.

And so it goes, for genus after genus of reptiles. In the aforesaid area, the yellow ratsnake (Elaphe) lives mainly in the trees, feeding heavily on birds; the red ratsnake mainly on the ground and in burrows, preying heavily on small mammals such as mice and shrews. The common hog-nosed snake (Heterodon) and the southern hog-nosed snake are occasionally found in the same place, but the former feeds chiefly on the southern toad (Bufo), the latter on the spadefoot toad (Scaphiopus).

Figure 63. Where two related reptile species inhabit the same area, they usually occupy different habitats. For example, where the brown kingsnake (upper) and the common kingsnake (lower) coexist, the former lives in dry fields and on barren clayhills, the latter in damper and better vegetated places. [Ross Allen's Reptile Institute]

The blacksnake (Coluber) dashes about in the damper situations, the coachwhip in the drier ones. When two related species of the same area are noncompetitive, or largely so, because of some difference in the respective ways of life, the two are said to be ecologically separated. The nature of the separation between two species need not be the same in every area where the two coexist. The clear-cut ecological separation of two related species is not limited to reptiles, but is of widespread occurrence among animals and plants.

The subjects of competition and ecological separation have many ramifications. Most of these need not be pursued here, but one of them is worth mentioning. Ecological separation often involves the avoidance not only of competition but also of hybridization. Remotely related species hardly ever attempt to interbreed. If they did so, the mating would probably come to nought, for reasons of genetic incompatibility among others. But, at least in the reptiles, two closely related species may be quite capable of interbreeding, of producing hybrid offspring that are fertile. Both the morphological and behavioral characteristics of a species have a genetic background, and have evolved as adaptations to some particular way of life; so, obviously a species is not likely to profit from the introduction into its genetic make-up of characteristics from another and differently adapted species. Living things have evolved so-called isolating mechanisms, ways of minimizing hybridization. Among reptiles, a common way, in fact probably the commonest way, is a clear-cut ecological separation. Two closely related reptile species, even though potentially able to hybridize, are not going to do so very often if they live in different habitats.

The concepts of ecological separation and of competition between species do much to clarify the distribution of living crocodilians. Nowhere do we find any large number of crocodilian species in one area; and where two species overlap in geographic range, they occupy different habitats for the most part. Furthermore, if the two crocodilian species, separated by habitat, are not very different in size, they will be markedly unlike in head shape; and a difference in head shape is correlated with unlike feeding habits. But more often than not, one of two habitat-separated crocodilians will be much larger than the other, and given to taking larger prey on the average.

Let us see how these generalizations apply in the vast expanse of the Asiatic tropics, with its diversity of crocodilians. One species, the estuarine crocodile, ranges widely over this area, from Ceylon and the southern coasts of India to the Philippines, Fiji, and the northern coast of Australia. A gigantic reptile, the largest of living crocodilians, it lives chiefly in estuaries and coastal waters, freely entering the sea; it also ranges inland, but mostly or exclusively along rivers. In northern Australia its range overlaps that of Johnston's crocodile, which is a much smaller reptile with a very narrow snout. Interestingly, local residents call the estaurine crocodile "alligator," and restrict the name "crocodile" to the smaller species. Johnston's crocodile lives mostly in the fresh water, occasionally about brackish ponds, and feeds upon small organisms. It is endemic—strictly confined—to northern Australia.

Just north of Australia, and separated from it by the Torres Strait, lies the great island of New Guinea. It harbors the estuarine crocodile, which as usual inhabits the coastal waters and the rivers. The ponds and lakes of the island's interior are the home of another species, the New Guinea crocodile. It does not differ much from the estuarine crocodile in head shape; but it is a small reptile, perhaps the smallest of the genus Crocodylus, scarcely a third the length of the estuarine giant. The New Guinea crocodile is endemic to the island for which it is named.

During the Pleistocene, sea level fluctuated with the waxing and waning of vast ice sheets in the high latitudes; and at times, a land bridge was formed between New Guinea and Australia. Thus, it is not surprising that many species of snakes, lizards, frogs, and other organisms are to be found on both sides of the Torres Strait. Yet, the New Guinea crocodile does not inhabit Australia, nor does Johnston's crocodile occur on New Guinea Evidently these species are too much alike, in needs and capabilities, to find separate habitats in either Australia or New Guinea. The two areas seem each to have ecological "room" only for a single small, freshwater crocodilian, along with the large, estuarine species.

Many islands of the southwestern Pacific, especially the smaller ones with limited freshwater resources, harbor only the estuarine crocodile. In the Philippines, the range of this species overlaps that of the Mindoro crocodile. The latter, endemic to a few islands of the Philippine group, is very similar to the New Guinea crocodile in size, head shape, and freshwater habitat. Borneo is unusual in having three crocodilians. One of these is the estuarine species; a second is the Siamese crocodile, smaller than the estuarine one, and more characteristic of fresh water; the third is a Tomistoma, the "false gavial," a fish-eater with exceedingly narrow snout. Java has the Siamese and estuarine crocodiles, Sumatra the "false gavial" and the estuarine crocodile.

Ceylon has the estuarine crocodile and the mugger. The latter is a swamp-dweller, essentially of the fresh waters. Although by no means rivalling the estuarine crocodile in size, the mugger is a large reptile, larger than the New Guinea, Mindoro, or Siamese crocodiles. It is remarkable among crocodiles for its broad, short, alligator-like snout. In India and Burma, the range of the mugger overlaps that of a gigantic, narrow-snouted fish-eater, the gharial. Overlap of the mugger, the estuarine crocodile, and the gharial is possible in or near East Pakistan.

At this point, the ecological separation of crocodilians will not be reviewed on a world-wide basis. The situation in the Asiatic tropics is typical: most areas have but one species of crocodilian, or else two that differ in habitat, size, and food; a few areas may have three species, all of them different in their respective ways of life. The Amazon drainage of South America has four different species of crocodilians. The Amazon, greatest of all river systems, contains one-fifth of all the running fresh water in the world, and offers a great diversity of freshwater habitats. This is why it can support four species of crocodilians, each of them ecologically separated from the others. North of the Amazon in South America, there may be localities that harbor one crocodile and three caimans, but proof of this is lacking.

Thus, if two crocodilian species are going to exist in the same area, they must be adapted to fill two different ecological niches; and the two separate niches must be present and open to crocodilians. If three crocodilian species are to coexist, then they must occupy three different niches, all three available. In the fresh and coastal waters there is a rather low limit to the number of really distinctive niches that could support a crocodilian species. If we look at the fossil record, we see goniopholids radiating from the Old World, followed by early pholidosaurs and hylaeochampsids; we see late phytosaurs burgeoning in Africa, gavialids spreading probably from a South American homeland, early tomistomines radiating from Eurasia and later ones from Africa, crocodylines and alligatorines both moving between the Old World and the New. But the various regions of the world did not simply come to harbor more and more crocodilians as the geological periods went by. Rather, a crocodilian group would spread only into areas where suitable niches were both available and open; or else, by virtue of superior adaptations, would take over niches by displacing some other group. Studies on competition and ecological separation help us to understand ancient episodes whose outcome is revealed by the fossil record.

The crocodilians once had open to them several ways of life that seem closed to them today. The teleosaurs were more thoroughly marine than any modern crocodilian, and the metriorhynchids were reptiles of the high seas. The atoposaurs, scarcely bigger than a hatchling alligator, have no ecological counterpart among the living crocodilians. The stomatosuchids, duck-billed giants, must have had feeding habits unlike those of

any modern species. In ancient days there were also terrestrial crocodilians. But as the Crocodilia were diversifying, other reptilian orders and
vertebrate classes were spreading on the land, in the fresh waters, and in
the seas. Crocodilians eventually relinquished many of the environmental
situations they once occupied. As we have already seen, the pygmy crocodilians did not survive past the Jurassic; the marine ones vanished around
mid-Cretaceous, and the duck-billed giants at the end of the Cretaceous.
Except in South America, terrestrial crocodilians did not persist long into
the Cenozoic. From the Eocene of Europe has come the virtually complete skeleton of a crocodilian with sturdy legs, and with a tail that was
rounded, not flattened in cross-sections; the toes were shortened and flattened at the tip, as though the claws had become hoof-like. This may have
been the last crocodilian, outside of South America, to run about on land.

Again excluding South America, the rather generalized crocodilians
were the only ones to survive well into the Cenozoic. That is to say, the
survivors were of medium to large size, semiaquatic, predaceous chiefly
upon aquatic organisms, and characteristic of fresh or coastal waters. This
description applies also to the majority of the crocodilians that survived
in South America; but in addition, that continent had terrestrial sebecids
and small, duck-billed nettosuchids, both of which persisted until the end
of the Miocene. The history of South America throws light on this circumstance. The present Isthmus of Panama, linking South America with
North America, first came into existence around the early Pliocene.
Throughout all the preceding portion of the Cenozoic, South America had
been isolated from the lands to the north by broad ocean barriers. During
the long period of Cenozoic isolation, South America developed a distinctive mammal fauna. This included five endemic orders of hoofed animals (all now extinct); the order Edentata, formerly diverse but today
represented only by anteaters, sloths, and armadillos; and a characteristic
lot of rodents. The larger carnivores were marsupials, comparatively primitive mammals. But while this fauna was developing in isolation, a vastly
different lot of mammals was evolving in North America, or in Eurasia
and then moving into North America. A few of these northerners may
have been able to reach South America across the water gap. When the
Isthmus of Panama rose, a land bridge was formed between North and
South America, a bridge that permitted the first major interchange of the
South American mammal fauna with the Eurasian-North American one.

A few of the southerners went north for varying distances, but most of the movement was into South America. From the north there came (eventually, not all at once) a shrew, deer, peccaries, sabertooths and true cats, a bear, skunks and weasels, raccoons and coatimundis, tapirs, mastodons and mammoth elephants, tapirs, and camels, along with various rabbits, squirrels, mice, and many others. With this irruption of more advanced northerners, the old South American mammal fauna dramatically vanished, leaving only a few scattered remnants. As the newcomers were able to displace even a great many mammalian stocks, it would not be surprising if they similarly displaced some reptilian ones. With the disappearance of South American sebecids and nettosuchids, the world was left only with those crocodilians that were predatory in fresh or coastal waters.

If the rise and spread of the mammals was largely responsible for the withdrawal of crocodilians from various environments, why was not the withdrawal complete? Why were crocodilians not replaced in the fresh and coastal waters by mammals? The question is not easy to answer, but a review of the living mammals reveals not a one that looks like a potential competitor with any crocodilian. Only a small number of mammals obtain a goodly portion of their food in the water. The platypus, the water-opossum, the giant water-shrew, several other shrews, and hare-lipped bats feed from the water, but they are much smaller than any crocodilian, and take comparatively small prey. Some of them inhabit brooks and upland streams where crocodilians are not found. The crab-eating macaque, a species of monkey, is restricted to Formosa, where it sometimes prowls the sea beaches in search of crabs, mollusks, and edible seaweeds. Several other monkeys hunt on the beaches, but also eat much vegetable food. The semiaquatic rodents—beavers, various water-rats, the muskrat, the capybara, and the coypu or nutria—are principally or exclusively vegetarian. The seals and their kin are largely marine, and concentrated in the waters that lie north or south of the tropics. The tiger, the jaguar, the fishing cat, the jaguarondi, and perhaps a few other members of the cat family will hunt at the water's edge or in the shallows, but also forage in terrestrial situations. Racoons, the crab-eating dog, and the raccoon-dog may hunt in the shallows, but they also prowl on land, and they take vegetable food as well as small prey. The otters, the minks, the otter-civets, and probably the little-known water-civet, capture small aquatic prey, but also hunt on land. The saro, largest of otters, rivals a small crocodilian in size and is thoroughly aquatic; but it feeds largely upon river mussels, along with crabs and a few fishes. The sea-otter feeds on marine organisms in cold waters. A few whales inhabit rivers, but they either pursue fishes in deep water or else grub in the mud for invertebrates. Finally, the tapirs, moose, and hippos are vegetarians, as are the more thoroughly aquatic sea-cows and their relative the dugong.

It is not clear why mammals have so rarely come to rely exclusively on animal food secured from ponds, lakes, rivers, and coastal shallows, the crocodilian habitats and hunting-grounds. Perhaps the food supply of such places is inadequate to support a population of mammalian carnivores. At any rate, crocodilians require far less food than mammals of comparable size. There are two main reasons for this circumstance. Of the energy derived by a mammal from its food, a high percentage goes to maintain a constant body temperature; while a reptile draws most of its body heat from the surroundings, and can utilize practically all the energy from its food for such things as movement, growth, and the maintenance of tissues and organs. Also, the total metabolism—the over-all exchange of materials and energy in the body—proceeds at a much higher rate in mammals. In general, smaller mammals require proportionately more food than large ones; some of the smallest mammalian carnivores may have to consume their own weight of food every twenty-four hours. The amount of food needed by an animal will vary with size, species, temperature, and other factors; so it is hard to generalize about mammalian vs. crocodilian food requirements. Of interest in this connection are studies contrasting the food intake of alligators with that of a domestic dog. The weight of food (mostly meat, some fish) consumed during a year by seven alligators, each weighing about 100 pounds, approximately equalled the weight of dog food eaten by one 95-pound dog during the same period of time. At the end of the year, the alligators appeared to be healthy and of normal proportions, not emaciated.

Crocodilians are also much better than mammals at adjusting to a temporary scarcity of food. If a drought or some other environmental condition drastically reduces the amount of available food, the crocodilians slow their growth rate. Not voluntarily, of course; one might say that in these reptiles, movement and maintenance have priority over growth when it comes to the utilization of the energy that is provided through the digestion of food. (Captive alligators, poorly kept, may continue to live but make almost no measurable growth, a circumstance that once misled even the scientists into believing that these reptiles require centuries to attain full size.) When food again becomes abundant, the crocodilians resume their growth. Among the mammals, in contrast, a long-continued reduction in the amount of available food will usually result in a reduction of the local population through death or emigration.

As suggested in Chapter 8, the survival of the crocodilians well into the Age of Mammals is a complex subject. It does seem quite likely that these reptiles were ousted from the terrestrial niches, at least, by the burgeoning of the mammals. The survival of crocodilians to the present only as predators in certain waters, fresh or coastal, hints at some adaptive advantage over mammals in these particular aquatic situations. One such advantage, perhaps a highly important one, is the ability to do with much less food at all times, and to pass unscathed through long periods of food shortage.

Many additional questions could be asked about the ancient crocodilians. For example, what are we to make of Dakotasuchus, a heavily armored crocodilian from the early Cretaceous of western North America? It seems to have been a goniopholid, although its remains are too fragmentary to make such identification a certainty. The reptile had a sturdily built scapula or shoulder blade; and as this structure serves for the attachment of muscles that operate the forearm, Dakotasuchus evidently was given to walking. Did some goniopholid offshoot become terrestrial, and did it leave the crocodilian footprints that have been found in an early Cretaceous stratum of Kansas? What kind of crocodilian left the strongly ribbed teeth that have been picked up at scattered localities from New Jersey to Florida? What was the age of two gigantic vertebrae, apparently crocodilian, discovered a century or so ago along the Aquiry River in the Amazon drainage of Brazil? What is the identity of fossil bones found by an early paleontologist in Europe, and described by him as being those of a "gavial"? Where did a New Guinea tribesman obtain the Pleistocene crocodilian vertebra that he sold to a Dutch scientific expedition? Such questions are presently unanswerable; they are mentioned here only to emphasize that the fossil history of the crocodilians is not a cut-and-dried affair, but one toward which many contributions will be made in years to come.

PART IV *Natural History of the American Alligator*

12 THE ALLIGATOR'S TAXONOMIC HISTORY AND GEOGRAPHIC RANGE

THE LEGENDS have been disavowed; the fossil history of the Crocodilia has been described, and parts of it interpreted in the light of broad biological concepts. Thus, the way has been paved for the detailed discussion of a crocodilian life history. For this purpose the American alligator has been selected. Not that there is much choice; the other crocodilians of the world are poorly known.

The alligator was mentioned by authors as far back as the sixteenth century, but not until the early nineteenth century did it receive an acceptable Latinized name. True, in 1788 the German ethnologist and naturalist, Johann Friedrich Blumenbach, probably thought he was naming the alligator when he erected the scientific name of *Lacerta alligator*. But in those days, when taxonomy was but an infant science, taxonomic categories were very broadly conceived, and the name coined by Blumenbach was not based primarily upon a specimen of the alligator. Herpetologi-

176

cal catalogues note that the first acceptable name for this reptile was proposed by F. M. Daudin in 1802. Behind that notation is an interesting story:

Long before he was elected President of the United States, Thomas Jefferson longed to know what natural wonders would be found west of the Mississippi, and by 1793 he had backed five abortive attempts to cross the continent. One of these, toward which George Washington also contributed a small sum of money, was led by André Michaux, a French botanist who had been collecting, studying, and scientifically naming the plants of eastern North America. Michaux brought to the attention of botanical taxonomists such trees as the longleaf and pond pines, the king-nut hickory, the quaking aspen, the winged and slippery elms, the great-leaf Magnolia, and the blue ash, as well as the overcup, laurel, and blue-jack oaks; along with smaller plants such as the white Trillium, the wild buckwheat, the dwarf larkspur, the dwarf pawpaw, the star anise, the wild sarsaparilla, the blue cohosh, the muscadine, the flame Azalea, the buffalo-nut, and dozens more. Michaux turned out to be not only a good botanist but also a spy for the French government. His activities in the latter capacity were revealed, and his expedition did not get far across the country. In his travels, Michaux obtained an alligator from the Mississippi. He preserved the specimen and sent it to his friend F. M. Daudin, a herpetologist in France.

Some years later, Daudin presented to the French Academy of Sciences the first two volumes of a great work on reptiles and amphibians; and in Volume 2 the American alligator was formally dubbed *Crocodilus mississipiensis*, meaning "the crocodile of the Mississippi River." The type specimen on which the name was based was the one that had been collected by the botanist-spy Michaux. The type locality, the place where Michaux got the type specimen, was given only as the banks of the Mississippi. Today we prefer a highly specific statement of type locality. In Daudin's time, "Mississipi" was the accepted spelling; "*mississipiensis*" was not a slip of the pen, and the name might well stand today as it was written, although some students have preferred to emend the original spelling.

Confusion has surrounded the date of Daudin's Volume 2. The French adopted a new calendar after the Revolution, and as far as they were concerned, a new era began on September 22, 1792; for on the preceding day the National Convention had abolished the monarchy and declared France a republic. Volume 2 was dated "*An X*," the tenth year of the Revolutionary calendar, overlapping 1801 and 1802. The meeting of the French Academy of Sciences, at which Daudin presented his first two volumes, was held on "*26 Frimaire, An X*," which is December 17, 1801 in the more familiar calendar. Thus, the name *mississipiensis* dates from 1801, not 1802 as commonly cited.

It might be asked why we should be concerned with the precise date of Daudin's publication. Zoological taxonomists wish to use for each species of animal life the first Latinized name that was proposed for it, at least the first that was advanced in an acceptable, Linnaean fashion. Names proposed in the early days of taxonomy are particularly troublesome, for at that time the world was being explored, and specimens were pouring in to the taxomists; the same species might be given two or three different names by as many zoologists who were working independently of each other. Today we often must decide which of several published names has priority over all others, and this may be hard to do. Some of the important early works may now exist only as one or two fragile copies carefully treasured in some library, and the information about their actual date of publication may be hard to come by after a lapse of 150 or 200 years.

Citizen Daudin was not greatly admired by his contemporary, Georges Chrétien Léopold Frédéric Dagobert, the Baron Cuvier. In 1807 Cuvier erected the genus *Alligator* for the sole reception of the American alligator, and, ignoring Daudin's name of *mississipiensis*, renamed the reptile *Alligator lucius*. "Lucius" was the Latin name of the pike, a fish with a snout shaped much like that of an alligator. Cuvier gave the type locality of his *lucius* only as the "Mississipi" River, but did say that the reptile ranged upstream as far as the mouth of the Red River. As *lucius* was the only species of alligator known to Cuvier, it became the "type species" of the genus *Alligator*. Today we regard the generic name *Alligator* as well founded, but see that Daudin's specific name *mississipiensis* has precedence over Cuvier's *lucius*. The scientific name of the American alligator therefore stands today as *Alligator mississipiensis* (Daudin). The authority's name, Daudin, would not usually be written, except in some formal account. The parentheses around "Daudin" indicate that the name he advanced, *mississipiensis*, was not originally proposed in the same genus with which it is now associated.

In 1815 the English naturalist William Leach got hold of an alligator from Dauphin Island in the mouth of Mobile Bay, Alabama. Thinking he had some previously undiscovered species, and wishing to honor Cuvier, Leach named his "new" reptile *Crocodilus cuvieri*. Today we would say that *Crocodilus cuvieri* Leach is merely a synonym of *Alligator mississipiensis* (Daudin).

By the middle of the nineteenth century, it was generally agreed that the alligator should be known scientifically as *Alligator mississipiensis*. Edward D. Cope, the American antomist, herpetologist, and paleontologist, concurred with this view, but thought he had discovered a second species of alligator. In 1865 he named his supposed new species *Alligator helois*. He had but one specimen, the type. It differed from the norm of other American alligators in several minor features of external anatomy, the most impressive being tail shape: the end of the tail was not much compressed, and not much serrated in its dorsal outline. The description of the specimen suggests that it was what reptile fanciers now call a "bathtub alligator." That is to say, it was probably an alligator that had been raised in some kind of tub in a house, where it received a poor diet, insufficient sunlight, and no exercise. Abnormalities of development are likely when an alligator is raised under such conditions. Cope's lone specimen was of unknown geographic origin, suggesting that it had been someone's "pet" before it was preserved as a scientific specimen. *Alligator helois* Cope is another synonym of *Alligator mississipiensis* (Daudin).

In modern times, the alligator acquired another synonym. Some years ago, visiting a splendid zoological park in Australia, I was amused to see that a huge American alligator was on display as an estuarine crocodile. (The confusion is understandable, for, as previously noted, the estuarine crocodile is called "alligator" in Australia.) A photograph of this big alligator was widely distributed, and, duly labeled as an estuarine or "saltwater" crocodile, was reproduced in several books about Australia or about the wildlife of that country. In 1953 a would-be contributor to the taxonomy of crocodilians decided, on the basis of this photograph, that Australia must harbor a very distinctive local race of the estuarine crocodile, *Crocodylus porosus*. We have not previously commented on the scientific naming of geographic races (or "subspecies" as they are more formally known). The name of a species is a binomial, consisting of two Latinized expressions; the name of a subspecies is formed by adding a third Latinized expression to the appropriate binomial. This was done in the case of the supposedly distinctive estuarine crocodile of Australia. But as the proposed name was actually based on a captive alligator, or its picture, "*Crocodylus porosus australis* Deraniyagala" is another synonym of *Alligator mississipiensis* (Daudin).

The foregoing account reveals the variety of problems that may confront the taxonomist in his effort to ascertain the proper scientific name for some organism. He must be not only a biologist but also something of a bibliophile.

Turning from taxonomic synonymy to a strictly biological problem, is there any possibility that the American alligator, now conceived to be a single species, actually is two species whose subtle differences have not been recognized? A situation of this kind would not be without parallel in herpetology. The "blue-tailed skink" of eastern North America turned out to be three different species, and the same thing happened with the "glass-lizard." More recently, the crowned snake (Tantilla) of Florida has proven to be a composite of at least two species. The whistling treefrog (Hyla) and the "gray treefrog" were long confused, and were disentangled only after it became evident that they had completely different calls; and then the "gray treefrog" itself proved to be a composite of two species.

E. A. McIlhenny, referring no doubt to the situation in Louisiana, stated, "There are two distinct types of alligators—one that grows long and slender, another that grows short and heavy. This fact is most noticeable in the males, and there is apparently no reason for it except a natural difference in stature." A comparable situation exists in Florida, where many male alligators stop growing in length when about 11 to 12 feet long, and there after begin to broaden. This broadening is not simply a matter of putting on weight, for the skull itself becomes very wide. Yet, all the really gigantic alligators known to me, males ranging from about 14 to 18 feet in length, had a comparatively narrow head and snout. (A short-headed and a long-headed alligator are shown in Fig. 64). In short, fully grown male alligators apparently can be sorted into two groups, which differ from each other in total length and in snout shape. They do not differ in habits and habitat, as they should if they represented two species. The significance of the anatomical dimorphism is unknown; it might have something to do with the evolutionary potentiality of splitting into narrow-snouted and broad-snouted lines of descent, a potentiality that was realized in various crocodilian lineages, ancient and modern.

Figure 64. Some adult alligators have a comparatively short, broad snout (upper), others a comparatively long and narrow one (lower). [M. L. Judd and Charles J. Belden]

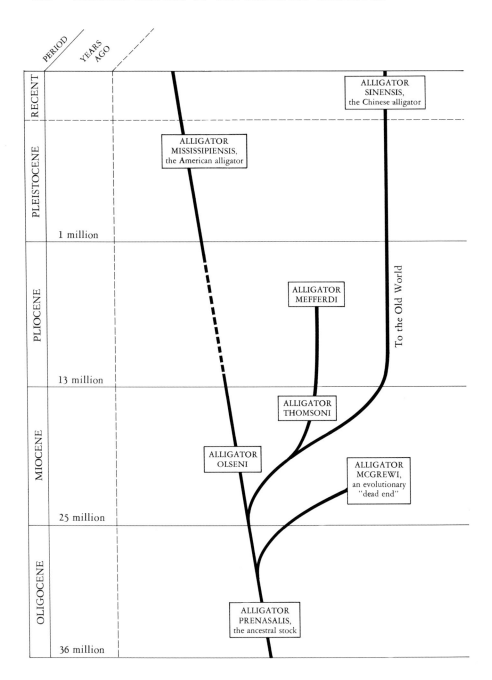

Figure 65. The evolution of the alligators. Dates are approximate.

All American alligators are regarded as belonging to one species, *Alligator mississipiensis*. The range of this species, stated broadly, includes the lowlands of the southeastern United States, from the extreme southeastern corner of Virginia southward through the Florida Keys, westward to the Rio Grande in eastern Texas, and northward up the Mississippi Valley as far as eastern Arkansas and northwestern Mississippi. (Modern man has extirpated the alligator from parts of this area, but we are concerned at this point with the original or natural range, as it was in the days before hide-hunting, random shooting, and the profound alteration of wetland ecology.) Early settlers in the southeastern United States were impressed by the alligator, and various towns or natural features were named to indicate the reptile's occurrence in the vicinity. If we review old place names based on the alligator, we find the northernmost to be Alligator Sink in the Dismal Swamp country of southeastern Virginia; the southernmost, Alligator Island in extreme southeastern Florida; the westernmost, Alligator Creek in eastern Texas; and the northernmost in the Mississippi Valley, Alligator Town in western Mississippi opposite the mouth of the Arkansas River. Within the area bounded by these four localities, there are dozens of other localities variously called Alligator Creek, River, Bay, Bayou, Lake, Swamp, Sink, Channel, Dead Lake, Island, Point, Harbor, Hole, Landing, or Town. While a few of these names did not allude to the presence of the reptile most of them did. The distribution of "Alligator" place names corresponds remarkably well to the range of the alligator itself.

Of course the original range of this reptile is not determined solely from place names. Published accounts of travel are useful in distributional studies, and so are museum specimens if they have locality data. Also, in some areas the alligator can still be seen today. We may consider this reptile's range in detail, state by state.

Along the Atlantic seaboard, the northernmost locality records were for Dismal Swamp. Originally this was a vast and swampy wilderness, about ten miles wide and thrice that in length, lying partly in southeastern Virginia and partly in North Carolina above Albemarle Sound. George Washington visited the area at least six times, and called it a "glorious paradise"; he had a canal dug to drain a part of the swamp, and organized a company to cut out the cedars. Much more of the tract has since been drained, the cedar and cypress logged out, the peaty soil in places burned away, canals cut to Chesapeake Bay and Albemarle Sound. The alligator has vanished from this northernmost outpost of its range, and it seems never to have been abundant there. Around the 1950s, a surprisingly large number of young alligators turned up here and there in southeastern Virginia. It cannot be held that the species was making a comeback in that area, for the reptiles probably had escaped from captivity, or had been liberated. (When locality records, however numerous, are based each on the discovery of a single individual, the existence of a reproducing population is not proven.) Yet, it was interesting to see the alligator apparently managing to survive in the northeastern tip of its former range. Since Washington's time, the United States has become somewhat warmer; and a good many animals, characteristic of the more southerly states, have slowly been extending their respective ranges northward. Today, southeastern Virginia may be climatically more suitable for the alligator than it was a few centuries ago.

South of Albemarle Sound, and so wholly in North Carolina, is another low-lying tract, which in recent times has been called Alligator Swamp. John F. D. Smyth, in a 1784 account of his North American travels, said that Great Alligator was

> indeed dismal far beyond description, and can only be exceeded by another, on the borders next to Virginia. . . . This one first mentioned is also called the Great Alligator Dismal Swamp. . . . This astonishing and horrible place is about forty miles in length, and about fifteen or twenty in breadth, with a large lake in the middle several miles in diameter. It is reported to be named from a monstrous Alligator or Crocodile that once was seen here, many of which of the common size still infest it.

From Alligator Swamp the range of the alligator extended southward through the lowlands of eastern North Carolina, and so into the lowlands of eastern and southern South Carolina. John Drayton, referring to South Carolina in an 1802 work, said, "Alligators are in abundance in our brackish and fresh tide waters, and from thence many miles up the rivers; but they are scarcely ever seen as high up as the falls." Of the range in Georgia, William Bartram remarked in 1791, "The alligator, a species of crocodile, abounds in the rivers and swamps, near the sea coast, but is not to be seen above Augusta." The Reverend Adiel Sherwood stated in 1827, "The alligator, a loathsome amphibious animal, infests the rivers of Georgia, but it does not frequent them more than 60 miles from the ocean." By 1837 Sherwood had modified his earlier opinion: "The alligator, a loathsome amphibious animal, and the ugliest creature that crawls or walks on this earth, infests the rivers of Georgia. It has been found in the neighborhood of Milledgeville, and even in Murder creek; but it does not frequent the upper parts of the state."

From southern Georgia the alligator ranged southward through Florida all the way to Key West. About 20 miles west of Key West lie the Marquesas Keys, and about 50 miles farther west are the Dry Tortugas. These two island groups, although reached by a few lizards and snakes of the Florida mainland, did not harbor the alligator. Nor did this reptile inhabit the Cay Sal Banks, which lie about 70 miles southeast of the Florida Keys. From Florida the range of the alligator extended westward through southern Alabama, and thence into southern and central Mississippi.

The northward extension of the range, up the Mississippi Valley, is a subject about which much has been written. In the early days of travel on the Mississippi River, passengers looked forward to their first glimpse of (and often their first shot at) an alligator; and many a downstream traveler noted the point at which these reptiles first began to appear. It was generally agreed that the mouth of the Arkansas River was roughly the northern limit of the alligator's range along the Mississippi. The 1810 narrative of Christian Schultz said of alligators, ". . . although commonly seen as high up as the Arkansas River, yet we saw none till we reached the Walnut Hills, upwards of two hundred miles below the mouth of that river. From thence to this city [New Orleans] we saw them every day." Henry R. Schoolcraft, in an 1821 account of travels, stated, "The Alligator is first seen below the junction of the Arkansas." In 1846 J. H. Hinton said that the alligator "is first seen in great numbers, in passing to the south, on the Arkansas, that is to say, a little north of 33°. . ." But Hinton's remarks were taken from those of earlier writers; and Hugh Murray in 1839 declared that the alligator's range on the Mississippi did not extend above the latitude of 32½° North. Murray and other authors lead us to think that the alligator rapidly vanished from the more northern portion of its range on the Mississippi; and by the 1830s downstream travelers were not likely to get a shot at one until Louisiana was reached.

Louisiana, like Florida, had alligators throughout. From Louisiana the reptile followed the Ouachita River northward into southern Arkansas.

In 1823 Edwin James described S. H. Long's trip from Pittsburgh to the Rockies. James wrote, "An alligator was seen . . . many miles above the entrance of the Saline Fork [the Saline River, a tributary of the Ouachita]." The alligator was once very common in the Red River of Louisiana. It followed this stream northwestward to reach the extreme southeastern tip of Oklahoma and the northeastern corner of Texas. West of Louisiana the alligator inhabited the coastal lowlands of eastern Texas, all the way to the Rio Grande. It also followed the Texas rivers, such as the Trinity, Colorado, Brazos, Aransas, and Nueces, for varying distances inland. In the northeastern part of Texas it ranged much farther inland than in the southeastern part. In the north it reached as far inland as (roughly) Dallas and Waco, even Hamilton; in the south, as far as (again roughly) Austin, San Marcos, and San Antonio. Still farther south in Texas, it did not range more than about 75 to 100 miles inland of the Gulf of Mexico, and not even this far along the Rio Grande. (There was, however, a 1907 report, possibly valid, of the alligator well up the Rio Grande, in the stretch between Del Rio and Eagle Pass. On this subject, more later.)

There was an 1884 record of the alligator for "Mexico," which could have meant nothing more than the Mexican side of the lower Rio Grande. Otherwise, there is no indication that the reptile lived south of the United States. Still, the northeastern part of Mexico has received little attention from reptile collectors, and could yield some herpetological surprises. In Tamaulipas, about 75 miles south of the Texas border, the Rio San Fernando winds through mesquite scrub to fall into the Laguna Madre. The Laguna breaks up northwardly into a labyrinth of channels and isolated basins, the latter strung out almost to the Rio Grande. Rainfall is about 25 to 30 inches annually, concentrated toward the late summer and fall. The local freshwater situations are sufficiently permanent to support at least two species of aquatic turtles (a softshell and a geographic race of the yellow-bellied turtle). Some attention has been given to the migrating waterfowl that arrive each winter at Laguna Madre, to the number of several million; but the other wildlife of the region has gone unstudied for the most part. In extreme southern Tamaulipas, around Tampico, the fauna becomes primarily a tropical one; and there the American crocodile and Morelet's crocodile have been found. But no one knows what kind of crocodilian, if any, lives in the stretch of country that lies between the Brownsville and Tampico regions. It would be interesting to search the

Laguna Madre area not only for the alligator but also for some other reptiles—the mud turtle, the diamondback terrapin, the green anole, the
ground skink, the six-lined racerunner, the slender glass-lizard, the Gulf
saltmarsh snake, and the cottonmouth, among others—whose respective
ranges have been traced westward into eastern Texas but not as yet into
Tamaulipas.

Some books indicate the alligator to have reached southwestern
Tennessee, an area well above the mouth of the Arkansas River. The
original basis for this view seems to have been an account of Tennessee
reptiles and amphibians offered in 1896 by Samuel N. Rhoads. In this work,
Rhoads merely said, "I was assured by Mr. J. A. Craig, of Samburg, that
he had seen Alligators in the Mississippi near Memphis." Perhaps Mr. Craig
had actually glimpsed an alligator gar, a huge and heavily armored fish
found in the Memphis vicinity; but in any event, Rhoad's comment is inadequate to outweigh the evidence that the alligator did not range up the
Mississippi beyond its junction with the Arkansas.

The so-called baby alligators now sold to tourists in Florida are actually hatchlings of the spectacled caiman; they are imported by the
thousands, especially from Colombia. Until recently, this traffic was indeed
based on the alligator. In the alligator's hatching season, commercial collectors would scour the ponds and swamps at night, taking the hatchlings
by the thousands. These were sold to tourists, who took them north and
rapidly tired of them. In highly urbanized areas, a great many returned
travelers would dispose of the unwanted little reptiles by flushing them
down the toilet (giving rise to the absurd legend, still current, that giant
alligators infest the sewers beneath New York City). But where lakes
or rivers were accessible, other people would simply liberate their baby
alligators; and many of the reptiles were later recaptured before they could
succumb to starvation, low temperatures, predators, water pollutants, or
other hazards. Recaptures were often noted in the newspapers, and sometimes even in the scientific journals; but such "locality records" are scarcely
worth repeating here. In these days of rapid mass transportation, of pet
shops and reptile fanciers, of traveling carnivals, roadside zoos, and other
shoddy exhibits, and of innumerable souvenir-minded tourists, a great
variety of reptile species are being transported about the country, and liberated here and there by accident or intent. In most cases, no distributional
significance can be attached to the discovery of a reptile at some point

outside its proven range, unless an actual breeding population of the reptile is found at that point.

A friend, upon being told that records of the alligator in Pennsylvania could rest only on escaped or liberated specimens, replied that there was no law against an alligator's going up to Pennsylvania if it took the notion to do so. But even ignoring the circumstance that an alligator can hardly be said to "take notions," there are inescapable laws of nature that confine a species to a given geographic area. Among all living things, only man can spread over the earth almost at will, and he does so mostly by virtue of cultural attainments, not his innate physical endowments. Factors that have some bearing on the distribution of a species include the circumstances of its origin, the environmental vicissitudes to which it has been exposed in the past, the present environment in which it must now exist, its innate needs, and its innate abilities to fill these needs. The distribution of a species, determined by these five factors, might then be altered by man's activities; thus, man could be listed as a sixth factor.

Let us consider the range of the alligator in the light of these factors. As noted in Chapter 9, the genus *Alligator* arose in North America during the Oligocene. The ancestral stock, typified by *Alligator prenasalis*, was broad-snouted, and so were all of its descendants. In the Oligocene, swamplands were widespread across North America. The Rocky Mountains, which had started to rise in the Cretaceous, were just beginning to cast a significant rain-shadow; east of the mountains, the first grasslands and open woodlands were beginning to develop. Climate, although mild, was cooler than in the preceding Period. Tropical forest, which in the Eocene had reached Wyoming and Vermont, fell back to central Mexico. The genus *Alligator* is unique among crocodilians in that its modern members live outside the tropics. This seems generally to have been the case with the extinct members, also.

In the Miocene, western and central North America became drier, extensive grasslands forming. There was a temporary reversal of the trend toward a cooler climate. Tropical plants pushed up to Oregon and Washington. As we have noted, the genus *Alligator* had diverged by the Miocene into three evolutionary lines. One of these, typified by *Alligator mcgrewi*, was exceedingly broad-snouted, no doubt very specialized; it did not survive past the Miocene. A second line, typified by *Alligator thomsoni*, thrived in western North America, and pushed across Bering Bridge to become an-

Figure 66. The range of the alligator as it was in the days before extensive hide-hunting and the destruction of the wetland habitats.

cestral to the Chinese alligator. (The bridge apparently was submerged in the Oligocene, but it was above water in the Miocene, which Period saw much interchange between the Eurasian and the North American faunas.) A third line, typified by *Alligator olseni*, existed in eastern North America. Unfortunately, we do not know how far this latter species ranged, for nonmarine fossil beds of Miocene age are very scarce in eastern North America. *Alligator olseni* is known only from Florida, which alone of eastern states (east of Texas) has yielded a goodly lot of Miocene, nonmarine vertebrates.

Toward the latter Miocene, the cooling trend was resumed; and the trend toward aridity continued in the rain-shadow of the Rockies. In the Great Plains, grasslands spread; lakes, ponds, swamps, and other aquatic situations became fewer; aquatic and swamp-dwelling animals began to vanish from the region. But eastern North America continued to be well-watered and mild, with subtropical forests extending northward to Virginia. In the Pliocene, central and western United States became even drier, losing the greater part of its aquatic and semiaquatic fauna. *Alligator mefferdi*, the Pliocene representative of the *thomsoni* line, became extinct; and before this Period was out, alligators survived in North America only as the *olseni* line of the east. The identity of the Pliocene member of this line is uncertain. (Nonmarine fossil beds of Pliocene age are about as scarce in eastern North America as Miocene ones.) Florida has yielded the fragmentary remains of a Pliocene alligator; it seems to be the modern species, *Alligator mississipiensis*. In other words, as far as present material will show, the Miocene species *olseni* had evolved into *mississipiensis* before the Pliocene was out.

Thus, evolutionary history helps to explain the distribution of the alligator. The living American species is the culmination of a line of descent that entered the southeastern United States as far back as the Miocene, and of several lines of descent within the genus *Alligator*, only this one survived to the present in North America, for it was the only one to occupy a part of North America that was not profoundly affected by the cooling and drying of the Miocene and Pliocene. Bnt evolutionary history does not explain why the modern limits of the alligator's range stand just where they do. Obviously the eastern and most of the southern limits are determined by the sea; for while it sometimes lives in brackish marshes, the alligator is not marine. But what determines the inland limits of the range?

During the Cretaceous, long before the genus *Alligator* had evolved, a great arm of the sea encroached upon central North America. The sea also covered what are now the lowlands of the eastern United States, and marine deposits of great thickness accumulated over this area. As the waters retreated, the former sea bottom was exposed as a low plain. Lines of dunes followed the retreating shoreline, and behind them came fresh-water swamps. The former Cretaceous shoreline is still well-marked in many places. Its more easterly stretch is often called the Fall Line, and separates two areas that are very different physiographically. In the geologist's terminology, the Fall Line separates the Coastal Plain, the formerly submerged area, from the Piedmont Plateau, which saw no Cretaceous or Cenozoic submergence. Piedmont and Coastal Plain offer very different environments for occupation by animals and plants. Of course some living things, tolerating a wide variety of ecological conditions, can range over both of these physiographic regions; but a great many cannot. Among reptiles, species of more northerly distribution often find the southern limit of their range at the Fall Line in Georgia and South Carolina, while reptile species of more southerly distribution often find the northern limit of their range along the same line.

The environmental differences between Piedmont and Coastal Plain are particularly sharp in eastern Georgia and western South Carolina. In this area the Piedmont landscape is primarily one of rolling, red-clay hills, sparsely vegetated or else covered with stands of shortleaf and loblolly pines. Here and there are patches of hardwood forest, with thick humus beneath oaks and hickories. The streams are comparatively swift, bottomed with firm sand and pebbles. Some of the creeks occupy valleys that are flooded in winter and meadow-like at other times; but in general, the streams have no large swamps along their courses, firm ground extending to the water's edge in most places. Natural lakes are few, although man has dammed many streams to make fishponds or millponds. The soil is full of quartz pebbles, and there are outcrops of flint, shale, sandstone, aplite, and other rocks. But below the Fall Line, in the Coastal Plain, the landscape is flatter. Sandhills form long ridges paralleling the Fall Line. Streams are slow and winding, with lagoons and backwaters along them. Stream bottoms often are silty, or covered with a thick accumulation of decaying plant material. Cypress swamps are common, as well as forests of swamp-dwelling hardwoods such as red maple, tupelo, and white bay. Rock outcroppings are limited to limestone and jasper. Although climate does not change as abruptly at the Fall Line as do soils, topography, and plant associations, there are climatic differences between Piedmont and Coastal Plain, the latter being warmer and rainier.

The herpetologist who is based in a Fall Line city can sample two different reptile faunas in a day's collecting. Take, for example, the situation near Augusta, Georgia. A few miles above the Fall Line the collector may find the brown kingsnake on the red-clay hills, the queen snake and midland watersnake along the rocky brooks, the worm snake beneath ground debris in the humus layer of the hardwood forest, the painted turtle in the lakes. A few miles below the Fall Line he would encounter none of these, but would find many species that do not enter the Piedmont: the gopher tortoise, red-tailed skink, and southern hognose snake on the sandhills; the rainbow snake in larger streams, the mud snake in ponds or bogs, the banded watersnake and the cottonmouth in a variety of aquatic situations, the alligator in lagoons and swampy lakes.

A series of waterfalls, or more often stretches of rapids, exist where rivers pass over the Fall Line. Pioneer settlers invaded the southeastern United States along the rivers, pushing upstream until the way was blocked by falls or rough water. At the head of navigation, in other words at the Fall Line, they disembarked to build their settlements. It is no coincidence that the course of a Cretaceous shoreline is today rather closely marked by Columbus, Macon, Milledgeville, and Augusta, in Georgia; and by Columbia and Camden in South Carolina. When early writers stated that the alligator did not range above the falls, or above such towns as Milledgeville and Augusta, they were in effect saying that this reptile was a species of the Coastal Plain, finding the inland limit of its distribution at the Fall Line, the old Cretaceous shoreline, the edge of the Piedmont Plateau.

The Coastal Plain extends northward from the Carolinas, ever narrowing. Richmond, Washington, Baltimore, Wilmington, Philadelphia, and Trenton mark the northward course of the Fall Line. However, only a minority of organisms that are confined to the Coastal Plain can follow this physiographic region to its northernmost tip. Many of the Coastal Plain reptiles require a milder winter and a longer warm season than they would find in, say, Delaware or the pine barrens of New Jersey. Reptile species differ among themselves in their tolerance for chilling and their ability to avoid climatic rigors. Thus, some Coastal Plain species range farther north than others. The black swamp snake, the banded watersnake, the southern hognose snake, the coral snake, and the eastern diamondback rattlesnake do not quite reach southeastern Virginia; the alligator, the yellow-bellied turtle, the chicken turtle, the red-bellied watersnake, the brown watersnake, the mud snake, and the cottonmouth do (or did) reach that area, but not significantly beyond; the Florida turtle and the rainbow snake reach somewhat beyond it.

The ocean tends to ameliorate the seasonal vagaries of temperature in bordering lands, and so areas along the Atlantic seaboard of the eastern United States will average warmer in winter than areas lying much farther inland at the same approximate latitudes and altitudes. The Dismal Swamp area, over a period of forty years, had an average temperature for January (the mid-winter month) of about 43 degrees Fahrenheit, and an average annual growing season (in other words, frost-free season) 230 days long. To find roughly comparable winter conditions along the Mississippi, one would have to go down about to the mouth of the Arkansas. This circumstance bolsters the belief that the northwardly distribution of the alligator was limited along the Atlantic coast and up the Mississippi Valley by winter temperatures.

Of use in distributional studies is the climatological concept of isotherms. An isotherm is simply a line connecting geographic localities that are the same in some aspect of temperature. For example, one might draw on a map a line connecting points that have an identical average annual temperature. On climatological maps, isotherms are often drawn at intervals of 5 degrees Fahrenheit. That is to say, one line will connect localities with an average annual temperature of 70 degrees, another line connects localities with an average annual temperature of 65 degrees, still another 60 degrees, and so on. The isotherms trace sinuous courses across the map, and they parallel each other only in very rough fashion, for temperature is affected not only by latitude and proximity to water but also by altitude and other factors. An isotherm map for the average temperature of July (the midsummer month) throws no light on alligator distribution, nor does the isothern map for annual maximum temperature. But on a map of average January temperatures, the isotherm of 45 degrees corresponds moderately well to a line marking the northern limit of the alligator's range; and on a map of average annual minimum temperatures, the isotherm of 15 degrees corresponds even better with the reptile's northerly range limits.

If winter temperatures have been important in determining how far north the alligator could range on the Atlantic Coastal Plain and in the Mississippi Valley, then the northernmost populations of this reptile must have been endangered by any winter that was colder than normal. The experiences of Captain Matthew Phelps, as detailed by Anthony Haswell in 1802, are of interest here:

There are likewise Alligator or Crocodiles in these rivers. . . . One peculiarity of these creatures, which fell within my observation, was their incapacity to bear excessive cold. I had seen in passing up the Big Black, at times, thirty or forty of these creatures, sleeping on the shore, or sunning on old logs, and generally killed a number, on the tails of which the inhabitants make an agreeable repast; but in going up the river after the hard winter of 1779 and 1780, I saw but one live one, while the shores were lined in a manner with dead ones, and the air perfectly tainted.

Figure 67. A lake in western Tennessee harbors many Coastal Plain organisms, including the bald cypress which is so common in the alligator's range; but the alligator itself does not inhabit this area, which is too cold in winter for the survival of that reptile. [Tennessee Conservation Dept.]

Phelp's account is consistent with the observation that captive reptiles of many kinds, including the alligator, will seemingly recover from accidental chilling, only to die a month or so later. Unfortunately, it is not known how far Phelps had proceeded up the Big Black River (in Mississippi) when he encountered the dead alligators.

One would not expect the range limit of the alligator (or any other organism) to correspond perfectly with any isotherm. This is because isotherms are drawn on the basis of temperature measurements made at weather stations. Local factors, such as a large body of water, a line of hills blocking off winds, or even a large stand of trees, may result in local readings unlike those made at nearby weather stations. Indeed, local conditions can alter not only the temperature but also the relative humidity, the rate of evaporation, the wind velocity, and the effectiveness of the local rainfall; so ecologists prefer to distinguish between "climate," which is described from data gathered at weather stations, and the "microclimate" to which a living thing is actually exposed in its normal habitat. The alligator overwinters in a water-filled "'gator hole," or beneath an overhanging bank, or in a horizontal tunnel. The construction of such dens is a subject for later discussion; at this point suffice it to say that in winter the microclimate of a den is much warmer than that of the ground surface nearby.

The western limit of the alligator's range is determined to some degree by precipitation, which begins to decline rapidly west of the Mississippi. Thus, while the New Orleans area receives an average annual precipitation of about 60 inches, the lower Rio Grande receives only 25 inches. However, no isopluve, no line connecting localities of equal precipitation, corresponds with the western limit of the alligator's range. The reptile can thrive in rivers, which are not necessarily dependent on local precipitation for their continued existence. A river flowing through an arid land may arise in some distant region of higher precipitation, or may draw its water from a very large area. The alligator, being able to follow rivers, can range westward beyond the limits that would be imposed if it were confined to the still waters. If it is to live in a river, however, it must have a considerable and constant flow of water. This requirement excludes it from streams that are small or but seasonal in their flow. Thus, it does not follow any of the western rivers to the headwaters. Furthermore, in the lands west of the Mississippi winter temperatures are not high enough for the alligator along the middle and upper courses of the rivers.

A great many organisms are distributed roughly like the alligator; that is, from the Coastal Plain of Virginia and the Carolinas southward into Florida, thence westward into eastern Texas, and northward up the Mississippi Valley for some distance. Several reptiles, distributed in that approximate fashion, do not follow the Texas coastal lowlands as far as the lower Rio Grande, yet range across that state to the Del Rio-Eagle Pass area farther up the river. Examples include the snapping turtle, two species of watersnakes, and the copperhead (which lives in stream valleys in the western part of its range). There are also some isolated records for the cottonmouth well up the Rio Grande. As various aquatic or streamside reptiles, components of a Coastal Plain fauna, definitely have reached the Del Rio-

Eagle Pass stretch of the Rio Grande, the alligator might have done so as well. Edgar A. Mearns, naturalist and army surgeon, was probably not in error when in 1907 he reported the alligator to occur at a locality "20 miles south" of Fort Clark, in Kinney County, Texas. Although we must suppose that he was guessing, a bit inacurately as it happened, at the distance and direction from Fort Clark, no doubt he was referring to some point on the same stretch of river that harbors other Coastal Plain reptiles.

With the coming of settlement, the numbers of the alligator were everywhere reduced, and the reptile actually vanished from, especially, the northern and western portions of its range. It has been extirpated, or nearly so, from Texas, Arkansas, Oklahoma, northern Louisiana, the greater part of Mississippi, nearly all of Alabama, the clay hill country of the Florida Panhandle, the upper Coastal Plain of Georgia and the Carolinas, and areas north of Albemarle Sound.

13 SUBSPECIES AND HABITAT OF THE ALLIGATOR

AS THE PRECEDING chapter has shown, the genus *Alligator* persisted in the southeastern United States after having been extirpated from other parts of North America by climatic rigors. This does not mean, however, that the entire Southeast was wholly unaffected by the late Cenozoic vagaries of temperature and rainfall. The Southeast clearly was affected by such vagaries in the Pleistocene, the period that followed the Pliocene. The Pleistocene is sometimes called the Ice Age, for it was marked by the formation of glaciers, vast ice sheets, in the higher latitudes. During the Pleistocene there were four major glacial advances, the most extreme of them bringing the north polar ice sheet well down into northern Europe and the northern part of the United States. Episodes of glacial advance were characterized by a shift toward a cooler and rainier climate. These four episodes were separated by interglacials, during which the ice retreated. Episodes of glacial retreat were characterized by a shift toward a warmer and drier climate. The last major glacial advance, which brought the north polar ice sheet down as far as Wisconsin, came to a halt as recently as about 10,000 years ago, and we now seem to be moving into a fourth interglacial.

The fossil record reveals some glacial cooling to have been felt as far south as Florida. The peninsular portion of that state has yielded the Pleistocene remains of the eastern porcupine, a marmot (probably the woodchuck), a lemming mouse, an elk, the meadow vole, the red fox, the Pleistocene ancestor of the tree swallow (as a breeding bird, not just a winter visitor), the ruffed grouse, and the worm snake. The modern representatives or relatives of these vertebrate species all live hundreds of miles north of Florida. Other vertebrates, as well as invertebrates and plants, probably moving into Florida during some time of maximum Pleistocene glacial chilling, later fell back far to the north, but also left surviving populations in the cool, deeply shaded ravines along Florida's Apalachicola River. The fossil record likewise shows the effect of interglacial drying to have been felt as far east as Florida, which at some time in the Pleistocene harbored two armadillos, the coyote, a pocket gopher perhaps allied to the present western ones, a peccary related to the western "javelina," the jaguar, the ocelot, the hog-nosed skunk, and the Pleistocene ancestor of the California condor. The modern representatives or relatives of these vertebrate species all live far west of Florida. It is likely that, during some interglacial episode, the decreasing rainfall permitted tongues of grassland and scrubland to extend far into the Southeast, forming corridors along which western animals could spread. A few essentially western plants, invertebrates, and vertebrates, probably moving into Florida during some time of maximum Pleistocene interglacial drying, later fell back to the west, but also left surviving populations in peninsular Florida areas where porous soils and rapid runoff lessen the effectiveness of the local rainfall.

In short, Pleistocene fluctuations of temperature and rainfall markedly altered the distribution of living things in the Southeast. (Support for this view also comes from states other than Florida.) It is interesting to ask what might have happened to the Coastal Plain fauna during the more extreme climatic vagaries. At a peak of glaciation, it is likely that some widespread but cold-intolerant members of that fauna were extirpated from all but the more southerly portion of the Coastal Plain. In the east, a cold-intolerant species of the Coastal Plain could have withdrawn only into peninsular Florida. Farther west, the same species could have fallen back into southern Texas and perhaps northern Mexico. Thus, a shift toward a cooler climate could have broken the geographic range of many a cold-intolerant species into two well-separated components, one Floridian and the other Texan (or Mexican). Similarly, an interglacial shift toward a decidedly drier climate could have broken the range of many an aquatic or semiaquatic Coastal Plain species into two major components; for a really extreme shift of this nature would leave only two extensive areas of wetlands: the lowlands of the Atlantic Coastal Plain and the delta of the Mississippi. The stretch of country between these two areas would not be rendered waterless, but its wetlands would be much reduced in extent and number. Therefore, the intermediate stretch would function as a barrier (perhaps in some cases not a wholly effective one) between the eastern and western components of an aquatic species. Also, during at least the first interglacial, the polar icecaps melted back beyond their present extent. The melt-water raised sea level well above its present stand, and the rivers of the Coastal Plain were embayed along their lower courses. A saltwater channel, along with its bordering saltmarsh or mangrove swamp, may not be an impassable barrier to a freshwater reptile; but it is much more of a barrier than the usual river. Thus, in many an aquatic species of the Coastal Plain, the genetic contact of an eastern population with its western counterpart could have been severely limited at certain times.

If a species is broken into two geographically separated populations, each of these goes its separate evolutionary way; and over the millennia, the two populations come to differ from each other in certain features of anatomy and life history. With time, the two may diverge into separate species which are no longer capable of interbreeding. Among reptiles, this divergence through geographic isolation seems to be the commonest way in which new species are formed. Often, however, environmental changes may permit the two components to spread, and to re-establish contact with each other at a time when they have diverged somewhat but are still capable of interbreeding. Under these conditions, the two may eventually form a narrow or a broad zone of intermediacy in the area of contact and interbreeding. In such a case the taxonomist would say that the two populations were not different species, but merely two subspecies or races of a single species.

How does this bear on the biology of the alligator? Aquatic or semi-aquatic reptiles, widespread in the Coastal Plain and commonly associated with the alligator, are usually represented by one subspecies in the eastern part of the Coastal Plain, and by a different subspecies in the western part and Mississippi Valley. For example, in the Atlantic Coastal Plain drainage of eastern Georgia, the alligator is associated with the eastern mud turtle, the Florida turtle, the yellow-bellied turtle, the eastern chicken turtle, the Gulf Coast spiny softshell, the banded watersnake, the red-bellied watersnake, the brown watersnake, the Florida green water-snake, the eastern mud snake, and the eastern cottonmouth. In the Gulf Coastal Plain drainage of western Louisiana, the alligator is associated with the western counterparts of the aforesaid turtles and snakes; in other words, with the Mississippi mud turtle, the Missouri turtle, the red-eared turtle, the western chicken turtle, the Texas spiny softshell, the broad-banded watersnake, the yellow-bellied watersnake, the diamondback watersnake, the green watersnake, the western mud snake, and the western cotton-mouth. Apparently no one has asked whether the American alligator similarly exists as distinct eastern and western subspecies; it might well be expected to do so.

The formal definition and naming of subspecies is properly done through the pages of some journal that is devoted to taxonomic studies. In the present book I note only that the alligators of Louisiana and Texas are trenchantly different from those of Florida, Georgia, and the Carolinas. Probably two subspecies are represented. The most obvious difference between the two lies in the coloration of the juvenile and young adult. In the more westerly population, the light elements of the pattern are pale yellow or whitish; and the whitish ventral coloration extends high onto the sides of the body, neck, and head. Especially characteristic is a whitish speckling that covers the side of the lower jaw, and that extends even onto the upper jaw. (Fig. 39, upper portrays a typical young adult of the western population.) In the more easterly population, the lighter elements of the pattern vary from a medium yellow to a rich orange-brown (depending on locality). The eastern juvenile has lateral light markings, but these are not the pale color of the venter. At no age is there conspicuous light speckling on the side of either jaw; the young adult has but a trace of light markings on the side of the body. (Fig. 36 portrays a typical young adult of the eastern population.) In both populations, old alligators may become quite dark laterally and dorsally; darkening with age proceeds more rapidly in the east. In either population, this darkening can be hastened by prolonged exposure to sunlight in an unshaded pen.

Now to review the habitat of the alligator. This reptile is primarily,

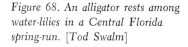

Figure 68. An alligator rests among
water-lilies in a Central Florida
spring-run. [Tod Swalm]

Figure 69. A habitat of the alligator:
a Central Florida cypress pond, often
flooded by a nearby creek.
[W. T. Neill]

although not exclusively, a species of the fresh water, rather than of the
brackish or the salt. It will live in both the flowing fresh water and the
still. Along the larger rivers, it is usually more common in the lagoons and
backwaters than in the stream proper. However, it can live in streams that
have no adjoining lagoons or swamps. For example, I have counted as
many as seventy alligators along three miles of a central Florida spring-
run, a run virtually without adjoining bodies of quieter water. (In many
parts of the country, a spring-run is brook-sized at best; but a central
Florida spring-run may emerge from the ground as a sizeable river.) The
alligator also thrives in large marshes, even those in which the water
table fluctuates considerably; for in such places, the adult reptile digs a
"'gator-hole" down to water. The hole is not a tunnel but a veritable pond.
In Okefinokee Swamp I have seen 'gator-holes 25 feet across. The alligator
can likewise exist in an area that has no large bodies of flowing or still

Figure 70. Alligators have often been seen in this ditch, a man-made channel choked with the introduced water-hyacinth (above). Alligators also rest in clumps of a native aquatic plant, water-lettuce (below). [W. T. Neill and Paul Lorck Eidem]

water, provided it does have a great number of small ponds among which the adults can move. Such an area is usually an expanse of low-lying pine flatwoods dotted with shallow basins, but in some large tracts of much higher ground, sinkhole ponds are sufficiently numerous to support a population of alligators.

Certain man-made aquatic situations are also suitable for the alligator. This reptile usually avoids small creeks, but will live in the lakes that are formed when these streams are dammed to provide power for a grist mill. Also, the long-abandoned rice fields of lower South Carolina provide a suitable habitat for the species.

A South American plant, the water-hyacinth, was deliberately introduced by man into the southeastern United States, with the intention of beautifying the swamps and waterways. The plant's purple flowers did just that, but the leaves and stems formed floating masses that soon choked lakes and blocked channels (Fig. 70, upper). Today, millions of dollars are spent each year to control this aquatic plant. The introduction of the water-

Figure 71. *The extremes of alligator habitat in Florida: a deeply shaded, swamp-bordered stream (at left), and an open marsh (above). The distant marsh seems prairie-like, but its grasses and sedges conceal waterholes (at right).* [W. T. Neill]

hyacinth proved favorable to certain small fishes, frogs, salamanders and aquatic snakes. Seemingly it was also favorable to the alligator. Both young and adult alligators frequently float among the water-hyacinth clumps. In such places the reptiles are extremely well concealed; and even a very large one is hard to see among the plants. Alligators also float among native aquatic plants, such as the water-lily, bonnet-lily, and water-lettuce (Fig. 70, lower).

The distribution of some aquatic organisms is controlled at least in part by the so-called *pH* of the water; that is, the degree of acidity or alkalinity. However, the *pH* of the water seems to have no bearing on the presence or absence of the alligator. On the one hand, this reptile exists in the central Florida spring-runs, which well up through limestone and which are notably alkaline. On the other hand, it exists in highly acid cypress ponds, and in the "blackwater" streams which are stained by plant acids to the color of strong tea. Activities of man have muddied various rivers to an excessive degree, and from such streams the alligator is generally absent. Very muddy streams have usually been profoundly disturbed in their ecology, and one could not assume that the turbidity of the water was directly responsible for the alligator's absence.

In all parts of the alligator's range, most individuals are comparatively inactive during the winter, which they spend in " 'gator-holes" or partly flooded burrows. The winter temperature of the water is no doubt important in setting limits to the alligator's geographic range, as previously noted. During the warmer part of the year, the alligator's active season, certain bodies of water vary among themselves in temperature. In the limestone country of Florida and southern Georgia, a big spring-run maintains a fairly constant temperature the year round, and in summer is cooler than nearby waters that are not spring-fed. Some of these spring-runs, especially the more northerly of them, maintain a cooler temperature than is optimum for the alligator in its active season. In Florida these runs offer sunny banks and islands on which the reptiles often rest, belly in the water and back to the sun. Perhaps this is true basking, the reptile utilizing the sun's warmth to elevate its temperature above that of the water. In Georgia some cool spring-runs are deeply shaded by vegetation, and offer no sunny islands or banks. Such a run will usually harbor no alligator, even though an old milldam lake on such a stream will usually have the reptiles in it.

During the alligator's active season, the water may become very warm in the shallow and nearly treeless marshes. In southern Florida, marsh-dwelling alligators often spend the day in the deep shade of an aquatic plant called Thalia. Thalias grow in ponds, lakes, marshes, and river shallows, where they often form extensive colonies. The Thalia leaves are the largest to be borne by any herbaceous plant that is native to the United States. Thick stems, six to ten feet long, hold the great leaves above the water; and a Thalia colony forms a sunshade beneath which the water stays cool. At some localities, alligators seem never to desert the Thalia colonies during the hottest part of the year.

There is no report of an alligator's swimming well out to sea. However, the reptile is occasionally found in brackish coastal waters. Invasion of such waters is most likely to take place where extensive inland marshes drain into the sea, establishing a gentle gradient from the fresh water to the salt. Actual nesting in the saltmarsh, or in some other brackish-water situation, has not been noted; and it is probable that most alligators seen in brackish water were but temporary visitors from some body of fresh water farther inland. Yet, there are some localities—for example, the vicinity of Key West, Florida—where alligators have been found in sufficient numbers, and at sufficient distance from fresh water, to suggest permanent residence in a saline habitat. In near-coastal situations, where the water is fresh but is subject to tidal rise and fall, the reptile can live permanently.

The alligator does not utilize all parts of a swamp or marsh. Its awareness is directed toward the surface of the water, the shallows, the nearby banks, and the bottom to a depth of about 10 or 15 feet, occasionally a bit more. On a few occasions I have seen an alligator, disturbed by man, dive to a depth of about 20 feet and make off across a lake bottom, its path marked by a stream of gas-bubbles liberated from bottom sediments by the reptile's passage. Of course, in the greater portion of the alligator's range there is not much really deep water; the streams, lagoons, oxbows, "dead lakes," and milldam lakes of the Coastal Plain are fairly or quite shallow for the most part. The greatest depth of water is in the huge sinkholes and springheads of Florida's limestone country. In recent years, scuba diving in these flooded shafts and caverns has become a popular hobby, but few divers ever see an alligator. I know of but one instance in which a diver, entering a headspring cavern, encountered an alligator. The reptile departed hastily as the man entered, the two brushing past each other at the cavern's mouth. Even in this case the cavern was not deeply submerged. In the Everglades, "'gator-holes" sometimes occupy basin-like cavities in the underlying limestone, but there is no reason to think that the reptiles utilize anything more than the surface, upper waters, and banks of the cavities.

The foregoing summary of the alligator's habitat is based on observations made up to about 1950. Since then, the reptile has been completely exterminated in many areas, and nearly so in most others. The numbers of the alligator have been decimated even in tracts theoretically set aside as inviolable sanctuaries for wildlife. Of course the species has suffered most in the habitats that are readily accessible to hide-hunters, or that are readily drained and filled by land developers. The herpetologist, if beginning his field experience after the midpoint of the present century, would never suspect that the alligator once abounded in almost every major aquatic situation of the Coastal Plain, with the exception of smaller streams and well-isolated small ponds.

14 COURTSHIP AND NESTING OF THE ALLIGATOR

IN ORDER to show how fallacies had crept into the literature, a few aspects of the alligator's life history were touched upon briefly in Chapters 1–4. These aspects may now be reviewed in greater detail, and the discussion of them integrated with other topics, to present an orderly account of the alligator's life. Where important gaps exist in our knowledge, attention is drawn to them.

The account may begin with the courtship. This takes place in the spring of the year, beginning around the first part of April throughout the greater part of the range. The literature would lead one to believe that the courting and mating season is very long, extending from March through July. However, the authors responsible for this idea did not actually witness courting but merely heard (or were told about) bellowing, and mistakenly assumed that bellowing was a sign of courtship. Actually, bellowing is done throughout the alligator's active season, and is most often heard after the eggs have already been laid. Most actual courting takes place in April. It is not known how the sexes locate each other at this time. Perhaps the anal glands lay a trail detectable by another alligator, but there is no proof of this. It is not known what role, if any, the throat glands may play in the courtship; nor is it known how one alligator determines the sex of another. At no time in its courting or mating does the alligator give off an odor detectable by man. It is impossible to say which sex is the more active in searching for a mate, but there is a little evidence suggesting that both sexes search during the courting season. There is not a shred of actual evidence to support the oft-repeated statement that "rival males" battle over a female at this season. Such an idea in part reflects anthropomorphism; it also reflects the triply mistaken assumption that bellowing is exclusively a male activity, that it is especially associated with courtship, and that it is a manifestation of aggression. After a male and a female have located each other, the former is the more active in pressing the courtship. The courting pair do not fight each other; courtship is a slow and quiet proceeding.

During the courtship period the male remains with the female until she is stimulated to permit copulation. It usually takes at least three days, and sometimes up to seventeen days, before the female is so stimulated. If the courting pair is badly disturbed by man during his time, they cease their courship activities and do not take them up again that year. If the female cruises about in deeper water, the male will swim after her; if she moves onto land, he will follow her there. Most of the courting is done in the water. When the female lies quietly on land or in shallow water, the male usually lies beside her; and from time to time he will use his forelimb to stroke her in the dorsolateral region (Fig. 72). The dorsolateral glands lie beneath the area that is stroked, so perhaps these glands are hedonic in function. Strokes are concentrated on the area just in advance of the female's rump. In water, the male eventually confronts the female, places his head beneath hers, rubs or butts her throat with the top of his head, and blows great streams of bubbles past her cheeks. These actions take place near the end of the courtship, and by them the female is finally stimulated to permit intromission, which takes place in shallow water. The male lies beside the female, facing the same direction. The female slightly elevates her tail and bends it away from the male. The male's penis is erected somewhat laterally and upwardly. There is no truth to the common belief that the female rolls onto her back, on land or in the water, to permit copulation. This belief stems from the difficulty in understanding how two alligators could copulate if both individuals stayed belly-down. Nevertheless, the male readily accomplishes intromission, which lasts for about two or three minutes.

In captivity, a male alligator directs his courtship toward one female only, even though several other females may be present. It is inferred that a similar situation exists in nature. In other words, a male alligator, unlike a bull or a buck deer, will impregnate only one female during the breeding season.

There is no indication that the male automatically remains near the female after coition has been accomplished, although in many cases his home range—the area to which he restricts himself—may be nearby. As spring passes into summer, the female begins to build a nest. It is not known exactly how much time elapses between copulation and the onset of nesting activities. Since mating is usually done during the first part of April, and since most nest-building begins around the first part of June, one supposes that the female begins to build a nest about two months after coition. The female does not first clear a large space on which a nest will later be constructed. If an area about a nest appears somewhat denuded of vegetation or ground debris, the circumstance reflects only the female's scraping up of nesting material, and perhaps some trampling incidental to nest-building activities. Usually, vegetation surrounds the nest and helps to shade it (Fig. 73). The coming and going of the female may form a trail between the nest and the water. This trail may be very noticeable if the nest is in a thick stand of herbaceous vegetation, which of course is easily trampled. In forest vegetation the trail may be inconspicuous among the tree trunks and shrubs. The nest is usually built about 10 or 15 feet from the water's edge, and is almost always placed in the shade. In river swamps, the nest is sometimes built at the base of a large

Figure 72. As courtship begins, the male alligator lies beside the female and begins to stroke her (below). The strokes are given more often and more vigorously along the hind part of the female's body (at right). [Ross Allen's Reptile Institute and W. T. Neill]

tree, usually a cypress; and the nesting material is piled partly against the tree trunk. In central Florida there are many sinkhole lakes whose shores are very sparsely vegetated; and a female alligator, living in a lake of this kind, will go as much as 250 feet away from the water in order to nest in the shade of trees. On rare occasions a nest is built on a grassy bank just above a large spring-run whose comparatively cold flow keeps the nearby bank cool and moist even on hot, sunny days; but this is the only circumstance under which a wild alligator was seen to nest in the full sunlight even though shade was nearby. In marshes, alligators tend to nest on small islands whose woody vegetation provides more shade than the herbaceous vegetation of the marsh proper. In general, the female builds her nest in the coolest available situation, within the limits imposed by the danger of flooding or drying.

In some habitats, for example broad marshes with few islands, the scarcity of suitable nesting sites may lead several females to nest near each other. I have seen four nests in an area about 30 feet long. There are early reports of larger nesting aggregations, with many attended and old nests in sight at the same time. I do not doubt such reports, for there

Figure 73. Usually, dense vegetation shades the alligator's nest. Often, a nest is built at the base of a tree. [Tod Swalm]

probably was more communal nesting in the days when the alligator was perhaps a thousand times more abundant than it is today.

A nesting site having been located, the female begins to build the nest. As emphasized in Chapter 2, she does not use her mouth to gather nesting material, nor does she bring material from some distant locality. It is unusual for her to gather ground debris that lies more than about 15 feet from the spot on which the nest will be built. With lateral movements of body and tail, she scrapes up whatever nesting material is immediately available (Fig. 9). Usually she scrapes up a mixture of dead leaves and mud. The dead leaves of the cabbage palm (which easily break into strips and bits) are often included in the nesting material. About the marshes, nests often contain sawgrass blades. In a swamp, the nest may include a variety of leaves fallen from the swamp hardwoods. If much plant debris is available, the nest may be constructed chiefly from it, with little ad-mixture of soil. If the ground is sandy, the female will build with a mixture of leaves and sand. Some nests are made up more of fresh vegetation than of ground debris. A nest of this kind is usually encountered in marsh-land, where many herbaceous plants are easily uprooted by the female's scraping movements. A captive female will construct her nest entirely of sand if nothing else is provided. I have seen a captive female work soggy pieces of cardboard boxes into a nest that was otherwise of sand. Thus, the nature of the nesting material would seem to depend mostly on habitat and availability. Yet, the female may exercise some degree of selectivity. I have never seen "Spanish moss" in a nest, although masses of this plant often lie on the ground in places where alligators nest.

The female crawls over the sides and top of the nest, packing the material. With a hindfoot she digs a cavity in the top of the nest. Both hindfeet may be used in digging the cavity, but they are not used simultaneously. The hindfoot manipulates the nesting material with dexterity. The female works leisurely and sporadically, taking usually two to three days (that is, 48 to 72 hours) to complete the nest. The greater part of the nest-building takes place by night, but it is not unusual to see a female at work in the morning also. The observation of Albert M. Reese (described in Chapter 11) suggest that the female, after having completed her nest, may withhold her eggs for at least two weeks if weather conditions are unfavorable. However, under normal conditions the completion of the nest cavity is followed in a few hours by the laying of the first egg therein. Unlike turtles, which usually lay their eggs at night, the female alligator may lay by night or by day.

When the female is ready to lay, she perches atop the nest in such a position as to bring her vent above the nesting cavity. The hindfeet are kept near the vent, where they break the fall of most of the eggs that are laid. She slightly elevates her tail while laying. The egg is bright white in color as it emerges from the female's vent; by day, a distant observer can easily count the eggs as they are laid. The number of eggs in a clutch will vary. Literature records suggest the range of variation to be from 20 to 70. However, most of the literature is unreliable in its treatment of the alligator's life cycle; and in any event, the usual number in a clutch is more important than the rarely encountered extremes of variation. A majority of clutches will be made up of about 30 eggs. It is unusual for a female to deposit significantly fewer eggs than this figure, but some females deposit many more. Almost all clutches would be encompassed by a range of 28 to 52. It is not known why a few of the clutches are so much larger than the remainder, but a suggestion might be offered on this point. In the wild, most nesting females are young adults, about 5 to 7 feet in length. These young adults should be responsible for most of the nests that contain the usual number of about 30 eggs. Other females, larger and older but not yet very aged, might therefore be responsible for most of the larger clutches.

The alligator's egg, unlike that of most birds, is not larger at one end. The average length of an alligator's egg is about 3 inches, the average width about 1¾ inches. However, there is considerable variation, some eggs being a little below the average in width but well above it in length. An exceptionally elongate egg may be nearly 3½ inches long. An unusually small egg will barely exceed 2½ inches in length. The literature includes reference to eggs that were only about 2 inches long, or that exceeded 3½ inches. But even if these figures are accurate, they deal with rare aberrations, and do not indicate the normal range of variation.

After laying, the female crawls carefully over the sides of the nest, closing the cavity. She does not bring her full weight to bear on the top of the nest after the eggs have been deposited. The completed nest is variable in size. In most cases, the height varies from about 18 to 30 inches, the basal diameter from about 4 to 5 feet. The early literature, straining one's credulity as usual, offers reports of nests more than 6 feet high. Perhaps in a low-lying tract with few eminences an old nest might serve as a foundation for a new one; and so nesting debris might seem piled to a much greater height than usual. However, this is speculation. It is possible that some early observers mistook wood-rat nests for those of the alligator. In the river swamps of the St. Johns drainage in Florida, the wood-rat may pile twigs, leaves, and sticks into an enormous heap, far larger than any alligator nest. These exceptionally large wood-rat nests are seen on river islands and banks, places where alligators would be expected to nest.

It has generally been assumed that a female alligator will nest every year, but this is not true in all cases. In captivity, young adult females have been known to nest each year for several successive years, and so we may be sure that the individual female does not nest only in alternate years (as do some reptiles). However, larger and older females in captivity will usually nest at irregular, unpredictable intervals of two, three, or four years. The oldest females cease reproductive activity entirely, and usually produce no young at all during the last fifteen or twenty years of life in captivity. It is probable that mating activities are often inhibited by the unnatural conditions to which a penned alligator is exposed; and the reproductive performance of older females is probably better in the wild than in captivity. Still, it is inferred that in nature the female's fertility will eventually begin to decline; and that very old females do little or nothing to increase the local population of alligators.

The female normally remains with her nest while the eggs are developing. Usually the guardian female rests with her throat on the nest (Fig. 74, upper), although at intervals she may lie about 5 to 10 feet away. If alligators are frequently hunted, they will become shy, and the females may no longer guard the nest, at least against man. Also, captive females may become inured to the presence of a keeper, and may lose the guarding impulse. However, under normal conditions the female will guard her nest, even against man. The guarding behavior looks like an attack, but it is not. As a person approaches the nest, the guardian female rises, turns rather slowly toward the intruder, and begins to inflate with air (Fig. 74, lower). If the person halts about 20 feet from the nest, the female may do nothing but hiss. If the person continues to approach, however, the reptile

Figure 74. A female alligator often rests with her throat on her nest (upper). Sensing an intruder, she begins to open her mouth (upper), and to turn upon him (lower). [Ross Allen's Reptile Institute]

will lunge open-mouthed in his direction. The open mouth is aimed upward, toward the person's face. The lunge is accompanied by a loud hiss. In this lunge, the alligator does not actually attempt to bite. If the person steps back a pace or two, the alligator advances and repeats its threatening gesture. If the person turns and flees, the alligator will follow for a short distance. In other words, the guarding behavior is a series of stereotyped actions which cause the alligator's potential enemy to retreat from the vicinity of the nest.

On one occasion I came upon an alligator nest that had been built in a river swamp at the base of a huge cypress tree. The guardian female, about 7 feet long, made the usual lunge, and I stepped around the tree trunk. She followed, and I started walking around the trunk at a pace she could maintain. She followed me for four circuits around the trunk, but did not pursue when I suddenly left the tree and made off through the under- brush. On another occasion I tried to see how far a guardian female could be lured from her nest. This nest was in dense brush about 15 feet from the edge of a shallow, mud-bottomed basin. The basin often held water, but at this time was nearly dry except at its lower end, where it opened into a stream. The coming and going of the female had left a well-worn path from the basin's edge to the nest. Brush and branches overhung the path, which was almost tunnel-like. The female, about 8 feet long, made the expected lunge as I approached along the path. I backed up a few paces and stopped. She promptly followed and made a second open-mouthed lunge, hissing loudly. Again I retreated a few paces, and again she followed to lunge. We went through the sequence a third time, bringing her to the edge of the basin. Two more repetitions of the sequence brought her well out into the basin, where she lay in the mud hissing but no longer lunging. I reached over and tapped her on the snout with a boat paddle I had been carrying. She fled immediately, not back toward the nest but along the basin and into the nearby water. Here she cruised back and forth, watching me. A few days later, the area received some long-delayed rain, heavy down- pours. The river rose, flooding the basin and even the lower part of the path that led to the nest. The nest seemed to be in no danger of flooding, how- ever, and the female was found to be beside it again.

It is by no means certain that a guardian female would actually bite a person if he failed to retreat. It may be significant that, while adult alli- gators have been known to attack swimmers in the water, there is no report

Figure 75. A footprint in the sand (at right) reveals a raccoon to have been the predator that opened this turtle nest. An alligator nest, if left unguarded by the female, might be similarly raided. [W. T. Neill]

of anyone's having been bitten by a female alligator who was defending her nest. It is certain that the female gives the intruder ample opportunity to escape. Ritualized confrontation, without actual bloodshed, is widespread among animals, as noted in an earlier chapter.

It is not known what predators, other than man, might raid an alligator's nest. Where alligators live, raccoons are usually very abundant. These mammals find and dig into a great many turtle nests (Fig. 75), and so might dig into an alligator nest if it were left unattended. The introduced wild hog would no doubt root into an unguarded nest. The black bear is often a swamp-dweller (Fig. 25); it does a great deal of rooting about, and will eat the eggs of reptiles and birds. However, the bear has become very scarce in most areas, and we do not know how often it menaced alligator nests in the days when it was abundant. In the early 1900s, Albert M. Reese was told by "reliable hunters" that "bears are persistent searchers for and eaters of alligator eggs." It should also be recalled that during the Pleistocene the alligator had to live with a variety of mammals that are now extinct; and some of these might have been confirmed egg-eaters. The Pleistocene fauna seems to have been in existence as recently as 12,000 years ago, and this does not seem very long ago when one considers the lengthy history of the crocodilians. The automatic response of a guardian female alligator to an intruder need not have evolved primarily as a defense against the few egg-predators that prowl the swamps and marshes today.

The alligator's nest is menaced by the possibility of flooding, drying, or overheating. The female has evolved behavior patterns that minimize these hazards to the eggs. The nest is nearly always placed in a spot that stays cool and damp, yet above the level of flood waters. It is not known whether any of the aforesaid environmental hazards can be further reduced by the female after she has built the nest. She does make frequent trips between the nest and the water, and dampens the nest area somewhat, not with urine as some would have it, nor with an occasional mouthful of water, but with the water that drips from her body. If a summer proved unusually hot and dry, her actions might be doubly advantageous to the eggs, the nest being both cooled and dampened by these drippings. On the other hand, frequent visits to the water by a nesting female may serve only her own needs for water, food, or cooling. Speculation aside, one observable circumstance hints that the female's movements between nest and water represent a behavior pattern directly related to the requirements of the eggs. This is the female's habit of resting with her throat on the nest. It is conceivable that the skin of the throat is particularly sensitive to temperature, moisture, or both. Perhaps the female is automatically stimulated to visit the water, and to return dripping wet, when the throat encounters a nest surface that is too hot or too dry. In several of the crocodilians many scales of the throat are provided with a tiny pit, or two such pits. These scale pits are thought to have a sensory function, but no one knows what they sense. Something similar could be present, although less evident externally, in the alligator.

The elevation of the eggs, well above the general ground level, helps avert the danger of flooding. To bring about this elevation, the female must build with available material, mostly plant debris. Damp, packed plant material generates and retains considerable heat as it decays. In spite of the frequent assertion that the alligator's eggs are "incubated" by the warmth of the decaying nest debris, I believe that this heat of fermentation is often a hazard to the eggs, and that the female's choice of a cool nesting site reflects an imperative need to minimize the ever-present danger that the eggs will become overheated. As noted in Chapter 2, the alligator embryo should not be significantly more heat-tolerant than the adult; and the temperature in a nest is very close to a body temperature that would be fatal to an adult. During the nesting season, the ground temperature at night does not fall low enough to jeopardize an alligator's life, or even to prohibit its activity. But no doubt the temperature does fall low enough to affect adversely the development of the alligator embryo. To judge from the raising of eggs in the laboratory, the only adverse affect would be the slowing of embryonic development. Eggs removed from the nest, and thereafter exposed only to the prevailing air temperatures, usually do not hatch until latter September or early October, long after most broods in the wild have made their appearance. The heat of fermentation in a nest could be said to incubate the eggs, in the sense that this heat to some extent counteracts the night-time temperature drop in the swamps and marshes. But the complexity of the situation is obscured by the simple comment that the eggs are incubated.

As suggested by a brief comment in Chapter 6, reptiles carry on what is called behavioral thermoregulation. A reptile has no effective internal mechanism for maintaining a constant body temperature, and so must take on the temperature of its environment. Yet, a reptile during its active season does maintain a fairly constant body temperature by restricting its activities to times when, and places where, certain favorable temperatures prevail. For each reptile species there is a voluntarily accepted range of temperatures; and within this range, there is one certain, optimum body temperature (called the eccritic temperature) that the reptile will strive to maintain as often as possible during the active season. A fatally low temperature lies well below the minimum temperature that is voluntarily accepted. Yet, the eccritic temperature lies not far below the maximum temperature that will be voluntarily accepted, and the latter in turn lies not far below a fatally high temperature. In other words, reptiles carry on most of their activities at a body temperature that is surprisingly close to the point of dangerous overheating. It is thus interesting to note that the alligator embryo—unless it be far more heat-tolerant than the adult, an improbability—similarly lives very close to a point of dangerous overheating.

Of special interest is the assertion that the female opens the nest when the eggs hatch, and so permits the young to escape. Two circumstances are consistent enough with this view. First, the female does guard the nest, and so might be present at hatching time; and second, the young can and occasionally do cry out while still in the egg, and so could attract the female's attention. Also, a newly hatched young sometimes yelps, as though with pain, when detaching itself from the egg membranes. However, at least four circumstances militate against the idea that the female opens the nest. First, this idea originated not from any observation, but from the transferral to the American alligator of beliefs about the Nile crocodile. Second, no reputable observer has reported opening of the nest by the female. Indeed, even the most fanciful legend-mongers do not claim actually to have witnessed a female in the act of nest-opening. Other details of the alligator's reproductive activities—the details of courting, copulating, nest-building, and nest-guarding—have been observed in captivity by many people, but no one has seen a captive female open a nest, or even seen a nest that looked as though it had been opened. Third, and perhaps most significant, old nests in the wild show no sign of having been opened. And finally, any organism, even one with keen hearing, would find it hard to track down the source of a faint cry that was given just once or twice, or at irregular intervals; but the same organism, upon hearing a repetitive call, could keep correcting its heading as it moved toward the caller, which would quickly be located. When an organism has evolved the impulse and ability to vocalize in a fashion that will attract another member of the same species, the vocalization is a repetitive effort (a "segmented" call, in the terminology of those who study animal behavior). The juvenile alligator's distress call is loud and repetitive, and does attract the adults; but the grunts from the eggs, being faint and nonrepetitive, probably do not attract any adult. The next chapter offers further distinctions between the juvenile grunt and the juvenile distress call of the alligator.

The alligator's hatching season is a prolonged one. A majority of the broods appear around the last of July and the first part of August, but a few do not appear until late August or even early September. During the hatching season, some clutches have hatched while others have not; but one cannot look at a nest and tell whether the young have emerged. A nest with empty egg shells looks quite like a nest with unhatched eggs. I believe that the hatchlings automatically and successfully work their way upward through the debris at the top of the nest, just as turtle hatchlings automatically and successfully work their way upward through the packed sand of their buried nest.

One circumstance implies that, whatever the female may normally do, the hatchlings can escape from the nest without her assistance. In Georgia it was not unusual for bands of hide-hunters, operating out of Florida, to raid an area where the alligators had gone comparatively unmolested for years. Such raids were usually made during the summer, the alligator's nesting season. Alligators are easily located at night by their brilliant eye-shine in the rays of a light, and the hunters would wipe out nearly all of the adult alligators in some large swamp, lake, or backwater. After the hunters had gone, I could not locate a single adult in the water, or a guardian female at her nest. All nests were left untended. Yet, around August hatchlings would appear in fair numbers. It seems clear that these young were emerging without assistance.

Wherever it persists in any numbers, with or without legal protection, the alligator is slaughtered heavily during its nesting season (as well as at other times). Today, a great many nests—I would say a majority of them —are left untended, the females having been killed by hide-hunters. In the fall, shortly after the hatching season, I have opened many nests, but have never found a dead brood in them. Such nests contain only egg shells, along with a few eggs that failed to develop. If hatchlings could not emerge from the nest without the assistance of the female parent, many nests should have contained dead young.

It is not known why some broods are late to emerge. It is possible that broods differ innately among themselves in the rate of embryonic development, and that development is slowed by temperature or moisture conditions that are tolerable but not optimum. However, late hatching of some broods is most likely to reflect late mating of some adults. Probably a few adults cannot locate mates as rapidly as most others.

Indeed, as a result of hide-hunting and the thinning of alligator populations, some of these reptiles probably cannot locate a mate in most years. Hide-hunters speak of a "blinker," an alligator that has been shot at many times, and that has become exceedingly wary. A "blinker" can no longer be approached to within gunshot range. It will submerge the moment a light falls on it, or the moment it hears the rapping of a boat paddle against a gunwale. Once submerged, it will seek some retreat and not reappear, or else reappear momentarily at some even more distant point. A "blinker" may survive for many years, usually acquiring a nickname among the local people, but it lives a solitary life, with no other alligators for miles around.

In some reptile species the female can produce two or more successive broods of young after just one mating, the male's sperm living in the female's reproductive tract for one to several years. For example, an indigo snake produced fertile eggs four years after the last possible copulation, and a night snake continued to lay fertile eggs for five years after a mating. Sperm storage and delayed fertilization have been found to exist among snakes, lizards, and turtles. No one knows whether crocodilians could be added to this list.

In captivity, the reproductive success of the alligator is not high, at least not in the southern states where the reptiles are usually displayed in outdoor pens. Many clutches die, especially at a time when the embryos are nearly full-term. I believe this simply reflects overheating of the nest as the summer proceeds. The captive female, unlike a wild one, does not have a free selection of a nesting site. She must accept whatever temperature conditions prevail in the pen, and must build her nest of whatever material she can find therein. As a rule, July is the warmest month in most of the United States (except along the Pacific Coast), and this seems to be the month in which so many clutches die in captivity. In the wild, the reproductive success is probably good, for it is unusual to open a nest and find a dead clutch. It is usual, however, to find a few eggs that never developed, probably because they were never fertilized. This is a normal situation among reptile species that lay a large number of eggs.

15 THE YOUNG
OF THE ALLIGATOR

WHILE SOME FEMALES are guarding their respective nests, all the other individuals of an alligator population, both males and non-nesting females, are carrying on various activities of their own. These activities seem to have little or no direct bearing on the eggs, nests, and guardian females, and so need not be described at this point in the review of the alligator's life cycle.

It might be asked what stimulates the guardian female finally to abandon her nest. It is possible that she departs upon hearing the grunting of the foetuses shortly before they are ready to hatch. However, I believe that the impulse to guard the nest simply wanes as the nesting season progresses. This is the case in captivity. Captive females guard the nest assiduously, and defend it energetically, during the first part of the nesting season, but much less so during the latter part. Captive females have generally lost interest in the nest by the time the eggs are ready to hatch, and have taken to spending most of their time in the water. In the wild, the impulse to search for food may gradually overcome the impulse to remain by the nest. It is possible that a nest, after about two months of exposure to the elements, is no longer identifiable by most egg-predators, and may no longer be in any great need of guarding.

When the alligator's egg is nearly ready to hatch, the foetus is itself coiled into a remarkably ovoid shape. Both head and tail are bent over upon the belly. At the tip of the foetus's snout is a tiny, hard, pointed structure. This is commonly (but inappropriately) called the caruncle, and with it the little alligator slits the egg shell at hatching time. As the point of the caruncle is directed somewhat downwardly, one supposes that the foetus cuts the shell by repeatedly raising the head and then bringing it down again, a nodding movement. It is not known whether the alligator's egg shell is weakened by enzymatic action at the time of hatching. Nor can it be said whether the caruncle is eventually absorbed, or whether it is shed. When the hatchling emerges and uncoils, it seems much too long to have come from so small an egg. Newly hatched alligators vary among themselves in total length. Most are about 8½ inches long at hatching. A few uncommonly small ones will fall just short of 8 inches, and a few uncommonly long ones will reach 8¾ inches. At the time of hatching, the alligator's

Figure 76. When an alligator hatches, its belly is distended by a mass of yolk. In this individual, the mass is larger than usual. [W. T. Neill]

Figure 77. The alligator hatchling is elaborately patterned with yellowish and black. [Ross Allen's Reptile Institute]

belly is greatly distended with unabsorbed yolk (Fig. 76). This material is utilized as nourishment by the hatchling during its first few days of life outside the egg shell. For a time a scar remains on the hatchling's belly, marking the point where egg membranes were formerly attached. This scar has nearly vanished by the time the hatchling goes into winter retreat, but in some cases may still be discernible the following spring.

In many vertebrate species, the newborn or newly hatched individual is quite different in coloration from the adult. In such cases, the distinctive coloration of the juvenile could be especially advantageous to its way of life, a way quite different from that of the adult. On the other hand, in various species the distinctive juvenile coloration seems to be primitive, hearkening back to the coloration of some ancestral stock. Related species may be colored differently when adult, yet almost identically when young. The juvenile coloration can provide a clue to taxonomic relationships, to lines of evolutionary descent. (For example, members of the thrush family are usually spot-breasted or speckle-breasted when adult, but this is not true of two members of that family, the American robin and the bluebird. Yet, robins and bluebirds reveal their relationship to other thrushes by being speckled-breasted when juvenile. Comparable examples could be cited among mammals and reptiles.) Thus, it is always potentially useful to describe in detail the juvenile coloration of a reptile. This has not previously been done in the case of the hatching alligator. The following description is based on typical hatchlings from Georgia.

At the moment of hatching, the alligator is plain, dull whitish on the under surfaces of the head, neck, and body. The side of the body is grayish-black, marked with four to six vertical, light bars which branch or coalesce irregularly. At this time, these light bars are dull whitish. The back is black, crossed by four whitish bars. A fifth whitish bar crosses the rump, and extends onto the upper part of the hindlimb. A sixth whitish bar crosses the back of the neck, just anterior to the level of the forelimb insertion. The neck also bears a seventh whitish crossbar, anterior to the sixth one. Unlike the other light crossbars, this seventh one in interrupted at the dorsal midline with dark. The side of the lower jaw is mostly whitish, but bears three indistinct grayish blotches in a horizontal row. The eyelid is whitish, and from it a whitish stripe extends backward to the hind margin of the head. This light stripe is bordered above by a blackish one. The tail is blackish with ten or eleven whitish crossbars. Within a day or two of hatching, the whitish markings of all the dorsal and lateral surfaces have begun to take on a yellowish tinge; and within a week or so, these markings have become distinctly yellow. In many reptiles, a yellow component of the coloration does not make its appearance until a day or two after hatching.

The young alligator is commonly said to display dorsal light crossbars on a blackish background. However, the light areas actually are part of the background coloration, a part that is not obscured by the extensive dark markings. In other words, a yellowish pigment underlies all the lateral and dorsal surfaces; but in places this pigment is hidden by an overlying blackish one. Once in a great while, as a rare genetic accident, an alligator comes into the world with a normal ground color but without the dorsal pattern. Such an individual is yellowish on all the dorsal and lateral surfaces, and the deep yellow crossbars stand out as the darkest markings of the body.

Albinism, a complete lack of pigmentation, is a widespread abnormality in the Animal kingdom. Pure albinos have not been reported in the alligator, but near-albinos are known. These do not exhibit the pearly whiteness of a fully albino reptile. There is some dark pigment in the skin, and the general coloration is a dirty whitish. In a near-albino hatchling, the pupil of the eye has a dark reddish cast. There exists among many organisms a color abnormality termed (somewhat inappropriately) vitiligo. This condition is characterized by the presence of irregular blotches from which some or all of the normal pigmentation is lacking. Vitiliginous alligators are known, and so are melanistic—abnormally blackish—ones. Alligators usually darken with age, but the reference here is to those that are deep, uniform blackish at the time of hatching. It is likely that in nature an aberrant coloration is a handicap to a hatchling, even if the condition is not genetically linked with other abnormalities, say of physiology or of behavior.

Many species of animal life, both vertebrate and invertebrate, normally exist in two color phases, one dusky and the other reddish. While something is known about the physiological basis of this color dimorphism, it is not known what determines the proportion of dusky to reddish individuals in nature. It has been suggested that the red phase tends to predominate in arid situations, but this is not so with various reptiles that exhibit the red-black color dimorphism. At any rate, once in a while there turns up a hatching alligator in which all the normally blackish areas are cinnamon-red. This color abnormality is so rare that one could scarcely speak of a "red phase" in the alligator. Reddish, whitish, and yellowish alligators do have the capacity to produce some dark pigment after prolonged exposure to sunlight; and they will, after years of captivity in a sunny pen, become about as dark as any others.

Of course, abnormalities of the alligator hatchling are not limited to those of pigmentation. One alligator, which has lived for years in captivity, has a small, weak, malformed fifth leg, dangling from the right hindleg. On rare occasions, in both reptiles and birds, a single egg will contain two embryos. A condition of this kind has once been reported for the alligator. Two-headed snakes and turtles have been reported with surprising frequency, but no two-headed crocodilian is known. "Freaks" have great appeal to the general public, but they are usually of very minor scientific interest. Let us return to normal hatchlings of the alligator.

Of special interest is the normal presence of vague black spots along the side of the hatchling's lower jaw. In juveniles and young adults of the black caiman, the smooth-fronted caimans, and the jacaré, the sides of the lower jaw are strongly spotted or blotched. In their position, the markings on the lower jaw of the hatchling alligator are an especially close counterpart of the spots that decorate the lower jaw of the black caiman. In the latter species, the prominent jaw spots serve as camouflage by interrupting the outline of the head. In the hatchling alligator, the spots are much too dim and too transient to serve as camouflage. It may be inferred that spotting of the lower jaw is a primitive character in alligatorids, a character nearly lost in the American alligator but still present in some caimans.

There is evidence from other sources suggesting that the American alligator is more highly evolved than the caimans. Dark spotting of the lower jaw is also present in Osteolaemus and some Crocodylus, as well as Tomistoma, and so the character may be a very ancient one, antedating the separation of the Crocodylinae and Alligatorinae.

Within a single brood of baby alligators there is some minor variation in details of pattern, and especially in the lateral light markings. As far as is known, there is no consistent difference between male and female in juvenile pattern. No one has determined what percentage of an alligator brood is male, and what female. One would suspect males and females to be produced in about equal numbers, but an investigation into the situation would be welcome. Little is known about the genetics of sex determination in crocodilians.

Upon hatching, the young alligators make their own way to water. It is not known how they find the water. It may be pertinent to note certain studies on freshwater turtles, for turtle hatchlings must also find their own way to water. Indeed, the usual brood of turtle hatchlings can reach water only by traveling much farther than is required of the usual alligator brood. The young turtles are hatched with an automatic impulse to climb upward, and this impulse brings them out of the buried nest. The impulse to climb begins to wane rapidly as soon as the hatchlings see light. Having emerged, the young turtles become sensitive to a strong humidity gradient, and will move in the direction of increasing humidity. However, such a gradient may not exist between the nesting site and the water. The turtle hatchlings also develop a marked impulse to turn away from a blocked horizon, and to move toward a brighter one. By "horizon" I do not mean any particular portion of the broad sky, but rather the limited portion of the landscape that can be seen by the young turtle. The position of the sun seems to have little to do with the matter. Movement in the direction of a brighter horizon will usually bring the turtle hatchlings to water, partly because such a horizon exists over and near water, and partly because the female parent of the hatchlings had an impulse to move away from the brighter horizon when seeking a nesting spot.

The foregoing comments on water-finding reactions of turtle hatchlings are but generalizations, and the reactions vary somewhat from one species to another. Of course, findings based on turtles cannot simply be transferred to alligators. However, these findings suggest that it is time to abandon the assertion, so often made without actual evidence, that the hatchling alligators are shepherded to the water by their mother; time, instead, to study alligators for evidence of reactions similar to those found in turtles. Does the female alligator, in her search for a nesting spot, automatically turn away from a comparatively bright and open horizon, and move toward a horizon that is blocked and darker? Whatever stimulates her to behave as she does, in effect her nesting impulse carries her from a brighter situation to a darker one; that is, from the water to a vegetated and usually deeply shaded spot. Does the newly hatched alligator have an automatic impulse to move toward a more brightly illuminated horizon? If it did, it would quickly reach the water, for at the usual alligator's nest the illumination over the nearby water might be several thousand times greater than in the woods that surround the nest on three sides. (The human eye can adjust to much variation in illumination, and the average person does not realize just how dark a vegetated area is in relation to open areas nearby.) If a nest were built on a small eminence in marshland, the illumination of the surrounding area might be about the same in all directions. If so, movement of the hatchlings in any direction would soon bring them to water.

Studies by Albert M. Reese, published in 1925, suggest that small alligators do have an impulse to move toward an area of greater illumination. As experimental animals, Reese used five alligators ranging from about 13 to 22 inches in length. These alligators were placed in a box that was illuminated at one end only. One might have expected the timid little reptiles to have huddled in the dark end of the box, but they did not. Thirty observations were made on the five alligators, 150 in all; and in 108 of these observations the reptile was in the bright end of the box. In only fifteen of the 150 cases was the reptile facing away from the light. The behavior of Reese's alligators could very well reflect a retention, slightly beyond the hatchling stage, of an early impulse to move in the direction of greater illumination.

Young alligators may also have an impulse to move in the direction of greater humidity. I have kept small alligators, about ten inches in total length, in a pen that offered a damp substratum, a pool of water, and an optimum temperature. When a fine mist from a garden hose was allowed to drift into the pen, the young reptiles would face toward it, move into it, and sit in it for hours. Such behavior might be expected of alligators that had become dehydrated in captivity, but these reptiles were not suffering from any such condition. I suspect that they retained a juvenile impulse to move in the direction of higher humidity. Of course, further experimentation is desirable.

As mentioned previously, adult alligators are known to dig out large, deep basins, the so-called 'gator-holes. Many authors call these holes "dens," and go on to state that the alligator brood, upon hatching, makes its way to the mother's den, and remains there under maternal care for eighteen months. Such prolonged attention to the young would be remarkable even in mammals. The figure "eighteen months" seems to have entered the literature through the misreading of another (and equally erroneous) statement that young alligators remain with their mother in her den until they are 18 inches long. Neither statement regarding care of the young in the mother's den would appear so frequently if all authors knew that adult alligators dig holes, the so-called dens, only in certain limited portions of the species' range. Basin-like holes are dug only where there are marked seasonal fluctuations of water table. In general, such holes are dug only in marshland and sinkhole country; and throughout the greater part of the alligator's range, these holes are unknown. A later chapter will consider holes dug by adult alligators. At this point, suffice it to say that the brood of alligators could not as a general rule move promptly into the mother's "den" for maternal care, because in most areas no such dens exist.

In marshlands a falling water table may leave water only in the 'gator-holes. It is not surprising that at such times young alligators congregate in the 'gator-holes, along with fishes, frogs, and aquatic salamanders. (In the more marshlike, eastern portion of Okefinokee Swamp at times of low water, the fisherman can make an almost unbelievable catch of speckled perch by dropping his bait into a 'gator-hole.) Toward the end of the hatching season, baby alligators may be quite numerous in certain marshlands; for each nest has produced about thirty or more hatchlings, and predators have not yet taken their full toll of these young. As the only available water might be in the 'gator-holes, it would not be surprising to find a number of young in a hole that was also occupied by an adult alligator. It is astonishing to see how frequently the myth of the maternal alligator has colored the thinking not only of armchair authors but also of people who have seen some alligators in the wild. Here is a typical comment from the supposedly scientific literature: "Each 'gator hole was normally occupied by several alligators—usually a breeding female, the sow, and her one- and two-year

broods. Older alligators up to a length of 4 or 5 feet were often present."
How does anyone know that any particular alligator, present in such an
aggregation, is a "sow," a female? How does anyone know that small alligators, seen in a 'gator-hole, are the progeny of any adult that happened to
be in the same hole? If alligators of various sizes—yearlings, two-year-olds,
4- or 5-footers, and one or more larger adults—are found in a single hole, it
is reasonable to suspect a randomly composed aggregation of whatever individuals are in the vicinity when aggregation becomes necessary.

As a matter of fact, more often than not there is no adult alligator in a
'gator-hole that harbors a number of young during a period of low water.
Not that an adult would in any manner keep the young out of its den;
but in any particular area, most adult alligators have been killed by hide-
hunters, and only a small minority of the local 'gator-holes are still occupied by their makers. Hatchlings, searching for water, are most likely to
chance upon a hole that is unoccupied. At times of low water, hatchlings
(and larger alligators) also aggregate in waterholes that were not dug
or deepened by the adults. During the 1940s, when alligators were still
common in places, some exceptionally large aggregations were formed in
natural basins of Hendry County, Florida. These basins, limestone-bot-
tomed, held deep water when all the surrounding marshes and swamps had
gone dry. The largest aggregation was made up of at least 72 alligators,
ranging from juveniles to 9-footers.

Captive broods, hatched in nearly natural surroundings, disperse rapidly
if their mother's pen is enclosed by coarse-mesh wire, or some other material through which the little reptiles can pass. Dispersal takes place so
soon after hatching that, even in captivity, one rarely has a chance to see
a brood while more than a few of its members are still together. In captivity,
dispersal takes place in the water, not over land; and the same is probably
true in the wild. In most parts of the alligator's range, those parts in which
holes are not dug, field work during the hatching season will reveal almost
all the hatchlings to be scattered, not aggregated. Ignoring aggregation that
is forced by low water, in most areas the herpetologist will see an aggregation of hatchlings only if he is fortunate enough to be on hand in the
first hour or two after hatching.

Although the "baby alligator" trade is today based in large part on
imported hatchlings of the spectacled caiman, there was a time not long
ago when countless thousands of baby alligators were gathered from the

Figure 78. Ward's great blue heron (perched here on the fence of an alligator pen) is a major predator on hatchling alligators. [Paul Lorck Eidem]

Florida swamps and marches for sale to tourists. Southern Florida was a favorite collecting ground. In those days the alligator was still moderately abundant in that part of the country, and the supply of hatchlings seemed inexhaustible. Great blue herons were also common in that region. These long-legged birds would stalk about in the shallows, occasionally lunging at small, aquatic vertebrates. Great blue herons (of the more southerly subspecies, often called Ward's great blue heron) are a major predator on alligator hatchlings; and commercial collectors soon learned that such hatchlings were dispersed chiefly over those lakes in which many of the herons were to be seen. A nocturnal visit to these lakes would usually be profitable, far more profitable than a visit to some lake that was not frequented by herons at this season. How different is this situation from the imaginary one supplied by most authors, who depict each brood as being safely ensconced in the mother's "den," a veritable reptilian nursery, for a year or more.

This is not to say that alligator hatchlings are ignored at all times by the adults. As mentioned in Chapter 2, a hatchling will voice a distress call when seized by some enemy; an adult will charge in the direction of the call, and attack the enemy if it does not flee. But such behavior is not to be called "maternal" or "parental," for the distress call attracts any adult that hears it.

The young alligator can make two similar but nonetheless distinguishable calls, in addition to a hiss. For convenience, one of these calls may be termed the juvenile grunt; the other, louder and higher-pitched, is the distress call. The vocalizing of a young alligator can be puzzling, but is clarified by the concept of behavioral "thresholds." Any given action of an alligator is not to be regarded as the result of forethought, of intelligent selection between alternatives, or of any other reasoning process. Rather, such an action is a well-nigh automatic response to a stimulus which may be internal (physiological) or external (environmental). Some responses are not easily triggered, being activated only by a certain strong and appropriate stimulus. A response of this kind is said to have a high threshold. Other responses are so easily triggered that they may be activated not only by a weak stimulus but sometimes by any one of a variety of stimuli. A response of this kind is said to have a low threshold. A low-threshold reaction may on occasion even be triggered uselessly, by some inappropriate stimulus. The juvenile grunt of the alligator is a response with a very low threshold. If many hatchling alligators are penned together, the listener will probably hear one or several of them grunting at irregular intervals. In such cases, the grunting is usually stimulated by a sound, often a sound so distant that the listener scarcely noted it. The slamming of a car door, the barking of a dog, the high-pitched squeal of a child at play—these are among the sounds that have been noted to evoke a grunt from a young alligator. However, a visual stimulus will also evoke the grunting response from a small alligator, which may vocalize when the observer moves. A nearby, heavy footfall may set off the grunting response, and so may the distant, earth-shaking rumble of heavy machinery. A little alligator may occasionally grunt if it has difficulty in scrambling over or among obstacles on the floor of its pen. The grunt of one juvenile may stimulate another to grunt. Small alligators, well adjusted to captivity and accustomed to being fed, often begin to grunt while rushing toward food as it is placed in their pen.

The impulse to grunt develops shortly before the alligator is ready to hatch. Perhaps tight confinement within the egg shell stimulates an un-hatched alligator to grunt; or the stirring of a foetus, somewhere in the compact mass of eggs, might stimulate another foetus; and conceivably, the grunting of one foetus might evoke a similar response from another. Jarring of the ground by the observer's footfall is yet another possible stimulus to foetal grunting. The juvenile grunt, as given by a hatchling, does not attract a nearby alligator. (This observation may bolster the belief that the female is not stimulated to open the nest when the eggs are ready to hatch.) The literature provides some absurdly anthropomorphic explanations of the ju-venile grunt, such as that the young alligator is expressing contentment, announcing its presence to the world, saying hello, and so on. The grunt probably functions to keep adults alerted to the nearby presence and approximate whereabouts of the young. The literature on animal behavior provides a number of instances in which an organism reacts to a certain stimulus not by any overt movement but by a heightened awareness. And there is nothing remarkable in the development, shortly before hatching, of a response that becomes useful shortly after hatching.

The literature also asserts that the mother alligator answers her grunt-ing brood with a similar grunt, and leads them in a parade around a lake. But as noted in Chapter 2, this was originally a Bartramian fantasy, and was enlarged by later legend-mongers. Not only do broods disperse rapidly after hatching, but the adult alligator, regardless of sex, does not voice either the juvenile grunt or the distress call. When an alligator reaches a length of about 4 feet, it ceases to grunt, or to "shriek" when seized, and begins to bellow for the first time. Concomitantly, some other behavior patterns of the alligator change completely. Grunting and shrieking in distress are pre-pubertal activities of the alligator, activities lost with the attainment of sexual maturity. When an alligator becomes an adult, and loses the impulse to voice the distress call, it develops the impulse to react to the distress call of another and younger individual.

Although the grunting of the juvenile alligator is an activity that has a very low threshold, the voicing of the distress call is an activity with a very high threshold. Nothing will stimulate the juvenile to give the distress call except actual seizure, and rough painful seizure at that. Many living things go through certain defensive actions only when seized roughly, perhaps actually hurt, as though by the teeth or claws of some predator. The alliga-tor's distress call, louder and sharper than the grunt, is given over and over again in rapid succession. The young alligator continues to shriek as long as it is under attack. Adult alligators, if not rendered unnaturally shy by man's activities, are galvanized into activity by the distress call. The action of an adult alligator in response to the juvenile's distress call is not a ritual confrontation but a true attack; and the would-be predator is bitten if it does not flee.

The distress call is doubly useful. In many organisms—various birds, frogs, salamanders, and rodents, for example—the adult emits a shrill cry when seized by a predator. It has been shown that this shriek alone will sometimes disconcert the predator, and cause it to drop its prey, which therefore has at least a chance to escape. In like fashion, some predators might be disconcerted by the surprising cry of a juvenile alligator. And the cry may attract an adult alligator, against which the usual predator would not or could not stand. Observations on frogs draw attention to a third possible function of a distress call. As is well known, frogs often set up a noisy chorus in or near some body of water. (Frog choruses are mating calls, and as such have no counterpart among crocodilians.) The field herpetologist in his nocturnal ramblings may encounter a chorus of bullfrogs around the border of a lake, and may wish to gather a few specimens for scientific or gastronomic purposes. If he secures the frogs with a gig (a multi-pronged spear), and one of them voices the loud, screaming distress call of the adult bullfrog, the other adults usually cease their mating calls, settle lower in the water, and suddenly become very difficult to approach. In this case, then, the distress call of one frog alerts others to the nearby presence of danger, and increases their wariness. It is not known whether the distress call of one juvenile alligator alerts other juveniles that happen to be in hearing range, but the possibility exists.

The action of the adult alligator in responding to the distress call of the young should not be likened to any human action; nor should it be described in a phraseology that suggests the linking of two alligators, respectively large and small, by some emotional bond. The behavior patterns of reptiles, as much as their anatomical characters, are to be viewed as adaptations that have evolved because they are favorable to the survival of the species. Even if the juvenile alligator were invariably killed by the predator before the adult alligator reached the spot, the action of the adult would be of survival value to the species; for the predator would be killed or driven away before it could attack other juvenile alligators in the vicinity. Also, some predators are known to avoid a certain kind of prey after having had an unpleasant experience with it; and a narrow escape from an adult alligator might cause a predator to stay away from small alligators in the future.

The adult's reaction to the distress call is the only direct interaction between adult and juvenile alligators. Except when reacting to the distress call, the adults ignore the juveniles completely, as far as one can judge from overt responses of the adult. Juveniles will occasionally crawl up on the snout or back of an adult, just as though it were a log (Fig. 12). There is no truth to the absurdly contradictory assertions that the young alligators are fed by their "mother" and preyed upon by their "father." An adult alligator, male or female, perhaps because it is already replete, will sometimes lie for hours with prey in its mouth, and under such conditions the nibbling of hatchlings at the prey might be ignored. But such an episode would be mere happenstance, and most unusual, too, for the examination of alligator stomach contents reveals the food of the juveniles to differ considerably from that of the adults. Even more unusual would be predation of an adult alligator, male or female, upon any juvenile in the wild. Feeding habits of the alligator are described in the next chapter.

16 THE FOOD
OF THE ALLIGATOR

THE FOOD of the alligator is another subject that has been treated very unscientifically in the literature. Almost every aspect of the alligator's feeding behavior has been subject to misinterpretation, and even the tabulation of alligator stomach contents has obscured the situation rather than clarified it.

The feeding habits of any reptile might be studied from several different standpoints. First, one might consider the food items that will be accepted in captivity. Certain foods that are not encountered in the wild will nonetheless be accepted in captivity by many reptilian species. For example, a captive ratsnake has been persuaded to eat hamburger, and a green anole to accept crumbs of chocolate cake. A captive alligator will eat meat of various kinds available in the butcher shop but not in the swamps and marshes. Like many other reptiles, a captive alligator may become accustomed to a certain feeding routine, a set procedure during which it is offered some fairly natural item of food; and under such conditions, it may also accept an unnatural item if this is proffered in the accustomed way. As an illustration, a Florida tourist attraction encourages its visitors to throw marshmallows to penned alligators, which take the confections as though they were pieces of meat. Thus, the feeding behavior of alligators in captivity gives no more than a rough idea of what foods would be accepted in the wild.

Observations in captivity may occasionally reveal an interesting refusal on the part of some reptile species to accept a certain kind of food. In peninsular Florida, garfishes are often unpopular with man. Two species of garfishes, the long-nosed gar and the Florida spotted gar, are commonly seined or otherwise removed from many bodies of water. Thus, at times large quantities of dead gars are available as food for captive alligators. If Florida spotted gars are thrown to penned alligators, the reptiles promptly seize the fish and eat them; but long-nosed gars, thrown to the same alligators, are refused. Usually the alligators recognize and reject long-nosed gars even before biting them. If, as occasionally happens, an alligator bites down on a long-nosed gar, the reptile immediately relinquishes its jaw-grip, and the fish is left to float uneaten about the pen. Interestingly, the Seminole Indians of the Florida Everglades eat the spotted but not the long-nosed gar, which they say is poisonous. Some gars are known to have poisonous roe.

On one occasion, I kept a black caiman, a spectacled caiman, and an American alligator together in a pen. The three reptlies, all juveniles, were fed cut pieces of beef and chicken wings chopped in a fashion to leave some bits of bone. All three crocodilians rapidly learned to recognize some aspect of the feeding procedure. They would dash to the plate of food as soon as it was offered, seizing and bolting the bits of meat. Knowing that crocodilians will eat fishes, once I interspersed the bits of meat with dabs of cat food, a strong-smelling, paste-like substance made from fishes. But not one dab of cat food was touched. All three of the crocodilians, in spite of their hasty gobbling, selected and ate only the chunks of meat. I suspect that it was the texture of the cat food that repelled the crocodilians. At any rate, the situation reveals crocodilians, including the alligator, to have certain fixed attitudes toward potential foods. Although a considerable number of items are accepted, other items are automatically rejected even when proffered under circumstances most favorable toward their ingestion. In most cases we do not know what triggers the acceptance or the rejection response, but at least we can see the undesirability of assuming, in the absence of direct and unequivocal evidence, that any particular organism is preyed upon by the alligator in nature.

Fresh problems emerge when we come to consider the kinds of food that would be taken by an alligator in the wild. Innate responses to potential food, the automatic impulses to accept or to reject any particular item, might be about the same in all alligators. Yet, alligators in a Louisiana marsh might in practice have a very different diet from that of alligators in a Georgia swamp, simply because these two geographic areas harbor different assemblages of prey species. The local abundance and availability of some particular prey organism should have much to do with the presence of that organism in stomachs of alligators.

The food of wild alligators is best determined from examination and identification of stomach contents. In his 1929 article, R. Kellogg listed the food items thus found in 157 stomachs. I center the discussion around Kellogg's article because it was more detailed than most accounts of the alligator's feeding habits, and because it has been widely quoted by later writers. Of the alligators whose stomachs were opened, 146 were from Louisiana, the others from southwestern Georgia or northern Florida. From Kellogg's tables of alligator stomach contents, it would seem that the alligator's feeding habits in Louisiana were remarkably different from those in Georgia and Florida. The more easterly alligators seemingly had been feeding largely upon vertebrates, especially fishes, aquatic turtles, and aquatic snakes; the more westerly alligators, although they had eaten some vertebrates, apparently had relied heavily upon invertebrate prey. Thus, the data at first glance suggest geographic variation in the alligator's feeding habits, perhaps reflecting regional differences in the availability of certain prey items. But unfortunately, not much information was given about the size of the alligators that were killed and opened. If the Louisiana specimens were mostly small ones, and if the few Georgia-Florida specimens were larger ones, the apparent regional difference in feeding habits might actually reflect no more than the tendency of larger alligators to take larger prey (most invertebrates being smaller than the fishes, waterfowl, turtles, and other vertebrates that fall prey to larger alligators). Later in this chapter, some comments will be offered about the effect of local ecology on the alligator's diet. But at this point it suffices to say that from mere tabulation of stomach contents one cannot decide why Louisiana alligators, much more than Georgia-Florida ones, had managed to ingest a variety of invertebrates.

Furthermore, various statements by Kellogg concerning the relative frequency which certain organisms are preyed upon have been interpreted in different ways by different authors. There might at first seem nothing unequivocal in the statement that, for example, "shrimps comprised 2.59 per cent of the total food" recovered from the 157 alligator stomachs. But what is meant by the figure of "2.59 per cent"? Does it mean that 2.59 per cent of the examined stomachs contained at least one shrimp? Or does it mean that when all individual prey items were counted, 2.59 per cent of the total were shrimp? Or that shrimp made up 2.59 per cent of the weight of the food? Although Kellogg's mathematics cannot be followed, clearly he was not concerned with proportionate weight of food items, and seemingly his percentages relate to the total of individual prey items. This approach led to an oft-quoted generalization: "The food of the alligator is made up chiefly of crustaceans (47 per cent), fishes, turtles, and other vertebrates (29 per cent), and insects and spiders (23 per cent), consisting for the most part of crabs, crawfishes, turtles, and water beetles." Such a generalization is not very meaningful, even when accomplished by an explanation of the way in which the percentages were computed. If a given series of stomachs contained, say, 15 crayfishes and 15 watersnakes, then crayfishes and watersnakes would make up equal percentages of the total food items found in the stomachs. But one watersnake might easily provide an alligator with 200 times as much nourishment as one crayfish would provide, and it could not be concluded that watersnakes and crayfishes were equally important in the diet of the alligator. Also, it could happen (and did happen in the case of the aforesaid shrimp) that one alligator contained many individuals of some prey organism. The percentage value assigned to that organism would therefore reflect the atypical feeding habits of one alligator, not the typical feeding habits of the alligator as a species.

There is an even more serious objection to Kellogg's data and the customary interpretations thereof. Not until 1956 was the concept of "secondary ingestion" introduced into the herpetological literature, and the concept has been slow to spread to those writers who deal with the alligator's feeding habits. The concept and its significance are easily explained. Imagine a reptile species that is psychologically adapted to catch, and physiologically adapted to digest, the frogs with which it is associated. The stomach of a frog usually contains, and is frequently packed with, various insects such as beetles and ants. When this reptile eats a frog, it also "secondarily ingests" the invertebrates on which the frog had preyed. The frog's flesh is quickly digested by the reptile, but not so the secondarily ingested invertebrates. The integument of an insect is composed of a substance called chitin; and this substance is relatively indigestible, at least by reptiles that feed primarily on vertebrates. In a short while, the reptile's digestive fluids will have dissolved the frog, or at least rendered its remains unidentifiable; but the beetles and ants will still be in excellent condition, identifiable to species in many cases.

The aforesaid chain of predation—frog upon insects, reptile upon frog— is cited because it is a particularly common one in nature. But of course other chains could similarly cause a predator to ingest, secondarily, some item that it would normally ignore, and that it could not readily digest. A pygmy rattlesnake eats a mud salamander, which in turn had crammed down a big centipede; an indigo snake eats a gopher-frog that chanced to be full of ground-beetles; a coachwhip snake engulfs a racerunner lizard, which had been eating spiders; a great blue heron catches a fish that had gorged on water beetles and dragonfly larvae; a snapping turtle in a farm pond takes a duckling whose crop is stuffed with corn. Secondary ingestion, although frequently ignored in the literature, must be very common in nature. The alligator is, of course, one predator that is especially likely to ingest many invertebrates secondarily; for the alligator gulps down its prey whole or in large chunks, and this prey includes fishes, frogs, turtles, and birds that are themselves often replete with insects, crayfishes, spiders, and other invertebrates.

On the basis of Kellogg's report, subsequent authors have concluded that the alligator was highly insectivorous. Certainly Kellogg reported a lengthy list of insects and other small invertebrates from the alligator stomachs that were examined. However, it is likely that most of the invertebrates were first eaten by a fish, frog, bird, or some other vertebrate, which in turn fell prey to an alligator. Alligator stomach contents were described as including one orb-weaver spider, many wolf-spiders, a roach, katydids and crickets, numerous ground beetles, a ladybird beetle, a darkling beetle, many dung-beetles and leaf-chafers, a cloverstem borer-beetle, a leaf-beetle and many weevils, a robber-fly, some kind of butterfly or moth, various ants, one bee, and one velvet-ant, among others. I believe an entomologist would agree that these invertebrates—arboreal, cursorial, secretive, or aerial species, in the main—are not likely to be taken as prey by an alligator, which forages in the water. These invertebrates are, however, the natural prey of certain frogs and birds, both of which are eaten by the alligator. Kellogg's list of stomach contents also included aquatic insects such as stonefly larvae, dragonfly nymphs, water-striders, back-swimmers, giant water-bugs, soldier-fly larvae, predaceous diving-beetles, and water-scavenger beetles. Some of these insects, perhaps all of them, could have been eaten by fishes, frogs, birds, or turtles, which in turn fell prey to alligators. In short, Kelogg's list does not support the conclusions that have often been based on it.

Now to review some of the organisms that reached alligator stomachs probably through direct predation, not secondary ingestion. Among the fishes are the Florida spotted gar, alligator gar, bowfin, bugfish, buttercat, tadpole madtom, sheepshead killifish, sailfin molly, glass minnow, striped mullet, largemouth bass, and redbelly. It must not be supposed that these are all eaten in equal quantity by the alligator, which does not often catch fast-moving, alert fishes. In marshlands fishes often aggregate by the hundreds in 'gator-holes during periods of dry weather. And if the water table continues to fall, many of these fishes die, probably because the oxygen supply of the water becomes depleted. Under such conditions, sunfishes and largemouth bass are the first to die, and their dead bodies probably would be eaten by any alligators that existed in the same hole. Also, in the alligator's range it is not unusual for large quantities of leaves and other plant debris to be blown by hurricane winds or washed by torrential rains into lakes and streams. Sometimes the decay of this plant material greatly lowers the oxygen content of the water, and the result is a massive fish-kill with mortality especially heavy among the sunfishes, basses, and other species that require well-oxygenated water. As a matter of fact, through forces of nature or the activities of man, a few sick, injured, or dead fishes are likely to be available to the alligator as food in almost any body of water.

Frogs taken by the alligator include the pig-frog, bullfrog, leopard frog, Florida cricket-frog, green treefrog, and narrow-mouthed frog. The last-named species is terrestrial as an adult, and breeds mostly in rainwater puddles, thus not often falling prey to the alligator, which usually forages in more nearly permanent bodies of water. (When a small alligator swallows a narrow-mouthed frog, the reptile is almost certain to ingest secondarily a number of ants, for ants are the principal food of the narrow-mouth.) The green treefrog usually lives in vegetation above water, but it is exceedingly common almost everywhere that alligators are to be found, and it must enter the water at least for breeding. So it is not surprising that an occasional green treefrog falls prey to an alligator. (The stomach of the green treefrog is often packed with spiders, along with flying and leaf-dwelling insects.) In Florida, the pig-frog is an important food item of the alligator. Tadpoles of the pig-frog, large tads nearly ready for transformation to the adult stage, are taken with great frequency by alligators up to about 4 feet long. Adult pig-frogs are also preyed upon. Several aquatic salamanders, large and small, coexist with the alligator, but are not known to be eaten by it. Various salamanders, of species that are largely terrestrial when adult, give off a highly astringent slime when molested. The slime is known to discourage some predators, and a captive alligator will not accept one of these salamanders as food. Perhaps the aquatic salamanders are similarly unpalatable.

The alligator preys heavily on other reptiles, especially turtles. Turtles eaten by the alligator include the mud turtle, loggerhead musk turtle, diamondback terrapin, Barbour's map turtle, Florida turtle, Florida red-bellied

Figure 79. The longnosed garfish (at right) is not eaten by the alligator, although other species of garfishes are. The striped swampsnake (at left) feeds on crayfishes; and so an alligator, eating a swampsnake, might secondarily ingest crayfish remains. [Louisiana Tourist Commission and Ross Allen's Reptile Institute]

Figure 80. *The green watersnake,*
shown here, feeds on the pig-frog
(at top); both species fall prey to the
alligator. [Ross Allen's Reptile
Institute]

Figure 81. *The Florida turtle (upper) and*
the Florida softshell (lower) are often
eaten by the alligator [W. T. Neill]

turtle, yellow-bellied turtle, and Florida softshell. Snakes eaten by the alligator include the Florida green watersnake, Gulf saltmarsh snake, broad-banded watersnake, Florida watersnake, banded watersnake, striped swamp-snake, and ribbon snake. All of these are nonvenomous snakes that live about the water. A captive alligator, kept in fairly natural surroundings, would eat the cottonmouth moccasin, a venomous snake frequently associated with the alligator in both swamps and marshes. Although a water-snake and a cottonmouth are superficially similar, the alligator distinguishes between the two, and attacks each in a different fashion. The nonvenomous watersnake is simply seized and devoured; but the venomous cottonmouth is bitten, tossed, and thrown about before it is consumed.

Figure 82. The venomous cottonmouth moccasin, shown here, is sometimes eaten by the alligator. [Ross Allen's Reptile Institute]

Figure 83. A large alligator gulps down a nonvenomous indigo snake. [W. T. Neill]

Species of lizards found within the alligator's range are not aquatic. Usually they enter water only through accident or the desperate avoidance of a predator. Thus, little significance can be attached to a few records of lizards (the ground skink and the green anole) in alligator stomachs.

Authors have been much taken with the idea that large alligators eat small ones. However, the alligator is far less cannibalistic than, say, man and some of his domestic animals. Very rarely does one alligator eat another even under the crowded and otherwise unnatural conditions of captivity. If in nature the remains of one alligator have been found in the stomach of another, the circumstance probably reflects carrion-eating. Alligators do not identify other organisms or objects by their form or shape;

and it is likely that a decomposing alligator would soon lose its original scent or other identifying characteristic. If a few alligator scutes are found in an alligator's stomach, they should probably be interpreted as gastroliths. Every dead alligator leaves behind a large number of bony and well-nigh indestructible scutes; and these, falling usually to a lake or stream bottom, are available for ingestion as gastroliths by living alligators.

Birds taken by the alligator include the pied-billed grebe, least bittern, mottled duck, king rail, coot, barred owl, and boat-tailed grackle. Various authors devote a disproportionately large amount of space to supposed predation on ducks by the alligator. Most ducks of North America are migratory birds, breeding and summering well north of the alligator's range. They arrive within that range only after the weather has turned cool, and after most alligators have gone into hibernation. Along the southern edge of the alligator's range, this reptile does feed, albeit sparingly, at a season when some migratory ducks are present in the swamps and marshes. However, throughout the alligator's active season in most parts of the range the only ducks present in any numbers are the mottled duck (of Florida, southern Georgia, and a coastal belt of Louisiana and Texas) and the wood duck (widespread in eastern North America). Actual predation on the wood duck has not been reported. The horned grebe and the short-eared owl have been reported as food of the alligator; but both of these birds arrive in the alligator's range during the winter, and are not likely to fall prey to the alligator except on rare occasions. I have seen alligators in the water beneath a rookery of little blue herons, and suppose the reptiles would eat anything that fell into the water from the nests, be it a nestling or a fish regurgitated by a parent bird. Sportsmen who shoot birds around marshes report that a dead bird is sometimes seized by an alligator before it can be retrieved; but little significance can be attached to such reports, for the same kinds of birds in life might consistently elude alligators.

Mammals taken by the alligator include the rice rat, cotton rat, cotton mouse, muskrat, round-tailed water-rat, Norway rat, marsh rabbit, swamp rabbit, and mink. There are a few records of predation on the coypu, or nutria, a troublesome aquatic rodent that has spread widely in the Gulf States after initial introduction (from South America) by E. A. McIlhenny. Domestic dogs are eaten by the alligator, but not as frequently as rustics usually assert. Dogs are usually taken while they are swimming. Hogs have also been reported in the diet of the alligator. In one case, a hog pen was enclosed on three sides only, the fourth side opening into a cypress pond of considerable extent; and one night a large alligator took a hog from the pen. The next night I found a large alligator lying in a nearby and much smaller cypress pond; it was still holding in its jaws the uneaten carcass of the hog. In the southeastern United States, hogs are often penned where they can root and wallow in the wet ground beside a body of water; and I suspect that most hogs, taken by an alligator, were penned under such conditions. Troops of feral hogs, so common in parts of the Southeast, are not often menaced by alligators, but I know of one case in which a wild hog was caught by a large alligator. Several times during the day, this reptile was seen with the dead hog in its jaws.

There are records of alligator predation on cattle. Today, of course, an alligator is usually killed before it grows large enough to take such prey. Cattlemen in Florida have commonly urged the extinction of the alligator, holding it to be a frequent predator on cows and calves; but of course such people, fearing for their livestock, are sometimes inclined to over-emphasize the frequency of such predation. Also, in some areas there is much cattle "rustling" (often by truck in this mechanized age), and in such areas it is possible to find people who are anxious to blame alligators for the decimation of a nearby cattle herd. From personal experience I know of one instance in which cattle were actually taken by a large alliga-tor. Following the prohibition of "open range" in Florida, an enormous tract of land was fenced as a cattle ranch. There were no large bodies of water on the tract, but many small sinkhole ponds. Into these ponds the cattle often waded belly-deep to munch water hyacinths and perhaps to keep cool. A large alligator lived on this tract, and occasionally pulled down a cow or a calf. Interestingly, the reptile never remained long in one sinkhole. It frequently moved from one pond to another, leaving its tracks in the mud. This alligator was eventually captured alive, and proved to measure a few inches under 12 feet in total length. There are a few early and possibly reliable records of alligator attacks on horses and mules. Preda-tion on man is a topic for the next chapter.

In various species of living things, marked sexual dimorphism in size is an adaptation that reduces the degree to which adult males and adult females must compete with each other for food. This is probably the case with the alligator, also. Large items of prey, such as hogs and cattle, are taken by very large alligators. These latter are usually males, for ten feet is close to a maximum length for female alligators, and females even of this size are not often encountered in captivity or in the wild. It is true that in modern times domestic animals have been about the only large prey that was readily available to well-grown male alligators. However, not long ago (geologically and biologically speaking), the Coastal Plain of the south-eastern United States harbored giant ground sloths, a giant tortoise-arma-dillo, a giant beaver, capybaras, a mastodon, mammoth elephants, horses, a tapir, peccaries, camels, and the long-horned bison, in addition to many large, predaceous mammals such as a dire-wolf, true wolves, a short-faced bear, the black bear, a grizzly-like bear, a puma, a jaguar, a giant jaguar-like cat, and a saber-tooth. Up until the end of the Pleistocene, large male alligators probably had much large prey available to them.

Returning to the alligator's food in modern times, I do not doubt that alligators, especially small ones, will take crayfishes. Nevertheless, crayfish remains must often arrive in an alligator's stomach as a result of secondary ingestion, for these invertebrates are fed upon by certain fishes, frogs, turtles, and birds that are in turn fed upon by alligators. In other words, in any given area the alligators do not feed directly on crayfishes as often as would be suggested by the uncritical tabulation of stomach contents. Perhaps a small alligator, when foraging on the bottom in shallow water, would occa-sionally take a dragonfly larva or a giant water-bug. In captivity hatchling alligators will accept crickets and roaches if these are tossed into the water where they kick and struggle; and so it is likely that small alligators in nature will take some insects. However, I have known young alligators, fed in captivity only on crickets and roaches, to die because the digestive tract was blocked with the undigested, chitinous bodies of these insects; and I do not think that the alligator, at any age, is supported to any important degree by insect prey.

A few other organisms might be added to the list of the alligator's prey if all the early writings were credenced. However, most of the early works are a mélange. In reading them, one cannot separate the actual ob-servations from the folk fallacies and the literary embellishments. Perhaps I should have rejected a larger portion of the literature relating to the alli-gator's prey. In any event, not much importance can be attached to alli-gator predation on species that are lacking at most times from the alliga-tor's range or habitat. What is needed is a list of the organisms that provide most of the food for the alligator. On such a list I would place garfishes (except the long-nosed gar); catfishes (but not the channel catfish, a fast-swimming fish of the rivers); the pig-frog, both tadpoles and adults; the Florida turtle, yellow-bellied turtle, and Florida red-bellied turtle; the Florida softshell; and the Florida, the banded, and the broad-banded watersnakes (all of them geographic races of a single species). Less frequently taken, but perhaps important food at restricted times and places, are the bowfin, bullfrog, Florida green watersnake, mud turtle, and coot. Carrion is eaten whenever it is available. Crayfishes may be eaten in small numbers by young alligators, but better evidence of such predation is needed. Secondary ingestion is responsible for some of the crayfishes, and almost all of the insects and spiders, that are found in alligator stomachs. Very large alligators will take livestock, and may have taken other large game in past ages.

In short, the alligator seems for the most part to be a predator on vertebrates. Given the opportunity, the alligator might take a wide selection of vertebrates; but in practice it usually catches slow-moving vertebrates that live in the water, or that often venture into the water from nearby land or vegetation. Alert and agile vertebrates do not often appear in the alligator's diet, nor do aquatic vertebrates that are highly characteristic of flowing water (as opposed to still water).

Kellogg and others provide a good bit of information about organisms that are ingested, primarily or secondarily, by the alligator in extreme southern Louisiana. This area is very low, sloping gently toward the sea, and within it there is a broad zone where fresh and salt waters intermingle in complex fashion. Normal tides, storm tides, and vagaries of rainfall frequently bring about changes in the salinity of the water. The ecological situation results in an unusual commingling of freshwater and brackish-water organisms. More to the point, the ecological situation in extreme southern Louisiana brings the alligator into contact with various organisms that are lacking from most other parts of its range. Shrimp, fiddler crabs, Sesarma crabs, blue crabs, and pipefishes are at times available in this area for the alligator to prey upon, take as carrion, or ingest secondarily as the case may be. On the other hand, the occasional encroachment of brackish water tends to exclude from this area certain fishes, frogs, snakes, and turtles upon which the alligator feeds in other parts of its range. The present account of the alligator's diet is not especially concerned with highly localized peculiarities thereof; but it seems desirable to emphasize the unusual nature of the ecological situation in southern Louisiana because that area has provided much of the available information about the alligator's feeding habits.

Kellogg reported a fine selection of gastrolithic material from alligator stomachs: pebbles, stones, gravel, sand, cinders, shotgun shells, cartridge cases, and a fragment of clamshell. He also reported a small quantity of vegetable debris from alligator stomachs. Some of this debris—burnt wood, hickory nutshells, sweetgum balls, and the rock-hard seeds of the lotus—was probably ingested as gastroliths. Other seeds could have been ingested secondarily, or accidentally as the reptile bit down upon some prey that was hiding in aquatic vegetation. In Florida, alligator stomachs often include fragmentary blades of eelgrass and of a submersed Sagittaria, plants that form "meadows" on the bottom of large spring-runs. The Florida turtle and the Florida red-bellied turtle (both largely vegetarian) graze in these underwater meadows; the mud turtle and the bowfin often hide there. It is probable that alligators accidentally ingest the blades of eelgrass and Sagittaria while snapping at turtles and fishes. On one occasion, masses of these aquatic plants were dumped into an alligator pen along with chunks of meat, and the alligators were not averse to consuming some of the plant material along with the meat. Alligators occasionally bite at floating clumps of water hyacinth, but are probably stimulated to do so by the scent or actual presence of a small food animal in the clump. The intentional ingestion of plant material as food is regarded as improbable, for biochemical studies have revealed the alligator to be incapable of digesting carbohydrates such as starches, sugars, and cellulose.

The chapter will close with remarks on the methods whereby alligators procure food. When a man elects physically to attack an enemy or some prey, he makes little use of his mouth. Instead, he uses his arms, striking a blow with the hand, the clenched fist, or some instrument. Perhaps this is why some people, even biologists who should know better, have been perfectly willing to accept the absurd notion that an alligator uses its tail to club prey, or to bat some prey into its mouth. One could as easily accept the idea that a lion charges rump-foremost at a gazelle. The exceptionally powerful jaws and formidable dentition are located on the front end of the reptile, not the hind. The same is true of the sense organs whereby the alligator finds prey and identifies it, and whereby it must determine, often in less than a second, the precise location of an animal that will try to make off the instant it spots an attacker.

Furthermore, man usually locates the exact position of any object, including an item of prey, by seeing it; and he usually identifies the item by its shape. Thus, it has been all too easy for man to assume that other predators, including crocodilians, locate and identify prey in the same fashion. Actually, there is no reason to believe that any reptile has the mental ability to identify any motionless object by form alone. In general, the reptilian predator may (depending on species) react to movement, sound, vibration, body heat, taste, or scent produced by the prey .

In capturing food, young alligators make little use of vision. Identification of prey is made by sense organs that are located along the sides of the alligator's snout. It would not be amiss to say that the alligator can taste with the sides of its snout. In man, organs of taste are concentrated on parts of the tongue and inner surfaces of the mouth; but this need not be so among lower vertebrates, some of which have the taste organs concentrated outside the mouth, for example on fleshy barbels or along the sides of the body. When foraging, the young alligator rotates the head so that one side of the snout is in contact with the substratum. As the reptile moves along, it sweeps the side of the snout in arcs over the substratum. Even a tiny bit of food is promptly identified, and the reptile takes the food into the side of the mouth. This method of foraging is used when the reptile is completely submerged, when it is in the shallows near the edge of the water, or when it is completely out of water. I have never known young alligators to forage out of water in the wild, but in captivity they are easily encouraged to do so. When a young captive alligator is fed chunks of meat on a plate, the reptile does not bite directly at any chunk, even though this food may lie a mere fraction of an inch away from the reptile's jaws. Instead, the alligator sweeps the side of the snout in arcs across the plate, seizing any chunk of meat only after the side of the snout has touched it.

Evidently the young alligator's taste organs are very sensitive. If the reptile happens to touch, with the side of its snout, some water to which a minute amount of blood has been added, the foraging reaction is immediately evoked from the reptile; the side of the snout is promptly swept back and forth across the substratum while the alligator crawls about.

Figure 84. Pimple-like protuberances along the edge of the alligator's upper and lower jaw are probably organs of taste. [Ross Allen's Reptile Institute]

In captivity a young alligator learns a feeding procedure with remarkable rapidity. If the reptile has been fed about three times, its reaction to the arrival of the observer will depend on whether or not the latter brings food. If he does not, the reptile will remain motionless or else will retreat; but if he brings a plate of food, the reptile will rush over to the plate almost before the observer can set it down and withdraw his hand. The foregoing remarks relate to small alligators that are properly penned and disturbed as seldom as possible. Pitiful little "pet" alligators, kept in a tub of chilly water and snatched up at frequent intervals, are more likely to languish and die than to reveal any characteristic behavior patterns of the species. It is suspected that the feeding behavior of the alligator in the wild is conditioned by early experiences, the young reptile having an innate impulse to repeat any foraging procedure that has proven successful. Little is known about the early conditioning of feeding behavior in any animal; but in the young alligator, the ease of such conditioning in captivity suggests comparable conditioning in the wild.

I know of one instance in which young alligators seemed to have learned, in the wild, a certain technique of foraging. In southeastern Georgia there was a milldam lake which had been enlarged and deepened, within historic times, by the collapse of underlying limestone. This lake, which I often visited, once harbored a few large alligators and many small ones. The grist mill at the edge of the lake was infested with rats, which subsisted for the most part on cornmeal. Well after dark, when human disturbance had ceased, the rats would scamper and chase each other over the mill's walls, often falling into the lake. In the water there were also likely to be one or two dead rats shot by the miller during the day. Almost every night in the warmer part of the year, several small alligators about 3 to 4 feet long would swim over to the millhouse. Here they would lie beneath its walls and seize any rat that fell into the water. They would also make off with dead rats. It is possible that the alligators were drawn to the millhouse by the smell of rats, living or dead. However, I think it more likely that an alligator, at first foraging randomly around the lake shore, and having taken a rat or two at the millhouse, would develop an impulse to hunt again in the area where food had been obtained. Interestingly, the larger alligators in this lake never came near the millhouse; they stayed in the opposite end of the lake where human disturbance was limited to an occasional fisherman.

In captivity when one young alligator begins to feed, others are stimulated to do the same. Even an alligator that has been refusing food for one cause or another will often be stimulated to feed if another one begins to do so. There is obvious survival value to a behavior pattern whereby the feeding of one stimulates that of another; for if one young alligator happens on or has been conditioned to seek out some particular kind of food, other young alligators may have their attention drawn to a locally available food resource. Incidentally, this behavior pattern is not peculiar to crocodilians, but is widespread among vertebrates. There is a good bit of truth to the old German saying that if a pig is penned alone it will never grow fat.

The alligator has some impulse to move toward another organism that is itself moving, or splashing water. However, the impulse is weak in small alligators, and understandably so; for the little reptile is itself preyed upon by various fishes, frogs, reptiles, birds, and mammals, and the alligator as a species would not have profited through the evolution of a behavior pattern that led the young automatically to investigate any disturbance in the water. Larger alligators, relatively immune to predation, have a stronger impulse to investigate distant movement or splashing if they have not been frequently shot at. It is not known whether an alligator can detect and identify the air-borne scent of some distant prey. I have seen large alligators, swimming in the water, try to stalk some potential prey that was on land or in bushes as much as 5 feet from the water's edge; but it is not known whether the reptile's attention was drawn by the prey's scent.

Figure 85. The smaller of these alligators, a well-grown female, will never reach the size of the male with which she is penned. Larger size enables adult males to take larger prey. [Ross Allen's Reptile Institute]

17 ALLIGATOR
ATTACKS ON MAN

ALTHOUGH SELDOM perturbed to any great degree by his own internecine activities, man is much aroused on those rare occasions when he himself falls prey to some lower animal. The importance of such occasions could easily be overemphasized. In discussing alligator attacks on man, I should like to note at the outset that this reptile is far less dangerous to man than is, say, the domestic dog. Rabid dogs, and even nonrabid ones, attack people far more often than do alligators; and the same can be said of domestic cattle and hogs. Alligator predation on man would not in fact merit lengthy discussion were not the literature so confused and contradictory in its treatment of the subject.

Some of the early writers regarded the alligator as dangerous to man, quick to attack anyone who stood on the bank or ventured into the water. Yet, other early writers took the opposite view, regarding this reptile as harmless, even safe to swim with. Later authors have taken similarly opposing stands on the alligator's tendency to attack man. Up until about 1948, people who knew the alligator in the wild—I mean the naturalists and field biologists, not the locals who mistrust all animal life—considered the reptile to be harmless if let alone. Until the late 1940s I shared the general herpetological opinion that the alligator would not deliberately attack man; that reported attacks (when not apocryphal) reflected only the female alligator's defense of her nest, the response of an adult to the juvenile's distress cry,

Figure 86. An alligator uses its jaws, not its tail, to capture prey or confront an enemy. Here a large alligator lunges threateningly at a person who intrudes on its domain. [Ross Allen's Reptile Institute]

or mere self-defense by a cornered or injured alligator. But then, around 1949 and the early 1950s, we had to revise our opinions. In most parts of the alligator's range the situation remained unchanged; but from Oke-finokee Swamp to southern Florida the reptile seemed abruptly to become less afraid of man. At scattered localities within this area, an alligator would attack a person, or would venture into a garden to eat some outdoor goldfish or the family dog. In this extreme southeastern corner of its range, the alligator remained surprisingly bold for about a decade; then once again it seemed to become consistently afraid of man. In short, there is good evidence, from the events of recent years, that the alligator's reaction toward man can vary with time and with place. The earlier literature becomes more intelligible in the light of this evidence. It is probably that some of the early writers really did find the alligator to be a predator on man, and that other early writers, in different times or places, found this reptile much inclined to flee from man. But what determines, at any given time or place, the alligator's reaction to man?

I spent a total of nearly five years at various localities throughout the range of the estuarine crocodile, the most notorious "man-eater" among the crocodilians, and I found great variation, from place to place, in the reaction of this reptile toward the presence of man. In some areas it was unquestionably dangerous; it attacked a good many people, and no doubt would have attacked more had not the local residents been wary of venturing into the reptile's habitat. Yet, in other areas it was exceedingly shy, even the larger adults submerging and vanishing at the approach of man. The local behavior of the estuarine crocodile was predictable in advance. Where the local people were relatively primitive tribesmen, armed only with the spear or perhaps the bow and arrow, the reptile was dangerous. It would take man as quickly as it would any other prey of comparable size. The same situation prevailed in areas where the people were culturally more advanced, but for some reason not inclined to molest crocodiles. Yet, in localities where the people were well provided with firearms, and especially where crocodiles were hunted extensively, the reptiles were very shy of man, and even by night I could not paddle a boat to within close range of any crocodile, large or small. Like the gun-shy alligators called "blinkers," these crocodiles would submerge the moment a light was shined upon them. The behavior of the estuarine crocodile provides a clue, I believe, to the way in which we should interpret observations on the American alligator. Modern observations, as well as those of the more reliable early writers, are consistent with the interpretation that at times and places where alligators were extensively hunted they became shy; but when and where the alligators could grow to maturity with little or no molestation the larger ones would sometimes attack man. It is of interest to review some early and modern observations in the light of this interpretation.

Of course many early accounts purporting to describe alligator attacks on man must be discounted. For example, Mrs. Trollope's 1832 account (quoted in Chapter 2) is obviously apocryphal. Europeans wanted to read about the "ferocious saurian," and there were always some authors who would cater to this demand. A theme that runs through many early writings, and that lessens their credibility by its very repetition, is the alligator's supposed "preference" for Negroes as an item of food. This theme probably originated with the 1565 account of Sir John Hawkins, the slave trader. In that work, it was stated that ". . . a Negro, who as he was filling water in the river, was by one of them carried clean away, and never seen after." This episode, if not wholly a fabrication, took place outside the range of the alligator, and must have involved the American crocodile. But as previously noted, the two reptiles were not distinguished from each other at that time, and were thought to be nearly or quite identical with the Nile crocodile. Later accounts of the alligator were influenced by narratives of Hawkins's expeditions. In the influential 1687 work of Richard Blome, we read ". . . a servant to the Consul of Alexandria, going to take up one of them, thinking it had been a piece of wood, was suddenly seized on, and drawn by it to the bottom of the river, and never seen more." It is not clear whether Blome was drawing attention to an episode in Egypt, but in any event he was writing primarily about Jamaica (which harbors the American crocodile) and about what he called the "alligator."

The 1808 account of Thomas Ashe related that "Two men, one black and the other white, [went] into the water . . . to push of a boat which had got fast on a bar [in the Mississippi]. An alligator attacked the African, and drew him under water by the leg . . . and crushed his bones in the presence of the white man, whom he neither attacked or regarded." Ashe's comments were scientifically worthless, but they helped to mold the ideas of later writers. Adam Hodgson in 1824 wrote, "A gentleman from Florida, who lives on the River St. John, told me, that they often carried away Negroes while bathing, and that a female slave . . . had been recently carried off, when drawing water from the river." This hearsay statement, contradicted by actual observations on the St. Johns (see below), is useful only in tracing the growth and spread of a folk belief. Of course, if alligators were inclined, at any locality, to attack people during slavery days, it is not surprising that attacks were most frequently directed toward those individuals who had to fetch water from the streams and lakes, and who visited such places in order to wash themselves and their clothes. But in 1832 Timothy Flint stated of the alligator, "It is said, they will attack a Negro in the water, in preference to a white." And from J. H. Hinton, 1846: "It is said they will attack a Negro in the water in preference to a white."

Frederick Marryat, on his trip to the United States, was not favorably impressed with contemporary accounts of the alligator, and was moved to pen a short satire about this reptile. In 1839 he wrote of some gigantic alligators—"from seventeen to twenty-one feet long"—that had been kept alive at a museum. One of the reptiles, "preferring death to the loss of liberty, . . . committed suicide by throwing himself out of a three-story high window. He was taken up from the pavement the next morning; the vital spark had fled, as the papers say, and, I believe, his remains were decently interred." In this and other comments, Marryat was ridiculing the exaggerations and the anthropomorphisms that had colored most accounts of the alligator. And ridiculing the folk beliefs that were so commonly presented as fact, Marryat continued, "One [of the alligators], as a memorial, remains preserved in the museum, and to make him look more poetical, he has a stuffed Negro in his mouth." The old idea that the alligator is an especial menace to Negroes still exists, and visitors to Florida can find it illustrated by a variety of tastelessly conceived postcards sold at roadside shops.

The earlier writers also accepted the notion that an alligator attacks with its tail. Several early accounts, purporting to describe alligator predation on man, begin with a sentence much like this: "With a blow of its powerful tail, the alligator knocked the boy into its waiting jaws." A remark of this kind reveals that its author did not personally witness the supposed episode, and was not above penning folk belief as fact.

Most of the early writers emphasize that the alligator was especially likely to attack children. There was probably some truth to this idea. When a predator encounters another animal, the outcome of the confrontation commonly depends upon the size relationship of the two. If there is a great discrepancy in size, the two will probably ignore each other. (Note Fig. 12, in which a large alligator ignores the tiny fishes that swim near its jaws.) If there is somewhat less discrepancy, the predator may dispatch the other animal with a mere snap. (Note Fig. 83, in which a large alligator bites and swallows a nonvenomous snake.) If the other animal is large enough or dangerous enough to put up a good struggle, the predator attacks it in some stereotyped fashion, a fashion that has evolved because it has usually permitted successful predation. If the predator and the other animal would make well-matched adversaries, they will probably do no more than confront each other with ritualized postures, displays, or sounds; and one of the two will make off before blood is shed. (The cinema often portrays a bloody struggle between two animals, but such combats are "stage-managed"; the animals fight because they are penned together and goaded by man into unnatural frenzy. Most naturalists, field biologists, and experienced outdoorsmen, even those in the richest game country, have never seen an animal combat in the wild, beyond the killing of some prey species by one of its usual predators.) Finally, the predator itself will flee before the approach of some much larger animal. This is not to say that size relationship is the only factor determining the reaction of an alligator to some other animal, for we have already noted that this reptile eats one species of gar while rejecting another, and does not attack the venomous cottonmouth in the same way it attacks a nonvenomous watersnake. But the reaction of an alligator to another animal is always affected to some degree by the size relationship of the two, and this reaction is probably of paramount significance except in cases where the other animal is unusually noxious, or is dangerous out of all proportion to its size.

It must be emphasized that the alligator never evaluates or responds to the totality of any situation, but merely reacts automatically to some particular stimulus that is provided by that situation. It is almost an overstatement even to say that the alligator's actions are modified in accordance with the size of the animal it confronts. Apparently the reptile reacts not to the bulk but simply to the vertical height of another animal. The available data suggest that alligator attacks upon man, when not directed toward children, have been directed toward adults who were recumbent, kneeling, crouching, sitting, or swimming. There is no good evidence that an alligator has attempted to prey upon an adult person who was standing erect.

(Perhaps the grotesquely long necks of many dinosaurs functioned to deter predators; even the great carnivore Tyrannosaurus might have been disconcerted by a comparatively inoffensive sauropod dinosaur when the latter reared its head 25 feet in the air. Perhaps a modern iguanian lizard, rising to bipedal stance, appears four or five times "larger" to a predator. Perhaps to man's prehuman ancestors, the first advantage of an upright posture was its effect upon fearsome mammalian predators of that day.)

Let us note a few early observations on the alligator's attitude toward man as an item of prey. It is fairly certain that Réné-Robert Cavelier, the Sieur de la Salle, lost a member of his entourage to an alligator. One account mentioned, "the loss of La Salle's servant, Dumesnil, who was seized by an alligator while attempting to cross the Colorado [in Texas]." Another account noted that this river was later dubbed La Maligne, "because in M. de la Salle's former journey, an alligator devoured one of his servants, who was swimming over it." The episode took place in 1685 or 1686. La Salle's group had already begun the practice, soon to become widespread, of shooting alligators on sight. From various writings we learn that in 1681–82 this group made a trip down the Mississippi from the mouth of the Arkansas to a locality in present Tensas Parish, Louisiana. They "killed several large alligators, on their way." In the period 1685–87, one of La Salle's men commanded a fort near the mouth of the Lavaca River in Texas, and here "he sometimes amused himself with shooting alligators." Another man, who was with La Salle at the time Dumesnil was killed, remarked of alligators, "I have shot many of them dead."

In the New Orleans area, the shooting of alligators probably began with the 1699 visit of Jean Baptiste Lemoyne de Bienville. In 1718 the town of New Orleans was founded; and three years later, Father Charlevoix found the local alligators to be shy.

> There are many caymans in this river. . . . Our French people nevertheless bathe in it as freely as they would in the Seine. As I declared my surprise at it, they replied that there was no cause for fear; that indeed when they were in the water, they saw themselves almost always surrounded with caymans, but they never came near them.

Charlevoix also mentioned a nearby lake abounding with fishes and waterfowl which could supply the New Orleans settlers with food "when they have destroyed the caymans, which swarm in it."

Another early visitor to the New Orleans area, A. S. Le Page Du Pratz, was told by a local resident that "all newcomers were afraid of those creatures [alligators], although they have no reason to be so." In 1774, writing of alligators along the lower Mississippi generally, Le Page Du Pratz stated, "I myself killed all that ever I met of them; and they are so much the less to be dreaded, in that they can neither run nor rise up against a man. In the water . . . they are dangerous, but in that case it is easy to guard against them." And it is probable that in Le Page Du Pratz's time, at localities well away from the settlements, there were still alligators that would attack a swimming man. But by the early 1800s, settlements had multiplied rapidly, and the alligator had been decimated all along the lower Mississippi. In 1814 H. M. Brackenridge could make the general statement that "The alligator . . . is not considered a ferocious or dangerous animal by the inhabitants." In 1817 E. Montule visited New Orleans, where he killed two alligators. He wrote, "Everything considered, the crocodile is much less feared at New Orleans and Louisiana than we imagine in Europe. It is only dreaded by hogs and dogs." Harriet Martineau, writing in 1837 of a trip up the Mississippi River, commented, "I was on the lookout for alligators all the way up the river, but could never see one. A deck passenger declared that a small specimen slipped off a log into the water one day when nobody else was looking; but his companions supposed he might be mistaken, as alligators are now rarely seen in this region." The foregoing references, and a few others not quoted, reveal how extensively the alligator was hunted along the lower Mississippi during the first 120 years of settlement there.

Turning now to the St. Johns River of Florida, we find that William Stork wrote in 1766: "Alligators are here in great numbers, they never attack men either in the water or upon land; all the mischief they do, is carrying off young pigs from the plantations near the rivers." This calm appraisal of the situation is very different from William Bartram's exciting description (quoted in Chapter 2), although Bartram's supposed observations were made on the same river and about a decade later. However, Stork probably had reference to the situation that existed on the lower (northern) St. Johns, not exactly a well-settled area at that time, but one with a good many large plantations, a fort or two, and a river ferry. When Bartram encountered aggressive alligators, he was much farther upstream (somewhere around the present Lake Jessup), in a nearly uninhabited, 60-

mile stretch of river between two trading posts. While Bartram's account was considerably embellished by fancy, I do not doubt that he found the alligators here to be disturbingly bold. By 1821 James C. Forbes could write of alligators in Florida generally, "though they are held in great dread by the timid, [they] are inoffensive, unless roused to protect themselves." And John Lee Williams, in an 1836 account of Florida, wrote,

> If any of our readers wish to become acquainted with the chivalric character of the male [alligator], let them consult William Bartram's Travels in Florida, page 129. These hideous reptiles are, however, more disgusting than dangerous. I have often seen people bathe within a few yards of them, with perfect safety; nor have they, as far as we have ever heard, attempted to injure any person. They often attack dogs and hogs, and have, rarely, attempted to seize cattle swimming in the water.

Some parts of the alligator's range were settled at a comparatively late date; and at the more sparsely inhabited localities, the reptile was still dangerous. In an 1817 letter, William Tell Harris wrote of an episode on the Catawba River in South Carolina. "A man and woman were crossing a swamp near the river, when an alligator darted forward, and endeavored to seize the woman's horse; this so alarmed the animal, that he threw her; the reptile then attacked the woman, and before assistance could be obtained, so much injured her, as to render her recovery doubtful."

The early writings are not as detailed as we might wish. However, the foregoing accounts, along with a good many others that I have not quoted, suggest that in the days before settlement, the alligator was occasionally dangerous to man; and that it became shy as its numbers were decimated.

Now to consider some events of modern times. In this consideration, I have been deliberately vague about identities, to spare possible embarrassment to a victim of alligator attack; and vague about localities, to spare certain embarrassment to Chambers of Commerce. The described episodes are adequately documented, with one exception which is noted at the appropriate place. As mentioned previously, for about a decade beginning with 1948 the alligators seemed to become dangerous in an area from Okefinokee Swamp to southern Florida. A park had been established in Okefinokee; the local alligators had been well protected, and some of them had reached a large size without having been molested by man. In 1949 at least two large alligators began stalking tourists and fishermen in the park, or behaving aggressively toward small boats on nearby waterways. The reptiles had to be removed before they harmed someone. Turning to Florida, it was in 1944 that the alligator first received legal protection in that state. In 1948 a woman was attacked by an alligator while she was swimming in a large spring-run near the Florida Gulf coast. The head springs had long been commercialized, and considerable effort had been made to protect all wildlife along the run. In this stream, alligators had grown to large size without molestation. The swimming woman was attacked by a large alligator, which seized her by the right arm, and bit down on it three times. Then the reptile released the arm to seize her left hand, with which she was trying to defend herself. Finally, the alligator desisted in its attack, and the woman made her escape to shore. Two men, both of them familiar with alligators, captured the offending reptile and then killed it. These men (both of them known to me personally) measured the alligator, found it to be slightly more than 9 feet in length, determined it to be a male, and opened its stomach to reveal turtle and fish remains, along with a gastrolith of wood and another of stone. The woman had been in the habit of swimming in the river almost daily; she had seen the alligator on previous occasions, in about the same spot each time, but had regarded it as harmless.

In 1950 a fifteen-year-old girl, swimming in a creek in southeastern Florida, was attacked by an alligator. Her brother, in a nearby boat, saw the reptile as it moved to attack; he cried a warning, but the girl could not reach the boat in time. The alligator seized the girl by one leg at the level of the knee, but relinquished its grip as the girl was pulled into the boat. Local residents said it had been forty-three years since anyone had been attacked by an alligator in that area.

In 1952 a nine-year-old girl was fishing for minnows in a flooded rock pit in extreme southeastern Florida. The pit had been inhabited for years by an alligator which had grown up there. The area was a suburban one, and the reptile's presence was well known to many local residents. The alligator seized the child by the arm, but then relinquished its grip. As the alligator returned to the attack, a ten-year-old boy dragged the girl to safety. Her arm had been mangled from wrist to shoulder, and both forearm bones broken. The incident attacted nation-wide attention, and President Harry S. Truman presented the boy with an award for his bravery. The alligator was captured, and proved to be slightly over 6 feet in length.

In 1951 an alligator began trying to catch swimmers in a large sinkhole lake in central Florida. This reptile never caught anyone, for its approach was always noticed in the clear, shallow water; but on several occasions it ran the swimmers out of the lake. The alligator was captured, and proved to be about 9 feet in total length. During that same year, a large alligator in like fashion chased swimmers away from a brackish-water beach on the Florida Gulf coast. It had been twenty-three years since anyone had been attacked by an alligator in the county where the beach was located. In 1928 a boy had stepped into a golf course pond, where he was seized and drowned by an alligator, and where a second youth, trying to help the first, was severely bitten. This coastal county had another attack in 1958, when a member of a road gang, clearing grass along a right-of-way, was charged by an alligator that had been concealed nearby. This episode is the one previously mentioned as being deficient in detail.

In 1957, at a locality in eastern Florida, a nine-year-old boy vanished, and his mangled body was eventually discovered in a creek. Several large alligators, seen in the vicinity, were shot and opened. Two stomachs were reported to contain portions of the body. It was never proven to the satisfaction of everyone that an alligator had actually killed the boy, but several physicians expressed such an opinion. In any event, local residents began shooting alligators on sight, and urging repeal of the law that had given the local alligators protection for over a decade.

In 1958 a man was swimming in a central Florida lake. Wearing

Figure 87. Hide-hunting threatens to exterminate the American alligator completely. As shown here, the alligator hide of commerce is the skin of the under surfaces only. [Ross Allen's Reptile Institute]

swim-fins and a face-mask with snorkel, he was swimming slowly in water about 6 feet deep. An alligator seized the man by the head, pulled him under water, and shook him. Twice he managed to surface for a breath of air, but each time was pulled under and shaken again. Struggling for shallow water, he got his feet on the bottom, and stood up. The alligator immediately released its hold, and swam off rapidly. The alligator's teeth had left puncture wounds on the man's neck, throat, corner of eye, jaw, ear, scalp above opposite ear, and back of head. Since 1958 there has been no alligator attack in Florida, to my knowledge.

In the latter 1950s and the 1960s, the price of alligator hides kept rising, for the supply was dwindling and the demand for them increasing. Also, a new method of preparation rendered them more amenable to certain commercial uses. Eventually a hide (which is usually the skin of the underparts only) came to bring as much as $6.50 to $9.00 per foot of length. The high prices lured many new people into the alligator poaching industry, and stimulated the old, well-established poachers to intensify their own activities. During the 1960s most alligator populations in Florida were thinned to a small fraction of what they had been in the latter 1940s and early 1950s. Even alligator "farms" were not safe from the midnight raids of poachers. It is thus not surprising that alligators seemed to become shy in Florida from the latter 1950s on, if I am correct in thinking that the hunting of alligators makes the survivors wary of man.

In the Coastal Plain of Georgia, outside Okefinokee Swamp, the alligators never became bold in modern times, even though sometimes they were in theory protected by game laws. Georgia, unlike Florida, did not have a great many resident hide-hunters. Georgia alligators were killed chiefly by local people, who did not overly concern themselves with game laws. Large alligators, especially, were killed lest they menace domestic animals. Enforcement of the game laws was often difficult. In an area where I frequently studied reptiles, one game warden had five counties to patrol. In Georgia and in some other parts of the Southeast, prosecution of offenders was at times ,difficult; for a good many judges, perhaps because they themselves came from local stock, were more sympathetic toward poachers than toward alligators. Although the alligator did increase in numbers when protected by Georgia law (and also profited when hunting was curtailed by the exigencies of World War II), in that state it never became nearly so common as it did in Florida. This situation may not have been solely a reflection of sociological differences between the two states; the alligator's ecological needs are probably filled better in northeastern and peninsular Florida than in most parts of the Georgia Coastal Plain. At any rate, during the time when alligators seemed to be growing bolder in Florida, comparatively few of them lived to reach a large size in Georgia, and these few did not escape being shot at.

No doubt constant hunting limits attacks by the removal of many large alligators, which are the only ones likely to menace man. Also, when alligators are hunted intensively, the shier are the ones most likely to survive. However, I have been impressed by the way in which whole populations of alligators can abruptly become shier after just a few of their number have been shot. As mentioned in Chapter 15, all the bullfrogs of a population may abruptly become wary when one of their number voices the adult distress call. However, adult alligators have no distress call. To what stimulus, then, might alligators be reacting when they seem to learn of nearby danger? Although this question cannot be answered with certainty, a clue is provided by recent studies on snakes. When a snake is hurt, or seized by a predator, it discharges the secretion of certain cloacal glands. It has generally been supposed, and perhaps correctly so, that this usually pungent discharge functions primarily to disconcert an enemy. But it has lately been discovered that the discharge of one snake will also cause another of the same species to exhibit apparent fright reactions, when the latter comes near the spot where the former had given off its scent. In short, here is a mechanism whereby some individuals of a reptile population could in effect be "warned" that a dangerous predator is in the vicinity. It will be recalled that an alligator, when seized or hurt, everts its throat glands for some unknown reason. As the glands do contain a waxy substance, presumably they liberate some kind of secretion when they are everted. No odor is produced by this eversion, as far as a person can detect. But perhaps the secretion, carried by wind or water, is detectable by other alligators at a considerable distance, many of them becoming warier as a result. This idea needs further investigation.

18 THE ALLIGATOR'S GROWTH, LONGEVITY, AND HIBERNATION

THE ALLIGATOR'S rate of growth can be widely variable, for it depends on the amount of food eaten. If food is in short supply, the reptile grows little. The relationship between feeding and growth is complicated by a third factor, temperature. The alligator needs more food, and has a stronger urge to forage, when its body temperature is comparatively high (within the range of temperatures that permit normal activity). Before the discovery of the temperature-feeding-growth relationship, experimenters kept alligators in cool surroundings, where the reptiles ate very little and so made poor growth. Thus, it was mistakenly concluded that a great length of time was necessary for an alligator to reach its full size. R. L. Ditmars was the first to challenge this fallacy. He collected some alligator eggs from a nest in South Carolina and shipped them to New York, where five of them hatched. Five years after hatching, the reptiles averaged about 5½ feet in length. Ditmars surmised that under ideal conditions the growth of the alligator in nature would be even more rapid.

It will be recalled that the alligator has a fairly well defined hatching season. This season appears even more sharply defined when attention is directed to one particular locality, for the local alligators, being exposed to the same environmental conditions, are likely to begin nesting at about the same time. Most of the local broods accordingly appear within one short period. And at any one particular locality most of the hatchlings should grow at about the same rate, for each is likely to receive about the same amount of food. During and immediately after the hatching season, the smaller alligators at one locality can easily be sorted into length groups, which correspond to age groups. Suppose this sorting were done during or immediately after the hatching season, somewhere in Georgia or northern Florida. The hatchlings would be about 8 inches long, yearlings about 20 to 25 inches, two-year-olds about 32 to 36 inches, three-year-olds about

42 to 46 inches. A few of the smaller alligators could fall outside the expected range of measurement, for they might have been stunted as the result of environmental vicissitudes, or through some innate lack of vigor. But an occasional aberrant alligator will not confuse the issue, the length groups being based on measurement of the normally-growing majority.

Small, captive alligators, if ideally provided for, grow at about the same rate as wild ones. These captives, in their fourth year of life, and at a length of about 48 to 52 inches, cease voicing the juvenile distress call when molested. They also make their first efforts at bellowing, responding in raspy fashion to the thunderous roars of large adults. Probably there are some other changes of behavior at this age in the wild. For example, alligators about 4 to 4½ feet long, presumably in their fourth year, are the ones most often to be found wandering about on land at a long distance from water. It would seem, then, that alligators become adolescent in their fourth year. They would not be expected to breed in that year, for they reach adolescence some months after the close of the breeding season. But observations are consistent enough with the idea that at least some of them begin to breed as they enter their fifth active season. By that time they should be at least 5 feet in length, and breeding females of that size are common.

In the foregoing account of the alligator's growth rate, it was necessary to mix observations made in the wild with those made in captivity, for beyond the third year the growth rate in nature is not determinable with all the desired accuracy. Individual variation in this rate will confuse the issue more and more as the years go by. There is usually no problem in distinguishing the three-year-olds from the older alligators, but there might be difficulty in distinguishing some fast-growing four-year-olds from some slow-growing five-year-olds. Length groups, corresponding respectively to the fourth and fifth years of life, could probably be identified without difficulty if large numbers of specimens could be measured. But the young adults are far less common than the juveniles, and less amenable to measurement. It would be possible to capture large alligators, measure them, mark them indelibly in a fashion that would permit individual identification, release them, recapture them on later occasions, and remeasure them. The literature includes certain measurements supposedly taken in this fashion. In nature the older adults are even harder to find and measure than the younger ones. To judge from observations on well-fed captive alligators, the growth rate begins to slow down in the eighth year, at which time the reptile is about 8 to 9 feet long.

Not much is known about the growth rate beyond the eighth year. One alligator reached a length of 10 feet in eleven years, and another reached 12 feet in sixteen years. These were captives, well fed on fishes and stockyard offal. It is likely that after the eighth year the growth rate slows down more in females than in males; but of this there is no actual proof. At any rate, most females seem not to grow beyond a length of 9 feet, and probably no female exceeds 10 feet.

As mentioned in Chapter 12, some males cease growing in length when no more than about 12 feet long, although continuing to broaden in head and body. Other males, comparatively elongate in build, will considerably exceed 12 feet in length. What is the maximum length reached by an adult male alligator? The largest alligator examined by me was a male killed in 1956 at Lake Apopka, Florida. My measurement, made a day after this reptile was killed, indicated it to be 17 feet 5 inches in total length. The length of the skull, from tip of snout to occiput, is now 594 mm., nearly 23½ inches. But the snout-to-occiput measurement does not give a good idea of the skull's huge size, for in the alligator some of the skull bones extend posteriorly beyond the occiput; and the lower jaw, when normally articulated, extends even farther posteriorly. In this alligator the total length of the head, carried from the tip of the snout back to the level of the posterior margin of the lower jaw, was 28¼ inches. The teeth were all present and in excellent condition. The reptile was in fine shape, heavily muscled, well-fleshed but not stout. Neither head nor body had broadened with age. The skin was without blemish. This alligator was not a senile oldster, and in all save its great size it had the appearance of a young adult. I believe it would have continued to grow, had not its life been ended by some local residents.

The snout-to-occiput skull measurement is useful for comparison with certain figures in the scientific literature. There is one authentic record of an alligator skull larger than that of the Lake Apopka specimen. In 1886 a huge alligator was killed on the Sebastian River in Florida. Its skull eventually reached the Museum of Comparative Zoology at Harvard College, where Thomas Barbour found it to measure 640 mm. from snout to occiput. Regrettably, the total length of this alligator was not recorded. The reptile need not have been proportioned exactly like the one from Lake Apopka, but it should have been a good 18 feet in length. At any rate, the actual measurements and seeming youthfulness of the Lake Apopka alligator, along with the size of the Sebastian River skull, have led me to suggest 18 feet as the approximate upper limit for the species—a limit reached by very few individuals. One can find unsubstantiated reports of larger alligators, especially in the writings that have kept the myths and legends alive. However, the maximum length of a reptile might well be determined in the same fashion whereby sportsmen determine size records for game animals: by actual measurement of available specimens, not by reference to unverifiable statements in the literature.

No doubt very large alligators were once far more common than they later became, but there is no evidence that the maximum size was ever greater than it has been in modern times. Florida is dotted with thousands of shell heaps accumulated by prehistoric Indians who subsisted largely on mollusks and other aquatic organisms. These refuse middens, collectively spanning something over 6,000 years, are rich in vertebrate remains, including the scutes, teeth, vertebrae, and limb bones of alligators. Many of the remains were from large alligators, probably about 12 feet long. But I have seen no midden material that would suggest a reptile as large as the Lake Apopka specimen. Also common in Florida are the scutes and teeth of Pleistocene alligators; and these remains, like those from the middens, are not exceptionally large.

Man has altered the alligator's ecology to different degrees depending on locality. Thus, it is hard to say just how much natural variation the alligator exhibited, from place to place, in its growth rate. Three environmental factors could affect this rate. First of these is water temperature. The effect of this factor should be negated to some degree by the alligator's impulse to maintain a constant body temperature. (Once warmed to its optimum temperature by the sun or the substratum, an alligator can forage in comparatively cool water, to which it does not lose heat rapidly. A large alligator, having less surface area in proportion to mass, loses heat more slowly than a small one.) A second factor is the length of the active season. However, this season is no more than ten or fifteen days longer in the southern part of the alligator's range than in the other parts. A third factor, the most important, is the kind of habitat. Within the alligator's range, freshwater marsh is an exceptionally rich habitat, far richer in living things than any lake, river, or swamp. Marshes often teem with turtles, aquatic snakes, frogs, tadpoles, and slow-moving fishes, along with other organisms that are less important in the alligator's diet. The three environmental conditions that might hasten an alligator's growth—warmer water,

Figure 88. Animal remains, potsherds, and flint points from a Florida Indian midden of about 1,000 A.D. At upper center is a fragment of alligator jaw with 5 empty tooth sockets; and just above, lying on a sherd, is the broken scute of an alligator. [W. T. Neill]

longer active season, and rich marshland habitat—are combined in the Everglades region of southern Florida. While available data are not as copious as might be wished, it appears that in the Everglades a juvenile alligator could add as much as 16 or 17 inches to its length in a year's time. It is also hard to say whether the maximum size of the alligator is geographically variable, for today nearly all the adults are killed before they are fully grown, and the older literature is unreliable in its description of large alligators. But in almost any widespread reptile species there are likely to be certain areas where adults reach an exceptionally large size, for uncertain reasons. Even the early writers never postulated really gigantic alligators in Georgia and the Carolinas. The species might have reached a greater size in northeastern and central Florida than in any other area. Southern Louisiana might also have harbored exceptionally large alligators, equalling the Florida ones in size; but contentions to this effect are not adequately documented.

Passing from the alligator's growth and size, we may next consider certain processes that accompany growth. As the alligator ages and increases in size, it must continually replace the thin outer layer of the epidermis, the so-called stratum corneum. In snakes at intervals the stratum corneum is sloughed from the entire body, and in most lizards it is shed in sizeable patches; but in the alligator this layer is normally shed in minute flakes. As the alligator grows, it also replaces its teeth. This tooth replacement is a complex process, and is not fully understood. In reptiles, the basic pattern of tooth replacement is an alternate one; that is to say, the odd-numbered teeth and the even-numbered teeth function as separate series, and all the teeth of one series are replaced at about the same time. This pattern seems to be established in the alligator foetus, but is not carried much beyond the point of hatching. In the adults of many reptile groups, a wave of tooth replacement will begin at the back of the tooth row, and move forward on alternate teeth. One wave will move forward, eventually replacing all the odd-numbered teeth; the next wave will replace all the even-numbered teeth, again in sequence from the back of the jaw to the front. In the alligator there seems to be an occasional replacement wave; but in this species, as in crocodilians generally, regularity of replacement breaks down quite early in life. It is customary to state that tooth replacement in a crocodilian eventually becomes quite random. However, "random" is perhaps too comprehensive a term to describe the situation. Since the old tooth is shed before the replacement tooth is fully grown and in position, a gap would be left in the tooth row if several consecutive teeth were replaced simultaneously; and if replacement became truly random, such gaps would be expected to occur now and then. However, one does not see growing alligators in which several consecutive teeth have been replaced simultaneously. Apparently some mechanism functions to prevent the development of a gap in the tooth series.

In a growing alligator, a tooth may remain functional anywhere from eight to sixteen months, but is most often replaced after about a year. It is not known whether a broken or loosened tooth is replaced promptly, or whether the progress of replacement is independent of accidents to the teeth. Several replacement teeth, lying in one jawbone, form a vertical series with a functional tooth. In young alligators, the base of the functional tooth is mostly reabsorbed at the time of replacement, and only the cap of that tooth remains to be shed when the replacement tooth grows into place. In older individuals, the base of the functional tooth is not reabsorbed to such a degree, but it develops a perforation, later a notch, that permits the replacement tooth to enter the pulp cavity of its predecessor. Tooth replacement ceases in old alligators, which may be nearly toothless during the last decade or so of life (Fig. 2).

It is often asserted that the reptiles, in contrast with the birds and mammals, are characterized by "indeterminate growth." That is to say, the individual reptile is supposed to keep growing throughout its entire life, although the growth rate may be very slow in latter years. I have never been able to discover the empirical basis for this assertion. Usually, a captive reptile grows rapidly for a time, then grows more slowly. Eventually it reaches the expected adult size of its species; and soon thereafter, it ceases to grow, at least to any measurable extent. Many a reptile makes no measurable growth in the last half or even two-thirds of its life in captivity. Some captive reptiles have lived a remarkably long time, yet a captive reptile that sets a record for longevity usually sets no record for size. Cessation of growth in reptiles is a subject that needs to be placed upon a firmer footing. With particular reference to the alligator, an old individual may live for years without growing measurably. In this reptile, old age is marked by a decline of vigor, the cessation of tooth replacement, loss of appetite, the cessation of reproductive activities, and sometimes the development of dorsal lesions which may expose the bony scutes. It seems fairly clear that in an old alligator the processes of catabolism, of systemic break-down, are outstripping the processes of anabolism, of systemic build-up; and given such conditions, it is hard to see how or why an old, senile alligator would nevertheless be adding something each year to its length or bulk.

The best evidence suggests that a male alligator, under normal conditions, grows rapidly for about the first eight years of life; grows more slowly, but still measurably, until about its sixteenth year; grows very slowly, almost imperceptibly, for another decade or so; then ceases growing, and begins instead to show signs of senility; becomes markedly senile in the third decade of its life, and dies before passing the half-century mark. Females parallel the males in their development for about the first decade of life, but grow very little thereafter. Females in captivity rarely reach the age of thirty, and so may not be as long-lived as males.

The alligator's growth and longevity are affected by the reptile's period of inactivity during the winter, and so the present chapter is a logical place to offer comments on hibernation. The literature relating to reptile hibernation is confused and contradictory. Some authors hold that most or all reptiles of the temperate climes will hibernate in winter, while other authors assert that hibernation is possible only to birds and mammals. Part of the confusion stems from a paucity of observations on the winter behavior and physiology of reptiles, but a larger part stems from a semantic difficulty. The term "hibernation" has been used in a variety of ways. For some authors, any sort of retreat from winter conditions could be termed hibernation. By this definition, reptiles of temperate climes certainly hibernate. With the onset of cool weather, they seek out a winter retreat in the ground, down a rocky crevice, or in the pulp of a rotting stump. But by a far more rigid definition, hibernation is a period of deep sleep with a lowering of body temperature and metabolic rate. A third definition emphasizes the presence of an internal, physiological, seasonally timed rhythm. By this last interpretation, a reptile would not be said to hibernate if its usual winter behavior involves little more than a cold-induced sluggishness, reproducible in the laboratory at any time of year. Putting aside conflicting definitions for the moment, let us see what alligators and other reptiles actually do to pass the winter.

If a reptile is progressively cooled, its movements are slowed; and by the time its body temperature has declined to 40 degrees Fahrenheit or thereabouts, effective locomotion may no longer be possible. The chilled reptile may do nothing more than writhe slowly, or move its limbs feebly and uselessly. If then warmed, the reptile will soon recover its motor abilities. There is considerable variation, from one species to another, in the amount of chilling that can be tolerated. In general, the more cold-hardy species are those of the colder climes, as might be expected. A reptile in the wild will usually overwinter where it will be cool but not frozen. When it is unearthed from its winter retreat, its body temperature is well below a level that would be accepted voluntarily during the active season. And the lower the body temperature of the unearthed reptile, the more sluggish and ineffectual are its movements. Motor abilities are quickly regained when the reptile is warmed. The effect of winter chilling seems to differ in no way from laboratory chilling, and the circumstance has led to a belief that the winter quiescence of a reptile involves little more than a lowering of the metabolic rate as a direct result of winter temperatures. But as a general rule this is not actually the case. Many snakes, at least some lizards, and the alligator, feeding normally in captivity, usually will lose appetite as winter approaches, even though the temperature in their pen is kept constant throughout the year. And in the wild most reptiles do not wait until the advent of cold weather before beginning activities involved with overwintering. At the least, they must seek out an overwintering retreat where they will be moderately safe from flooding, freezing, and predators; and they must begin the search before their movements are hampered by falling temperatures. It is late summer, and still very hot, when the canebrake rattlesnake in Georgia begins its annual trek (often a long one) to its winter den. Toward the latter part of the warm season, many snakes begin to forage very actively, often invading habitats and utilizing food resources that are avoided at most other times. Shortly before the arrival of winter, the eastern diamondback rattlesnake in Florida usually manages to build up a heavy deposit of fat under the skin and in the mesenteries. Thus, it is not an over-generalization to say that in reptiles overwintering commonly involves much more than a simple and immediate response to lowered temperature.

Fortunately, some studies have been made on the alligator, revealing significant seasonal changes in its physiology. Captive alligators were kept all winter at a constant warm temperature equalling the local average for a day in June. In these experimental reptiles, the approach of winter was found to be accompanied by a drop in the glycogen level of the blood. Glycogen, sometimes called "animal starch," is found chiefly in the liver and the muscle cells. When needed, it can be converted into glucose and carried to the tissues by the blood. Glucose is one of the most readily available sources of body energy. The glucose level of one experimental reptile dropped in October or November, and rose again in February or March. (The inactive season of the wild alligator extends roughly from mid-November to mid-March.) The approach of winter was also accompanied by the alligators' loss of appetite. The lowering of the glycogen level and the loss of appetite did not result one from the other. The two were shown to be independent developments as winter approached. In nature many behavioral and physiological changes of various animals are governed at least in part by day length, which decreases in the fall and increases in the spring. But further experimentation on the captive alligators revealed that the lowering of the glycogen level and the loss of appetite were independent of illumination, just as they were independent of temperature. Parallel experiments were carried on with certain caimans, which, being tropical, are not called upon in nature to retreat from winter temperatures. The caimans, kept warm in winter, developed no lowering of blood glycogen level, and no loss of appetite.

A reptile that is dug from its winter retreat, or that is chilled in the laboratory, may be incapable of crawling off, but it is mentally alert, and will usually go through some procedure that functions to avert enemy attack. For example, a snake, chillled almost to rigidity, on the approach of an enemy may flatten its head and body, and void the pungent contents of the anal scent glands. A chilled lizard may writhe and gape. A box turtle might be too cold to walk, but it will withdraw the limbs and head into the shell, and close the shell tightly by moveable, bony flaps. A severely chilled alligator will hiss, writhe, and gape, and will bite down slowly but strongly on an object that is brought within range of its jaws. If hibernation must involve deep sleep, then the only true hibernators are various small mammals (a majority of them rodents) and one or two birds. But there seems no strong reason why the term "hibernation" should not be applied to the overwintering behavior of the alligator, and probably to that of most reptiles in temperate climes.

Some aspects of the alligator's hibernating behavior have gone virtually uninvestigated. Little is known about the body temperature in hibernation, although some inferences might be drawn from water temperatures in winter. Will an alligator, in the comparatively warm southern part of its range, occasionally interrupt its winter quiescence to take food? How does an alligator breathe when its winter retreat is full of water, as it usually is? What stimulates the reptile to resume activity in the spring? Does it begin to feed as soon as it breaks its four-months' rest, and if so, does it forage with exceptional pertinacity at this time? Must it build up depleted energy reserves before its reproductive urges are aroused? Such questions must go unanswered for the present. At least it is possible to describe the dens, in which the winter is spent.

In the following discussion, the term "den" is used to mean any excavation made by the alligator for its own occupancy, regardless of the excavation's shape or the season during which it is occupied. Three types of den are constructed, according to the needs and opportunities presented by the local environment. One type, the so-called 'gator-hole, is a large, deep basin. This type of den is constructed in bodies of water where the bottom is a very thick deposit of soft, peaty material, easily dug out by the reptile. A basin may simply be dug into the bottom of a large, marshy tract, as is so in parts of Okefinokee Swamp. In central Florida a basin may be dug into the bottom of a sinkhole pond. As late as the 1940s there were large tracts where almost every sinkhole pond had a 'gator-hole in it.

Such ponds are saucer-shaped depressions, nearly circular in outline, and shallow in proportion to their width. The alligator digs its basin in the approximate center of the pond, the deepest point. The rim of the basin is an approximate circle, in most cases. The blackish, peaty material, excavated by the reptile, forms a low parapet encircling the basin's rim. As long as the alligator is in residence, the basin is kept completely free of aquatic vegetation, although plants grow thickly on the encircling parapet. Usually the parapet is shallowly submerged, and overgrown with so-called emergents: plants (such as cattail and pickerel weed) that are rooted in bottom debris, and that send their stems and leaves well above the surface of the water. When the alligator is killed, the soft material of the parapet may slump back into the basin, which then may be encroached upon by some kind of water lily or other aquatic plant. In the sinkhole country of central Florida one can tell at a glance when a basin is no longer occupied by its maker.

As the result of an unusual geological situation, another and distinctive kind of basin is constructed by the alligator in the Florida Everglades. The Everglades are essentially a sawgrass marsh with a peaty bottom, but the deposit of peaty material rests on a vast sheet of limestone. This stone lies near the surface, and in fact is exposed in many places. The limestone, whether submerged or not, is much eroded and sculptured, with many deep cavities as well as smaller pockets. If an Everglades alligator is going to dig a deep basin, it usually must do so over and within some cavity of the underlying rock. Thus, a basin in the Everglades is likely to be a limestone cavity that the reptile has cleaned out to some degree.

Probably, the impulse to dig a basin was originally evolved not as a method of coping with low temperatures of winter, but with lowering of water table in a dry season. In the southern part of the alligator's range, winter temperatures probably do not endanger the reptile when it is in the deep water of the basin, especially since a deep pool is comparatively slow to change temperature. Thus, in some areas, notably the Everglades, there is no need for the alligator to dig any kind of den other than the basin, which shelters from both drought and cold. There are several reasons why basins are not dug in most parts of the alligator's range. In most areas the seasonal fall of the water table is not so pronounced as to leave an alligator quite without water. Even in a period of extreme drought, water remains in the rivers and in the river-fed lakes and backwaters. Also, in most areas the aquatic situations usually offer only a thin deposit of bottom debris, beneath which may be compacted soil with the cable-like roots of swamp trees. An alligator digs only by pushing soft material aside, using lateral movements of the flanks and of the broad snout. Finally, in some areas a basin might not adequately protect the reptile from winter cold.

As noted previously, a large alligator is oblivious of small ones at most times; and during periods of cold or drought juveniles can find refuge in the basins, if such are dug by the local adults. Whatever their age, the juveniles are not shepherded to a basin by an adult, and they may or may not end up in a basin that is still occupied by its maker. In peninsular Florida, the region wherein basins are most often dug, there is a winter dry season; and the falling of the water level gradually concentrates much aquatic life in the basins. Whether a drought occurs in winter or some other season, and whether it results from natural causes or from man's control of run-off by means of dams and levees, the basins function to preserve much of the local wildlife. During a dry spell in the Everglades, the 'gator-holes may provide the only water for miles around. When the Glades go dry, the deer, raccoons, and other mammals find their drinking water in the basins. Egrets and other wading birds hunt around the edges of the basins. Various fishes, frogs, and aquatic salamanders would probably die out locally if basins were not excavated by alligators.

A second type of den is dug by alligators that live in rivers. "Dug" is perhaps not the correct word, for the reptile simply noses its way under an overhanging bank, working through the mucky soil and the tangle of plant roots. In constructing this type of den, the alligator usually moves at least some dirt, which drifts away in the water. When an alligator is nosing under a bank, its tail swings back and forth in strong lateral arcs, roiling the water. I do not subscribe to the view, advanced in the literature, that the primary function of this tail movement is to waft away the excavated dirt. The reptile can nose into the soil and root tangles only by using the propulsive power of the tail. Once in place beneath a bank, the alligator often seems to hump its back a few times; the top of the bank may be lifted slightly, and saplings shaken; the water is clouded with loosened earth. It is in late summer or autumn that one most often sees an alligator preparing a riverside den. This kind of den is used only for hibernation. It is not known whether small alligators may hibernate in the riverside den of an adult. There is no particular reason why they should do so. Beneath the overhanging bank of a Coastal Plain river, the ground is usually honey-combed, and small reptiles can find a retreat there without having to dig at all. (The brown watersnake, a river-dwelling reptile for the most part, custo-marily hibernates in this network of cavities; and the cottonmouth moccasin sometimes does so.)

A third type of den is a long, horizontal burrow. Much of this burrow is tunnel-like, its diameter not much greater than that of its maker. Usually, however, there is a small chamber—presumably a turning-around place—near the rear of the burrow. At certain levels of waters, the chamber may also provide an air space. Sometimes a burrow has one or two short side branches. These probably exist because the reptile, beginning to dig a bur-row, ran into large roots or other obstructions, and had to change its course. Burrows are most often found in certain areas that are seasonally inundated: the flatwoods especially, but also the floodplains of the large rivers. (By "flatwoods" I mean only the slash pine and wiregrass flatwoods, with nu-merous ponds and with a hardpan of clay-like material. Other types of flat-woods, such as those with a limestone hardpan, are excluded.) The burrow is dug at a time when the water is high, the ground softened by flooding. Usually a burrow mouth is disclosed only after the water table falls.

In most parts of the country where alligators dig burrows, the flatwoods and the river bottomlands are inundated in winter. The winter rains, even though perhaps not as heavy as the summer ones, are the more effective in flooding the lowlands; for evaporation is less in cool weather, and more importantly, the water table established by summer rains has not fallen very low by the time the winter rains begin. In a broad belt across the south-eastern United States, winter flooding must long have been the rule, for many events in nature are adjusted to this annual, cold-weather inundation. An example, of special interest in herpetology, is the movement of various amphibians to breeding ponds in the flooded flatwoods and bottomlands.

Thus, a burrow is usually flooded when occupied by a hibernating alli-gator, and is not frequented by the reptile during its active season. I do not know whether small alligators might overwinter in the burrow of a larger one. In contrast with the more conspicuous basin, the alligator's burrow is not well known to the locals, and has rarely (or perhaps never) been men-tioned previously in the literature. Most burrows seen by me were in the belt of flatwoods that crosses the middle and lower portion of the Coastal Plain in Georgia. However, I know of one burrow that was dug by an alligator at the edge of a shallow slough adjoining a large spring-run in central Florida. Both the habitat and the geographic location were surprising in this latter case.

Further study may reveal the desirability of recognizing a fourth type of den. Here and there, where topography permits, an alligator digs a large hole into the base of some high bank. This hole may extend downward into the bank at an angle of about 45 degrees from the horizontal, or may first angle downward but soon level off and become approximately horizontal. Such a den is large, holds much water, and is useful to the alligator both in winter and in times of low water. Perhaps, then, it should be regarded as a variety of basin, dug not straight down but at an angle. In the Everglades, a cavity in the underlying limestone may lead downward at an angle; and an alligator, in constructing a basin, may clean out such a cavity.

A large lake, one with a fairly stable water level, may harbor many alligators, yet have no discoverable dens in or beside it. Presumably some alligators simply overwinter in natural surroundings, or else modify these surroundings only to a minor and undetectable degree. Juvenile alligators seemingly do not construct any kind of den, nor is there evidence that they overwinter in an adult's den save in those limited areas where basins are dug. Thus, it seems likely that the juveniles, especially, often hibernate in natural surroundings, although the exact nature of these surroundings is usually problematical.

It is easy to understand why an alligator does not grow very much during its winter months in a basin, riverside den, or burrow. Hibernation is a fasting period of about four months' duration, at least in most parts of the alligator's range. Perhaps during a mild winter in peninsular Florida, an alligator might feed sparingly upon the fishes or other organisms that share its basin. It is clear that in peninsular Florida, alligators that hibernate in basins are not torpid; for they can usually be lured to the surface by an imitation of the juvenile's distress cry, a circumstance taken advantage of by hide-hunters. However, even under the most favorable of conditions alligators are disinclined to feed much in winter, and we have noted that growth is dependent upon feeding. Less obvious is the effect of hibernation on longevity. In reptiles, hibernation is a period not only of fasting but also of rest, of lowered body temperature, of reduced metabolic rate, and of minimum demand on most systems of the body. One might say that months spent in hibernation are not deducted from the potential life span of an individual reptile. The months of activity are the ones that "age."

Captive reptiles, coming from temperate climes, are often kept warm and encouraged to feed the year around. But according to several experienced keepers, these reptiles stay healthier when allowed a few months of cool quiescence. The alligator is among the species that have been observed to profit by a winter respite from activity.

19 THE ALLIGATOR'S SOCIAL ORGANIZATION, DEMOGRAPHY, AND ENEMIES

NOW WE COME to the knotty problem of territoriality, and its possible existence in the alligator. Centuries ago, man observed territorial behavior in certain domestic and wild animals. An old proverb, "Every cock to his own dunghill," neatly summarizes territorial behavior: each rooster pre-empts some particular area, in which he will take up a conspicuous position and vocalize loudly. He may tolerate hens and chicks in this area, but will chase another rooster away. Not until the 1940s was the concept of territoriality clearly enunciated in the scientific literature, and disentangled from related concepts. In the 1950s and 1960s, the attention of the general public was drawn to territorial behavior; according to several popular books of that period, man's genetic heritage includes territorial impulses, often manifested as possessiveness and aggression.

Some reptiles (for example, the green anole) are territorial; others (such as the banded watersnake) show no sign of territorial impulses. What about the alligator? Most recent authors have asserted that it (and by extension, the Crocodilia generally) is indeed territorial. However, the assertion has rested chiefly on an interlocked series of erroneous beliefs: that only the male alligator will bellow; that bellowing is done chiefly in the spring; that it is associated with courtship; that it is a prelude to combat; that wild alligators often fight with each other; that fighting is principally an activity of spring, the time of courtship; and that males are particularly combative. The problem of alligator territoriality needs to be reconsidered. Let us look briefly at the main pattern of territorial behavior, and then see if the alligator's observed activities will conform at all to this pattern. The discussion of territoriality might well center around the birds, but with occasional side glances at the mammals, for territorial behavior reaches its most elaborate and clear-cut development in these two groups.

Living things are not "born free." Each species is confined to a certain area, or series of areas, beyond which the individual will not stray. For convenience, this area or series of areas is often described in geographic terms, and dubbed the "range" of the species. But the species does not occupy all of this range; individuals are actually restricted to a certain habitat within the geographically described area. Thus, the alligator is said to occupy a given range in the southeastern United States, although the individuals are actually confined to certain aquatic situations, such as freshwater marshes, swamps, lakes, and rivers. But usually a species does not utilize all parts of what we choose to call its habitat. Consider, for example, the alligator and the green treefrog. When swamps or marshes harbor alligators, they almost always harbor green treefrogs; thus, in many areas the alligator and the green treefrog occupy the same habitat. But most of the time the frog does not venture into the water or onto the bank. It lives a yard or two above the surface of the water, clinging to the stems of emergent vegetation or the branches of shrubs. In contrast, the alligator is bound to the water and the banks, and has little to do with the vegetation level where the treefrog lives. The term "biotope" is often used to denote that portion of the habitat to which some organism is confined. The biotope of the alligator is essentially the surface of the water, the shallow water and its bottom, and the banks—all within some suitable expanse of habitat. In many species—and this is the problem toward which we have been heading —the individual is not even free to roam throughout its biotope. Rather, the biotope is parceled out into territories, and at most times the individual restricts its activity to its own territory. There could be a further limitation on its movements: parts of the territory might be visited only at certain times of day or only at the appropriate season.

In many birds of temperate climes, the adult male establishes its territory in the spring of the year. It has an automatic impulse to make itself conspicuous within this territory; and so it may show itself boldly, sing loudly, or do both. A mockingbird or a nightingale sings not to gratify man but to demarcate its territory. The skylark, spiraling upward while singing, has caught the fancy of poets from Shelley and Wordsworth to Bashō and Onitsura; but the "flood of rapture" voiced by the "blithe spirit" simply functions to demarcate a territory on the ground below, a territory to which the bird is invisibly tethered. When the adult male advertises its presence within its territory, other adult males are stimulated to keep away, but adult females are attracted. If an adult male happens into the territory of another, the intruder is set upon by the occupant. The outcome of a territorial struggle is usually predetermined. The male is inclined to fight when in his own territory, but much less so when outside it; and whether or not the struggle involves some physical contact, it is usually the intruder who turns and flees, often to be pursued a short distance by the occupant of the territory. In some cases, a territorial confrontation may involve only ritual display and vocalization, without physical contact. In any event, the invader of another's territory has arrived therein through automatic responses, is not "bent on conquest," and departs if the area proves to be occupied by an individual of normal vigor.

Although the male occupant of a territory will repel another male, he will permit the entrance of a female. It would be a slight misstatement to say that the male can determine the sex of an intruder. It would be more nearly accurate to say that the territorial male's response to an invader is determined by the latter's behavior, coloration, or both. Studies were made on the common flicker, a kind of woodpecker. In this species the sexes are colored alike except for a black facial marking in the male. If the facial marking of a male is plucked away, the bird is treated like a female by others of its kind. If a female is provided with a black facial mask of glued-on feathers, she is treated like a male by others of the species, and will be chased away even by her own mate. Courtship begins after the female has been permitted to the male's territory, and mating is eventually accomplished.

From one animal group to another, territorial behavior has a variety of ramifications, but most of these need not be considered. It is germane that birds, which rarely have a keen sense of smell, demarcate a territory by being visible and audible within it; but mammals, in which a sense of smell is often highly developed, may demarcate a territory by imparting an odor to it or its boundaries. The odor may arise from the urine, the feces, the content of special glands, or some combination of these. A territory is usually defended only against an intruder of the same species; but in some animals, the male will defend its territory against intruders of related species as well.

The alligator's behavior suggests that the reptile has certain territorial impulses, but the details of that behavior do not conform very well to the pattern of territoriality as outlined above. The following interpretation of the situation is offered tentatively.

Although it is useful at times to subsume certain activities of diverse organisms under the rubric "territoriality," it is likely that territorial behavior has evolved independently on a number of different occasions. A fiddler-crab and a baboon are both territorial, but hardly as the result of common inheritance from a territorial ancestor. An elaborate behavior pattern, like a complicated anatomical structure, has evolved from something simpler. The territorial behavior of a bird is integrated with many evolutionary advances, such as well-developed parental care, perfection of flying ability, acuity of vision, and the vivacity that comes from a constantly high metabolic rate. A crocodilian should not be expected to show the advanced and specialized form of territoriality that exists in birds. In the alligator we may be seeing territoriality in a comparatively simple form, perhaps even a basic archosaur form.

An adult alligator, whether male or female, takes up residence in a certain area, and at most times of year is inclined to defend this area against any large intruder, whether the latter is another adult alligator or an animal of a different species. The alligator shown in Fig. 86 is not "attacking" the man, in the usual sense of the word; nor is it attempting predation. Rather, the reptile is confronting the man, an intruder of another species, with open mouth, upward lunges, and loud hisses. Fig. 89 shows another confrontation. Birds have evolved a sharper distinction between defense of an area against an intruder of the same species (true territoriality), and defense of an area against an intruder of another species. Birds have also evolved sexual differences in the defense of an area. It is the male bird who locates a territory, demarcates it, and does more to defend it against invaders of the same species, although both sexes may defend the nest against some egg-predator, or join forces to drive off an intruder such as a cat or owl.

Territoriality is often said to function primarily as a mechanism whereby a male and a female of some particular species can carry on courtship and copulation without disturbance from other members of the same species. But territoriality can have other functions as well. When the individuals of a given species are not aggregated but are well spaced throughout the biotope, competition among these individuals is minimized, and the resources of the biotope are utilized to the fullest extent. Also, since the occupant of a territory tends to be more aggressive than the invader, territoriality makes for a degree of social stability; and if (as so often happens) a territorial confrontation involves only some threatening noises and displays, this stability is attained without physical harm to the individuals. Other important functions of territoriality are conceivable; for example, the maintenance of population density at an optimum level within any given expanse of habitat. The point is that in birds, much more than in the alligator, territorial behavior has become interwoven with reproductive activities. Birds may court, copulate repeatedly, build a nest, tend the eggs, and rear the young in a territory that is located, demarcated, and defended by the male. This statement is not applicable to all birds, but I am not here concerned with all the ramifications of territoriality from one bird group to another.

By narrow definition, stemming chiefly from studies on birds, a territorial animal is one in which the male is the more active in setting up and defending a territory, and one in which the defense is primarily against an intruder of the same species. By this definition, the alligator is not territorial. Yet, it performs some acts that are very suggestive of territorial behavior. "Incipiently territorial" is perhaps the best term for the behavior

Figure 89. A large alligator, penned under fairly natural conditions, confronts an intruder. [Tod Swalm]

of the alligator. Birds and crocodilians are of common ancestry, but birds have evolved much greater departures from the ancestral, archosaurian stock; and it is not perturbing that the elaborate territorial behavior of birds should merely be foreshadowed, not duplicated, in a crocodilian.

Certain activities of the alligator, so far discussed independently of each other, may be reviewed in sequence for the light they throw on incipient territoriality. The sequence is anchored to known facts, but admittedly some gaps exist in it. In the spring, upon emergence from hibernation, the adult alligator's principal activity is not the establishment of a territory but the search for a mate. Both sexes engage in this activity. The anal glands, present in both sexes, function at this time to leave a trail whereby one alligator can find another. The location of a mate is likely to be a time-consuming task; for even if one alligator tracks down another, the two may be mismatched as regards sex, size, or physiological and psychological readiness for mating. The spring activities of the alligator, as so far related, find a parallel in the activities of other reptiles, for example various snakes. There is a small amount of bellowing by alligators in the early spring. This vocalization does not function to bring the sexes together, for if it did, it would be indulged in far more often at the beginning of the breeding season. Bellowers do not move toward each other; and the chief function of the bellow is to keep individuals apart, not bring them together. A small amount of seemingly functionless bellowing in early spring is not surprising; in many animals, some seasonally timed activity may be preceded by half-hearted "false starts" earlier in the year. These "false starts" may actually serve to bring the animal to a condition of psychological readiness for the full-scale activity at the appropriate season. After mating, the male alligator seeks out an area in which he will concentrate his activities. The female's area of activity is predetermined by the location of her nest, from which she will not go very far. After the eggs are laid, both sexes begin to bellow in earnest. This vocalization enables the alligators to distribute themselves evenly over the biotope, a desirable spatial arrangement as noted above. The bellow is a "segmented" call, a series of roars repeated with almost mechanically precise timing; and a call of this kind functions to reveal the location of the caller to others of the same species. The bellow is not normally a manifestation of hostility or aggression toward another individual (note Fig. 1). Bellowing is not followed by combat, and bellowers remain in the position they were occupying when a chorus began.

There are literature references to a captive alligator that bellowed in response to a loud musical tone of a certain pitch, and that supposedly became aggressive immediately after the bellowing. However, the original publication reveals the reptile to have been penned by itself in a bathtub. I do not doubt that this alligator automatically bellowed in response to a sound of the proper pitch and volume, or that it exhibited violent activity after a loud blast was sounded practically in its ear. But the reptile's tail-thrashing, misinterpreted as an aggressive gesture, was simply the normal reaction of an alligator trying desperately to swim its way out of an unpleasant situation.

The alligator is unusually alert, not aggressive, for a few moments after bellowing. The dilation of the pupil, evident at the time of bellowing, is probably a manifestation of this alertness; for many animals display a dilated pupil when excited or stimulated. Pupil dilation is not prima facie evidence of aggressiveness, and in fact has most often been reported to accompany fright, or excitement over the arrival of food.

After mating, a male alligator sometimes establishes itself in the same area it had occupied the previous year. A large alligator in an undisturbed tract may reappear, year after year, in about the same location. But most alligators are growing, changing rapidly in their requirements and abilities; most environments change, too. Thus, an alligator may shift its area, not only from year to year but even every few months. A female, when her nest-guarding urge has waned, may change or enlarge her area of activity. Thus, during the summer the adults are moving about quite a bit, each one advertising its whereabouts by an occasional bellow. This situation has a counterpart in waterfowl. In certain geese, the territory is "portable," so to speak; the individual moves about, but remains constantly ready to defend an area about itself. This shifting about of adult alligators cannot always proceed smoothly, for space in which to move is not limitless; the expanse of suitable habitat is bounded by the water's edge, and sometimes an alligator may not find for its use an area that is both unoccupied and sufficiently large. Accordingly, two adults may occasionally confront each other. The confrontation is ritualistic: each gapes widely, lunges upward, and attempts to overtop the other, all the while hissing loudly (not bellowing). If one of the contestants has already been established in the area, the newcomer will probably turn and flee. If a freshly caught adult alligator is introduced into a pen where several adults already reside, one of the residents will usually chase the newcomer. Even though the latter may be the larger of the contestants, it will flee desperately, and do its best to scramble out of the enclosure. In the wild, when an ousted adult finds no area that it can dominate within a given swamp, marsh, or stretch of river, it leaves that expanse of habitat; and by so doing, it has at least some chance of finding an area that it can pre-empt. Once established in an area, the adult alligator will confront not only another adult of its kind, but any large animal that appears on the scene, except, of course, an animal that is identified as potential prey, to be seized rather than confronted ritualistically.

The juvenile alligators are not affected by the adult's partitioning of the biotope into individual areas. The juveniles cruise about and forage in the territory of any adult. Their occasional grunts alert the adult to their nearby presence; and if one of the juveniles runs afoul of a predator, its distress cry brings the adult promptly, not to confront the predator ritualistically but to attack it directly. Otherwise, the juveniles are ignored until they are in their fourth year. Then they become adults, begin to join in bellowing choruses, and are moved to stay out of an area that is already occupied by an adult. Some alligators, newly turned adult, can find a pre-emptable area, but many cannot. Accordingly, those in their fourth year are the ones that most often travel overland, with a chance of finding a swamp or marsh in which they can take up residence.

The partitioning of the biotope into individual areas should be very effective in maintaining an alligator population at an optimum density. If an adult dies, the area it formerly occupied will soon be taken over by another one; yet, overcrowding is prevented, for an adult leaves the vicinity if it cannot pre-empt an area. Within a given expanse of suitable habitat, all parts of the biotope are utilized to support adult alligators; and since juveniles are admitted into an adult's territory, they can take small items of prey that would be ignored by the adult. Also, the outward movement of surplus young adults, and an occasional old adult, serves to introduce the species into every available expanse of habitat.

So much, then, for the alligator's incipient territoriality, as conceived in the light of available data. The social behavior of vertebrates has another aspect, that of hierarchy. As early as 1911, a two-leveled social hierarchy was recognized to exist in an Old World lizard of the genus Lacerta: when many males were penned together, one of them dominated all the others. In 1913 attention was first drawn to an elaborate social hierarchy in domestic fowls. One individual ("Alpha") in a flock could peck any of the others, and was not itself pecked by any; a second ("Beta") could peck all but Alpha, and was itself pecked only by Alpha; a third could peck all but Alpha and Beta, and was pecked only by them; and so on down the line. Social hierarchies, varying in complexity and in overt manifestations, were subsequently found to exist in many vertebrate species. An outstanding student of social hierarchies was led to compare flocks of hens to "certain college faculties in the U.S.A.," and today we may speak of a peck-order in a human aggregation. In reptiles, territorial and hierarchical behavior overlap to some degree. There is evidence of hierarchical levels in the alligator. The usual "alligator farm" will include a pen in which several or many large adult alligators lie about placidly, appearing to ignore each other completely; but the situation is not as it seems. In the group there is an Alpha individual; the rest are Betas. When the Alpha and any Beta are moving about the pen on a collision course, it is the Beta who turns aside. There may be no other clue to the Alpha's status, although it is sometimes evident that the Betas do not crowd the Alpha as closely as they do each other. The Alpha is usually the largest of the lot. However, previous residence within an area has something to do with hierarchical level. It is the Alpha who chases any newcomer that is introduced into the pen; and the Alpha, by virtue of prior establishment there, will dominate even a larger individual. A keeper, wishing to introduce a freshly caught adult alligator to a pen where other adults have long been established, may provide himself with a doubled-over length of rubber hose, or some other weapon that will not actually harm an alligator. Using the hose, he belabors the Alpha, chasing it around the pen until it becomes desperate in its efforts to escape. If thoroughly cowed, the ertswhile Alpha will usually remain subordinate for at least a few days, during which time the newcomer becomes established in the pen. The Alpha and the newcomer will eventually set up a dominance-subordinance relationship with each other, perhaps on the basis of size. But neither will suffer physical harm, as might have been the case if the Alpha had chased the newcomer around a pen from which the latter could not escape.

We have nearly exhausted the range of subjects relating to the alligator's life history. Not that the account verges on completeness; many subjects could receive no more than scant mention, for they have gone nearly uninvestigated. One subject, very important but very little known, is the alligator's demography. How many alligators may be expected in a tract of a given size? How many will be male, how many female? What is the composition of the population as regards age-groups? Such demographic questions cannot be answered comprehensively; the best we can do is offer a few scattered observations. On several occasions during the latter 1940s and the 1950s, a census was made of alligators along a large spring-run in central Florida. At that time alligator hides did not bring the price they later commanded, poaching had not yet become a major industry, and the alligators in this run were rather well protected. Censuses were made in summer, before the hatching season, at night when every alligator is easily spotted by its eye shine. The run, about five miles long, consistently harbored 70 to 75 alligators along its length, a majority of them juveniles and young adults. In the Everglades National Park, aerial and other surveys revealed 'gator-holes (not necessarily occupied in every case) to exist with an approximate frequency of one to every three acres. Studies in Georgia revealed that the number of hatchlings present in a lake or a sharply delimited expanse of low flatwoods was reduced by about nine-tenths between the end of the hatching season and the beginning of the following active season. These observations were made at fairly undisturbed localities, and at a time when hatchling alligators were not collected by man. The decimation of the hatchlings was the result of natural hazards and perhaps innate defects. This is about all that can be said on the subject of alligator demography.

Another subject, about which all too little is known, is that of orientation in the alligator. Orientation is currently of much interest to students of animal behavior. How do homing pigeons find their way home from a distant locality? What serves to guide various migratory mammals on their long treks, the migratory birds on their flights? How do far-wandering sea turtles manage to find the very limited areas where they breed? Less spectacular navigational abilities exist in many organisms, including some amphibians and reptiles. Attention has lately focused on so-called light-compass reactions of animals. The sun, moon, and stars move in scheduled ways, and so over any particular spot on the face of the earth they occupy a predictable position for any season and time of day. Location on the face of the earth can be determined from the position of celestial bodies—if the time of day is known, and the day of the year. There is reason to believe that various animals, somehow transported a long way from home, can return

Figure 90. The well-marked trail of an alligator through a marsh. [Ross Allen's Reptile Institute]

to that home because they have requisite time sense, and an impulse to move in a given direction according to the position of the celestial body. Crocodilians have not been used in an investigation of orientation, but a light-compass reaction, comparable to that in certain freshwater turtles, is to be expected in them.

Under appropriate conditions, alligators make long treks. These treks are seasonal, and might be termed migrations. As the water table falls, the reptiles may move into lower situations, in which more water remains. Or, where there is a gentle gradient from the fresh water to the salt, the reptiles may move farther into the brackish situations as these are freshened by run-off during the rainy season. Along the lower edge of the Everglades, the long trails of alligators are conspicuous features. Trails are often deeply worn, and presumably are used over and over again. In other parts of the alligator's range, a deeply worn trail is occasionally encountered (Fig. 90). Such trails must represent a seasonal shift of territory, not the movement of an individual within a single, large territory.

Another poorly known subject is that of the alligator's enemies. By "enemy" is meant an organism that is adapted to prey upon the alligator, compete with it, or parasitize it harmfully. The raccoon, the black bear, and the (introduced) wild hog have been suggested as possible mammalian predators on the alligator at some stage in its life history. An early writer said that the panther would kill young alligators.

The great blue heron is an important predator on alligator hatchlings. Audubon portrayed a whooping crane attacking such hatchlings, but he may have been exercising artistic license. An early writer stated that baby alligators are eaten by "buzzards." No doubt he was using the latter term in the British sense, to mean hawks of the genus Buteo. The red-tailed hawk, red-shouldered hawk, and broad-winged hawk are known to take snakes and lizards, and so they might take a small alligator as well; but proof of this is lacking. The bald eagle (now verging on extinction) often catches turtles, and a captive individual would kill snakes, including the cottonmouth; so perhaps this bird, which in Florida frequently nested beside a large body of water, was once a predator on small alligators. Again, proof is lacking. The caracara, a long-legged hawk that strides about on the so-called "prairies" of southern Florida, is definitely known to kill and eat young alligators. The cottonmouth is the only reptile observed to prey on alligator hatchlings, although the snapping turtle might do so at times.

As for amphibian predators, on several occasions a baby alligator has been found in the stomach of a bullfrog. The big frogs of the genus Rana take larger prey than is generally realized. This is well illustrated by Fig. 29, in which a river-frog, by no means a large example of its species, chokes down a 14-inch rattlesnake. Collecting reptiles and amphibians by night with a flashlamp, I have often spotted a baby alligator and one or more river-frogs, both species in sight from the same vantage point; and I suspect this frog takes an occasional small alligator. On one occasion, some captive leopard frogs swallowed six (out of a brood of twenty-eight) week-old alligators placed in a pen with them. The leopard frogs were from southwestern Florida, where their species reaches an exceptionally large size: but even so, they were not as large as an adult river-frog, bullfrog, or pig-frog. Among fishes, the large-mouthed bass is the only one definitely known to eat small alligators.

As for competitive relationships, there are fishes, large salamanders, frogs, turtles, snakes, birds, and mammals whose feeding habits overlap those of the alligator to a greater or lesser degree. Thus, this reptile has many competitors for food. It is not known whether the alligator encounters really severe competition from any of its associates. When many predators compete with each other in nature, the result is an intricate web of relationships, rarely amenable to precise analysis. The alligator does not compete significantly with any other crocodilian. Its range overlaps that of only one other crocodilian, the American crocodile; and the area of overlap is a very restricted one, the brackish water situations along the extreme southwestern tip of Florida.

For convenience, the alligator's parasites may be considered as its enemies, although in reality most parasites do little damage to their hosts. Sometimes parasites multiply harmfully when their host has been weakened by some other agency. There is one report of a leech that was found on an ailing alligator. The internal parasites of the alligator are numerous, but most of them need not be mentioned, for little is known of them beyond their taxonomic characters. Many internal parasites have a complex life history, involving two or more hosts. Take, for example, some minute flatworms called trematodes. An internally parasitic trematode may have a free-swimming larva, which finds a snail and bores into it. Within the snail, the larva reproduces asexually, giving rise to many larvae of a second type, which return to the water, swim to a suitable place, encyst themselves, and remain encysted until swallowed by some vertebrate. In the vertebrate, the cyst opens, the larva matures, and sheds a vast number of eggs. The eggs pass into the water, hatch there, and begin the cycle anew. Some trematodes must invade four different hosts in order to complete the life cycle. The alligator, the snapping turtle, and various watersnakes all commonly acquire trematodes. Often a fall of water level will leave a struggling mass of bullfrog tadpoles, large ones, entrapped in a puddle. The herpetologist may be tempted to collect these tadpoles as food for captive watersnakes and alligators; but if he does so, the reptiles may soon develop an extraordinarily heavy infestation of trematodes.

Of much interest is the green alga that sometimes grows on an alligator. This alga has not been identified to species, as far as I know. However, several algae are known to be epizoic; that is, to grow on animals. The alligator's alga is probably one of the several species that grow more often on turtles. A healthy alligator in the wild is not attacked by the alga. An alga-infested alligator is usually ailing, senile, or penned improperly. As many an aquarium keeper has discovered, a green, aquatic alga, whether growing on animate or inanimate objects, will flourish best in clear, sunny water. If an alligator is kept almost constantly in water, especially water exposed to direct sunlight, the reptile may develop an algal infestation. A heavily infested alligator is usually very emaciated, and may develop deep lesions on the areas of the body where the alga grows (mostly the upper surfaces of the body, limbs, and tail). A heavily infested alligator can hardly ever be saved. It is uncertain whether death results directly from the alga, or whether the latter grows more thickly as the reptile loses vigor from some other cause.

On one occasion, a small alligator was kept in a pen that was constantly humid. The air and substratum temperatures, even in the coolest and shadiest parts of the pen, were above a level that the reptile would have accepted

Figure 91. In an experimental pen, an alligator (at left) manages to sun while yet avoiding much contact with too-hot substratum. Black caiman (at right) can tolerate a higher temperature than can the alligator, but is disinclined to leave the cool shade completely. [W. T. Neill]

in nature. Nevertheless, after a week or so of constant humidity, the alligator took to seeking out a shaft of sunlight that struck the floor of its pen each afternoon. Here it would adopt a stance (Fig. 91) that made for minimum contact with the substratum. (A reptile derives its body temperature more from the substratum than from the circumambient air.) I suspect that the alligator's impulse was one that functioned to dry the body. For a fresh-water reptile, an occasional drying may be very important in keeping the skin clear of algae and perhaps other organisms. (Freshwater turtles often rest with the limbs extended, the digits spread apart to stretch the webbing. The turtles are commonly said to be "sunning" when doing this, but in captivity they will go through the same activities at night, especially if a breeze is blowing.)

The alligator can harbor a virus that produces a "sleeping sickness" in man and the horse. (This is not the notorious African sleeping sickness.) But the alligator cannot be specifically blamed for occasional, highly local-ized outbreaks of this disease in Florida, for the virus often is present in many other swamp-dwelling organisms. Various birds, lured to birdbaths and feeders, are probably responsible for bringing the virus into suburban areas, where mosquitoes transfer it from one host to another.

Aspergillosis is known in alligators. This disease is produced by a fungus that grows in the lungs. Birds of prey and domestic ducks are likewise susceptible to aspergillosis.

Of course, man is the greatest enemy of the alligator, and of the crocodilians generally. The order Crocodilia survived for 200 million years, an immense span of time during which the major land masses of the earth were rearranged, mountain chains thrown up and leveled again, vast areas drowned beneath the waves or uplifted from the sea bottom. But the Crocodilia are not likely to survive much beyond the end of the present century, if that long. The tropical crocodilians have no better chance for survival than does the American alligator. Some of them are even nearer to extinction at the present time than is the latter species.

Here and there, efforts have been made to save the alligator. However, this reptile could be saved, as a reproducing species in nature, only if the general public desired so, and strongly. By and large, the public is apathetic to the destruction of wildlife. Stronger legislation against the killing of alligators did not deter hide-hunting. The alligator could be saved for an extra decade or two if laws were passed making it illegal to sell or buy any item made of crocodilian leather. I doubt that any such laws will be passed. Most people are still so close, mentally, to their primitive ancestors that they must wear or carry—often as status symbols!—items made from the furry pelts of mammals, the gaudy plumage of birds, and the scaly hides of reptiles. Parks and "preserves" will not save the alligator. Such places, even though theoretically inviolate, and set aside for the enjoyment and edification of all, in practice are encroached upon more and more by commercial interests. Also, a park is not immune to the effects (for example, pollution and the control of run-off) of commercialization outside its boundaries.

Other conditions militate against the preservation of the alligator for very long. The reptile could not be saved unless expanses of suitable habitat were also saved, along with a selection of the prey animals on which the alligator feeds. Today, many lakes and rivers are polluted far beyond anything an alligator could tolerate. Pollution is greatest in highly urbanized parts of the country outside the alligator's range, but is increasing rapidly within that range. The general public has been apathetic toward the deterioration of man's own environment, and is not likely to keep a stretch of marsh or swamp undefiled just for the sake of the wildlife. Large wet-lands, sparsely inhabited by man, have provided the last refuge for the alligator and much other wildlife. But today it is comparatively easy to drain or fill such tracts, and this is being done rapidly as the human popu-lation multiplies and so requires more living space.

Today there are outcries and reactions against the heedless destruction of nature. Man is not likely to breed, fight, or pollute himself completely out of existence. Some day he will stabilize his own population and reach an equilibrium with the environment. But not much wildlife will survive to that day.

In the meanwhile, it would be well to discover as much as possible about the ways of imperiled organisms. The present section of this book has covered the ways of the American alligator, as far as I have been able to discover them. It may be felt that I have been unduly skeptical of the early literature, say from the 1600s through 1935. If much credence is given to this early literature, the alligator emerges as an extraordinary animal, a chimaera, a combination of barnyard bull, mother hen, and ravening wolf, with faint overtones of dragon and decided overtones of human personality. If one disavows most of the older literature, and concentrates instead on objective findings, the alligator (along with other crocodilians) appears plainly to be a reptile, with the behavior patterns appropriate thereto. This situation should not disturb the herpetologists, who long ago concurred with the anatomists and paleontologists in classifying the crocodilians as reptiles.

PART V *The Modern Crocodilians*

20 THE CHINESE
ALLIGATOR AND THE CAIMANS

THE AMERICAN alligator has been discussed at some length. No other crocodilian could be treated in such detail, for all the others are poorly known. In the following review, the living crocodilians are considered species by species. Many life history topics have been omitted for want of information. Comments on taxonomic history have been intentionally abbreviated, such history usually being of concern only to the specialist. Mention is made of a few synonyms that happen to be of interest beyond the purely nomenclatural.

The American alligator's closest living relative is the Chinese alligator, mentioned in Chinese literature as far back as the early Third Century A.D. Chinese names for the species have been given as *yow lung* and *tou lung*, both combinations signifying a dragon. Marco Polo was the first Westerner to write of the Chinese alligator. He did not carefully distinguish it from the crocodiles of tropical Asia, but his more detailed comments probably were based on the Chinese species. He said the reptile was found in the province of "Karazan" (somewhere in southern or south-central China, apparently). It lived in springs, lakes, and rivers, hiding in "caverns" by day, and emerging by night to feed, leaving deeply worn trails along the shores. It was hunted for the hide and the meat, Polo continued. The contents of the gall bladder were thought to ease parturition, disperse boils or skin eruptions, and cure the bite of a mad dog.

The priest M. Martini, in his 1656 book on China, mentioned the alligator and provided the first specific locality record for it, saying that it infested the Yangtze River at Chinkiang, where it was much feared by the local residents. In 1869 some Englishmen saw an alligator on exhibit in Shanghai, and were told that it had come from Kiangsi Province. There are several later records of alligators on exhibit, and it is said that Buddhist priests could acquire merit by purchasing the captive reptiles and freeing them. There is one notice of a tame alligator kept in a temple pool at Nanking, and of others in temple pools near Chinkiang. In 1870 the naturalist R. Swinhoe wrote of seeing an alligator on display (as a dragon) in Shanghai. The reptile, about 4 feet long, was kept in "tepid water." Realizing that this crocodilian was probably unknown to science, Swinhoe tried to buy it; but the exhibitors, making much money off the display, would not sell. This alligator was supposed to have been caught in Shensi Province.

A. A. Fauvel, of the Imperial Chinese Maritime Customs, first gave the Chinese alligator a scientific name. The name, published in 1879, stands today: *Alligator sinensis* Fauvel. A few natural history notes were offered by Fauvel, who, as an honorary curator of the Shanghai Museum, was in a good position to review Chinese and Western writings. His locality records were for Wuhu and Chinkiang. The taxonomy of the Chinese alligator has since suffered only a few vicissitudes. The species has a bony plate in the upper eyelid, a character present to a greater or lesser degree in caimans but supposedly not in the American alligator. This circumstance led to the suggestion, in 1947, that the Chinese alligator did not belong in the same genus with the American one, but stood midway between the latter and the caimans. This view runs contrary to the paleontological evidence that *sinensis* is an Asiatic offshoot of the *thomsoni* line of descent, within the genus *Alligator*. Also, the American alligator does occasionally have a bony plate in the upper eyelid: a plate was well developed in at least one large female American alligator from central Florida. In living and fossil alligators of North America, the plate is probably present more often than is generally believed. After an alligator's death, and the decay of the softer tissues, the plate falls free of the skull, to which it has no bony attachment. Even in the Chinese alligator and the caimans, the plate is seldom preserved with the skull. Thus, the genus *Caigator* Deraniyagala, erected for the sole reception of the Chinese alligator, is but a synonym of *Alligator*.

The modern range of the Chinese alligator is the valley of the lower Yangtze River, with locality records concentrated in Anhwei and Kiangsi (not Kiangsu) provinces. No doubt the range was once much larger, and there is no particular reason to doubt Chinese references to the presence of the species in Shensi or even Kwangtung Province in former centuries. Fauvel discovered references to the alligator in the Korean literature, and wondered if the species also inhabited Korea. But Korea was more or less under Chinese domination for 2,000 years, and the Korean literature often parallels the Chinese. If the Chinese alligator could tolerate a Korean winter, it would have to be far more cold-hardy than the American species. And the shallow, rapid, twisting rivers of Korea do not offer much bottom-land of the kind seemingly required by the Chinese reptile.

The Chinese alligator, like so many other reptiles and also some amphibians, may exhibit certain reflex movements for hours after having been fatally wounded. The heart of a turtle may beat for a day or more after removal from its owner, and frog-legs have been known to hop out of the frying pan when salt was sprinkled on them. Such reflexes led the Chinese to believe that some mysterious strength-giving principle lay in the alligator and its parts. The scales were thought to cure fevers, nosebleed, toothache, female disorders, diseases of the heart and intestines, and disorders arising from fears; and large pieces of the hide were used to head war drums. Evidently man was responsible for reducing the range of this alligator. The

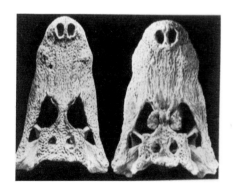 

Figure 92. Two skulls of the Chinese alligator. In an older individual (at right in the left-hand figure, at bottom in the right), the snout is broadened and upturned to a degree rarely seen in the American alligator. Note also the bony plate of the upper eyelid, preserved with one of these skulls. From Robert Mertens, 1943, Senckenbergiana 26, No. 4.

survival of the species along the lower Yangtze is explained by the ecological situation there. The Yangtze drains a vast expanse of uplands, and picks up numerous tributaries along its 3,500-mile course to the sea. The lower part of the river is subject annually to great floods, which convert the bottomlands into marshes and render them uninhabitable by man. In these grassy marshes the alligator persisted, along with other wildlife. Also, adjoining the lower Yangtze are large areas with labyrinthine waterways and deep lakes, natural refuges for wildlife.

The young of the Chinese alligator are brightly patterned with yellow and black, much as in the American species. The yellow crossbands number about five on the body and eight on the tail. Black spotting of the lower jaw is more pronounced in the Chinese species than in the American (ignoring some Florida juveniles of the latter). The pattern of the Chinese reptile becomes obscure with age. Some adults are light-flecked about the sides of the head and body, in a fashion recalling young adults of the American alligator from Louisiana and Texas. Growth rate appears to be about the same in the two alligator species, to judge from observations on captives. However, the Chinese alligator rarely or never exceeds a length of 5 feet. At least this is true today. Old Chinese annals regarded the maximum length as nearer 10 feet. The Chinese reptile has proportionately a broader and shorter snout, chunkier body, and shorter tail than its American congener. In captivity, a fat old adult often leads an onlooker to make some

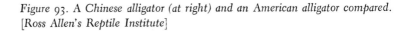

Figure 93. A Chinese alligator (at right) and an American alligator compared. [Ross Allen's Reptile Institute]

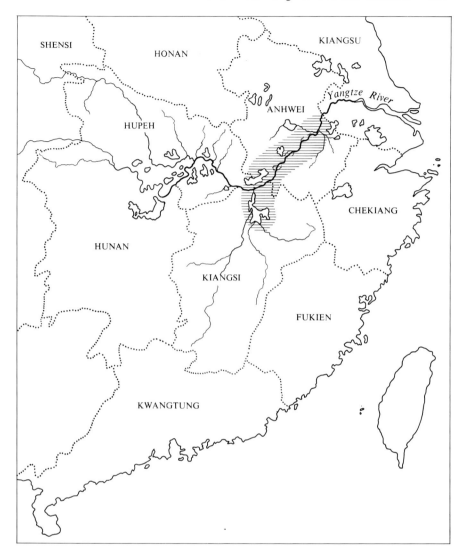

Figure 94. Eastern China. In modern times, most specimens of the Chinese alligator have come from parts of Anhwei and Kiangsi provinces (hatched area), but the range may formerly have extended to many other parts of the area mapped here.

reference to a pig. A Chinese source claims that the female grows larger than the male, but this may be doubted.

The broad, powerful jaws of the Chinese alligator suggest predation on turtles. This is not proven, but China has a considerable variety of fresh-water turtles. A Chinese legend from Anhwei Province relates that a turtle will crawl upon the back of a floating alligator as it would upon a log; the alligator, slowly sinking tail-first, raises its head and opens its mouth; the turtle climbs to the tip of the alligator's snout—and tumbles into the wait-ing jaws. Although of no scientific value per se, the legend may have been inspired by the alligator's predation on turtles. One would expect other small game to be taken, also. About 1920 local residents in the Yangtze region said that the alligator, as a result of constant persecution by man, no longer showed itself in the open during the day, but would prowl at night to take chickens and small dogs.

The Chinese alligator digs at least one kind of a den. This is a hiber-nating burrow, about 1 foot in diameter and 5 feet in length. Some indi-viduals, dug from their hibernating burrows in mid-March, were cold and sluggish; but one of them was capable of hissing loudly. In the lower Yangtze region, winter is the dry season; and the overwintering alligators are in dry burrows, not flooded ones. On one occasion, a wildcat was dis-covered in a burrow from which local residents had previously removed an alligator. A Chinese source claims that males hibernate singly in simple burrows, the females communally in complex burrows; but this may be doubted.

A captive female guarded a pile of nesting material against the approach of other Chinese alligators and of man. On one occasion the bellow of an American alligator stimulated captive Chinese alligators to voice a series of short, explosive roars.

Little else can be said about the Chinese alligator. At best, it is verg-ing on extinction; perhaps it is already extinct. As late as 1959, animal dealers in Kowloon and Shanghai were receiving a few—a very few—speci-mens from Communist China, but such specimens may not have been ob-tained from the wild.

We may turn next to the caimans, representatives of the subfamily Alligatorinae in the New World tropics. The name "caiman" (of Carib Indian origin) is rarely used for these reptiles in their homeland. Throughout most of Latin America, a *caiman* is a crocodile, or even a lizard. Only in books (including the present one) are the tropical alligatorines called caimans. Alligators are distinguished from caimans by the presence in the former of a strong, bony septum that extends longitudinally through the nasal cavity of the skull. The only obvious function of the septum is the strengthening of the end of the snout, which must receive considerable pressure when used shovel-fashion during the excavation of a burrow. The septum characterizes living and fossil alligators, and is foreshadowed in the Eocene genus *Procaimanoidea*, possibly ancestral to the genus *Alligator*. In the American alligator, the back of the neck is armored by four enlarged, bony scutes, and in the Chinese alligator by six; but in the caimans, the number is eight or more. Also, in the alligators (at least the living ones) the bony plates of the back do not form such a tightly interlocked shield as they do in the caimans.

Of all the caimans, the most alligator-like in appearance is the black caiman, *Melanosuchus niger* (Spix). It is, however, no more closely related to the alligators than is any other caiman. *Melanosuchus*, the genus whose only member is the black caiman, is closely related to the genus *Caiman*, the latter including the spectacled and the broad-nosed caiman as well as extinct species. The black caiman was first described scientifically by Johann Spix, a German naturalist-explorer who encountered the reptile on the Solimões (upper Amazon) River. He dubbed it *Caiman niger;* but in 1862 the English taxonomist John Gray erected the genus *Melanosuchus* for the sole accommodation of the species Spix had found. The generic names of South American caimans were in a state of flux for many decades, but the situation need not be reviewed. The zoological question is whether the black caiman is sufficiently distinct from the species of *Caiman* to warrant a genus of its own. It seems to be. One of its skull characters (the vomer exposed on the palate) is unusual in crocodilians. Also characteristic of the black caiman is a very large orbit. The orbit is the skull cavity that contains the eyeball and associated structures. In the living reptile, the large size of the eye is obvious. The head shape is unusual among crocodilians; the snout is broad, yet tapers abruptly to a sharper point than one would expect in a broad-snouted crocodilian. The species of *Melanosuchus* and of *Caiman* have a bony ridge that borders the orbit above, and that crosses the top of the snout just in advance of the eyes. The function of this ridge is unknown.

Figure 95. A juvenile of the black caiman (above), showing the bright facial pattern. The abruptly pointed snout of the adult (at right) is unusual among crocodilians. [W. T. Neill]

The black caiman is essentially a species of the Amazon Basin. It ranges from Marajo, the vast island in the mouth of the Amazon, and from nearby Ilha Mexiana, westward across northern Brazil, and so into southern Colombia, northeastern Peru, and eastern Ecuador. To the south it reaches the Brazilian state of Guaporé (Rondônia), and the northern part of the state of Mato Grosso. It has been reported to occur north of the Amazon drainage, on the upper Essequibo in southern British Guiana; the record has been questioned but is probably valid, for assuredly the species inhabits the upper reaches of the Rupununi River, west of the upper Essequibo in British Guiana. However, reports of the species south of the Amazon Basin, specifically along the Paraguay River, rest on a misconception. Early explorers in the Paraguay drainage found two species of caimans there, one of them very dark in color; and reference was thereafter made to the "black" caiman of the Paraguay. This reptile is the jacaré, a member of the genus *Caiman*. It should also be noted that in South America the adjective "black," or some equivalent such as *negro* or *preto*, is often applied to the darkest of the local crocodilian species, whether or not this is *Melanosuchus*.

When two or more species of crocodilians occupy the same area, they are ecologically separated. I had long supposed the black caiman, by far the largest of the four Amazonian crocodilians, to be a species of the large rivers and lakes. The reality of the situation turned out to be surprisingly different. The reptile will inhabit the shallows and margins of large lakes, but is more characteristic of areas with many small ponds. Low-lying, grassy savannas, periodically inundated, are probably the optimum habitat. The extraordinary feeding behavior, unique among crocodilians, should be highly effective within the pond and shallow-water habitat. The black caiman relies on hearing and vision to locate an animal that is moving in the shallows or at the water's edge. The reptile dashes through the shallows to lunge at the prey. At the time of attack, the caiman's body is carried well off the ground and the snout points straight ahead, the tip of the snout, not the side, seizing the prey. The style of attack is that of a terrestrial predator, even though prey is not hunted far from water. In the black caiman, the sense of hearing is very keen; the reptile will promptly swing about to face any distant splashing. The sense of vision is keen, too. At night, a captive black caiman may jump nervously when a hand is waved over its pen, although other species of crocodilians in the same pen take no notice.

The literature provides little information about the black caiman. In one account these reptiles are described as being "too lazy to swim away" when shot at; "too lazy to attack any large animal." But of course the term "lazy" is not descriptive of any reptile, whose movements are

Figure 96. The range of the black caiman (hatched area).

predetermined by the stimuli that reach it. The black caiman is seldom active in bright sunlight, but begins to move about at dusk. Its principal item of food is the capybara, a pig-sized rodent that spends much of its time in the shallows. Where black caimans live, one may occasionally find masses of capybara hair lying in the shallows or at the water's edge. Local residents hold that the black caiman will regurgitate the hair of a capybara, or of some other mammal that is eaten. In a crocodilian's digestive tract, mammalian hair will certainly remain in fairly good condition after most other traces of the engulfed mammal have vanished. However, regurgitation has not been reported in any crocodilian, and it is more likely that a mass of hair is defecated in such good condition that local residents would not suspect its passage in the usual direction through a digestive tract.

Toward the lower Amazon Basin, there develops a marked seasonal variation in rainfall, the rainy season beginning near the end of the calendar year. Shortly before the rains arrive, when the ponds and lakes are at their lowest, fishes are often concentrated, and fall prey to the black caiman. This reptile, like the alligator in Florida, is often blamed for the disappearance of cattle. In some areas the black caiman is much feared, but I could learn of no well-authenticated attack on man. In the herpetological literature, the black caiman has been described as "the only dangerous member of the alligator family," but the description seems to have been influenced by folk beliefs. In South American writings the species is often called "ferocious" or "dangerous," but an eye-witness account of an attack is not forthcoming.

There is a report of a 10-foot black caiman that was taken from a flooded den in savanna country near a river. The end of the reptile's snout could be seen dimly when someone looked into the den. The caiman was alert; it "roared" (hissed loudly, I suppose) and caused water to slop out of the den. It cannot be concluded that the reptile dug the den in which it was found. The giant armadillo, a mammal with a range something like that of the black caiman, lives near rivers and digs a burrow that could accommodate a large crocodilian.

The black caiman builds a nest of vegetable debris. The nest averages larger and higher than that built by an alligator, although much depends on the kind of material available for nesting. Several females may nest near each other. The length of the egg varies from about 3¼ to 3½ inches, the diameter from about 2 to 2¼ inches. The juvenile is deep black above, with narrow crossbands of pale yellow. Some of the bands may be broken or incomplete, so that a crossband count cannot be given exactly. Usually there are about nine crossbands on the body, although the first of these, just behind the head, may be indistinct. The bright facial pattern of the juvenile is shown in Fig. 95, left. The juvenile grunt is much like that of the alligator. I do not know whether there is a juvenile distress call. The juvenile does have a distinctive kind of call, which I term the warning growl. When approached by an enemy, a small black caiman will utter a deep, prolonged, throaty growl, a surprising noise to come from a reptile. This call sounds much like a dog's growl. The juvenile will also hiss when disturbed.

The maximum size of the species is problematical. I have seen a good many 10-footers and one approximate 13-footer. A specimen photographed years ago at Leticia, Colombia, measured slightly over 13 feet. Several publications in English give the maximum length as 15 feet, and several in Spanish or Portuguese as 5 meters; but the basis for the assertions does not appear. As might be expected, "travelers' tales" mention black caimans about twice as long as any actually measured. At any rate, there is no empiric basis for the frequent assertion that the black caiman exceeds the American alligator in length. This caiman does not lose its bright pattern as rapidly as does the alligator. The light-yellow crossbands of the black caiman eventually turn white, but remain conspicuous even in large adults.

There is one good record of predation on an adult black caiman by an anaconda. Otherwise, man is the only known enemy of this crocodilian. The Amazon Basin has been encroached upon by man to a much greater degree than is likely to be realized by persons who have not visited that region. The species has been hunted to supply the demand for hides and zoo specimens. In recent decades, many low-lying, grassy tracts within the Basin have been turned over to cattle ranching; and on the ranches special effort is made to eradicate all caimans regardless of species. Ranch hands are sometimes paid a small bounty for every caiman egg that is destroyed. While sizeable populations of the black caiman persist in some areas, the species is an endangered one. In recent years there has been a decline in the number of hides brought to dealers, and in the number of young black caimans taken alive.

Figure 97. Anacondas, giant constrictors of South America, are not well known; there may be several species. The kind shown at left will prey on the black caiman; the kind below it on Schneider's smooth-fronted caiman. [Ross Allen's Reptile Institute]

Figure 98. The broad-nosed caiman is characterized by a very wide skull, the widest of any living crocodilian. From K. P. Schmidt, 1928, Field Museum of Natural History Publication 252.

Now to the genus *Caiman*. The naturalist Spix, exploring the Rio San Francisco in southeastern Brazil, collected a broad-nosed caiman. In 1825 he erected the genus *Caiman* to accommodate this reptile, and he dubbed the species *Caiman fissipes*. But as it turned out, Daudin had previously (1802) applied the name *Crocodilus latirostris* to an example of the same species. Spix's generic name was well-founded, while Daudin's specific name is the oldest one given to the broad-nosed caiman. Thus, the reptile is known today as *Caiman latirostris* (Daudin). It has been found to occupy an extensive part of eastern and southern South America, outside the Amazon drainage. The range extends from the Brazilian state of Pernambuco southward to the state of Rio Grande do Sul, and westward into the Gran Chaco. In the extreme southern part of its range it is known chiefly from the drainage of the Paraná, records being few in the Paraguay drainage farther west. In the extreme southwestern part of its range, the broad-nosed caiman is exposed to an occasional freeze as cold fronts sweep northward out of Patagonia. The southerly limit of the range is probably determined by the amount of cold the species can tolerate. However, the exceedingly broad head and powerful jaws of this caiman must reflect some dietary specialization, presumably turtle-eating; and many areas might not provide the necessary food. Within its range, the broad-nosed caiman is present in some drainages but not others, a circumstance implying some special requirement that is filled only at scattered localities. The distribution overlaps that of the jacaré, but it is unusual to find the two at the same locality.

Remains of a giant toad (listed as *Bufo marinus* but probably *Bufo*

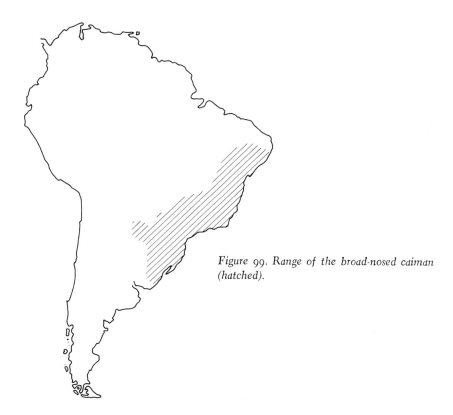

Figure 99. *Range of the broad-nosed caiman (hatched).*

Figure 100. A broad-nosed caiman in life. [Ross Allen's Reptile Institute]

ictericus) and of a small bird were found in the stomach of one broad-nosed caiman, along with about a dozen stones that served as gastroliths. A captive broad-nosed caiman produced forty-eight eggs. The egg measures about 2¼ to 2½ inches in length, about 1¾ inches in diameter. The maximum adult length is between 6½ and 7 feet. The adult usually is light-colored for a crocodilian of its size; the yellowish-green or yellowish-brown of the back fades laterally into the yellow of the belly. Vernacular names for the species are *jacaré verde* and *jacaré de papo amarelo*.

The genus *Caiman* includes one other living species, the spectacled caiman, which is broken into several geographic races or subspecies. Before considering the subspecies, first we may consider the species as a whole. The spectacled caiman has been a source of much nomenclatural dispute. This common, widespread species came to scientific attention in the days when taxonomy was an infant science. At that time, generic and specific limits were very broadly drawn. Linnaeus, founder of the system of zoological nomenclature, had several species of crocodilians at his disposal, among them the spectacled caiman; but he lumped all of these reptiles simply as a crocodile. When in 1758 he used the name *Lacerta crocodilus* for this composite assemblage, he focused his attention on the spectacled caiman, even though he thought he was describing the crocodile that was mentioned so often in Classical writings. Modern European taxonomists often adhere to the letter of the nomenclatural law, especially in dealing with New World species; and so the spectacled caiman appears under the name of *Caiman crocodilus* (Linnaeus) in the writings of many European workers and their American followers. But the name *crocodilus* is so inept that a majority of workers in the United States have rejected it in favor of the next oldest specific name, provided in 1801 by J. G. Schneider, who dubbed the reptile *Crocodilus sclerops*. With the establishment of the genus *Caiman*, Schneider's species was transferred to it. Thus, the spectacled caiman stands as *Caiman sclerops* (Schneider) in many works, including the present one. The type locality of Schneider's species is unknown.

Figure 101. *An example of the common South American race of the spectacled caiman.* [Ross Allen's Reptile Institute]

The common name, spectacled caiman, refers to the bony ridges that border the orbit and extend across the top of the snout.

The spectacled caiman occupies an enormous range, from the Mexican state of Oaxaca to the Paraguay River in southern South America. Within this range, the species is broken into four geographic races or subspecies, each with its own English and scientific name. Most distinctive of these races is the southernmost one, the jacaré, which may prove to be a fully distinct species. However, the jacaré and the common Amazonian race of the spectacled caiman neatly replace each other geographically, a spatial arrangement suggesting that the two are races of a single species. Following a conservative course, I list the jacaré as a race of *Caiman sclerops*. I use the name "spectacled caiman" for the species as a whole, and refer to the widespread race of the Amazon-Guiana region as the "common caiman." The latter may itself be broken by taxonomists into two or more subspecies when enough specimens have been examined.

In reptiles, the various races of a single species may differ considerably among themselves in habits as well as appearance; and so it is well to consider separately each race of the spectacled caiman. Of the four currently recognized races, by far the best known is the common caiman, *Caiman sclerops sclerops* (Schneider). It ranges from Venezuela and the Guianas southward through the Amazon Basin, excluding the upper Rio Apaporis, where a different subspecies is found. It also reaches Trinidad and some other islands off the northern coast of South America. It inhabits a variety of aquatic situations, including ponds, lakes, swamps, marshes, streams, and even saltmarsh on occasion. It is more characteristic of the still water than of the flowing; more common in open situations than in deeply shaded ones.

The nest is often built of vegetable debris scraped from the surface of the ground. In some areas the debris is full of palm spines. The nest is usually constructed no more than a yard from the water's edge. Several females may nest near each other. An occasional nest is in full sunlight, but most are built in thickets or beneath bushes and trees. An exposed nest may be made of fresh, green material. The surface of an exposed nest may crust over, thus shielding the contents from desiccation. The female crawls over the side of the nest to give it a final shaping. Most investigators say the nest is not defended, and they cannot be blamed for holding such a view; for this caiman is shy, and flees to the water if a person is in the vicinity. Nevertheless, a large female, in a fairly undisturbed area, will defend her nest even against man. The nest is defended with fair frequency against Amazonian Indians (who are small people on the average). The size of the nest is variable. Loose material, if present in abundance, may be piled into a nest larger than that of the American alligator; but damp, finely divided material may be fashioned into a small, tightly compacted nest. Having finished the nest, the female may withhold her eggs, presumably until climatic conditions become more favorable for laying. May is the month of egg-laying, although this might not be the case in peripheral parts of the range.

Most clutches are made up of twenty-five to thirty eggs. The smallest reported clutch included eighteen eggs, the largest forty. Of course, local residents often claim to have seen much larger clutches than any that have actually been counted. Egg size is notably variable. The length varies from about 1¾ to 2¾ inches, the diameter from about 1 inch to 1½ inches. The shell is white at the time of laying, but is soon stained by the debris of the nest. An occasional egg is blunter and larger at one end than at the other, an unusual circumstance among crocodilians. A few days after it is laid, the egg develops a whitish band around its smaller circumference; the band is more nearly opaque than the rest of the shell. A similar band exists in the egg of the American alligator and of some turtles. In the wild, most caiman eggs hatch, old nests rarely containing more than a few abortive eggs.

The hatchling, not much over 6 inches long, is yellowish or yellowish-brown, with black crossbands. There may be six bands on the body (counting one just behind the head), and seven on the tail. However, the bands are often broken or incomplete, some of them present on one side of the body only. Amusingly, in several parts of South America the local residents may recognize three "kinds" of common caiman, according to whether the crossbands are complete, broken at the midline of the back, or broken and alternately arranged. The three varieties are given completely different names, although all three may turn up in a single brood of hatchlings. There is a dark spot on the posterior part of the hatchlings lower jaw, but otherwise the side of the head is not strongly patterned. The juvenile grunt is voiced, and the impulse to grunt has a very low threshold; when many hatchlings are kept together, some grunting may be heard at almost any time. In the Amazon drainage, these diminutive hatchlings have to live with an extraordinarily large and diverse assemblage of aquatic predators; and so the common caiman, more than most other crocodilians, might profit from a behavior pattern that kept the adults constantly alerted to the whereabouts of the young. When the juvenile is seized by an enemy, it voices a distress call. A captive juvenile may not cry out when seized up by its keeper; but the attack of a predator is more violent, and is accompanied by actual physical hurt to the little reptile. The distress call is a segmented cry, much like the distress call of the alligator but higher in pitch.

Although the common caiman is widespread and often abundant, its feeding habits in the wild have gone almost uninvestigated. Captive individuals forage like small alligators, rubbing the side of the snout over the substratum, and biting sideways at any food that is discovered in the process. However, at times the caiman will also rely on other senses to locate food; it does not forage with the side of the snout as consistently or determinedly as does a small alligator. No doubt small aquatic organisms make up the bulk of the food. Dr. Frederick Medem, who has contributed so greatly to our knowledge of South American crocodilians, photographed a common caiman whose lower jaw had been pierced by two spines of a catfish; the fish itself was found in the reptile's stomach.

A wonderfully detailed old engraving portrays a common caiman in the act of defending its eggs against a bead-snake (Anilius). The engraving may have been based on a painting made in Surinam around the year 1700 by the artist-naturalist Maria Merian. At any rate, the creator of the picture certainly knew the common caiman, its eggs, and the bead-snake. The latter species, nonvenomous, is thought to be a burrower, and a predator on snakes and lizards. I would not be surprised if it turned up around a caiman's nest, or if it were eaten by the nesting female .

The maximum size of the common caiman is reported to be 8½ feet. I have known several captive ones whose measurable growth stopped when about 1 foot short of the aforesaid record. Seldom does one see a 7-footer in the wild, although 5-footers are not rare. This species is unusual in that the stratum corneum may be shed in small patches, each about ¼ to ½ inch in diameter. In two or three days' time, the stratum corneum of the entire body may be shed in the form of these patches. In a population of common caimans, the individuals are not as widely spaced as alligators would be.

The natural enemies of the common caiman are unknown. Man is the chief enemy. Each year when the hatchlings emerge, thousands of them are sent to the United States as "pets," or are mounted for local or foreign sale as curios. South American cattle ranchers, trying to eradicate caimans, do not distinguish the black caiman, which might on rare occasions take a calf, from the inoffensive common caiman which takes small prey. There has been some demand for the hides of the common caiman. The survival of this reptile in fair numbers may reflect its ability to live in a great variety of aquatic situations, and probably an ability to subsist on a variety of small animals.

I have wondered, however, if the hatchling of the common caiman was somehow protected aaginst certain predators by a secretion, or an odor, that man does not readily detect. This idea came to mind when I learned of a woman who was allergic to baby caimans. She did not fear or dislike the little reptiles; in fact, she thought they were rather appealing. She worked in a post office where large numbers of baby caimans were mailed to pet fanciers. If there was a baby caiman in the building, even though it might be packed away in a container, she would break out with a rash, develop swollen eyes and a "runny" nose, and find it hard to breathe. Other reptiles did not affect her in this fashion. Of course her reaction could have been idiosyncratic. But on the other hand, a species would profit if the individuals had the ability to release a fast-acting allergen when disturbed. In this connection, it may by significant that the Amazonian Indian tribes, without exception as far as I can learn, will not eat the common caiman, although the same tribes eat the smooth-fronted caimans and declare them to be excellent.

The biology of the common caiman has another puzzling aspect. In at least some areas, this reptile has the ability to "change color" rapidly. Metachrosis or "color change" in reptiles involves so-called melanophores, concentrations of dark pigment in the cells of the skin. A given expanse of a reptile's skin may appear green, yellow, or some other color when the melanophores are in a contracted state; but when the melanophores expand, they obscure the aforesaid color, and impart a dark cast. Metachrosis exists in many lizards and at least a few snakes. In some lizards, metachrosis may be involved primarily with camouflage (that is, background-matching), or with alteration of the image that is presented to a predator; but a more widespread function of metachrosis is that of defense from extremes of temperature. In most metachromatic species, the melanophores expand when the individual is chilled, and contract when it is warm. Thus, the reptile darkens when it becomes cold, lightens when it becomes hot. As is well known, a dark color absorbs heat while a light color reflects it. A common caiman, normally marked with black bands on a background of olive or yellowish-brown, will darken as it is chilled, becoming so dark that the crossbands are no longer distinguishable. When fully darkened, it looks remarkably like an individual of the Central American subspecies, which throughout the greater part of its range is uniformly dusky at all times. Warmed again to normal temperature, the common caiman rapidly assumes its normal coloration. It would not be surprising if a reptile from some temperate clime should darken rapidly when chilled. But why should a tropical caiman have this ability? At least one other tropical reptile, the boa constrictor, for unknown reasons has the ability to darken with cold.

Leaving the common caiman, we may turn to a more northerly race of *Caiman sclerops*: the brown caiman of Central America and southern Mexico. Throughout the greater part of the Cenozoic, South America was separated from Central America by a wide seaway, dubbed the Panama Portal. Not until around the beginning of the Pliocene was the seaway bridged by what is now the Isthmus of Panama. The spectacled caiman is a powerful swimmer, and could have crossed into Central America from South America before the seaway was bridged. But even if it did, there surely was not much genetic intercourse between the Central American and the South American populations of the species; and so the two went separate evolutionary ways. The appearance of the Isthmus permitted the two populations to flow together again, and to interbreed in the zone of contact.

The brown caiman is commonly stated to range from the Atlantic coast of Colombia northward through Central America into extreme southwestern Mexico; but this statement is misleading. Northward of Nicaragua, the species becomes restricted to the Pacific slope, and so is lacking from a large part of Central America. The range does not overlap that of Morelet's crocodile, which inhabits the Caribbean slope of southern Mexico, British Honduras, and Guatemala. The Mexican distribution of the brown caiman is limited to the states of Chiapas and Oaxaca. A supposed Michoacan record seems to rest only on a misunderstanding; local residents indeed speak of the *caiman*, but by this they mean the American crocodile. There may be some truth in a report of a true caiman on the Pacific slope of Colombia.

The original description of the brown caiman came about in unusual fashion. A strange crocodilian was found in the Rio Magdalena of Colombia. On one side of the reptile's head, the fourth tooth of the lower jaw fit into a pit in the upper jaw, an arrangement characteristic of alligatorines. On the other side of the head, the upper jaw was notched in a fashion that left the lower fourth tooth exposed when the mouth was closed; this is more of a crocodyline arrangement. Only two of the fingers were clawed. There was no bony plate in the upper eyelid, and no ridges on the head. The tail was notably low-crested. The total length was a little less than

Figure 102. A spectacled caiman from Colombia's Rio Magdalena (above) is obscurely marked. In Central America and Mexico, the same species is uniform brown (at right). [Ross Allen's Reptile Institute]

29 inches. In 1868 E. D. Cope described the specimen as representing a hitherto undiscovered genus and species, and named it *Perosuchus fuscus*. I could not guess what the reptile actually was, beyond the likelihood that it was highly aberrant, a "freak." In 1928 K. P. Schmidt decided that the name *fuscus* could be used for the Mexican and Central American caiman. Since then, this caiman has generally been called *Caiman fuscus* (Cope) or *Caiman sclerops fuscus* (Cope), depending on whether it was considered a full species or merely a race of the spectacled caiman. By either interpretation, the type locality of the brown caiman would seem to be the Rio Magdalena. The lower Magdalena, around Barranquilla, is the chief source of the caimans that are sent to Florida by the thousands every year. The lower Magdalena population appears to be intermediate between the brown caiman and the common caiman. Thus, I have granted the brown caiman subspecific standing only, referring to it as *Caiman sclerops fuscus* (Cope).

The brown caiman occupies a variety of aquatic situations, but reaches maximum abundance in fresh, open, quiet waters. At the mouth of the Magdalena, it enters brackish waters, feeding there upon mollusks and crabs. Its habits are poorly known. A nest is built of vegetable debris. In Chiapas, the nesting season is said to be sometimes between April and July. The eggs and hatchlings of true, fully differentiated *fuscus* are not known. Eggs from the Rio Magdalena region do not differ from those of the common caiman. Hatchlings from the Magdalena are much like those of the common caiman, although the black crossbands are more interrupted. Magdalena caimans darken as they grow older, and eventually become dull olive with only a trace of pattern. However, they do not develop the rich, uniform brown coloration that characterizes the Central American and Mexican population. If a young caiman from the Magdalena is chilled, it darkens rapidly, thus coming to look more like the norm of the subspecies. A melanistic juvenile was seen from the Magdalena. It was completely black above and below, except for an irregular grayish area along the midline of the belly; even the iris of the eye was black.

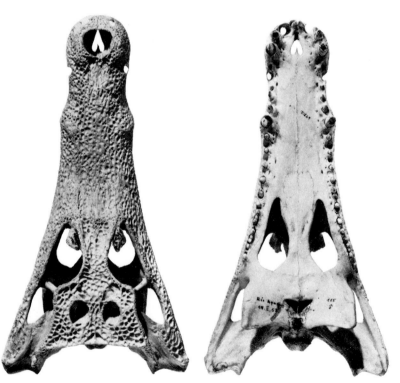

Figure 103. The Apaporis River caiman has a narrower snout than does any other race of the spectacled caiman. Shown is the skull of the type specimen. From Fred Medem, 1955, Fieldiana: Zoology 37.

The brown caiman voices the juvenile grunt and the juvenile distress call. Adults can be lured by an imitation of the latter cry. Both young and adult will hiss when cornered. The maximum size is reported to be 6 feet, but I have not seen one that would exceed 5. At any rate, the brown caiman is a smaller reptile than the common caiman. The range of the brown caiman is overlapped by that of the American crocodile, but the two species, separated by habitat, are not in competition with each other to any significant degree. The crocodile, a much larger reptile, inhabits principally the large rivers, estuaries, and coastal lagoons—situations in which the brown caiman rarely occurs.

A third subspecies of the spectacled caiman is the Apoporis River caiman. Described as recently as 1955, it stands as *Caiman sclerops apaporiensis* Medem. It is confined to the upper Rio Apaporis of Colombia, as far as is known. It has a remarkably slender snout for a member of the *sclerops* complex. The coloration of the adult is also distinctive: blackish spots and vermiculations on a bright yellowish-brown background. The smaller juveniles are not readily distinguished from those of the common caiman. The maximum length of the Apaporis River caiman is close to 7 feet. The tail seems to have been mutilated in a surprisingly high percentage of the known specimens. A mutilation of this kind is most likely suffered when the reptile is a hatchling. Possible competitors of the Apaporis River caiman are the two smooth-fronted caimans (*Paleosuchus*) whose ecological niche will be discussed later. The black caiman ranges to the lower Apaporis but not the upper. (The upper reaches of the river are separated from the lower by a series of waterfalls.)

Even though the Apaporis River caiman is strikingly distinct by virtue of its narrow snout, this reptile is surely a race of *Caiman sclerops* and not a separate species. Away from the Rio Apaporis, but still within Colombia's Comisariato Amazonas, the common caiman may show a narrower snout and more vermiculate pattern than usual, a circumstance probably betokening the genetic influence of *apaporiensis*.

A fourth race of the spectacled caiman is the jacaré, *Caiman sclerops yacare* (Daudin), first described far back in 1802. Daudin knew it to inhabit Paraguay and parts of Brazil. The range of the jacaré centers in the Mato Grosso of Brazil, and extends southward of the Mato Grosso along the Paraguay River. The upper Paraguay is an area of vast marshes, in which are formed mats of water hyacinth and aquatic grasses. The mats, known as *camelotte*, break up at times of high water, and many of the fragments drift down the Paraguay River. Such a floating island carries many organisms with it, and may reach Buenos Aires or even Montevideo before it falls to pieces. Jacarés, both large and small, have been found on these natural rafts, as well as snakes and lizards. The continuous range of the jacaré extends southward about to Corrientes, near the Paraguay-Argentina border; records farther south may be based on individuals that were carried down-river on floating masses of *camelotte*.

There are several references in the literature to the supposed occurrence of the jacaré in the Parnaíba, at the western border of the state of Piaui in northeastern Brazil. Investigation reveals the record to have been based on nothing more than a 1905 illustration of a caiman's skull. The skull was broader than is usual in the common caiman, and so was like that of the jacaré. However, in the common caiman the skull may broaden with age. I have seen old captives of the common caiman that had become broader of head than a jacaré. There seems no reason to postulate the presence of the latter far outside the general region of the Paraguay drainage.

The biology of the jacaré is almost unknown. Stomach contents have included fishes, crabs, river snails, and a snake, along with accidentally swallowed vegetation. Gastroliths have not been found in the few stomachs that have been opened. The maximum length has been given as 8 feet, and the figure seems accurate. I have known some captive adults that ceased growing measurably when about 7½ feet long.

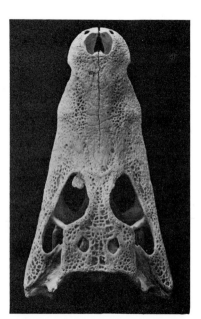

Figure 104. In this skull of a jacaré, note two small holes near the end of the snout. Two teeth of the lower jaw originally protruded through these holes. The bony plate of the upper eyelid has been preserved on the left side of the skull only. From K. P. Schmidt, 1928, Field Museum of Natural History Publication 252.

The dentition of the adult jacaré differs on the average from that of the other caimans in that several enlarged teeth of the lower jaw may completely penetrate the upper jaw. There may be a large hole extending vertically through the side of the upper jaw and accommodating the enlarged lower fourth tooth. In some individuals this hole may also be broken completely through to the lateral surface of the upper jaw, so that the lower fourth tooth is exposed when the mouth is closed. This situation may exist on just one side of the head, or on both.

Finally, we come to the genus *Paleosuchus*, the smooth-fronted caimans. They are so called because, unlike the species of *Caiman* and *Melanosuchus*, they lack ridges around and in front of the eye. The upper eyelid of a smooth-fronted caiman is ossified throughout; thus, a bony flap completely covers the eye when the latter is closed. Another peculiarity of the smooth-fronted caimans is the completely dark iris of the eye. In this genus, there is a heavy armor of bony scutes dorsally, and elsewhere there are many bony platelets each imbedded in a scale. Thus, a smooth-fronted caiman is completely armored, as were some very early crocodilians. Perhaps John Gray had this situation in mind when in 1862 he coined the name *Paleosuchus*, meaning "ancient crocodilian." The two species have been called rough-backed caimans, in allusion to the coarseness of the dorsal armor. Efforts have been made to call one of the species "smooth-fronted" and the other "rough-backed"; but these usages are confusing, and both have been inconsistently employed.

Cuvier's smooth-fronted caiman, now standing as *Paleosuchus palpebrosus* (Cuvier), was described by the Baron Cuvier in 1807 on the basis of a specimen from Cayenne, French Guiana. The distribution involves the Guianan region, the Amazon Basin, and the Mato Grosso. Schneider's smooth-fronted caiman was known to science as far back as 1768, when it and several other crocodilians were thought to be one and the same. It stands today as *Paleosuchus trigonatus* (Schneider), 1801, and is the type species of the genus *Paleosuchus*. Schneider gave no type locality. The range is nearly identical with that of Cuvier's species, but may not be quite as extensive. Schneider's smooth-fronted caiman is not known to break out of the Amazon Basin to enter the Mato Grosso, or to follow the Amazonian headwaters quite as far westward as does Cuvier's species.

What an ecological puzzle is presented by the smooth-fronted caimans!

Figure 105. Range of the brown caiman (horizontal hatching), the common caiman (diagonal hatching), the jacaré (vertical hatching), and the Apaporis River caiman (dot). The four are regarded as geographic races of the spectacled caiman.

Figure 106. The smooth, ridgeless snout and the heavy dorsal armor are shown in this photograph of Cuvier's smooth-fronted caiman. A lateral view of another individual (at far right) reveals the chunky build and dark iris. [Ross Allen's Reptile Institute]

How are the two ecologically separated from other crocodilians, and from each other? The ecological separation of *Melanosuchus* and *Paleosuchus* affords no problem; the former is a much larger reptile, given to foraging about the banks and shallows, and taking comparatively large prey. The two South American species of *Crocodylus* are very large reptiles of coastal situations and major streams, from which *Paleosuchus* is lacking. The real problem is the ecological separation of the smooth-fronted caimans from the spectacled caiman. The smooth-fronted caimans seem to be relict species, unable to compete with the spectacled caiman, and able to survive only in situations avoided by the latter. In my experience, smooth-fronted caimans are characteristic of deeply shaded waters. This is why virtually all locality records are in rainforest. Smooth-fronted caimans rarely leave the water, and are not seen lying in the sun. Most records of smooth-fronted caimans are for swiftly running or turbulent waters, which are usually avoided by the spectacled caiman. When smooth-fronted caimans and the spectacled caiman inhabit the same stream, the former will be found around rapids, waterfalls, and whirlpools, while the latter will inhabit the lagoons and the stretches of quiet water. Nevertheless, I think that the fundamental separation between the smooth-fronted caimans and the spectacled caiman is not a matter of the water's turbulence. In the first place, both species of *Paleosuchus* have at times been reported in quiet lagoons and swamps. In the southern end of Comisariato Amazonas, Colombia,

Cuvier's smooth-fronted caiman was found in the absolutely still, deeply shaded waters of floodplain ponds. These bodies of water may be flooded when the Amazon rises, but otherwise they are isolated. The ponds were full of dead leaves. The mottled jaws and reddish cranial table made the head of the floating reptile very difficult to locate among them. No spectacled caiman was seen in these densely shaded ponds.

In nature, the smooth-fronted caimans often bear a growth of filamentous green algae, which seemingly infest the normal, healthy reptiles. The relationship may be one of mutual advantage; the caiman is camouflaged, and the alga finds a substratum on which it does not have to compete with other algal species. A similar relationship seems to exist between epizoic algae and turtles in the United States. When smooth-fronted caimans are sent to the United States and kept in exposed pens, the reptiles are likely to be attacked by their own or some native alga; the infestation soon becomes heavy, and the reptile dies.

The ecological separation between the two smooth-fronted caimans is not clear. Most writers, describing the habitat of these caimans, have not tried to distinguish between the two species. In most areas, Schneider's smooth-fronted caiman is by far the more conspicuous of the two, and I think this species is the one that has so often been noted in swift waters. Schneider's smooth-fronted caiman has a comparatively long and narrow snout, the kind of "streamlining" one expects in a crocodilian of strongly flowing waters. In contrast, Cuvier's smooth-fronted caiman has a fairly short, broad snout, suggesting residence in quieter water. A dietary difference between the two species is also to be expected.

Cuvier's smooth-fronted caiman is reported to conceal itself by day in a burrow beneath the water level. One was taken from a burrow about 5 feet long in a dried-out swamp. The nest is built of leafy debris, and is guarded by the female. She will not try to defend the nest against man, however. Clutches include about fifteen to twenty-five eggs. Small pebbles are swallowed as gastroliths.

Schneider's smooth-fronted caiman is also said to conceal itself by day in a burrow beneath the water level. Three individuals, tethered in a brook in their natural habitat, never showed themselves by day, but emerged about 9:00 P.M. to pursue fishes. Unfortunately, some life-history notes on the smooth-fronted caimans do not make clear which species was under consideration. Stomach contents have been reported to include small ro-

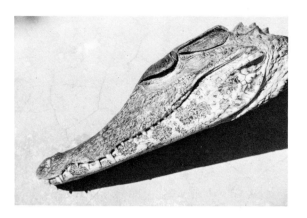

Figure 107. In Schneider's smooth-fronted caiman, the snout is comparatively long and slender. In both species of smooth-fronted caimans, the eye is completely protected by a bony flap when the upper eyelid is closed. [W. T. Neill]

dents, a snake, small crocodilians of undetermined species, and numerous fishes, along with a scattering of fresh-water shrimp, crabs, aquatic beetles, and aquatic spiders. As nearly as I can determine, this list of prey is a composite one, based on stomach contents of both Cuvier's and Schneider's smooth-fronted caimans. The beetles and spiders probably were secondarily ingested, having first been eaten by a fish. It may be mentioned that South America has a freshwater fish fauna of extraordinary diversity, the number of catfish species alone exceeding the total number of North America freshwater species. It would not be surprising if both of the *Paleosuchus* turned out to prey chiefly on fishes, with *trigonatus* pursuing the more active fishes, and *palpebrosus* nosing about for the slower bottom-dwellers.

Individuals of *Paleosuchus* are said not to occur in groups. This observation was made in an area where the habitat was swift streams. Such a habitat does not produce a great deal of prey of the kind acceptable to crocodilians; and under such conditions, wide spacing of individuals is to be expected. Cuvier's smooth-fronted caiman is the smallest of the New World crocodilians, the maximum reported length being about 4 feet 9 inches. (The species is sometimes called "dwarf caiman.") Schneider's smooth-fronted caiman is a good bit larger, reaching a maximum recorded length of about 7½ feet. An anaconda, very much distended by a recent meal, was discovered half out of water on the Rio Ucalayi in eastern Peru. The snake proved to measure 19½ feet in length, and to contain a 6-foot Schneider's smooth-fronted caiman. The snake's digestive juices had begun to bleach and corrode the skin of the engulfed crocodilian. (The large species of anaconda may feed primarily on caimans of some kind.) Man is the only other known enemy of the smooth-fronted caimans. The Indians harpoon the reptiles, using a special kind of an iron harpoon point with two

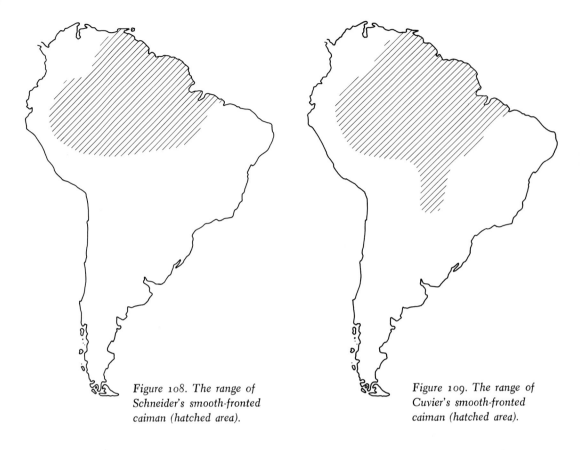

Figure 108. The range of
Schneider's smooth-fronted
caiman (hatched area).

Figure 109. The range of
Cuvier's smooth-fronted
caiman (hatched area).

barbs. Living specimens of the two smooth-fronted caimans are also taken
for eventual sale to zoos and reptile fanciers.

Many naturalists have explored South America and written about their
experiences in that country. However, I have relied but little on this body
of literature, in which it is often hard to separate observation from hearsay.
We are told, for example, that the females of the jacaré will form a ring
about their young to fight off the hungry males; and that the mother jacaré
will carry her baby by the scruff of its neck, like a mother cat with her
kitten. We are further told that the broad-nosed caiman will eat the
tender roots of aquatic plants. And when the edibility of a caiman is discussed, mention is often made only of the reptile's tail. The writings of the
naturalist-explorers also include some probably accurate accounts of caiman
behavior; but regrettably in many cases one cannot decide just what species
was under observation.

21 THE AMERICAN CROCODILE

THE FOUR New World species of crocodiles are all poorly known. The American crocodile, by virtue of its wider range, has received more study than any of the other three. Like some other crocodilians, the American crocodile came to scientific attention in the early days of taxonomy. In 1768 the Austrian physician Joseph N. Laurenti (not "Laurentus," as sometimes given) erected the genus *Crocodilus* (which we now prefer to spell *Crocodylus*), its type-species being *niloticus*. Laurenti also mentioned a "*Crocodilus americanus*." Whatever Laurenti thought he was describing under this name, he based the description not on an actual specimen but on an old and quite unrecognizable drawing that was published by Albertus Seba in 1734. While some of Laurenti's successors used the name *americanus* for the common crocodile of the New World, herpetologists during the last 40-odd years have rejected the name. (In a 1954 paper on *Gavialosuchus*, the name *Crocodylus americanus* was revived for the American crocodile, but I think through accident rather than intent.) Modern herpetological preference has been for the unequivocal name *Crocodylus acutus* Cuvier, 1807. Cuvier's type-specimen was from "Santo Domingo," by which was meant the Dominican Republic.

This crocodile's distribution, mainly a coastal one, centers in the Caribbean region. There are populations on Cuba, the Isle of Pines, Hispaniola, and Jamaica. In past decades, a few individuals turned up on Grand Cayman, Cayman Brac, and Little Cayman. The species also inhabits the Caribbean coast of Venezuela and Colombia. On the mainland northward of Colombia, the distribution follows the entire Caribbean coast of Central America, and then swings around the coasts of the Yucatán Peninsula to reach the Gulf coast of Mexico. Northward along the Mexican Gulf coast, the distribution extends approximately to Tampico in extreme southern Tamaulipas, as far as is known. The American crocodile also inhabits the tropical Pacific coasts, from Ecuador and Colombia northward to southern Sinaloa, Mexico. The Tres Marias Islands, in the Pacific about 75 miles

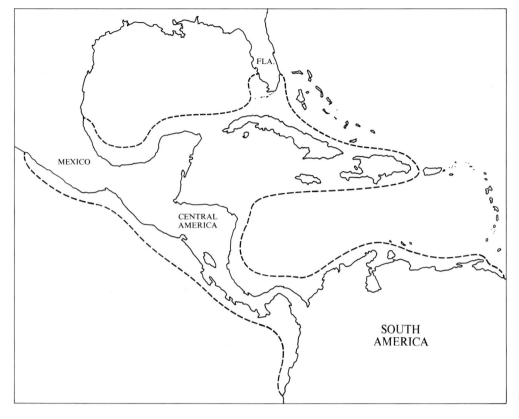

Figure 110. *The range of the American crocodile. Range boundaries are indicated by a broken line. The species follows some larger rivers to points well inland.*

off Mexico's Nayarit coast, likewise have yielded a few individuals. Finally, the distribution extends to the lower coasts of Florida. (Vague records for the Bahamas, if at all valid, are based on wandering individuals, not populations.)

For a long while, the presence of a true crocodile in the United States, in southern Florida, went unrecognized. Constantine S. Rafinesque-Schmalz, a colorful naturalist and traveler, in 1822 wrote of crocodilians in the southern United States, "The most common species is the *Crocodilus lucius* of Cuvier [the American alligator]; there is a sharp-snout alligator in Florida which must be his *Crocodilus acutus*." Rafinesque was quite right, but his surmise was overlooked for decades. (Or disavowed, more likely. While Rafinesque's occasional amours and inebrieties would scarcely lift the eyebrow of a modern worker, they scandalized the pedants of the past century.) In 1869 a natural history journal made note of a crocodile skull, exhibited in Boston. The skull had been obtaiend earlier that year by Jeffries Wyman, pioneer student of Florida archeology. This crocodile, and another like it, had been killed at the mouth of the Miami River, near the point where the stream emptied into Florida's Biscayne Bay. At that locality was a tiny settlement—half-a-dozen houses clustered around Brickell's Store—about which Miami would soon grow. Wyman's crocodiles were correctly identified as *Crocodylus acutus*, and the skull he brought back provided the first tangible proof that Florida harbored a true crocodile. The sportsman C. J. Maynard, who knew of Wyman's discovery, in 1873 claimed to have killed a 10-foot crocodile in Florida, at a locality between Lake Harney and the head of the Indian River. The locality record has since been cited as the northernmost one for the American crocodile. I find it improbably far north, some 170 miles above the northernmost verifiable record on the Florida east coast; and Maynard's approach was more entertaining than scientific. In any event, herpetology is beset with dubious locality records, most of them based on fabrications, misidentifications, introductions, or errors of cataloguing; and in general, far-outlying locality record for some particular species is not worth considering unless based on the discovery of an actual population of the species at that locality. Within modern times, crocodiles have existed on the Florida east coast as far north as the general vicinity of Palm Beach.

The range of the crocodile on the Florida west coast has been a matter of dispute. In 1953 there was published a study of crocodile distribution in and near the Everglades National Park. At that time there were many rumors but no definite identification of a crocodile north of Cape Sable, which forms the southwestern tip of Florida. Verifiable records seemed limited to a coastal strip east of Cape Sable, the islets in Florida Bay, and the upper Keys. Since in the early 1950s no crocodile could be located on the Florida west coast, the conclusion was drawn that the species never lived there. However, crocodiles have been hunted extensively both inside the park and outside it; and it is temeritous to declare, on the basis of investigations around 1950, just where *Crocodylus acutus* lived a decade or two earlier. I have seen a young specimen collected near Everglades, Collier County, Florida, and do not question a record from the Imperial River, Lee County. Charlotte Harbor may represent the northernmost limit of the species' range on the Florida west coast. But it is certainly true that reports of the species on that coast are heresay in most cases. The distribution did extend to the lower Keys, there being good records for Key West and Stock Island. There are no records for the Marquesas or Tortugas groups.

Reptiles, even large ones, escape from captivity, or else are liberated, with surprising frequency. Sometimes they are liberated quietly, and recaptured with great fanfare, in order to publicize an exhibit or its operator. No biological significance can be attached to the reported capture of a crocodile at a bathing beach near Sarasota, Florida; to the shooting of another in the upper Coastal Plain of South Carolina, at Swansea (according to a newspaper account); or to records for Alabama and Texas.

The fossil history of the American crocodile seems to be unknown. However, I have wondered about the identity of slender, "ribbed" teeth of crocodilians, found along the eastern seaboard from New Jersey into southern Florida. These have been given a name of their own (*Pliogonodon priscus* Leidy, from New Jersey), or more recently in Florida have been compared with the poorly known South American genus *Charactosuchus*. Paleontological attention has not been drawn to the existence of ribbed teeth in many Florida specimens of the American crocodile, in which there is a strong rib on the anterior face of the tooth, matched by an equally strong one on the posterior face. Between the two strong ribs there are usually nine lesser ribs on the outer face of the tooth, and eight (rarely nine) lesser ribs on the inner face. The distinctness of the lesser ribs depends on the position of the tooth in the jaw, and on the size of the crocodile. The anterior teeth are the more strongly ribbed, and the ribbing is usually more obvious in the young adult than in the old adult or the juvenile. Dental ribbing has been reported for the African sharp-nosed crocodile, and exists in several other crocodile species. The most heavily ribbed teeth I have seen were those of a New Guinea crocodile. However, ribbing is not limited to crocodiles. It is weakly developed in Schneider's smooth-fronted caiman, and very strongly developed in some spectacled caimans. Thus, this dental character does not necessarily place the South American *Charactosuchus* as a *Crocodylus* or even a crocodyline. However, it does suggest the direction in which one might look for the identification of slender, ribbed, crocodilian teeth from the Pliocene of Florida. Such teeth are surely not those of the alligator, and probably not those of a *Gavialo-*

Figure 111. On a cold winter day, an American crocodile (from Florida) follows a little patch of sunlight about its pen. [Ross Allen's Reptile Institute]

suchus. They might logically represent a *Crocodylus,* perhaps even the direct ancestor of the American crocodile. (The alligator tooth has a well-developed fore-and-aft ribbing, but little or no trace of the lesser ribs.)

At one time during the last glaciation, with so much water locked into the glacial ice, the sea level was about 370 feet below its present stand. The level has been rising (not continuously, but with occasional halts and brief reversals of direction) for about the last 17,000 years. During most of this time, American crocodiles in Florida (if present) must usually have left their remains at localities that are now submerged (recalling that the species is essentially coastal and estuarine in distribution). It is also possible that the American crocodile could not survive in Florida during a peak of glaciation. In modern times, with the last glaciation still melting back, this essentially tropical species has been barely able to maintain a foothold in the southern tip of the state. At an elevation of about 25 feet on the Florida Gulf coast, in Citrus County, I found a Pleistocene fossil bed with slender, ribbed teeth which I regard as those of the American crocodile. Also present were blunter, ribless teeth which could have been those of crocodile or alligator. The deposit also included remains of watersnake, extinct giant tortoise, softshell turtle, snapping turtle, large box turtle, and the ancestor of the yellow-bellied turtle. This assemblage dated probably from a Pleistocene interglacial stage, when sea level was above its present stand. Such an interglacial stage presumably had a climate that was a bit warmer than the present one, thus permitting the crocodile to range farther north on the Florida Gulf coast than it now does.

Figure 112. South American individuals of the American
crocodile, such as the one shown here, have a very long,
narrow snout (upper). The snout is broader in an American
crocodile from Cuba's Cienaga de Zapata (lower). This
latter individual is the one mentioned in the text as having
responded vigorously to an imitation of the juvenile
distress cry. [Ross Allen's Reptile Institute]

Observations on a captive crocodile revealed how winter temperatures might determine the northern limit of the species' range. The specimen, an adult from Palm Beach County, Florida, was kept in an artificial but outdoor pen, where it was exposed to Central Florida air temperatures. Water, at a temperature of about 71 degrees Fahrenheit, was kept running strongly through a pool in the pen. On a cold day in winter, the reptile would move into a patch of sunlight that struck the pool (Fig. 111). It would even move out of the water to follow this patch of sunlight, rapidly becoming chilled and numbed by the cold substratum and air. Placed back in the pool, it would be warmed by the water therein—and would promptly

Figure 113. A Guatemalan juvenile of the American crocodile. [W. T. Neill]

Figure 114. A young American crocodile in close-up view. [Ross Allen's Reptile Institute]

crawl back into the little patch of sunlight. In other words, the crocodile had the impulse to move, when chilled, not to the warmest situation but simply into sunlight. This behavior pattern could be highly useful in the tropics, where a crocodile could move into morning sunlight if chilled by the nightly fall of temperature, or could crawl onto a warm and sunny bank if chilled from prolonged immersion. But in an area where winter temperatures fall low enough to numb the reptile, such a behavior pattern would prove fatal. In contrast with this crocodile, captive alligators would take to the comparatively warm water as soon as the substratum and air grew cool. The alligators would in fact sink to the bottom of the water and lie there motionless for hours if the air was quite cold. As noted previously, hibernation in the alligator involves some seasonal changes of physiology, but such changes might be evolved more readily than the behavior patterns that are necessary for a crocodilian's survival in a temperate climate.

The American crocodile is also unable to live for long in cold water. If kept in water with a temperature below about 65 degrees Fahrenheit, the crocodile becomes torpid, sinks to the bottom, and eventually drowns. It may be mentioned in passing that 65 degrees Fahrenheit is approximately the body temperature below which tropical reptiles in general are likely to be killed outright or weakened and rendered susceptible to respiratory infections.

Earlier workers did not realize how widespread the American crocodile was, or how variable in some of its anatomical features. Thus, the species was "discovered" and named—more accurately, renamed—on several occasions. Some of the synonyms may be worth reviving to designate local races of the single species *Crocodylus acutus*. In 1870 Auguste Duméril and Marie-Firmin Bocourt described the crocodile of the Rio Magdalena, Colombia, as *Crocodilus lewyanus*. For a brief while in the 1940s this name was revived, as *Crocodylus acutus lewyanus* Duméril and Bocourt, to designate a South American subspecies whose range limits were undetermined. In my experience, American crocodiles from northern South America have an extremely long and narrow snout (Fig. 112). They are occasionally difficult to distinguish from the Orinoco crocodile, *Crocodylus intermedius*, a long-snouted species.

The Florida population of the American crocodile was once thought taxonomically distinctive. In 1875 C. E. Jackson and W. T. Hornaday killed two adult crocodiles at Arch Creek, a tributary of Biscayne Bay in what is now North Miami. That year, Hornaday dubbed the Florida population *Crocodylus floridanus*. Today it is surmised that the Florida population of the American crocodile is not taxonomically distinct from the West Indian one. A thoroughgoing review of the American crocodile, with abundant material from all parts of the range, might reveal the existence of two or more races; but for the present, the American crocodile must stand simply as *Crocodylus acutus*.

The principal habitat of this species is the coastal waters and brackish estuaries. Individuals are most common in channels and coastal lagoons, although some (usually small ones) are found in shallower water of tidal flats and mangrove swamps. Florida Bay provides an unusual habitat, a broad expanse of fairly shallow, brackish water dotted with islands. The American crocodile will also range up the larger rivers. It does not invade large, freshwater rivers in Florida, for such streams are not present in the southern part of that state. The streams of the southwest coast are embayed and brackish along their lower courses, while those of the southeast coast are small (and canalized by man in most cases). But in other parts of the range, the crocodile follows the tropical rivers far inland, especially if these rivers offer large lakes along their courses. If a tropical, freshwater lake harbors crocodiles, it is likely to be not only large and connected with a river, but also teeming with fishes and provided with sandy beaches. No doubt the American crocodile takes a variety of prey, but its principal food is fishes, for the pursuit of which the reptile is anatomically and behaviorally adapted. Beaches seem necessary if the crocodile is to nest.

Some anomalies in the crocodile's distribution (for example, absence from the Bahamas) may be explained by the ecological requirements of the hatchlings, which can live in the fresh or the brackish water but not the strongly saline. Although the adults (which will swim at sea) might reach some particular island, they could not establish a population on it unless it offered freshwater streams or heavy runoff.

In 1898 H. L. Willoughby offered what is taken to be the first description of the crocodile's nest. He claimed to have examined two nests in the Everglades, and said that the nest was merely a hole scooped in the sand at the water's edge. The eggs were deposited in layers, and the clutches numbered 50 and 75 respectively. The sand over the nest was smoothed to the general ground level. His account was evidently influenced by legends, such as that of the multitiered nest with a great number of eggs. Also, his description suggests that he may really have examined turtle nests. Nevertheless, Willoughby's account has provided the basis for many subsequent remarks on the nest of the American crocodile.

Actually, the American alligator and the American crocodile are not very different in their methods of building a nest. The female alligator scrapes up vegetable debris to make a nest, but will scrape up sand along with it if such material is present. In captivity she will build a nest of sand alone if no vegetable debris is provided. The female crocodile scrapes up sand alone, and makes no effort to incorporate vegetable debris into the nest. However, her nest may include some vegetable debris if this is already mixed with the sand. The crocodile's nest may also include gravel if present in the sand. The alligator piles vegetable debris into a high mound, while the crocodile piles sand into a lower but wider mound. In both species the female digs a nesting cavity in the top of the elevation she has constructed; and in both, the hind feet are used to dig the cavity as well as to help shape the nest. One literature account states that the female crocodile throws more sand over the completed nest, using "both front legs" for this

Figure 115. A sight that can no longer be seen: a crocodile on the beach at Key West, Florida, 1935. The species has vanished from many parts of its Florida range. [W. T. Neill]

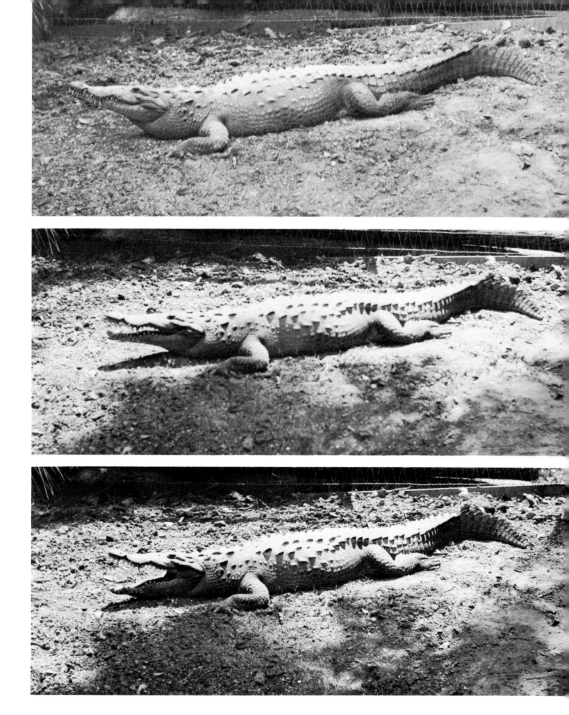

Figure 116. A Florida specimen of the American crocodile rests with mouth closed (upper); but upon sensing the approach of an intruder, it opens the mouth (center). Thereafter, it will lie for a long while with jaws agape (lower). [Ross Allen's Reptile Institute]

Figure 117. *Above, a Florida haunt of the crocodile: the mangrove-bordered lower reaches of a stream near the coastal edge of the Everglades. In Florida, the crocodile often nests in "sand" that is really pulverized shell. Shown at right is a Florida Gulf beach that is entirely of shell.* [W. T. Neill]

purpose. This conclusion was not based on actual observation but on an attempted interpretation of tracks left by one female crocodile at her nesting site. In my experience, the female crocodile reached forward with a hind leg (much larger and stronger than a foreleg) to throw sand over the nest. Finally, the female crocodile, like the female alligator, crawls over the sides of the nest to give it a final shaping. In most areas the finished nest of the crocodile is not like that of a sea turtle, smoothed over and virtually undetectable; it is a definite eminence, about 12 to 18 inches high and 10 to 12 feet across. A few crocodile nests are nearly flat. Such nests are in areas where the sand is firmly packed, except for an upper inch or two where it is drier and looser. In such an area the female scrapes out the nesting cavity, but cannot find much loose sand to throw atop the nest; what little she throws may be washed down later by rains. Even under these conditions a nest can be detected, for its material is looser than the surrounding sands, and around it are signs of the female's scrapings.

I have followed common usage in describing the nesting material as "sand"; but in the Florida range of the crocodile the coastal "sands" are

often thick deposits of pulverized shell. Over the centuries the shells of marine mollusks have been ground up by wave action and piled along the shores of peninsular Florida (Fig. 117, right), forming a substratum in which plants will grow and reptiles nest. (A turtle nest, shown in Fig. 75, is in this shell "sand.")

The female crocodile guards her nest; but being very shy, she will not guard it against man. If a person is in the vicinity, the nesting female will slip away to hide in the water nearby. Nevertheless, it is easy to prove that she remains with her nest, for her fresh tracks are usually to be seen at the edge of it. On one occasion, a wire fence was erected around a crocodile's nest in the wild, with the hope of containing the hatchlings when they appeared; but during the night the female not only tore away the fence but also twisted it into a veritable wire rope. The female crocodile may have to travel 20 yards or more from water to find a sandy nesting ground; and her movements, between the nest and the water, may produce a well-worn trail.

The egg-laying season of the crocodile in Florida extends from about mid-March to mid-May, with most of the eggs deposited in April. The number of eggs in a clutch ranges from 21 to 56, as far as records show. The egg varies in length from about 2½ to a little over 3 inches, and in width from about 1¾ to a little over 2 inches. Crocodilian egg measurements are here given in general terms, even though measurements to a fraction of a millimeter, so often met with in the literature, would doubtless appear more scientific. A reptile egg will change its size. Probably every reptile egg is smaller at the moment of deposition than at the moment of hatching. Also, if an egg is kept in comparatively dry surroundings it will absorb water when these surroundings are finally dampened, and will increase markedly in all dimensions. As the nesting hole is not wide, the eggs must pile up in it; but as the eggs tumble into the hole, they do not arrange themselves into distinct tiers. The width of the hole is such that the eggs are piled two and three deep, in irregular fashion.

In Florida, most hatchlings appear around late July and early August. The hatchling is about 9½ inches in total length. The dorsal ground color is greenish-gray. The pattern consists of four or five blackish crossbars on the body, and eight to ten blackish crossbars on the tail. The crossbars are often broken up into spots, especially on the tail (Fig. 118). Aberrant hatchlings have not been described, although double-yolked eggs have been reported. According to one account, Colombian hide-hunters saw two whitish, presumably albinistic, adult crocodiles "in the Palenque River." American crocodiles from Cuba occasionally lack all traces of crossbars, being a uniform light gray above.

The small American crocodile voices the juvenile grunt, which like the alligator's is occasionally given even before hatching. If mauled by some predator, the small crocodile voices the juvenile distress call, a repetitive note much like the alligator's distress call but higher in pitch. The adult crocodile is more rapidly galvanized into action by the distress call of its young than is the adult alligator under comparable conditions. Even a freshly caught crocodile, which would normally stay hidden for weeks in the mud and water of its pen, will charge at an imitation of the distress cry, and can be made to leap or scramble over a fence that would contain the reptile at other times. If someone is skilled at imitating crocodilian distress calls, he can rouse an American crocodile without evoking any response from an alligator; or he can do the reverse.

In Honduras, stomach contents of the American crocodile were re-

Figure 118. A hatchling of the American crocodile, from Florida. [Ross Allen's Reptile Institute]

Figure 119. A hatchling of the American alligator (at left) and of the American crocodile. Both specimens are from Florida. [W. T. Neill]

ported to include top minnows; other fishes; a ball of hair; hooves, perhaps of peccary; and fragments of turtle shell. Bones of a crocodilian were also found in the stomach of a large crocodile, and from this find the assumption of cannibalism was made. Believing that a behavior pattern has evolved because it is beneficial to the species that exhibits it, I favor the less sensational (and less anthropomorphic) interpretation that one crocodile perhaps indulged in a bit of scavenging, or picked up a few crocodilian bones as gastroliths. One Honduran crocodile was seen whirling "what appeared to be a smaller one" in the air. But as the locality harbored iguanas and basilisks, both given to swimming at times, the prey could have been a lizard. All the crocodile stomachs contained small stones. Captive American crocodiles will ingest hard objects that are thrown into their pen. I have known pop bottles, beer cans, and tobacco pipes to be ingested by captive crocodiles. The food of the species in Jamaica has been reported to include fishes, crabs, birds, and dogs.

The American crocodile is popularly believed to be far more dangerous than the alligator, but this belief reflects the influence of stories about Old World crocodiles, some of which are occasional predators on man. The American crocodile is not known to have attacked anyone in Florida, either in the course of predation or in defense of the nest. On one occasion, a badly wounded crocodile bit a tormenter who took it for dead; and on another a crocodile bit a canoe after the occupants had belabored the reptile about the head with boat paddles in order to rouse it to action. On a third occasion, a reptile collector paddled a canoe up to a crocodile that was resting on the bank. The reptile, possibly roused from sleep, dashed for the water, and bit at the canoe in passing. There are a few accounts of crocodile attacks on man in the tropical lands south of Florida, and one or two of these may be truthful. But in general, the American crocodile is a very shy reptile, much harder to approach than the alligator. The crocodile's senses seem to be very keen. The nocturnal collector of crocodiles may let his canoe drift down very quietly upon the floating reptile, but the latter will usually dive before a noose pole can be brought into play. An entire local population of crocodiles will become exceptionally shy if hide-hunters have been operating in the area.

During the first few years of life, the crocodile's growth rate at least equals that of the American alligator, to judge from observations on captives. A month after hatching, a Florida juvenile had reached a length of 11½ inches. A male crocodile from the Florida Keys, 39 inches long when caught, added 16 inches to that length in as many months. Old crocodiles grow slowly, however. Around 1925 a crocodile was captured at Lantana, Florida, on Biscayne Bay. The reptile at that time was a sizeable adult, although its exact length was not recorded. In 1947 it measured 13 feet 8 inches in total length. In 1952 it pushed its snout through a line of cypress posts that separated its pen from that of a very large alligator, and was fatally injured by the much heavier alligator. I measured this crocodile at the time of its death, and obtained the following figures: total length 14 feet; head length 28½ inches; from the anterior margin of the eye to the tip of the snout, 16¾ inches; head width 17 inches; hind foot length 12 inches; midbody width 27 inches. In five years time this crocodile had added very little to its length, and its tooth replacement was slowing down or had ceased. Only 48 teeth were present, as follows: upper jaw, 11 on the right side and 13 on the left; lower jaw, 13 on the right side and 11 on the left. The normal tooth complement of the American crocodile, prior to the onset of senility, is generally given as 70. In Florida, at least, it is usually 66 (18 teeth on each side of the upper jaw, 15 on each side of the lower).

The largest American crocodile known to me was one of the two killed by Jackson and Hornaday at Arch Creek, in what is now North Miami. The specimen, a male, was 15 feet 2 inches in length, with an estimated 6 inches missing from the end of its tail. The maximum length of the species is commonly given as 23 feet, but this figure stems from an old account that was never amenable to verification. As the Lantana specimen (Fig. 120) had about ceased growing at a length of 14 feet, and was showing signs of senility, I would expect the maximum possible length in most areas to be very nearly approached by the Arch Creek crocodile.

The American crocodile has several times been reported to inhabit some kind of basin-like depression. It is uncertain whether such depressions are of wholly natural origin, or whether they are modified to some degree by the crocodile. A captive crocodile will dig into bottom mud, and occasionally emerge with the mud plastered over its snout and back (Fig.

Figure 120. A 14-foot crocodile from Florida, photographed shortly after its accidental death in captivity. [W. T. Neill]

121). In the wild a crocodile will make a kind of burrow, a short tunnel that runs more nearly horizontally than vertically. It is sometimes possible to catch a crocodile by blocking off the entrance of the burrow, and then digging down to the reptile. It is not clear why a tropical crocodilian should construct a burrow, but the habit must be of considerable importance. The spectacled caiman, the black caiman, and the two smooth-fronted caimans, along with the American crocodile, have all been reported to inhabit burrows at times. Almost any captive crocodilian, having been fed to repletion, will seek a retreat (usually the pool in its pen) and lie there for about 36 to 40 hours; and so in the wild the reptiles might seek a burrow or other shelter in which to lie quiescent while digestion proceeds.

In the usual habitat of the American crocodile, there is a scarcity of firm, open spots on which the reptile can crawl out of water. The spots that do exist are much frequented; and from them well-marked trails (so-called slides) may lead to water. A crescent of lake beach may be occupied by a dozen or more crocodiles of all sizes. Even in the water, the crocodiles do not seem to be territorial (unless the indiivdual's territory is very small). By night, one sweep of the headlamp over the water may reveal as many as 35 crocodiles, their eyes glowing redly. Leon L. Walters, using binoculars by day, counted 75 of these reptiles in sight at one time in an embayment of a Honduran lake.

In its fourth year, at a length between 4 and 5 feet, the American crocodile loses the impulse to voice the juvenile distress call, and begins instead to voice a series of roars. This series is the equivalent of the alligator's bellow, although it does not have the deep, thunderous quality of the alligator's effort. The "bellow" of the adult crocodile is made up of about three to six "roars," each roar actually a loud hiss. On one occasion, blasting at a distant limestone quarry set off a chorus of bellowing among captive alligators, and an adult crocodile was stimulated to respond. The crocodile, floating in the water, adopted the posture that would be expected of an alligator under the same conditions: head uplifted, tail arched and waving. In this position, the crocodile banged its jaws together several times. (An alligator, drifting in the water, may indulge in some loud jaw-banging, but not in connection with bellowing.) The crocodile then dived, and "bellowed" under water, raising streams of bubbles with every exhalation. This episode took place in north-central Florida on February 8, in the coldest part of the year. I have also seen and heard American crocodiles

Figure 121. *A captive crocodile emerges with mud on its snout and back, evidence that the reptile had been digging into the muddy bottom.* [*Ross Allen's Reptile Institute*]

"bellowing" above water. On one occasion four captive adults held their heads as high out of water as they could, and "bellowed" with their snouts almost touching. It seemed to me that each was trying to rear above the others; and three of them promptly ceased "bellowing" and began to move a few feet away when they were overtopped by the largest of the group. Yet, these crocodiles showed no actual hostility toward one another, each becoming quiescent as the chorus died down.

Known enemies of the American crocodile are few. In Florida, raccoon tracks have been found around disturbed nests of the crocodile, and a black bear was once actually seen to raid a nest. In the tropics, the jaguar is said to dig into the crocodile's nest, and to prey on the juveniles as well. Of this I have no proof, but the jaguar does often forage along the edge of a stream or lake. Man is the chief enemy of the American crocodile. The numbers of the species have been greatly thinned in all parts of the range, including Florida. The last records of the crocodile on the Florida east coast were in the 1930s, and the same is true of the last records for the Lower Keys. In 1951 I found one adult at a locality on the Upper Keys near Key Largo, but the Florida population today seems to be restricted to Florida Bay and the mainland shores south of Cape Sable.

22 THE ORINOCO, CUBAN, AND MORELET'S CROCODILES

THE ACCOUNT of the American crocodile may be followed by that of the Orinoco crocodile, for the two seem to be closely related. In 1819 the physician Robert J. Graves applied the name *Crocodilus intermedius* to a long-snouted crocodile whose geographic origin he did not know. It was the Orinoco species, which stands today as *Crocodylus intermedius* Graves. Its range is the Orinoco Basin at lower elevations. Thus, the distribution is primarily Venezuelan, although the species also reaches Colombia, where it has been reported from the Rio Meta.

There is no certainty that the Orinoco crocodile is a species distinct from the American crocodile, of which it might be only a geographic race. The Orinoco crocodile is noteworthy for a very long and slender snout. If the snout be considered as extending as far back as the forward margin of the eye, then the snout's length is well over twice the maximum width. The snout rises toward its tip, and so the profile is concave. On the back of the neck, the Orinoco crocodile has six enlarged scutes. The foregoing characters of head conformation and neck scalation are supposed to distinguish the Orinoco crocodile from the American crocodile. They do so on the average, but not consistently. In many American crocodiles, the snout length is no more than twice the snout width; but the ratio does not hold for some South American individuals, in which the snout length is about 2.2 times greater than the snout width. The profile of the American crocodile is often straight, or even slightly "humped" just in advance of the eyes; but sometimes it is strongly concave as in the Orinoco species. The American crocodile commonly has only four enlarged scales on the back of the neck; but six may be present, in the same arrangement that characterizes the Orinoco crocodile. Perhaps the most consistent distinguishing feature of these two crocodiles is the length of the symphysis, the junction of the right and left halves of the lower jaw. In the Orinoco crocodile, the symphysis extends back to the level of the sixth tooth or even farther back, while in the American crocodile it extends back only to the level of the fourth or the fifth tooth.

Many aquatic organisms, including some that cannot move overland or live out of water, have managed to pass between the Orinoco and the Amazon drainages. The two river systems are closely interdigitated, especially in Venezuela's Amazonas Province where the Casiquiare is said at times to link them. One supposes that the high elevation of the Sierra Pacaraima, and of other uplifts in and near southern Venezuela, has barred the spread of the Orinoco crocodile southward into the Amazon. But it is strange that no crocodile exists along the coast of the Guianas and Brazil. It will be recalled from Part II that in the New World the genus *Crocodylus* has been primarily North American, and the incursions of the genus into South America were never very successful, to judge from the fossil record. The American crocodile probably arose in Mexico or Central America and moved south. It may have had insufficient time to spread southward coastally beyond Colombia, Venezuela, and Ecuador. It is tempting to believe that *Crocodylus acutus*, having ranged eastward along the northern coast of South America as far as the mouth of the Orinoco, then moved up that drainage, where it gave rise to *intermedius*. Before this conclusion could be accepted, more must be learned about the crocodiles of the lower Orinoco and the nearby Venezuelan coast. In any event, *intermedius* is a *Crocodylus* that has evolved precisely the characteristics one would expect of a crocodile that had to coexist with a variety of caimans, for it is very large, agile, long-snouted, a river-dweller, ecologically unlike any of the living caimans.

In 1910 a crocodile turned up on Grenada, a little island about 150 miles north of the Venezuelan coast. The reptile was reported to be of the Orinoco species. The great flood of the Orinoco River carries masses of floating vegetation to the sea, so perhaps the crocodile made a part of the voyage on a "floating island."

The natural history of the Orinoco crocodile is known mostly from

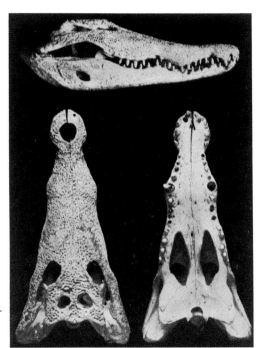

Figure 122. An extraordinary specimen from the crocodilian collection of the Senckenberg Museum: the skull of a large Orinoco crocodile, collected in Venezuela in 1885. From Robert Mertens, 1943, Senckenbergiana 26, No. 4.

travelers' tales, which are of limited value, often based largely upon legends relating to the Nile crocodile. We are told that the eggs of the Orinoco crocodile are buried in the ground. Presumably, then, the species does not pile vegetation into a nest, but nests in a fashion like that of the American crocodile. There is no reason to accept early, excited claims that the Orinoco crocodile often menaced man. A verifiable attack on man has not been reported, and one would expect this reptile primarily to be a fish-eater. The maximum size is commonly given as "22 feet and four inches" or "20 to 24 feet." These records are based on a literature statement made in the 1820s; and in the century and a half that have gone by since then there has been no tangible evidence that the species can reach so great a size. The largest measureable specimen falls a little short of 13 feet. The maximum size is probably about equal to that of the American crocodile.

The numbers of the Orinoco crocodile have been greatly reduced by hide-hunting, and the species has been difficult to obtain in recent years. It might be mentioned that, where crocodiles and caimans are both available to hide-hunters, the crocodiles are generally hunted much more intensively. A caiman is likely to be small. Its dorsal armor (unsaleable, usually) forms a wide strip, and the ventral scales may contain bony platelets, which lessen the value of a hide. The caiman's habitat may be difficult of access. In contrast, the large crocodile, with so much eminently saleable skin on its belly and sides, lives in a river or large lake, on which a boat can easily bring the hide-hunter within gunshot range.

Now to the Cuban crocodile. In 1807 the Baron Cuvier applied the name *Crocodilus rhombifer* to a crocodile whose geographic origin he did not know. It turned out to be the Cuban species, which stands today as *Crocodylus rhombifer* Cuvier. In historic times, the Cuban distribution has

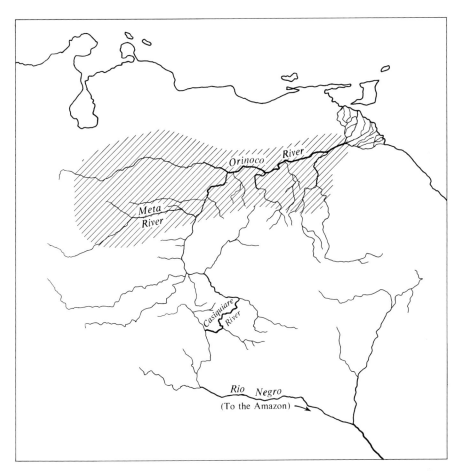

Figure 123. *The range of the Orinoco crocodile (hatched area) covers the lowlands of the Orinoco drainage in Venezuela, and reaches Colombia along the Meta River. The Orinoco and Amazon drainages are actually linked by the Casiquiare River, but the Orinoco crocodile does not reach the Amazon.*

been very limited. Published records have all been for Santa Clara Province (now called Las Villas Province, saints being out of fashion in Communist Cuba). These records cluster in the Ciénaga de Zapata, but some lie a little farther east, just east of the Bahía de Cochinos (the Bay of Pigs). In historic times the species has also existed on the Isle of Pines, seemingly confined to the Gran Ciénaga de Lanier in the southern part of the island. The sportsman C. J. Maynard claimed to have killed two different kinds of crocodiles on Little Cayman Island, which lies about 145 miles south of Cuba. Later workers, apparently accepting Maynard at face value, assumed that he had found both the American crocodile and the Cuban crocodile on Little Cayman. However, the American crocodile is variable individually, especially from young adult to old; and, regardless of the extent to which Maynard's adventures were fictionalized, the American crocodile is probably the only crocodilian ever to have reached the Cayman group of islands.

Fossils reveal *Crocodylus rhombifer* formerly to have had a wider range in Cuba. The name *Crocodilus pristinus* Leidy, 1868, was based on a fossil vertebra from Ciego Montero in Las Villas Province. In later years, more diagnostic bones were obtained from the vicinity of Ciego Montero, and seemed to be those of *rhombifer*. Fossils, probably of this latter species, have also been found at Casimbas de Jatibonico, in the same province. The Cuban fossils are of Pleistocene age, and they date from a time when freshwater marshland was more extensive in Cuba than it is today. In 1966 Luis S. Varona erected the name *Crocodylus antillensis* for some Pleistocene skull fragments from Cueva Lamas, a cave near Santa Fé on the north coast of Cuba, in La Habana Province. The description suggests *rhombifer* more than *acutus,* and *antillensis* may represent the Pleistocene stock from which modern *rhombifer* was derived.

In the days before modern hide-hunting with firearms, there seems to have been a strong ecological separation between the Cuban crocodile and the American crocodile, the former inhabiting freshwater swamps and marshes, the latter occupying large rivers and coastal situations. Early writers in Cuba agreed that the *caiman* (vernacular for the American crocodile) and the *cocodrilo* (vernacular for the Cuban crocodile) were never to be found at the same locality. But the activities of modern man rapidly altered the ecological situation. With the development of a charcoal-burning industry, swampy tracts were deforested; even mangrove swamps were cut over.

The *caimaneros*—professional hide-hunters—concentrated their efforts on the American crocodile, which was easier to locate and which had a more valuable hide than the more heavily armored Cuban crocodile. When hide-hunting died down (as it did for a time), the latter species moved into coastal situations from which it had previously been excluded. In 1917 Thomas Barbour found only the Cuban crocodile around the Bay of Pigs, in the coastal situations where the American crocodile would normally be expected; and the local residents knew that the circumstance was anomalous.

Figure 124. Young Cuban crocodiles, showing the stout build and the enlarged scales of the legs. The elevation behind the eye will become more prominent with age. [C. J. Hylander]

Figure 125. The range of Morelet's crocodile (horizontal hatching) and of the Cuban crocodile (diagonal hatching).

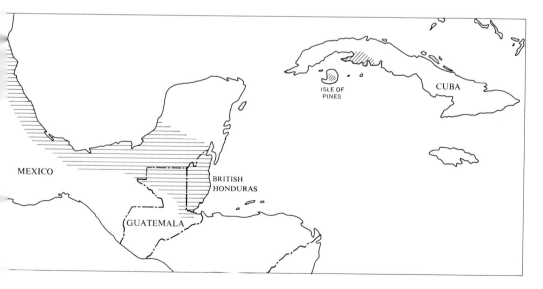

An earlier chapter suggested that among both reptiles and amphibians the ecological separation of two closely related species may function not only to minimize competition but also to prevent interbreeding. There are a number of instances in which modern man has altered the environment, producing ecologically abnormal areas in which two closely related species will begin to interbreed. In the United States, such hybridization has most often been reported among toads of the genus *Bufo*; and among reptiles, the red ratsnake now frequently hybridizes with the Everglades ratsnake in southern Florida, or with the yellow ratsnake in central Florida, in the unnatural milieu that is provided by farms and suburbs. It is possible that the American crocodile and the Cuban crocodile, as a result of ecological changes in Cuba, now hybridize there. The Cuban *caimaneros* report hybrid crocodiles which they call *mixturados* or *cruzados*. These reptiles are not the so-called *chinos*, which are typical American crocodiles except for a lack of dark markings. The hunters say that when a male crocodile cannot find a female of his own species he will mate with a female of the other species. In general, the opinions of hide-hunters are not scientifically important; but the *mixturados* themselves are impressively intermediate between the two crocodile species that inhabit Cuba. In *Crocodylus rhombifer* the build is very stout. The head is high posteriorly, meeting a thickened, muscular neck. The dorsal shield is made up of six longitudinal rows of bony plates (three rows on each side of the midline); and this shield is continuous with the neck armor, which is made up of six large plates. The legs of the Cuban crocodile are covered with enlarged scales, enlarged far beyond anything met with in other crocodilians. There is a high, bony elevation behind and a longitudinal ridge in front of the eye. The colors are yellow and black, and the pattern is primarily one of small spots. In contrast, *Crocodylus acutus* usually is slimmer of build, and without the high head or thickened neck. The dorsal shield is made up of four longitudinal rows of bony plates, this shield being well separated from the four plates that armor the neck. The leg scales are small. The colors are greenish-gray and black, and the pattern is one of crossbands which may be broken into blotches. In all the aforesaid features, the *mixturados* are intermediate. Reptile hybrids tend to be intermediate between the two parent stocks.

The Cuban crocodile courts in shallow water, not far from shore. A captive male was reported to make guttural noises while courting. The male also emitted *"resoplidos,"* which perhaps were exhalations. Copulation takes place in the shallows. The copulating male lies beside and partly atop the female, who bends her tail aside to facilitate intromission. According to several modern articles, the female digs a nesting hole in the ground near water, and after she has deposited her eggs she covers the hole with the dirt she has excavated. However, this statement, with only minor changes of phraseology, can be traced back to an 1880 work by Juan Gundlach. In his discussion of crocodiles, Gundlach supplied a few minor notes on three captive juveniles, along with some hearsay and anecdotal material. He also parroted the legends of his day: the American crocodile gives off an odor of musk; the Cuban crocodile cries like a child in order to attract attention; at mating time, the male crocodile bellows like a bull; a crocodile's dorsal armor will deflect a musket ball; the Cuban crocodile defends itself with its tail; the edible portion of a crocodile is its tail, and in the American crocodile even this appendage may have a musky flavor—the same old legends that eighteenth- and nineteenth-century writers, whatever their nationality, fastened upon the local crocodilian, whatever its identity. Gundlach's brief remark on crocodile nests could easily have been derived from some *campesino* who actually had seen or heard about a nest of the American crocodile. Among crocodilians, the basic pattern of nest-building is the scraping up of vegetable debris. A slight departure from this pattern, the scraping up of and digging into sand, is a likely specialization in a species that nests on beaches, as does the American crocodile. If the Cuban species, essentially a reptile of freshwater marshes, nested in the specialized fashion of a coastal and river-dwelling crocodile, the situation would be very interesting; it would also be very puzzling.

The egg of the Cuban crocodile measures about 3 inches in length and 2 inches in diameter. The hatchling is not known. The juvenile voices the distress cry when hurt. This distress cry is much like that of the American alligator and the American crocodile, being a repetitive series of high-pitched grunts. At the Parque Zoológico in Habana, adults of these three crocodilian species were penned together; and there it proved possible, by experimentally imitating a crocodilian distress cry at various pitches, to make all three charge at and practically over the fence that surrounded their pen. As far as I could learn, Cuban hunters do not know that it is possible to lure an adult crocodilian by imitating the juvenile distress cry. Such knowledge seems to have been confined to the southeastern United States and the Amazon Basin (although lately spread more widely by herpetologists and the books they write).

The present food of the Cuban crocodile is not known. Some recent

Figure 126. Skeleton of a Cuban ground sloth, displayed in 1916 by its discoverer, Carlos de la Torre y Huerta. Fossil bones of this sloth often bear tooth marks of the Cuban crocodile. [*La Sociedad de Historia Natural "Felipe Poey."*]

works have described it as preying on waterfowl, wild pigs, dogs, and people. The statement can be traced to Gundlach, who actually said that the Cuban crocodile could be baited with a dead bird. Pigs and dogs were not mentioned by Gundlach in unequivocal connection with the Cuban crocodile. He probably had in mind the food of the American crocodile, as he clearly did when he mentioned predation on man. The posterior teeth of the Cuban crocodile being stout and blunt, it has been assumed that the reptile preys on crabs and mollusks. I would suggest predation on turtles, however. A turtle, closely related to the yellow-bellied turtle of North America, inhabits almost all freshwater situations in Cuba. But the Cuban crocodile also has enlarged, sharp teeth in the forward portion of the jaw. The lower fourth tooth, and the upper tenth, are veritable "canines." This reptile would not need such huge teeth in order to capture, or to defend itself from, any of its modern associates in the freshwater marshes of Cuba (ignoring man and his domestic animals, comparative newcomers). Fossil deposits throw some light on the original feeding habits of the Cuban crocodile. As mentioned, remains of this reptile were found at Casimbas de Jatibonico and Ciego Montero. These localities, and others nearby, became famous for the remains of three genera of giant ground sloths. Some of these ground sloths were big as a bear (Fig. 126). Although probably vegetarian for the most part, the ground sloths were armed with powerful claws and teeth. It is believed that these mammals fed by pulling down tree branches or digging up plants. A Cuban crocodile, with huge teeth, strong neck, and heavy armor, would be well adapted for predation upon bulky ground sloths. Fortunately, we do not have to guess that such predation

Figure 127. An adult of the Cuban crocodile. Note the spotted pattern
and the bony ridge behind the eye. [Ross Allen's Reptile Institute]

took place. Not only are the bones of ground sloths and Cuban crocodiles
intermingled at some localities, but the sloth bones often bear the tooth
marks of crocodilians. It is interesting that fossil beds provide the only
clue, aside from hearsay and speculation, to the diet of the Cuban crocodile.

The Cuban crocodile is remarkably aggressive toward other crocodilians.
A 6-foot Cuban crocodile will chase a 9-foot American crocodile around
a pen, and maul the larger reptile if the latter is not rescued. The Cuban
crocodile also is, in proportion to its size, one of the most difficult of all
crocodilians for the herpetologist to handle. For one thing, this reptile
is heavily muscled, and therefore both strong and weighty. A firm grip on
the reptile's neck is hard to maintain, for the bony armor of that region

will hurt one's hands. If the reptile thrashes or "rolls" when seized, the outwardly tilted teeth can do damage even after the jaws are tied. But more importantly, the Cuban crocodile has an exceptionally strong impulse to fight when molested. This circumstance may reflect the evolution and long isolation of the species on Cuba. Not until the arrival of man did that island harbor any organism sufficiently large, and sufficiently predatory, to menace a crocodile that was above juvenile size. (I assume that the two local species of crocodiles, being ecologically separated, rarely fought with or preyed upon each other.) *Crocodylus rhombifer* never evolved much impulse to flee, for there was nothing from which flight was necessary, not until the American Indians reached Cuba a few thousand years ago.

This is not to say, however, that the Cuban crocodile has been a menace to man. The impulse to fight a man when cornered and the impulse to seize a man as an item of food are two very different behavior patterns Speaking very generally, the mere size of a man will discourage attack by any crocodilian that is under 9 feet long, even if the reptile belongs to a species that will take large prey, and comes from an area where the crocodilian population has not been rendered wary by hunting. A child, or an adult of some small race of people, might be attacked by a somewhat smaller crocodilian. I doubt that the Cuban crocodile has often reached the length of 9 feet. Gundlach gave 16½ feet as the maximum length of the species, but his record has generally been disavowed by recent workers. Modern books give 12 feet as the maximum length. This figure apparently stems from Thomas Barbour, who saw a mutilated hide "nearly twelve feet in length." When a crocodile is skinned in the usual fashion, the hide is not stretched very much; but a hide can be stretched if the skinner so desires. It is possible to take a 12-foot hide from a 9-foot crocodile, although the skin is likely to be torn here and there in the process of stretching. The mutilated hide seen by Barbour may well have been torn by stretching. The largest Cuban crocodile known to me was a captive adult that measured about 9 feet. The specimen was very stout, broad-headed, and with scattered gaps in the tooth row; it seemed to be fully grown, and senile. In the last two decades, it has been unusual to see a Cuban crocodile that exceeded 7 feet in length.

According to the Cuban literature, the adult of the Cuban crocodile produces "*un mugido sordo,*" presumably a sound analogous to what I have termed the bellow. Not surprisingly, Gundlach, who was steeped in the crocodilian legends of his day, wanted to believe that the sound was produced only by the male, and in the mating season. Gundlach, having been one of the few sources of comments, accurate or otherwise, on the Cuban crocodile, has been uncritically paraphrased by many subsequent writers on this little-known reptile. I once heard a captive Cuban crocodile voice its "bellow," the call actually being a mechanically repetitive series of loud hisses. This "bellow" was much like that of the American crocodile, but was more prolonged, no less than ten roar-like hisses making up the completed "bellow." The sex of the bellower was not determined. The date was December 5, a bright, cool day, and hardly a time of mating.

The Cuban crocodile has many peculiarities. While any crocodilian may walk about with the body held off the ground, the Cuban species does this more often than any other crocodile. It has exceptionally strong and muscular legs. While almost any juvenile crocodilian might occasionally adopt a squatting posture (like the alligator in Fig. 91), with the hindlimbs flexed and the forelimbs extended, the Cuban crocodile is the only species in which the adult often assumes this stance. The Cuban crocodile is the only member of its genus in which the iris of the eye is dark brown, so dark that the pupil is not readily distinguished. Elsewhere among crocodilians, a dark iris is met with only in caimans of the genus *Paleosuchus*, the Tomistoma, and the dwarf crocodiles of the genus *Osteolaemus*. It is not clear why the Cuban crocodile should have a heavily pigmented iris, in contrast with other members of its genus. Nor is it clear why this species should have, in adults, a high, bony prominence behind each eye. The same structure, but more highly developed, characterized the extinct "horned alligator" from the Paleocene of North America. Perhaps during courtship the prominences of one individual are rubbed against the gular surfaces of the other; but this is speculation.

No doubt the Cuban crocodile will vanish before anyone can unravel the mysteries of its life history. In fact, the species may already be extinct. In 1949 Ross Allen and I went into the Ciénaga de Zapata, reputedly the last home of *Crocodylus rhombifer*; but we found only some *Crocodylus acutus*, these wary from constant hunting. In the 1950s quite a few fine, large adults of the Cuban crocodile reached the United States, but the reptiles were not taken from the wild; they had long been in captivity.

The account of New World crocodilians closes with a description of Morelet's crocodile. For more than half a century, the literature has asserted that Morelet's crocodile, a species of southern Mexico and northern Central America, is closely related to the Cuban crocodile. The assertion must be re-examined, for it rests chiefly on a series of mistaken suppositions. Well over a century ago, the biological collector P. M. A. Morelet visited the Yucatán Peninsula. As any enthusiastic collector would do, Morelet picked up interesting specimens at stops along the way. In Cuba he collected some mollusks, and when these eventually reached a museum they were incorrectly labeled as coming from Yucatán. In modern days, with so much emphasis on precise locality data, it is hard to realize that even as late as the 1930s at least one major museum labeled incoming specimens only with the point of shipment, even though this might have no bearing whatsoever on the point of collection. Arriving at his destination, Morelet collected some crocodiles of a species that had previously gone undiscovered. The reptiles were taken at what Morelet called "Lac Flores, Yucatan." This was Lake Petén Itza, also called Lake Petén or Lake Flores, in what is now the Petén of Guatemala. Morelet's material, properly labeled, was made the basis of a new species, *Crocodilus moreletii*. The description was published in 1851 by Auguste Duméril and André M.-C. Duméril, who selected a specific name that would honor the collector. Today the species stands as *Crocodylus moreleti* Duméril and Duméril. However, the reality of its existence was not immediately granted. In 1919 Thomas Barbour drew attention to Morelet's "Yucatan" mollusks that really came from Cuba, and guessed that the name *moreleti* was based on a *Crocodylus rhombifer* similarly carried by Morelet from Cuba to the Yucatán Peninsula. Barbour had not actually seen the type specimens, or any other specimens, of the Yucatán species. Nevertheless, his guess was seized upon by later workers, who promptly listed *moreleti* as a synonym of *rhombifer*. In 1924 Karl P. Schmidt showed that *moreleti* was a distinct species, which he found to be abundant in the vicinity of Belize (City), British Honduras. As that time, Schmidt had never seen a *rhombifer*; but of course he was constrained to compare *moreleti* with *rhombifer*, wanting to show that his predecessors had improperly synonymized the two. Thus although *moreleti* was restored to the scientific listings, it had become linked with *rhombifer* in the literature, and so in the minds of later workers.

The Cuban crocodile and Morelet's crocodile resemble each other in certain details of skull conformation. In both species the skull is wide, and deep posteriorly, when compared with the skull of the American crocodile.

The outward tilt of the teeth, so conspicuous in *Crocodylus rhombifer*, is approached in just a few of the largest *moreleti* skulls. The two species agree with each other, but not with *acutus*, in a feature of the palate: the premaxillaries form an approximately transverse suture with the maxillaries. In *acutus*, the premaxillaries are prolonged posteriorly, and the aforesaid suture forms an arc. The young *moreleti* is spotted with yellow and black, although not as brightly patterned as a *rhombifer*. So much for the similarities between the Cuban crocodile and Morelet's crocodile. The differences between the two are impressive if attention is turned to living specimens rather than the literature. Widely divergent from the crocodilian norm, *Crocodylus rhombifer* is one of the most distinctive members of its genus. On the other hand, *Crocodylus moreleti* is a very generalized crocodile: in most individuals of the latter species, the snout is neither impressively long and narrow, nor impressively wide. The dorsal armor is not as reduced as in *acutus*, nor as heavy as in *rhombifer*; the same might be said of the neck armor. In Morelet's crocodile there is no approach to *rhombifer's* horn-like prominence behind the eye. The legs of *moreleti* are covered with small scales; there is no approach to the extraordinary leg armor of the Cuban species. The build of Morelet's crocodile is neither as slim as that of the American crocodile nor as massive as that of the Cuban crocodile. Nor does the dark iris of *rhombifer* have a counterpart in *moreleti*, whose iris is pale silvery-gray, as is the case with most crocodilians. The spotted pattern of the young Morelet's crocodile soon vanishes, the adult being a drab, uniform grayish-brown above. This is unlike the Cuban species, which remains brightly patterned even as a large adult.

Morelet's crocodile has one skeletal feature unique among crocodilians: the maxillary bone, where it is enlarged to accommodate the base of the tenth upper tooth, may form an angulate rather than a rounded swelling. The angulation of the maxillary was once used to define a Pleistocene subspecies, *Crocodylus moreleti barnumbrowni* Mook, from the Petén of Guatemala, but the character exists in old adults of living *moreleti*. In the Cuban crocodile, as in crocodiles generally, the maxillary is swollen to accommodate an enlarged tooth, but the swelling is rounded rather than angulate.

While Morelet's crocodile and the Cuban crocodile may be more closely related to one another than either is to the American crocodile or to the Orinoco crocodile, the relationship has not been shown to be as close

Figure 128. The Cuban crocodile (at left) and Morelet's crocodile (right) are very different in build, snout shape, dorsal armor, leg scalation, and other features. [Ross Allen's Reptile Institute]

Figure 129. The skull of an old adult of Morelet's crocodile (at left in both photos) is characterized by outwardly tilted teeth. Such tilting is actually more characteristic of the Cuban crocodile, even though not evident in the skull of a fairly young individual of the latter species (at right in both figures). From Robert Mertens, 1943, Senckenbergiana 26, No. 4.

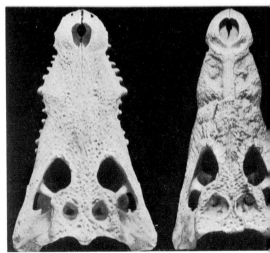

as one might infer from the literature. Morelet's crocodile may be the comparatively unchanged remnant of an ancient, generalized, continental stock from which was derived the highly specialized, insular *Crocodylus rhombifer*. However, it is not out of the question that some similarities between *moreleti* and *rhombifer* represent parallel adaptation instead of relationship.

The juvenile of Morelet's crocodile, with its fairly broad snout and its yellow and black pattern, is very reminiscent of a young brown caiman. The adult of Morelet's crocodile, usually about 6 or 7 feet long and of a uniform brownish color, looks much like an adult brown caiman. The primary habitat of Morelet's crocodile—the open, quiet waters—again recalls *Caiman sclerops*. These two species do not overlap geographically, but occupy mutually exclusive ranges. In northern Central America and southern Mexico the brown caiman is confined to the Pacific drainage, Morelet's crocodile to the Caribbean drainage. The similarity between these two reptiles, a crocodile and a caiman, does not indicate close relationship, but may well reflect the circumstance that the two are ecological counterparts of each other.

Two problems exist with reference to the distribution of Morelet's crocodile. First, how far does the species range into the Yucatán Peninsula? In British Honduras, the range extends northward through Orange Walk District and thence into Corozal District. I have seen one specimen that

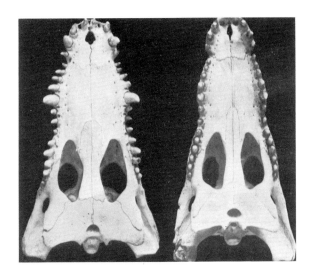

Figure 130. The young Morelet's crocodile is reminiscent of a young brown caiman in color, pattern, and head shape. [Ross Allen's Reptile Institute]

was caught just across the northern border of British Honduras, near Chetumal, Quintana Roo, Mexico. Elsewhere in the Mexican portion of the Yucatán Peninsula, the range extends northward into central Campeche. Apparently, then, the species enters only the basal part of the Yucatán Peninsula. This is not surprising, for in the central and outer parts of the peninsula the rainfall becomes scantier and more seasonal, the fresh-water situations widely separated. A second question: how far southward does Morelet's crocodile range? Does it reach the Caribbean drainage of Honduras? Published references to the species in "Honduras" actually relate to British Honduras. The distribution extends southward through the forested southern half of British Honduras, and there is no reason to question an old record farther south, in the Rio Polochic of Guatemala. Southward of the Polochic there lies the comparatively dry Motagua Basin, and beyond it the Espíritu Santo uplift. Across the uplift, in northern Honduras, the Chamelecón drainage is inhabited by *Crocodylus acutus*, to the exclusion of *moreleti*. Crocodiles have been seen in Lake Yojoa, a large, isolated lake near the Ulua River in northern Honduras. Their identity as *acutus* has been assumed in the literature, although no specimen has been examined. The elevation of Yojoa, and its isolation from a large river, render it an unlikely locality for the American crocodile. The presence of Morelet's crocodile in Honduras cannot be demonstrated, but the species might turn up in the extensive marshes that lie at opposite ends of Lake Yojoa.

The optimum habitat of Morelet's crocodile is ponds and lakes of the savanna. However, the species does live in rainforest country, in lakes (Fig. 131, upper). Large, permanently flowing rivers are not frequented, but the species occurs in intermittent rivers that break up into isolated stretches of water during the dry season. The species is also present in swampy, labyrinthine waterways which exist along some rivers. Although Morelet's

Figure 131. Lakes of the dense rainforest (upper), ponds of the open savanna (center), and slow streams (lower) were formerly inhabited by Morelet's crocodile in British Honduras. [W. T. Neill]

crocodile has been found very near the coast, there is no record for mangrove swamp, saltmarsh, or other truly saltwater situations.

Nothing is known about the courtship, nest, eggs, or hatchlings of Morelet's crocodile. In the days before extensive hide-hunting, large numbers of individuals could be found within a very limited expanse of water. Stomach contents were found to have included beetles, water bugs, snails, small crustaceans, a fish, and a mass of gray mammal hair. It is interesting to see once again that the fur of a mammal proved more difficult than the flesh or bones for a crocodilian to digest. Also present in the stomachs was a little accidentally ingested vegetable matter, along with a hard nutlet and some quartz gravel presumably swallowed as gastroliths. The aforesaid beetles included some aquatic kinds, but also some ground-beetles and scarabs. I suspect that the insects were secondarily ingested for the most part. At the locality (Belize) where a gray-furred mammal had been eaten, I have seen the common opossum, which is gray-furred.

As the rear teeth are stout and blunt in the adult of Morelet's crocodile, the assumption has been made that the species preys heavily on crabs and mollusks. However, I doubt that really hard-shelled crabs or mollusks occur in the usual habitat of this crocodile. The rivers may harbor thick-shelled clams, and be invaded by large crabs; but the *aguadas*, the scattered ponds of the savanna, have only thin-shelled snails, and no crabs at all as far as I have seen. The *aguadas* and the intermittent rivers together harbor an abundance and a variety of turtles, on which Morelet's crocodile is likely to prey. According to a probably reliable account, on one occasion a crocodile attacked a young child. The episode took place in the Petén of Guatemala, at a locality where I would expect Morelet's crocodile to be the only crocodilian present. But normally this crocodile is very shy; and, because of its small size, it is disinclined to take any but small prey.

The maximum size of Morelet's crocodile is generally given as 8 feet, a figure which appears acceptable. I have not seen an individual exceeding 7 feet, nor a skull more than 11 inches long. Natural enemies of the species are unknown. Competition with the American crocodile is minimal; Morelet's crocodile does not inhabit the large rivers and saltwater situations where its larger congener exists. Man has nearly exterminated Morelet's crocodile. In 1923 K. P. Schmidt saw hundreds of individuals in sight from the causeway that links Belize with the higher ground. But by the time I first visited British Honduras, in 1959, crocodiles no longer existed anywhere near the causeway, even though the swamps themselves remained about as Schmidt described them. Several later trips, to all districts of British Honduras and to nearby parts of Guatemala and Mexico, revealed Morelet's crocodile to have been killed off almost everywhere, although professional hunters claimed to know of a few remote areas where specimens could still be obtained. Among the exceedingly impoverished people of British Honduras and nearby areas, the sale of just one crocodile hide is an important financial transaction; and the location of a surviving crocodile population is a closely guarded secret.

23 THE NILE CROCODILE

TURNING NOW to the Old World, we may consider the Nile crocodile, Africa's most widespread crocodilian, and one known since Classical times. The legends and myths that grew up around it, and that were later transferred to other crocodilians, beset the literature even today. Herodotus, a Greek historian of the fifth century B.C., has received much of the credit, or blame, for drawing attention to the Nilotic reptile. Herodotus wandered over Greece, Egypt, and Asia Minor, and wrote a so-called history. This was actually a mass of legendary, local, antiquarian, geographical, and ethnological lore, derived partly from predecessors but also supplemented by his own travels. He was not completely credulous; he questioned, for example, what he had been told about that remarkable bird, the phoenix. But he did believe that a mare gave birth to a rabbit; and that there was a distant land of headless people, each of whom had one large eye in the center of the chest. In short, his biological concepts were naive, more myth than science.

Herodotus said that an old name for the Nile crocodile was *champsae*, meaning "from the egg." Centuries later, taxonomists made good use of this word when naming crocodilians. Such generic names as Champse, Champsa, Pristichampsus, Thecachampsa, Brachychampsa, and Hispanochampsa adorn the literature. A later Greek historian-geographer, Strabo, added that the name *suchis* was applied to a tame crocodile in Egypt; and so today many crocodilian generic names end in *-suchus*.

Herodotus, Pliny, and others wrote that the crocodile would open its jaws, acquire a mouthful of insects, and snap down on them. But this habit was sometimes the crocodile's undoing (the old writers continued), for a beast called the ichneumon would leap down the crocodile's throat and eat the reptile's stomach, thus keeping the numbers of the crocodile down. As we have already seen, the legend of the insect-catching crocodilian was later transferred to the American alligator and the Cuban crocodile. Happily, the ichneumon was forgotten, at least as a mammalian predator that ate the crocodile from within.

With the Renaissance, and the rediscovery of the Classical writings, the old legends were brought back to life and worked into the philosophical framework of the times. In Elizabethan days, natural history was thought to provide an insight into the human condition, or into the Creator's intent. The life of a beast was thus lent great "human interest." Probably this is why the old legends have been so hard to eradicate even from scientific thought. Take, for example, Edward Topsell's bestiary, an influential work which claimed to reveal "of every Beast . . . their severall Names, Conditions, Kindes, Vertues (both naturall and medicinall), Countries of their breed, their love and hate to Mankinde, and the wonderfulle worke of God in their Creation, Preservation, and Destruction." Of crocodilians, Topsell had this to say:

> The nature of this beast is to be fearefull, ravening, malitious, and trecherous. The tayle of a Crocodile is his strongest part, and they never kill any beast or man, but first of all they strike him downe and astonish him with their tailles. The males of this kind do love their females above all measure, yea even to jealousie. And it is no wonder if they made much of one another, for beside themselves they have few friends in the world.

Today, even the most scholarly works on crocodiles assert that the reptile strikes a blow with its tail, and that the male crocodiles fight one another in the breeding season! The assertions, for all their repetition, trace back not to objective studies but only to Elizabethan fancies built in turn upon legends from the dawn of history.

The Latin name of *Crocodilus niloticus* was used as early as 1699 by

Oligerius Jacobaeus. But this usage has no taxonomic standing, for it antedates the tenth, or 1758, edition of Linnaeus's *Systema Naturae*. Today we consider that the genus *Crocodylus*, and its type-species *Crocodylus niloticus*, stem from Joseph Laurenti (although Laurenti actually used the spelling *Crocodilus*). Laurenti considered the Nilotic species to inhabit India and Egypt, although the range does not actually reach India. He mentioned India because he did not distinguish the Nile crocodile from Schneider's smooth-fronted caiman, which he mistakenly thought was Indian. Efforts have been made to transfer the name *niloticus* from a Nilotic crocodile to a South American caiman; but fortunately, common sense has so far prevailed. The name *Crocodylus niloticus* Laurenti acquired at least fourteen synonyms between the year of its publication (1768) and 1948. Most of these synonyms need not be listed here, but a few of them merit comment. The name *Crocodilus robustus* L. Vaillant and C. Grandidier, 1872, was based on a large, stout, and comparatively broad-headed crocodile from "Amboulintsatre" (Ambositra?) in Madagascar. Also in 1872, Vaillant applied the name *Crocodilus madagascariensis* to a Madagascan crocodile. It soon became evident that *madagascariensis* was a synonym of *niloticus*, but the name *robustus* was retained for a good many years as a validly founded one, the proportion of the snout (its breadth contained only about 1.5 times in its length) apparently setting *robustus* apart from any crocodile inhabiting mainland Africa. However, *robustus* also turned out to be the Nile crocodile. The synonyms *robustus* and *madagascariensis* draw attention to the occurrence of *niloticus* in Madagascar (the Malagasy Republic), a large island separated from the African mainland by a channel 250 miles wide. The Madagascan population might prove to be subspecifically distinct from the mainland one.

Of interest are two synonyms published in 1827 by Etienne Geoffroy St. Hilaire. In the first century B.C., Strabo had written of the city of Arsinoé, which the Greeks called Crocodilopolis, a place where the Egyptians held crocodiles in veneration, and kept tame ones in a lake. For many centuries thereafter, Egypt was studied (if at all) only through Classical writings about it. But Napoleon's battles in that land of impressive ruins, and the discovery of the Rosetta Stone, focused early nineteenth-century attention on the actual relics of Egyptian civilization. It was discovered that at some time in the archeological past the Egyptians had mummified not only the bodies of their rulers but also of crocodiles large and small. Ancient portrayals of a crocodile, or of a crocodile-headed god on monuments and coffins and papyri, along with a hieroglyph resembling a crocodile, hinted further at some early cult involving this reptile. Geoffroy St. Hilaire went to the site of ancient Thebes (Luxor), some 650 river miles up the Nile, and spent 23 days hunting for mummified crocodiles in the tombs. The hunt was successful. He thought he had discovered two distinct species of mummified crocodiles, neither of them the common species of the Nile. His views were influenced by Classical writings, which suggested the presence of several kinds of crocodiles in Egypt. In 1827 he erected the names *Crocodilus lacunosus* and *Crocodilus complanatus*, based on mummified remains. However, the mummies were those of Nile crocodiles, and the two names eventually passed into the synonymy of *niloticus*.

In later years, Flinders Petrie translated an Egyptian papyrus which stated that in the days of the Fourth Dynasty the term "great" was applied to any crocodile over 7 cubits long (10½ feet). The largest mummified crocodile is about 15 feet long, and there is no evidence that the ancient Egyptians encountered Nile crocodiles larger than the ones that exist today. A cult of the crocodile persisted into modern times in many parts of Africa, having been noted in such diverse places as Angola, Nigeria, the Congo Basin, Uganda, and Tanzania. At Ibadan in Nigeria, an albino crocodile (Fig. 132) was kept in a low-walled pool and attended by a priest; and at Lagos Lagoon, human victims were once offered to sacred crocodiles in the hope of averting a flood. But in most parts of Africa, the Nile crocodile is hunted for its hide.

The African range of the Nile crocodile, in the days before hide-hunting, was very extensive in large rivers and along coasts. Specifically, the range extended from the present Federation of Mali (formerly Senegal and Soudan), from Niger and Chad, and from the delta of the Nile, southward practically to the Cape of Good Hope in South Africa (excluding highlands and deserts, of course). The very large African area from which the reptile was lacking—the northern part of the continent, west of the Nile—is an arid land for the most part, much of it mountainous. Fossil remains of the Nile crocodile have been found at localities that are today too dry for the species. Such remains date from a period of less arid climate than the modern one. From continental Africa, the range of the Nile crocodile extended eastward to the Comoros, Madagascar, and even the Seychelles. The reptile is supposed formerly to have ranged a short distance into south-

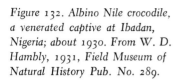
Figure 132. Albino Nile crocodile, a venerated captive at Ibadan, Nigeria; about 1930. From W. D. Hambly, 1931, Field Museum of Natural History Pub. No. 289.

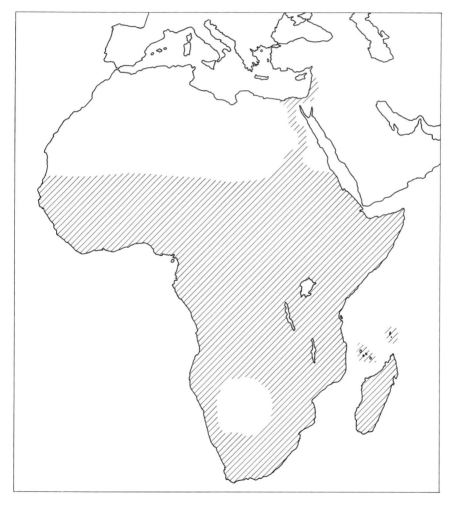

Figure 133. The range of the Nile crocodile (hatched area).

western Asia, following the eastern shore of the Mediterranean. The Asiatic locality records (Israel and the Palestine area of southwestern Syria) are based on eggs, as far as I can learn. One might wish for better evidence of the species' presence in Asia. There have also been suggestions that the Nile crocodile followed the islands and shores of the Mediterranean westward as far as Sicily and Tunisia, but it may be doubted that the species ever ranged so far beyond the tropics; this suggestion can be traced back to an undocumented assertion or guess. The original range of the Nile crocodile has been much reduced by man. An Asiatic population of the species no longer exists. Crocodiles had vanished from the Seychelles by about 1800. By the latter 1700s, the species was gone from the delta of the Nile, but was still to be found a short distance above Cairo. By 1870 it had practically vanished from all of the Nile below Aswan, in other words from below the first cataract on the river. In the 1890s the crocodile persisted in fair abundance between the first cataract and the second. But in that stretch of river, and even farther upstream, the numbers of the crocodile declined rapidly in the twentieth century. In the 1950s, Dr. Hugh B. Cott made important ecological studies on the Nile crocodile along a stretch of the Victoria Nile between Murchison Falls and the Lake Albert delta. He found a concentration of crocodiles probably unrivaled elsewhere in Africa at that time, but within a few years there came the news that even this population was declining. In South Africa, Kenya, Uganda, and Tanzania (formerly Tanganyika), the annual crop of crocodile hides declined markedly through the 1950s and 1960s, simply because few crocodiles remained to be shot.

The optimum habitat of the Nile crocodile probably was the larger rivers. However, there are habitat records for coastal situations, not just river mouths and estuaries but also mangrove swamps. There are hearsay accounts, possibly valid, of crocodiles swimming in the sea off the coast of Zululand, South Africa. Also inhabited by this species are large, freshwater marshes, such as the Sudd of the Upper Nile and the Okovango Swamps of Botswanaland (formerly Bechuanaland).

During the last twenty years or so, with the numbers of the Nile crocodile obviously declining, there have been efforts to discover something of its biology, and some objective studies in the modern scientific tradition have been made. By far the most important of these have been studies by Cott, around whose 1961 paper I have centered much of the following discussion.

Various studies, otherwise admirable, have reported the opinions of game wardens, professional hunters, and local residents concerning the activities of the Nile crocodile. Regarding these opinions, I can do no better than quote a remark by that outstanding student of crocodilians, the late K. P. Schmidt: "The fact is that whether in civilized or in quite uncivilized countries the native lore of natural history is a mixture of acute observation of fact and an elaborate structure of misinterpretation and myth, and in every case requires shifting and criticism by the scientific method. . . ." Students of the Nile crocodile have also drawn attention to numerous accounts of travel and adventure in Africa. It appears to me that these accounts, like the early narratives of travel in the alligator country of North America, are useful chiefly in revealing that some currently accepted beliefs about crocodilians can be traced back not to actual observation but merely to some guess, bit of hearsay, or ancient legend.

The courtship of the Nile crocodile is little known. Just below Murchison Falls, Cott witnessed the termination of a courtship. The female, in shallow water, reared her head into the air, opened her mouth, and emitted some kind of a sound. The male, who had been lying awash, approached the female from the rear, and mounted her in the usual crocodilian mating posture. After copulation, the pair moved off into deeper water. This episode took place on January 1. In Africa it is widely believed that the female rolls onto her back in order to facilitate copulation, and although there are supposed "eye-witness" accounts of such behavior, they may be regarded as apocryphal. In Uganda the eggs are laid mostly around December or January, and in northern Rhodesia around late August or September. In this species, egg-laying may be timed with the seasonal fall of the water table, which exposes suitable nesting places. In general, the eggs are laid after the dry season has gotten under way, and the water table has continued to drop for about three weeks. The incubation period (normally about twelve or thirteen weeks) corresponds in part to the period of lowest water, and the eggs hatch after the lakes and rivers have begun to flood again.

An interesting situation was discovered by Cott at Lake Victoria. This vast basin (26,000 square miles in extent) has two dry seasons each year. Some of the local crocodiles were laying near the beginning of the first dry season (around August and September), but others near the beginning of the second dry season (around December and January).

The Nile crocodile does not scrape plant debris into a nest, but leaves her eggs in the ground. The actual process of nest-building has not been studied, and it is not known whether she scrapes up sand before she begins digging the cavity that will contain the eggs. The nest is usually in the coarse sand of a river bank, bar, or lake beach. Nests in gravel have also been noted. Usually the nest is dug near water and near shade. Although Nile crocodiles are often photographed on sunny river banks and bars, they cannot long abide the heat of such places; and the female crocodile, while sometimes lying at her nest, more often lies hidden in the shade nearby. A Nile crocodile strives to keep its body temperature between the approximate limits of 75 and 81 degrees Fahrenheit. At localities without sand or gravel near the water, the female may climb a high bank, or travel overland as much as 200 yards or more, to find a suitable nesting spot. Communal nesting has been reported at scattered localities, anywhere from three to as many as 25 or 30 nests having been found clustered near each other. No doubt in past times when crocodiles were more numerous, communal nesting was more frequent.

The nesting hole of a large female is about 2 feet deep, and in it the eggs are piled to a depth of about a foot (not in two neat layers as legend would have it). It is often asserted that the female lays her eggs at night, but of this there is no proof; and the assertion at least in part reflects an effort to draw, or force, a parallel with the nesting behavior of some turtles. On one occasion, a Nile crocodile was glimpsed digging at her nest in the early morning, a circumstance suggesting that the eggs could be laid in the daylight hours. After the eggs have been covered with sand, the nest is smoothed over to the ground level by the female, but the female's tracks, and the imprint of her ventral scales, may reveal the location of the nest. Sometimes the female rests with her throat pressed to the ground immediately above the nest, a behavior pattern that recalls a nesting female of the American alligator.

The number of eggs in a clutch will vary from 25 to 95. However, most nests contain between 45 and 75 eggs, and the average number is 55 to 60, depending on locality. There is some evidence to suggest that on the average the larger females deposit larger clutches (but not larger eggs) than the smaller females. The writers of Classical antiquity described the egg of the Nile crocodile as equaling the egg of a goose in size. It is amusing

Figure 134. *A monitor lizard of Africa. Many species of monitors inhabit the Old World tropics, some of them preying on crocodile eggs.*
[Ross Allen's Reptile Institute]

to find, in the nineteenth- and twentieth-century literature, at least fourteen assertions that the crocodile's egg is about the size of a goose egg—but no mention of an actual measurement!

The female Nile crocodile remains with her nest night and day, and eats little or nothing during the period of guarding. There are very few observations of an attack by the female upon some organism that approached her nest. This is not surprising, for the nest is well concealed. The species would profit if the female had an impulse to charge from her nearby covert only when some egg-predator actually began to dig into the nest. The studies of Cott suggest that a large lizard, the Nile monitor, is a would-be egg-predator, and is kept away from crocodile nests only by the presence of the guardian females. The eggs of the Nile crocodile are also menaced by mongooses, water-mongooses, baboons, hyenas, warthogs, and bush-pigs. Once a crocodile nest has been torn open, the eggs may be eaten by vultures and marabou storks. Even a crocodile may eat an egg once it has been dug from the nest. Such behavior is not dysgenic, for the egg would otherwise be completely wasted. When a female crocodile is found with her throat on the nest, she usually seems reluctant to leave, even at the approach of man.

It is widely asserted, both in Africa and in the literature, that the female uncovers the young at the time of hatching. Yet, no one has ever seen such behavior. In the case of the Nile crocodile, as of the American alligator, not even the most unreliable of the legend-mongers claims actually to have seen liberation of the young by the female; rather, such liberation is inferred for a variety of reasons, none of them impelling. The Nile crocodile voices the juvenile grunt. This is sometimes given shortly before hatching. The call is not a repetitive one, but a single note given at irregular intervals. In the Nile crocodile, as in crocodilians generally, there is no evidence that the juvenile grunt attracts the female or any other adult. Some nests of the Nile crocodile become rather hard-baked by the sun, and this circumstance has helped bolster the idea that the hatchlings must be helped out of the nest. Nevertheless, I think they work their own way out if they get out at all. If a nest is constructed of such a material, or placed in such a spot, that the hatchlings cannot escape unaided, probably they die; evolution is at work, limiting the reproductive success of an individual female who lacks the impulse to select a safe nesting site. After the eggs hatch, the former nest collapses to a circular crater, the empty egg-shells being flattened as the sand falls and takes up the space left by the emergence of the brood.

The hatchling is about 12¼ to 12½ inches in length. It is grayish above, with poorly defined, darker crossbands. Ten to twelve crossbands, most of them broken into blotches, can usually be discerned on the tail; but the crossbands of the body are reduced to irregular flecking, and cannot be counted (Fig. 135). At the time of hatching, the little crocodile still has the caruncle, with which it slits the egg-shell.

Herodotus said that the female crocodile exercises some kind of supervision over her young. This is the origin of the assertion, still to be found in the scientific literature, that the female of the Nile crocodile (and of various other crocodilians) cares for her brood. Some absurd myths have entered the literature: the young Nile crocodiles, upon hatching, attach themselves to the dorsal serrations of the female's tail, and so are trans-

Figure 135. A young Nile crocodile. [Ross Allen's Reptile Institute]

ported to water; the hatchlings are conveyed to water upon the mother's back. We are told that a man once saw a female crocodile with 17 or 18 recently hatched young, all sunning on a bank. As he approached, the "parent" went into the water, followed by her "offspring." But if young crocodiles are glimpsed near an adult, there is no way to determine that the adult is their mother, or even a female. I do not doubt that a person once saw "young crocodiles all around an adult in the water," or that some other people saw "babies resting on a crocodile's back"; but the interpretation of these associations has been unduly anthropomorphic. Man, in whom the mammalian care of young reaches its highest development, is quick to imagine some parent-young interaction when he sees young organisms with an adult of their own kind. Young Nile crocodiles on land might rest beside an adult just as they would beside a rock or a fallen tree; and young crocodiles in the water (like the young alligators in Fig. 12) might crawl upon the back of a floating adult just as they would crawl upon a floating log. Naturally, the members of a brood are to be found near each other for a brief while after hatching. It is said that the members of a brood "quickly disperse when frightened, but soon pack again, calling to each other loudly with a chirruping cry," but the description fits a juvenile distress cry, which would be heard if a member of a brood were seized by an enemy. There is no reason to believe that hatchlings will regroup once they have dispersed (unless some of them later end up in the same water-hole during a drought); and no reason to think that the juvenile vocalizations function to reassemble a scattered brood.

In 1800 the pioneer herpetologist C. N. S. Sonnini de Manancourt described the receipt of some baby crocodiles. The Egyptian who brought the reptiles claimed to have been attacked while collecting them. In the modern literature, Sonnini's old account, mere hearsay from the start, has been used to document the contention that, "At hatching time, the female becomes bolder than usual, in defence of her offspring." But once again, not even Sonnini's Egyptian informant could have known the sex of the attacking crocodile, or its familial relationship to the juveniles that were collected. Nor can a single attack, even if well documented, be used to demonstrate a seasonal change in the boldness of even one female crocodile, much less of the females in general. I would expect any juvenile of the Nile crocodile to voice the distress cry when hurt, and any nearby adult to charge in the direction of the sound. The season has nothing to do with the matter, nor the sex of the adult, nor the familial relationship of the adult to the shrieking juvenile. A contrary situation would represent an extraordinary departure from the norm of crocodilian behavior, if such behavior be defined from observation rather than hearsay, speculation, and legend.

In the scientific literature dealing with the Nile crocodile, the juvenile grunt has not been distinguished from the juvenile distress cry. The former sounds very much like the juvenile grunt of the American alligator, and is given occasionally, at irregular intervals. When the young Nile crocodile is hurt, it voices a higher, louder note, a cry that is given over and over again. The juvenile distress cry is very much like that of the American alligator.

Young Nile crocodiles are said frequently to climb into vegetation. Having kept a baby alligator that persisted in climbing upon, and even sleeping upon, the petiole of a Philodendron leaf, I should perhaps not question any claim of scansorial ability in a crocodile. However, we are told that young Nile crocodiles climb upon grass blades, where they are seen "hanging on like chameleons"; and that they climb reeds to a height of as much as 8 feet, whence they drop off into the water when someone approaches. I believe that these observations were based on young monitor lizards rather than baby crocodiles. In general conformation, pattern, and coloration, a monitor is very suggestive of a crocodile; and almost anywhere that the Nile crocodile is found, some species of monitor also exists. As a further source of possible confusion, a native name may be applied to the crocodile in one area, to a monitor lizard in another. While baby crocodiles climb well, they do not grasp reeds, twigs, or grass blades; rather, they scramble upward through vegetation by the same movements with which they would scramble up a bank. In contrast, a climbing monitor actually seizes a plant stem, and is supported in large part by its sharp, recurved claws, which dig into the stem.

Although baby crocodiles may be numerous during and immediately after the hatching season, somewhat larger juveniles are rarely seen; at least, they are rarely seen by African hunters and local residents, who remark on the apparent scarcity of 2-, 3-, and 4-footers. Such juveniles frequent heavily vegetated shallows and backwaters, or even isolated ponds at some distance from a main body of water. It is disappointing to read in the scientific literature that the apparent secretiveness of these juveniles "has been forced upon them by the habit of cannibalism"; that the juveniles hide in the reeds and shallows because they would be eaten by an adult if they ventured into the biotope where the latter resided. Once again, an interpretation of crocodilian behavior is unduly anthropomorphic. Among the vertebrates, man has been an exceptionally cannibalistic species; perhaps this is why he is quick to impute cannibalism to other organisms. Cott has pointed out that the juvenile crocodiles are seldom seen in the daytime, but are abroad at night in the expected numbers and in the biotope of the adults. As the adult crocodiles forage mainly by night, a purely diurnal secretiveness would not save the juveniles from falling prey to their elders (if such predation were really likely to take place). Reported predators on crocodiles include catfishes, monitor lizards, softshell turtles, marabou storks, fish hawks, fish eagles, ground hornbills, leopards, and lions; and Africa harbors a great many other predators which probably kill crocodiles. If the Nile crocodile has evolved an impulse to be exceptionally secretive when young, and by so doing avoid predation, one might expect the predators to be something other than adult crocodiles.

Actually, a great many reptiles are very difficult to find until they become young adults, and this is particularly true of species that are vulnerable to predators when juvenile but much less vulnerable when adult. For example, among many turtle species, the hard-shelled and well-protected adults may be common, but the small, thin-shelled juveniles almost impossible to find. In many parts of the eastern United States, the box turtle may be exceedingly abundant as an adult, yet the herpetological collector will rarely encounter a juvenile. Although adults of the gopher tortoise are often conspicuous in parts of the southeastern United States, the thin-shelled juvenile—a potential morsel for many predators—remained unknown to science until 1953. Also, in many of the large, nonvenomous snakes, the comparatively defenseless young are rarely seen, in contrast with the adults which can escape, discourage, or fight off many predators. Thus in Florida, adult indigo snakes between 5 and 7 feet long, and adult southern pine snakes between 4 and 6 feet, are often encountered; but smaller individuals of either species are rarely seen, and the respective juveniles of these two snakes were not made known to science until 1951. The comparative secre-

Figure 136. In many reptiles, the highly vulnerable juveniles are secretive as compared with the adults. Thus the juvenile of the indigo snake (at left), a mere handful, eluded scientific description until 1951; but the large adult (below) is often encountered in Florida. [W. T. Neill and Ross Allen's Reptile Institute]

tiveness of many young reptiles probably involves something more than the minimization of predation at a vulnerable time of life. Among crocodilians, particularly, the ecological separation of juveniles from adults functions to minimize competition between the two age groups, and to permit a fuller utilization of local food resources.

Cott made important observations on the feeding habits of the Nile crocodile at various localities from Uganda to the Zambesi, with some data from Zululand also. Stomach contents (reported in greater detail than I here supply) included tiger beetles, ground beetles, diving beetles, predaceous diving beetles, whirligig beetles, darkling beetles, scarabs, longhorn beetles, and weevils; assassin bugs, giant waterbugs, backswimmers, and other true bugs; bees and ants; dragonflies and maidenflies; roaches, crickets, longhorn grasshoppers, shorthorn grasshoppers, mole crickets, and other orthopterans; earwigs; termites; a moth caterpillar; and flies of three families. Also present in stomachs were spiders, crabs, shrimp, snails, and clams. Fish prey of the crocodiles included a shark, elephant fishes, characids, dace, catfishes of four families, an eel, a killifish, a plectrorhynchid, a centropomid, and various cichlids including five species of Tilapia. Likewise found in the crocodile stomachs were amphibians and reptiles, as follows: toads, ranid frogs, sedgefrogs, narrow-mouthed frogs, snake-necked turtles, crocodiles and crocodile eggs, Nile monitors, rock pythons, four genera of colubrid snakes (including the egg-eating snake), a black-necked cobra, and a puff adder. Bird remains recovered from crocodile stomachs included cormorants, anhingas, a pelican, a heron, two or three kinds of ducks, two kinds of gallinules, a dove, a goatsucker, and a plover. Mammal remains included a manis, a jackass, a zebra, hippos, riverhogs, domestic cattle, domestic sheep and goat, antelope of four or five genera, marsh mongooses, a genet, a porcupine, an octodont rodent, mice of three or four genera, baboons, guenons, and human beings.

Referring to insects from the crocodiles' stomachs, Cott noted that "a surprising feature of the collection is the large number of terrestrial forms . . . land beetles number 196 as compared with 148 water-beetles." I do not think the terrestrial insects were taken by crocodiles that foraged on the land or in the bushes. If every insect found in a crocodile's stomach is deemed to have arrived there as the result of direct predation by the crocodile (the currently accepted view), then we must assume that every insectivorous toad, frog, lizard, and bird found in a crocodile's stomach arrived there with an empty digestive tract! No doubt these Nile crocodiles, which had taken a variety and abundance of insect prey, secondarily ingested a large part (probably the greater part) of the reported insects. There is no reason to believe that young crocodiles forage on land. On the contrary, they are highly aquatic.

Stomach contents included abundant gastroliths: gravel in the case of juveniles, stones in the case of larger individuals. Crocodiles acquired a burden of gastroliths sooner in a very stony area than in a less stony one. When the weight of accumulated gastroliths reached about 1 per cent of the crocodile's weight, no more gastroliths would be ingested. Bits of glass and crockery were found, and quite properly interpreted as gastroliths. Gastroliths were regarded as functioning to increase the crocodile's weight in the water. "When a large animal, such as a buffalo or waterbuck, has been captured, there follows a prolonged struggle. . . . Stomach stones cannot fail to favor the predator in these circumstances." As suggested in the section dealing with the American alligator, this interpretation of gastroliths can be traced back to an old legend. Granting an exceptionally large crocodile to weigh 1,000 pounds, it is unlikely that 10 pounds of stomach stones would help the reptile in a struggle with a buffalo. Although the old literature described the struggle of a crocodilian and its prey as a mere tug-of-war, it is a far more complex encounter. The weight of gastroliths was also regarded as functioning to permit longer submergence and greater vertical stability in the water. If such effects exist, they must be very insignificant, for crocodilians without gastroliths are wonderfully maneuverable, and can sink straight down. The lungs are, of course, the hydrostatic organ. The flattened tail functions as a vertical stabilizer. However, a young crocodilian will also extend its limbs as balancers in the water (see Fig. 139 in the next chapter). It is not surprising that various parts of a crocodilian's body should be utilized in controlling aquatic movement; but it would be surprising indeed if crocodilians had evolved a mechanism that left a part of this important control to the haphazard discovery of stones or other heavy objects. As pointed out by Cott, it is the juvenile crocodile that at times seems a little awkward in the water, as though in need of more vertical stability; but the juvenile, even where gastrolithic material is available in abundance, will not pick up anything like 1 per cent of its body weight in stomach stones. The adults, which by virtue of mass and swimming experience are in less need of stabilization, nevertheless pick up a proportionately greater weight of gastroliths than do the juveniles.

As the hydrostatic theory of gastrolith function has been evoked in connection with several crocodiles, including some that are yet to be discussed, the theory might be laid to rest at this point. Crocodilians in general, the Nile crocodile among them, do not have an impulse to ingest heavy objects as gastroliths. The impulse is to ingest hard objects, even if these are so light as to float. Captive Nile crocodiles have been known to ingest floating objects such as light bulbs, photographers' flashbulbs, and tightly capped thermos bottles. A crocodilian will ingest a hard, light chunk of wood that floats at the surface, yet will ignore a heavier but softer, water-logged chunk that has settled to the bottom. It will swallow stones when they are available, and stony gastroliths persist in the reptiles' stomach longer than do gastroliths of wood, bone, or shell. In a stony region the crocodilian's "standard load" of gastroliths might come to include nothing but stones. But when stones are scarce or lacking, the gastrolithic burden is made up of other hard objects, especially pieces of wood and charcoal. If crocodilian gastroliths were primarily hydrostatic in function, one would have to argue that they function to make the American alligator more buoyant and less stable in the water! But more importantly, gastroliths are ingested by various members of the birds and the crocodilians, the two living groups of organisms that have descended from the thecodontians. They were also ingested by various extinct archosaurian and non-archosaurian reptiles, some of them not aquatic. It seems reasonable that an explanation of gastroliths should be applicable at least to all the stone-swallowing descendants of the thecodontians. Although crocodilians do not have a highly specialized organ, the gizzard, of the avian sort, they are unique among living reptiles in that the stomach does exhibit some specializations reminiscent of a gizzard. Thus, the primary function of crocodilian gastroliths seems to be digestive. If a crocodile profits from the extra weight that is provided by stony gastroliths, or from the buoyancy provided by woody ones, the profit is a secondary one. This is not to say, however, that the digestive function of crocodilian gastroliths is solely the abrading of ingested food. To speculate from studies on other vertebrates, the physical presence of objects in the stomach, even those without nutritive value, can have an effect on the flow of digestive secretions, and on the impulse to seek food.

The adult Nile crocodile, like the adult American alligator, usually seizes large prey by the leg, or occasionally by the head. The literature commonly asserts that the prey is dragged into deeper water and there drowned, but I expect this assertion is based wholly on the old legends. While I have not personally witnessed the foraging technique of a large Nile crocodile in nature, I know from experience that two other large crocodilians (the American alligator and the estuarine crocodile) begin to "whirl" immediately after seizing some large prey. When the remains of a large animal appear in the stomach of a Nile crocodile, they are likely to consist only of a foot or leg, a circumstance suggesting that the prey's limb had been torn off by the widespread crocodilian technique of "whirling." The Nile crocodile is known to "whirl" when tearing meat from the body of a dead animal. In deeper water, the crocodile will swim rapidly toward the surface to take some prey that is resting or swimming there; and a small individual will actually leap partly out of water to snap at some volant prey. There is no convincing evidence that either juvenile or adult will hunt living prey on land, and it is amusing to read in the supposedly scientific literature the statement that Nile crocodiles "lie in ambush beside game trails" and take passing prey by "the deadly tail-stroke." The concept of the "deadly tail-stroke" might be of interest to students of human psychology and of ancient legend, but should be dismissed from the field of crocodilian biology.

As Cott has pointed out, the Nile crocodile does not often prey on man. Yet, it does attack man occasionally. Human remains have been found in crocodile stomachs, and adequately documented attacks on man are not lacking. Crocodilians apparently have an impulse to repeat a foraging technique that proves successful; and there is considerable evidence that a large Nile crocodile, having attacked man successfully, may repeat the attack in about the same place and in the same fashion. In one fairly well-documented case of recent years, a very large crocodile eventually seized eight people, most of them children, at a single locality on a river in southern Mozambique. But in most parts of Africa the crocodile has been extensively hunted; few individuals now live to reach a very large size, and the surviving populations are wary of man.

Cott has remarked, "As scavengers, [Nile] crocodiles fill the same niche as that occupied by vultures, marabous, and hyenas. . . . They readily assemble . . . to feed on a carcass . . . and have frequently been observed in the water dismembering buffaloes, zebra, waterbuck, or the carcasses of crocodiles discarded by skinners." Here is evidence that cannibalism cannot be inferred simply because crocodile remains turn up in crocodile stomachs occasionally. Where crocodiles live in numbers they must die in numbers, leaving their rotting carcasses as carrion; leaving, also, numerous scutes and other bones to be ingested as gastroliths.

The literature includes conflicting statements about the growth of the Nile crocodile, some workers claiming the rate to be only an inch a year, others claiming a foot a year. Cott found that in the wild one could not with certainty distinguish year-groups beyond the third year. Data from a few captives, including one that was penned under fairly natural conditions, revealed the growth rate to be about 11 inches a year for the first seven years. Thereafter, the rate slowed abruptly to about 1½ inches a year, and this rate was maintained for another fifteen years at least. The maximum size of the Nile crocodile is difficult to determine. Modern herpetologists have usually, and quite properly, disavowed the early claims of 25- and 30-foot giants, and have settled upon 16 feet as the maximum length that can be validated. The last figure is probably close to the maximum length in most parts of Africa. It would not be surprising, however, if there were a few localities where the crocodiles, for genetic or environmental reasons, attained an unusually large size. In the early 1960s, some exceptionally large Nile crocodiles were imported into the United States from a locality somewhere in the southern part of Africa; and one of these, as nearly as I could measure the uncoöperative reptile, was closer to 17 feet than to 16. There are also some areas where a Nile crocodile over 12 feet is unknown, probably because the local individuals have almost no chance of escaping a hunter's bullet for many years. Much has been made of so-called pygmy Nile crocodiles, supposedly never over 6 feet in length, in the Aswa River of northern Uganda; but the story of these "pygmies" can be traced to writings that are a good deal less than scientific. The African popular literature provides many entertaining arguments about pygmy elephants, hippopotamuses, chimpanzees, leopards, crocodiles and people.

The Nile crocodile is said to "estivate," but this term seems never to have been defined, at least with reference to reptiles. Old works credit the crocodile with digging long burrows, but these apparently have not been observed by recent workers. There is scant evidence of territoriality in this species. If territorial impulses exist, surely they are in abeyance during the day, when a number of adults will lie beside or even atop one another on river banks and islands. (Cott figured 23 adults crowded onto a little islet, with others in the water nearby.) According to books on life and travel in

Figure 137. A very young
individual of the Nile crocodile.
[Ross Allen's Reptile Institute]

Africa, male crocodiles often fight each other "fiercely," especially in the
breeding season; and unfortunately, such comments have been accepted
uncritically into the scientific literature. Even if battles took place (and of
this there is no convincing evidence), the sex of the battlers could not be
determined, nor the occasion for combat. And it might also be doubted
that the courting season of the species was widely known. As with the
American alligator, so with the Nile crocodile: legend, anthropormorphism,
and literary embellishment have combined to paint an inaccurate picture of
crocodilian biology. Nile crocodiles are often scarred, a circumstance not
remarkable in a land full of predators. As Cott appropriately remarked,
"Direct evidence as to the agents responsible for the damage is generally
wanting." There is no justification for assuming that mutilations are the
work of other crocodiles. Most mutilations were probably sustained by
hatchlings, which thereafter bore the signs of a narrow escape from some
predator. Not only do many predators menace the crocodiles; the adults
of this species are also attacked by elephants, and more frequently by
hippos. Apparently, hippos and crocodiles often dispute the occupancy of

some stretch of water, the aggressor usually being a male hippo who attempts to drive crocodiles away. There are reports of large crocodiles that were bitten in two by hippos.

A common mutilation in the Nile crocodile is the loss of the tail tip. Such a mutilation is often ascribed to predation by another crocodile, but of course a hatchling could easily lose its tail tip to a softshell turtle or one of the hard-beaked wading birds that inhabit the African marshes. There is also a possibility that tail tips are lost in ways other than narrow escapes from predators. In the United States, snakes of many species, some aquatic but others terrestrial, often lose the tail tip. For years herpetologists speculated vainly on the identity of the predators that were abbreviating so many snakes. As it turned out, predation was hardly ever involved. Snakes are susceptible to a disease called tail-rot. In this very common reptilian malady, the tail tip loses its blood supply, dries up, decays, and breaks away, leaving a stub that heals cleanly. As far as I can learn, the causative agent of tail-rot has not been identified (or looked for; reptile diseases have received little attention). Tail-rot is also known to attack monitor lizards. In the part of Africa where Cott was working, the Nile monitor often has a rotten tail tip that eventually breaks away. It would not be surprising to find tail-rot in the Nile crocodile and other crocodilians.

In previous chapters, it was useful to speak of a crocodilian's "bellow," made up of a series of "roars." Cott described the roar of the adult Nile crocodile as "a growling rumble, very deep in pitch, rattling, vibrant and sonorous, like distant thunder [and persisting] for six or seven seconds." The description suggests a sound much like the roar of the American alligator. Curiously, no author mentions the Nile crocodile as voicing a series of roars, and we are left to wonder at what intervals these sounds are given. At any rate, Cott photographed an adult roaring by day from a river bank, so we may dismiss claims that the call is given only by night or only from the water. I would also dismiss claims that the roar is heard only in the breeding season; that the female calls the male by a roar quite different from his; and that a wounded crocodile will "utter a bellow of pain" other than a loud hiss. These notions trace back to folk belief, not scientific investigation. The Nile crocodile voices a warning hiss when cornered. According to hearsay, a trapped crocodile, or a female guarding her nest, may also utter a warning growl when someone appears. Cott heard certain basking crocodiles, somehow identified as males, voice an abrupt, hollow sound, which he termed a bark or cough. I have occasionally heard a large alligator make such a noise, and have considered it merely an eructation, the sound being incidental to the passage of gas. The diet of a crocodilian, mostly meat bolted in chunks, must be quite conducive to flatulence.

The studies of Cott throw some light on the crocodile's custom of resting with jaws agape. Gaping crocodiles have immediately available to them a wide range of environmental temperatures, from the cool river to hot land in full sun. Some crocodiles would lie on the bank but leave the tail in the water, probably maintaining precise control over the body temperature. Shady places also provided an environmental temperature between the extremes of the water and the full sun on land. Thus, it is unlikely that gaping is done in order to lose heat. Although some organisms gape when in the last stages of heat prostration, presumably to facilitate the carrying off of heat by way of the breath, a gaping crocodile is not severely overheated, and does not pant. In some organisms, for example the dog, heat is lost by evaporation of moisture from the tongue and mouth; but the crocodile's tongue and mouth are poorly provided with glands, and are dry. On a chilly day, a captive crocodile will crawl into the sunlight and lie there gaping, even though the body temperature is below, not above, the voluntarily accepted level. Gaping seems to be done when the reptile vaguely senses a potential enemy somewhere in the vicinity. Cott found crocodiles to gape less often in the shade than in the sun, and less often in the early morning than later in the day. I would expect a crocodile to be exceptionally alert when in the open; and would not be surprised if a population of crocodiles, under observation from a nearby blind, became increasingly "uneasy" as the day wore on. Many organisms, especially those that live in groups, became increasingly leery of a blind as the hours go by. Cott provided a fairly close-up view of a crocodile that was resting on a bank yet not gaping; but this individual was badly emaciated, and normal reactions are not to be demanded of so sickly a crocodile.

There are one or two reports of a leech actually in a crocodile's mouth, but gaping to dry an occasional leech is improbable, for such gaping exposes the tongue and mouth of the Nilotic reptile to the much more troublesome tsetse fly. If gaping is anything more than warning behavior, perhaps it also functions to minimize fungal or algal attack. A variety of aquatic reptiles, including crocodilians, turtles, and snakes, have an impulse to dry the skin at intervals; and if they are prevented from so doing, they often develop skin lesions or infestations. Crocodilians are unusual in that the mouth cavity is closed off at most times from the remainder of the digestive tract, and is not provided with much salivary flow. Thus crocodilians, more than other aquatic reptiles, may need to dry and sun the lining of the mouth as a means of discouraging algal or fungal infestation thereon. But I consider such drying to be at the most a secondary function of gaping, which is primarily warning behavior.

Predators and large enemies of the Nile crocodile have been mentioned An external parasite of this reptile is the "tsetse fly" (actually a comprehensive name for several species of flies). This blood-sucker, which as a carrier of African sleeping sickness and nagana has rendered many localities virtually uninhabitable by man and his domestic animals, is disinclined to bite mammals as long as crocodiles are available. The African area of heaviest tsetse infestation (roughly Guinea and Gabon eastward to the Great Lakes, with scattered smaller areas farther east and south) corresponds remarkably well to the area of greatest diversity among African crocodilians. Thus, economic gains from the sale of crocodilian hides are offset when the fly, in the absence of crocodiles, turns to man and livestock. Other external parasites of the Nile crocodile are leeches of two or three species. Internal parasites include roundworms (nematodes), as well as a haemogregarine (a miscroscopic protozoan) transmitted by the bite of a tsetse fly.

Herodotus stated that certain unidentified birds would enter the open mouth of a crocodile and pick off the blood-sucking insects. This story, like Classical writings generally, was regarded as gospel about 1,100 years later, although given moralistic overtones: the ravening crocodile profited by restraining his rapacity toward the seemingly insignificant bird. Later, the tale was dismissed as a flight of fancy. Still later, it appeared that birds actually entered the crocodile's mouth; and the scientists were chided for undue skepticism. The original story, its rejection, and the refutation of the rejection have all received an unwarranted amount of attention and anthropomorphization. The Nile crocodile is associated with many birds. The reptile (stereotyped in its behavior, like all crocodilians) has no impulse to snap at birds when it is resting out of water. Crowned cranes may sleep among basking crocodiles, as they would sleep among so many rocks. Knob-billed geese and white-faced ducks walk over the crocodiles, as they would walk over so many logs. The Goliath heron, white heron, little egret, Egyptian goose, a pratincole, the Hagedash ibis, the sacred ibis, and the

African skimmer—all may be seen walking about oblivious to nearby resting crocodiles. The situation is not unusual in nature. A visit to Africa's game-fields will reveal zebras and antelopes grazing placidly while their enemy, the lion, rests or strolls about nearby. Under certain fairly exacting conditions a lion will pull down a zebra, or a crocodile will seize a waterfowl; but under other conditions, predator and prey ignore each other. The circumstance emphasizes, once again, that we should regard the behavior of a wild animal as a well-nigh mechanical response to a certain aspect of an immediate situation. A spur-winged plover, a thick-knee, a wagtail, and a sandpiper may flit about a crocodile, occasionally picking a leech or (more often) a tsetse fly from the reptile's skin or mouth, just as these birds would pick food from a log, rock, or any other substratum. In this relationship, a bird is not "brave" when it enters a crocodile's mouth, nor is the reptile "forebearing" when it fails to snap down upon the visitor.

The relationship becomes of biological interest if a bird is associated with the crocodile so frequently as to derive a significant portion of its food from the skin and mouth of the reptile, and if the crocodile is thus freed of a significantly large number of parasites. Both a spur-winged plover and a thick-knee have several times been reported to accompany the Nile crocodile, and to pick a good many parasites from the crocodile's skin and mouth. These keen-eyed birds take alarm easily. Their cries of fright, and perhaps their abrupt departure, are said to rouse the crocodiles when someone approaches. I do not know how it is determined that crocodiles, dashing for the water upon the arrival of a man, were roused by birds rather than some attribute of the man. The thick-knee has several times been reported to make its nest near nesting crocodiles. Perhaps a mutually advantageous relationship has developed, or is in the process of developing, between the Nile crocodile and one or two of its avian associates. Perhaps the reptile is freed of parasites and alerted to danger, while the birds are fed and protected from egg-predators. But a definite statement is hard to make, for studies are too few to reveal whether crocodile and bird are associated consistently or just occasionally. The situation may parallel that of the giant tortoises and the day-geckos (small lizards of the genus *Phelsuma*) in the Aldabras. The lizards often scamper over the shells of the moving tortoises in search of insects, but the lizards and the tortoises can thrive separately as well as together.

The various ecological relationships of the Nile crocodile are not likely to be understood much better than they are today, for the reptile is obviously vanishing. The great demand for crocodilian hides, and the recent increase in the price that is paid for them, have led to the decimation of the Nile crocodile even in parts of Africa that have been called "remote." In Africa, as in Florida, when the local crocodilian is extirpated from unprotected areas, poachers turn their attention toward parks and game reserves, where they make a rich haul of skins. Also, the emergence of a nation from colonial status is likely to be an occasion for winking at (if not overtly rescinding) the local game laws, and the continued survival of the Nile crocodile is not likely.

24 SOME LITTLE-KNOWN CROCODILIANS OF AFRICA AND AUSTRALIA

THE CROCODILIAN fauna of Africa is limited. Only four species of crocodilians inhabit that continent, and only one of these, the Nile crocodile, is really widespread. Contrary to popular fancy, Africa is not primarily a well-watered land of swamps and lush rainforest. Most of the continent is desert, scrubland, steppe, savanna, open woodland, or uplands. A rainforest belt extends from the Congo Basin westward to Cameroun, and thence still farther west (but only as a coastal strip) to Guinea. Three out of Africa's four crocodilians live mostly if not entirely within this rainforest belt. There is not much African rainforest outside the aforesaid belt. Many groups of organisms, represented abundantly in the New World tropics, and again in the great stretch of tropics from southern Asia to northern Australia, are not very well represented in tropical Africa. For example, the tropical flora of Africa is unexpectedly scanty, and this is particularly true of the rainforest component of that flora. Botanists have long remarked on Africa's meager showing of orchids, palms, bamboos, and aroids—plant groups that abound in other tropical lands. It is suspected that in past ages drastic shifts to a drier climate

Figure 138. Africa's main rainforest belt (horizontal hatching), and the range of the African sharp-nosed crocodile (vertical hatching). Dots indicate outlying locality records for the crocodile.

have eradicated many organisms from Africa; and that the vast Sahara Desert has limited the reinvasion of the continent by organisms coming from the Asiatic tropics. At any rate, crocodilians may be added to the list of tropical groups with but poor representation in Africa. The New World tropics have nine species of crocodilians, and the Australasian tropics eight; but Africa has only the Nile crocodile, the African sharp-nosed crocodile, and the two dwarf crocodiles (Osteolaemus).

The African sharp-nosed crocodile was known to science as far back as 1789, but at that time was confused with the gharial of India. In 1825 Baron Cuvier described the African sharp-nosed crocodile as *Crocodilus cataphractus*. ("*Cataphractus*" means "clad in armor.") Cuvier did not know the geographic origin of the species, which stands today as *Crocodylus cataphratus* Cuvier. The name acquired two synonyms, and one of these, *Crocodilus leptorhynchus* Bennett, 1835, merits comment as being based on material from Fernando Póo, a Spanish-owned island in the Bight of Biafra. The island lies about 30 miles off the coast of Cameroun, and the occurrence of the species so far from the mainland is of interest. The range of the African sharp-nosed crocodile covers the African rainforest belt, but also extends beyond it. Specifically, this reptile ranges from Senegal eastward into the Congo, and southward into Angola. The species has also been reported at Lake Tanganyika, a locality record isolated from (farther east than) the principal area of occurrence. Scattered expanses of rainforest exist in eastern Africa, east of the main rainforest belt; and a good many organisms, distributed more or less continuously throughout the main belt, exist also as isolated populations farther east. Presumably there was a former continuity of the main belt with what are now easterly outliers. At any rate, the Lake Tanganyika record for the sharp-nosed crocodile is not out of keeping with what is known of animal and plant distribution across central Africa. This is not to suggest that the crocodile is directly dependent on plants of the rainforest. Rather, environmental conditions necessary for the development of tropical rainforest—continuous warmth and high rainfall, for example—are likely to be ideal for crocodiles.

To judge from its streamlined build and its very narrow snout, the sharp-nosed crocodile is a stream-dwelling predator upon small fishes. However, neither the habitat nor the principal food is known with certainty. Several locality records mention rivers: the Benué, the Niger, and the Ogooué. Although largely confined to rainforest country, the species also reaches areas where the principal vegetation is savanna woodland or grassy savanna.

The nest is made of plant debris. Little is known of the eggs or hatchlings. I have heard, and been astonished by, the juvenile distress cry. As far as I have learned, this is the only crocodilian whose distress cry is highly distinctive. When seized, the young of the African sharp-nosed crocodile voices not the usual crocodilian series of shrieks, but a medley of loud squawks, squeaks, honks, and yaps. The adult of this crocodile, being seldom over 6 feet in length, and having narrow jaws, is probably incapable of fighting off the larger predators that menace the young; and it may be that the extraordinary vocal efforts of the molested juvenile function to surprise or frighten a predator into discontinuing an attack, at least for the few moments necessary for the little reptile to vanish in the water. Many small, inoffensive organisms will cry out loudly when seized, and such vocalization is definitely known to discourage some mammalian predators. When seized, the juvenile sharp-nosed crocodile will also evert the throat glands; but no visible secretion is produced by this action, nor any odor that can be detected by man.

The juvenile of almost any crocodilian may occasionally use the feet to make small adjustments of position in the water; but the juvenile of the African sharp-nosed crocodile (Fig. 139) does this more often, and more capably, than any other species known to me. Both fore and hind feet are used to maintain vertical stability, to pivot abruptly in the water, and to provide braking action when the swimming reptile nears an obstruction.

The juvenile of the sharp-nosed crocodile is patterned with deep black

Figure 139. A juvenile of the African sharp-nosed crocodile uses its limbs to maintain or change position in the water. [Ross Allen's Reptile Institute]

Figure 140. The skull of the African sharp-nosed crocodile (at right) is somewhat like that of Johnston's crocodile (at left), but the similarity reflects parallel evolution rather than close relationship. From Robert Mertens, 1943, Senckenbergiana 26, No. 4.

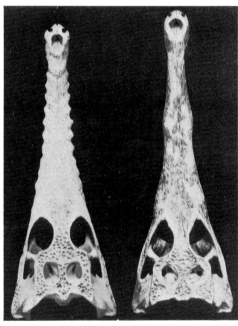

blotches and crossbands on a greenish-gray or greenish-yellow background. The snout of the juvenile, although narrow, is fairly short. The snout lengthens with age (Fig. 140), and the pattern becomes duller. In both juvenile and adult, there are four or five dark blotches on the side of the lower jaw, recalling similar markings in various caimans. It is unusual to see an African sharp-nosed crocodile much over 5 feet in length. The maximum length is said to be 8 feet. Competition with the Nile crocodile should be minimal, what with the differences between the two in size and (probably) diet.

Although the living species of *Crocodylus* have not yet been covered in their entirety, a brief departure from taxonomic arrangement will be made in order to dispose of the two remaining crocodilians of Africa. These are the dwarf crocodiles, genus *Osteolaemus*. In 1860 Edward D. Cope described an unusual crocodilian from the "Ogobai" (Ogooué) River in what was then called French Equatorial Africa (now Gabon). It was the West African dwarf crocodile. Cope considered it to represent a previously unknown genus and species. The name he proposed stands today, and the West African dwarf crocodile is known as *Osteolaemus tetraspis* Cope. The generic name means "bony throat," the reference being to bony platelets in the scales of the throat. The species acquired several synonyms, but these need not be reviewed. The distribution of this dwarf crocodile seems limited to a small part of western Africa, with locality records for Sierra Leone, Guinea (formerly French Guinea), Ghana (formerly the Gold Coast), Togo, Nigeria, Cameroun, and Gabon. The species is largely, and perhaps exclusively, a rainforest one, but it may also inhabit savanna country not far from the rainforest belt. According to the literature, this crocodile "is often found in salt or brackish-water where its upturned snout is useful in keeping its head above choppy waves"; but the statement may be regarded as a fabrication, inspired by the pronounced development of an "aquatic profile" in the adults of *Osteolaemus tetraspis*. The biology of the species is almost unknown. A captive reptile laid eggs around the end of June, and the length of an egg was about 2¾ inches, the width about 1¾ inches. The maximum length of the adult is regarded as 6 feet, but most adults do not exceed 5 feet. The species must be fairly common at some localities, for a good many specimens have reached zoos and reptile collections. According to the literature, African tribesmen "erect palisades around their bathing spots in the rivers so as to ensure a tranquil bath"

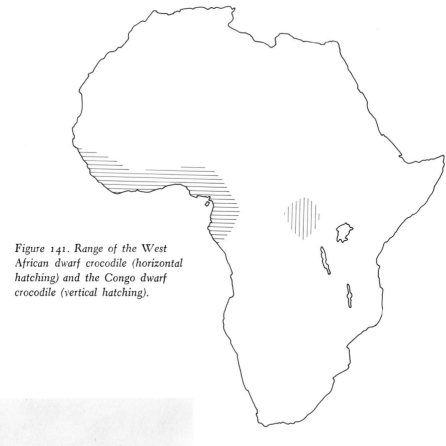

Figure 141. Range of the West African dwarf crocodile (horizontal hatching) and the Congo dwarf crocodile (vertical hatching).

Figure 142. In head shape and heavy armor, the West African dwarf crocodile (at right) resembles a smooth-fronted caiman. The lower jaw of this dwarf crocodile (above) is blotched like that of a smooth-fronted caiman, also. [W. T. Neill]

in areas where this dwarf crocodile lives; but the species is an inoffensive one, and if palisades are really erected, they are intended to keep out Nile crocodiles.

A second species of dwarf crocodile, the Congo dwarf crocodile, was first made known to sicence by K. P. Schmidt in 1919. This reptile had been collected by an American Museum expedition to the Congo. Schmidt regarded the Congo dwarf crocodile to be so different from the West African one as to warrant separate generic status, and he dubbed the Congo reptile *Osteoblepharon osborni.* The name *Osteoblepharon* means "bony eyelid"; both of the dwarf crocodiles have a small, bony structure in the

Figure 143. The Congo dwarf crocodile.

upper eyelid. *Osteoblepharon* was thought to differ from *Osteolaemus* in the arrangement of several bones of the skull; *Osteolaemus* also had a better-developed nasal septum, and a more upturned snout. These characters were later deemed inadequate to separate two genera, and *Osteoblepharon* became a synonym of *Osteolaemus.* The Congo dwarf crocodile stands to-day as *Osteolaemus osborni* (Schmidt). In 1953 it was guessed that the two dwarf crocodiles were no more than geographic races of a single species, but United States workers, at least, have not generally adopted this view; and the gradually accumulating facts support the idea that two species are represented, separated by a thousand miles or more. The two species are

Figure 144. The up-turned snout of the West African dwarf crocodile will remain up-turned throughout life. [Ross Allen's Reptile Institute]

easily distinguished by external features. In the West African dwarf crocodile, the tip of the snout is upturned, strongly so in adults; and the enlarged supracaudal scales, anterior to the point where the tail crest becomes single, number eleven pairs. In the Congo dwarf crocodile, the snout is straight, and there are twelve to fourteen pairs of supracaudals anterior to the non-paired supracaudals.

The type-specimen of the Congo dwarf crocodile came from Niapu, in what was then the Belgian Congo (now the Republic of the Congo). The locality is in the northeastern part of the Republic, far up the Itimbiri River, a tributary of the Congo. One or two other locality records exist, well up in the headwaters of the Congo River drainage. To judge from locality records, the habitat is probably the swift, upland streams of the rainforest. The fossil history of the genus *Osteolaemus* is unknown, although anatomically the genus is primitive, more primitive than *Crocodylus*. Of the two dwarf crocodiles, the Congo species is somewhat the more primitive, seeming to be a relict species, surviving only in a small area of very high rainfall, and in a habitat not invaded by any species of *Crocodylus*. The biology of the Congo dwarf crocodile is little known. The collector of the type-specimen, Herbert Lang, discovered that the nest was made of vegetable debris. The maximum proven length of the Congo dwarf crocodile is only 3 feet and 9 inches.

Both of the dwarf crocodiles look remarkably like the smooth-fronted caimans of the New World. In *Osteolaemus*, just as in *Paleosuchus*, the snout is smooth, the dorsal armor heavy, the iris dark, the maximum size small for a crocodilian. The bony eyelids and ventral platelets of the dwarf crocodiles also recall the smooth-fronted caimans. But the dwarf crocodiles have the "crocodyline notch" of the upper jaw, exposing the fourth lower tooth, a character which suffices to distinguish these reptiles at a glance from any caiman. It is suspected that the dwarf crocodiles are much like the smooth-fronted caimans in habits and habitat. Another interesting prob-

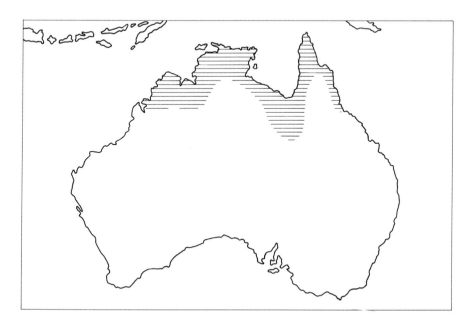

Figure 145. Australia, showing range of Johnston's crocodile (hatched).

lem relates to the broad gap between the respective ranges of the two dwarf crocodiles. Further collecting might narrow this gap.

Returning now to the genus *Crocodylus*, it is convenient here to discuss Johnston's crocodile, the only crocodile confined to Australia; thus the remaining chapters can deal with an essentially Asiatic group of crocodilians. Early in the 1870s, Robert A. Johnston collected a slender-snouted crocodile at Cashmere, on the upper Herbert River in northern Queensland, Australia. J. E. Gray thought the reptile to be a *Tomistoma*, but G. Krefft rightly decided that it was a previously unknown species of *Crocodylus* (or rather *Crocodilus*, the spelling that prevailed in Krefft's day). Krefft intended to dub the species in honor of its collector, but through some error the name he published, in 1873, was *Crocodilus johnsoni*. Most taxonomists have agreed that the original spelling could be emended, and today the species usually stands as *Crocodylus johnstoni* Krefft. However, some taxonomists, especially European ones when dealing with non-European species, have regarded original spellings as sacrosanct; and so Johnston's crocodile is called *Crocodylus johnsoni* in lists prepared by various Old World workers and their few American followers.

Johnston's crocodile has been found to range widely across northern Australia, from northeastern Queensland westward into the Kimberley Division of Western Australia. The range corresponds roughly to the extent of the tropics in Australia. All but the northern part of that continent lies in the south-temperate zone. This species could probably range farther south in Australia if temperature alone controlled its distribution. But, with the exception of a strip along Australia's east coast, the subtropical part of the continent is too dry to support a freshwater crocodilian. The spread of the species to the north, into New Guinea, probably has been prevented by the prior establishment there of the New Guinea crocodile, *Crocodylus novae-guineae*, another small crocodilian of the fresh waters.

Savanna woodland, not rainforest, predominates throughout the range of Johnston's crocodile. The habitat of the species seems to be the smaller rivers or creeks, which may occasionally be followed down to brackish water. In general, this reptile avoids the sizeable bays, estuaries, and river mouths, in which the much larger estuarine crocodile, *Crocodylus porosus*, is to be found. Johnston's crocodile is seemingly unrelated to Palimnarchus, a fossil crocodilian from Australia. Palimnarchus may prove to be a tomistomine rather than a crocodyline.

R. A. Johnston not only collected the type-specimen of the crocodile that was named for him, but also provided most of the information we have about its life history. He discovered that the female builds a nest by scraping up dead leaves and grass, along with some earth. The food consists primarily of small fishes, but other small organisms may be taken at times. Johnston opened a good many stomachs, never finding anything larger than a water-rat in them. Australia harbors large rats of the genus *Hydromys*. These rodents, highly specialized for an aquatic existence, live about streams, swamps, and estuaries, where they feed on snails, clams, and crayfishes. Stomach contents of the crocodiles also included fragments of mollusk shells, and some plant material that probably had been accidentally ingested. Gastroliths in the form of pebbles were likewise present. The smallest known specimen of Johnston's crocodile, presumably a hatchling, was scarcely over 9 inches in total length. The maximum length of the species is considered to be 8 feet, although most individuals are under 6 feet. Australian aborigines recognized the harmless nature of Johnston's crocodile, and were not averse to bathing in its haunts.

As shown by an accompanying photograph (Fig. 140), Johnston's crocodile somewhat resembles the African sharp-nosed crocodile. The similarity is not indicative of relationship. Nor is either of these two species particularly related to the Orinoco crocodile, another narrow-snouted species. Narrowing of the snout has taken place independently in various lines of crocodilian descent, apparently as an adaptation for the more efficient pursuit and capture of fishes.

25 THE FRESHWATER CROCODILES OF THE SOUTH-WEST PACIFIC ISLANDS

WE MAY NOW TURN to the tropical Asiatic region, using this geographic term very broadly to include the islands that lie between Asia and Australia, and the islands that are strung out east of New Guinea, as well as the tropics of mainland Asia.

Within the tropical Asiatic region, the New Guinea crocodile, the

Mindoro crocodile, and the Siamese crocodile apparently form a related series of freshwater species, and so may be considered in sequence. Johnston's crocodile is sometimes considered a part of this series, to which it may indeed be related. However, the New Guinea, Mindoro, and Siamese crocodiles form a compact group, from which Johnston's crocodile stands somewhat apart as being more specialized.

The large, widespread estuarine crocodile, *Crocodylus porosus*, was reported from New Guinea at quite an early date; but for a long while the presence of a second and smaller crocodile on that island was not recognized. In 1908 George A. Dorsey collected anthropological material in New Guinea. At Ibundo on the lower Sepik River, in what is now the Territory of Papua and North-East New Guinea, he obtained the skull of a small crocodile; and somewhere in New Guinea, probably also on the lower Sepik, he obtained another but somewhat larger skull. Crocodile skulls, along with skulls of wild hogs and human beings, were often kept about native longhouses in New Guinea. The two skulls obtained by Dorsey reposed for years in the collections of the Field Museum at Chicago. In 1922 C. W. A. Monckton, long a Resident Magistrate in New Guinea, published the opinion that there were two species of crocodiles in New Guinea, one large and dangerous to man, but the other small and inoffensive. In 1928 K. P. Schmidt concluded that the two skulls, brought by Dorsey from the lower Sepik, represented a previously undiscovered species of crocodile, a species smaller than the estuarine crocodile, and probably an inhabitant of fresh water. Schmidt named the new species *Crocodilus novae-guineae*. The English name of "New Guinea crocodile" is suggested by the Latin name he chose for this reptile. The validity of the species was not promptly granted, however. In 1931 the name *novae-guineae* was tossed into the synonymy of *porosus*. Schmidt later went to the Sepik River country, where his party shot two specimens of the New Guinea crocodile, obtained two more from native collectors, and acquired twenty-two skulls in exchange for knives and plane blades. Some of the skulls were gaudily painted and tasseled. Armed with this fresh material, in 1932 Schmidt reaffirmed the validity of *novae-guineae*. Nevertheless, in a 1945 account of the reptiles of the Pacific Islands, the species was vouchsafed mention only in a footnote, with the hint that the name might have been based only on some inconstant variation in young individuals of the estuarine crocodile. Meanwhile, in 1943 and 1944 I had had abundant opportunity to study the New Guinea crocodile in Papua, procuring enough material and information to prove its distinctiveness from the estuarine crocodile in both anatomy and habits. Some of my observations were published in 1946. The New Guinea crocodile now stands as *Crocodylus novaeguineae* Schmidt. (Modern taxonomic usage frowns on hyphens in Latin names.)

The distribution of the New Guinea crocodile is still not well understood. Apparently the species exists as a number of isolated populations that correspond in the main to extensive areas of freshwater swamps and marshes. In Papua there is (or was) a population in the Port Moresby area. Another population extends along the coastal lowlands roughly from Kerema (not to be confused with Karema near Port Moresby) westward across the Fly River delta to Daru or perhaps Buji. One would expect the range to be continuous from southwestern Papua into southeastern Irian Barat (the former Dutch New Guinea); yet there seems to be no record for the latter area, and at Merauke in 1944 I could find only the estuarine crocodile although searching especially for the smaller species. Years later, a party of well-armed Indonesians, operating from a boat in waters near Merauke, were shooting crocodiles for leather, curios, and nostrums. I examined their kill, finding only the estuarine species. West of Merauke, in the country drained by the Bian, Digul, Mapori, and Eilanden rivers, the estuarine crocodile occupies the coastal strip of mangrove swamp, but the New Guinea crocodile should be present farther upstream. The Papuan range of the New Guinea crocodile also extends far up the Fly and its tributary the Strickland. Until recent years, the species abounded in the vast marshes of Lake Murray, Papua.

Mountain ranges, trending approximately in a southeast-northwest direction, occupy much of the interior of the island of New Guinea. The crocodilian populations so far mentioned are on the south side of the mountains. The New Guinea crocodile also occurs on the north side. There is a population in the area between Bogia and Wewiak, this population also extending up the Sepik as far as Ambunti and probably much farther. On the north side of the dividing ranges, as on the south, there seems to be no record for Irian Barat. It is probable that scattered populations of this crocodile exist at fairly high elevations in the interior of New Guinea. The reptile is known to some of the upland tribes, who regard it as both inoffensive and edible. To the east-northeast of Port Moresby, at a distance of about 14 miles, there is an abrupt drop from interior highlands to coastal

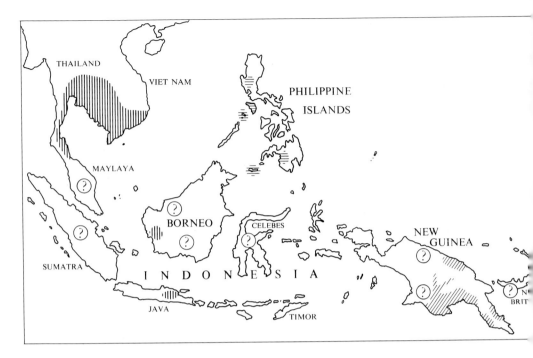

Figure 146. Distribution of the New Guinea crocodile (diagonal hatching), Mindoro crocodile (horizontal hatching), and Siamese crocodile (vertical hatching). Question marks indicate areas in need of more study.

lowlands, the drop being marked by such impressive topographic features as Rouna Falls and the escarpment called Hombron Bluff. As a large New Guinea crocodile once fell over Rouna Falls, I suppose that a population of the species exists above the cataract.

The habitat of the New Guinea crocodile is various. I describe two localities where it was abundant. Lake Murray is a vast basin, shallow for the most part, with a very indented shoreline. Two streams enter it, and one flows from it. Forested islands dot the lake. The surrounding country is mostly rainforest, but near and bordering the lake are also patches of sago swamp and of curly-bark (Melaleuca) swamp. In many places the edges of the lake are occupied by marsh, the conspicuous plants of which include rice, jungle-rice, a reed, a sugarcane, and a nut-rush. The last often forms small islets in the lake. At a second locality, the Waigani Swamp area (7 to 12 miles north of Port Moresby), there exist a medium-sized basin and a number of small lakes. Waigani Swamp has some large expanses of open, deep water, narrowly edged with reeds and patches of lily-pads. However, the New Guinea crocodiles seemingly avoided these open areas, being concentrated in deep, sluggishly flowing channels and in small lakes overgrown with herbaceous aquatics. The channels were bordered for the most part with curly-bark, palms, figs, gums, and Casuarina, along with much thick brush. The surrounding country was a savanna woodland with much *kunai* grass, and with scattered curly-barks and gums. In the savanna woodland, not far from Waigani, were numerous small, isolated ponds, often choked with grasses and sedges. These isolated ponds seemed not to harbor crocodiles, although water-lizards and monitors were often common about the borders. In general, the swift, rocky stretches of a river are not inhabited by the New Guinea crocodile; nor the broad, deep stretches away from lagoons, marshes, or labyrinthine waterways. The species is said to follow coastal wetlands down into brackish water, but of this I have no proof.

At Waigani and vicinity, the nesting site was usually 20 to 30 feet back from the water, often on higher ground bordering a lagoon or sluggish channel. The nests were always in dense brush, and completely shaded; many were built at the base of a tree. A well-worn path, made by the female, led tunnel-like through the thick brush from the water's edge to the nest. The path was always wet and muddy, for it received drippings each time a female emerged from the water to visit her nest. Several times I could see water pouring off a female as she lunged up a bank atop which she had nested. Guardian females took to water as I approached, and then floated at the surface, watching me. When I approached a guardian female for the first time, she would allow my small boat to get within about 30 feet before she would scuttle into the water. But having once been disturbed at the nest, she would become warier, and would slip into the water when I was a good 50 feet away. Having been disturbed two or three times, a female would become so wary that I could hardly get a distant glimpse of her before she vanished into the water. If someone had followed my route a few days after I had been studying the crocodiles, he would probably have concluded that nests were not guarded in this species.

Once I paddled to shore and went back to examine a nest. The guardian female, about 6½ feet long, left the water and approached me along the tunnel-like path that led to the nest. She stopped when about 10 feet away and began to hiss, also to thrash laterally; but when I took one

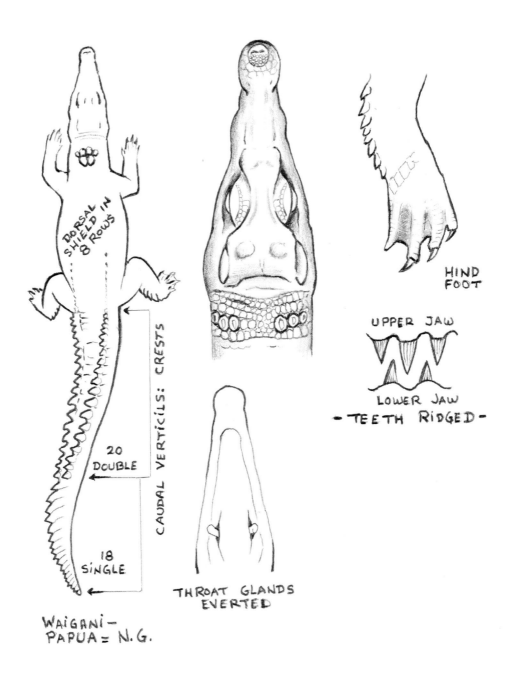

DORSAL IN SHIELD 8 ROWS

CAUDAL VERTICILS: CRESTS

20 DOUBLE

18 SINGLE

WAIGANI- PAPUA = N.G.

THROAT GLANDS EVERTED

HIND FOOT

UPPER JAW

LOWER JAW

-TEETH RIDGED-

Figure 147. The New Guinea crocodile in Papua: sketches from the author's field journals.

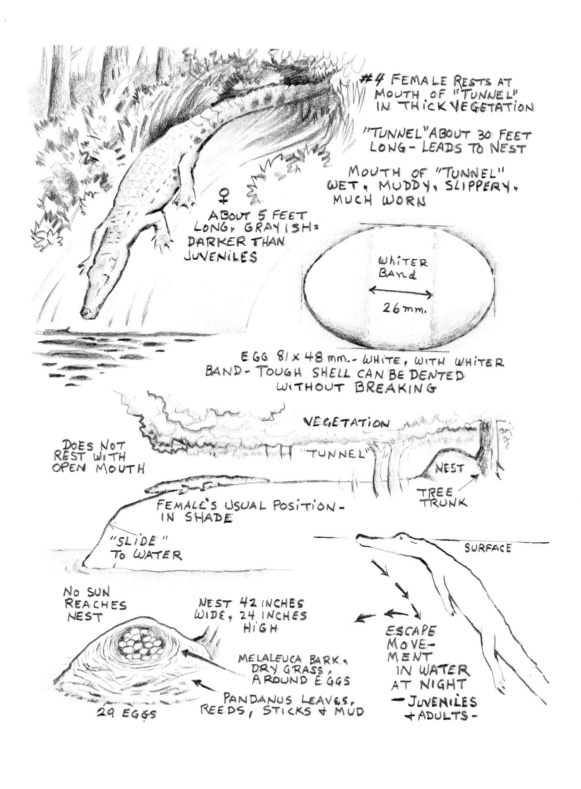

#4 FEMALE RESTS AT MOUTH OF "TUNNEL" IN THICK VEGETATION

"TUNNEL" ABOUT 30 FEET LONG - LEADS TO NEST

MOUTH OF "TUNNEL" WET, MUDDY, SLIPPERY, MUCH WORN

♀ ABOUT 5 FEET LONG, GRAYISH= DARKER THAN JUVENILES

WHITER BAND

26 mm.

EGG 81 x 48 mm. - WHITE, WITH WHITER BAND - TOUGH SHELL CAN BE DENTED WITHOUT BREAKING

DOES NOT REST WITH OPEN MOUTH

VEGETATION

"TUNNEL"

NEST

TREE TRUNK

FEMALE'S USUAL POSITION - IN SHADE

"SLIDE" TO WATER

SURFACE

NO SUN REACHES NEST

NEST 42 INCHES WIDE, 24 INCHES HIGH

MELALEUCA BARK, DRY GRASS, AROUND EGGS

ESCAPE MOVEMENT IN WATER AT NIGHT — JUVENILES + ADULTS -

29 EGGS

PANDANUS LEAVES, REEDS, STICKS & MUD

step in her direction, she fled back to the water. All crocodilian species will hiss when confronting an enemy, but thrashing is a display less often noted. If a crocodile thrashed when someone stood nearby, the movement would probably be misinterpreted as a "tail-stroke"; but my distance from the reptile revealed such thrashing merely to be a part of the warning behavior.

Nests with eggs were seen in November. The nests were roughly hemispherical, about 4 feet in diameter and 2 feet in height, and composed of scraped-up plant debris. The nest is unique among crocodilians, as far as has been reported, in that it has a "lining" of comparatively soft material around the egg. The lower half of the nest consisted of coarse Pandanus leaves, reeds, and sticks embedded in a matrix of mud. The upper half, containing the eggs, had a thin shell of mud and twigs; but inside the shell, surrounding the eggs, was a soft, dry mixture of grass, leafy debris, and strips of bark from curly-bark trees. (Strips of soft, papery bark fall naturally from the curly-bark tree.) Those better known descendants of the thecodontians, the birds, usually build a nest of some comparatively coarse material and then line it with something softer; and it is interesting to discover comparable nest construction in the crocodilians. The eggs of the New Guinea crocodile lie very near the top of the nest, and the hatchlings should have no trouble in escaping unaided through the thin layer of material that covers the clutch above. In most nests the temperature was about 96 degrees Fahrenheit. I visited one nest several times, each time lifting up a bit of the nesting material in order to see the eggs. From this nest I got a temperature reading of 103 degrees Fahrenheit. I now suspect that my disturbance of the nest did something, perhaps let in moisture, to encourage fermentation of plant debris, thus raising the nest temperature higher than it would normally have gone. But it might be noted that the Port Moresby area, where this nest was found, is unusually hot, the air temperature not infrequently exceeding 103 degrees during the crocodiles' nesting season. The number of eggs in a clutch ranged from 23 to 35. The egg was about 3 inches in length, and a little less than 2 inches in diameter.

The dorsal ground color of the hatchling and older juvenile is an olive-yellow. This color darkens with age, becoming a dull grayish. In the young crocodile, the back bears five or six blackish crossbands broken into rows of spots. There are a few small, rounded, blackish spots on the sides of the body, and similar but larger spots on the sides of the tail's basal third. On the last two-thirds of the tail, there are seven or eight blackish, broken crossbars. The under surface of the tail is brown, except toward the whitish basal third of that appendage. Other ventral surfaces are whitish. The juvenile voices a distress cry, very loud and shrill but not substantially different from the distress cry of most crocodilians. Juveniles and young adults were caught by hand at night. On one occasion I seized a juvenile, and it began shrieking. A nearby adult charged promptly at my boat, but submerged while yet a few yards away.

On another night, a friend and I paddled in pursuit of a juvenile that we had frightened. Instead of vanishing in deep water, as most of these crocodiles did when clumsily stalked, this one made for a straight, shallow channel scarcely wider than the boat. Not until later did I realize the nature of this channel: rising water had flooded the oft-used trail of a gigantic estuarine crocodile. The trail crossed a little islet, on the opposite side of which the estuarine crocodile was lying in its trail, facing away from us, and unnoticed by us at that time. As I grabbed the little New Guinea crocodile, it began to shriek. The adult estuarine crocodile immediately threw itself back in our direction. Had it not been for vegetation, the large reptile could possibly have reversed its direction with a single lunge. (The estuarine crocodile is very agile even when adult.) But as it happened, the crest of the islet was overgrown with saplings, and the big crocodile crashed into several of these. We paddled away hastily, and were not followed. It is probable that the distress cry of the small New Guinea crocodile, while momentarily arousing the estuarine crocodile, was too high-pitched to stimulate the big reptile into an actual attack. When seized, the juvenile of the New Guinea crocodile also everts the throat glands, but no odor is produced that human nostrils can detect.

Stomachs of New Guinea crocodiles often contained masses of black feathers, which I took to be those of the locally abundant gallinules and coots. One stomach contained a fledgling of the willie-wagtail, a common small bird. One night, the beam of my headlamp fell on a small New Guinea crocodile just as it leaped almost completely out of water to seize a water-lizard that was sleeping on a reed. The night was very dark, and it was surprising that a crocodile could locate a motionless lizard. As several kinds of birds, lizards, and frogs were to be found at night on vegetation overhanging the water, perhaps this crocodile often leaps for its prey. Juveniles of the New Guinea crocodile ingest gravel, and adults ingest small stones, to serve as gastroliths.

I once came upon two large mounds of vegetation, which I first took to be crocodile nests. Each proved to be *kunai* grass piled over a dead and rotting hog. In 1946 I reported such mounds probably to be the work of New Guinea crocodiles; but now I would ascribe them to estuarine crocodiles, for reasons that will become apparent when that species is discussed.

At the time the adult females of the New Guinea crocodile were guarding their nests, the smallest juveniles I could find were about 2 feet long, and probably yearlings. Most guardian females I estimated to be about 5 feet in length. I am told that in some other parts of New Guinea nesting females are seldom under 6 feet long. One female, 5 feet and 3 inches in length, upon examination proved to be sexually immature. The largest New Guinea crocodile measured by me was 5 feet and 8 inches long. According to the literature, the species reaches a length of 9 feet and 4 inches.

Little was learned about social organization in the New Guinea crocodile. The spatial distribution of individuals suggested territoriality. They were well spaced, and never two together. In the deep, sluggish, canal-like waterways, two might occasionally be separated by no more than 50 to 75 feet, but greater separation was the rule. The same crocodile would appear in the same place night after night. However, after heavy floods all the reptiles would take up new positions, although still maintaining wide separation from one another. The floods often washed away many fallen logs and branches, and altered the configuration of the shore line. Every night for a period of eight months I paddled along about two and a half miles of waterways that were inhabited by New Guinea crocodiles, yet I never heard a roar, a bellow, or a juvenile grunt. The distress cry of the juvenile, and the warning hiss that is given at all ages, are the only sounds I heard from this species. Nor did I ever see a New Guinea crocodile "bask"; that is, take up a position out of water and in the sunlight. A few crocodiles were found out of water by day, but they were in deep shade, hiding in thick vegetation or under piles of fallen timber in low-lying spots that had previously been flooded. When disturbed in such places, they would dash into the nearest remaining water and hide in patches of aquatic vegetation. Most of the reptiles were in the water by day or night. I saw some females guarding their nests by night as well as by day.

The New Guinea crocodiles, even the young ones, had impressively good control of their buoyancy and stability in the water. The resting position in the water was never horizontal. The crocodile's body was kept at an angle of about 45 degrees from the surface, and the neck was bent over so that the head alone was horizontal. In this position, the crocodile would often swim a foot or two, or change its heading, by swimming with the legs rather than the tail. If alarmed, the crocodile would pull downward and backward a foot or two, and then, well beneath the surface, would dive still deeper, swimming with the tail. It was surprising to see a crocodile move downward and backward through the water, as rapidly as though jerked by a string. Presumably this abrupt submergence is made possible by a rapid exhalation of breath.

Wherever I found the New Guinea crocodile, there too I found the estuarine crocodile, an unanticipated circumstance. However, at a locality where I found New Guinea crocodiles, the estuarine crocodiles would all be large, mostly 9 to 12 feet in length, and some even larger. If this situation is a usual one, then the two species are not in much competition for food, the huge estuarine crocodiles probably ignoring the small game that supports the New Guinea crocodiles. Also, the adult estuarine crocodiles were mostly in large lakes, not channels. In southern Papua I found young estuarine crocodiles, those equaling a New Guinea crocodile in size, to occupy certain small, narrow basins that led off the larger streams. Thus, the young estuarine crocodiles were separated ecologically from adults of their own kind as well as from New Guinea crocodiles.

New Guinea is often thought of as one of the few regions that remain ecologically unspoiled, but the New Guinea crocodile has lately been hunted as persistently as the American alligator. In 1967 no crocodiles of any kind could be found on the Fly River below d'Albertis, and no more than about four a night in the stretch between d'Albertis and the Avu River. The aforesaid localities are far up the Fly, in country that was almost unknown as late as the 1940s. In many areas along both the Fly and the Sepik, both the New Guinea and the estuarine crocodiles have been killed out. On Lake Murray, where New Guinea crocodiles once abounded, an evening's search revealed only one. In 1969 some game officials estimated that in another four or five years the New Guinea crocodile would be extinct, and the estuarine crocodile extirpated from the Territory of Papua and North-East New Guinea, unless special measures were taken to save the reptiles.

Closely related to the New Guinea crocodile is the Mindoro crocodile. The latter has been a source of much perplexity. When K. P. Schmidt was returning in 1923 from a visit to New Guinea, he stopped briefly at Manila, on Luzon in the Philippines. There he was given three small crocodiles from Mindoro, an island just south of Luzon. In 1935 Schmidt concluded that these three specimens, and a comparatively large skull without collecting data, represented a previously undescribed species, which he named *Crocodylus mindorensis*. The type-locality was simply the island of Mindoro, an exact locality record being unavailable. The species was stated to differ from the New Guinea crocodile in having, among other things, a broader and heavier skull, with heavier pitting of the skull bones, and with more pronounced ridges in front of the eyes. Nearly a half-century before Schmidt focused scientific attention on the Mindoro crocodile, Joseph B. Steere had proceeded up Mindoro's Catuiran River. After two days' travel upstream, he shot the first known specimen of the Mindoro tamarao, a kind of wild cattle. Skinning the tamarao, he used its flesh to bait some crocodiles. In this way he caught a crocodile about 8 feet in length. In 1891 Steere described the incident. In 1935 it became evident that the skull of Steere's crocodile was the one to have reached Schmidt, minus its collecting data. For more than a decade after its description, the Mindoro crocodile was generally excluded from the scientific lists, being regarded, like the New Guinea species, as probably a variant of the estuarine crocodile. Once *Crocodylus novaeguineae* was conclusively distinguished from the estuarine crocodile, the similar distinctiveness of *Crocodylus mindorensis* was generally granted, although no one had had chance to study the Mindoro reptile in nature.

The exact taxonomic position of the Mindoro crocodile was still not settled, however. In 1953 an outstanding German student of reptiles, Heinz Wermuth, suggested that the New Guinea crocodile and the Mindoro crocodile be considered as geographic races of a single species. Accordingly, he listed the two as *Crocodylus novaeguineae novaeguineae* and *Crocodylus novaeguineae mindorensis*. This nomenclature has been followed by subsequent German workers, and by some others. To further complicate the situation, in 1955 an important taxonomic review of the living Crocodilia assigned the Mindoro crocodile to Luzon, Mindanao, and the Sulu Archipelago, but not to Mindoro. Finally, in a 1968 review concerned primarily with fossil crocodilians, Mindoro was apparently taken to be a part of New

Guinea; both the New Guinea crocodile and the Mindoro crocodile were considered to inhabit the island of New Guinea.

There the matter has rested. Actually, one cannot decide on wholly objective grounds whether the New Guinea crocodile and the Mindoro crocodile should be considered subspecies or full species. It is possible that a single species of freshwater crocodile once spread widely over the islands of the southwestern Pacific; and that the range of this crocodile was eventually split into two or more fragments, each of which went its separate evolutionary way. If the New Guinea and the Mindoro crocodiles represent two such fragments, and if the two managed to re-establish geographic contact with each other, would they interbreed freely (as subspecies should do)? Would they interbreed just sporadically? Or would they behave as full species, and fail to interbreed? One cannot guess. The respective ranges of the two are separated by about 1,500 miles. All specimens of the Mindoro crocodile can be distinguished from all specimens of the New Guinea crocodile. In some diagnostic features, the variation in one of these reptiles does not overlap the variation in the other. While little is known of the fossil history of this particular group of crocodiles, paleontological studies on other organisms (for example, the gopher tortoises and some other turtles of North America) have shown that one can fall into gross error when assuming a subspecific relationship between fairly similar but geographically remote kinds of reptiles. Paleontological studies also reveal that certain details of crocodilian skull structure reflect habits and habitat; and so the similarities between the New Guinea and the Mindoro crocodile, while in part indicative of relationship, may well have been exaggerated by the restriction of both these reptiles to lifeways that minimize competition with the estuarine crocodile. Finally, if the New Guinea and Mindoro crocodiles are to be ranked as subspecies on the basis of guess, one could make out a good case for guessing the Mindoro crocodile to be a subspecies of the Siamese crocodile, which is very similar to the Mindoro reptile in many ways. Schmidt's views on the Mindoro crocodile, first published in 1935, and amplified in 1956 when more specimens had become available, today seem close to the reality of the situation. I list the Mindoro crocodile as *Crocodylus mindorensis* Schmidt. The known distribution includes the Philippine islands of Luzon, Mindoro, Mindanao, Busuanga, and Jolo.

The biology of the Mindoro crocodile is almost unknown. Since the species has been found in the interior of Mindoro and Luzon, it probably

Figure 148. A young specimen of the Siamese crocodile. [W. T. Neill]

occupies a habitat that is not often reached by the estuarine crocodile. Most adults of the Mindoro crocodile seem to be in the size range of 5 to 6 feet; and Steere's specimen, about 8 feet long, is the largest reported.

The Siamese crocodile is better known. Unlike its relatives, the New Guinea and Mindoro crocodiles, it is not wholly a species of the south-western Pacific islands, but occurs also on the southern Asiatic mainland. Near the end of the eighteenth century, it was discovered by French missionaries in Siam (now Thailand). The missionaries sent a skull back to Europe; and J. G. Schneider, on the basis of this skull, erected the species *Crocodilus siamensis*. The Siamese crocodile stands today as *Crocodylus siamensis* Schneider. It has acquired one unimportant synonym, based on Siamese material. Another synonym, based on a fossil, will be discussed later. The Siamese crocodile has at times been confused with the mugger, *Crocodylus palustris*; but such confusion is possible only with juveniles, for the two species differ greatly in head shape when adult. On the Asiatic mainland, the Siamese crocodile inhabits Thailand, Cambodia, and South Viet Nam, as well as the Malay Peninsula southward to the Patani River. An old record for China is not regarded as valid, but, what with the Chinese emphasis on the use of crocodilian parts as nostrums, it would not be sur-

Figure 149. Head of an adult Siamese crocodile. Ridge-like elevation behind the eye is characteristic of the species. From M. A. Smith, 1919, Journal of the Natural History Society, Siam 3 (3).

prising if skins or skulls of the Siamese crocodile had been imported into China. In the islands that lie south of the Asiatic mainland, the Siamese crocodile has been taken on Java and Borneo.

The distribution of the species in Thailand is extensive, with locality records thinly but widely scattered over the country. Thailand records of especial interest include the Mae Nam Khong (upper Mekong) at Khenmarat; the vicinity of Sai Yoke, on the Mae Nam Kawae Noi in extreme western Thailand; the vicinity of Chumphon, on the Isthmus of Kra in the Malay Peninsula; and the upper Mae Yom above Phrae in northern Thailand. Cambodian records of particular interest include the northern part of the Tonle Sap, and a small lake at an elevation above 3,000 feet on the Luang Bian Plateau. The distribution of this crocodile tends to follow rivers, but the reptiles are more often found in bordering swamps and lagoons than in the streams proper. Some of the locality records are much farther inland, and at much higher elevations, than any record for the estuarine crocodile. The Siamese crocodile seems not to have been reported in salt water. In most parts of this species' range, there are marked wet and dry seasons. Where seasonal differences of rainfall are pronounced, large areas may be dry a part of the year, and then be flooded when the rains come. On the Asiatic mainland, especially, the Siamese crocodile's existence must be adjusted to marked seasonal fluctuations of the water table.

Observations on the biology of this species all come from Thailand. The nest is not known. Eggs are said to be laid during the rainy season, early in that season I would suspect. The egg is about 3 inches long and 2 inches in diameter. Hatching has been reported in August. Hatchlings are a little under 10 inches in length. The juvenile grunt is voiced. The juvenile distress cry has not been reported, but should exist. The coloration of the hatchling is unreported. The pattern of the larger juvenile or young adult consists of four or five blackish crossbars on the body, and about ten wide, blackish crossbars on the tail. Laterally there are blackish blotches on the body and the basal third of the tail. As compared with the Mindoro and New Guinea crocodiles, the Siamese species is noteworthy for broader crossbars and larger spots. Presumably the growth of the Siamese crocodile is rapid, at least during the first few years of life, for a three-year-old was 39 inches long. A peculiarity of the adult is an elevated, bony ridge behind the eye. A similar but higher ridge characterizes the Cuban crocodile of the New World. The Siamese and the Cuban crocodiles are the only members of their genus in which this ridge is strongly developed. The largest recorded Siamese crocodile was 11 feet and 4 inches in length. At this size, senility is evident.

The Thai, or some of them, distinguish between the estuarine crocodile and the Siamese crocodile, regarding the latter as edible but the former not. There may be some objective foundation for this belief. The diet of an organism can affect the flavor of that organism's flesh. Certain ducks and coots may be savory if bagged from the fresh waters, but intolerably "fishy" when shot on saltwater feeding grounds. The estuarine crocodile might indeed be unpalatable if it had been feeding in coastal situations, something the Siamese crocodile rarely or never does. The Thai, noting the webbing of the toes to be more extensive in the estuarine than in the Siamese crocodile, refer to the former as "duck-footed" and the latter as "chicken-footed."

For convenience in discussion, the term "freshwater crocodiles" may be used in the present chapter, without implication of complete restriction to fresh water, for the series of *Crocodylus* that is made up of the species *novaeguineae, mindorensis,* and *siamensis.* It will be seen from the foregoing account that freshwater crocodiles are widely but thinly distributed over the southwestern Pacific region, and are apparently lacking from many islands as well as many mainland areas. Past geologic and climatic episodes —for example, a rise of sea level, a subsidence of land, a local shift toward a drier climate—could have eradicated such crocodiles from some areas. Also, the freshwater species would probably be of wider geographic and ecological occurrence were they better able to compete with the highly successful estuarine crocodile. However, I think that the freshwater crocodiles have been removed from many localities through the activities of man. By this I do not mean just modern hide-hunting, but also earlier hunting by native peoples. The freshwater crocodiles, comparatively inoffensive, have been a ready source of meat, as well as hides, teeth, trophy skulls, and other items. These reptiles seem to have persisted chiefly in areas where the local people, until very modern times, were armed only with such ineffective weapons as the wooden-tipped arrows and spears of New Guinea; or where there was some religious sanction against the killing of animal life. The spread of iron-tipped weapons, and later of firearms, probably served to extirpate the freshwater crocodiles from many localities.

It is possible that in a few remote spots some relict populations of freshwater crocodiles remain to be discovered. It is even possible that taxonomically nameworthy populations remain to be discovered. In 1935 Schmidt suggested that a freshwater crocodile should be found on Borneo, an island known at that time to harbor only the estuarine crocodile and the Tomistoma. A freshwater crocodile was eventually found on Borneo, and identified as *Crocodylus siamensis.* If enough specimens ever become available to permit a convincing comparison, the freshwater crocodile of Borneo might turn out to be distinct from mainland *siamensis.* Also in 1935, Schmidt expressed the opinion that there should be a freshwater crocodile in the Celebes. In 1954 Dr. D. A. Hooijer described some fragmentary crocodilian remains from the Pleistocene of the Celebes; these appeared to represent an undescribed species of *Crocodylus,* not *porosus, siamensis,* or *palustris.* Special search might well be made for surviving freshwater crocodiles in the lakes of the Celebes. In the latter nineteenth century, Eugene Dubois, discoverer of the prehuman "Java ape-man," also found Javanese remains of a Pleistocene crocodile, and named them *Croco-*

dylus ossifragus. The species was later identified as Crocodylus siamensis. Not until 1915 did it become evident that the Siamese crocodile still existed on Java, where one or two specimens were collected.

In 1956 I reported sight records of small crocodiles about the upland lakes of New Britain. The habitat is an improbable one for the estuarine crocodile, and the reptiles I saw were probably the New Guinea crocodile or some undescribed close ally thereof. The New Guinea crocodiles I examined from Papua, south of the New Guinean central ranges, differed slightly from Schmidt's description of specimens from the Sepik, north of the ranges; and it may be that two different subspecies are involved.

The apparent absence of freshwater crocodiles from the great island of Sumatra is hard to believe. Yet, from that island have so far come only the Tomistoma and the estuarine crocodile. The Siamese crocodile is probably more widespread in the Malay Peninsula than available specimens would indicate. Captive individuals have been seen in Penang (and in Singapore off the southern tip of the Malay Peninsula), but I could not be sure that they were taken locally.

On Luzon, in the Philippines, the Mindoro crocodile seems to exist only in the interior, away from the heavily settled coastal lowlands. Strangely, Mindoro is the only Philippine island from which more than one or two specimens of a freshwater crocodile have been taken. It is odd that only one specimen of a Mindoro crocodile has been reported from Mindanao, an island so much larger than Mindoro, and ecologically so much more diverse. According to R. Woltereck, in a 1941 paper, hidehunters on Mindanao sold 12,243 crocodile skins to an American buyer in a period of six months. If only a herpetologist could have examined those hides for the presence of a *Crocodylus* that was not *porosus!* Even a belly skin suffices to distinguish the estuarine crocodile from the Mindoro crocodile. In the former, the ventral scales are comparatively small; between the level of the axilla and the level of the groin, these scales are arranged in about 23 to 30 transverse rows. In the Mindoro crocodile—also in the New Guinea crocodile and Johnston's crocodile—the ventral scales form only about 16 to 18 transverse rows between the level of the axilla and the level of the groin.

The freshwater crocodiles of the southwestern Pacific accordingly offer very attractive problems for the student of crocodilian taxonomy. Unfortunately, the New Guinea and Mindoro crocodiles, never very abundant in modern times, have probably been dealt the coup-de-grace by the hide-hunting industry. Thailand may be able to preserve the Siamese crocodile for a few decades after its Philippine and New Guinean allies have vanished.

26 THE MUGGER AND THE ESTUARINE CROCODILE

TWO SPECIES of the genus *Crocodylus* remain to be discussed: the mugger and the estuarine crocodile. It is not intended to suggest that the two are closely related to each other. The mugger is related to the group that includes the Siamese, Mindoro, and New Guinea crocodiles. Just as this group has a highly specialized, narrow-snouted relative, Johnston's crocodile, to the south, so does the same group have a highly specialized, broad-snouted relative, the mugger, to the north. The closest living relatives of the estuarine crocodile may be the members of the Asiatic freshwater group, but the relationship is distant. Crocodile relationships are discussed in fuller detail at the end of the present chapter.

In 1831 B. P. Lesson applied the name *Crocodilus palustris* to a crocodile from India. The name *palustris* means "of the marshes," and emphasizes the habitat of the species. Several synonyms, based likewise on Indian material, need not be listed. The range extends from West Pakistan eastward across India as far as Assam, and perhaps as far as Burma, although records from the latter country are lacking. This crocodile also inhabits Ceylon, the large island that lies off the southern tip of India. An old record for the Malay Peninsula is probably based on a misidentification. There is also a single old record of the mugger for Java. This record has generally been disavowed by modern workers, and rightly so, as Java lies about 2,000 miles outside the known range of the species. Yet, a 1967 issue of *Life* magazine, in a photographic essay on a wildlife reserve at the western tip of Java, included an illustration of what appears to be an adult mugger. This reptile is often called the "sacred crocodile of India," for in the latter country it is often kept and pampered in temple pools and local marshes. For centuries there was a movement of Indian people, religious

Figure 150. Range of the Indian mugger (diagonal hatching) and the Ceylonese mugger (horizontal hatching).

beliefs, and temple architecture into Java, and it may be that the mugger was introduced there, persisting in a few places.

In 1936 P. E. P. Deraniyagala concluded that the Ceylonese population of the mugger should stand as a separate subspecies, which he named *Crocodylus palustris kimbula*. But in 1933, Franz Werner had erected the name *Champse brevirostris* for a supposedly African crocodile. As it turned out, Werner's lone specimen was actually a Ceylonese mugger. Thus, *brevirostris* had precedence over *kimbula* as a name for the Ceylonese subspecies. The geographic races of the mugger therefore stand now as *Crocodylus palustris palustris* Lesson, inhabiting the mainland part of the species' range, and *Crocodylus palustris brevirostris* (Werner), confined to Ceylon.

The two may respectively be called the Indian mugger and the Ceylonese mugger. The name "mugger," incidentally, is not of English origin but is a borrowing from Hindustani. Easily pronounceable vernacular names, such as gharial, jacaré, and mugger, are colorful additions to the English language, and relieve the monotony that otherwise characterizes the list of English names for crocodilians. The two subspecies are distinguished by certain features of scalation. In the Ceylonese mugger, the scales of the throat are broadened laterally to form what looks like a series of collars. The bony scales that make up the dorsal armor are arranged in six longitudinal rows for the most part (three rows on each side of the dorsal midline); and the row that lies nearest the midline is not conspicuously wider than the other rows. In the Indian mugger, the scales of the throat are closer to the crocodile norm in size and arrangement, and do not particularly suggest a series of wide collars. The bony scales of the dorsal armor are arranged in four rows (two rows on each side of the dorsal midline), and the row that borders the midline is distinctly broader than the one that does not. It is interesting to note the collar-like arrangement of the scales in the throat region of the Ceylonese mugger. Among various reptile groups, ventral scales may be enlarged on a part of the underside that suffers the most impact or abrasion when the reptile crawls; often this is the chest, throat, or both. A collar-like arrangement of enlarged throat scales is the norm in the alligatorines, which generally do less swimming and more crawling than the majority of crocodylines. In the estuarine crocodile, which is the most highly aquatic species of *Crocodylus*, the throat

Figure 151. A young Ceylonese mugger. [Ross Allen's Reptile Institute]

scales are but very slightly enlarged. The mugger, which resembles an alligatorine in head shape, habits and habitat, seemingly has begun to evolve collar-like throat scales of alligatorine appearance. The habitat of the mugger includes marshes and swamps as well as lakes and rivers. Fresh water is usually frequented, but the species is occasionally to be found in brackish coastal marshes and swamps.

The literature may include some actual facts about the mugger's life history. However, these facts are interwoven with the usual old legends and with Ceylonese folklore, and I am inclined to regard the life history of the species as virtually unknown. We are told that the mugger catches fishes by opening its mouth and waiting for them to swim in; that it cruises open-mouthed through the water in order to catch frogs; that the female uses her forefoot to dig a nest in a sandbank; that the hatchlings call their mother, who digs them out of the nest; that the little ones receive maternal care; that during the dry season the mugger goes back into the jungle and hides under a rock; that the mugger uses its tail to deliver a blow. Much of this material is plainly apocryphal, and doubt is cast over the remainder.

The mugger's egg is about 2½ inches in length, 1½ in width. The female guards her nest, remaining beside or in contact with it most of the time. The hatchling is about 10 inches long. The juvenile pattern, not described in any detail, includes dark crossbands on the tail and dark spots on the side of the body. The pattern becomes obscure with age, the old adult being almost uniformly dark above. The juvenile grunt is given. So is the juvenile distress cry; it will summon an adult, as is usual among crocodilians. India is another part of the world where some people know how to lure the adult crocodilian by imitating the juvenile distress cry. The food of the mugger includes fishes, frogs, and sizeable aquatic mammals, with lesser numbers of smaller mammals and birds. The literature frequently repeats the story that a mugger will eat the corpses as they float downstream from the burning ghats of India, and that a reptile, so fed, may then become a man-eater. The story has persisted on account of sensational rather than factual quality. There is no evidence that a mugger eats dead or living people in India, and the reptile is not feared there. It is claimed that an occasional Ceylonese mugger will take to attacking man, but one might suspect some confusion with the estuarine crocodile, which also frequents Ceylon. In many parts of the mugger's range, the shallow bodies of water vanish during the dry season, and at this time the reptiles may wander in search of waterholes. I regard as improbable the story that the mugger passes the dry season by burying itself in the mud and "estivating." Earlier workers regarded the maximum length of the mugger as exceeding 15 feet, and modern workers have reduced the figure to 13 feet. A specimen about 13 feet long has actually been measured. However, even a 10-footer is rare today. The usual adults, between 6 and 8 feet long, are remarkably alligator-like in head shape, but of course display the "crocodyline notch" of the upper jaw.

Finally we come to the estuarine crocodile. This is another reptile whose discovery is credited to J. G. Schneider, who in 1801 dubbed it *Crocodilus porosus*. Schneider regarded the species to inhabit India (a geographic term that was defined broadly and loosely in his day). Actually, the estuarine crocodile had been named earlier, in 1795, by F. A. A. Meyer, who had called it *Crocodylus natans*. However, the name erected by Meyer was overlooked until 1960. The resurrection of this obscure old name, to replace the well-known and oft-used name *porosus*, has seemed inadvisable. The code of the zoological nomenclature provides a sort of limbo, into which may be dropped certain validly proposed names whose present use might confuse matters. Thus, the estuarine crocodile stands as *Crocodylus porosus* Schneider. Schneider's concept of the species was based in part on a 1734 drawing by Albertus Seba, but also on some actual museum specimens, at least one of which is still in existence. The Ceylonese population is distinguishable from other populations of the species, and it is clear that Ceylonese specimens reached Schneider. Also, Seba used the adjective *Ceilonicus* in connection with his own drawing. Thus, Schneider's type-locality has been restricted to Ceylon. A determination of Schneider's type-locality has been important because Deraniyagala, in 1955, suggested that the Ceylonese population of the estuarine crocodile should be regarded as a distinct subspecies. If this view is followed, then the name *Crocodylus porosus porosus* Schneider is to be restricted to the Ceylonese population. In 1807 Cuvier applied the name *Crocodilus biporcatus* to an estuarine crocodile that did not come from Ceylon, and the name has been resurrected from the synonymy to designate the non-Ceylonese subspecies, which stands today as *Crocodylus porosus biporcatus* Cuvier. No precise type locality was given by Cuvier. When an early taxonomist failed to supply a type-locality, a later worker may designate one in the interest of nomenclatural stability. In this fashion the type-locality of *biporcatus* has been designated as Java.

The two subspecies of the estuarine crocodile are not very different from one another. The Ceylonese subspecies usually has a transverse row of somewhat enlarged scales (the postoccipitals) following the dorsal junction of the head with the neck. Outside of Ceylon, the estuarine crocodile rarely has postoccipitals; and the dorsal scales immediately behind the head are quite small. Crocodiles usually have postoccipitals, and the estuarine species has often been considered noteworthy for its loss of these scales as part of a general reduction of armor. The estuarine crocodile has become the most thoroughly aquatic and most frequently marine of living crocodiles; and in this species, which swims far and frequently, reduction of armor probably functions to lighten the body weight and lessen friction with the water. The presence of postoccipitals in Ceylonese specimens suggests that Ceylon may harbor a comparatively primitive population of the estuarine crocodile. For this reason it seems useful to recognize two subspecies. These may be called the Ceylonese estuarine crocodile and the Indonesian estuarine crocodile.

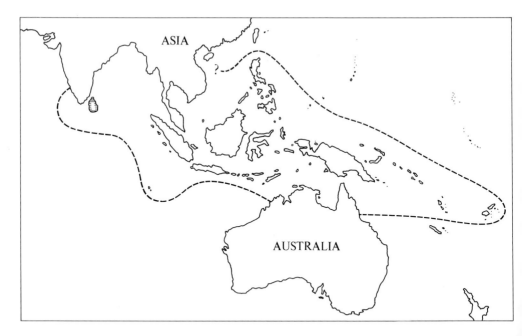

Figure 152. The range of the estuarine crocodile. Limits of the range are indicated by a broken line. Large rivers, reaching the sea within these limits, may be followed upstream for dozens of miles by this crocodile. The Ceylonese population (hatched) may be a distinct subspecies.

The range of the Ceylonese estuarine crocodile includes only the island of Ceylon, as far as is known. The range of the Indonesian estuarine crocodile is very wide. The west coast of India is inhabited northward only to the vicinity of Cochin; but the east coast of that country is probably inhabited throughout its length, for locality records are scattered from Pondicherry, India, in the south, to Barisal, East Pakistan, in the north. There is also a record for the Burmese portion of the upper Malay Peninsula. On the Asiatic mainland, the species probably exists as scattered populations rather than as a single continuous one. There are old records for southern China, although the species no longer lives there. Records for the Indo-Chinese Peninsula are surprisingly lacking. Indonesian locality records include Sumatra, Java, Borneo, Labuan, Sulawesi, the Moluccas, Batjan, Simeulue, the Riau Archipelago, Ambon, Ternate, Flores, the Mentari Islands, Timor, and Irian Barat, among others. North of Indonesia the estuarine crocodile reaches the Philippines, Singapore, the southern Malay Peninsula, and the Palau Islands. East of Indonesia, the species reaches the Territory of Papua and New Guinea, the Aru Islands, the Kei (Ewab) Islands, the Bismarck Archipelago, the Solomons, the New Hebrides, and the Fijis. The northern coast of Australia is also inhabited by this widely ranging reptile. Some far-outlying locality records, for example the Fijis, the Palaus, and the New Hebrides, might be based on wandering individuals rather than breeding populations. An estuarine crocodile once arrived in the Cocos (Keeling) Islands, which lie a good 600 miles from any other land. Evidently an individual crocodile of this species can cross a wide expanse of ocean.

The presence of the estuarine crocodile in salt water was revealed at an early date, and the idea grew that it was not to be found above tidewater limits. Eugene Dubois, working in Sumatra, pointed out in 1896 that the species also ranges up the large rivers for a long distance. In general, the estuarine crocodile does not invade swift streams or very small ones. Nevertheless, in New Guinea I found good-sized adults, those in the 9- to 12-foot range, in smaller streams than I had anticipated. I saw four adults at a point about 30 miles up the Markham River in northeastern New Guinea. The Markham here is a braided stream, occupying a broad and sparsely vegetated valley. At the point where the crocodiles were seen, the stream was so shallow, and so stony of bottom, that a truck could be driven across it. I also saw and caught estuarine crocodiles on

Figure 153. *A young estuarine crocodile from Malaysia.* [*Ross Allen's Reptile Institute*]

the Laloki, a Papuan river of no great size. In places this stream became narrow, deep, and forest-bordered; in other places broader, shallow, rocky of bottom and high of bank, with savanna woodland atop the bank. In Papua, the large adults (but not smaller adults or juveniles) were also present in large basins which offered swamps and lakes as well as sluggish channels. Along the rivers of Papua, there appeared to be some ecological separation of young from adult. The adults were to be found in the stream proper, or in nearby large basins. The young occupied small, gully-like depressions leading into the main stream. These depressions—"draws" they would be called in alligator country—may be produced by erosion. At any rate, a typical "draw" would be mud-bottomed in the dry season, but with a vegetation-choked pool near its head; and in this pool a young estuarine crocodile would often live, vanishing in the water, mud, and plant stems when anyone approached. Even by night the young crocodiles were sometimes present in the pools. However, one of the young reptiles would occasionally go down to the river by night, as shown by its tracks in the mud and its absence from the pool where it was usually to be found. One large adult, seen in the surf near Port Moresby, Papua, had been badly injured by native spearmen. In Ceylon, Deraniyagala considered the estuarine crocodile to be characteristic of areas with mangroves, or else with a somewhat cattail-like herbaceous plant (Lagenandra).

In spite of its wide range, the estuarine crocodile has not become well known. The literature relating to it provides a few facts, interspersed with scraps of native folklore and more often with the same old legends that have been fastened upon most of the larger crocodilians. For example, in connection with this species we are again given the absurd story that the "unwary stroller at the water's edge" will have "his legs swept suddenly from beneath him by a deftly wielded tail" of an estuarine crocodile. We are told that the males of this reptile are made "more ferocious" by injuries received in fights over the females during the breeding season. "During this season the males are said to grunt throughout the night." I suggest that males of the crab-eating frog, *Rana cancrivora* and closely allied species, grunt all night during the rainy season in places where crocodiles have been seen. This group of frogs, widespread over a large part of the area that is occupied by the estuarine crocodile, tolerates brackish water to a degree that is unusual among amphibians. Deraniyagala related a Ceylonese legend to the effect that the male and female estuarine crocodile would confront each other in a sort of wrestlers' embrace, rise higher and higher in the water, and copulate belly-to-belly. It is amusing to see that local residents in many parts of the world do not understand how crocodilians manage to copulate with the female belly-down, and do not observe the reptiles keenly enough to discover the truth of the matter.

I know the estuarine crocodile best from New Guinea, but have encountered it casually in various other parts of its range, from the Malay Peninsula and the Philippines southward through Indonesia to northern Australia. The life history can at least be sketched in broad outline. The female builds a nest by scraping plant debris into a pile. Sometimes she builds with dead plant material, but more often she scrapes up tall green grasses, or else herbaceous aquatic plants that are easily uprooted or defoliated. According to the literature, the nesting site is far from water, but this comment merits amplification. In an area with well-marked wet and dry seasons, the eggs are laid at a time when the water table is at least fairly high. If the slope of the ground is gentle, and if the water table falls, the nest may be left 50 yards or more from a body of water. But in an area or habitat where the water table does not fall very much, the nest is seldom over 25 or 30 feet from the water's edge. I have seen several nests that were built atop a fairly high bank, down which the female could slip immediately into the water, even though the water table might have fallen by several feet. There is mention in the literature of nests 4 or 5 feet high, but some exaggeration may be suspected. Nests I have seen (in the Philippines, several parts of Indonesia, and Papua) were about 25 to 30 inches high, and about 4 to 5 feet in diameter. In these nests, the plant material —mostly the blades of large grasses and of long-leaved aquatic plants— was loosely piled. The nesting material is not as tightly compacted as in the nest of most other crocodilians. When the female estuarine crocodile lurches out of water and walks to her nest, streams of water pour off her, soaking the path that she follows. It is amusing to note that in Ceylon, as in many other countries, the local people seemingly have never observed the

Figure 154. Hatching egg (below) and nest (at right) of the estuarine crocodile; Java. From Felix Kopstein, 1938, Bulletin of the Raffles Museum, No. 14.

simple and inevitable method whereby a crocodilian's nesting path becomes soaked, and choose instead to ascribe the soaking to some elaborate behavior pattern on the part of the nesting female. According to the Ceylonese legend, the female estuarine crocodile scoops out two basins near her nest, waits until these basins are full of water, and then with her tail splashes this water over the nest. It is easy to see how the legend of the two basins could have developed: the female uproots and scrapes up vegetation from a small area in which her nest will be located, and in so doing might easily leave depressions in which rainwater or seepage could accumulate.

The female estuarine crocodile lies beside her nest to guard it; she will guard it against man. The number of eggs in a clutch ranges from 25 to 72. The egg is a little over 3 inches long, and about 2 inches in diameter. Of all the living species of *Crocodylus*, this one exhibits the greatest reduction of the black markings. The hatchling is greenish-gray above, with small, scattered, black spots on the body and tail. The arrangement of the spots on the body may suggest crossbands. Spots become larger, and therefore more reminiscent of crossbands, on the last quarter of the tail. Adults become uniformly dark above, but may retain a trace of spotting on the sides of the body and tail. In other species of crocodiles, the bony

plates of the dorsal armor are squarish in outline, and fit closely together; but in the estuarine crocodile, these plates are reduced in size, ovoid in outline, and separated one from another. In both small and large estuarine crocodiles, the shape and separation of the dorsal scutes is evident externally. Well over a century ago, John Gray, who was much inclined to split crocodilian and other genera, held that a crocodile with reduced, ovoid, bony scutes should be placed in a separate genus, *Oöpholis*. Today this proposal has little to recommend it. In the juvenile estuarine crocodile, the scales of the dorsal armor, as well as the six clustered scales that protect the back of the neck, each bear a very sharp, almost knife-edged, longitudinal keel. Both the juvenile grunt and the juvenile distress call are voiced, neither departing significantly from the crocodilian norm.

The behavior of a cornered, tormented hatchling has inspired many an anthropomorphism in the literature: ". . . vicious disposition . . . ferocity . . . fiendish little brutes . . . uncontrollable rage . . . positively the most vicious reptiles . . . exhibition of rage." Of course, such phrases might better be limited to interpretations of human behavior. To describe the crocodilians' behavior in more scientific fashion, one might say that the hatchling or juvenile of the estuarine crocodile, cornered in a pen or box, has an automatic impulse to confront an enemy, even a very large enemy; and if the young reptile is prodded with a stick, it has an automatic impulse to bite at the source of its torment.

The food of the estuarine crocodile is not well known. In captivity, both small and large individuals will leap upward from the water's surface to snap with unerring aim at a piece of food that is being dangled. Probably estuarine crocodiles, like New Guinea crocodiles, will leap upward to pick sleeping vertebrates from branches that overhang the water. The juvenile estuarine crocodile has a rather slender, streamlined snout, a head shape to be expected in a crocodile that pursues fishes. When the juveniles leave the "draws" to visit the nearby river, probably they do pursue fishes; but fishes could hardly be pursued in the little, vegetation-choked pools along the "draws." There are treefrogs of the genus *Hyla* on this vegetation, and various tadpoles in the pools. On the damp ground or grass of the "draws" there are frogs of the genus *Rana*, and often a small, harmless snake (*Natrix mairii*). Perhaps the young estuarine crocodile preys upon some of these vertebrate associates. According to the literature, the young individuals eat water beetles, shrimps, crabs, fishes, frogs, and small turtles;

but I do not know whether the basis of this statement is wholly factual.

As mentioned in the preceding chapter, in Papua I came upon two mounds of *kunai* grass, resembling crocodile nests, but each mound covering a dead pig. Both mounds were near the edge of a marsh, and beside one of them were crocodile tracks leading to water. In 1946 I described the mounds as probably being the work of the New Guinea crocodile; for the estuarine crocodile, although present just a mile or so away, had not been noted in that exact stretch of marsh. However, I now feel that the estuarine crocodile was the species responsible for the mounds. In the first place, the New Guinea crocodile feeds upon small organisms, and is not likely to take a pig, while the estuarine crocodile as an adult will prey upon large animals. Second, the estuarine crocodile can and often does gather a mound of *kunai* grass in which to nest, and so might well employ a similar technique when building a mound to cover the body of a dead animal; but the New Guinea crocodile does not gather *kunai* grass when nesting. Third, Kingsley Fairbridge, in two of his works, among them an autobiography, tells how a man was caught by a predaceous estuarine crocodile in New Guinea. Injured and nearly helpless, the man was covered up by the crocodile, which built over him a mound much like the one I found. The man, who was still able to cry for help, was heard by Fairbridge and his native associates, and was rescued. (The two works of the elder Fairbridge were brought to my attention through the kindness of Rhodes Fairbridge and Robert J. Tilley.) Wild pigs are abundant throughout most of the range of the estuarine crocodile. In New Guinea, pig trails crisscross the forest and grassland, often bordering a river or leading into the shallows of a lake or swamp. Rusa deer are frequently seen near the water, also. On the Asiatic mainland, and in the island arc that includes the Greater Sundas and the Philippines, the lake shores and river banks are frequented by a greater variety of large mammals. Nevertheless, throughout the range of the estuarine crocodile there are almost no reliable records of predation on large animals other than man, although domestic cattle and horses are said to be attacked.

The estuarine crocodile is the only crocodilian that has demonstrably preyed on man with considerable frequency. At times and places where governments have kept official statistics on the local causes of death, a good many deaths from estuarine crocodile attack have been tabulated. There are also a number of well-documented, eye-witness accounts of attacks.

Attempted predation on man has been witnessed by professional biologists. The zoologist P. J. Darlington, Jr., was seized by a 10-foot estuarine crocodile in New Britain. Darlington had made his way along a submerged log, and was dipping up a test tube of swamp water when the reptile rose to the attack. It seized Darlington by the arms, and began to "whirl." Darlington was whirled over and over as he was carried to the bottom, but the crocodile released its grip, and he was able to escape. In Papua I witnessed two attacks on man. These attacks took place less than two weeks apart, and at localities less than a mile apart along a single stretch of lake shore. Both attacks were probably made by the same estuarine crocodile. Three men, in a small boat scarcely adequate for two, were clowning, and shooting wildly at waterfowl. Their antics attracted a considerable audience of people, who watched from a high bank overlooking the lake. The men overturned the boat; and two of them, who could swim, grabbed the third man whose inability to swim was well known. Perhaps some prank was involved in the upset, for the two swimmers towed their nonswimming companion not toward shore but in a direction parallel with it. However, a large estuarine crocodile came up behind them and seized the legs of the man who was being towed. The crocodile whirled the man over a time or two and then disappeared with him, while the two swimmers made their way rapidly and safely to the bank. The next day, I tried unsuccessfully to find the victim's body, but think now that I was looking in the wrong place. At that time I did not realize how much fiction had entered the herpetological literature, and I accepted the common assertion that a crocodile would cache large prey below the surface of the water, under an overhanging bank or submerged log. No crocodilian, anywhere in the world, has even been shown to do such a thing.

About twelve days later, I paddled a small boat along the lake, paralleling the shore line. Native tribesmen had once lived near the lake, but they had long since moved away because their ritual cannibalism had kept them in trouble with the authorities. Now, however, small hunting parties were visiting the lake, which, along with its adjoining swamps and marshes, was a rich hunting ground. Something less than a mile from the spot where the previously mentioned attack took place, I stopped my boat to watch the distant actions of two Papuan tribesmen who were on the lake in a small dugout. Each man was armed with a spear, not the huge, black-palm wooden spear of aboriginal manufacture, but the shorter iron spear obtained from a trading company. Between my boat and that of the natives, the lake shore was widely bordered with water-lilies, whose floating leaves were thickly clustered. The man in the bow of the dugout stood erect, holding his spear and gazing intently at the lily-pads as his companion paddled the dugout into the water-lilies. Probably the men were looking for turtles, as a side-necked turtle of the genus *Emydura* abounded in the lake. But the moment the boat began to shake the water-lily leaves and stems, a large estuarine crocodile moved to the attack. The reptile had been lying submerged among the stems, and the hunters had passed it without seeing it. The crocodile lunged at the man in the bow, overturning the boat but nevertheless catching the man by the ankle, and beginning to "whirl" with him. The other man made for the nearby bank; but, glancing back, he saw the plight of his companion, and rushed back to seize a spear and plunge it into the crocodile's body. The reptile released its victim, who was dragged to shore by his companion. As I paddled over, the crocodile vanished. The injured man wanted only to stop his bleeding with a compress of mud and grass, but he was taken to a medical station where the ragged remnant of his foot was amputated. About two weeks later I saw him again, hobbling about cheerfully with a crutch he had made from a tree branch. In later years, at various localities in Papua, Irian Barat, and North-East New Guinea, I encountered many natives, both men and women, who had lost a foot or a hand to an attacking crocodile.

In the attack described above, the crocodile could hardly have made any identification of its prey. Rather, it charged instantly in the direction of a disturbance among the lily-pads. Crocodilians of several species will automatically move in the direction of some disturbance in the water, but the estuarine crocodile does so with exceptional directness. One might say that it will seize prey first, and then identify it. Outside the Philippines, the Greater Sundas, and the Asiatic mainland, the adult estuarine crocodile is not likely to encounter any native animal that could not be overcome. In New Guinea, for example, there are no tigers, leopards, or other cats; no bears or wolves; no elephants or rhinos; no native cattle. The mammal fauna, ignoring domestic species, is made up of small or inoffensive marsupials, rodents, bats, and echidnas, along with pigs and deer, both of which may have been introduced by prehistoric man.

The estuarine crocodile ingests stones, as gastroliths. If the function of gastroliths is to add weight, there seems no reason why they should be

ingested by a species that has lessened its weight through evolutionary reduction of bony armor.

The growth rate of the estuarine crocodile is rapid. In captivity, young
ones have been reported to add as much as 18 or 20 inches to their length in
a year's time. Young estuarine crocodiles feed readily in captivity if kept at a
proper temperature. I suspect that most other crocodiles would grow this rapidly in captivity were not their feeding impulses somewhat inhibited by
nervousness or by unnatural surroundings. A three-year-old estuarine crocodile
may be 4 feet long. But as might be expected, adults grow more slowly. A
captive adult, 15½ feet long, added 10 inches to that length in two years'
time. It has often been assumed that the estuarine crocodile and the Nile
crocodile, by virtue of their large maximum size, should require a century to
become full-grown. However, the American alligator and the Chinese alligator
are the only crocodilians definitely known to live more than fifty years; in
captivity at least, crocodiles usually die in their second or at the most third
decade. It is probably significant that the two alligators, inhabiting temperate
regions, have a long season of winter inactivity, which adds to their longevity;
while crocodiles, coming from tropical climes, are active most or all of the
year. Perhaps one or two crocodile species, in areas of seasonal rainfall, are
quiescent for a short while at the peak of the dry season, but on this point
there is more speculation than information. The maximum size of the estuarine crocodile is uncertain. There is a literature account of an estuarine crocodile that measured 33 feet in length, and of another that measured 29 feet.
However, the skulls of these crocodiles reached museum collections, and
do not substantiate any such lengths. I have seen several 19-footers. K. P.
Schmidt regarded 20 feet as the probable maximum length, and the figure
seems well chosen.

The activities of the adult estuarine crocodile, outside of nesting and
of predation on man, are practically unknown. The adult voices a prolonged roar. This is loud and has a vibrating quality, but does not equal
the deep thunder of the alligator's roar. I heard the call of the estuarine
crocodile only once, on the north coast of Mindanao in the Philippines.
Possibly stimulated by some man-made noises on land, a crocodile roared
in a nearby brackish bay, and was promptly answered by about four others.
As nearly as I could judge, some of these crocodiles roared more than once,
but not with the pumping regularity that characterizes an alligator's bellow.
It cannot be said whether or not the estuarine crocodile is territorial. In-

dividuals do not gather on river banks or sand bars, as do Nile crocodiles and American crocodiles. During about five years' total residence at various localities within the range of the estuarine crocodile, I saw only two individuals lying in the open. One of these, a huge adult, was seen several times in a nearly dry swamp during the dry season. The other, a smaller adult about 11 feet long, lay in the brush of a stream bank, and did not move when I approached. Probably it had been seriously wounded by gunshot. Yet, in most of the areas that I visited, I could find estuarine crocodiles in the water at night. According to hearsay accounts in the literature, the estuarine crocodile lies open-mouthed on a river bank, where a sandpiper picks its teeth and the willy-wagtail picks insects off its skin; but I think the accounts represent nothing more than a transfer to the estuarine crocodile of old stories about the Nile crocodile. In New Guinea I was told by a native tribesman that a large crocodile would take up residence in a bamboo thicket on land, and charge forth to seize prey. Today, knowing more about crocodiles (and about native tribesmen), I believe my informant had in mind the mythical crocodile—as real to him as a flesh-and-blood one—that figures prominently in New Guinea superstition; for in New Guinea, as in ancient Egypt, modern Africa, and India, there is some kind of religious cult involving the crocodile. At any rate, *Crocodylus porosus* is the most thoroughly aquatic member of its genus, the least likely to come onto land for anything but nesting or the occasional passing between lakes during the dry season.

Within the vast expanse of tropics that stretches from southern Asia to northern Australia, the range of the estuarine crocodile overlaps that of every other crocodilian. The area of overlap is not wide in some cases, but the estuarine crocodile has been able to exist at least somewhere within the range of the mugger (both subspecies); the New Guinea, Mindoro, Johnston's, and Siamese crocodiles; the Tomistoma; and the gharial. Yet, the estuarine crocodile is not in much competition with any of the others. The gharial rivals the estuarine crocodile in bulk, but differs greatly from it in feeding habits. The mugger is a large, heavy crocodile, but is a broad-headed species of shallow marshes. The Siamese, Mindoro, New Guinea, and Johnston's crocodiles, as well as the Tomistoma, are freshwater species, all smaller than the estuarine crocodile. Johnston's crocodile and the Tomistoma are also very narrow-snouted, given to feeding upon small fishes.

Man is the greatest enemy of the estuarine crocodile, and the species

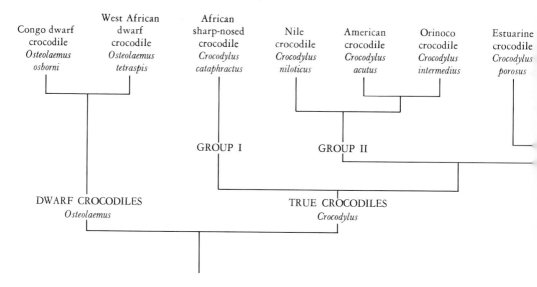

Congo dwarf
crocodile
*Osteolaemus
osborni*

West African
dwarf
crocodile
*Osteolaemus
tetraspis*

African
sharp-nosed
crocodile
*Crocodylus
cataphractus*

Nile
crocodile
*Crocodylus
niloticus*

American
crocodile
*Crocodylus
acutus*

Orinoco
crocodile
*Crocodylus
intermedius*

Estuarine
crocodile
*Crocodylus
porosus*

GROUP I   GROUP II

DWARF CROCODILES   TRUE CROCODILES
Osteolaemus   *Crocodylus*

is rapidly being exterminated. The large average size, as well as the reduced
armor, assures the hide-hunter of a handsome profit. In fact, the estuarine
crocodile yields the most valuable skin of any crocodilian. As the species
usually inhabits large rivers and estuaries, it is easily hunted at night from
a powerboat by men with lights and firearms. In the 1950s and 1960s, with
the price of crocodilian leather skyrocketing, hundreds of thousands of
estuarine crocodiles were killed annually. In many areas once thought remote—for example, parts of the Territory of Papua and North-East New
Guinea—the species has been wiped out, and its disappearance from all parts
of its range is to be expected within a very few years.

The account of the estuarine crocodile concludes the review of the
genus *Crocodylus*. It is now possible to suggest certain relationships within
this, the largest genus of crocodilians. The African sharp-nosed crocodile
is not closely related to any other surviving member of the genus. Its
Tomistoma-like snout is only superficially similar to that of Johnston's
crocodile. The sharp-nosed crocodile has several unique features of skeletal
anatomy. Its pattern—deep black smudges—is also unique among living
crocodilians. It might seem that pattern is not a guide to relationship, and
in many groups of organisms it might not be. But all the crocodilians have
a basically similar crossbanded pattern, which must be exceedingly ancient
and genetically very stable; and any departure from the crocodile norm is

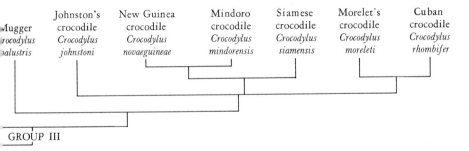

Figure 155. *Suggested relationships among living members of the subfamily Crocodylinae. The diagram is intended to show only the nature and approximate degree of relationship, without reference to the precise time period during which any line began to branch.*

thus likely to be significant. As the juvenile distress cry is similar in most of the crocodilians, attention is drawn to the curiously different cry of the juvenile sharp-nosed crocodile. This species is referred to what I shall call Group I within the genus *Crocodylus*, and is the only living member of this group. Fossil members of the group are unknown, unless the South American *Charactosuchus* turns out to belong to it.

The Nile crocodile is related to the American crocodile. Anatomical similarities between these two were noted decades ago by Charles C. Mook. The two species agree in crossbanded pattern and general conformation. Both nest in sand. Both lie about communally on river banks, often with jaws agape. The significance of the similarity between these two has been obscured by the widespread custom of imputing to any crocodilian the real or fancied habits of the Nilotic species. Both the Nile and the American crocodile probably radiated from some Eurasian stock. An Eocene species, *Crocodylus megarhinus*, may represent the arrival of this group in Africa, and may be ancestral to the Nile crocodile. The group probably reached the New World no later than the Oligocene. I regard the Orinoco crocodile as an offshoot of the American crocodile or its ancestor. At any rate, it is a member of the group that includes the American crocodile. The Nile, American, and Orinoco crocodiles are surviving members of what may be called Group II.

The rest of the world's living crocodiles form Group III, which also probably radiated from Eurasia. This third group seems to have diverged into two components, one strongly of the fresh waters but the other very tolerant of brackish and saltwater situations. The latter component culminated in the estuarine crocodile. In spite of its large size and reduced armor, the estuarine species is similar to the surviving freshwater crocodiles of Asia. Capable of moving readily through tropic seas, the saltwater component never had its distribution broken into thoroughly isolated fragments, and so never diverged into several species. In contrast, the distribution of the freshwater component was easily broken by stretches of sea, by arid expanses on land, and by uplands. Thus, the freshwater component eventually produced a variety of species in the Australasian tropics. This component has two subdivisions. The first of these subdivisions is represented today only by the mugger, a broad-headed marsh-dweller; it has filled a niche left open by the absence of alligatorines from tropical Asia. *Crocodylus sivalensis*, from the Pliocene of India, may be an ancestor of the mugger. The second subdivision of the freshwater component has one specialized member, Johnston's crocodile. This latter inhabits an area that is climatically less than ideal for crocodilians; and where most of the local aquatic situations, of a kind that might support crocodiles, are occupied by the estuarine species. Johnston's crocodile has evolved to fill the only niche left open to it, that of a narrow-snouted fish-eater in small streams. The Siamese, Mindoro, and New Guinea crocodiles are comparatively unspecialized within the second subdivision of the freshwater component. The Siamese crocodile, especially, is quite generalized. The second subdivision also reached the New World, where its most primitive living representative is Morelet's crocodile. The Cuban crocodile is a specialized derivative of the stock that gave rise to Morelet's crocodile. The living members of Group III, six species in the Old World and two in the New, are all characterized by a trend toward the breaking up of the pattern into spots. Some members of this Group are definitely known to build a nest by scraping up plant material, and I think all of them do so.

An accompanying diagram (Fig. 155) portrays probable relationships within the living Crocodylinae. A good fossil record would be an ideal ideal basis for such a portrayal, but the immediate ancestors of the living crocodiles have gone undiscovered for the most part. Certain anatomical, pattern, and behavioral similarities or differences among the living species of crocodiles suggest the groupings that have been erected. The groupings are consistent with what is presently known of crocodilian evolutionary history and with the general principles of zoogeography, the scientific study of animal distribution. It will be interesting to see how well the suggested groupings are bolstered by further work in paleontology, as well as by more detailed investigations into crocodile anatomy and habits.

27 THE TOMISTOMA
AND THE GHARIAL

THE SUBFAMILY Crocodylinae having been reviewed, we may turn to the subfamily Tomistominae. In 1838 S. Müller applied the name *Crocodilus (Gavialis) schlegelii* to a long-snouted crocodilian from southern Borneo. Müller thought the reptile to be more closely related to the gharial of India than to the true crocodiles. In 1846 he erected the genus *Tomistoma* (roughly meaning "slit-mouth") for the sole accommodation of his Bornean species. Today the reptile stands as *Tomistoma schlegeli* (S. Müller). (An initial is used in order to distinguish S. Müller from F., I., J., K., and L. Müller, all of whom published herpetological studies.) For a long while the taxonomic position of the species was not clear. It was often called "Malayan gavial," under the supposition that its nearest relative was the Indian "gavial." Not until the 1950s was there general agreement that S. Müller's species belonged in the family Crocodylidae; and not until the 1960s did it seem desirable to place *Tomistoma*, along with its extinct relatives such as *Gavialosuchus*, in a separate subfamily, Tomistominae, within the Crocodylidae. A suitable common name for Müller's species has not emerged from the literature. "False gavial" has been suggested, but the spelling "gavial" has little to recommend it. Generic names longer than *Tomistoma*—for example, *Chrysanthemum* and *Washingtonia*—have come into the common speech, and so the reptile will here be called a Tomistoma.

In the Tomistoma, the mandibular symphysis (the line of junction between right and left halves of the lower jaw) is very long, extending back

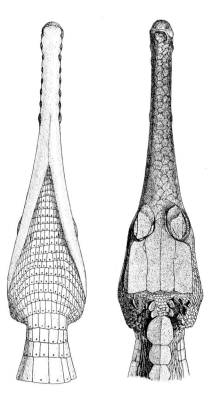

Figure 156. Head of a young Tomistoma. From Nelly De Rooij, 1915. The Reptiles of the Indo-Australian Archipelago.

to the level of the fourteenth or fifteenth tooth. In the narrow-snouted species of crocodiles, the symphysis does not extend backward beyond about the eighth tooth. The Bornean distribution of the Tomistoma includes Indonesian Borneo and Sarawak. The species also inhabits Sumatra and the southern part of the Malay Peninsula. In 1866 A. Strauch mentioned seeing a museum specimen labeled as coming from Java, but a population of the species has not been discovered on that island.

In 1915 Nelly de Rooij published the first volume of a work dealing with the reptiles of Indonesia and some adjoining lands. This volume included an unexcelled illustration of the Tomistoma, and provided what little information we have about the natural history of this crocodilian. The habitat is said to be freshwater rivers, and this is probably correct, for a high percentage of the available locality records mentioned rivers (for example, the Baram, Sadong, and Kapuas rivers in Sarawak; the Musi, Blindaban, Singilino, and Inderapura rivers in Sumatra). The nest is unknown. The egg is remarkably large, about 4 inches in length and 3 inches in diameter. The young Tomistoma is olive above, with blackish crossbands on the back, blackish spots on the lower sides, and broad, blackish crossbands on the tail. The iris of the eye is yellowish-brown, a point of difference from all other living crocodilians. The sides of the jaws are blotched with dark brown. The food is said to consist of fishes, and this is probably correct, for the long and slender snout is regarded as a specialization for fish-eating. Although the snout is slender, it widens posteriorly, and is not set off abruptly from the remainder of the head. In other words, the head is streamlined, and it is inferred that the reptile actively pursues its prey. This is in contrast with the gharial, which creeps upon, or lurks in wait for, its prey. The maximum size of the Tomistoma is generally given as 16 feet, a figure which probably stems from De Rooij, who gave the total length as 4.7 meters (about 15 feet and 5 inches).

Figure 157. An adult Tomistoma in life. [Ross Allen's Reptile Institute]

Several recent works state that the Tomistoma is called *buaia senjulong* in the Malay Peninsula, *buaia sapit* in southern Borneo, and *bediai sampit* in the Dyak country of Borneo. The statement derives from De Rooij, and its frequent repetition suggests that a bit of explanation would be welcome. *Buaya* (English-influenced spelling) or *boeaja* (Dutch-influenced spelling) or *buaja* (modern Indonesian spelling) is the Malayan word for crocodile. The word is widespread in southeastern Asia; I have heard it as far northeast as the Iloco-speaking and Pangasinan-speaking areas of Luzon, as far southeast as Irian Barat. In the Malayan language, the Tomistoma is *buaya sepit*; I have heard the name in both Sumatra and the Malay Peninsula.

Sepit means "pinched," and refers to the reptile's curiously narrowed snout. *Senjolong* (or *sendjolong* in the Indonesian spelling) is the name of a marine fish with a slender, toothed snout. When the Tomistoma is called *buaya senjolong*, as it is on both sides of the Straits of Malacca, it is being compared with a gar-like fish of the sea. In the Malay Peninsula, the Tomistoma is also called *buaya jolong-jolong*, a curious name perhaps reflecting a superstition; *jolong-jolong* means "first" or "beginning." But it may be that inland people, not knowing the marine fish called *senjolong*, changed the name *buaya senjolong* into something more meaningful to them.

Finally, we come to the gharial, the only surviving member of the family Gavialidae. "Gharial" is a vernacular name for this crocodilian in the Ganges Valley of India. Back in 1789, C. C. Gmelin gave this reptile the scientific name of *Lacerta gangetica*. Gmelin thought it inhabited not only the Ganges River of India, but also the region of Senegal in Africa. The erroneous ascription of the species to Senegal came about through confusion with the African sharp-nosed crocodile. Later in 1789, P. J. Bon-

Figure 158. The range of the Tomistoma (diagonal hatching) and of the gharial (horizontal hatching).

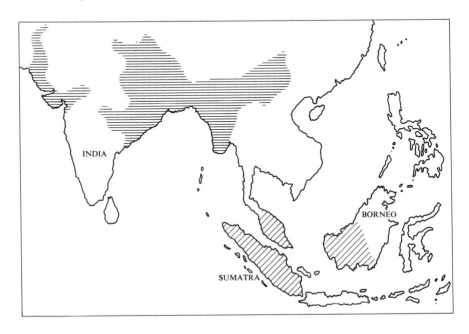

naterre christened the gharial *Crocodilus gavial.* Bonnaterre, one of his informants, or his printer evidently had misread the word "garial," taking it to be "gavial." European taxonomists of tbat day were not often familiar with Hindustani, and the error stood for a while without comment. In 1811 M. Oppel erected a genus of which the gharial was the type, and, following the lead of Bonnaterre, Oppel called this genus *Gavialis.* Not until the 1930s did it become generally evident that the gharial merited a family of its own, and of course this family was dubbed the Gavialidae. In the meanwhile, the gharial came to be called, or rather miscalled, a "gavial," at least in the English, German, Italian, Spanish, and French languages. Gmelin's specific name acquired several synonyms before Oppel erected the genus *Gavialis,* but these synonyms are of little interest today, and need not be discussed. In 1876 there was a stillborn effort to emend Oppel's generic name to *Gharialis,* but the rank and file of the taxonomists have opposed tampering with generic names, even the most ill-conceived ones. Today the gharial stands as *Gavialis gangeticus* (Gmelin). There seems no reason why a linguistic error of the taxonomists should be foisted upon the general public, and it is to be hoped that the name "gharial" will supplant the erroneous "gavial" in forthcoming reptile books.

The name *gangeticus* means "inhabiting the Ganges," which river may be regarded as Gmelin's type-locality. The range is now known to include several river systems: the Indus of West Pakistan; the Mohanadi and the Bhima of India; the Ganges of India and East Pakistan; the Brahmaputra of East Pakistan and Assam (India east of East Pakistan); the Kaladan of western Burma; and the Irawaddy of central Burma. The species also reaches Nepal in the Ganges drainage. The distribution is compatible with the idea of spread from India. Spread to lands west of the Indus is blocked by mountains and deserts.

Although the taxonomic history of the gharial began with Gmelin in 1789, the reptile was known, at least vaguely, at a much earlier date. In the third century A.D., a Roman writer on natural history, Claudius Aelianus (also called Aelian), mentioned a distant river, perhaps the Ganges, in which there lived a distinctive crocodilian. Aelianus described this crocodilian's snout as though it might have been a horn growing from the reptile's head. Centuries later, after the Reformation and the reawakening of intellect, the Classical writings were revered, and for a time were regarded as well-nigh infallible. Aelianus was credited with knowing the

Figure 159. The persistence of legend as shown by a nineteenth-Century illustration of the gharial: the portrayal is accurate in many details, but the reptile's nasal appendage existed only in the imagination of early writers.

Ganges and its gharial, and if he said that the gharial had a horn on its head, then some kind of horn it must surely have. Even well into the nine-teenth century, when the external conformation of the gharial had become known, writers refused to abandon the idea that it had some kind of horn-like appendage on its snout. As late as the 1880s, books on natural history were likely to include an oft-used illustration of a gharial, fairly accurate except for its portrayal of a great, bladder-like structure on the tip of the reptile's snout. According to the literature of that day, the gharial has at the end of its snout "a large, cartilaginous protuberance, in which the nostrils are situated." Even as late as 1915, the scientific literature asserts that the gharial has "a large, fleshy lump" at the end of its snout. And in a 1936 reptile book, mention was made of the "lumpy tip of the snout . . . a swollen and lumpy nob [*sic*] of flesh, surmounted by the nostrils." Many dictionaries published in the first quarter of the twentieth century include a woodcut of a "gavial" with some kind of horn-like prominence at the end of the snout. The circumstance affords more proof, if such were needed, that crocodilian legends die hard, and that their demise is not necessarily hastened by plain evidence negating them. The gharial has nothing on the end of its snout beyond a nostril area, and this resembles the nostril area of any other crocodilian (see Fig. 42). In all the living crocodilians, the hard, bony upper surface of the snout is interrupted by a small area of softer tissue surrounding the valvular nostrils.

The natural history of the gharial is almost unknown. It is said to dig a nesting hole in the sand of a river bank. Perhaps it does, as the restriction of the species to rivers would make such nesting behavior probable. However, we are also told that in the nesting hole the female gharial lays exactly 40 eggs arranged in two layers of 20 each, the layers separated by a foot of sand. This comment probably reflects nothing more than the old legend of the two-layered nest. Obviously there is a need for a modern, objective investigation into the nesting habits of the gharial. The reptile might actually scrape up plant debris, as do the majority of crocodilians. The young are said to appear in March or April, but there is need for better evidence on this point. Throughout the greater part of India, rain is brought by the southeast monsoon, which reaches the coasts and the inland regions during the period from May to October. In many areas, if the young gharials hatched in March and April the eggs would be in the nest during the driest part of the year. The hatchling is said to be "15.8 inches long." The juveniles are said to inhabit shallows, backwaters, and even isolated floodplain ponds, leaving the rivers proper to the adults. This is probably the case; with so great a discrepancy in size between juvenile and adult, it would be surprising if the two did not utilize separate portions of the habitat. Cannibalism has not been imputed to the gharial, and the biotopic separation of juvenile from adult may be viewed in the light of ecology rather than of

Figure 160. A young gharial, about 4 feet long. [Ross Allen's Reptile Institute]

legend. The gharial's food consists primarily of fishes, but adult gharials have occasionally been known to take waterfowl and small mammals. Supposedly, the stomach of a gharial is likely to contain numerous metal armlets, anklets, and similar ornaments of human manufacture. Accordingly, this inoffensive reptile was once portrayed as a man-eater. The currently accepted version of the story, perhaps slightly less sensational, is that the gharial will eat the corpses that drift down the Ganges from the burning ghats. I would suggest that if ornaments ever really occur in a gharial's stomach, they were ingested as gastroliths. The bottom of the Ganges must be littered with such ornaments, what with the countless thousands of bedecked corpses that have been dumped into the river. It would be an even better idea to dismiss the whole topic as apocryphal. The story of the numerous ornaments cannot be traced back to any objective observations on the gharial, but rather to old writings on the Nile crocodile. There was a time when almost every natural history book would tell how many metal armlets and anklets had been found in the stomach of a Nilotic saurian.

Some young gharials, about 3 to 4 feet in length, were kept outdoors in a roomy pen with a large pool of flowing water. They spent all of their time in the water, and were never seen lying on the pen floor. They fed readily upon shiners, fast-swimming fishes of the family Cyprinidae. The shiners, placed in the gharials' pool, would form a school, which would swim back and forth. A gharial would quickly spot the school, and begin to creep toward it across the pool bottom. Reaching a position near the school, the reptile would stop and remain motionless. As the school swam by, the gharial would snap at it with a sideways jerk of the head, a movement too fast for the eye to follow. Only the gharial's head and neck were involved in this movement; the body remained motionless. By this sideways snap the gharial would usually capture one fish, occasionally two simultaneously, rarely none at all. After two or three shiners had been caught, the fishes would become wary, avoiding the gharials. R. L. Ditmars aptly likened the outline of a gharial's head to a frying pan, the snout being the handle. (The description applies to the adults, somewhat less so to the juvenile.) In other words, the snout meets the rest of the skull at something of an angle; the head is not well streamlined, nor ideally adapted for swift forward movement of the reptile through water. Rather, the snout is reduced to as small a cylinder as is compatible with the retention of effective teeth. If a man tries to strike a sharp blow with a submerged stick, he will have some idea of the mechanical forces that a gharial must overcome in snapping at a fish.

Observations were also made on a gharial that was penned singly. It, too, fed readily on shiners. In catching the fishes, it almost always snapped to the right. If the swimming school passed to the reptile's left, it was usually ignored. The fishes passed to the right about as often as to the left, and my observations reflect not their activities but those of the gharial. I examined the reptile carefully to see if it had sustained some injury to the either side of its head or neck, but it was without blemish. In the human

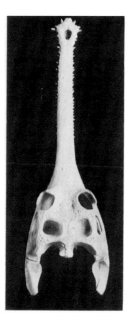
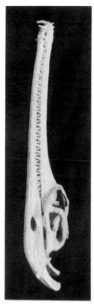

Figure 161. *The skull of an adult gharial. The snout is set off rather abruptly from the remainder of the skull.* [U. S. National Museum]

Figure 162. In the gharial, as shown here, the bony armor of the back is continuous with that of the neck. [Ross Allen's Reptile Institute]

being, one hand is usually favored over the other, especially in work that requires exceptional dexterity; and one eye is the "master eye." Bears also exhibit "handedness," a tendency to use one forearm much more frequently than the other; and certain arena bulls are said to "hook" rather consistently toward the left or toward the right as the case may be. It would not be surprising to find as far down the evolutionary scale as the crocodilians, or even further down, a tendency to strike out laterally in one direction far more often than in the opposite direction.

I regard as improbable the story that the adult gharial moves long distances overland in the dry season. There is no reason why it should do so, for it is nearly or quite restricted to large rivers which do not go dry. In parts of India the name "gharial" is occasionally misapplied to the mugger, which might desert the shallow marshes in the dry season. Perhaps stories about the mugger have been transferred to the gharial. In the adult gharial, the hindlimb (and to a lesser degree the forelimb) is more paddle-like in shape than in any other living crocodilian. I suspect that the adult gharial hardly ever leaves the water except to nest. The literature includes tales of gharials measuring more than 30 feet in length. If length records are accepted only when verifiable, the species reaches about 21½ feet. Enemies of the gharial, other than man, are not known. Competition with the estuarine crocodile is largely precluded by the gharial's dietary specialization. Also, the gharial follows rivers upstream to points far above the range of the estuarine crocodile. Both habitat and dietary specialization remove the gharial from competion with the mugger.

And so the review of the Crocodilia has come to an end. How much remains to be learned about these reptiles! The fossil history of the group should emerge into clearer light as paleontological studies continue, and there is not much that one can say to hasten such emergence. It might be useful to mention that, while the early history of the Crocodilia offers challenging gaps, there is also a remarkable lack of knowledge about the immediate ancestors of the living species. The American alligator is the only species whose ancestry can be traced in considerable detail. The taxonomy of the modern crocodilians also needs further investigation, with partciular reference to the recognition of geographic races within a few of the species. Taxonomically nameworthy races probably exist in the American alligator and the American crocodile; and as noted earlier, additional races of the spectacled caiman are also thought to exist. Four Trinidad examples of the spectacled caiman, collected and brought to my attention by Richard Thomas, were marked with paired dorsal spots, and with lateral spots in lineate arrangement. These and other characters of the specimens suggest that a distinctive subspecies may occupy Trinidad. Differences are detectable between the more northerly and the more southerly populations of Morelet's crocodile, suggesting at least the possibility of subspeciation. In 1948 Deraniyagala suggested that a distinct race of the Nile crocodile lived in Lake Rudolph, northern Kenya; and another in the curiously isolated Lake Baringo of western Kenya. The Nile crocodile probably has several races, but their formal recognition must await a study of specimens from most parts of the species' range. Southeastern Africa, with its complexity of large lakes, rivers, and mountainous barriers, is an exceptionally interesting (and inadequately investigated) area from the standpoint of animal distribution; and attention might be given here not only to the Nile crocodile but also to the sharp-nosed crocodile of Lake Tanganyika.

A subspecies has been defined as a geographic race, and so problems of raciation are closely tied to those of geographic distribution. Several parts of the tropics are poorly explored with reference to crocodilian distribution. This is true, for example, of the Asiatic mainland east of India. There are very few crocodilian records for Burma, the Malay Peninsula, and South Viet Nam. On the big islands of Sumatra, Java, and Borneo, crocodilian records are likewise few and at times puzzling. Freshwater crocodiles, especially, should provide distributional and perhaps taxonomic surprises on the mainland and the islands of tropical Asia. In South America, an interesting area for investigation would be the north coastal stretch, especially toward the Guianas. Nor is much known about the crocodilians of the Pacific coast of Columbia and Ecuador.

But more pressing than problems of raciation and distribution are those of habits. Studies on life histories and ecology must be undertaken speedily, for most and probably all of the living crocodilians are doomed. It is to be hoped that we can at least learn a few basic facts about each species before it becomes extinct: how the nest is built, the approximate number of eggs in a clutch, the detailed appearance of the hatchling, the vocalizations of juvenile and adult, the kinds of dens that are dug (if any). Of course, we need information on many other aspects of crocodilian natural history, such as exact geographic range, habitat, guarding of the nest, aggregation, food, social organization, demography, and enemies, but these aspects have in most cases changed by the activities of modern man. Even these aspects might be usefully studied if the investigator would reject legend and every variety of local opinion, while espousing the findings of evolutionary biology, animal behavior, and herpetology of the more exacting sort. The gharial, the Tomistoma, and the African sharp-nosed crocodile merit particular attention, for each of them will probably be found to exhibit some striking departures from the crocodilian norm in details of the life cycle. The Orinoco crocodile, Mindoro crocodile, Morelet's crocodile, and Cuban crocodile warrant immediate attention, for they are already at the point of extinction, and seem likely to vanish before much is recorded of their natural history. The Chinese alligator, brown caiman, jacaré, broad-nosed caiman, Apaporis caiman, smooth-fronted caimans, Johnston's crocodile, and dwarf crocodiles are poorly known; and only slightly better known are the black caiman, South American spectacled caiman, American crocodile, New Guinea crocodile, mugger, estuarine crocodile, and Siamese crocodile. A fair amount of life history data is available for the Nile crocodile, and a larger amount for the American alligator; but the habits even of the latter species are not fully understood.

The present book has but little to say about the conservation of crocodilians. To conserve a crocodilian as a reproducing species in a state of nature, it is necessary also to conserve many of its associates and a sizeable expanse of its habitat. At present, the protection of organisms and their habitat must be attempted within the limits that are set by attitudes toward wildlife conservation in general. Thus, the protection of a crocodilian is but one facet of a broad subject, conservation, which cannot be discussed in any detail here. But since the basic problems of conservation are similar everywhere, and the crocodilians provide a particularly clear insight into those problems, a few generalizations might be usefully advanced.

At one time it was hoped that a commercially valuable wild species, such as a crocodilian, could be managed in a fashion that permitted commercial exploitation while yet maintaining an adequate population of the species in nature. But with reference to crocodilians, and I think to much other wildlife, the time is past when a species in nature could be equated with a corn crop in a field or with a herd of cattle in a pasture. If a wild species is commercially valuable, its breeding stock will be cut into more and more as the years go by; and whether the species is commercially valuable or not, the expanses of habitat open to it will be reduced progressively, year by year. The time is also past when crocodilians and other large organisms could be preserved satisfactorily in a system of so-called sanctuaries, parks, and reserves. Such places, theoretically inviolate, in practice are progressively encroached upon by commercial interests. I do not refer here to poaching (although this is also a problem), but rather to condoned encroachment. The "setting aside" of an area as some kind of wildlife sanctuary commonly means its opening to exploitation. A road or causeway is usually built into it; branch roads are built throughout it; fishing is encouraged, and perhaps even hunting in season. At the least, vending concessions spring up; at the most, the area is opened to timbering, oil exploration, the leasing of waterfront property, and mining for road ballast. In short, the setting aside of an area commonly means the disruption of ecological relationships, and the destruction of those values for which the area was ostensibly set aside. With those values destroyed, no one can suggest why the area should not be converted to a fully commercial one. People who profit through the destruction of our natural heritage, whether through the sale of crocodilian leather goods or through the conversion of pristine tracts into housing subdivisions, are often found championing a conservation measure or a proposal to set aside some particular area. From their point of view, such behavior is reason-

able; but the circumstance underlines the ineffectuality of the currently accepted approach to conservation.

Just as the word "save" in an advertisement usually means "spend,"
so does the word "conservation" usually mean "destruction." That is to say,
the fundamental aim of most conservation measures, at least those that
have to do with commercially valuable organisms such as crocodilians, is not
the preservation of the species; rather, it is either the slowing of the decimation of that species, in order that a commercial "crop" can be reaped for a
few years more, or else the temporary halting of the decimation in order
that the species may be exploited again as soon as its numbers have somewhat recovered. Dedicated conservationists probably did not intend such an
outcome of their efforts, but that is beside the point. The important agen-
cies, the ones that can actually exert a strong influence on the rate at which
our wildlife heritage is squandered, are for the most part oriented toward the
commercial interests. For centuries, commercial interests of one sort or
another have had practically carte blanche to exploit the wildlife of the
world. As a result, we are left today with but a remnant of a formerly spectacular flora and fauna. For the most part, conservation measures are
designed to make even this remnant somehow available to commercial
exploitation. By "measures" I mean the few proposals that are actually
implemented, as contrasted with the many that are uselessly advanced at
meetings or fruitlessly distributed in mimeographed form. If the surviving
remnant of our wildlife heritage is to be utilized to the maximum advantage
of all, it will be necessary to abandon the concept of conservation, and to
adopt in its stead the concept of preservation. The latter concept has as its
heart the idea that the continued *survival* of a living organism, be it an alligator, a Sequoia tree, or whatever, is the paramount concern. A species is preserved because a large (but usually silent) percentage of the people believe it
should be, for reasons that are ethical, esthetic, and scientific. By definition,
a preserved species is completely shielded from commercial exploitation.
With the emphasis truly and sincerely on the permanent preservation of a
species, a protected area would be secure against the presently legal forms
of commercial encroachment, and could be rendered secure against the law-
less forms. For example, the poaching of crocodilians, which cannot be controlled under existing statutes and the attitude they reflect, would be
stopped abruptly if it were made illegal for anyone to possess, sell, or offer
for sale any item of crocodilian leather.

It is not intended here to blame any particular group of people for the extermination of crocodilians and other wildlife, or for the deterioration of the physical environment. Hide-hunters are usually needy people, and they are heirs to a tradition that regards wildlife as having been "put here" for man's utilization. Hide and leather-goods dealers supply a demand created by the public. Developers clear land and drain swamps in order to supply housing needed by a burgeoning population. Politicians in democratic societies are expected to respond to the wishes of the majority, and only a small percentage of their supporters would often put wildlife preservation ahead of commercial interests. Nor is it intended to decry the dedication of conservationists who have struggled heroically on behalf of us all, and who have lately taken the significant step of bringing their causes before a court of law. The rubric "Environment" may now be seen in magazines, and the word "ecology," shorn of much of its scientific connotation, is creeping into the common speech. Television shows dramatize the need for wildlife preservation, and radio talks promise effective action. But if one ignores the written and spoken words, and goes instead to see what is actually happening, one finds that the swamps are still being drained or filled, land cleared, sanctuaries despoiled, roads and canals cut in unending succession across the countryside, air and water further polluted, habitats destroyed, crocodilians and other wildlife utilized in the manufacture of many luxury items.

Accordingly, I do not suppose that any efforts will really succeed in preserving the crocodilians or much other wildlife for any great length of time. The resources of nature will continue to be used, at a constantly increasing rate, to serve man's needs of the moment; and in man's heavily populated and highly technological world there will be little room for wildlife. But with an emphasis on preservation, some of the presently remaining wild species will neither be wiped out immediately, nor conserved into extinction within a decade or so. Rather, they will be given a fresh, albeit brief, lease on life, during which time they can be enjoyed by enlightened people, and studied by scientists, for two or three more human generations.

BIBLIOGRAPHY

FOR TWO REASONS, the following biblio-
graphic arrangement of topics does not rigidly parallel the preceding text
arrangement. First, many a published work covers a variety of subjects, and
chapter-by-chapter documentation of the text would necessitate much cross-
referencing or the repetition of many entries. Second, the bibliography is
intended to be of somewhat wider scope than the text, directing the reader
not only to works upon which certain parts of the text were based, but also
to other works that are of interest in the study of crocodilians. Accordingly,
the bibliography is broken into ten sections, designated A through J respectively. Of these, Section A, "The Growth of Fallacies," serves mostly
to document Part I of the text, and is concerned primarily with the early
channels whereby myths and legends entered into later writings about the
American alligator. Section B, "The Fossil History and Anatomy of the
Crocodilians," relates chiefly to Part II of the text. Many of the entries in
Section C, "The Activities of Reptiles," pertain especially to Part III of the
text, but others provide background information that may also be useful in
connection with Parts I, II, or IV. On the one hand, this section does not
attempt to cover the whole field of reptile activities; but on the other hand,
it is not limited to works that deal specifically with crocodilians. Rather, it
provides a selection of works that help to interpret the observed activities

448

of crocodilians. Section D, "The Physiology, Genetics, Embryology, and Parasitology of the Crocodilians," does not correspond to any single part or chapter of the text. Section E, "The Natural History of the American Alligator," relates especially to Part IV of the text. It is not meant to imply that the entries of Section A are all fanciful, and those of Section E all factual, in their treatment of the alligator's activities. Some of the early writers have said much that is still of value, and few of the later ones have managed to eschew all the old legends. Most entries in Section F, "The Taxonomy of Living Crocodilians," cover the taxonomy of a variety of crocodilians, and so may be useful in connection with several of the chapters that make up Part V of the text. Excluded from this section are taxonomic papers whose limited scope permits their inclusion in Sections G, H, or I. Section G, "The Chinese Alligator and the Caimans," relates especially to Part V, Chapter 20; Section H, "The Crocodiles of the New World," to Part V, Chapters 21–22; and Section I, "The Crocodilians of the Old World," to Part V, Chapters 23–27. Section J, "The Crocodilians Generally," is made up of works that do not fall readily into any of the preceding categories, usually because they overlap several taxonomic groups, geographic areas, or approaches toward the study of crocodilians. The bibliography is selective, not exhaustive.

A. THE GROWTH OF FALLACIES

Alexander, J. E. *Transatlantic Sketches.* London, 1833.

Antoine, F. P. D'E. *Voyages du Capitaine Robert Lade,* II. Paris, 1782.

Ashe, Thomas. *Travels in America, 1806.* London, 1808.

Audubon, J. J. "Observations on the Natural History of the Alligator," *Edinburgh New Philosophical Journal,* new series, Vol. 2 (1927), pp. 270–80.

Baily, Francis. *Journal of a Tour in Unsettled Parts of North America in 1796–7.* London, 1856.

Bartram, John. "Journal Kept by John Bartram of Philadelphia, Botanist [etc.]," Appendix in William Stork's *A Description of East Florida,* 3rd ed. London, 1769.

Bartram, William. *Travels through North and South Carolina, Georgia, East and West Florida* [etc.]. New York, 1791. (There are many later editions.)

Bernard, John (editor). *Retrospections of America 1797–1811.* New York, 1887.

Blome, Richard. *The Present State of His Majesty's Isles and Territories in America.* London, 1687.

Bogert, C. M. "The Influence of Sound on the Behavior of Amphibians and Reptiles," pp. 137–318 in "Animal Sounds and Communications," *American Institute of Biological Sciences,* Publ. No. 7 (1960).

Bossu, J. B. *Noveaux Voyages dans l'Amerique Septentrionale.* Paris, 1777.

Bothwell, Dick. *The Great Outdoors Book of Alligators.* St. Petersburg, Fla., Great Outdoors Publishing Co., 1962.

Brackenridge, H. M. *Views of Louisiana.* Pittsburgh, 1814.

Brickell, J. *The Natural History of North Carolina* [etc.]. Dublin, 1737. (Reprinted, Raleigh, N. C., 1911.)

Buckingham, J. S. *The Slave States of*

America. Paris (no date).

Byrd, William. *The Westover Manuscripts Containing the History of the Dividing Line betwixt Virginia and North Carolina* [etc.]. Petersburg, 1841.

Carr, A. F., Jr. "A Contribution to the Herpetology of Florida," *University of Florida Publ., Biological Science Series,* Vol. 3, No. 1 (1940).

Carrington, R. "Edward Topsell and Elizabethan Natural History," *Zoo Life,* Vol. 8, No. 2 (1953), pp. 66–67.

Carroll, B. R. *Historical Collections of South Carolina.* New York, 1836.

Catesby, Mark. *The Natural History of Carolina, Florida* [etc.]. London, 1731.

Cist, Charles. *The Cincinnati Miscellany or Antiquities of the West.* Cincinnati, 1846.

Cuming, F. *Sketches of a Tour to the Western Country.* Pittsburgh, 1810.

Dana, E. *Geographical Sketches on the Western Country.* Cincinnati, 1819.

Darby, William. *A Geographical Description of the State of Louisiana.* Philadelphia, 1816.

Daubeny, Charles. *Journal of a Tour through United States and in Canada (1837-8).* Oxford, 1843.

De Sola, C. R. "The Crocodilians of the World," *Bulletin of the New York Zoological Society,* Vol. 36, No. 1 (1933), pp. 3–24.

Dewees, W. B. *Letters from an Early Settler of Texas.* Louisville, Ky., 1852.

Ditmars, R. L. *The Reptile Book.* New York, Doubleday, Page and Co., 1907.

—— *Reptiles of the World.* New York, The Macmillan Co., 1910. (Later edition, 1933.)

—— *The Reptiles of North America.* Garden City, N. Y., Doubleday, Doran, and Co., 1936.

Drayton, John. *A View of South Carolina.* Charleston, 1802.

Dubois, Jay (editor). *Travellers' Tales.* New York, Everybody's Vacation Publishing Co., no date. (Includes the travels of John Hawkins.)

Dunton, John. *Letters from New England.* Boston, Prince Society, 1867.

Ellicott, Andrew. *Journal.* Philadelphia, 1803.

Flint, Timothy. *Recollections.* Boston, 1826.

—— *The History and Geography of the Mississippi Valley.* Cincinnati, 1832.

Fontaneda, Do. d'Escalante. *Memoir of Do. d'Escalante Fontaneda Respecting Florida* [etc.]. Washington, D. C., 1854. Also Coral Gables, Fla., 1945.)

Forbes, J. G. *Sketches, Historical and Topographical, of the Floridas, More Particularly of East Florida.* New York, 1821.

French, B. F. (editor). *Historical Collections of Louisiana.* New York, 1846.

Gadow, Hans. *Amphibia and Reptiles.* Cambridge Natural History, Vol. 8. Cambridge, 1901.

Georgia Historical Society Collections. Savannah, 1840.

Gosse, P. H. *Letters from Alabama (U.S.), Chiefly Relating to Natural History.* London, 1859.

Gurney, Joseph. *A Journey in North America.* Norwich, 1841.

Hakluyt, Richard. *The Principal Navigations, Voyages, Traffiques, and Discoveries of the English Nation.* 12 vols. Glasgow, 1904.

Hallock, Charles. *Camp Life in Florida: a Handbook for Sportsmen and Settlers.* New York, 1876.

Harper, Francis. "Alligators of the Okefinokee," *The Scientific Monthly,* Vol. 31 (1930), pp. 51–67.

Harris, W. T. *Remarks Made during a Tour through the United States of America in the Years 1817-19.* London, 1821.

Haswell, Anthony. *Memoirs and Adventures of Captain Matthew Phelps.* Bennington, Vt., 1802.

Heriot, George. *Travels through the Canadas.* London, 1807.

Hewatt, Alexander. *An Historical Account of the Rise and Progress of the Colonies of South Carolina and Georgia.* London, 1779.

Hinton, J. H. *A History and Topography of the United States of North America.* 2nd ed. Boston, 1846.

History of North America. London, 1776.

Hodgson, Adam. *Letters from North America.* London, 1824.

James, Edwin (editor). *Account of an Expedition from Pittsburgh to the Rocky Mountains, by S. H. Long (1819–20).* Philadelphia, 1823.

Janson, C. W. *The Stranger in America.* London, 1807.

Jeffery, T. *History of the French Dominions in North and South America.* London, 1760.

Jones, C. C. *Antiquities of the Southern Indians, Particularly of the Georgia Tribes.* New York, D. Appleton and Co., 1873.

Kellogg, R. "The Habits and Economic Importance of Alligators," *U. S. Dept. of Agriculture, Technical Bull.* No. 147 (1929).

Kendall, G. W. *Narrative of Texan Santa Fe Expedition.* New York, 1844.

Ker, Henry. *Travels through the Western Interior of the United States, 1808–1816.* Elizabethtown, N. J., 1816.

Lahontan, Baron. *New Voyages to North America.* London, 1703.

Latrobe, C. J. *The Rambler in North America, 1832–3.* 2nd ed. London, 1836.

LeBuff, C. R., Jr. "Observations on Captive and Wild North American Crocodilians," *Herpetologica,* Vol. 13, Part 1 (1957), pp. 25–28.

Legge, R. E. "Mating Behaviour of American Alligators," *International Zoo Yearbook,* Vol. 7 (1967), pp. 179–80. (Droplets of water, vibrating on the back of the bellowing alligator, are regarded as jets of water ejected from unknown anatomical structures.)

LeMoyne, Jacques. *Narrative of LeMoyne (Translated from the Latin of De Bry).* Boston, 1875.

Le Page du Pratz, M. *History of Louisiana.* London, 1774.

Lewis, George. *Impressions of America and the American Churches.* Edinburgh, 1845.

Levasseur, A. *Lafayette en Amerique en 1824 et 1825.* Paris, 1829

Lorant, Stefan (editor). *The New World:* *The First Pictures of America* [etc.]. New York, Duell, Sloan and Pearce, 1946. (Includes LeMoyne's narrative, and the first known illustration of an American alligator.)

Lyells, Charles. *Travels in North America.* 2nd ed. London, 1855.

McCall, G. A. *Letters from the Frontiers.* Philadelphia, 1868.

McIlhenny, E. A. *The Alligator's Life History.* Boston, Christopher Publishing House, 1935. (This has been the most widely cited publication in the field of crocodilian natural history, but it draws so heavily upon myth and legend as to be inadequate for scientific documentation.)

Mackay, Charles. *Life and Liberty in America.* New York, 1859.

Markham, C. R. "The Observations of Sir Richard Hawkins, Knight [etc.]," *Hakluyt Society Report* No. 57 (1878), pp. 89–349.

Marryat, Frederick. *A Diary in America.* Philadelphia, 1839.

Martineau, Hariet. *Retrospect of Western Travel.* New York, 1838.

Montule, E. *A Voyage to North America and the West Indies in 1817.* London, 1821.

Murray, A. Matilda. *Letters from the United States, Cuba and Canada.* New York, 1856.

Murray, Hugh. *An Historical and Descriptive Account of British America.* Edinburgh, 1839.

Oldmixon, J. *The British Empire in America.* 2 vols. London, 1741.

Olson, J. E., and E. G. Bourne (editors). *Original Narratives of Early American History.* New York, 1906–07.

Peck, J. M. *Guide for Emigrants Containing Sketches of Illinois, Missouri* [etc.]. Boston, 1831.

Pennsylvania Magazine of History and Biography. Philadelphia, 1897.

Phillipo, J. M. *The United States and Cuba.* London, 1857.

Pickett, A. J. *History of Alabama.* Charleston, 1851.

Pittman, Philip. *European Settlements on the Mississippi.* London, 1770. (Also Cleveland, 1906.)

Pope, C. H. *The Reptile World*. New York, Alfred A. Knopf, 1955.

Pope, John. *A Tour through the Southern and Western Territories of the United States of America*, Richmond, 1792.

Power, Tyrone. *Impressions of America* (1833–5). Philadelphia, 1836.

Ramsey, David. *History of South Carolina from 1670–1808*. Charleston, 1809.

Relation of the Invasion and Conquest of Florida. London, 1686.

Rich, Obadiah. *A General View of the United States of America*. London, 1833.

Roberts, William. *An Account of the First Discovery and Natural History of Florida*. London, 1763.

Savage, J. M. "Crocodilia," *McGraw-Hill Encyclopedia of Science and Technology*, pp. 551–53. New York, McGraw-Hill Book Co., 1960.

Schmidt, K. P. "The American Alligator," *Field Museum of Natural History*, Leaflet No. 3 (1922).

Schoolcraft, Henry R. *Narrative Journal of Travels*. Albany, 1821.

Schultz, Christian. *Travels on an Inland Voyage*. New York, 1810.

Shea, J. C. (editor). *Early Voyages up and down the Mississippi*. Albany, 1861.

Sherwood, Adiel. *A Gazetteer of the State of Georgia*. Charleston, 1827. (Later editions include 1829; Washington, 1837; and Atlanta, 1839.)

Sloane, H. *A Voyage to the Islands Madera, Barbados, Nieves* [etc.] 2 vols. London, 1707, 1725.

Smith, Hugh M. "Notes on the Alligator Industry," *U. S. Fisheries Commission Bulletin*, No. 11 (1891), pp. 343–45.

Smyth, J. F. D. *A Tour in the United States of America*. London, 1784.

Swanton, J. R. "Indian Tribes of the Lower Mississippi Valley and Adjacent Coast of the Gulf of Mexico," *Bureau of American Ethnology, Bulletin*, No. 43 (1911).

—— "The Indians of the Southeastern United States," *ibid.*, 137 (1946).

Taylor, William R. *The Discovery of the Great West: La Salle*. New York, Rinehart and Co., 1956. (An annotated edition of Francis Parkman's 1869 work of the same name.)

Thwaites, R. C. *Early Western Travels 1748–1846*. 2 vols. Cleveland, 1904, 1905.

Trollope, Mrs. F. E. M. *Domestic Manners of the Americans* [etc.] New York, 1832.

True, F. W. *The Fisheries and Fishery Industries of the United States*. Part 2. Washington, 1884.

Viconte de Pagès, P. M. F. *Voyages autour du Monde et vers les deux Poles*, I. Paris, 1782.

Visit to Texas, being the Journal of a Traveller. New York, 1834.

Wakefield, Priscilla. *Excursions in North America*. London, 1806.

Wansey, Henry. *An Excursion to the United States in 1794*. Salisbury, 1798.

Williams, J. L. *The Territory of Florida, or Sketches of the Topography, Civil and Natural History* [etc.]. New York, 1837.

Wortley, Lady E. S. *Travels in the United States* [etc.]. New York, 1850.

B. THE FOSSIL HISTORY AND ANATOMY OF THE CROCODILIANS

Abelsdarff, G. "Notiz über die Pigmentierung des Schnerven bei Theiren (Alligator)," *Archiv für Augenheilkunde*, Vol. 53 (1905), pp. 185–86.

Ahrenfeldt, R. H. "Two British Anatomical Studies on American Reptiles (1650–1750). 1. Hans Sloane: Comparative Anatomy of the American Crocodile," *Herpetologica*, Vol. 9, Part 2 (1953), pp. 79–86. (Includes bibliographic reference to many early papers on crocodilian anatomy.)

Andrews, C. W. *A Descriptive Catalogue of the Marine Reptiles of the Oxford Clay*. Part II, pp. 80–206. London, British Museum (Natural History), 1913. (The portion cited deals with Jurassic crocodilians.)

Antunes, M. T. "*Tomistoma lusitanica*, crocodilien du Miocene du Portugal," *Revista de Faculdade de Ciencias (Lisboa)*, Ser. 2, Vol. 9 (1961), pp. 5–88.

—— "Sur quelques Caractères Archaïques des Crocodiliens, à propos d'un Mesosuchien du Lias Supérieur de Tomar (Portugal), Remarques sur l'Origine des Crocodilia," in "Evolution des Vertebres: Problemes Actuels de Paleontologie," *Colloques Internationaux du Centre National de la Recherche Scientifique*, No. 163 (1966).

Auffenberg, Walter. "Additional Specimens of *Gavialosuchus americanus* (Sellards) from a New Locality in Florida," *Quarterly Journal of the Florida Academy of Sciences*, Vol. 17, No. 4 (1954), pp. 185–209.

—— "Notes on Fossil Crocodilians from Southeastern United States," *ibid.*, Vol. 20, No. 2 (1957), pp. 107-13.

—— "Fossil Crocodilians of Florida," *The Plaster Jacket*, No. 5 (1967).

Axelrod, D. I., and H. P. Bailey. "Cretaceous Dinosaur Extinction," *Evolution*, Vol. 22, No. 3 (1968), pp. 595–611.

Bagley, C., and O. R. Langworthy. "The Forebrain and Midbrain of the Alligator with Experimental Transsections of the Brain Stem," *Archives of Neurology and Psychiatry*, Vol. 16, No. 2 (1926), pp. 154–66.

Barbour, T. "A Note on Tertiary Alligators," *Copeia*, No. 151 (1926), pp. 109–11.

Baur, George. "The Proatlas, Atlas and Axis of the Crocodiles," *American Naturalist*, Vol. 20 (1888), pp. 288–93.

Beddard, F. E., and C. P. Mitchell. "On the Structure of the Heart of the Alligator," *Proceedings of the Zoological Society of London*, 1895, pp. 343–49.

Bertan, Martin. "Zur Entwicklungsgeschichte des Geruchsorgans der Krokodile," *Zeitschrift für Anatomie und Entwicklungs*, Vol. 104, No. 2 (1935), pp. 168–202.

Bischoff, T. L. W. "Über den Bau des Crocodil-Herzens, besonders von Crocodilus lucius," *Archiv für Anatomie und Physiologie* (1836), pp. 1–12.

Brazaitis, Peter. "The Determination of Sex in Living Crocodilians," *British Journal of Herpetology*, Vol. 4, No. 3 (1968), pp. 54–58.

Brockman, H. L., and J. P. Kennedy. "Interventricular Septal Defect in *Alligator mississipiensis* Daudin," *Texas Reports on Biology and Medicine*, Vol. 20, No. 4 (1962), pp. 719–20.

Brodkorb, Pierce. "The Avifauna of the Bone Valley Formation," *Florida Geological Survey, Report of Investigations*, No. 14 (1955). (Of interest in connection with the ecology of Gavialosuchus.)

Broili, F. "Die Gattung *Alligatorium* im Oberen Jura von Franken," *Sitzungsberichte des Bayerische Akademie des Wissenschaft (München)*, Part 2 (1931), pp. 63–74. (*Alligatorium* is an atoposaurid crocodilian.)

——"Beobachtungen an *Geosaurus*," *Centralblatt für Mineralogie, Geologie, und Paläontologie*, Part B (1931), pp. 232–42. (*Geosaurus* is a metriorhynchid seacrocodile.)

Broin, F. de, and P. Taquet. "Découverte d'un crocodilien nouveau dans le Crétacé Inferieur du Sahara," *Comptes Rendus, Academie de Sciences (Paris)*, No. 262 (1966), pp. 2326–29. (Describes a gigantic pholidosaurid crocodilian.)

Broom, R. "On a New Crocodilian Genus (*Notochampsa*) from Upper Stromberge Beds of South Africa," *Geological Magazine*, new series, Vol. 1 (1904), p. 580.

—— "On *Sphenosuchus* and the Origin of the Crocodiles," *Proceedings of the Zoological Society of London*, 1927, No. 1, pp. 359–70.

Brown, Barnum. "The Largest Crocodile," *Natural History*, May, 1942, pp. 260–61. (On Phobosuchus, now called Deinosuchus.)

Brühl, C. B. *Das Skelet der Krokodilinen*. Vienna, 1862.

Burmeister, G. "Examen Crítico de los Mamíferos y Reptiles Fósiles Denominados por D. Augusto Bravard y Mencionados en su Obra Precedente," *An-*

nales de Museo Nacional (Buenos Aires), Vol. 3 (1885), pp. 95–173 (Includes description of a South American gharial.)

Camp, C. L. "A Study of the Phytosaurs," *University of California Memoirs,* No. 10 (1930).

Case, E. C. "Abnormal Sacrum in Alligator," *American Naturalist,* Vol. 30 (1896), pp. 232–34.

Chiasson, R. B. *Laboratory Anatomy of the Alligator.* Dubuque, Iowa, William C. Brown Publishers, 1962.

Coe, M. D., and K. V. Flannery. "Early Cultures and Human Ecology in South Coastal Guatemala," *Smithsonian Contributions to Anthropology,* Vol. 3 (1967). (Includes archeological records of the brown caiman and American crocodile.)

Colbert, E. H. "*Sebecus,* Representative of a Peculiar Suborder of Fossil Crocodilia from Patagonia," *American Museum of Natural History Bulletin,* No. 87 (1946), pp. 217–70.

—— "The Eustachian Tubes in the Crocodilia," *Copeia,* 1946, No. 1, pp. 12–14.

Colbert, E. H., and R. T. Bird. "A Gigantic Crocodile from the Upper Cretaceous Beds of Texas," *American Museum Novitates,* No. 1688 (1954).

Colbert, E. H., and C. C. Mook. "The Ancestral Crocodilian *Protosuchus,*" *American Museum of Natural History Bulletin,* No. 97 (1951), pp. 143–82.

Crosby, E. C. "The Forebrain of *Alligator Mississippiensis,*" *Journal of Comparative Neurology,* Vol. 27 (1916).

D'Alton, J. S., and H. Burmeister. *Der Fossile Gavial von Boll in Württemberg, mit Bezugnahme auf die Lebenden Krokodilinen.* Halle, 1854.

Davenport, C. B. "Note on the carotids and the Ductus Botalli of the Alligator," *Bulletin of the Museum of Comparative Zoology,* Vol. 24, No. 2 (1893).

De Vis, H. "On Remains of an Extinct Saurian," *Proceedings of the Royal Society of Queensland,* Vol. 2, (1885), pp. 181–91. (Description of Palimnarchus, a Pleistocene crocodilian of Australia.)

Dietz, R. S., and W. P. Sproll. "Equal Areas of Gondwana and Laurasia (Ancient Super Continents)," *Nature,* Vol. 112 (1966): 1196–98.

Edgworth, T. H. *The Cranial Muscles of Vertebrates.* London, 1935.

Edmund, A. G. "Tooth Replacement Phenomena in the Lower Vertebrates," *Life Sciences Division, Royal Ontario Museum, Contributions,* No. 52 (1960).

Eisler, P. "Zur Kenntnis der Histologie des Alligatormagens," *Archiv für Mikroscopische Anatomie,* Vol. 34 (1889), pp. 1–10.

Estes, Richard. "Fossil Vertebrates from the Late Cretaceous Lance Formation [,] Eastern Wyoming," *University of California Publications in Geological Sciences,* Vol. 49 (1964).

Forbes, T. R. "Studies on the Reproductive System of the Alligator," *Journal of Experimental Zoology,* Vol. 78, No. 3 (1938).

Fraas, E. "Die Meerkrokodilier (Thalattosuchia) des Oberen Jura unter Specieller Berücksichtigung von *Dacosaurus* and *Geosaurus,*" *Paleontographica,* Vol. 49 (1902), pp. 1–72.

Fürbringer, M. "Zun Vergleichenden Anatomie der Schultermuskeln. III," *Morphologie Jahrbuch,* Vol. 1 (1876), pp. 636–816. (Deals with the shoulder musculature of lizards and crocodilians.)

Gadow, H. "Untersuchungen über die Bauchmuskeln der Krokodile, Eidechsen und Schildkröten," *Morphologie Jahrbuch,* Vol. 7 (1882), pp. 57–100.

Gans, C. (general editor); A. Bellairs and T. Parsons (volume editors). *Biology of the Reptilia. Vol. 1. Morphology.* London, Academic Press, 1969.

Gehlbach, F. R. "Amphibians and Reptiles from the Pliocene and Pleistocene of North America: A Chronological Summary and Selected Bibliography," *Texas Journal of Science,* Vol. 17, No. 1 (1965), pp. 56–70.

Gervais, P. "Crocodile Gigantesque Fossile au Bresil," *Journal of Zoology,* Vol. 5 (1876), pp. 232–36.

Giles, L. W. "Polydactylism in an Alligator," *Copeia,* 1948, No. 3, p. 214.

Gilmore, C. W. "*Leidyosuchus sternbergii,*

a New Species of Crocodile from the Ceratops Beds of Wyoming," *Proceedings of the United States National Museum,* Vol. 38 (1910), pp. 485–502.

—— "A New Fossil Alligator from the Hell Creek Beds of Montana," *ibid.,* Vol. 41 (1911), pp. 297–302. (Description of a Brachychampsa.)

—— "A New Aetosaurian Reptile from the Morrison Formation of Utah," *Annals of the Carnegie Museum,* Vol. 16 (1926), pp, 325–42. (This supposed aetosaur, Hoplosuchus, has proven to be a crocodilian, possibly an atoposaur.)

Goodrich, E. S. *Studies on the Structure and Development of Vertebrates.* London, The Macmillan Co., 1930.

Gulliver, G. "On the Blood Corpuscles of the Crocodilia," *Proceedings of the Zoological Society of London,* Vol. 8 (1840), p. 131.

Hair, P. "On the Arrangement of the Muscular Fibres of the Alligator," *Journal of Anatomy and Physiology,* Vol. 2, No. 2, Series 1 (1868), pp. 26–41.

Harlan, R. "Some Observations on the Anatomy and Physiology of the Alligator of North America," *Transactions of the American Philosophical Society, New Series,* Vol. 2 (1825), pp. 216–28.

Haughton, S. "On the Muscular Anatomy of the Alligator," *Annals and Magazine of Natural History,* 4th Series, Vol. 1 (1868), pp. 232–62.

Heilman, G. *The Origin of Birds.* London, 1926. (Includes much on the archosaurs and their osteology.)

Hochstetter, H. "Beiträge zur Anatomie und Entwickelungsgeschichte der Blutgefässsystemes der Krokodile," in A. Voeltzkow, *Reise in Ostafrika,* Vol. 4, pp. 1–139.

Hoffstetter, R. "Thecodontia," in J. Piveteau (editor), *Traité de Paléontologie.* Paris, Masson and Co., 1955.

Holland, W. J. "*Deinosuchus hatcheri,* a new genus and species of crocodile from the Judith River Beds of Montana," *Annals of the Carnegie Museum,* Vol. 6 (1909), pp. 281–94.

Howes, G. B. "On the Probable Existence of a Jacobson's Organ among the Crocodilia," *Proceedings of the Zoological Society of London,* 1891, pp. 149–56.

Huber, G. C., and E. C. Crosby. "On the Thalamic and Tectal Nuclei and Fiber Paths in the Brain of the American Alligator," *Journal of Comparative Neurology,* Vol. 40, No. 1 (1926).

Huene, F. von. "Ein Versuch zur Stammesgeschichte der Krokodile," *Centralblatt für Mineralogie, Geologie, und Paläontologie,* Vol. II (1933), pp. 577–85.

—— *Die Fossilen Reptilien des Südamerikanischen Gonwanalandes [Etc.].* Munich, 1944.

Iordansky, N. N. "Peculiarities of the Crocodilian Skull Related to the Feeding Function and Origin of Gavialidae," *Zoologicheskii Zhurnal,* Vol. 46 (1967), pp. 567–75.

Joffe, J. "The 'Dwarf' Crocodiles of the Purbeck Formation, Dorset: a Reappraisal," *Paleontology,* Vol. 10, No. 4, pp. 629–39.

Kälin, J. A. "Uber den Brustschulterapparat der Krokodile," *Acta Zoologica,* Vol. 10, (1929), pp. 343–99.

—— "Über die Stellung der Gavialiden im System der Crocodilia," *Revue Suisse de Zoologie,* Vol. 38 (1931), pp. 379–88.

—— "Beiträge zur Vergleichenden Osteologie des Crocodilidenschädels," *Zoologische Jahrbuch, Abteil für Anatomie und Ontogenie der Tiere,* Vol. 57 (1933), pp. 535–714.

—— "*Hispanochampsa mulleri* Nov. Gen. Nov. Sp. [,] ein Neuer Crocodolide aus dem Unteren Oligocän von Tarrega (Catalonien)," *Abhandlungen für Schweizerische Paläontologische Gesellschaft,* Vol. 58 (1936), pp. 1–40. (Hispanochampsa is regarded as an alligatorine.)

—— "Ein Extrem Kurzschnauziger Crocodilide aus den Phosphoriten des Quercy: *Arambourgia* (Nov. Gen.) *gaudryi* De Stefano," *ibid.,* Vol. 62 (1939), pp. 1–34. (Arambourgia is regarded as a crocodyline of Eocene age.)

—— "Crocodilia," in J. Piveteau (editor), *Traité de Paléontologie.* Paris, Masson and Co., 1955. (This important work summarizes previous studies and advances new ideas on the fossil history of the Crocodilia.)

Kennedy, J. P., and H. L. Brockman, "Open Heart Surgery in *Alligator Mississippiensis* Daudin," *Herpetologica*, Vol. 21, No. 1 (1965), pp. 6–15.

Kermack, K. A. "An Ancestral Crocodile from South Wales," *Proceedings of the Linnean Society of London*, Session 166, Parts 1–2 (1956). (Describes a late Triassic crocodilian possibly related to Protosuchus.)

Kingsley, J. S. "The Bones of the Reptilian Lower Jaw," *American Naturalist*, Vol. 39 (1905), pp. 59–64.

Kramer, G., and F. Medem. "Über Wachstungsbedingte Proportionsanderungen bei Krokodilen," *Zoologische Jahrbuch, Allegemeine Zoologie* (Jena), Vol. 66 (1955), pp. 62–74.

Krebs, B. "Der Jurakrokodilier *Machimosaurus* H. V. Meyer," *Paläontologische Zeitschrift*, Vol. 41 (1967), pp. 46–59. (*Machimosaurus* is a goniopholid crocodilian of latter Jurassic age.)

Kurtén, Björn. "Holarctic Land Connexions in the Early Tertiary," *Commentationes Biologicae, Societas Scientiarum Fennica*, Vol. 29, No. 5 (1966).

—— "Continental Drift and the Palaeogeography of Reptiles and Mammals," *ibid.*, Vol. 31, No. 1 (1967).

Kuhn, O. "Die Tier- und Pflanzenwelt des Solnhofener Schiefers," *Geologica Bavarica*, No. 48 (1961), pp. 1–68. (Reviews the many crocodilians from a famous latter Jurassic deposit.)

Lambe, L. M. "On a New Crocodilian Genus and Species from the Judith River Formation of Alberta," *Transactions of the Royal Society of Canada*, Vol. 1 (1907), pp. 219–44. (Describes *Leidyosuchus canadensis*, a Cretaceous crocodyline of zoögeographic interest by virtue of its northerly distribution.)

Langston, W. "The Sebecosuchia: Cosmopolitan Crocodilians?" *American Journal of Science*, Vol. 254 (1956), pp. 605–14.

—— "Fossil Crocodilians from Colombia and the Cenozoic History of the Croco-

dilia in South America," *University of California Publications in Geological Sciences*, Vol. 52 (1965). (An important work, reviewing previous studies and describing new material. Charactosuchus, two gharials, the Nettosuchidae, and a giant Caiman are among the crocodilians discussed.)

—— "Mourasuchus Price, Nettosuchus Langston, and the family Nettosuchidae (Reptilia: Crocodilia)," *Copeia*, 1966, No. 4 (1967), pp. 882–85.

Larsell, O. "The Cerebellum of Reptiles: Chelonians and Alligators," *Journal of Comparative Neurology*, Vol. 56, No. 2 (1932).

Liem, K. F., and H. M. Smith. "A Critical Reevaluation of the So-called 'Angular' in the Crocodilian Mandible," *Turtox News*, Vol. 39, No. 6 (1961), pp. 146–48.

Lortet, L. "Les Reptiles Fossiles du Bassin du Rhône," *Archives du Museum d'Histoire Naturelle* (Lyon), Vol. 5 (1892), pp. 3–139. (On atoposaurs, especially.)

Lydekker, R. "On the Occurrence of the Crocodilian Genus *Tomistoma* in the Miocene of the Maltese Islands," *Quarterly Journal of the Geological Society of London*, Vol. 42 (1886), pp. 20–22.

Mathur, P. N. "The Anatomy of the Reptilian Heart. Part II. Serpentes, Testudinata and Loricata," *Proceedings of the Indian Academy of Science, B*, Vol. 23 (1946), pp. 129–152.

Meek, A. "On the Occurrence of a Jacobson Organ, with Notes on the Development of the Nasal Cavity, the Lachrymal Duct and Harderian Gland in *Crocodilus porosus*," *Journal of Anatomy and Physiology* (London), Vol. 27, No. 10 (1892).

—— "The Olfactory Organ of the Crocodile and the Homologies of the Ethmoid Region," *Proceedings of the University of Durham Philosophical Society*, Vol. 3 (1908).

Mehl, M. "*Caimanoidea vischeri*, a New Crocodilian from the Oligocene of South Dakota," *Journal of Geology*, Vol. 24 (1916), pp. 47–56. (Caimanoidea is an alligatorine, close to Alligator.)

—— "*Dakotasuchus kingi,* a Crocodile from the Dakota of Kansas," *Denison University Bulletin, Journal of the Science Laboratories,* Vol. 36 (1941), pp. 47–65. (Dakotasuchus was a Cretaceous goniopholid (?) crocodilian, possibly terrestrial.)

Miall, L. C. *The Skull of the Crocodile. A Manual for Students.* London, The Macmillan Co., 1878.

Milani, A. "Beiträge zur Kenntnis der Reptilienlunge (Alligator und Crocodile)," *Zoologische Jahrbuch,* Vol. 10 (1897), pp. 133–56.

Moens, N. "Die Peritonealkanale der Schildkröten und Krokodile," *Morphologische Jahrbuch,* Vol. 44 (1911), pp. 1–80.

Mook, C. C. "Skull Characters and Affinities of the Extinct Florida Gavial, *Gavialosuchus americanus* (Sellards)," *Bulletin of the American Museum of Natural History,* Vol. 44 (1921), pp. 33–42.

—— "*Brachygnathosuchus brasiliensis,* a New Fossil Crocodilian from Brazil," *ibid.,* pp. 42–49.

—— "Individual and Age Variation in the Skulls of Recent Crocodilia," *ibid.,* pp. 51–66.

—— "Notes on the Postcranial Skeleton in the Crocodilia," *ibid.,* pp. 67–100.

—— "*Allognathosuchus,* a New Genus of Eocene Crocodilians," *ibid.,* pp. 105–10.

—— "Skull Characters of Recent Crocodilia with Notes on the Affinities of the Recent Genera," *ibid.,* pp. 123–268.

—— "A New Species of Alligator from the Snake Creek Beds," *American Museum Novitates,* No. 73 (1923). (Description of *Alligator thomsoni.*)

—— "Further Notes on the Skull Characters of *Gavialosuchus americanus* (Sellards), *ibid.,* No. 155 (1924).

—— "A Revision of the Mesozoic Crocodilia of North America," *Bulletin of the American Museum of Natural History,* Vol. 51 (1925), pp. 319–432.

—— "The Skull Characters of *Crocodilus Megarhinus* Andrews," *American Museum Novitates,* No. 289 (1927).

—— "A New Species of Crocodilian from the Torrejon Beds," *ibid.,* No. 447 (1930). (Describes a Leidyosuchus from the Paleocene of New Mexico.)

—— "New Crocodilian Remains from the Hornerstown Marls of New Jersey," *ibid.,* No. 476 (1931).

—— "A Study of the Osteology of *Alligator prenasalis* Loomis," *Bulletin of the Museum of Comparative Zoology,* Vol. 74 (1932), pp. 19–41.

—— "A Skull with Jaws of *Crocodilus sivalensis* Lydekker," *American Museum Novitates,* No. 670 (1933).

—— "A Crocodilian Skeleton from the Morrison Formation at Canyon City, Colorado," *ibid.,* No. 671 (1933).

—— "A Skull of *Crocodilus clavus* Cope in the U. S. National Museum," *ibid.,* No. 678 (1933).

—— "The Evolution and Classification of the Crocodilia," *Journal of Geology,* Vol. 42 (1934), pp. 295–304.

—— "A New Crocodilian from the Lance Formation (*Prodiplocynodon langi* Gen. et Sp. Nov.)," *American Museum Novitates,* No. 1128 (1941).

—— "A New Crocodilian *Hassiacosuchus kayi* from the Bridger Eocene Beds of Wyoming," *Annals of the Carnegie Museum,* Vol. 28, No. 12 (1941), pp. 23–25.

—— "A New Fossil Crocodilian from the Paleocene of New Mexico," *American Museum Novitates,* No. 1189 (1942). (Describes Navajosuchus.)

—— "A New Pliocene Alligator from Nebraska," *ibid.,* No. 1311 (1946). (Describes *Alligator mefferdi.*)

—— "A New Pleistocene Crocodilian from Guatemala," *ibid.,* No. 1975 (1959). (Describes a Pleistocene specimen of *Crocodylus moreleti.*)

—— "Preliminary Description of a New Goniopholid Crocodilian," *Kirtlandia,* 1967, No. 2, pp. 1–10.

Müller, L. "*Crocodilus siamensis* Schneid. und †*Crocodilus ossifragus* Dubois," *Paleontologia Hungarica,* Vol. 1 (1923), pp. 109–122.

—— "Beiträge zur Osteologie der Rezenten Krokodilier," *Zeitschrift für Morphologie und Ökologie der Tiere*, Vol. 2, Parts 3–4 (1924), pp. 427–60.

Nash, D. "A Crocodile from the Upper Triassic of Lesotho," *Journal of Zoology*, Vol. 156, No. 2 (1968), pp. 163–79.

Neill, W. T., H. J. Gut, and P. Brodkorb. "Animal Remains from Four Preceramic Sites in Florida," *American Antiquity*, Vol. 21, No. 4 (1956), pp. 383–95. (Archeological remains of the American alligator.)

Nopcsa, F. von, "Über die Namen eineger Brasilianischer Fossiler Krokodile," *Centralblatt für Mineralogie, Geologie und Paläontologie*, 1924, p. 378.

—— "Neue Beobachtungen an *Stomatosuchus*," *ibid.*, 1926, pp. 212–15.

—— "Paleontological Notes on Reptiles. VII. On the Classification of the Crocodilia," *Geologia Hungarica, Paleontological Series*, Vol. 1 (1928), pp. 75–84.

Owen, R. "On the Communications between the Cavity of the Tympanum and the Palate in the Crocodilia (Gavials, Alligators and Crocodiles)," *Philosophical Transactions of the Royal Society of London*, 1850, pp. 521–27.

—— "A Monograph on the Fossil Reptilia of the Cretaceous Formations," *Paleontographical Society of London*, 1864, pp. 1–57.

—— "Monograph on the Fossil Reptilia of the Wealden and Purbeck Formations. Supplement 8. Crocodilia (*Goniopholis, Petrosuchus*, and *Suchosaurus*)," *ibid.*, Monograph 32 (1878). (Describes goniopholid and pholidosaurid crocodilians.)

Panizza, B. "Sulla Strutura del Cuore e Sulla Circolazione del Sangue del *Crocodilus lucius*," *Biblioteca Italiano* (Milano), No. 70 (1833), pp. 87–91.

Parker, W. K. "On the Structure and Development of the Skull in the Crocodilia," *Transactions of the Zoological Society of London*, Vol. 11 (1883), pp. 263–310.

Patterson, B. "Occurrence of the Alligatorid Genus *Allognathosuchus* in the Lower Oligocene," *Field Museum of Natural History, Geological Series*, Vol. 4 (1931), pp. 221–26.

—— "*Caiman latirostris* from the Pleistocene of Argentina, and a Summary of South American Cenozoic Crocodilia," *Herpetologica*, Vol. 1, No. 2 (1936), pp. 43–54.

—— "Remarks on South American Fossil Crocodiles," *Copeia*, 1943, No. 2, pp. 123–24.

Pilgrim, G. "Paleontologia Indica. The Vertebrate Fauna of the Gaj Series in the Bugti Hills and the Punjab," *Memoirs of the Geological Survey of India, New Series*, Vol. 4, No. 2 (1912), pp. 1–83. (Includes description of a fossil gharial.)

Price, L. I. "Os Crocodilideos de Fauna Formaçao Bauru, do Cretaceo Terrestre do Brazil Meridional," *Annales do Academia Brazil, Ciencias*, Vol. 22 (1950), pp. 473–90.

—— "Novos Crocodilideos dos Arenitos da Serie Bauru. Cretaceo do Estado de Minas Gerais," *ibid.*, Vol. 27 (1955), pp. 487–98.

—— "Sobre o Craneo de um Grande Crocodilideo Extinto do Alto Rio Jurua, Estado do Acre," *ibid.*, Vol. 36 (1964), pp. 59–66.

Reese, A. M. "The Nasal Passage of the Florida Alligator," *Proceedings of the Philadelphia Academy of Natural Sciences*, 1901, pp. 457–64.

—— "The Vascular System of the Florida Alligator," *ibid.*, 1914, pp. 413–25.

—— "The Blood of *Alligator Mississippiensis*," *Anatomical Record*, Vol. 13, No. 1 (1917), pp. 37–44.

—— "The Structure and Development of the Integumental Glands of the Crocodilia," *Journal of Morphology*, Vol. 35, No. 3 (1921), pp. 581–611.

—— "The Structure and Development of the Intromittent Organ of the Crocodilia," *ibid.*, Vol. 38, No. 3 (1924), pp. 301–13.

—— "The Cephalic Glands of *Alligator Mississippiensis*, Florida Alligator, and of *Agkistrodon*, Copperhead and Moccasin," *Biologia Generalis*, Vol. 1, Nos. 3–5 (1925), pp. 482–500.

—— "The Ductless Glands of *Alligator Mississippiensis*," *Smithsonian Miscel-*

laneous Collections, Vol. 82, No. 16 (1931), pp. 1–12.

Reig, O. "Archosaurian Reptiles: a New Hypothesis on Their Origins," *Science,* Vol. 157, pp. 565–68.

Romer, A. S. "Crocodilian Pelvic Muscles and Their Avain and Reptilian Homologues," *Bulletin of the American Museum of Natural History,* Vol. 48, Art. 15 (1923), pp. 533–52.

—— *Osteology of the Reptiles.* Chicago, University of Chicago Press, 1956. (A major work on the skeletal anatomy, fossil history, taxonomy, and pertinent bibliography of the Crocodilia and other reptile groups.)

—— *Vertebrate Paleontology.* 3rd ed. Chicago, University of Chicago Press, 1966.

Runcorn, S. (editor). *Continental Drift.* New York, Academic Press, 1961.

Rusconi, C. "Observaciones Criticas sobre Reptiles Terciarios de Parana (Familia Alligatoridae)," *Revista de Universidad Nacional (Cordoba),* Vol. 20, Nos. 7–8 (1933), pp. 1–52.

—— "Observaciones sobre los Gaviales Fosiles Argentinos," *Anales de Sociedad Cientifico de Argentina,* Vol. 119 (1935), pp. 203–14.

Schmidt, K. "New Crocodilians from the Upper Paleocene of Western Colorado," *Geological Series of the Field Museum of Natural History,* Vol. 6, No. 21 (1938), pp. 315–21. (Describes Ceratosuchus and a Leidyosuchus.)

—— "A New Fossil Alligator from Nebraska," *ibid.,* Vol. 8, No. 4 (1941), pp. 27–32. (Describes *Alligator mcgrewi.*)

Sellards, E. H. "A New Gavial from the Late Tertiary of Florida," *American Journal of Science,* 1915, pp. 135–38. (Description of what is now called *Gavialosuchus americanus,* a tomistomine.)

—— "A New Tortoise and a Supplementary Note on the Gavial, *Tomistoma americana,*" *ibid.,* 1916, pp. 235–40.

Shiino, K. "Das Chondrocranium von *Crocodilus* mit Berücksichtigung der Gehirunerven und der Kopfgefässe,"

Anatomische Hefte, Vol. 50 (1914), pp. 253–382.

Sill, W. D. "*Proterochampsa Barrionuevoi* and the Early Evolution of the Crocodilia," *Bulletin of the Museum of Comparative Zoology,* Vol. 135, No. 8 (1967), pp. 415–46. (Describes the earliest known crocodilian.)

—— "The Zoogeography of the Crocodilia," *Copeia,* 1968, No. 1, pp. 76–88. (A recent, important summary of the fossil history of the Crocodilia.)

Simpson, G. G. "*Allognathosuchus mooki,* a New Crocodile from the Puerco Formation," *American Museum Novitates,* No. 455 (1930).

—— "New Reptiles from the Eocene of South America," *ibid.,* No. 927 (1937).

Sluiter, E. "Das Jacobsonsche Organ von *Crocodilus porosus* (Schn.)," *Anatomischer Anzeiger,* Vol. 7 (1892), pp. 540–45.

Soule, J. D. "Oxytalan Fibers in the Periodontal Ligament of the Cayman and the Alligator," *Journal of Morphology,* Vol. 122, No. 3 (1967), p. 169.

Staley, F. "A Study of the Gastric Glands of *Alligator Mississippiensis,*" *Journal of Morphology and Physiology,* Vol. 40, No. 1 (1925).

Sternberg, C. M. "A New Fossil Crocodile from Saskatchewan," *Canadian Field Naturalist,* Vol. 46 (1932), pp. 128–33. (Describes a Leidyosuchus.)

—— "A Skull of *Leidyosuchus canadensis* Lambe," *American Midland Naturalist,* Vol. 13 (1932), pp. 157–68.

Symposium: "Gondwanaland Revisited: New Evidence for Continental Drift," *Proceedings of the American Philosophical Society,* Vol. 112, No. 5 (1968).

Virchow, H. "Über die Alligatorwirbelsaule," *Archiv für Anatomie und Physiologie,* 1914, Parts 2–3, pp. 103–42.

Walker, A. D. "*Protosuchus, Proterochampsa,* and the Origin of Phytosaurs and Crocodiles," *Geological Magazine,* Vol. 105, No. 1 (1968), pp. 1–14.

Walls, G. "The Vertebrate Eye and Its Adaptive Radiation," *Bulletin of the Cranbrook Institute of Science,* Vol. 19 (1942), pp. 1–785.

Wassersug, R. J. and M. K. Hecht. "The Status of the Crocodylid Genera *Procaimanoidea* and *Hassiacosuchus* in the New World," *Herpetologica*, Vol. 23, No. 1 (1967), pp. 30–34.

Webb, S. D., and N. Tessman. "A Pliocene Vertebrate Fauna from Low Elevation in Manatee County, Florida," *American Journal of Science*, Vol. 266 (1968), pp. 777–811. (Describes crocodilian teeth resembling those of Charactosuchus.)

White, T. E. "A New Alligator from the Miocene of Florida," *Copeia* 1942, No. 1, pp. 3–7. (Description of *Alligator olseni*.)

Woodburne, M. O. "A Fossil Alligator from the Lower Pliocene of Oklahoma and Its Climatic Significance," *Papers of the Michigan Academy of Sciences, Arts, and Letters*, Vol. 64 (1959), pp. 47–50.

Zangerl, R. "*Brachyuranochampsa Eversolei*, Gen. et Sp. Nov., a New Crocodilian from the Washakie Eocene of Wyoming," *Annals of the Carnegie Museum*, Vol. 30, (1944), pp. 77–84.

Zappler G. "Fossil Bonanza," *Natural History*, Vol. 64, No. 8 (1960), pp. 18–30. (Includes photograph of a well-preserved crocodilian, possibly a terrestrial species.)

C. THE ACTIVITIES OF REPTILES

Allee, W. C. *Animal Aggregation. A Study in General Sociology.* Chicago, University of Chicago Press, 1931.

—— *The Social Life of Animals.* New York, W. W. Norton & Co., 1938.

—— "Social Dominance and Subordination among Vertebrates," *Biological Symposia*, No. 8 (1942), pp. 139–62.

—— *Cooperation among Animals.* New York, Henry Schuman Co., 1951.

—— "Dominance and Hierarchy in Societies of Vertebrates," in P.-P. Grassé (editor), "Structure et Physiologie des Sociétés Animales," *Colloques Internationaux du Centre National de la Recherche Scientifique*, No. 34, 1950 (1952), pp. 157–81.

Allen, E. R., and W. T. Neill. "The Vertical Position of the Pupil in Crocodilians and Snakes," *Herpetologica*, Vol. 6, No. 3 (1950), pp. 95–96.

Barach, J. P. "The Value of the Skin Secretions of the Spotted Salamander," *ibid.*, Vol. 7, No. 2 (1951), p. 58. (An alligator refused this species of salamander as food.)

Beach, F. A. *Hormones and Behavior; a Survey of Interrelationships between Endocrine Secretions and Patterns of Overt Response.* New York, Hoeber and Co., 1948.

Birch, L. C. "The Meaning of Competition," *American Naturalist*, Vol. 91, No. 856 (1957), pp. 5–18.

Blair, W. F. (editor). *Vertebrate Speciation.* Austin, University of Texas Press, 1961.

Bogert, C. M. "Thermoregulation in Reptiles, a Factor in Evolution," *Evolution*, Vol. 3, No. 3 (1949), pp. 195–211.

—— "How Reptiles Regulate Their Body Temperatures," *Scientific American*, Vol. 200, No. 4 (1959), pp. 105–8, 111–12, 115–16, 118, 120.

Bogert, C. M., and R. B. Cowles. "Results of the Archbold Expeditions. No. 58. Moisture Loss in Relation to Habitat Selection in Some Floridian Reptiles," *American Museum Novitates*, No. 1358 (1947).

Brazaitis, P. "The Occurrence and Ingestion of Gastroliths in Two Captive Crocodilians," *Herpetologica*, Vol. 25, No. 1 (1969), pp. 63–64.

Brisbin, I. L. "Evidence for the Use of Postanal Musk as an Alarm Device in the King Snake, *Lampropeltis getulus*," *ibid.*, Vol. 24, No. 2 (1968), pp. 169–70.

Brown, F. A. "Biological Clocks," *Biological Sciences Curriculum Study Pamphlet*, No. 2 (1962).

Brown, W. L., and E. O. Wilson. "Character Displacement," *Systematic Zoology*, Vol. 5, No. 2 (1956), pp. 49–64.

Bullock, T. H. "Compensation for Temperature in the Metabolism and Activity of Poikilotherms," *Biological Reviews of the Cambridge Philosophical Society*, Vol. 30 (1955), pp. 311–42. (Deals with physiological compensations, not behavioral thermoregulation.)

Bullough, W. S. *Vertebrate Sexual Cycles*. London, Methuen and Co., 1951.

Burghardt, G. M. "The Primacy Effect of the First Feeding Experience in the Snapping Turtle," *Psychonomic Science*, Vol. 7, No. 11 (1967), pp. 383–84.

Burt, W. H. "Territoriality and Home Range Concepts as Applied to Mammals," *Journal of Mammalogy*, Vol. 24 (1943), pp. 346–52.

—— "Territoriality," *ibid.*, Vol. 30 (1949), pp. 25–27.

Burton, Maurice. *Animal Courtship*. New York, Frederick A. Praeger, 1953.

Busnel, R. G. (editor). *Acoustic Behavior of Animals*. New York, American Elsevier Pub. Co., 1963.

Cagle, F. R. "An Outline for the Study of a Reptile History," *Tulane Studies in Zoology*, Vol. 1, No. 3 (1953). (An important summary, with extensive bibliography, of life history topics that might profitably be investigated.)

Carpenter, C. C. "Opportunities for Animal Behavior Research in Oklahoma, with Selected References on Animal Behavior," *Proceedings of the Oklahoma Academy of Sciences*, Vol. 39 (1959), pp. 87–98. (Similar opportunities exist in most other areas, and the bibliography is widely useful.)

Carthy, J. D. *Animal Navigation*. Charles Scribner's Sons, 1957. (Long-distance navigation is possible to some turtles and birds, and should be looked for among crocodilians.)

Collias, N. E. "Animal Language," *Biological Sciences Curriculum Study Pamphlets*, No. 20 (1964).

Comfort, A. "The Life Span of Animals," *Scientific American*, Vol. 205, No. 2 (1961), pp. 108–19.

Cott, H. B. *Adaptive Coloration in Animals*. New York, Oxford University Press, 1940.

Cunningham, B., and A. P. Hurwitz. "Water Absorption by Reptile Eggs during Incubation," *American Naturalist*, Vol. 70 (1936), pp. 590–95.

Davis, D. D. "Behavior of the Lizard *Corythophanes cristatus*," *Fieldiana: Zoology*, Vol. 35, No. 1 (1953).

Dessauer, H. C. "Hibernation of the Lizard, *Anolis carolinensis*," *Proceedings of the Society for Experimental Biology and Medicine*, Vol. 82 (1953), pp. 351–53.

—— "Effect of Season on Appetite and Food Consumption of the Lizard, *Anolis carolinensis*," *ibid.*, Vol. 90 (1955), pp. 524–26.

Dunson, W. A. "Some Aspects of Electrolyte and Water Balance in Three Estuarine Reptiles, the Diamondback Terrapin, American and 'Salt Water' Crocodiles," *Comparative Biochemical Physiology*, Vol. 32 (1970), pp. 161–74.

Dunson, W. A., and A. M. Taub. "Extrarenal Salt Excretion in Sea Snakes (Laticauda)," *American Journal of Physiology*, Vol. 213, No. 4 (1967), pp. 975–82. (Summarizes knowledge of salt glands in reptiles, and suggests the presence of such a gland in the American crocodile.)

Edgren, R. A., M. K. Edgren, and L. H. Tiffany. "Some North American Turtles and Their Epizoöphytic Algae," *Ecology*, Vol. 34 (1953), pp. 733–40.

Fraenkel, G. S., and D. L. Gunn. *The Orientation of Animals: Kineses, Taxes, and Compass Reactions*. Oxford, Clarendon Press, 1940 (Also New York, Dover Pubs., 1961, a reprint with additional notes and bibliography.)

Frost, S. W. "Frogs as Insect Collectors," *Journal of the New York Entomological Society*, Vol. 32 (1934), pp. 193–94.

Gibbons, J. W. "Possible Underwater Thermoregulation by Turtles," *Canadian Journal of Zoology*, Vol. 45 (1967), p. 585.

Gleason, K. K., and J. H. Reynierse. "The Behavioral Significance of Pheromones in Vertebrates," *Psychology Bul-*

letin, Vol. 71, No. 1 (1969), pp. 58–73.

Gordon, M. S., G. A. Bartholomew, A. D. Grinnell, C. B. Jorgensen, and F. N. White. *Animal Function: Principles and Adaptations* New York, The Macmillan Co., 1968.

Gossette, R. L., and A. Hombach. "Successive Discrimination Reversal (SDR) Performances of American Alligators and American Crocodiles on a Spatial Task," *Perception and Motor Skills*, Vol. 28 (1969), pp. 63–67.

Gottlieb, G. "Prenatal Behavior of Birds," *The Quarterly Review of Biology*, Vol. 43, No. 2 (1968), pp. 148–74. (Decribes the sequence in which sensory systems of the avian embryo become functional. Comparable studies on the crocodilians are much needed.)

Gray, J. *Animal Locomotion*. New York, W. W. Norton & Co., 1968.

Hediger, H. *Wild Animals in Captivity*. New York, Dover Pubs., 1964.

—— *The Psychology and Behaviour of Animals in Zoos and Circuses*. New York, Dover Pubs., 1968.

Hollingsworth, M. J. "Environmental Temperature and Life Span in Poikilotherms," *Nature*, Vol. 218, No. 5144, pp. 869–70.

Howard, W. E. "Innate and Environmental Dispersal of Individual Vertebrates," *American Midland Naturalist*, Vol. 63, No. 1 (1960), pp. 152–61.

Jackson, C. H. "The Analysis of an Animal Population," *Journal of Animal Ecology*, Vol. 8 (1939), pp. 238–46.

Kayser, C. *The Physiology of Natural Hibernation*. New York, Pergamon Press, 1961.

King, W. "The Occurrence of Rafts for Dispersal of Land Animals into the West Indies," *Quarterly Journal of the Florida Academy of Sciences*, Vol. 25, No. 1 (1962), pp. 45–52.

Klauber, L. M. *Rattlesnakes: Their Habits, Life Histories, and Influence on Mankind*, 2 vols. Berkeley, University of California Press, 1956. (Includes much useful information on reptile natural history generally.)

Krogh, A. *Osmotic Regulation in Aquatic Animals*. New York, Dover Pubs., 1965.

Lack, D. *The Natural Regulation of Animal Numbers*. New York, Oxford University Press, 1954.

Lanyon, W. E., and W. N. Tavolga (editors). *Animal Sounds and Communications*. American Institute of Biological Sciences, Pub. No. 7 (1960).

Maier, N. R., and T. C. Schneirla. *Principles of Animal Psychology*. New York, Dover Pubs. 1964.

Maturana, H. R. "A Study of the Species of the Genus *Basiliscus*," *Bulletin of the Museum of Comparative Zoology*, Vol. 128, No. 1 (1962).

McGinnis, S. M. "The Adaptation of Biotelemetry Techniques to Small Reptiles," *Copeia*, 1967, No. 2, pp. 472–73. (Such techniques could easily be adapted to the study of crocodilians and their movements.)

Mertens, Robert. "Die Warn- und Droh-Reaktionen der Reptilien," *Abhandlungen der Senckenbergische Nuturforschenden Gesellschaft*, No. 471 (1946), pp. 1–108.

—— *The World of Amphibians and Reptiles*. New York, McGraw-Hill Book Co., 1960. (An exceptionally fine popular review of the living amphibians and reptiles of the world. Also in German and French editions.)

Neill, W. T. "The Occurrence of Amphibians and Reptiles in Saltwater Areas, and a Bibliography," *Bulletin of Marine Science of the Gulf and Caribbean*, Vol. 8, No. 1 (1958), pp. 1–97.

—— "The Reproductive Cycle of Snakes in a Tropical Region, British Honduras," *Quarterly Journal of the Florida Academy of Sciences*, Vol. 25, No. 3 (1962), pp. 234–53. (Summarizes what is known of the timing of the reptile reproductive cycle in tropical regions.)

—— "Viviparity in Snakes: Some Ecological and Zoogeographical Considerations," *American Naturalist*, Vol. 98, No. 898 (1964), pp. 35–55. (Discusses environmental factors involved with the evolution of reptilian viviparity.)

—— "Isolating Mechanisms in Snakes,"

Quarterly Journal of the Florida Academy of Sciences, Vol. 27, No. 4 (1965, imprinted 1964), pp. 333–47. (Snakes are the only reptile group in which the mechanisms of reproductive isolation have been discussed in detail.)

Neill, W. T., and E. R. Allen. "Algae on Turtles: Some Additional Considerations," *Ecology,* Vol. 35, No. 4 (1954), pp. 581–84.

—— "Secondarily Ingested Food Items in Snakes," *Herpetologica,* Vol. 12, Pt. 3 (1956), pp. 172–76.

—— "*Deiroptyx,* Cuba's Reptilian Oddity," *Nature Magazine,* Vol. 50, No. 1 (1957), pp. 39–41, 52.

Noble, G. K. "The Sense Organs Involved in the Courtship of *Storeria, Thamnophis* and Other Snakes," *Bulletin of the American Museum of Natural History,* Vol. 73 (1937), pp. 673–725.

Noble, G. K., and H. T. Bradley. "The Mating Behavior of Lizards: Its Bearing on the Theory of Sexual Selection," *Annals of the New York Academy of Sciences,* Vol. 25 (1933), pp. 25–100.

Noble, G. K., and A. M. Breslau. "The Senses Involved in the Migration of Young Fresh-Water Turtles after Hatching," *Journal of Comparative Psychology,* Vol. 25, No. 1 (1938), pp. 175–93.

Noble, R. C. *The Nature of the Beast.* New York, Doubleday, Doran and Co., 1945.

Odum, E. P., and H. T. Odum. *Fundamentals of Ecology.* Philadelphia, W. B. Saunders Co., 1959.

Oliver, J. A. " 'Gliding' in Amphibians and Reptiles, with a Remark on an Arboreal Adaptation in the Lizard, *Anolis carolinensis* Voigt," *American Naturalist,* Vol. 85, No. 822 (1951), pp. 171–76.

—— *The Natural History of North American Amphibians and Reptiles.* Princeton, N. J., D. Van Nostrand Co., 1955.

Park, O. "Nocturnalism—The Development of a Problem," *Ecological Monographs,* Vol. 10, No. 3 (1940), pp. 486–536.

Parker, G. H. *Animal Colour Changes and Their Neurohumours.* Cambridge, England, 1948.

—— "Background Adaptations," *Quarterly Review of Biology,* Vol. 30, No. 2 (1955), pp. 105–15.

Pieron, H. *Le Problem Physiologique du Sommeil.* Paris, Masson and Co., 1913. (Includes much on sleep in reptiles, and criteria whereby the sleeping state may be defined.)

Potts, W. T., and G. Parry. *Osmotic and Ionic Regulation in Animals.* New York, Pergamon Press, 1964.

Rand, A. L. "Secondary Sexual Characters and Ecological Competition," *Fieldiana-Zoology,* Vol. 34, No. 6 (1952), pp. 65–70. (Although this work is concerned mainly with birds, its conclusions seem applicable to crocodilians.)

Riddle, O. "The Rate of Digestion in Cold Blooded Vertebrates. The Influence of Season and Temperature," *American Journal of Physiology,* Vol. 24 (1909), p. 447.

Roe, A., and G. G. Simpson (editors). *Behavior and Evolution.* New Haven, Yale University Press, 1958.

Schoener, T. W. "The Ecological Significance of Sexual Dimorphism in Size in the Lizard *Anolis conspersus,*" *Science,* Vol. 155, No. 3761 (1967), pp. 474–77.

Scott, J. P. *Animal Behavior.* Chicago, University of Chicago Press, 1958.

—— *Aggression.* Chicago, University of Chicago Press, 1958.

Schmidt-Nielsen, K., A. Borut, P. Lee, and E. Crawford. "Nasal Salt Excretion and the Possible Function of the Cloaca in Water Conservation," *Science,* Vol. 142 (1963), pp. 1300–1.

Scott, J. P., and R. Fänge. "Salt Glands in Marine Reptiles," *Nature,* Vol. 182 (1958), pp. 783–85.

Sebeok, T. A. (editor). *Animal Communications: Techniques of Study and Results of Research.* Bloomington, University of Indiana Press, 1968.

Shafland, J. L. "Functional Anatomy of Suction Feeding in *Chelys Fimbriata* and *Pipa Pipa,*" *Anatomical Record,* Vol. 160, No. 2 (1968), p. 552.

Smith, H. M. "Survival Value of Voice in

Small Mammals," *Journal of Mammalogy*, Vol. 25, No. 4 (1944), p. 407.

Snyder, R. C. "Bipedal Locomotion of the Lizard *Basiliscus Basiliscus*," *Copeia*, 1949, No. 2, pp. 129–37.

Stebbins, R. C., and R. M. Eakins. "The Role of the 'Third Eye' in Reptilian Behavior," *American Museum Novitates*, No. 1870 (1958).

Storm, R. M. (editor). *Animal Orientation and Navigation*. Corvallis, Oregon, State University Press, 1967.

Svihla, A., and R. D. Svihla. "Bipedal Locomotion in the Iguana, *Iguana Tuberculata*," *Copeia*, 1952, No. 2, p. 119.

Tinbergen, N. "Social Releasers and the Experimental Method Required for Their Study," *Wilson Bulletin*, Vol. 60 (1948), pp. 6–51. (Includes a review of the pertinent herpetological literature.)

—— " 'Derived' Activities; Their Causation, Biological Significance, Origin, and Emancipation during Evolution," *Quarterly Review of Biology*, Vol. 27 (1952), pp. 1–32.

—— *Social Behaviour in Animals*. London, Methuen and Co., 1953.

Williams, J. T. "Reversal-Learning in the Spectacled Caiman," *American Journal of Psychology*, Vol. 81, No. 2 (1968), pp. 258–61.

Young, J. Z. *The Life of Vertebrates*. 2nd ed. New York, Oxford University Press, 1962.

D. THE PHYSIOLOGY, GENETICS, EMBRYOLOGY, AND PARASITOLOGY OF THE CROCODILIANS

Akers, T. K., and C. N. Peiss. "Comparative Study of Effect of Epinephrine and Norepinephrine on Cardiovascular System of Turtle, Alligator, Chicken, and Opossum," *Proceedings of the Society for Experimental Biology and Medicine*, Vol. 112 (1963), pp. 396–99.

Allen, E. R., and W. T. Neill. "Some Color Abnormalities in Crocodilians," *Copeia*, 1956, No. 2, p. 124.

Andersen, H. T. "Physiological Adjustments to Prolonged Diving in the American Alligator *Alligator Mississippiensis*," *Acta Physiologia Scandinavia*, Vol. 53 (1961), pp. 23-45.

Benedict, F. G. "The Physiology of Large Reptiles with Special Reference to Heat Production of Snakes, Lizards, and Alligators," *Carnegie Institution of Washington*, Pub. No. 425 (1932).

Brissin, I. L. "Reactions of the American Alligator to Several Immobilizing Drugs," *Copeia*, 1966, No. 1, pp. 129–30.

Brockman, H. L., and J. P. Kennedy. "The Surgical Occlusion of the Left Aortic Orifice in *Alligator Mississippiensis* Daudin," *Journal of Surgical Research*, Vol. 4, No. 11 (1964), pp. 500–3.

Burns, A. H., and D. C. Goodman. "Retinotugal Projections of *Caiman Sclerops*," *Experimental Neurology*, Vol. 18, No. 1 (1967), pp. 105–15.

Byrd, E. E., and R. J. Reiber. "Strigeid Trematodes of the Alligator, with Remarks on the Prostate Gland and Terminal Portions of the Genital Ducts," *Journal of Parasitology*, Vol. 28, No. 1 (1942), pp. 51–73.

Cameron, T. W. *Parasites and Parasitism*. New York, John Wiley and Sons, 1956.

Clarke, S. F. "The Habits and Embryology of the American Alligator," *Journal of Morphology*, Vol. 5 (1891), pp. 181–214.

Cloudsley-Thompson, J. L. "Water Relations of Crocodiles," *Nature*, Vol. 220, No. 5168 (1968), p. 708.

Cohen, M. M., and H. F. Clark. "The Somatic Chromosomes of Five Crocodilian Species," *Cytogenetics*, Vol. 6, Nos. 3–4 (1967), pp. 193–203.

Conant, R., and R. G. Hudson. "Longevity Records for Reptiles and Amphibians in the Philadelphia Zoological Garden," *Herpetologica*, Vol. 5, Pt. 1 (1949), pp. 1–8.

Coulson, R. A., and T. Hernandez. "Glucose in Crocodilia," *Endocrinology*, Vol. 53, No. 3 (1953), pp. 311–20.

—— "Renal Excretion of Carbon Dioxide

and Ammonia by the Alligator," *Proceedings of the Society for Experimental Biology and Medicine*, Vol. 88 (1955), pp. 682–87.

—— "Source and Function of Urinary Ammonia in the Alligator," *American Journal of Physiology*, Vol. 197, No. 4 (1959), pp. 873–79.

—— *Biochemistry of the Alligator*. Baton Rouge, University of Louisiana Press, 1964. (An important summary.)

—— "Site of Synthesis of Amino Acids in the Intact Cayman," *American Journal of Physiology*, Vol. 213, No. 2 (1967), pp. 411–17.

Coulson, R. A., T. Hernandez, and H. C. Dessauer. "Alkaline Tide of the Alligator," *Proceedings of the Society for Experimental Biology and Medicine*, Vol. 74 (1950), pp. 866–69.

Davis, L. F., and B. Schmidt-Nielsen. "Ultrastructure of the Crocodile Kidney (*Crocodylus Acutus*) with Special Reference to Electrolyte and Fluid Transport," *Journal of Morphology*, Vol. 121, No. 4 (1967), pp. 255–76.

Dill, D. B., and H. T. Edwards. "Physicochemical Properties of Crocodile Blood (*Crocodylus Acutus* Cuvier)," *Journal of Biology and Chemistry*, Vol. 90 (1931), pp. 515–30.

—— "Respiration and Metabolism in a Young Crocodile (*Crocodylus Acutus* Cuvier)," *Copeia*, 1931, No. 1, pp. 1–3.

Evans, H. E. "Notes on Panamanian Reptiles and Amphibians," *Copeia*, 1947, No. 3, pp. 166–70.

Ewer, R. F. "Haemodynamic Factors in the Evolution of the Double Circulation in the Vertebrates," *American Naturalist*, Vol. 84 (1950), pp. 215–20.

Fischman, H. K., J. Mitra, and H. G. Dowling. "The Karyotype of the Chinese Alligator (*Alligator Sinensis*)," *Mammal Chromosomes Newsletter*, Vol. 9, No. 2 (1968), pp. 81–82.

Gaunt, A. S., and C. Gans. "Diving Bradycardia and Withdrawal Bradycardia in *Caiman crocodilus*," *Nature*, Vol. 223, No. 5202 (1969), pp. 207–08.

Gilchrist, F. G. *A Survey of Embryology.* New York, McGraw-Hill Book Co., 1968.

Goin, O. B., and C. J. Goin. "DNA and the Evolution of the Vertebrates," *American Midland Naturalist*, Vol. 80, No. 2 (1968), pp. 289–98.

Greenfield, L. J., and A. G. Morrow. "The Cardiovascular Hemodynamics of Crocodilia," *Journal of Surgical Research*, Vol. 1, No. 2 (1961), pp. 97–103.

Hensley, M. "Albinism in North American Amphibians and Reptiles," *Michigan State University, Publications of the Museum, Biological Series*, Vol. 1, No. 4 (1959).

Hernandez, T., and R. A. Coulson. "The Effect of Carbonic Anhydrase Inhibition on the Composition of Urine and Plasma of the Alligator," *Science*, Vol. 119, No. 3087 (1954), pp. 291–92.

—— "Sympathomimetic Action of Xanthine Diuretics in the Alligator," *American Journal of Physiology*, Vol. 185, No. 1 (1956), pp. 201–4.

—— "Renal Clearance in the Alligator," *Federation Proceedings*, Vol. 1, No. 1 (1956).

—— "Metabolic Acidosis in the Alligator," *Proceedings of the Society for Experimental Biology and Medicine*, Vol. 99 (1958), pp. 525–526.

—— "Effect of Insulin on Amino Acid Tolerance," *Federation Proceedings*, Vol. 19, No. 1, Pt. 1 (1960). (The American alligator is the experimental animal used.)

—— "Amino Acid Excretion in the Alligator," *Comparative Biochemistry and Physiology*, Vol. 23, No. 3 (1967), pp. 775–84.

Heymons, R. "Pentastomida," *Bronn's Klassen und Ordnungen des Tierreichs*, Vol. 5, Section 4, Book 1. (Pentastomids, called linguatulids in older literature, in some cases parasitize crocodilians.

Higgens, G. M. "Development of the Primitive Reptilian Vertebrae Column as Shown by the Study of *Alligator Mississippiensis*," *American Journal of Anatomy*, Vol. 31, No. 4 (1923), pp. 273–408.

Huggins, S. E., L. C. Parsons, and R. V. Pena. "Further Study on the Spontaneous Electrical Activity of the Brain of *Caiman Sclerops*: Olfactory Lobes," *Physiological Zoology*, Vol. 41, No. 3 (1968), pp. 371–83.

Hughes, R. C., J. R. Baker, and C. B. Dawson. "The Trematodes of Reptiles, Part 2, Host Catalogue," Proceedings of the Oklahoma Academy of Sciences, Vol. 21 (1941), pp. 37–43.

Jasmin, A. M., J. M. Carroll, and J. N. Baucom. "Pulmonary Aspergillosis of the American Alligator *(Alligator Mississippiensis)*, American Journal of Veterinary Clinical Pathology, Vol. 2 (1968), pp. 93–95.

Karstad, L. "Reptiles as Possible Reservoir Hosts for Eastern Encephalitis Virus," *Transactions of the 26th North American Wildlife and Natural Resources Conference* (1961), pp. 186–202.

Kleinholz, L. H. "Behavior of Melanophores in the Alligator," *Anatomical Record*, Vol. 81, Supplement (1941), p. 121.

Llinas, R., C. Nicholson, J. A. Freeman, and D. E. Hillman. "Dendritic Spikes and Their Inhibition in Alligator Purkinje Cells," *Science*, Vol. 160, No. 3832 (1968), pp. 1132–35.

Llinas, R., C. Nicholson, and W. Precht. "Preferred Centripetal Conduction of Dendritic Spikes in Alligator Purkinje Cells," *ibid.*, Vol. 163, No. 3864 (1969), pp. 184–87.

Makino, S. *An Atlas of the Chromosome Numbers in Animals.* 2nd ed. Ames, Iowa, Iowa State College Press, 1951.

Mookerjee, H. K., and R. N. Battacharya. "On the Development of the Vertebral Column in *Alligator Mississippiensis*," *Zoological Society of Bengal*, Pub. 1 (1948), pp. 71–78.

Morgan, B. B. "The Physaloptera (Nematoda) of Reptiles," *Naturaliste Canadienne*, Vol. 70 (1943), pp. 179–85.

Parker, G. H. "The Time of Submergence Necessary to Drown Alligators and Turtles," *Occasional Papers of the Boston Society of Natural History*, No. 5 (1925), pp. 157–59.

Penhos, J. C., C. H. Wu, M. Reitman, F. Sodero, R. White, and R. Levine. "Effects of Several Hormones after Total Pancreatectomy in Alligators," *General and Comparative Endocrinology*, Vol. 8, No. 1 (1967), pp. 32–43.

Rand, A. S. "Desiccation Rates in Crocodile and Iguana Eggs," *Herpetologica*, Vol. 24, No. 2 (1968), pp. 178–80.

Randall, W. C., D. E. Stullken, and W. A. Hiestand. "Respiration of Reptiles as Influenced by the Composition of the Inspired Air," *Copeia*, 1944, No. 3, pp. 136–44.

Reese, A. M. "Artificial Incubation of Alligator Eggs," *American Naturalist*, Vol. 35, No. 411 (1901), pp. 193–95.

—— "A Double Embryo of the Florida Alligator," *Anatomische Anzeiger*, Vol. 28, Nos. 9–10 (1906), pp. 229–31.

—— "Embryology of the Alligator," *Proceedings of the 7th International Congress of Zoology*, 1907.

—— "The Development of the American Alligator," *Smithsonian Miscellaneous Collections*, No. 1791 (1908), pp. 1–66.

—— "Development of the Brain of the American Alligator: Paraphysis and Hypophysis," *ibid.*, No. 1922 (1910), pp. 1–20.

—— "Development of the Digestive Canal in the American Alligator," *ibid.*, No. 1946 (1910), pp. 1–25.

—— "Histology of the Enteron of the Florida Alligator," *Anatomical Record*, Vol. 7, No. 4 (1913), pp. 105-29.

—— "Development of the Lung of the American Alligator," *Smithsonian Miscellaneous Collections*, Pub. No. 2356 (1915).

—— "The Origin of the Notochord in *Alligator Mississippiensis*," *Anatomical Record*, Vol. 64, No. 3 (1936), pp. 405–8.

Reichenbach-Klinke, H., and E. Elkan. *The Principal Diseases of Lower Vertebrates.* New York, Academic Press, 1965.

Rider, J., and A. H. Bartel. "Electrophoretic Analysis of Young Caiman and Crocodile Serum," *Comparative Biochemistry and Physiology*, Vol. 20, No. 3 (1967), pp. 1005-8.

Röse, C. "Über die Zahnentwicklung der Crocodile," *Morphologische Arbeiten,* Vol. 3 (1894), pp. 195–228.

Schapiro, H. "Vomiting Responses in *Caiman Sclerops* Elicited by Central Nervous Stimulation," *Anatomical Record,* Vol. 160, No. 2 (1968), pp. 421–422.

—— "Retching Responses in *Caiman Sclerops* Elicited by Central Nervous Stimulation," *Proceedings of the Society for Experimental Biology and Medicine,* Vol. 129, No. 3 (1968), pp. 917–20.

Schneider, K. M. "Von dem Entleerungen einiger Panzerechsen," *Zoologische Anzeiger,* Vol. 142, Nos. 5–6 (1943), pp. 95–101.

Siminoff, R. "Quantitative Properties of Slowly Adapting Mechanoreceptors in Alligator Skin," *Experimental Neurology,* Vol. 21, No. 3 (1968), pp. 290–306.

Simkiss, K. *Calcium in Reproductive Physiology, A Comparative Study of Vertebrates,* New York, Reinhold Pub. Corp., 1967.

Stevenson, O. R., R. A. Coulson, and T. Hernandez. "Effects of Hormones on Carbohydrate Metabolism in the Alligator," *American Journal of Physiology,* Vol. 191, No. 1 (1957), pp. 95–102.

Symposium: "Physiological Mechanisms in Animal Behavior," *Society for Experimental Biology,* Pub. No. 4 (1950).

Travassos, L. "*Sebekia* du Poumon des Crocodiles d'Amerique," *Comptes Rendus, Societe Biologique, Paris,* Vol. 90 (1924), pp. 239–40. (Pentastomids parasitic in New World crocodilians.)

Van Tienhoven, A. *Reproductive Physiology of Vertebrates.* Philadelphia, W. B. Saunders Co., 1968.

Voeltzkow, A. "Biologie und Entwicklung der Ausseren Korperform von *Crocodilus madagascariensis* Grand.," *Abhandlungen der Senckenbergische Naturforschenden Gesellschaft,* Vol. 26, Part 1 (1889), pp. 1–149.

—— "On the Oviposition and Embryological Development of the Crocodile," *Annals and Magazine of Natural History,* Vol. 9 (1891), pp. 66–72.

—— "Embryology, Epiphysis, und Paraphysis bei Krokodilen und Schildkröten," *Abhandlungen der Senckenbergische Naturforschenden Gesellschaft,* Vol. 27 (1903), pp. 163–77.

Wallach, J. D., C. Hoessle, and J. Bennett. "Hypoglycemic Shock in Captive Alligators," *Journal of the American Veterinary Medicine Association,* Vol. 151, No. 7 (1967).

White, F. N. "Circulation in the Reptilian Heart *(Caiman Sclerops),*" *Anatomical Record,* Vol. 125, No. 3 (1956), pp. 417–31.

Wilbur, C. G. "Cardiac Responses of Alligator Mississipiensis to Diving," *Comparative Biochemistry and Physiology,* Vol. 1 (1960), pp. 164–66.

E. THE NATURAL HISTORY OF THE AMERICAN ALLIGATOR

Allen, E. R. "Ward's Great Blue Heron and the Alligator," *Florida Naturalist,* Vol. 23, No. 2 (1950), pp. 38–39.

Allen, E. R., and W. T. Neill. "Increasing Abundance of the Alligator in the Eastern Portion of Its Range," *Herpetologica,* Vol. 5, No. 6 (1949), pp. 109–12.

—— "The American Alligator," *Florida Wildlife,* Vol. 6, No. 5 (1952), pp. 8–9, 44.

Allen, E. R., and R. Slatten. "A Herpetological Collection from the Vicinity of Key West, Florida," *Herpetologica,* Vol. 3, No. 1 (1945), pp. 27–28.

Allen, H. "Do Glades Poachers Have Wildlife Officers on Run?," *Tampa Tribune,* Dec. 1, 1969, pp. 1–B, 6–B.

Anonymous. "Poachers Kill 50,000 Gators," *ibid.,* July 31, 1966, p. 22–A.

Anonymous. "The Law, the Courts, and the Alligator," *Audubon Magazine,* Vol. 70, No. 5 (1968), pp. 4–5.

Arthur, S. C. "Report of the Division of Wild Life: Alligators," *Louisiana Department of Conservation, Biennial Report,* 1925–26 (1926), pp. 174–75.

—— "The Fur Animals of Louisiana: the Alligator," *Louisiana Department of Conservation*, Bulletin No. 18 (1928), pp. 165–86.

Audubon, J. J. *The Birds of America*. New York, The Macmillan Co., 1937. (Includes a painting of baby alligators being attacked by a whooping crane.)

Baird, S. F. "Reptiles of the Boundary," *United States and Mexican Boundary Survey*, Vol. 2, Part 2 (1859).

Barbour, T. "A Large Alligator Skull," *Copeia*, 1933, No. 1, p. 43.

Barton, A. J. "Prolonged Survival of a Released Alligator in Pennsylvania," *Herpetologica*, Vol. 11, No. 3 (1955), p. 210.

Barwick, R. E., and P. J. Fullagar. "A Bibliography of Radio Telemetry in Biological Studies," *Proceedings of the Ecological Society of Australia*, Vol. 2 (1967), pp. 27–49.

Beach, F. A. "Response of Captive Alligators to Auditory Stimulation," *American Naturalist*, Vol. 78 (1944), pp. 481–505.

Beyer, G. E. "Louisiana Herpetology," *New Orleans Society of Natural History, Proceedings* 1897–99 (1900), pp. 25–46.

Blair, A. P. "The Alligator in Oklahoma," *Copeia*, 1950, No. 1, p. 57.

Brandt, Leonore. "Attack by a Pet Alligator," *Herpetologica*, Vol. 4, Part 6 (1948), p. 218.

Brimley, H. H. "Alligators and Crocodiles. 'Gator' Hunting in North Carolina," *North Carolina Wildlife Conservation*, Vol. 6, No. 4 (1942), pp. 8–11; Vol. 6, No. 5 (1942), pp. 5–8, 14.

Brown, B. C. *An Annotated Check List of the Reptiles and Amphibians of Texas*. Waco, Texas, Baylor University Press, 1950.

C., S. C. "An Upland Alligator," *Forest and Stream*, Vol. 12 (1879), p. 307.

Chabreck, R. H. "The American Alligator —Past, Present and Future," *Publications of the Louisiana Wild Life and Fisheries Commission* (1967), pp. 1–11.

Chamberlain, E. B. "Notes on the Stomach Contents of an Alligator," *Copeia*, 1930, No. 3, pp. 83–84.

Clark, S. F. "The Nest and Eggs of the Alligator, *Alligator lucius*," *Zoologische Anzeiger*, 11 *Jahrgeschichte*, No. 290 (1888), pp. 568–70.

—— "The Habits and Embryology of the American Alligator," *Journal of Morphology*, Vol. 5 (1891), pp. 182–214.

Clarke, R. F. "Alligator Escapees in Southeastern Virginia," *Herpetologica*, Vol. 9, No. 2 (1953), pp. 71–72.

Colbert, E. H., R. B. Cowles, and C. M. Bogert. "Temperature Tolerances in the American Alligator and Their Bearing on the Habits, Evolution, and Extinction of the Dinosaurs," *American Museum of Natural History*, Vol. 86, Art. 7 (1946), pp. 329–73. (A particularly important work; activities of the alligator must be compatible with its temperature requirements.)

Coles, R. J., "Alligators in Winter," *Copeia* No. 17 (1915), n. p. (Includes records of the alligator near Morehead City, North Carolina.)

Conant, R., and A. Downs. "Miscellaneous Notes on the Eggs and Young of Reptiles," *Zoologica*, Vol. 25, Part 1 (1940), pp. 33–48.

Cope, E. D. "Third Contribution to the Herpetology of Tropical America," *Proceedings of the Academy of Natural Sciences of Philadelphia*, Vol. 17 (1865), pp. 185–98.

Cox, B. "Dry Spell Has Florida on Verge of 'Disaster'," *Tampa Tribune*, May 6, 1967, pp 1A–2A. (Includes photographs of alligators, birds, and dead fishes about drying waterholes.)

Craighead, F. C. "The Role of the Alligator in Shaping Plant Communities and Maintaining Wildlife in the Southern Everglades," *Florida Naturalist*, Vol. 41, No. 1 (1968), pp. 2–7; Vol. 41, No. 2 (1968), pp. 69–74.

Cragin, F. W. [Account of Alligators up the Arkansas River], *Editorial Notes, Bulletin of the Washburn College Laboratory of Natural History*, No. 1 (1835), p. 111.

Crosby, Oliver. *Florida Facts Both Bright*

and Blue [etc.]. New York, 1887. (Remarks at this early date, that there are left in Florida "hardly alligators enough to show the tourists.")

Dorf, E. "Climatic Changes of the Past and Present," *Contributions from the Museum of Paleontology, University of Michigan,* Vol. 13, No. 8 (1959), pp. 181–210.

Dowler, B. "Contributions to the Natural History of the Alligator, *Crocodilus Mississippiensis*," *New Orleans Medical and Surgery Journal,* Vol. 3 (1847), pp. 311–36.

Duellman, W. E., and A. Schwartz. "Amphibians and Reptiles of Southern Florida," *Bulletin of the Florida State Museum, Biological Sciences,* Vol. 3, No. 5 (1958).

Engels, W. L. "Vertebrate Fauna of the North Carolina Coastal Islands. II. Shackelford Banks," *American Midland Naturalist,* Vol. 47, No. 3 (1952), pp. 702–42.

Evans, L. T., and J. Quaranta. "Vocality, a Factor in the Ecology of the Alligator," *Anatomical Record,* Vol. 105 (1949), pp. 101–2.

Feilden, H. W. "The Nest of the Alligator," *Zoologist,* 2nd Series, Vol. 5 (1870).

Funk, B. "'Gators in Drying Waterholes Being Picked Off by Poachers," *Tampa Tribune,* April 7, 1968, p. 9–B. (Includes photograph of many alligators in a drying waterhole.)

Gannon, R. "Let's Save the Alligator," *Readers Digest,* 1968, pp. 223–24, 226–28.

Giles, L. W., and V. L. Childs. "Alligator Management on the Sabine National Wild Life Refuge," *Journal of Wildlife Management,* Vol. 13 (1949), pp. 16–28.

Guidry, E. V., "Herpetological Notes from Southeastern Texas," *Herpetologica,* Vol. 9, Pt. 1 (1953), pp. 49–56.

Harper, F. "Some Works of Bartram, Daudin, Latreille, and Sonnini, and Their Bearing on North American Herpetological Nomenclature," *American Mid-*

land Naturalist, Vol. 23, No. 3 (1940), pp. 692–723.

Hernandez, T., and R. A. Coulson. "Hibernation in the Alligator," *Proceedings of the Society for Experimental Biology and Medicine,* Vol. 79, No. 1 (1952), pp. 145–49.

Hock, R. J. "The Alligator in Arizona," *Copeia,* 1954, No. 3, pp. 222–23.

Hoy, W. E., J. T. Penney, H. W. Freeman, W. R. Kelley, and N. H. Subeck. "New Distributional Records for Reptiles and Amphibians in South Carolina," *Copeia,* 1953, No. 1, pp. 59–60.

Jackson, W. H. "A Tremendous Alligator," *Forest and Stream,* Vol. 49 (1897), p. 204.

Kellett, J. H. "Time Runs out for the Gator," *Florida Naturalist,* Vol. 41, No. 3 (1968), pp. 115–16.

Kinder, T. "Alligators in the Colorado River," *Arizona Wildlife and Sportsman,* Vol. 6, No. 3 (1945).

Laycock, G. "The Gator Killers," *Audubon Magazine,* Vol. 70, No. 5 (1968), pp. 76–93.

Lee, D. S. "Possible Communication between Eggs of the American Alligator," *Herpetologica,* Vol. 24, No. 1 (1968), p. 88.

Leech, J. W. "Alligator Hunting in Texas," *American Field,* Vol. 103 (1925), pp. 224–25.

Legge, R. E. "Mating Behaviour of American Alligators, *Alligator Mississippiensis,* at Manchester Zoo," *International Zoo Yearbook,* Vol. 7 (1967), pp. 179–80.

Mason, C. R. "Boycott Alligator Product [*sic*], Audubon Society Recommends," *Florida Naturalist,* Vol. 40, No. 1 (1967), p. 2.

Mittleman, M. B., and B. C. Brown. "The Alligator in Texas," *Herpetologica,* Vol. 4, Part 6 (1948), pp. 195–96.

Myers, G. S. "Amphibians and Reptiles from Wilmington, North Carolina," *Copeia,* No. 131 (1924), pp. 59–62.

Ralph, J. *Dixie; or Southern Scenes and Sketches.* New York, 1896. (Mentions, at this early date, that vast numbers of small alligators and quantities of alligator novelties were being offered for sale in Florida.)

Ratterer, E. "Du Rein d'un Alligator," *Comptes Rendus, Societe de Biologie, Paris,* Vol. 83 (1920), pp. 586–99.

Rhoads, S. N. "Contributions to the Zoology of Tennessee. No. 1, Reptiles and Amphibians," *Proceedings of the Academy of Natural Sciences of Philadelphia* for 1895 (1896), pp. 376–407.

Reese, A. M. "The Breeding Habits of the Florida Alligator," *Smithsonian Miscellaneous Collections,* Vol. 48, Part 4, No. 1696 (1907), pp. 381–87.

—— "The Home of the Alligator," *Popular Science Monthly,* October, 1910, pp. 365–72.

—— *The Alligator and Its Allies.* New York, G. P. Putnam's Sons, 1915. (Devoted chiefly to the anatomy and embryology of the American alligator.)

—— "Alligators as Food," *Science,* New Series, Vol. 47 (1918), p. 641.

—— "Some Reactions of *Alligator Mississippiensis,*" *Journal of Comparative Psychology,* Vol. 3, No. 1 (1923), pp. 51–59.

—— "Phototactic Reactions of *Alligator Mississippiensis,*" *ibid.,* Vol. 5, No. 1 (1925), pp. 69–73

—— "The Ways of the Alligator," *Scientific Monthly,* Vol. 3 (1931), pp. 321–55.

—— "Hibernation of the Alligator in an Artificial Environment," *Herpetologica,* Vol. 4, No. 4 (1948), pp. 127–28.

Smith, G. "Alligator or Caiman?" *Florida Wildlife,* Vol. 22, No. 2 (1968), pp. 20–21. (Includes method of distinguishing alligator leather from that of caiman.)

Smith, H. M. "Notes on the Alligator Industry," *Bulletin of the U. S. Fish Commission,* 1891, Vol. 11 (1893), pp. 343–45.

Springer, S. "On the Size of *Rana Sphenocephala,*" *Copeia,* 1938, No. 1, p. 49. (Reports leopard frogs eating baby alligators.)

Stevenson, C. H. "Utilization of the Skins of Aquatic Animals," *U. S. Fish and Fisheries Commission, Report* for 1902 (1904), pp. 281–352.

Stirling, J. *Letters from the Slave States.* London, 1857. (Relates how a hunting party bagged 75 alligators.)

Strecker, J. K. "*Alligator Mississippiensis* (Daudin) in McLennan County, Texas," in W. J. Williams (editor), "Notes on the Zoology of Texas," *Baylor Bulletin,* Vol. 38, No. 3 (1935), pp. 24–25.

Svihla, A. "Description of an Alligator Nest," *Science,* Vol. 70, No. 1818 (1929), p. 428.

Sweet, F. H. "Some Alligators I Have Known," *American Forests and Forest Life,* Vol. 30 (1924), pp. 465–69, 484.

Swift, F. R. *Florida Fancies.* New York, G. P. Putnam's Sons, 1903. (The text is fictionalized, but the alligator photographs are interesting.)

Vandiver, C. A. "The Florida Alligator," *American Field,* Vol. 107 (1927), pp. 334–35.

Van Hyning, O. C. "Batrachia and Reptilia of Alachua County, Florida," *Copeia,* 1933, No. 1, pp. 3–7.

Viosca, P. "The Tale of 'Old Fire Eyes'," *Natural History,* Vol. 25, No. 4 (1925), pp. 400–6.

—— "External Sexual Differences in the Alligator, *Alligator Mississippiensis,*" *Herpetologica,* Vol. 1, Part 6 (1939), pp. 154–55.

Wright, A. H., and W. D. Funkhouser. "A Biological Reconnaissance of the Okefinokee Swamp in Georgia. The Reptiles. I. Turtles, Lizards, and Alligators," *Proceedings of the Academy of Natural Sciences,* Vol. 67 (1915), pp. 107–9.

F.   THE TAXONOMY OF THE LIVING CROCODILIANS

Boettger, O. *Katalog der Reptilien-Sammlung im Museum der Senckenbergischen Naturforschenden Gesellschaft in Frankfurt a. M. I. (Rhynchocephalen, Schildkröten, Krokodile, Eidechsen, Chamäleons).* Frankfurt a. M., 1893.

Boettger, O., and E. Pechuel-Loesche. "Die Kriechtiere und Lurche," in *Brehm's Tierleben,* Vol. 3. Leipzig, 1893.

Boulenger, G. A. *Catalogue of the Chelonians, Rhynchocephalians, and Croco-*

diles in the British Museum (Natural History). London, 1889. (An important early catalogue.)

Buffon, G. L. de, L. J. Daubenton, P. G. de Montbeillard, G. L. Bexon, and G. B. de Lacépède. *Histoire Naturelle, Generale et Particuliere, avec la Description du Cabinet du Roi.* 44 vols. Paris, 1749–1809.

Cuvier, G. L. "Sur les Differentes Especes de Crocodiles Vivans et Sur Leur Caracteres Distinctifs," *Annales du Museum d'Histoire Naturelle,* Vol. 10 (1807), pp. 8–66.

—— *La Règne Animal.* 4 vols. Paris, 1817.

Daudin, F. M. *Histoire Naturelle, Générale et Particuliere des Reptiles.* 8 vols. Paris, 1801–1803.

Duméril, A. M.-C., G. Bibron, *Erpétologie Generale ou Histoire Naturelle Complète des Reptiles.* 9 Vols. [in 10] plus Atlas. Paris, 1834–1854.

Dunn, E. R., and M. T. Dunn. "Generic Names Proposed in Herpetology by E. D. Cope," *Copeia,* 1940, No. 2, pp. 69–76.

Fitzinger, L. J. *Neue Classification der Reptilien nach Ihren Natürlichen Verwandtschafter.* Vienna, 1826.

Geoffroy Saint Hilaire, E. "Recherches sur l'Organisation des Gavials [etc.]," *Memoirs du Museum d'Histoire Naturelle,* Vol. 12 (1825), pp. 97–155.

Gray, J. E. *Catalogue of the Tortoises, Crocodiles, and Amphisbaenians in the Collection of the British Museum.* London, 1844.

—— "A Synopsis of the Species of Crocodiles," *Annals and Magazine of Natural History,* Vol. 10, No. 3 (1862), pp. 265–74.

—— "A Synopsis of the Species of Alligators," *ibid.,* pp. 327–31.

—— "Synopsis of the Species of Recent Crocodilians or Emydosaurians [etc.]," *Transactions of the Zoological Society of London,* Vol. 6 (1867), pp. 125–69.

—— *Catalogue of the Shield Reptiles in the Collection of the British Museum, II. Emydosaurians, Rhynchocephalia, and Amphisbaenians.* London, 1872.

Günther, A. C. *Biologia Centrali-Americana. Reptiles and Batrachia.* London, Porter and Dulan Co., 1902.

Lacépède, B. G. de. *Histoire Naturelle des Quadrupédes Ovipares et des Serpens* [etc.]. 2 Vols. Paris, 1788–1789.

Laurenti, J. N. *Specimen Medicum, Exhibens Synopsis Reptilium.* Vienna, 1768.

Linnaeus, C. *Systema Naturae per Regna Tria Naturae* [etc.]. 10th ed. Stockholm, 1758.

Merrem, B. *Tentamen Systematis Amphibiorum.* Marburg, 1820.

Mertens, R. "Die Rezenten Krokodile des Natur-Museums Senckenberg," *Senckenbergiana,* Vol. 26, No. 4 (1943), pp. 252–312.

Mertens R., and H. Wermuth. "Die Rentzen Schildkröten, Krokodile, und Brückenechsen," *Zoologische Jahrbücher (Systematik)* Vol. 83, No. 5 (1955), pp. 323–440. (The most important taxonomic summary of recent crocodilians, with extensive synonymies and pertinent bibliographic references.)

Mook, C. C., and G. E. Mook. "Some Problems in Crocodilian Nomenclature," *American Museum Novitates,* No. 1098 (1940).

Nopcsa, F. "The Genera of Reptiles," *Palaeobiologica,* Vol. 1 (1928), pp. 163–88.

Oppel, M. *Die Ordnungen, Familien und Gattungen der Reptilien* [etc.]. Munich, 1811.

Schneider, J. G. *Historiae Amphibiorum Naturalis et Literariae.* Vol. II. Jena, 1801.

Seba, A. *Locupletissimi Rerum Naturalium Thesauri Accurata Descriptio* [etc.]. Amsterdam, 1734.

Stejneger, L. "Crocodilian Nomenclature," *Copeia,* 1933, No. 3, pp. 117–20.

Wagler, J. *Natürliches System der Amphibien* [etc.]. München, 1830.

Wermuth, H. "Systematik der Rezenten Krokodile," *Mitteilungen der Zoologische Museum (Berlin),* Vol. 29 (1953), pp. 376–514.

Werner, F. "Die Lurche und Kriechtiere [etc]," in *Brehm's Tierleben,* 4th Ed., Vol. 4, Leipzig, 1912.

—— *Das Tierreich, Reptilia Loricata,* Lieferung 62 (1933).

G. THE CHINESE ALLIGATOR AND THE CAIMANS

Alvarez del Toro, M. "Breeding the Spectacled Caiman, *Caiman crocodylus*, at Tuxtla Gutierrez Zoo," *International Zoo Yearbook*, Vol. 9 (1969), pp. 35–36. (Avers that at hatching time, the male not only opened the nest but also broke the eggs by rolling on and biting them, in order to liberate the young! But also note Hunt, 1969, in this section of the bibliography.)

Anonymous. "A Surinam Portfolio," *Natural History*, Vol. 71, No. 10 (1962), pp. 28–41. (The spectacled caiman and an aniliid snake.)

Azara, F. d'. *Essais sur l'Histoire Naturelle des Quadrupédes de la Province du Paraguay*. Paris, Charles Pougens, 1801.

Barbour, T. "A Note Regarding the Chinese Alligator," *Proceedings of the Academy of Natural Sciences of Philadelphia*, Vol. 62 (1910), pp. 464–67.

—— "Further Remarks on the Chinese Alligator," *Preoceedings of the New England Zoological Club*, Vol. 8 (1922), pp. 31–34.

Blohm, T. "Observaciones sobre los Caimanes Traidos del Rio Orinoco en Abril de 1946," *Memorias de Sociedad de Ciencias Naturales de La Salle*, Vol. 8, No. 22 (1948), pp. 129–32.

Boulenger, G. A. "Remarks on the Chinese Alligator," *Proceedings of the Zoological Society of London for 1890* (1890), pp. 619–20.

Carvalho, A. L de. "Os Jacarés do Brasil," *Arquivos do Museu Nacional*, Vol. 42 (1951), pp. 127–39.

Chin Fu-Jen. "There Are Many Rare Animals in Peking Zoo," *Zoo Life*, Vol. 11, No. 3 (1956), pp. 93–94.

Cope, E. D. "On the Crocodilian Genus *Perosuchus*," *Proceedings of the Academy of Natural Sciences of Philadelphia* Vol. 20 (1868), p. 203.

Fauvel, A. A. "An Account of the Chinese Alligator," *Journal of the North-China Branch of the British Royal Asiatic Society*, Vol. 13 (1879), pp. 1–36.

Fittkau, E. J., J. Illies, H. Klinge, G. H. Schwabe, and H. Sioli (editors). *Biogeography and Ecology in South America*. Vol. I. The Hague, W. Junk Pub., 1968.

Fowler, H. W. "On the Identity of *Perosuchus* Cope with *Caiman* Spix," *Proceedings of the New England Zoological Club*, No. 5 (1915), pp. 103–6.

Goeldi, E. A. "Die Eir von 13 Brasilianischen Reptilien, nebst Bemerkungen über Lebens- und Fortpflanzungsweise Letzterer," *Zoologische Jahrbücher (Systematik)*, Vol. 10 (1897), pp. 640–76.

Hagmann, G. "Die Eir von *Caiman Niger* [etc.]," *ibid.*, Vol. 16 (1902), pp. 405–10.

—— "Die Eir von *Gonatodes humeralis, Tupinambis nigropunctatus,* und *Caiman sclerops* [etc.]," *ibid.*, Vol. 24 (1906), pp. 307–16.

—— "Die Reptilien der Insel Mexiana, Amazonenstrom," *ibid.*, Vol. 28 (1909), pp. 273–304.

Hsiao, S. "Natural History Notes on the Yangtze Alligator," *Peking Natural History Bulletin*, Vol. 9, No. 4 (1935), pp. 283–92.

Hunt, R. H. "Breeding of Spectacled Caiman, *Caiman c. crocodylus*, at Atlanta Zoo," *International Zoo Yearbook*, Vol. 9 (1969) pp. 36–37. (Neither male nor female tried to free the hatchlings from the nest, and neither was attracted by the grunting of the hatchlings as they emerged from the eggs.)

Kreyenberg, M. "Briefe aus China." *Wochenscrift für Aquarien und Terrarien Kunde*, Vol. 3 (1906), pp. 64–65, 420–21, 584.

Krieg, H. "Biologische Reisestudien in Südamerika. VIII. *Caiman Sclerops* (Schmalschnautziger Brillenkaiman)," *Zeitschrift für Wissenschaftliche Biologie*, Part A, Vol. 10 (1928), pp. 162–73.

Luederwalt, H. "Chava para a Determinaçao dos Crocodilideos Brasileiros com una Listade Especies do Museu Paulista," *Revista do Museu Paulista*, Vol. 14 (1926), pp. 387–92.

Martini, M. *Atlas Sinensis*. Amsterdam, 1656.

Medem, F. "*Palaeosuchus trigonatus* (Schneider) en Colombia (Noticia Preliminar)," *Lozania*, No. 5 (1952), pp. 1–12.

—— "Contribuciones a la Taxonomía y Distribucion del Yacaré Negro, *Palaeosuchus palpebrosus* (Cuvier), en Colombia," *Revista Colombiana, Antropologia*, Vol. 1 (1953), pp. 409–19.

—— "A New Subspecies of *Caiman Sclerops* from Colombia," *Fieldiana: Zoology*, Vol. 37 (1955), pp. 339–44.

—— "The Crocodilian Genus *Palaeosuchus*," *ibid.*, Vol. 39, No. 21 (1958), pp. 227–47.

—— "Osteologia Craneal, Distribucion Geographica y Ecologia de *Melanosuchus Niger* (Crocodylia: Alligatoridae), *Revista de la Academia Colombiana*, Vol. 12, No. 45 (1963).

Mook, C. C. "Skull Characters of *Alligator sinense* Fauvel," *Bulletin of the American Museum of Natural History*, Vol. 48 (1923), pp. 553–62.

Müller, L. "Zur Nomenklatur der Sudamerikanischen Kaiman-Arten," *Zoologischen Anzeiger*, Vol. 58 (1923), pp. 315–20.

Nicéforo Maria, H. "El Caiman Jacaré Negro (*Melanosuchus Niger* Spix) en Colombia," *Caldasia*, Vol. 7, No. 32 (1955), pp. 167–71.

Peters, J. A. "Herpetology in Modern China," *Copeia*, 1969, No. 1, pp. 214–15.

Pope, C. H. "The Reptiles of China," *Natural History of Central Asia*, Vol. 10 (1935).

Reese, A. M. "Caiman Hunting in South America," *Natural History*, Vol. 20, No. 4 (1920), pp. 424–27.

—— "Habitat of the Crocodilia of British Guiana," *Ecology*, Vol. 4, No. 2 (1923), pp. 141–46.

—— "Notes on the Crocodilia of British Guiana," *Bulletin of West Virginia University Scientific Association*, Vol. 2, No. 1 (1923), pp. 3–11.

Rivero-Blanco, C. "El Caiman y Su Valiosa Piel," *Lineas*, 1968, No. 136, pp. 11–13.

Schmidt, K. P. "Notes on Chinese Reptiles," *Bulletin of the American Museum of Natural History*, Vol. 54 (1927), pp. 467–551.

—— "Notes on South American Caimans," *Field Museum of Natural History, Zoological Series*, Vol. 12, No. 17 (1928), pp. 205–31. (An important paper on caiman taxonomy.)

Spix, J. B. de. *Animalia Nova sive Species Novae Lacertarum* [etc.]. Monachii (Franc.) Hübschmanni, 1825.

Swinhoe, R. "Notes on Reptiles and Batrachians Collected in Various Parts of China," *Proceedings of the Zoological Society of London for 1870*, (1870), pp. 409–12.

Vaillant, L. "Du Nom Générique des Caimans á Plastron Osseux," *Bulletin du Societe Zoologique de France*, Vol. 18 (1893), pp. 217–19.

—— "Contribution á l'Etude des Emydosauriens. Catalogue Raisonné des *Jacaretinga* et *Alligator* de la Collection du Muséum," *Nouvelle Archives du Muséum de l'Histoire Naturelle*, Vol. 10, No. 3 (1898), pp. 143–212.

Wright, T. (editor). *The Travels of Marco Polo the Venetian*. Garden City, N. Y., Doubleday and Co., 1948.

H. THE CROCODILES OF THE NEW WORLD

Allen, E. R. "Alligators and Crocodiles," *All-Pets Magazine*, April 1938, 4 pp.

Allen, E. R., and W. T. Neill. "The Florida Crocodile," *Nature Magazine*, Vol. 45, No. 2 (1952), pp. 77–80.

Allen, R. P. *The Flame Birds*. New York, Dodd, Mead and Co., 1947.

Anonymous. "Gone Gator," *Florida Times-Union*, July 1, 1960, p. 48. (Portrays a crocodile supposedly from South Carolina.)

Barbour, T. "A Contribution to the Zoogeography of the West Indies, with Special Reference to Amphibians and Reptiles," *Memoirs of the Museum of Comparative Zoology at Harvard*, Vol. 44, No. 2 (1914), pp. 209–359.

—— "The Crocodile in Florida," *Occasional Papers of the Museum of Zoology, University of Michigan*, No. 131 (1923), pp. 1–6.

—— "Third List of Antillean Reptiles and Amphibians," *Bulletin of the Museum of Comparative Zoology at Harvard*, Vol. 82, No. 2 (1937), pp. 75–166.

Barbour, T., and C. Ramsden. "The Herpetology of Cuba," *Memoirs of the Museum of Comparative Zoology at Harvard*, Vol. 17, No. (1919), pp. 71–213.

Bean, N. M. "Crocodile Nest at Trout Creek," *Everglades Natural History*, Vol. 1, No. 3 (1953), pp. 100–2.

Cochran, D. M. "The Herpetology of Hispaniola," "*United States National Museum, Bulletin* No. 177 (1947), pp. 1–398.

Cockerell, T. D. "A Little Known Jamaican Naturalist, Dr. Anthony Robinson," *American Naturalist*, Vol. 28, No. 333 (1894), pp. 775–80.

Cory, C. B. *Hunting and Fishing in Florida*. Boston, 1896.

Coscolluela, J. A. *Cuatro Años en la Ciénaga de Zapata*. Habana, 1918.

De La Sagra, R. *Historia Fisica, Politica y Natural de la Isla de Cuba*. Habana, 1838.

De Sola, C. R. "The Cuban Crocodile: An Account of the Species *Crocodilus Rhombifer*, with Notes on Its Life History," *Copeia*, 1930, No. 3, pp. 81–83.

Dickinson, W. E. "In Quest of an Adult Crocodile," *Everglades Natural History*, Vol. 1, No. 4 (1953), pp. 151–56.

Dimock, A. W., and J. Dimock. *Florida Enchantments*. New York, 1918.

Dunkle, D. H. "Note on *Crocodylus Moreletii*. A. Duméril from Mexico," *Copeia*, 1935, No. 4, p. 182.

Gardiner, J. "Alligators in the Bahamas," *Nature*, Vol. 34, No. 884 (1886), p. 546. (Unverified report of a crocodilian on Inagua, to which island the American crocodile might rarely stray.)

Garman, S. "Reptiles and Batrachians from the Caymans and from the Bahamas," *Bulletin of the Essex Institute*, Vol. 20 (1888), pp. 101–13.

Grant, C. "The Herpetology of the Cayman Islands," *Bulletin of the Institute of Jamaica, Science Series*, No. 2 (1940), pp. 1–56.

Gundlach, J. *Contribución a la Erpetologia Cubana*. Habana, G. Montiel, 1880.

Hornaday, W. T. [Note on the Florida Crocodile], *American Naturalist*, Vol. 9 (1875), p. 504.

LeBuff, C. R. "The Range of *Crocodylus Acutus* along the Florida Gulf Coast," *Herpetologica*, Vol. 13, Part 3 (1957), p. 188.

Lewis, C. B. "Alligators vs. Crocodiles," *Natural History Notes, Natural History Society of Jamaica*, No. 8 (1942), pp. 6–7; also in *Glimpses of Jamaican Natural History*, Kingston, 1949, pp. 13–15.

Lynn, W. G., and C. Grant. "The Herpetology of Jamaica," *Bulletin of the Institute of Jamaica, Science Series*, No. 1 (1940).

Maynard, C. J., [Chapter 1] in C. Hallock (editor), *Camp Life in Florida; a Handbook for Sportsmen and Settlers*. New York, 1876.

Moore, J. C. "A Mound on a Key in Florida Bay," *Everglades Natural History*, Vol. 1, No. 2 (1953), pp. 66–75.

—— "The Crocodile in the Everglades National Park," *Copeia*, 1953, No. 1, pp. 54–59. (A brief but important account of the natural history of the American crocodile in Florida.)

Müller, L., and W. Hellmich. "Mitteilungen über Kolumbianische Panzerechsen," *Ibero-amerikanische Studien*, Vol. 13 (1940), pp. 127–52.

Neill, W. T. "New and Noteworthy Amphibians and Reptiles from British Honduras," *Bulletin of the Florida State Museum*, Vol. 9, No. 3 (1965), pp. 77–130.

Neill, W. T., and R. Allen. "Studies on the Amphibians and Reptiles of British Honduras," *Publications of the Research Division, Ross Allen's Reptile Institute, Inc.*, Vol. 2, No. 1 (1959), pp. 1–76.

Patrick, R. W. (editor). "William Adie Whitehead's Description of Key West," *Tequesta*, 1952, No. 12, pp. 61–67. (Interesting description of a locality that formerly harbored the American crocodile.)

Powell, J. H. "The Status of *Crocodylus moreletti* in Yucatan" *International Union for Conservation*, 1965, No. 16, p. 6.

Rafinesque-Schmalz, C. S. [First mention of a crocodile in Florida], *Kentucky Gazette, New Series*, Vol. 1, No. 29 (July 18, 1822), p. 3.

Schmidt, K. P. "Notes on Central American Crocodiles," *Field Museum of Natural History, Zoological Series*, Vol. 12, No. 6 (1924), pp. 79–92.

Shattuck, G. C., and 13 Collaborators. "The Peninsula of Yucatan: Medical, Biological, Meteorological and Sociological Studies," *Carnegie Institution of Washington*, Pub. No. 431 (1933).

Stejneger, L. "Cuban Amphibians and Reptiles Collected for the United States National Museum from 1899 to 1902," *Proceedings of the United States National Museum*, Vol. 53, No. 2205 (1917), pp. 259–91.

Stimson, L. A. "Off the Map," *Florida Naturalist*, Vol. 13, No. 4 (1940), pp. 80–82.

Stuart, L. C. "A Contribution to a Knowledge of the Herpetology of a Portion of the Savanna Region of Central Petén, Guatemala," *University of Michigan, Museum of Zoology, Miscellaneous Publications*, No. 29 (1935).

—— "Some Further Notes on the Amphibians and Reptiles of the Petén Forest of Northern Guatemala," *Copeia*, 1937, No. 1, pp. 67–70.

Swanson, P. L. "Herpetological Notes from Panama," *ibid.*, 1945, No. 4, pp. 210–16.

Underwood, G. [Note on the American Crocodile], *Natural History Notes, Natural History Society of Jamaica*, No. 44 (1950), pp. 161–63.

—— "The Distribution of Antillean Reptiles," *ibid.*, No. 67 (1954), pp. 121–29.

Varona, L. S. "Notas Sobre los Crocodílidos de Cuba y Descripción de una Nueva Especie del Pleistoceno," *Poeyana*, Series A, No. 16 (1966), pp. 1–34. (An interesting paper on the Cuban and American crocodiles in Cuba.)

Wyman, J. [Note on the Crocodile in Florida], *Proceedings of the Boston Society of Natural History*, 1869, p. 78.

—— [Note on the Crocodile in Florida], *American Journal of Sciences and Arts*, Vol. 49 (1870), p. 105.

I. THE CROCODILIANS OF THE OLD WORLD

Adams, A. L. *The Wanderings of a Naturalist in India*. Edinburgh, 1867.

Aelianus, C. *De Historia Animalium*. Geneva, 1616.

Alexander, J. E. *An Expedition of Discovery in the Interior of Africa* [etc.]. London, 1838.

Anderson, A. "An Account of the Eggs and Young of the Gavial (*Gavialis Gangeticus*)," *Proceedings of the Zoological Society of London for 1875* (1875), p. 2.

Anderson, J. *Zoology of Egypt. Vol. First. Reptilia and Batrachia*. London, Bernard Quaritch, 1898. (Includes an interesting account of the Nile crocodile.)

Angel, F. "Sur un Squelette Céphalique de *Crocodilus Cataphractus* Cuvier," *Bulletin du Museum d'Histoire Naturelle*, 1926, pp. 125–26.

—— "Sur une Tete Osseuse de Crocodile de Madagascar (*Crocodilus Robustus* Grand. et Vaill.," *ibid.*, 2nd Series, Vol. 1, No. 3 (1929), pp. 186–87.

Anonymous. "Rhino Vs. Crocodile," *Northern Rhodesia Journal*, Vol. 1, No. 2 (1950), p. 13.

Anonymous. "Outsize Crocodiles," *ibid.*, No. 5 (1952), p. 45.

Anonymous. "No Crocodiles from India," *Oryx*, Vol. 9, No. 3 (1967), p. 184.

Anonymous. "Farming of Crocodiles New Project in Uganda," *African Wildlife News*, Vol. 3, No. 1 (1968), p. 9.

Anonymous. "Nile Crocodile in Danger," *Kingfisher*, Vol. 4, No. 2 (1968), pp. 12–13.

Attwell, R. I. "Crocodiles Feeding on Weaver-birds," *Ibis*, Vol. 96 (1954), pp. 485–86.

—— "Crocodiles at Carrion," *African Wildlife*, Vol. 13 (1959), pp. 13–22.

Banks, E. "Some Measurements of the Estuary Crocodile (*Crocodilus Porosus*) from Sarawak," *Journal of the Bombay Natural History Society*, Vol. 34 (1931), pp. 1086–88.

Barbour, T. "An Historic Crocodile Skull," *Copeia*, No. 126 (1924), p. 16.

Barrett, C. *Reptiles of Australia*. London, Cassell and Co., 1950. (An included photograph, p. 13, of an American alligator, misidentified as a "saltwater crocodile," was the basis of the invalid subspecies "*Crocodylus porosus australis*.")

Beccari, O. *Wanderings in the Great Forests of Borneo*. London, A. Constable Co., 1904.

Birt, G. R. "It Was a Crocodile," *Walkabout*, Vol. 34, No. 3 (1968), p. 5.

Boake, B. "The Nest of the Crocodile," *Zoologist*, Vol. 5, No. 2 (1870), pp. 2002–4.

Boulenger, G. A. *A Vertebrate Fauna of the Malay Peninsula from the Isthmus of Kra to Singapore Including the Adjacent Islands*. London, Taylor and Francis, 1912.

Boutan, L. "Le Crocodile des Marais (*Crocodilus Palustris*)," *Mission Scientifique Permenente d'Exploration en Indo-China, Decades Zoologique*, Hanoi, 1906.

Brander, A. D. "Stones in Crocodile's Stomach," *Field*, Vol. 146 (1925), p. 537.

—— "An Enormous Estuary Crocodile (*Crocodilus Porosus*), *Journal of the Bombay Natural History Society*, Vol. 34 (1931), pp. 584–85.

Brongersma, L. D., and G. F. Venema. *To the Mountains of the Stars*. Garden City, N.Y., Doubleday and Co., 1963. (Mentions the New Guinea crocodile and a fossil crocodile.)

Bustard, H. R. "Rapid Learning in Wild Crocodiles (*Crocodylus Porosus*)," *Herpetologica*, Vol. 24, No. 2 (1968), pp. 173–75.

—— "The Future of Australasian Crocodiles," *Wildlife of Australia*, Vol. 6, No. 2 (1969), pp. 40–43.

Cansdale, G. *Reptiles of West Africa*. London, Penguin Books, 1955.

Cloudsley-Thompson, J. L. "Diurnal Rhythm of Activity in the Nile Crocodile," *Animal Behaviour*, Vol. 12, No. 1 (1964), pp. 98–100.

Corbet, P. S. "Notes on the Insect Food of the Nile Crocodile in Uganda," *Proceedings of the Royal Entomological Society of London*, Section A, Vol. 34 (1959), pp. 17–22.

—— "The Food of a Sample of Crocodiles (*Crocodilus Niloticus*) from Lake Victoria," *Proceedings of the Zoological Society of London*, Vol. 133 (1960), pp. 561–71.

Cott, H. B. "The Status of the Nile Crocodile in Uganda," *Uganda Journal*, Vol. 18 (1954), pp. 1–12.

—— "Ecology and Economic Status of the Crocodile in Uganda," in "Record of Symposium on African Hydrobiology and Inland Fisheries," *Commission of Technical Cooperation in Africa South of the Sahara*, Publication No. 6 (1954), pp. 119–22.

—— "The Crocodile's Decline," *Listener*, Vol. 58, No. 1479 (1957), pp. 168–69.

—— "Scientific Results of an Inquiry into the Ecology and Economic Status of the Nile Crocodile (*Crocodilus Niloticus*) in Uganda and Northern Rhodesia," *Transactions of the Zoological Society of London*, Vol. 29, Part 4 (1961), pp. 211–357. (Includes actual observations of much importance, along with the entertaining opinions of nonscientific residents. The photographs of wild crocodiles are unexcelled.)

—— "The Status of the Nile Crocodile below Murchison Falls," *I. U. C. N. Bulletin*, Vol. 2, No. 8 (1968), pp. 62–64.

—— "Nile Crocodile Faces Extinction in

Uganda," *Oryx*, Vol. 9, No. 5 (1968), pp. 330–32.

De Jong, J. K. "Über eine Abnorme Bezahnung bei *Crocodilus Porosus* (Schn.)," *Miscellanea Zoologica Sumatrana*, Vol. 31 (1928), pp. 1–5.

De La Torre, R. *Skull Characters of Crocodilus Siamensis*. Piñar del Rio, Cuba, La Comercial, 1939. (8 pp.)

Deraniyagala, P. E. "The Crocodiles of Ceylon," *Ceylon Journal of Science*, Vol. 16, No. 1 (1930), pp. 89–95.

—— "Neoteny in *Crocodylus Porosus*," *Spolia Zeylanica*, Vol. 19 (1934), pp. 97–100.

—— "A New Crocodile from Ceylon," *Ceylon Journal of Science*, B, Vol. 19 (1936), pp. 279–86.

—— *The Tetrapod Reptiles of Ceylon. Vol. 1. Testudinates and Crocodilians.* Colombo, 1939.

—— *A Colored Atlas of Some Vertebrates from Ceylon*, 2. Colombo, Ceylon Nature Museum, 1953. (Includes a description of a Pliocene Crocodilian.)

—— "A New Race of the Estuarine Crocodile from Ceylon," *Spolia Zeylanica*, Vol. 27 (1955), pp. 277–79.

De Rooij, N. *The Reptiles of the Indo-Australian Archipelago, I. Lacertilia, Chelonia, Emydosauria.* Leiden, 1915.

Dharmakumarsinghi, K. S. "Mating and the Parental Instinct of the Marsh Crocodile (*Crocodilus palustris* Lesson)," *Journal of the Bombay Natural History Society*, Vol. 47 (1947), pp. 174–76.

Dubois, E. "On the Occurrence of *Crocodilus porosus* Far Above the Tideway in the Sumatran Rivers," *Notes of the Leyden Museum*, Vol. 18, No. 2 (1896), p. 3.

Dunsterville, M. "Crocodile and Gull," *Lammergeyer*, 1968, No. 8, p. 53.

FitzSimons, V. "Scientific Results of the Vernay-Lang Kalahari Expedition, March to September, 1930," *Annals of the Transvaal Museum*, Vol. 16 (1935), pp. 295–397.

Flower, S. S. "Notes on the Recent Reptiles and Amphibians of Egypt, with a List of the Species Recorded from That Kingdom," *Proceedings of the Zoological Society of London, for 1933* (1933), pp. 153–281.

Fowler, H. W. "A Few Reptiles and Fishes from Batanga, West Africa," *Copeia*, No. 45 (1917), p. 53.

Grabham, G. W. "A Crocodile's Nest," *Nature*, Vol. 80 (1909), p. 96.

Günther, A. C. *The Reptiles of British India*. London, Ray Society, 1864.

Hambly, W. D. "Serpent Worship in Africa," *Field Museum of Natural History, Anthropological Series*, Vol. 21, No. 1 (1931), pp. 1–83. (Includes remarks on sacred crocodiles in Africa.)

Hippel, E. V. "Stomach Contents of Crocodiles," *Uganda Journal*, Vol. 10, No. 2 (1946), pp. 148–49.

Hoare, C. A. "Studies on *Trypanosoma Grayi*. 3. Life-cycle in the Tsetse Fly and in the Crocodile," *Parasitology*, Vol. 23 (1931), pp. 449–84.

—— "On Protozoal Blood Parasites Collected in Uganda; with an Account of the Life Cycle of the Crocodile Haemogregarine," *ibid.*, Vol. 24 (1932), pp. 210–24.

Honegger, R. E. "Beobachtungen an der Herpetofauna der Seychellen," *Salamandra*, Vol. 1–2 (1966), pp. 21–36.

Hooijer, D. A. "Crocodilian Remains from the Pleistocene of the Celebes," *Copeia*, 1954, No. 4, pp. 263–66. (Describes remains seemingly not of the estuarine crocodile.)

Howcroft, T. P. "Crocodile and Geese," *Lammergeyer*, 1968, No. 8, p. 53.

Hubbard, W. D. "Crocodiles," *Copeia*, No. 165 (1927), pp. 115–16.

Inger, R. F. "The Systematic Status of the Crocodile *Osteoblepharon Osborni*," *Copeia*, 1948, No. 1, pp. 15–19.

Kimura, W. "Atagawa Tropical Garden and Alligator Farm Research Report No. 1, Crocodiles of Palau Islands," *Research Reports of the Atagawa Tropical Garden and Alligator Farm*, 1968, No. 1, pp. 1–40.

—— "Atagawa Tropical Garden and Alligator Farm Research Report No. 2, On the Hatching of Crocodile Eggs of Palau," *ibid.*, No. 2, pp. 1–32

King, W. "Palaeolithic Reptile and Amphibian Remains from Niah Great Cave," *Sarawak Museum Journal*, New Series, Vol. 10, Nos. 19–20 (1962), pp. 450–52. (Mentions remains probably of the estuarine crocodile.)

Kopstein, F. "Ein Beitrag zur Eierkunde und zur Fortpflanzung der Malaisschen Reptilien," *Bulletin of the Raffles Museum*, No. 14 (1938), pp. 81–167. (Describes nest and eggs of the estuarine crocodile.)

Kymdell, W. "Crocodile, Dogs and Waterbuck," *Lammergeyer*, 1968, No. 8, p. 53.

Lang, H. "Congo Crocodiles, Lizards, and Turtles," *Copeia*, No. 69 (1919), pp. 29–30.

Longman, H. A. "*Crocodilus Johnsoni* Krefft," *Memoirs of the Queensland Museum*, Vol. 8 (1925), pp. 95–102.

Loveridge, A. "The Nilotic Crocodile," *Copi*, No. 168 (1928), pp. 74–76.

—— [Attack on man, by an estuarine crocodile], *Copeia*, 1944, No. 2, p. 128.

—— *Reptiles of the Pacific World*. New York, The Macmillan Co., 1945.

—— "New Guinean Reptiles and Amphibians in the Museum of Comparative Zoology and the United States National Museum," *Bulletin of the Museum of Comparative Zoology*, Vol. 101, No. 2. (1948), pp. 305–430.

Marden, L. "Madagascar: Island at the End of the Earth," *National Geographic*, October, 1967, pp. 443–87. (Includes descriptions of a crocodile cult, and notes that the Nile crocodile has been hunted almost to extinction on Madagascar.)

Mertens, R. "Zur Synonymie von Zwei Krokodilnamen," *Senckenbergiana*, Vol. 30 (1949), pp. 9–10.

—— "Die Amphibien und Reptilien Südwestakrikas," *Abhandlungen der Senckenbergischen Naturforscenden Gesellschaft*, Vol. 490 (1955), pp. 1–172.

—— "Zur Systematik und Nomenklatur der Ceylon-Krokodile," *Senckenbergiana* (*Biologische*), Vol. 41, Nos. 5–6 (1960), pp. 267–72.

—— "Putzer-Vögel bei Krokodilen," *Natur und Museum*, Vol. 98, No. 5 (1968), p. 216.

Meyen, F. J. *Reise um die Erde* [etc.]. Berlin, 1835.

Modha, M. L. "The Ecology of the Nile Crocodile (*Crocodylus Niloticus* Laurenti) on Central Island, Lake Rudolf," *East African Wildlife Journal*, Vol. 5 (1967), pp. 74–95.

Monckton, C. A. *Some Experiences of a New Guinea Resident Magistrate*. New York, Dodd, Mead and Co., 1920. (First suggestion that New Guinea harbored a crocodile other than the estuarine species.)

Neill, W. T. "Notes on *Crocodylus Novae-guineae*," *Copeia*, 1946, No. 1, pp. 17–20.

Owen, T. R. "Notes on the Feeding and Other Habits of the Crocodile," *Sudan Wildlife and Sport*, Vol. 2, No. 2 (1951), pp. 33–35.

Pitman, C. R. "About Crocodiles," *Uganda Journal*, Vol. 8 (1941), pp. 84–114.

—— "Pigmy Crocodiles in Uganda," *ibid.*, Vol. 16, No. 2 (1952), pp. 121–24.

Pooley, A. C. "Preliminary Studies on the Breeding of the Nile Crocodile, *Crocodylus Niloticus*, in Zululand," *Lammergeyer*, 1969, No. 10, pp. 22–44.

—— "The Burrowing Behaviour of Crocodiles," *ibid.*, pp. 60–63.

Raven, H. C. "An Incident in the Feeding Habit of *Crocodilus Niloticus*, *Copeia*, No. 95 (1921), pp. 33–35.

—— "Crocodiles in Borneo," *Chicago Naturalist*, Vol. 9, No. 1 (1946), pp. 12–16. (Describes predation on man by the estuarine crocodile.)

Robinson, St. J. "The Crocodile at the Nest," *North Queensland Naturalist*, Vol. 16, No. 88 (1948), pp. 3–4. (Relates to the estuarine crocodile.)

Rose W. *The Reptiles and Amphibians of Southern Africa*. Cape Town, Maskew Miller, 1950.

Schinz, H. *Deutsch-Südwest-Afrika*. Oldenburg, 1891.

Schmidt, K. P. "Contributions to the Herpetology of the Belgian Congo [etc.].

Part 1. Turtles, Crocodiles, Lizards, and Chameleons." *Bulletin of the American Museum of Natural History*, Vol. 39 (1919), pp. 385-624.

—"A New Crocodile from New Guinea," *Field Museum of Natural History, Zoological Series*, Vol. 12 (1928), pp. 175-81.

—— "Notes on the Herpetology of Indo-China," *Copeia*, No. 168 (1928), pp. 77-80.

—— "Notes on New Guinea Crocodiles," *ibid.*, Vol. 18, No. 8 (1932), pp. 167-72.

—— "A New Crocodile from the Philippine Islands," *ibid.*, Vol. 20, No. 8 (1935), pp. 67-70.

—— "History of a Paratype of *Crocodylus Mindorensis*," *Copeia*, 1938, No. 2, pp. 67-70.

—— "On the Status and Relations of *Crocodylus Mindorensis*," *Fieldiana: Zoology*, Vol. 33, No. 5 (1956), pp. 535-39.

Schuette, G. W. "Crocodile's Prey," *Lammergeyer*, 1968, No. 9, p. 52.

Schultze, W. "Notes on the Nesting Place of *Crocodilus palustris* Lesson," *Philippine Journal of Science*, D 9 (1914), pp. 313-15.

Shelford, R. W. *A Naturalist in Borneo*. London, Fisher Unwin, 1916.

Shockley, C. H. "Herpetological Notes for Ras Jiunri, Baluchistan," *Herpetologica*, Vol. 5, No. 6 (1949), pp. 121-23.

Shortt, W. H. "A Few Hints on Crocodile Shooting," *Journal of the Bombay Natural History Society*, Vol. 28 (1923), pp. 76-84.

Smith, M. A. "*Crocodilus Siamensis*," *Journal of the Natural History Society of Siam*, Vol. 3, No. 3 (1919), pp. 217-21.

—— "The Reptilia and Amphibia of the Malay Peninsula," *Bulletin of the Raffles Museum*, No. 3 (1930).

—— *The Fauna of British India Including Ceylon and Burma. Vol. 1. Loricata, Testudines*. London, Taylor and Francis, 1931.

Tennett, J. E. *Sketches of the Natural History of Ceylon*. London, 1861.

Towers, H. C. "Crocodiles Answer Keeper's Call," *Zoo Life*, Vol. 11, No. 1 (1956), p. 15. (Describes muggers in an Indian lake.)

Tweedie, M. W. "Marine Reptiles," in G. L. Kestenen (editor), *Malayan Fisheries*. Singapore, Malaya Publishing House, 1947.

Villiers, A. "Tortues et Crocodiles de l'Afrique Noire Francaise," *Institute Francaise d'Afrique Noire, Initiations Africaines*, No. 15 (1958), pp. 1-354.

Waite, E. R. "Notes on the Range of *Crocodilus* and *Brachylophus*," *Proceedings of the Linnaean Society of New South Wales*, Vol. 24, Pt. 2 (1889), pp. 283-85.

Waytailingam, S. "Notes on the Breeding of *Crocodilus Palustris*," *Proceedings of the Zoological Society of London for 1880* (1880), p. 186.

Welman, J. B. *Preliminary Survey of the Freshwater Fisheries of Nigeria*. Lagos, 1948.

Welman, J. B., and E. B. Worthington. "The Food of the Crocodile," *Proceedings of the Zoological Society of London*, Vol. 113 (1943), pp. 108-12.

Wermuth, H. "Zur Nomenklatur und Typologie des Leistenkrokodils, *Crocodylus Porosus* Schneider 1801," (*Mitteilungen der Zoologische Museum (Berlin)*, Vol. 30 (1954), pp. 483-86.

—— "The Identity of the Name *Crocodylus Natans* Meyer 1795. A Second Contribution to the Nomenclature and Typology of the Estuarine Crocodile, *Crocodylus Porosus* Schneider 1801," *Spolia Zeylanica*, Vol. 29 (1960), pp. 23-27.

Werner, F. "*Champse Brevirostris*, ein Neues Krokodil aus Afrika, nebst einigen Bemerkungen über die Systematik der Loricaten," *Zoologischen Anzeiger*, Vol. 102 (1933), pp. 102-7.

Wettstein, O. v. "*Champse Brevirostris* Werner 1933 is a *Crocodylus Palustris Kimbula* Deraniyagala 1936," *Annals of Zoology* (Agra), Vol. 2 (1958), pp. 241-42.

Yadav, R. N. "Breeding of the Mugger Crocodile, *Crocodylus palustris*, at Jaipur

Zoo," *International Zoo Yearbook*, Vol. 9 (1969), p. 33. (A captive female cov-ered her nesting hole with sand and dry leaves, and guarded the nest.)

J.   THE CROCODILIANS GENERALLY

Alvarez del Toro, M. *Los Reptiles de Chiapas*. Tuxtla Gutierrez, Mexico, 1960. (Discusses the brown caiman, American crocodile, and Morelet's crocodile.)

Barbour, T. *Reptiles and Amphibians*. Boston, Houghton Mifflin Co., 1926.

Brazaitis, P. "Endangered!", *Animal Kingdom*, August, 1967, pp. 122–27.

Carr, A., and the Editors of *Life. The Reptiles*. New York, *Time*, Inc., 1963.

Cope, E. D. "The Crocodilians, Lizards and Snakes of North America," *Annual Report of the United States National Museum for 1898* (1900), pp. 155–1269.

Darlington, P. J. *Zoogeography: The Geographical Distribution of Animals*. New York, John Wiley and Sons, 1957.

Ditmars, R. L. *Reptiles of the World*. New York, The Macmillan Co., 1910.

Dunn, E. R. "Los Generos de Anfibios y Reptiles de Colombia. IV. Reptiles, Ordenes Testudineos y Crocodilinos," *Caldasia*, Vol. 3, No. 13 (1954), pp. 307–35.

Effeldt, R. "Die Reptiliensammlung der Herren Effeldt und Wagenführ," *Zoologische Garten*, Vol. 14 (1873), pp. 67–70.

Figuier, R. A. *Reptiles and Birds*. London, Bickers and Sons, 1869.

Gilmore, R. M. "Fauna and Ethnozoology of South America," in J. N. Steward (editor), *Handbook of South American Indians*, Vol. 6. Washington, 1950, pp. 345–464.

Kimura, W., and H. Fukada. *Crocodiles of the World*. Tokyo, 1966.

Kramer, G., and F. Medem. "Über Wachstumsbedingte Proportionsänderungen bei Krokodilien," *Zoologischen Jahrbücher (Allgemeine Zoologie)*, Vol. 66 (1955), pp. 62–74.

Medem, F., and H. Marx. "An Artificial Key to the New-World Species of Crocodilians," *Copeia*, 1955, No. 1, pp. 1–2.

Neill, W. T. *The Geography of Life*. New York, Columbia University Press, 1969.

Pope, C. *Reptiles Round the World*. New York, Alfred A. Knopf, 1957.

Reese, A. M. "Bibliography of the Crocodilia," *Herpetologica*, Vol. 4, Part 2 (1947), pp. 43–54. (Consists principally of anatomical and embryological titles. Many of Reese's entries have been omitted from the present book.)

Schmidt, K. P. "Crocodiles," *Fauna*, Vol. 6, No. 3 (1944), pp. 66–72.

—— "On the Zoogeography of the Holarctic Region," *Copeia*, 1946, No. 3, pp. 144–52.

Schmidt, K. P., and R. F. Inger. *Living Reptiles of the World*. Garden City, N. Y., Hanover House, 1957.

Smith, H. M. "Summary of the Collections of Snakes and Crocodilians Made in Mexico under the Walter Rathbone Bacon Traveling Scholarship," *Proceedings of the United States National Museum*, Vol. 93 (1943), pp. 393–504.

Spix, J. B. de, and C. F. Martius. *Reise in Brasilien* [etc.]. 3 Vols. and Atlas. Munich, 1823–1828.

Wermuth, H. "Das Verhältnis zwischen Kopf-, Rumpf- und Schwanzlänge bei den Rezenten Krokodilen," *Senckenbergiana (Biologie)*, Vol. 45, Nos. 3–5 (1964), pp. 369–85.

Wermuth, H., and R. Mertens. *Schildkröten-Krokodile-Brückenechsen*. Jena, G. Fischer Verlag, 1961. (This work is essentially an expansion of Mertens and Wermuth, 1955, cited above in Section F of the present bibliography. To the 1955 work, the 1961 one adds keys and illustrations.)

Wettstein, O. von. "Crocodilia," *Handbuch der Zoologie*, Vol. 7, No. 1 (1937), pp. 175–276.

INDEX

THE PRINCIPAL text reference to each living species or subspecies of crocodilian is in bold-faced type. Page numbers in italics are those of illustrations.

481